Shanghai Delta

This is China's richest part. Jiangsu long led the provinces in both industrial and agricultural production mainly because of "Sunan," i.e., the counties put under Suzhou, Wuxi, Changzhou, and Nantong. The Shanghai delta also includes the ten counties shown under the metropolis, plus Zhejiang counties under Hangzhou, Jiaxing, Huzhou, Shaoxing, Ningbo, and Zhoushan. Shanghai was populated from the delta; many of its families retain ties there, and these grew in economic importance during the 1970s and 1980s. But about a quarter of Shanghai's families come from Subei—i.e., all Jiangsu north of Sunan. No map legend can do justice to the lakes, gardens, poems, wines, or operas the flat delta bred. People meet in autumn at teahouses to enjoy chrysanthemums and freshwater crabs, discussing art and politics as well as business. Many small canals, not shown on the map, join all parts of this area.

CHINA
Heilongjiang
CHANGCHUN
Jilin
SHENYANG
Liaoning
Xinjiang
Nei Mongol
BEIJING
Hebei
Tianjin
Ningxia
Shanxi
Shandong
Qinghai
Gansu
XI'AN
Shaanxi
Henan
Jiangsu
Xizang
Anhui
SHANGHAI
Sichuan
Hubei
HANGZHOU
CHONGQING
Zhejiang
CHANGSHA
Hunan
Jiangxi
FUZHOU
Fujian
Guizhou
XIAMEN
Yunnan
Guangxi
Guangdong
HONG KONG
0
km
800
0
miles
500

UNSTATELY POWER

VOLUME I

Local Causes of China's Economic Reforms

LYNN T. WHITE, III

Written under the auspices of
the Center of International Studies, Princeton University
and
the Centre of Asian Studies, University of Hong Kong

An East Gate Book

M.E. Sharpe
Armonk, New York
London, England

An East Gate Book

Library of Congress Cataloging-in-Publication Data

White, Lynn T.
Unstately power : local causes of China's economic reforms /
Volume I
Lynn T. White III.
p. cm.
"An East gate book."
ISBN 0-7656-0044-7 (cloth : alk. paper); ISBN 0-7656-0045-5 (pbk : alk. paper)
1. China—Economic policy—1976– . 2. Local government—China.
3. Entrepreneurship—China. I. Title.
HC427.92.W514 1997
338.951—dc21 97–26804
CIP

Printed in the United States of America

The paper used in this publication meets the minimum requirements of
American National Standard for Information Sciences—
Permanence of Paper for Printed Library Materials,
ANSI Z 39.48-1984.

∞

EB (c) 10 9 8 7 6 5 4 3 2 1
EB (p) 10 9 8 7 6 5 4 3 2 1

For my family

Generally speaking, our rural reforms have proceeded very fast, and farmers have been enthusiastic. What took us by surprise completely was the development of township and village industries. . . . This is not the achievement of our central government. Every year, township and village industries achieved 20 percent growth. . . . This was not something I had thought about. Nor had the other comrades. This surprised us.

— Deng Xiaoping

We have had difficulty perceiving change because we have looked for the wrong kind of conflict (conflict *within* the government) and have underestimated the extent to which *the government itself as a whole* has been in conflict with other power systems.

— E. E. Schattschneider

Unstately Power: Local Causes of China's Economic Reforms

Contents

Shanghai Delta Map frontpaper
Provinces of China Map opposite title page
Central Shanghai Map endpaper
Abbreviations ix
Romanizations xi
A Note about Wordings xiii
Tables xv
Acknowledgments xvii

Introduction: Post-Revolutionary Politics as Largely Local 3

Four Ways of Answering Causal Questions About Large Correlations 5
Defining the Reforms: Functional Periodization vs. High Politics 8
Defining the State: Boundaries vs. Network Nodes 17
Defining Power: Lions vs. Foxes, with Local Synaptic Leaders in Both Groups 27
Defining the Public: Ways of Speaking vs. Ways of Acting 37
Defining Rationality: Political Causation and Circumspect Evidence 43
Scope of the Book and Sources 53
Appendix: Diagram of a Field of Functions and Activities 57

Part 1, Extraction: Local Entrepreneurs Reform the Political Economy—Prosperity Beyond the State 81

1.1 Rural Political Networks Beyond the State 84
a. Agriculture as the Root of the End of the Revolution 85
b. Rural Industry: Replacing State Socialism with Local Socialism 112

1.2 Business Management Beyond the State 166
a. The Raw Materials Crisis as the Origin of Urban Industrial Reforms 167
b. Taxes and Local Powers 196

1.3 Business Incentives Beyond the State 257
a. Ownership, Corruption, and Entrepreneurship 258
b. Credit, Savings, and Depreciation 298

1.4 Business Outreach Beyond the State 341
a. Local Technical Innovation to Market Quality Products 341
b. The Rise of Horizontal Trade and Regionalism 353

1.5 Local Situations Beyond the State 407
a. Migration and Residence Controls 407
b. Services and Collective or Private Enterprises 433

Sources 461
Index 509

Abbreviations

BR — *Beijing Review*
CCP — Chinese Communist Party
CD — *China Daily,* Beijing
CNA — *China News Analysis,* Hong Kong
CPSU — Communist Party of the Soviet Union
CR — Cultural Revolution
CYL — Communist Youth League
DGB — *Dagong bao* (L'Impartial), Shanghai, Tianjin, or Hong Kong
ECMM — *Extracts from China Mainland Magazines,* Hong Kong
EE — *Eastern Express*, Hong Kong
FBIS — *Foreign Broadcast Information Service,* Washington
FDXB — *Fudan xuebao* (Fudan Journal), Shanghai
FEER — *Far Eastern Economic Review*, Hong Kong
GMRB — *Guangming ribao* (Bright Daily), Beijing
GRRB — *Gongren ribao* (Workers' Daily), Beijing
HQ — *Hongqi* (Red Flag), Beijing
JFRB — *Jiefang ribao* (Liberation Daily), Shanghai
JJRB — *Jingji ribao* (Economic Daily), Beijing
JJYJ — *Jingji yanjiu* (Economic Research), Beijing
JPRS — *Joint Publications Research Service*, Washington
KMT — Kuomintang (Nationalist Party; a.k.a. Guomindang)
LDB — *Laodong bao* (Labor News), Shanghai or Beijing
LSYFZ — *Lüshi yü fazhi* (Lawyer and Law), Hangzhou
LW — *Liaowang* (Outlook), Beijing
MFN — Most favored nation (whose exports enjoy low tariffs)
MZGBDS — *Meizhou guangbo diansh*i (Radio and TV Weekly), Shanghai
NCNA — *New China News Agency*, Shanghai unless noted
PLA — People's Liberation Army
Post — *South China Morning Post,* Hong Kong

PRC	People's Republic of China
QNB	*Qingnian bao* (Youth News), Shanghai and Beijing
RMRB	*Renmin ribao* (People's Daily), Beijing
RMRBHWB	*Renmin ribao haiwai ban* (*RMRB* Overseas Edition), Beijing
SASS	Shanghai Academy of Social Sciences
SCMM	*Selections of China Mainland Magazines*, Hong Kong
SCMP	*Survey of China Mainland Press*, Hong Kong
SF	*Shanghai Focus* (*China Daily* weekly supplement), Shanghai
SHGG	*Shanghai gaige* (Shanghai Reforms)
SHGYJJB	*Shanghai gongye jingji bao* (Shanghai Industrial Economy)
SHHJKX	*Shanghai huanjing kexue* (Shanghai Environmental Sciences)
SHJJ	*Shanghai jingji* (Shanghai Economy)
SHJJDB	*Shanghai jingji daobao* (Shanghai Economic Herald)
SHJJNJ##	*Shanghai jingji nianjian, 19##* (Shanghai Economic Yearbook, 19##)
SHJJYJ	*Shanghai jingji yanjiu* (Shanghai Economic Research)
SHKXB	*Shehui kexue bao* (Social Science News), Shanghai
SHTJNJ##	*Shanghai tongji nianjian,* 19## (Shanghai Statistical Yearbook, 19##)
SHWB	*Shanghai wanbao* (Shanghai Evening News)
SHWL	*Shanghai wenlun* (Shanghai Literary Theory)
SHWXJ	*Shanghai wenxue jiao* (Shanghai Literary Corner)
SHXW	*Shanghai xinwen* (Shanghai News)
SJJJDB	*Shijie jingji daobao* (World Economic Herald), Shanghai
WHB	*Wenhui bao* (Wenhui News), Shanghai [or Hong Kong, if noted]
WHZY	*Wenhui zhi you* (Friend of Wenhui), Shanghai
XDRB	*Xingdao ribao* (Singapore Daily), Hong Kong
XMWB	*Xinmin wanbao* (Xinmin Evening News), Shanghai
XWB	*Xinwen bao* (News Report), Shanghai
XWJZ	*Xinwen jizhe* (Journalist), Shanghai
XWRB	*Xinwen ribao* (News Daily), Shanghai
ZGQN	*Zhongguo qingnian* (China Youth), Beijing
ZGQNB	*Zhongguo qingnian bao* (China Youth News), Beijing
ZGTJNJ##	*Zhongguo tongji nianjian, 19##* (Chinese Statistical Yearbook, 19##)
ZW	*Zhanwang* (Prospect), Beijing

Romanizations

This book generally romanizes Chinese in pinyin. This system may at first seem odd to English readers, because it uses frequent q's, x's, z's, and zh's with unexpected sounds. It is even more counterintuitive than the Wade-Giles system, the older alternative that was developed by British diplomats and missionaries. Pinyin has become standard in the People's Republic of China and in most publications. It is used in this book except for terms (and abbreviations such as KMT) associated with the Nationalist government or Taiwan. A brief table can help readers gain confidence about saying names in pinyin. The system is difficult mainly because of five consonants, listed below, that can be practiced.

The basic unit of this language is the syllable (which is always written with a single character). When you see a romanization, it should generally be either one or two syllables long. (If it is two, the division will usually be obvious in the lettering.) Pronounce each syllable as a unity; do not extend dipthongs so that they sound like two syllables.

Chinese, like any other tongue, has a distinctive sound system. Exact equivalences to English are difficult to reproduce on a printed list, but the aim here is only to give readers who specialize in other languages a sufficient accuracy so that they can be brave when referring to Chinese words in speech. On the next page are only the letters that most differ from what English readers expect. The first five are consonants, always occurring at the beginnings of syllables. After these, four syllable endings are also listed. A reader who follows this table—and says all other pinyin as if it were English—can feel confident the pronunciation will not be very far wrong.

***Pinyin* = Sound**

five sounds to start syllables:

c- = ts-
q- = ch-
x- = sh-
z- = dz-
zh- = j-

four sounds to end syllables:

-ian = -ien
-ong = -ung
-ui = -way
-i = -ee (sometimes -r, or -uh)*

Pronounce all other letters as in English. Assume most romanized words have two syllables. The most problematic symbol in this system is *-i.* A viable policy for most readers is to ignore its irregularities, although these are described in a note below.

---

*The pinyin *-i* varies in sound. Usually pronounce it as "-ee." But it is like "-r" after the initial consonants *ch-*, *r-*, *sh-*, and *zh-*. It is a deep "-uh" after *c-*, *s-*, and *z-*. This *-i* is the main technical flaw of pinyin, the most frequent case in which a single printed symbol does not map uniquely to a single sound. Because some have praised pinyin for its distinction between palitals and retroflexes, the pinyin blitheness about *-i* is odd. English readers who do not know Chinese can learn sounds for the *c-*, *q-*, *x-*, and *zh-* initials that seem most fearsome; then they can respectably neglect any further problems.

A Note about Wordings

Since this book is in English, its terms are chosen to approximate their usual meanings for many English-language readers. "Public prosecutor" is sometimes used here instead of "procurator" (*jiancha yuan*). When China's administrative jurisdictions are discussed here, the three "directly ruled municipalities" (*zhixia shi*; Shanghai, Beijing, and Tianjin) are called "provinces" along with the other provinces and "autonomous regions" (*zizhi qu*, such as Tibet), because they all operate similarly as branches of the central government. "High school" is preferred to "upper middle school" (*gaozhong*), and "junior high" to "lower middle" (*chuzhong*). Sometimes the term "State Cabinet" is inserted in the text near "State Council," when it is clear they refer to the same body, in an attempt to approximate for common readers what that body is. No solution to these problems is perfect, but this approach may help to demystify terms, despite real differences in national institutions. China hands will know the referents anyway.

Tables

Table 1.1-1 Indices of State Procurement Prices for Grains and Industrial Crops 99
Table 1.1-2 Songjiang County, Shanghai, 1965–1987 104
Table 1.1-3 Development in Qingpu County, Shanghai, 1970–1987 105
Table 1.1-4 Rural Industrialization in Tangqiao, Sunan, 1967–1985, and in All of Jiangsu, 1970–1985 116
Table 1.1-5 Rural Industry or Rural Agriculture: The Trade-off 131
Table 1.1-6 Gross Value of PRC Industrial Output by Ownership Type 132
Table 1.2-1 Percentage of Raw Materials for Steel Making in Shanghai Allocated by State Plans 176
Table 1.2-2 Shortages of Materials in Shanghai, 1985 177
Table 1.2-3 Sources of Shanghai National Income 177
Table 1.2-4 State Extraction, by Province 199
Table 1.2-5 Shanghai's Relative Non-use of Budgeting 207
Table 1.2-6 Budgetary Revenues Over Budgetary Expenditures and Budgetary Revenues Minus Expenditures per Person for Cities Near Shanghai 210
Table 1.2-7 Shanghai's Budgetary Expenditures and Revenues Through the Early Reforms 215
Table 1.2-8 Shanghai Revenues 216
Table 1.2-9 Provincial Revenue Retention and Subsidy Rules, 1980–1983 224

Table 1.2-10 Profits and Taxes Realized from State-owned Local Industries per 100 Yuan of Capital 234
Table 1.2-11 Income and Realized Profits and Taxes per 1 Yuan of Capital in Cities That Govern All Jiangnan Rural Counties, 1985 236
Table 1.2-12 Shanghai Revenues Decline 238
Table 1.3-1 Shanghai and Other Provinces' Industrial Output Growth by Ownership Type, 1980 and 1990 268
Table 1.3-2 Ownership Sector Change in Shanghai by GNP, 1978–1984 269
Table 1.3-3 Quick Rise of the Economic Responsibility System, 1979–82, in Some Shanghai Industries 283
Table 1.3-4 Declining Vertical and Rising Horizontal Integration in PRC Urban Economies 296
Table 1.3-5 State Investment in Shanghai 303
Table 1.3-6 Interest Rates on Different Shanghai Bank Loans 305
Table 1.3-7 Composition of Fixed Capital Investment 307
Table 1.3-8 Interest Offered to Different Shanghai Bank Depositors 315
Table 1.3-9 Consumption and Disposable Income, by Province 316
Table 1.3-10 Private Deposits of Shanghai Residents in Banks 317
Table 1.4-1 Declining Shanghai Share of China's Exports 347
Table 1.4-2 1983 Economic Indices for Provinces in the Expanded Shanghai Economic Zone 379
Table 1.4-3 Shanghai Delta Growth Rates 389
Table 1.5-1 Registered Migration to and from Shanghai 410
Table 1.5-2 Migration to and from Shanghai Delta Cities: Shaoxing and Xiashi 418
Table 1.5-3 Transient Populations of PRC Cities in Midreforms 426
Table 1.5-4 Labor Productivity in Shanghai by Sector 434
Table 1.5-5 Fall and Rise of Shanghai's Service Sector, 1952–1992 437

Percentages in this work are usually rounded from the sources.

Acknowledgments

The list of institutions and people to whom I owe thanks for help with this project is so long, there would be no way to record it fully. To begin with individuals: I am deeply grateful to my academic hosts Coonoor Kripalani-Thadani, Carol Chan, Edward K. Y. Chen, and Wong Siu-lun at the Centre of Asian Studies, University of Hong Kong; to my sometime co-authors Li Cheng and Zhou Xiao; and to teachers ranging from Helen Funnell in grade school to my graduate school mentor Chalmers Johnson (who first suggested in 1966 that it might be a good idea to study Shanghai). Many other instructors and colleagues since then also have my thanks for contributions to this project that are in some cases diffuse but have been crucial.

Generous people have provided tremendous help for this project. Parts of the manuscript at various stages were read by Alison Conner, Philip Huang, Li Cheng, Susan Hockaday Jones, Kevin O'Brien, and Thomas Rawski—although these friends are all completely absolved of the remaining errors and sins in this book. Peter and Sarah Cunich, Galen and Carol Fox, Anthony J. Hedley, John and Penny Lawton, Koenraad J. Lindner, Norman and Roberta Owen, Gerard Postiglione and Selene Lee, Priscilla Roberts, Ian Scott, and Brian and Sally Stewart have all been munificent on the logistical side. Barbara Aurelien, Betty Harris, and Margaret Thomas have helped with secretarial work at Princeton. Some of these, like others listed below, have also helped with academic questions that I put to them. The footnotes also contain names that could be added to this list. It is a real pleasure here to express my warm thanks to those mentioned above and to: Michael Agelasto, David Bachman, Joseph Bosco, John P. Burns, Chai Ling, Chan Kam-wing, Chan Man-hung, Chen Dingyue, Chen Haowen, Chen Shenshen, Chen Xiaoping, Chen Yuqun, Cheng Chaoze, Cheng Kaiming, Cheng Xiaonong, Chiao Chien, Gregory Chow, Roger Cliff, Audrey

Donnithorne, Fei Xiaotong, Fu Qiangguo, Mary Gallagher, Rick Glofcheski, Julia Gramer, Gu Mingyuan, Guo Xiaolin, Carol Hamrin, Chad Hansen, Norma Harris, He Deyu, Claire Hollingworth, Marlowe Hood, Huan Guocang, Philip C. C. Huang, Hung Shufen, London Kirkendall, Kuah Khun Eng, Y. Y. Kueh, H. K. Kwan, Reginald Y. W. Kwok and his family, Lee Chin-chuan, Elida Lee, Lee Ying-fen, Beatrice Leung, C. K. Leung, Li Wuwei, Li Xiaodong, Li Xuecheng, Liao Nien-fu and Chen Lu-ning, Lin Hao, Lin Lu, Lin Quanshui, Liu Ching-chih, Lu Feiyun, Lü Zheng, Ma Da, Meng Hongwei, Lyman Miller, Tom Moore, John Norris, Pei Minxin, Peng Dajin, Peng Wen-shien, Judith Polumbaum, Qin Jianxun, Stanley Rosen, David Shambaugh, Shi Qingkai, Shi Qingsheng, Shih Hsiao-yen, Shu Hanfeng, Shu Renqiu, Sia Yin-ching, Ronald Skeldon, Song Jun, Su Chi, Su Songxing, Antony Tatlow, Wang Chongfang, Wang Gungwu, Wang Shaoyun, Wang Xu, Philip Wickeri, Adam Williams, Wu An-chia, Wu Guoguang, Xia Jinxiong, Yang Bucai, Yang Dali, Yang Meirong, Yang Sizheng, Yao Liang, Yao Tinggang, Yen Chengzhong, Yu Shutong, Zhang Jian, Zhang Linlan, Zhang Yongwei, Zheng Yongnian, Zhou Ji, Zhou Jianping, Zhou Ruijin, Zhu Xingqing, Zhuang Ming, Zou Fanyang, and several PRC citizens who prefer not to be listed. My gratitude to Joan Lebold Cohen for permission to use three plates from her marvellous book about *The New Chinese Painting, 1949–1986* is also recorded in the second volume, where they will appear.

My debt to institutions is heavy: Princeton University made leave time available; and special thanks for this go to the Woodrow Wilson School, to the Politics Department, and to the Center of International Studies.

In Shanghai, during early parts of the project, my base was at the Shanghai Academy of Social Sciences. Some of the research and most of the writing was completed at the Centre of Asian Studies, University of Hong Kong, several of whose scholars contributed to the project substantively. On the other side of the Taiwan Straits, I also am very grateful to the Institute of International Relations of National Chengchi University and its former Director Lin Bih-jaw, as well as to Dr. Hsiao Hsin-huang of the Academia Sinica's Institute of Ethnology. Universities Service Centre at the Chinese University of Hong Kong, especially Ms. Jean Hung there, also helped with library materials.

Financial help for this project came from many sources. Princeton University, through its Woodrow Wilson School, has been bountiful with research support. At the inception of the project, while the author was also finishing a book about the Cultural Revolution, to which this project is the sequel, munificent support came from the Harry Frank Guggenheim Foundation. The Chiang Ching-kuo Foundation supported this book project generously during a central period in which it was written. I am extremely grateful to each of these institutions and to the people who administer them.

My warmest thanks go also to colleagues at M. E. Sharpe, especially to Douglas Merwin who has been a tremendous help to me as to many other authors in the China field. Mai Cota, Angela Piliouras, James Flannery, Bryan

Lammers, Joan Zurell, especially the copy editors Susan Warga and Debra Soled, and others at M. E. Sharpe put great effort into the production of this book, and I am extremely grateful to them.

I am nonetheless solely guilty as the perpetrator of this book, even though it would not exist without the help of those named above. The paradigms and definitions used in parts of the book are different from those used by some other China scholars. Many academics have a regrettable tendency to take their own analytic categories as realities, rather than as scopes through which realities can be viewed. I have tried to take alternative paradigms to task only for suggestions. They may be exclusively valid ways of seeing things that can actually be seen in many ways. I hope that no such suggestions are made or implied for the approach used here. I greatly respect the positive contributions that all other authors in this field have made to it, and I have learned from their good work.

Families are important even to writers. This includes the older generation: my mother, my mother-in-law, my sons Jeremy and Kevin, daughter-in-law Fiona, and new grandson Aidan, and the memory of my father were all important in this project. The dedication signals only part of my debt to them. My wife Barbara-Sue has put up with this book for so long, she has written one of her own and edited another in the interim. Our voyages have been together, and much the better for that.

Lynn T. White III
Princeton, New Jersey
May 1997

UNSTATELY
POWER

Introduction

Postrevolutionary Politics as Largely Local

Tian gao, huangdi yuan.
Heaven is high, and the Emperor is far away.
—*Chinese proverb*

This book aims to answer two closely related questions. First, why did Chinese reforms begin, especially in Shanghai and the delta surrounding that city? Second, what maintained the cycle of reforms and reactions thereafter? The hypothesis here is that local leaders wanted the changes. No unified plan from the center of the state in Beijing fully guided them, either at the start of reforms or later.

When explaining any major historical event such as China's reforms, it is useful to distinguish several kinds of causes and to search for evidence that might confirm their importance. It would be arbitrary to offer any single type prematurely as a full account, unless all the facts clearly supported that.[1] One kind of reason for any big political event is an immediate, short-term spark; this can often be identified with action by a specific leader. Readers who begin a book about China's reforms might expect to see information mainly about one man, Deng Xiaoping, and about a few other politicos around him. But the approach of this book casts a wider net, not just because fine accounts about Deng are available elsewhere. China's population is much larger than one state leader, larger even than a hundred of them. Western thinking about the PRC was deeply influenced by the actual power of one protagonist (Mao) by the middle of the 1950s, and that initial period was the era to which a one-man model of politics best applied.[2] At later times, and surely by the reforms, this situation became more complex. Spark causes, including decisions by central leaders, certainly help to precipitate events. Even large syndromes of correlation that involve many diverse political changes, such as China's reforms, depend partly on state-level decisions.[3] An emphasis on just a few leaders, however, can seldom provide convincing reasons why an event becomes widespread or why it lasts for a long time.

Another kind of explanation refers to long-term cultural and ecological factors, which also can help to shape such a major set of reforms. China, the oldest continuous polity in the world, arguably has the richest store of endemic or "inevitable" cultural causes to account for almost anything that happens there. Just as reliance on spark reasons at the center of the state may explain too little, very long-term factors often explain what precedes or follows a specific event as much as they explain the occurrence itself. Any widespread correlation such as China's reforms becomes too fuzzy to conceive clearly if a cultural approach is taken as the sole one. Both short- and long-term explanations have their uses. But a stress on spark causes tends to overspecify the explanation of large events. An emphasis on long-term context tends to overgeneralize the story being told.

Each of these types of explanation is really double, involving two different dimensions that can define more circumspect, better, multi-period accounts. Stories based on short-range factors generally stress individuals or small groups (e.g., a leader or a party). But they also generally begin with norms or decisions; they presume that intentional motives, rather than unintended contexts, mainly drive action. On the other hand, explanations based on long-term factors tend to consider very large groups, including many people together—e.g., the whole Chinese nation—and they often refer to unintended situations rather than to any kind of immediate idea as the fundamental sort of effective cause. An analytic decision to posit large groups, or instead to posit individuals, as the hypothetical cause of an effect is not the same as an analytical decision to posit situations rather than intentions as effective causes. In evaluating causal hypotheses, it will prove useful to distinguish the separation between individual or collective subjects from the separation between intentional or contextual data that bolster predicates.

This book will argue that recent changes in the basic structure of Chinese politics can generally be better accounted for by medium-term mass factors than by either short-term elite causes or cultural traditions. This can be presented only as a tentative conclusion until data are marshaled to show the respects in which it is true. To find such information in a manner that would allow alternative types of causes to be considered, this book explores both contexts and intentions, and both individuals and large groups. The only way to prove the case is to make a full search. So despite the main thesis here about local situations, collective (including state) intentions are explored too.

Unstately Power is a title meant to counter continuing endemic biases this author sees in most thinking and documentation about Chinese politics. But the term is meant to stir thought, to balance earlier unbalanced premises, not by itself to provide a complete view. *Local Causes of Chinese Reforms* is a less polemic and more accurate description of this book's message. The Chinese state is largely disunited, especially during recent years—but even many academic writers who understand and cite that fact continue to refer to "the state" with nearly the same esteem as do most of their sources. Reverence for the state is taken as a datum here about intentions. Contextual data show that policies actually exist in many sizes of groups in the Chinese system, that bureaucrats balance their private interests with pressure from their sometimes-nominal superiors and their local clients, and that the mix of rationalities among all these parties together is complex. Actual people react to both positive and negative incentives, and their ways of speaking about authorities do not mesh exactly with the unintended contexts of these influences. The state is a notion, in contemporary China, at least as much as it is a coherent organization. Power, insofar as it brings major effects, is not solely a matter of consciousness, but also of resources. Unstately power is too sweeping an idea to capture all the causes of Chinese reforms, but the far more common emphasis on the effective influence of the high state is problematic in exactly the same way.

Four Ways of Answering Causal Questions About Large Correlations

Short-term explanations in practice tend to stress the efficacy of individuals or small groups rather than the whole nation, but they also tend to seek changes in the context in which these individuals act that can be linked to their behavior. Long-term explanations in practice have a tendency to refer to all of China, rather than to single people or small factions; but they also tend to refer to the cultural habits and institutions by which people understand motives in communities. Despite these tendencies, a distinction between individuals and whole groups is not the same as a distinction between the immediate situations and the habitual cultures in which people act. So there are four main types of information to be explored when looking for the reasons behind a large historical event such as China's reforms.

Unintended context, causing action by individuals and small groups, has recently in political science been the most favored sort of explanation. Persons one by one are the center of attention, and their collective action is treated by summation. These "rational-action" logics clarify a great deal—and they make particular sense in China's reforms, which are largely economic. Many people and families have improved their livelihoods and liberties in recent decades. Reforms in some fields, and in the early 1970s, arose almost exclusively among nonintellectuals and were mainly driven by concrete, politically unarticulated interests. For example, the account here of early-reform agriculture and rural industry will follow this sort of reasoning. Shanghai suburban peasants once received little compensation for their increasingly arduous work under triple-cropping. So local leaders who founded rural factories and searched for new economic structures tended to gain widespread support. This was a seminal reform. The main substantive finding of this book, that local leaders and their small power networks have been crucial to the PRC reform process since the early 1970s, is largely based on evidence collected by this view of the situation. But rational-action logics do not explain everything—and in theory they need not do so, despite the expansive and futurist claims made for them by rational-choice enthusiasts. Many aspects of the reform syndrome, in fields ranging from painting to prisons, are mainly dismissed as legitimate subjects of inquiry by the rational-action approach, which cannot handle them. But any means to gather data is different from any substantive finding.

Intended habits, causing action by individuals and small groups, are the basis of the most common journalistic accounts of reforms, since readers often readily understand the motives of individuals, who are humans like themselves. The Chinese individuals may be either leading figures (Deng Xiaoping, Zhao Ziyang, Zhu Rongji) or types conceived as individuals acting on their own subjective ideals that are more specific than universal preferences for benefit. It can be shown, for example, that crucial aspects of China's reforms were caused by individuals' and families' introspective memories of the Cultural Revolution; attempts to understand them separate from subjective values would strain the evidence badly. But this approach, like the rational-action one, starts only from individuals or small groups. It assumes incoherence between the motives of different actors. That is a purely analytic premise—sometimes justified by data, sometimes not—which immediately suggests the need to try also the opposite surmise: that data might be understood to cohere, perhaps even like functions, as if a large group might act together.

Intended habits, causing action by the large collective, especially as represented by the Chinese state, are of course the most officially touted generators of reform.[4] The government suggests in propaganda that a communal public will motivate everything that its high, wise leaders do. This notion is not analytically silly, just because it is idealistic and ceremonious. For example, all four of the types of explanation outlined here, as they effect actual reforms in China, can be periodized by whether the intentions of "reformers" or "conservatives" prevail locally or in Beijing. Strictly economic or psychological approaches, seeking to explain events solely in terms of preferences found in individuals, would have to ignore the fact that large group motivations are perceived by many Chinese political actors themselves. Their shifting dominance helps account for much behavior. The leader Hu Qiaomu once described his country's reforms as a high-frequency cycle in which even-numbered years after 1978 were periods of reformist "loosening" (*fang*) while odd-numbered years were times of conservative "tightening" (*shou*). Such a simple even-odd pattern is not entirely accurate but can be widely documented.[5] This cycle of return is not just a national habit of speech; it is also a habit of national action, of the kind Pareto identified in terms of concurrent needs for elite integrity and elite recruitment.[6] Neither the reformist loosening nor the reactionary tightening is likely to disappear soon. These have been among the most constant aspects of China's reform. They are not just normative or just collective, but many data about them are most readily available as expressions of the unified whole polity.

Unintended context, causing action by the whole collective, especially by the state, is the logical remaining way to look at the origins of reform. This approach is nonvoluntarist but collective. It stresses ecological factors, such as the countervailing of threats to China from other states. In this view, the intentions or memories of actors are of secondary importance; the context can explain their ideas. Requisites of military security or economic competition from abroad, for example, are said to create an unavoidable need for reform in China. Many aspects of governance—the formal constitutional structure of the country, the informal political relations between intellectuals and rural entrepreneurs, and much else—may be treated under such a rubric. This kind of story, while explaining a good deal of what has happened, is as controvertible as the alternatives discussed above. China's size, from the forests of Heilongjiang to the jungles of Hainan, provides security against all but a handful of military competitors, for example. Yet reforms in many ways strengthen China, and this result is a plausible reason why some changes occur.

The order of this two-volume book, outlined in the table of contents, gathers information about each of these four types of explanations for China's political reforms. But no abstract trait of action—no adjective or function or cause—is the same as the concrete institutions that provide convenient references for organizing data. It is chancy to reify functions, to make them into things. That is a manageable problem, even though it has no perfect solution. Deductivists have claimed that identifying a function with an institution is an unforgivable sin. They are right that functions are analytic and merely adjectival—but the ideas for functions originally came from concrete structures (markets, governments, police, churches, and other institutional habits). There is no practical way to embed functions in structures without simultaneously speaking of them in terms of those structures.[7]

"Concrete theory," which has attracted attention especially among people who study individual rationality in comparative politics, is an oxymoron of the fruitful kind.[8] Functions or any other predicates are not reified as things; yet they are always seen as embedded in institutions. The opposite concerns about reification and embeddedness are both valid, so long as neither is forgotten. This too often happens. The present book runs some risk of being misread to imply that the institutions covered by its chapters perform only the sorts of activities that the table of contents suggests, whereas in fact they perform many. Other scholars speak of ideal types, e.g. Weber's three kinds of legitimate authority, as logically excluding each other in structures; but they could do so only concretely.[9] Forgetting about embeddedness is the opposite problem, as devoted deductivists show if they fail to link their organized sets of adjectives with anything concrete. But the old functionalists came up with four categories that, if seen as embedded in structures, cover a great deal of waterfront in any effort at social explanation. Use of them all together may leave few stones unturned in the effort to detect how China's reforms happened.

Defining the Reforms: Functional Periodization vs. High Politics

Two diametrically opposite definitions of reform are both very common in previous comparative writings about this subject. Some authors presuppose that "reform," properly speaking, is always a national policy; others think of it as a behavioral syndrome. Samuel Huntington represents the first view, claiming, "Reform is rare, if only because the political talents necessary to make it a reality are rare."[10] He conceives reform as something that only a high elite can do. A different definition, treating reform as a behavioral pattern, would leave open the issue of what or who caused it. If the word "reform" is restricted a priori to mean a syndrome begun by the state, then no question of other origins for it can be asked.

There is nothing wrong with defining reform as central policy, and this has been a basis for interesting historical comparisons.[11] But there is also nothing wrong with using for research an alternative definition—in which reforms are taken to be a behavioral syndrome, not a set of central policies—to find the extent to which they mainly resulted from central policies or from other factors. The fact that such a definition may set fuzzier boundaries of meaning than does the usual approach, in which the state declares reforms, is an advantage rather than the opposite.[12] Late Communist political change can be studied as a correlation, involving many state and nonstate actors. That will be the approach to China's reforms in this book.

"Reforms," according to a definition by János Kornai, must involve reductions of three things: a lessening of the "position of the state and quasi-state ownership," less "influence of the official ideology," and less "bureaucratic coordination."[13] Kornai designed his approach to describe economic changes, but it can be broadened to other fields too. The first three parts of this book are in general devoted to Kornai's three topics respectively, and the fourth part treats the state itself. Reforms are conceived here as a comprehensive change, involving many kinds of political relations. Perhaps they are "revolutionary" in effect—but it is clearest to avoid calling them revolutionary, because reformers generally lack any intent to overturn the existing order (even if that is what they end up doing despite their motives), and in fact they oversee the ebbing of the previous centralist revolution. The syndrome Kornai describes can be separated from the policies that caused it. But that syndrome could not be analyzed in many political networks beyond the central state if "reform" were predefined as an activity of the high politicians mainly.

"The top has policy, but the bottom has countermeasures" (*shang you zhengce, xia you duice*), says a very common PRC motto. The cumulative influence of countermeasures from many localities, acting in parallel, often became national policy not fully intended by the government. Reform may well have emerged at the top level largely from the opportunities of state leaders who met local leaders' needs. An impetus for change in Beijing arose not just from liberal changes of heart by Deng Xiaoping, but also from the fact that after the deaths of Zhou and Mao, Deng was identified in public with broad policy options that neither the Gang of Four nor Hua Guofeng adopted. This political platform was a good basis for Deng to claim Mao's old throne—not in a democratic vote, but in a process involving many leaders. Deng's elevation abetted the policies that many political actors favored, while still maintaining the traditional legitimacy that comes from having a single top leader as the organizational focus for central discipline and the supposed source of stately wisdom.

"The immediate cause of reform was the existence of a reform faction within the Chinese Communist Party, its successful struggle to gain supremacy over more conservative rivals, and its skillful strategy for launching and sustaining a bold program of political and economic renewal," as Harry Harding has written.[14] "Objective problems at the time of Mao's death still do not explain the extent of the reforms." Radicals in the Gang of Four opposed the reform syndrome, as did some Party conservatives, but the Beijing leaders were never united. Over time, reforms occurred because leaders at the top dealt with more local leaders at many levels who faced political, economic, and social problems after the main violence of the Cultural Revolution during the 1960s. Reformist and reactionary cadres were found in all sizes of Chinese jurisdictions.

A Definition of Reforms to Explore Their Diversity

The reforms began from no single origin, but from several types of causes that need to be compared and weighed together. A purpose of the present book is to complement others by showing that reforms, like the conservative reactions they bred, were both central and local. China's reforms came from state policies, but they also arose from the unintended results of previous state policies. They can often be traced to parallel situations in many localities, which resulted in local solutions to which Beijing politicians later acquiesced for the sake of monitoring and taxing. This fragmentation of China's state has itself become a factor shaping reforms, as Party leaders have nostalgically tried to maintain the unified solidarity they recall from the 1950s and the days of revolutionary victory. Technological change has been another crucial impetus for reforms in some fields and will be explored below. For example, agricultural mechanization instigated rural industry, and the spread of television was important for expanding the sources of public information and diversifying public views. Central leaders often founded the means for later political results that, despite their intentions, became reforms.

Rural industry is the best example of this process, and it merits early attention in this book because it is at the very center of PRC reforms. Rural manufacturing localized China's finances. Countryside factories and markets on the Shanghai delta in the early 1970s began to take raw materials away from the state sector, destroyed planning, and started to send Beijing's budget into the red. This source of reform is usually attributed to the wisdom of Deng Xiaoping. But Deng himself, in a candid 1987 mood, contradicted the popular emphasis on the power of the top leader by admitting that "one of the most significant achievements *which we had not expected* is that the township and village enterprises would develop so rapidly. This growth in output has been over 20 percent every year, and thus the rural employment problem has been solved."[15] Deng confessed frankly that he had not foreseen this sharpest reform. His intentions were not its main cause, as he openly confessed.

Deng Xiaoping was a linchpin of China's reform movement, but he was one person among a billion and some of his commitments were inconstant. When the urban changes of 1984 were announced, for example, he approved them publicly but said the details had all been arranged by others.[16] The reforms were not instructions from Deng. In fact, it is sometimes difficult to be sure where any top PRC leader stands on any policy issue.[17] None has an obvious reason to foreclose future actions or alliances until unintended circumstances compel this. They keep their options open. The most senior leaders, such as Mao Zedong or Deng Xiaoping, shifted their coalitions so often during their careers, it would be difficult to find in either a consistent set of principles. High second-rung leaders, such as Zhou Enlai under Mao (or Zhu Rongji and Jiang Zemin under Deng), also did ideologically different things at different times—even if apologists for these leaders tried to interpret the evidence to deny this. Top spokespeople who are not in sympathy with a policy sometimes deliver the highest-profile announcements of it, to preserve the appearance of united government. These high leaders are serious politicians, and politics is not philosophy.

No one decision, in any case, could sustain so complex a syndrome as China's reforms. Local changes can be so gradual and incremental as to be outside the purview of formal decision making.[18] Centrally mandated reforms can generate such severe economic and social problems that they have to be reversed by their initiators—as has happened several times in Hungary and other Eastern European countries. Alternatively, they can be so thorough that they create political pressures that change the system quickly, as in Poland.[19] The top of the state has no natural monopoly on defining reforms. They involve political change, but this can occur in localities and markets long before the state acknowledges the constraints on decisions that national officials make.

Since this book asks what caused the reforms, it cannot use the most common definition of reforms: that they were a policy. That definition would already answer the question; for if they were a government policy, then indeed the government caused them. This usual conception of the phenomenon of reforms has prevented sufficient probing of what lies behind the syndrome of reforms (including the high politics of them and official announcements about them). In order to find what started the reform syndrome, what keeps it going, what slows it down, and what is its fate, there is a need to define reforms as policies from many political networks, not just from the central state. This redefinition will disturb some readers. Even those who accept it, at least as a mere definition for the sake of argument and research, may take a while getting used to it.

High CCP leaders have often shown a broad disposition to reform. But a conservative disposition is an equally viable option at that level—and reaction does not entirely stop the reform process, as Brezhnev proved after Khrushchev in the USSR, and then Chernomyrdin after Gaidar in Russia.[20] Reformist foxes and conservative lions define each other politically. This happens in eras that are called periods of "reform" not because hard-line forces are absent then, but because they cannot constantly rule. The two opposing tendencies are mutually dependent in political terms. A great deal of reaction punctuates any time of reform.

Periodization as Integral to Definition

According to the official story, China's reforms began in 1978 when the CCP Central Committee affirmed Deng Xiaoping's leadership. The Cultural Revolution is said to have taken ten years, from 1966 to 1976, followed by a two-year transitional era under Hua Guofeng, before the reforms began in 1978 under Deng. The main event is conventionally called a "ten-year calamity"[21]—and it was indeed a tragedy, but it was not uniform, and not so exactly for the number of years that matches our fingers. The decade periodization might make some sense, especially if reform were defined as coming from the top of the state. Otherwise, it can be questioned.

Journalists, government analysts, and scholars—outside China as well as inside, and in Taiwan and Hong Kong too—practically all take this decade periodization as a given.[22] It is the standard premise from which research then proceeds. For example, an official history of Shanghai Party and government organizations, covering the years 1949 to 1986, had little to convey about either the late 1960s or the early 1970s.[23] The Cultural Revolution continued during the latter period in some respects—in political harassment of intellectuals and factional conflicts at some places.[24] In other respects, the 1970s were a new decade.

So the usual way of periodizing the Cultural Revolution refers to the decade ending in 1976, when Mao went to see Marx. Another period is then defined by another central leader, Hua Guofeng, as lasting until 1978 when Deng donned what was left of the dead charismatic Mao's mantle. This all carries a strong presumption, which might or might not prove best for organizing behavioral data, that reform is an act of the top state leaders, resulting mainly from their intentions and bright ideas. Such powerful people are often thought to know clearly what they want, and almost always to get it.

Information in most chapters of this two-volume book will show that the reform syndrome by 1978 was a continuation (after a 1975–76 halt, for some indices) of trends already evident in the period from 1971 to 1974—when "reforms" by this book's definition began, after the Cultural Revolution had ended. Especially in rich rural areas such as the Shanghai delta, where high-state monitoring was spotty relative to local talents, data show that crucial aspects of reform—e.g., output from autonomous factories—grew faster during several of those early years than during most years since 1978. If a decline of nationally state-owned heavy industries is understood as a crucial aspect of reforms, statistical data show this decline was strong by the early 1970s.[25] Other aspects of reform, even those in cultural fields for which change was faster later, were also beginning to alter fundamentally during the first years of the 1970s.

The shift of 1978 was less a matter of what people did than of what they said. The turn was less situational than normative. A few rich parts of China, prominently including the whole delta surrounding Shanghai, were changing throughout the 1970s much faster than people were refining their discourse to match what was happening. Chinese were actually making reforms for several years before they began to acquire legitimate words to talk squarely about them.[26] The political watershed of 1978 can be overestimated if policy is defined too narrowly. If policy is understood as something not always made in full public view, and if it is not taken as totally a matter of articulated state-level norms, then the following chapters will show many reform policies in the Shanghai area long before 1978.

The official chronology also obscures much about the Cultural Revolution. This holocaust was, in most of the local political networks it affected, far more violent during the 1960s than in the early 1970s—despite real sufferings by intellectuals at both those times. After the change of decade, the climate of chaos lessened, even though the formal high leadership in most localities was fairly stable after the earlier purges. In Shanghai, for example, Party committees were reestablished for all the urban districts and suburban counties during 1970.[27] Unjust brutalities in public did not end, but they had been far more widespread between 1966 and 1969. Most involved the continued repression of intellectuals. Workers had been organized into militia groups by radicals to neutralize the influence of more conservative professional soldiers, and some conflicts among worker groups were sporadically reported in large cities.[28] The legacies established by pre-1970 violence were still very much in evidence; and intellectuals, including youths and cadres sent to the countryside, continued to suffer from these holdovers far more than did other groups. But fewer people, and fewer types, were involved in new outrages during the early 1970s than during the late 1960s.

Pre-1978 reforms can also be found in quantitative measures, as evidenced by tables in many chapters of this book. A graph of China's gross value of industrial output after 1971, for example, suggests that overall growth was exponential until 1975, but then merely linear (at a high rate) at least until 1982.[29] Such data are not always easy to interpret, but they will be offered and mooted in many fields—from migrations to publications—in the chapters that follow. This book suggests the Cultural Revolution, properly conceived, was already ending by the early 1970s, especially by the period 1971–74. It disputes the usual periodization under which the Cultural Revolution is said to cover the whole decade from 1966 to 1976. That way of thinking about the early 1970s hides too many aspects of Chinese political development, because it neglects the real power of avowedly "weak" local networks, which gained more resources then.

The argument here is that China's changes were gradual enough to cast doubt on the years 1976 or 1978 as particularly crucial watersheds (especially in comparison to other years such as 1971, 1984, and perhaps 1995–96)—not to say that the early 1970s were exactly like later times. The choice of Mao's death year as the Cultural Revolution's end reveals more about the CCP's hopes for new legitimacy than about any other question of political history. In fact, a peak of organizational centralization had been reached about 1969, after the army stamped out many forms of political expression that arose during the Cultural Revolution.[30] But states never fully succeed in centralizing their societies, especially when infrastructure is as underdeveloped as in China. The period 1969–70 was probably the high tide of China's revolution, in the sense that political "commandism" began a slow and bumpy decline then. In high politics, the main evidence of this is Lin Biao's purge and the decline of army budgets. In rural areas, county budgets even in some inland places during the early 1970s took over roles that had in the 1960s been financed more centrally.[31]

In cities, the early 1970s are an era that has not yet received enough good research, and the evidence for a turnaround was then obscured by continuing newspaper campaigns. Urban industry grew quickly in these years. In the cultural sphere, newspapers were still limited in content (with the exception of *Reference Information*, a periodical that became very widespread then). Mao's death, delayed until 1976, was not the sole beginning of the reform period. The leadership clock then ticking in Beijing was related to the many clocks ticking in society more broadly, but it was particularly slow in this period. The Cultural Revolution had mainly ended by 1969, and the narrowly based (army) centralization was already being broadened by 1971. Adumbrations of quicker reforms, and a decline of random violence, were clear for five years before Mao's death.

The proposed watershed about 1971, although it is far more significant than most Chinese or Western periodizations suggest, shows reforms only in a nascent state. On some important indices, such as the rate of light industrial investment, most public reports would suggest that the early 1970s did not show reforms at all.[32] Others suggest they did. In any case, periodizations of behavioral change often do not capture then-current uncertainties about the significance of events. For example, the Gang of Four was put in jail on October 6, 1976. But a full ten months passed before Hua Guofeng announced (on August 12, 1977) that their arrest had been a historic landmark ending the Cultural Revolution.[33] If 1976 was really the Cultural Revolution's end, then the government was remarkably slow to acknowledge it as such. In terms of much local rural politics, the Cultural Revolution had ended much earlier. Such public waffling at the top raises doubts about whether historical events in China should be defined so usually in terms of court politics. High leaders had in fact suggested the end of the Cultural Revolution on several previous occasions since 1969.[34]

In Shanghai's municipal government, the fall of the Gang of Four might have been expected to bring other immediate major changes—but in fact (as part 4 of this two-tome book details) it brought surprisingly few. Not until the Revolutionary Committee gave way to a new municipal government, in 1979–80, did the structure or many personnel change. A 1983 set of shifts in the city government was at least as striking as anything that happened in 1976 or 1978. Yet much common wisdom concerning leadership changes is that vertically organized factions in the high state are crucial to everything. If so, when a powerful faction in central politics falls, as the Gang of Four did in October 1976, there ought to be obvious and extensive changes of administrators in their most important geographical base, Shanghai, especially since the top of the city government there has been demonstrably more central than local. Yet this did not happen.[35] What is wrong is not the history, but the presumption that the theory of extended clientelist hierarchy applies to all of it infallibly. Factions are not so hermetic or permanent as they are often described to be—especially by their members. The periods of their dominance become hard to determine, as individual participants are often able to hive off to other factions.

Political scientists, many of whom rely most heavily on government documents for footnotes, have been slow to stress how much the official 1966–76 periodization hides. Other scholars have suggested this, however, for their particular fields. Economist Barry Naughton, looking at state capital construction statistics over many years, has shown that the government put a truly startling portion of all its investment money (two-thirds of its total construction budget) into inland Great Third Front projects from 1964 to 1971. Naughton's references to 1964 rather than 1966, and to 1971 rather than 1976, cut across the official periodization with a blitheness that would be unthinkable without a straightforward approach to looking at behavioral time series.[36] Many tables throughout this book carry such time series from about 1970 to the press deadline. Watershed accelerations of reforms appear at least as frequently in the early 1970s, mid-1980s, and mid-1990s as they do near the official 1978 time. But numerical and economic data are not the only evidence for this reperiodization.

In the study of poetry, Bonnie MacDougall has retained the usual 1966 and 1976 dates but has also stressed the need for her fellow literary analysts to realize that subperiods within these ten years were crucial: a 1966–69 period of extensive violence, a 1969–71 transition, and a 1972–76 recovery.[37] More recently, sociologist Anita Chan has shown that conservatives after 1989 had a current political stake in obscuring the differences between the late 1960s and early 1970s.[38] Deng Xiaoping's very hard-line attitudes at many historic stages of Beijing politics (e.g., watershed 1957) may have prevented him from taking credit for having supported reforms before 1978—even for having done so in

1972–75, when he actually gained power in a period usually described as radical, serving for a while as de facto premier. The post-1978 top leaders of the Party kept the 1966–76 decade as the Cultural Revolution, and 1978 as the start of reforms, because this periodization saved for their own use what was left of Mao's charisma. It dated reforms to the year when their supremo Deng came to reign alone.[39]

The 1966–76 periodization of the Cultural Revolution needs to be rethought in many particular fields. For several kinds of behavior and attitudes, it is not obfuscatory. Many humanist intellectuals, repressed during that whole decade, understandably think of those years together. But the 1966–76 periodization must be reconsidered because it encourages presumptions that prevent making sense of data about many reforms in its latter five years. For specifiable kinds of behavior, the official periodization does not cover much of the historical evidence well.

A correlation of changes that is especially evident for 1971–75 in many Chinese spheres at once—notably including rural industry, state capital location, foreign policy, migration to middle-sized cities, fertility reduction, and media technology—will be set forth in various parts of this book. In some fields, e.g. in media content or in the treatment of high intellectuals, this trend may be identified but was very unstable. Sometimes it arose secretly, just in some rich rural parts of China, in the dark, or separately in different organizations. But few of these reforms served the long-term interests of the central Party elite in Beijing, even though some central leaders were often more reformist than many local leaders (whose interests in such cases usually prevailed). The government over time tolerated and then legitimated such changes, because they could not be stopped.

How can political reform be measured? It is possible to document behavior or decisions about many topics: new locations of major investments, lower defense spending, new industrialization in the rural economy that affected the daily work of millions, new links of trade or technical exchange between cities and countryside, shifts of military commanders, commercial support for the most popular media, somewhat expanded variety in newspapers and broadcasting, and even shifts among personalities running the top of the state. When these and much else all change together, massively and in some cases against explicit pressures coming from the state apparatus, then there *is* big political change—even if all top politicians choose to deny it, and even if lower ones have no interest in publicizing it or even conceiving it as a change. That is generally what happened in China from about 1971 to 1975 and then again at some later times. Because the power networks that most benefited were local and nonintellectual, the press seldom reported the political effects of these changes.

The baselines for measuring quantitative changes shown on many tables below might be questioned on the ground that data about quick economic and other changes in the early 1970s show only natural revivals after the Cultural Revolution. But *all* the reforms, including those after 1978, were in that sense understandable partly because of the Cultural Revolution. Furthermore, if the Cultural Revolution is deemed not to have ended until 1976, but if the important changes in the 1971–74 period are considered a reaction to it, then most of a cause has been put later than most of an effect. This would be logically awkward. Conservative and reformist forces have been in conflict in China for a very long time; in no period is either of them wholly absent. The periodization of 1966–76 for the Cultural Revolution and after 1977–78 for reforms obscures far too much behavioral evidence about Chinese politics both before and after Mao's death. It treats the Chinese polity as small, and it hides decisions taken by many Chinese potentates including local leaders.

Finally, geographical provisos must be added to the periodization proposed here. Most, though not all, of this book concerns the area surrounding China's largest city, Shanghai. Rural areas in Shanghai's delta had atypically early reforms, compared to most of China. And the economic reforms in central Shanghai (because of its role in China's fiscal system) were atypically late. This book does not argue that all China's reforms, *throughout* the country, began about 1971. By the same token, it does not argue that the Cultural Revolution ended uniformly everywhere. Instead, it argues that no single year suffices to date this change for all fields in all places—and that the effort to fix a date based on central politics alone hides dramatic shifts. In many areas, local forces for reform long remained much weaker than did local reactionaries. This was singularly true of Shaanxi province, but it generally applies to most of the north—and some parts of Shanghai.[40] The process of change shows far less homogeneity over space in China than the national government pretends. The Cultural Revolution, in some places and some respects, lasted for many years after Beijing declared it finished. Local leaders in those places remained conservative "leftists," opposing the new entrepreneurialism as a basis for wealth or power. But also, some kinds of reform began in many rich rural areas earlier than 1978.

Terminology can help make words match evidence better, so this book avoids using "Cultural Revolution" to describe the 1966–76 decade, instead using that phrase to describe the particularly chaotic period before 1970–71. It often refers to "reforms" in the early 1970s. Old locutions are used here in new ways, with apologies to readers familiar with previous habits, to highlight facts that have usually been obscured. China's reforms were political, not just more generally social. They occurred not just at the behest of state leaders, and not according to the official timetable. Their essential content was to change the structure of China's elites, making the central state less important and local networks more powerful. To proceed further, the word "state" needs a definition sensitive enough to comprehend both its institutional integrity and the fact that it is also a network of particular individual leaders.

Defining the State: Boundaries vs. Network Nodes

Americans tend to avoid speaking colloquially about "the state." Chinese, by contrast, show no such reticence. Even nonacademics refer often to the *guojia* (literally, "state-family"), by which they sometimes mean the ideal nation and sometimes just the official apparatus. The government, *zhengfu,* has an equally homely but exalted name, whose characters literally mean something like "rule-residence." The state is not the only institution that attempts to guide relations between people or claims legitimate authority over them.[41] But in China, it receives a lot of attention.

What is the state? Weber defined it as the institution claiming a monopoly of legitimate social coercion. There is at least one other kind of authority, that of parents over their children, that has a similar albeit more local claim. Actual coercion in a country as large as China is wielded by a great many different state and nonstate agencies. A variety of institutions, from gangs to corporations, can have coercive power that strongly resembles that of the state in immediate situations. Some of these employ force very effectively in the eyes of their followers, whether it is legitimate in high politicians' eyes or not.

State Networks and Hinge Leaders in a Postrevolutionary Context

How does the state relate to society? Some claim that "the definition of the state always depends on distinguishing it from society."[42] This seems questionable because society is a loose organization made up of others, including the state. The state may allege its monopoly of coercive powers, but this is no more than a claim, and the government is actually not unique in making it. At various times families, economic companies, revivalist cults, established churches, landholders' groups, secret societies, and other corporate groups have also assumed legitimacy for their ownership of any of the factors of power.[43] States often have enough force so that they can make their claims effective over many kinds of human action, of course; but there are other times, and other sorts of action, for which states do not even make this attempt, or do not succeed at it, or must be content with lip service to it rather than behavioral compliance. In revolutionary situations, a state's claims generally fail, so that another corporate organization begins to call itself the state instead. A successful new regime is soon recognized by other states—which have an interest in maintaining the same pretensions and so tend to recognize them universally. The extent of a state may be taken to depend on the effectiveness with which its claims are met, not on any essential difference between it and other corporate power networks.

This book describes an increasingly postrevolutionary situation in which the effective power of the PRC state leadership has contracted to a space that is less extensive than is suggested by the symbols of organization charts or public verbiage. Nonstate institutions in China are now extremely influential in structuring the state. They do this more obviously now than before reforms. Alfred Stepan describes the Southern Cone in Latin America, where several states in recent periods waxed far beyond the formal sphere of "government" and even beyond the task of setting relations between themselves and "civil society." They determined "many crucial relations within civil society as well."[44] The Chinese state did that increasingly during the early years of the PRC, reaching a level of influence outside the boundary of its regime more than has probably ever been achieved in most Latin American nations, or in most countries elsewhere. But since 1970, the Chinese state has had less success in structuring relations among nonstate power networks; the contrary has been more usual. The level of such power is hard to measure, but the trend of institutional change is easy to show. "Bringing the state back in" to studies of democratic societies is highly appropriate, since the state's autonomous role there is greater than official ideologies pretend. This emphasis is also fine for state organizations whose resources are expanding quickly, e.g. during high tides of centralist institutional revolutions.[45] But the PRC now faces quite a different situation; it is a country whose government regularly overstates what it can do. Its nonstate networks are quietly—without admitting as much—shaking off the heavy imposts and influences of a centralist regime. The present book is not subtitled *Kicking the State Back Out,* because that idea could never have been more than an analytic. It could not possibly have been something that happens always in all states. In China now, it happens to be exactly what de facto nonstate institutions have begun to do.

Authors tend to use the word "state" differently when they treat polities in different kinds of transformation. When the state's role is effectively expanding, they wish to show that its influence is broader than its chartered boundaries. When it is contracting, they can stress that it does not even control all the actors who are nominally its minions. These differences of word usage can highlight the political realities they describe. And they highlight that the boundary of the state must be found in behavior. Legal formalities do not set it.

Just as the tide of China's revolution, peaking about 1969, expanded the boundaries of the PRC state in many ways, its ebb beginning in the early 1970s sporadically pushed back the effective boundaries of the state. The Chinese government had failed to do much ordinary decisional work for a long period, while the Cultural Revolution and its aftermath disenfranchised many of its most highly educated bureaucrats. This phenomenon showed many diverse aspects: a backlog of good students who could not take university entrance exams until 1977, a backlog of ordinary civil cases for which street mediation had failed to satisfy the parties and for which real courts and judges subsequently were needed, an acute need to recruit better staff (and to remove labels such as "rightist" that kept many competent people from government work), a loosening of controls on shack construction to meet the pent-up demand for housing, more jobs for the ex-rural youths who had returned massively to medium-sized cities in the early 1970s, and many other specific governmental tasks. The official 1978 onset of reforms was the state's announcement of an intention that it would again begin to mind shops it had neglected for many years.

This was not the main substance of reform; it was a reactive and belated admission by central authorities that they had an accumulation of problems to address. Especially in the economic sphere, local authorities had already taken over many responsibilities. Hua Guofeng, no less than the radicals who preceded him in Beijing, was sincerely uninterested in many practical functions of government. Police control, especially of cultural opposition, occasionally fascinated Hua and his predecessors. But many economic matters they had often left to others (e.g., Deng Xiaoping during his partial mid-1970s comeback)—or to no one at a high level. So the shift of 1978 was in many spheres not so much a change of policy in Beijing as a hopeful assertion that there should be a policy in Beijing, that the state should marshal its resources to perform practical functions it had neglected.

By that late date, many cats were out of the bag, because local authorities had already assumed many roles the central government had only haltingly tried to perform after the mid-1960s. High state leaders had no obvious choice but to acquiesce, especially when they knew the Cultural Revolution had debilitated their ministry staffs so badly that they could no longer monitor compliance with many kinds of orders they issued.[46] This reaction by officials had to be presented in public as proactive: a new policy of derogating power to places and to markets. It was said to result from the 1978 wisdom of the new leader, Deng Xiaoping. But its impetus did not come from politicians in Beijing, most of whose particular interests it disserved.

National leaders, like most other people, think states should be coherent hierarchies. A state, properly speaking, is a unified organization. Although a coercive network that is recognized but not controlled by central leaders might be called a "local state," it is (nearly by admission in its name) not part of *the* state. The state is the central government elite whose glue holds. In China currently, that is the high state, and it does not include every cadre.[47] To define everyone with an official title as a member of "the state" in China today would violate that very concept. This book uses the word *local* to mean *nonstate,* with the understanding that nonstate entities come in many small and medium sizes.

The polity in socialist China has at least two layers: government cadres, and cadres outside government. Among China's eight million cadres in "leadership strata" (*lingdao jieceng*) during the early 1980s, only 11 percent were actually in government offices. Fully 68 percent were in enterprise units above the workshop director level, and 21 percent were in the CCP and mass organizations of towns, streets, and rural units.[48] The vast majority of these leaders were only nominally part of the state. They had great political (not just social) prestige, and usually they were Party members. There is a great deal of circumstantial evidence, however, that Leninist discipline failed to constrain most of them as thoroughly during reforms as before then.

An old debate among China scholars concerns whether most PRC collectivities are coordinated or cellular. Audrey Donnithorne wrote a 1972 article entitled "China's Cellular Economy," and many other authors have stressed the extent to which rural leaders have tried to protect their communities against impositions by higher levels of bureaucracy.[49] Still others have stressed that rural leaders are both "agents and victims" of administrative superiors.[50] Many Chinese organizations, some as high as the province level, have increasingly resembled "parastatals."[51] These institutions are power networks like the state, and they are also related to the state. Their leaders have two constituencies: a more central network and a more local network. They are best discussed as "synaptic" or "hinge" politicians, who are not completely beholden to either kind of network but maintain their positions by adjusting to both.[52]

These local hinge leaders are related to national state elites in some ways but remain autonomous from them in others. Comparativist Joel Migdal refers to them as "key switchmen," on whom the success of any party-state depends.[53] Actually, local leaders are important in all regimes, not just those with Leninist parties. Their resources can explain much about the career of any central government, as its influence ebbs and flows in comparison to that of their own networks.

The old metaphor about the state as a collective Leviathan or quasi-human body is too similar to the new story about strictly individual choices with which rational-action theorists would replace it. Both tend to underestimate the separate importance of midlevel leaders and the structures they create. These chiefs make decisions, individually but for collective groups that are not the whole regime. In a postrevolutionary system, especially a polity of China's size, metaphors about hinges or synaptic gaps can capture more information than either a whole-group or an ideally individualist approach can capture alone.

Hinge leaders have chances for great personal power, but they also risk personal shame. There is an old "paradox of power" in China. Traditional respect for teachers, for example, is balanced by other traditions that make these high-status individuals subject to collective norms—and vulnerable to public humiliation.[54] Top-down authority in China is largely wielded by "selectocracy," the choosing of local leaders rather than detailed or continuous central oversight. Bottom-up authority is largely wielded because local officials, thus selected, can by themselves decide any issue on which they can bargain a sufficient local consensus.[55] As Cultural Revolution politics richly illustrated, however, these powerful agent-and-victim leaders are subject to painful criticism if they fail to meet the interests of their more and less stately constituencies. Hinge leaders are especially important after peaks of revolutionary violence (e.g., in China about 1969). They gain experience in periods of postrevolutionary decompression, even if they do not appear prominently in expressive politics until later. In Russia, under the conservative Brezhnev before 1980, a midlevel official in Stavropol named Gorbachev or another in Georgia named Shevardnadze could try reforms and build their networks for years quietly, without challenging the still-conservative Soviet state. In China, too, midlevel leaders seldom announce themselves just as soon as they begin to achieve political positions.

Theorists mooting the "claim of coherence" by states have written: "Whether it makes pragmatic theoretical sense to impute interests, expectations, and the other paraphernalia of coherent intelligence to an institution is neither more nor less problematic, a priori, than whether it makes sense to impute them to an individual."[56] Sometimes states act coherently; often they do not. There is no need to adopt an analytical framework that would guarantee, before research, a neglect of data about either case.

State Network Capacities and Nonstate Networks' Capacities

The term "state capacity" is often used by political scientists, but qualifications have to be made about both these words when used in real situations. The polity can be a set of fragmented networks led by many hinge leaders, when it takes so lanky a form as in the PRC. State capacity apparently involves a search for evidence of occasions in which designated high state leaders have their way against resistance from other networks. So the state is defined in terms of its coherent leadership, and capacity by evidence of effective uses of power. When both these conditions become less salient, as is demonstrably the case in reform China, then state capacity goes down—but that analysis does not tell about the networks that partially take over as more capable. It does not tell how to evaluate these substitutes.

How should a decline of the state be appraised? Wang Shaoguang and others see "state capacity" as "the ability of a government in getting its jobs done."[57] Following an old functionalist tradition, Wang uses terms that subdivide these abilities into "extractive," "legitimative," "coercive" and "steering" capacities.[58] A regime can try to define its job narrowly when its resources decline—as is the situation in reform China. But people at large may not accept this redefinition. So when would a decline of state capacity be good, and when bad? This question is usually not asked, with the result that the statist answer (such a decline is always bad) is assumed true. A plausible answer would depend on whether such a change helped or hindered large numbers of people to realize both their collective and individual potentials. On that premise, it would be right to cheer a rise of state capacity under some conditions (perhaps those that precede revolutions) and to cheer its decline under other conditions (e.g., in China's reform, after coercive centralization had earlier harmed the capacities of many nonstate groups and individuals).[59] Traditional functionalists, and others such as Samuel Huntington in the late 1960s, put so much stress on order as a value, they would almost always view a rise of state capacity as good. A new version of this approach, however, could consider small groups and individuals too, specifying the conditions under which a decline of state capacity might benefit people.

A strong state, according to Stephen Krasner, is "one that is able to remake the society and culture in which it exists."[60] A tall order! No such state has ever existed. If cultures were somehow measured as relatively statist or not, then Chinese social traditions despite their mixture could show that nation to be notably statist in comparison to other countries. Of course, the national government has an interest in maintaining this legacy. Governments, like many other institutions (families, churches, schools, labor hiring organizations), are strong enough to have some influence on social culture over time, but none can "remake" it in a span short enough to allow for any serious notion of their political will. Stalin's state from 1929 to 1953, the likeliest contender for the title of going furthest in this direction, acted along with Russian tsarist and fatalist traditions, an external invasion by the German army, and other contingencies not designed by Stalin to make his changes. Mao's state was less strong in comparison. Most others are weaker. Political scientists need not be swept away by the claims that ambitious leaders make, even when state chiefs actually do have some effect.

The main recent news from China is that the state's extractive capacity, in particular, has plummeted relative to that of other political networks. But that does not mean *all* offices in China, taken together, receive less obedience or real revenue than they did prior to reforms, only that central ones do so. Local and central public budgetary and extrabudgetary funds, summed and then considered as a portion of the national income, rose slightly at least during the middle reform years: from 41 percent in 1967–77, for example, to 45 percent in 1987–89. So it might be argued that the "public" sector expanded then. But the central state budget, as a reported portion of all government levels' budgets and extrabudgets, decreased sharply between these two periods, from 50 to 28 percent.[61] More of the "public" sector by this measure became local, particularist, and less fully public.

The effective boundary of the PRC state is a band somewhere inside the limits of the formal administration. This band has moved during the whole reform era, but it fluctuates over short time periods and in response to immediate problems. As Dorothy Solinger has written, "Any differences existing among the elite as to how great a role to accord the market dissolved, when state power and state capacity to dominate the management of state assets and revenue were challenged."[62] The top elite was in agreement on this point, although their consensus was often countermanded by the interests of more local elites. A great deal of evidence shows a long-term decline in the reform state's capacity to control local notables and maintain revenue. This pattern can be phrased in the classic form of behavioral power: The state wanted and ordered one thing, local networks apparently wanted another, and the local thing is what generally happened. There were exceptions in particular places and at some times, but the overall pattern is clear.

Joel Migdal emphasizes the importance of ideal as well as material factors when he describes state capacity as a power to "penetrate society, regulate social relationships, extract resources, and appropriate or use resources in determined ways."[63] Theda Skocpol approves the Tocquevillian view that "states matter not simply because of the goal-oriented activities of state officials. They matter because their organizational configurations, along with their overall patterns of activity, affect political culture, encourage some kinds of group formation and collective political actions (but not others), and make possible the raising of certain political issues (but not others)."[64] States certainly try to do all this. Government leaders would have everybody believe that they alone possess such powers. But the motives of officials are insufficient evidence of what they can do. In practice, the state never has a monopoly over other groups that form, issues that arise, or the culture that is inherited or imported to undergird local politics.

Nonstate power networks in China now demonstrably perform many of these roles. Universities, upholding hoary traditions among Chinese intellectuals, have in practice provided bases for "some kinds of group formation and collective political actions" in city squares, protesting the state elite's incompetence and rapaciousness. The upsurge of rural entrepreneurs has made possible "the raising of certain political issues," for example concerning materials flows. As Skocpol suggests, analysts can also look "more macroscopically at the ways in which the structures and activities of states unintentionally influence the formation of groups and the political capacities, ideas, and demands of various sectors of society."[65] By the same token, other networks also structure the state. Often these powers were first created by the state, but with surprising frequency they come hurtling back at it like boomerangs. The unintentional effects of official methods of organization have had big repercussions in PRC history.[66] Now that nonstate political networks have increasing capacities, their intended and unintended effects on the state also must be parsed.

In China, the trend that more concrete resources go to nonstate networks has been furthered by an ideal norm that the state could not possibly be weak. For example, as Solinger notes, the central government undertook "reform as merely a *means,* a set of tools to be manipulated in the service of a few fundamental and statist ends: the modernization, invigoration, and enhanced efficiency of the national economy, and its consequent heightened capacity to boost both productivity and returns to the central state treasury."[67] This is true, and the results were not uniformly the intended statist ends. High government coffers during middle and late reforms received fewer of China's resource flows than in Mao's time, and high government leaders garnered somewhat less public respect than before. The benefits of heightened productivity and new organizational ideals have gone mostly to local power networks and not to the larger state. Presuming it is possible to exclude any argument that state leaders had an elitist kind of false consciousness, which might cause them to act against their own interests, the likeliest conclusion is that they indeed conceived reform as a means to serve statist ends—but they were wrong. The tool did not fit the task they intended. An equally relevant viewpoint would be that of the actors whom the reforms' result demonstrably strengthened, i.e., local leaders. This approach may redefine reforms, though it does not deny either that state leaders vainly hoped reforms could strengthen the CCP regime or that many local norms (not most situations) throughout the Chinese polity remained profoundly statist.

Reformers among PRC high politicians—i.e., those willing to have new entrepreneurial experts bring fresh blood into the political elite—nonetheless had to justify their policies as helping the state. For example, new bankruptcy laws, had they been enforced, would have reduced drains on the official budget. Sales of stock from nationalized firms, similar sales of housing, and enterprise mergers were all supposed to streamline the efficiency of the government-owned sector. When they first appeared, these policies often proved to be hopeful announcements rather than implemented laws. It may not greatly matter whether such measures were conceived as statist or whether Western journalists generally mistook them as individualist. When norms are not effectively applied, their ambiguities become moot. But in the short run, "the capitalistic measures being injected into or, perhaps more accurately, overlaid atop the administratively planned state owned economy in China are more apt at this stage to take on the features of that old system than to remold it."[68] Similarly, Leninist policies for electoral reform partially reconfirmed, rather than reformed, the nondemocratic system.[69] Reform was not just marketizing, and certainly it was not Western; but the growing powers of this time were nonetheless outside the state.

Some analysts of China have done much good work debunking foreign presumptions about the reforms, but a danger in this emphasis is to underestimate the extent of changes. Other scholars have stressed the breadth of institutions that have the capacity to affect top politicians' resources and policy outcomes. David Bachman finds the origins of investment leaps in the politics of large bureaucracies, not just the whims of top leaders.[70] Avery Goldstein says the PRC's hierarchy before 1966 encouraged "bandwagoning" strategies and ideological cooperation, while the Cultural Revolution's anarchy encouraged "balance-of-power" strategies for survival against rivals.[71] The same institutional and structural logic that makes these approaches useful can be extended to show the long-term effects on the Chinese state of the evolving political networks outside it.

Intentions and Situations in a Structural Definition of the State

Defining the state has been a problem in political science ever since legalistic explanations gave way to accounts that were more behavioral. Especially in the 1950s, analysts tended to stress the state's functions, and to seek a "boundary" between state and society sufficiently clear to be used in research. This trend, which Gabriel Almond and David Easton especially led, tended to account for most of the state's traits ultimately in terms of external social forces. By the 1980s, Theda Skocpol and others "brought the state back in," stressing its autonomy from and direction of other structures. Recently, a postmodernist critique has rejected both these trends, preferring to treat the state "as an effect of detailed processes . . . which create the appearance of a world fundamentally divided into state and society. The essence of modern politics is not policies formed on one side of this division being applied to or shaped by the other, but the producing and reproduction of this line of difference."[72]

Problems can be found in most proposals for finding a sharp line between state and society. If "society" is what overthrew the old Communist regimes of Eastern Europe, it certainly included a great many "state" cadres. In this book, they are more simply called local leaders—and are treated as political, not more vaguely social, because of their power. They are called local no matter what they may commonly say of the state, and no matter what high state bureaucrats may commonly claim of them. Clearly the state is an institution, but the old legalistic definition caught only its formal aspects. Functionalist definitions captured some similarities between the state and other decision-making institutions, but many such theories still suggested the state was essentially different from other structures for "goal attainment." Early works "bringing the state back in" also stressed the special resources that might tend to give the state a special autonomy to shape politics. Recent postmodernists claim that the state is not an "actual organization" but instead an apparent "structural effect."[73]

This book takes another approach to the definitional problem, drawing on each of the traditions outlined above but accepting none of them wholly. First, there would be no way of studying the causes of any political reforms without looking at their ecology and internal correlations, and even a flexible version of that procedure is unavoidably functionalist. Second, following the institutionalists' tendency, the definition of the state used here is that of a concrete structure—that is, an entity most easily specified in terms of its members (and sometime members, including "hinge leaders" who connect it to other concrete structures), even though functions are not the same as structures. In this approach the state is not just an analytic construct, even though its definition of course requires attributes.[74] Third, the interpretive approach takes facts about intentions seriously; and to answer the questions here about China's reforms, there is no good reason to discard intentions as potential causes. So:

1. The state is a group of people with corporate interests, holding together to the extent their order is enforceable. They try, sometimes unsuccessfully, to confirm this order by all means, even though they never have a full monopoly of the ideal and concrete resources to do so. Only for these purposes is the state a legal institution; its formal organization is not its definition.

2. The state performs social functions, making some decisions—but it is not the only agent for attaining goals.

3. The state claims exclusive rights to some kinds of resources and legitimacy, and this claim almost always makes it a powerful actor in politics, not just an emanation of other social forces. But many sources of goods and prestige are held by other powerful actors that collectively may constrain the state. (This could also be taken as an empirical, not a definitional, issue; the autonomy of the state is never total.)

4. The state has interests that induce it to nurture outside of itself a "cultural nexus of power."[75] It fosters habits that require politics to be studied far

beyond formal state institutions—but other powerful institutions in society also breed norms to their advantage, and the state is not so omnipresent that it can control them all.

The point of using such a definition is not to find that all of society penetrates the state as often as vice versa, but to explore how extensively specific kinds of *political* networks interpenetrate each other. The boundary of the state is likely to be drawn, at any time for any issue, through medium-level leaders, most of whom serve both the government and other groups too. The state cooperates and conflicts with alternative powers.

Divisions solely within the government elite can lead to official statements and ready evidence for footnotes. On this basis, scholars sometimes imply it is sufficient to look only at state institutions in order to see political change. The issue of which power institutions need to be examined, and which do not, is simply a matter of where the analyst decides to stop asking questions. There is no method, before reconnoitering, to say where that should be. It would be marvelously efficient to know in advance that large classes of potentially germane data were actually irrelevant to a causal sequence in politics. Despite some efforts and many claims, nobody has come up with an a priori procedure to be sure of that. The path chosen here, which looks into byways not far beyond power networks, is institutionalist; but it looks broadly, because its subject (China's reform) provides evidence widely from many kinds of networks. For smaller questions, less circumspection might befit.

The state is being pushed back out of many Chinese situations where it had more power before the 1970s. But the PRC state remains puissant in many fields of action. Any other possibility will scarcely occur to China scholars, who tend to err in the opposite direction, suggesting with footnotes the government kindly provides that no other powers exist there. The Chinese state is certainly not becoming a cipher for other institutions—any more than they are for it. It seeks maximum independence, and its search for autonomy during the reform period has often fallen short of success. But this is not to say it is withering away, has no spirit or resources of its own, or fails to recruit at least some new elites in hopes of maintaining itself as a mighty corporation.

The state is sometimes strong and sometimes fickle, always important, but not nearly so autonomous or unified as its propagandists claim. At different times and places, its policies vary. Many of the state elite's possible constituents are pleased by the growth that comes from diverse people trading efficiently. Others are pleased by controls on market depredations against human time, the environment for people, and citizens' earnings.[76] These two groups' policy interests conflict, whether or not they are articulately organized. This difference between espousing market efficiency or socialist control crosscuts the differences between central and local actors.

Leaders thus decide substantively different basic policies in different places and different administrative levels. Large coherent programs are difficult to plan officially, despite a widespread patriotic sense that China should have them. "A consensus must," as Lieberthal and Oksenberg write, "be sought both vertically and horizontally in the system. Lower level units have important resources they can bring to bear, and wide-ranging efforts are therefore made to strike balances that permit each major actor to support an effort or project with some enthusiasm."[77] The state includes China's preeminent leader, the few elders who second-guess his policies (including top military commanders), ministry heads, and other leaders of major agencies in Beijing. The state often extends fairly far beyond this group, but there is some evidence that local officials as high as provincial governors occasionally have views that differ from the central mainstream. At low administrative levels, "the state" can become a now-you-see-it-now-you-don't organization. In the public language of officials, ideals of hierarchic order are widespread; so an analysis of language alone would suggest that the state permeates all Chinese society from the top. But especially in practical matters of resource allocation, the central state's purview is recently becoming more limited. Even in cultural matters, the PRC government in reforms has haltingly become far less influential than its predecessors. Rumors of the state's demise in China would be distinctly premature. Old states do not die; they just fade away or change forms.

Defining Power: Lions vs Foxes, with Local Synaptic Leaders in Both Groups

What evidence can be presented to show that a person is under the influence of the state or is acting alone? The standard behavioral definition of power, which provides the best means to answer this question, explicitly includes both situational and ideal elements. Robert Dahl puts it famously, because algebraically: "A influences B to the extent he gets B to do something that B would not otherwise do."[78] It is often difficult to know the intentions of either leader A or follower B. The subjective wishes of these lettered gentry are, however, as essential to whether power has been exercised as is the behavioral datum about what B does.

This definition of influence—B does something only because A wants it—becomes especially problematic when A (e.g., state leadership) is not lucidly consistent on what it wants. This also runs into problems when B (e.g., local leadership) can react to unintended situations created by what A wanted previously. Furthermore, top leaders in China have often made ambiguous statements, presumably because they were of two minds. This can occur even at times when there is no solid evidence they are divided into two policy factions.

Examples from some fields are particularly rich, e.g., concerning top Party leaders' alternating policies toward intellectuals. Scientists during the Cultural Revolution often had been excluded from the ranks of "the people," but as Deng Xiaoping put it in a 1978 speech to the National Science Conference: "We must give full play to democracy and follow the mass line, trusting the judgement of scientists and technicians in such matters as the evaluation of scientific papers, the assessment of the competence of professional personnel, the elaboration of plans for scientific research, and the evaluation of research results."[79] CCP leaders in reform moods have sometimes acted like "foxes," to use Machiavelli's and Pareto's metaphor, recruiting talents that could increase Party resources and legitimacy. The same Communist elites in other phases have been conservative "lions," as when Deng Xiaoping in late 1989 claimed that, "China's problem overwhelmingly is the need for stability. Without stable circumstances, we can do nothing, and we also will lose what we have achieved."[80] Changing mandates from central leaders led to flexibility for local ones. As a foreign analyst has written, "When the principals are divided, the agents can get away with more (as every child knows)."[81] When a dominant principal is undecided or unclear, local captains take charge.

Top reformers' policies have often let things run their course, without much direction. A slogan helped to justify this: "feeling for stones when crossing the river" (*mozhe shitou guohe*). Zhao Ziyang, propounding rural reforms, was said to advocate a policy of official ignorance toward illegal or unauthorized local innovations. This too was sloganized as the "Four Don'ts": don't publicize unofficial reforms, don't oppose them, don't support them, and don't stop them.[82] Such a laissez-faire approach was implicit in many directives reaching local leaders, who could in practice often do whatever they wished. Insofar as reform came from the top, it was not a coherent policy even though many politicians suggested otherwise. Every aspect of it can be quite fully explained, from the evidence, as part of a diverse array of justifications for short-run accommodations to farmers, intellectuals, workers, and local networks whose support or neutrality the reform state could use.

At times of political crisis, divisions between conservative lions and reformist foxes were obvious in all political jurisdictions, including the central state. During the student demonstrations of May 1989, for example, Politburo member Li Tieying at one point characterized the student movement as "good and patriotic," so it should be "positively assessed." At the same time, he said it had a "negative impact on the dignity of the country."[83] Like everybody else in the world, China's leaders often have second thoughts. Power is easiest to ascribe to them when it is clear what they desire, but their need to maintain the Party's integrity conflicts directly with their need to recruit more talent for the regime as the revolution winds down. What they want is systematically ambiguous, along this dimension.

Uncertainties of state policy might embarrass China's top leaders more if public discourse did not attribute nearly supernatural subtlety to them. Their dicta are always reported in China as inherently wise and powerful. In January 1990, Deng Xiaoping toured Shanghai "to underline his support for the open door policy." During his normal winter vacation in the metropolis, he tarried at a high-technology factory involving American capital, giving "personal instructions" to speed up reforms.[84] Again in January 1994, Deng was seen by tourists at the new wing of the Jinjiang Hotel; he took an elevator up its tower to survey the city from on high.[85] Is this why Shanghai developed? It is not the only reason. Individual leaders such as Deng or Mao have some effects, and the state has an interest in obscuring the extent to which they are constrained by circumstances they do not control.

Influence, by definition, implies the possibility that B might *not* do what A wants. Postmodern radical thinkers have pushed this option to stress that potential resistance is not just the test of power (in either electricity or politics); resistance is also an inevitable trait of the concept. Capability is always against something, and that thing is potentially strong too. As interpreters have written: "Foucault holds that power needs resistance as one of its fundamental conditions of operation. It is through the articulation of points of resistance that power spreads through the social field. But it is also, of course, through resistance that power is disrupted."[86] The possibility of resistance, as those algebraic folk A and B teach, is essential to the idea of power.

Articulation, despite Foucault, is not essential to it. The analyst may need to know A's and B's wishes in order to tell when influence has occurred; but if they remain silent, it may still happen and only the social scientist is out of luck because it cannot be proven. When local powers in contemporary China merely evade the state's influence without resisting it in public, they weaken it just as surely. The prime example is rural industrialization—the most crucial of all China's reforms. Rural factories are giving sharply increased amounts of resources to networks led by kinds of people who have seldom played a role in that country's politics. These are mostly nonintellectuals who are able to prosper in localities—so long as they do *not* confront officialdom symbolically. This evolution is political, but it is not usually seen as such because most analysts tend to define political change as if it always implies large new ideas, organizations, and spokespeople. As Piven and Cloward have written, "the effect of equating movements with movement organizations—and thus requiring that protests have a leader, a constitution, a legislative program, or at least a banner before they are recognized as such—is to divert attention from many forms of political unrest and to consign them by definition to the more shadowy realms of social problems and deviant behavior."[87]

Synaptic Captains and Traditional Authority

"The key relationships are vertical relationships," according to one analyst of Chinese politics. "Society remains segmented along vertical lines, and within each vertical segment most relationships are inherently unequal."[88] Even so, vertical lines go in two directions. Leaders at each level are affected by people who usually follow them, not just by the ones who try to command them and to whom they practically always give verbal obeisance (no matter what else they do). A realistic paradigm is presented by G. William Skinner, who shows that the strength of any hinge leader in such a hierarchy depends on how convincingly that local chief can represent subordinates to superordinates and vice versa. The intermediate captain's status in each realm, one administratively high and the other low, depends on how well that synaptic leader can control and deliver the other constituency.[89]

The traditional Chinese state did not perform most functions using its own employees. Instead, it authorized local agents to collect taxes, run waterworks and granaries, and round up criminals. Payment to these helpers, and even to formally appointed magistrates, was mostly unofficial; the agents could rake off compensation informally. Major mandarins were rotated from place to place. Their courts' permanent local helpers, who included many not formally affiliated with the state at all, were important holders of power over most people. In the twentieth century, especially after 1950, the state recruited its own agents more regularly. Task brokering had been usual for so long, however, that it was difficult to eliminate that pattern. Distinctions between state and nonstate employees had long been fuzzy, and they did not suddenly become clear under communism. The collective sector, by the 1970s and 1980s, was the main inheritor of these ambiguities.

The PRC has depended on hinge leaders for years. University administrators were supposed to keep intellectuals in line—while urging scholars to explore ideas freely. Farm leaders paid grain imposts—while arranging for peasants to retain enough. Editors tried to report the news—while not reporting so much that the weaknesses of the state would show. Planners had to reduce the state's wage and benefits budgets—while nonetheless trying to assure workers that the "proletarian dictatorship" would ultimately put workers' interests foremost. Managers tried to send the government taxes and state profits—while investing against deterioration in their factories, loss of their markets, obsolescence of their technologies, and discontent among their workers.

Such leaders became the officially designated patrons within their local units. To create large and powerful political organizations in a modern setting, however, patronage proves inadequate. Span-of-control problems bedevil a boss who wants to maintain a very large number of direct relations with clients. So patrons use intermediate power brokers. As in their traditional form, these hinge mediators are not just clients; they are simultaneously clients and patrons, and that fact gives them some autonomy. Their patrons owe them resources and prestige for the work they do among their own followers. These local constituents owe them resources too; as proper middlemen, they naturally take a generous cut. They are dependent—but in two directions, not one. They are loyalists to two kinds of masters. If they manage affairs sufficiently well for both the boss to whom they allege unswerving fealty and for their own constituents over whom they allege constant protection, they can gain great wealth and autonomous power.

This is all very traditional in China, but it is a more subtle structure than neotraditional Leninism describes, for at least three reasons: First, it shows bidirectional authority, both top-down and bottom-up; it makes the distinction between who commands and who obeys an empirical matter that deserves research, not a premise that structures behavior. Second, this approach makes no assumption that positive incentives in either direction are more effective than negative punishments. Again, it is necessary to look at data before deciding whether carrots trump sticks. Third, it is an ideal type, an analytic predicate only, which does not exclude the possible relevance of charismatic totalism or legal-rational pluralism.

The main theorist of Communist neotraditionalism in China says it creates an "extraordinary ability to prevent organized political activities ever from reaching the stage of collective action."[90] But parallel activities, growing out of similar local situations, can together be more powerful than a Leninist party. As Zhou Xueguang argues, "The institutional structure of state socialism reduces the barriers to collective action, by producing 'large numbers' of individuals with similar behavioral patterns and demands that cut across the boundaries of organizations and social groups."[91] The state tries to prevent autonomous organization—but it cannot prevent interests. The state may unintentionally strengthen nonstate power networks, when its leaders use Leninist precepts to strengthen just their own state networks. Truly traditional and local institutions increasingly reap the rewards of the modern resources and communications patterns that the centralist revolution generated earlier.

Collective action does not always involve public expressions. Power, properly speaking, is not restricted to its openly articulated form. The opposite view suggests a unique role for the articulators, who are largely intellectuals. While a stress on the political importance of morally educated people is certainly traditional in China, there is now a divergence between that legacy and most actual politics. State patronism, organized at high levels by individuals with a considerable amount of education, is slowly giving way to many other forms of political organization. Local patronism, based on really traditional authority, is prominent among these, but there is also more mixing of different types of legitimacy than prevailed earlier, under Mao.

The Leninist state in China after 1970 failed to prevent many political activities that eroded its basic interests. Practically all Chinese people have constantly avowed the regime's legitimacy. Local cadres tend to hold a sincere view that the best administration must always come from the state.[92] This was, of course, their job, but it was also their belief. Local synaptic leaders think of themselves as part of the state, as well as protectors of their places. But they widely ignore the regime's mandates in practice.

Basic-level offices of the central state are now harder to fill than they were before reforms, because business enterprises and local posts bring more rewards. The courts, and sometimes even the police, lack enough resources to do their jobs. Taxes are commonly evaded, so that the national budget is in the red. The neotraditionalist state's capabilities have become far less extraordinary during the reform era than they earlier seemed. The quiet power of diverse local networks has remade China's political structure. Unarticulated parallel collective actions have eroded Communist neotraditionalism as a tool of the government.

At the same time, local leaders not only swear allegiance to the central state. Some of their actions complement it. Power and revenue are not zero-sum.[93] They are especially flexible beyond the short term. The number of jurisdictions should also be expanded beyond just "the center" and "the provinces," since China is not merely a two-tier polity. Families, lineages, villages, townships, and counties have also been very important for specific purposes. Only allocation over all sizes of jurisdiction, on an immediate basis, has a finite sum. Long-term resources are expansible. "Parasitism" by local networks on the state is a topic of much recent study, and it is a real phenomenon.[94] But the state is also parasitic on local authorities for taxes, and on familylike styles of authority for legitimacy. There is mutual parasitism between different sizes of political networks. There are mutual relations between relatively central and local units that strengthen both at the same time. This pattern is no more like parasitism than like symbiosis.

Top-down assumptions about authority often do not fully account for the resources of clients. For that reason, they have trouble reporting reforms. Similarly, "agency theory," as used by economists to study the conditions under which agents serve principals, tends to take a legalistic view of interpersonal links that are often fluid and political. Such a theory neglects actors who are simultaneously agents and principals. Hinge leaders, who are patrons in one context and followers in another, succeed in each of their constituencies to the extent they simultaneously succeed in the other. Agency theorists could expand their view to deal with this very common type of politician.

There is nothing uniquely modern or traditional about such captains; they are familiar in many kinds of organizations. "Synaptic leaders" have been studied in Thai and Lao villages, for example, "between the local community and the state, under pressure from both and mediating the interests of both." Even in contexts that are barely modernized, the "articulation of interests frequently involves replacing a single multi-purpose synaptor by specialized or competitive synaptors, or by individual accessibility between national and rural persons."[95] If the kinds of decisions that need to be made become more specialized, such captains adapt, to justify their powers. Small networks remain important, as do their chiefs no matter what kind of authority they mainly use.

In sum, concepts such as "local autonomy" or "state capacity" are best put in perspective by the older idea of power. Autonomy can be the power of a network to resist interference from others, and capacity is the power of a government to implement its policies. These are the same thing in different guises. Neither, however, fully suggests the onionlike structure of bands formed by the state and surrounding networks. Boundaries between the state and other networks are everywhere uncertain, because hinge leaders serve both at once. Many in practice disobey what state bureaucrats decree, e.g. by hiding production so as to avoid taxes, while swearing symbolic allegiance to the government. State capacity and local autonomy are alternative concepts that suggest quite simple tests, unlikely to capture all the resourcefulness among leaders.

Chinese Reforms vs. Communist Neotraditionalism

The structure of local leadership is often discussed in terms of hierarchic dyadic relations between single patrons and their clients. The role of Communist precedents imported from the USSR, and the role of the state in creating patron-client links, has been stressed to the point of minimizing the role of centuries-old Chinese habits in creating these results. There are many problems with this paradigm, if it is understood to rule out alternative analyses:[96]

- To the considerable extent that patrimonial authority organizes the behavior of individual Chinese, it remains difficult to prove that Communist/Leninist neotraditions, rather than Chinese old traditions, are the basis of patronist behavior. It is often possible to show what the state did, but it is not easy to explain whether actors followed Communist or fully Chinese traditions when they acted as the patrimonial model would predict.
- Not all authority relations in the PRC take the patrimonial form, even though many evidently have done so. Charisma has been powerful in the Maoist past, and it remains more important on both the national and local scenes than is often appreciated. Legal-rational norms are increasingly effective; nothing inherent in China, as compared with many countries that have strongly antirationalistic mores, prevents this trend. Totalitarian charismatic campaigns and legal categorizations of people into labeled status groups have been crucial motivators of events as large as the Cultural Revolution.[97] Patrimonial-"traditional" authority, personified by monitoring bosses, has also been endemic—but not exclusively so.
- Neither China nor Communism can be accurately identified with any single authority type. There are charismatic and legal-rational aspects of *both* the imported Leninist and the inherited Chinese old-traditional forms of organization. These aspects are "ideal types," different but not fully exclusive of each other, partially concurrent adjectives rather than nouns.
- Not all Chinese interpersonal networks are hierarchic. Many market relations (though not all, despite market theory) are horizontal. Often in China, people who are not at the top of nominal administrative hierarchies are powerful informally. When formal rank structures can be found, they may not necessarily correspond with the arrangement of real influence.
- Not all such networks in Chinese politics involve exchanges of a patron's

protection for a client's positive obedience. Some networks (e.g., among intellectuals) almost exclusively exchange social prestige. Others (among businesspeople) trade economic commodities. Still others (e.g., between PRC pop stars and their young audiences) are involved in very symbolic interactions whose content can be wholly normative and antihierarchic. These networks come to affect politics, even though their origin is not in power relations.

- Each authority type creates negative (not just positive) incentives to political action. In charismatic campaigns, activists make their careers, but also their targeted victims have often been scared and punished, suffering negative sanctions against later dissent. In patrimonial monitoring, subordinates who like their assigned bosses follow any instructions that come down, but also subordinates who dislike their bosses store up negative reactions until these have a chance to explode (as, for temporary reasons, they did in August 1966). In legal-rational labeling, members of interest groups with politically good names appreciate the affirmative action that favors them, but also those with negative "hats" combine to change the system. The sanctions created by each of the three authority types can be both positive and negative.
- There is finally the problem of China's size. Explanations that rely on logics of individual rational action, in patrimonial dyadic links only, work best when the leader and the followers know each other face-to-face. For a country of more than a billion people, this atomistic model needs considerable refinement if it is to go very far. It is especially useful for describing small collectivities, but these operate in broad contexts of many kinds of power networks. Patrimonial factions nest inside one another, and the notion of local "hinge leaders" developed here is an attempt to make the model of traditional authority, to the extent it applies, applicable to an environment in which any individual has contacts with only a tiny portion of the whole loose system.

Under what conditions do midlevel leaders, who are simultaneously patrons to some and clients to others, follow their patrimonial heads? Under what conditions do they evade the wishes of authorities "above" them and instead serve the interests of their own clients? If local leaders have two positions, as leaders and followers simultaneously, how do these roles relate to each other? Skinner has suggested the answer.[98] His topic may at first seem far-flung: the "captains" of traditional Southeast Asian overseas Chinese communities. These were simultaneously leaders of all local Chinese but also agents of the state bureaucracies in Spanish Manila, Dutch Semarang, French Phnom Penh, or by extension Bangkok in the 1950s. The "paradox" of leadership in these places has a logical form that is very useful for describing the links between nested factions in the PRC: The top Chinese local leaders usually had titles of nobility in the traditional courts, and their authority to run their own group was enhanced by the regard shown them in the state.[99] But at the same time, their credibility with the government depended on their ability to deliver their followers.

If the regime above a synaptic leader imposed too much (e.g., levied unreasonable taxes), it could easily destroy such a leader's position; then the state could end up hurting its own ability to benefit from that community. If a leader's constituents were openly rebellious toward the government, on the other hand, his position could also be ruined in that way. Preventing these dual dangers could lead to great prosperity. If the hinge captain could keep both his larger-community and smaller-community associates reasonably satisfied with each other, he gained legitimacy and wealth from each, because of his position in the other. If he was a sufficiently competent agent for each side, he would become a victim of neither.[100] A hinge chief had always to be Janus-faced, faithful not just to the government but also to the local network—which in any behavioral sense was also "above" him in power, because discontents there might gain the potential to destroy him politically.

In China, the hinges between networks are not usually ethnic, but political. Their "layers" or "levels" are many (these words are inexact because they suggest a different, vertical dimension) in a country of such extraordinary size. Communications are unreliable, so "higher" levels often do not obtain comprehensive information. There are political, not just technical, reasons that prevent a full transfer of information, as Susan Shirk has suggested.[101] Using a very different approach, Prasenjit Duara has described early-twentieth-century Chinese local power brokers, who are similar to these hinge captains. Duara describes China's "cultural nexus of power." Follow-the-leader ethics are certainly strong there. The high culture serves the high elite. This "cultural nexus" is a style of talking and writing that does not, however, inform all action.[102] The cultural nexus of evasion is also commonplace. Hinge leaders practically never have an interest in challenging their official patrons openly; on the contrary, the language they speak is exquisitely patrimonial. They in practice can nonetheless avoid behaving in accord with the wishes of these nominal higher-ups. Not all effective morals come to hinge leaders from a single source, not even from a Leninist party-state.

Authority during reforms has become more localized. First, small-group and family enthusiasms have tended to displace charismatic claims from the recent state leaders, many of whom have been rather uninteresting sober technocrats. National charisma, campaigns, and normative compliance were means of political organization before 1970; the substitute for them during reforms is a mixture of other normative interests in fields ranging from pop music to religions, but now no longer so often led by the state. Second, local patron-client groups have become collectively more important than the centralized Leninist party. More immediate petty tyrants, mindful of the power of the state but wily enough to maintain new exploitative powers of their own, have tended to supplant officially organized boss-monitors and centralized coercion or incentives. Third, allocations based on coordinated market entrepreneurship have taken over at least somewhat from the allocations that Mao's state tried to rationalize through class labeling, despite the strength of habitual connections that the socialist state fostered. Some utilitarian compliance has been created by price changes even in very imperfect markets.[103] None of these alterations is total, but each is a trend for which later chapters provide more evidence. State authority of all three kinds has been on a slippery slope down from its peaks in the 1960s, and local authority of all these kinds has partially replaced it.

This book will adduce data to suggest that, although the future destroyers of China's neotraditionalist Party will almost surely emerge from within its ranks (as they did in the USSR), the behavior of local leaders, who are the crucial people in contemporary Chinese politics, is not mostly neotraditionalist. Following some inherited Chinese and legal-rational modern political habits, and often enjoying a great deal of quasi-charismatic prestige within their own networks, these local leaders have already deeply undermined Leninist centralization. Neotraditionalism is explicitly presented as exclusive of other analyses, which parse different data and show weaknesses in the patronist state. When the Communist Party of China frays in public or is replaced—as will happen eventually, perhaps within a decade or two—the narrowness of this paradigm will become even more obvious.

The Strength of Local Leaders as a Revolution Ebbs

"The weak" are not *just* weak.[104] There is no need, when studying them, to focus on minor political results (crop stealing, Luddism, sullen attitudes) rather than on events that affect the structure of politics as a whole. In China during the Cultural Revolution, the "weak" damaged not just each other, but also important political elites. In the reforms, they have together been strong enough to enfeeble a Leninist state. Their attack on it continues so endemically that its future is, even in the private views of some high Party leaders, in considerable doubt.

Local leaders in this situation do not just engage in "infrapolitics" (as James Scott calls it).[105] Power in small collectivities is as effective, in the long term, as power in the national government, which has more obvious coercive sanctions. Networks are a more useful object of political study than is power conceived as merely centralized or decentralized, supra- or infrapolitics. Networks come in many types. Some are vertical; others, horizontal. Many networks exchange protection and sustenance for obedience and service; others exchange commodities or reputation. They can be isolated or widely connected. Some are official; others are not. Links between people and groups, as described by networks, are institutions that frame most exercises of power and also serve many other human purposes. It would be difficult to study politics while ignoring these platforms in which they are based. Organized horizontal relationships between networks were hardly new in China before reforms came, and they are not necessarily modern in any country.[106] But nonstate networks, both productive and corrupt, have expanded rapidly during reforms. They might be said to engage in infrapolitics; but if so, the bottom certainly constrains the top.

Actually, hinge leaders occur not just at "low" levels in the Chinese system, but throughout it even at top echelons in Beijing. Key leaders represent their sectors in high councils, standing for whole ministries and systems of agencies.[107] "Supreme helmsmen" such as Mao or Deng do not always control agencies as high as ministries in Beijing, and the main aim of nonstate leaders is not overall social efficiency, but usually the mobilization of more resources they can control: "The local, provincial, and even ministerial bureaucracies which own these firms are not concerned about the rationality of the state economy as a whole, or about profit maximization. They are concerned about input and revenue maximization, and job creation within their own bailiwicks."[108]

Some analysts emphasize that "the government" supports reforms. High reactionaries, however, have also been evident. The government is increasingly disjointed, and low-level officials spur reform policies that benefit them—even if many local leaders are also thoroughly tyrannical reactionaries in their immediate contexts, to preserve their local status there against rivals. Victor Nee makes a complex statement suggesting this tension: "Because the socialist state is the *primary* organizational actor in initiating market reforms, the *voluntary* compliance of middle- and lower-level state officials and functionaries is necessary for the successful completion of reform policies."[109]

Among local leaders, there is no agreement on the rate at which new blood should be recruited into the CCP elite—but localists may tend to be slightly less conservative about new recruitment than centralists, because the Beijing politicians have already made the official grade. Central states should be "brought back in" to explanations of politics. The PRC state is nonetheless permeable, lanky, and thoroughly co-opted by diverse interests that command resources including coercion. Local politics have now deeply penetrated the Chinese state, not just vice versa. Smaller networks also need to be "brought back in" to analyses of postrevolutionary politics.

Defining the Public: Ways of Speaking vs. Ways of Acting

Central PRC networks have attracted nearly exclusive attention, mainly because they are articulate. When political scientists look for power, they show an odd inability to conceive it separately from eloquence. Politics, in this overly narrow view, requires open utterance. Widely expressed norms and symbols are too often taken as necessary for power to exist. The only tale to tell is supposed to be the choice between political wills that are recounted in public. Hidden transcripts are the business of "the weak"—they become the hallmark of feebleness. Only open transcripts are seen as possibly strong. The myths of the weak may be human and thus fascinating, but they are thought to be fundamentally inconsequential for real politics. This book will try to show, however, that in China's reforms inarticulate power has been very strong.

Causation is implicit in every use of the word "power": a leader's desire causes a follower's action. Since the desires are intentions and the result is behavior, ideals and situations are equally essential to the very idea of power. Although this concept involves cause and effect, it does not necessarily involve articulation. The follower often guesses what the leader wants. In that case, the leader's power is as sure as if the orders had been shouted in public.

A state leadership presumably intends to benefit itself; the alternative premise, that it might intend to hurt itself, would be dubious. So proof that the state's influence is decreasing requires evidence that its interests are no longer served as well as they once were. Its intentions are no longer very effective. *When local networks gain at the expense of the central elite, proof of the change does not require evidence of local opposition to higher authorities, open or hidden, articulate or not.* It only requires behavior that actually weakens the state. There is no need to show the existence of an organized, self-conscious opposition—or to show that the local leaders' intentions were rebellious. Usually they are loyalist. Nonfulfillment of the central state's interest is sufficient to show that central intentions and resources are unavailing. The issue is clearest when put in terms of networks. The Chinese state has plenty of voluble friends, but that does not solve all its problems.

Who makes new institutions? What networks or groups? What kinds of enthusiastic or reliable or other leaders? If "the people" are the makers of new institutions, then who represents or speaks for them? Have the people decided who they are yet? Who can claim to represent them? Cultural or modernization hypotheses are usually proposed as answers to these questions, but the results can often be boiled down to findings about the relative powers of specific leaders in identifiable networks. Intellectuals, of course, like to become spokespeople for "the people"—but it is unclear which intellectuals can legitimate their rule. Political entrepreneurship, ideologies in Leninist or national traditions, international influences, and many other factors have their effects, but all through a mechanism of political strife. That is how institutions are built. Samuel Huntington is only the most prominent of modernization theorists to have shown that institutional development is not automatic.[110] He and others (in both the functionalist and Leninist schools) tend to sideline the main question: Whose interests are the institutions built to serve? In China, there has been a tendency for establishment intellectuals, in practice, to answer this question with platitudes about the people—and with offices for themselves.

No matter whether in local villages or in the Forbidden City, Chinese leaders now come to terms with a greater variety of people than they did before reforms. Yet the immediate implementers of this change have wreaked it with very little political articulation, scant demand making, no obvious ideology, and minimal publicity. It would be inaccurate to speak of China's high state and local networks as conflicting openly, except on rare occasions. But there are cracks (and very unusually, Tiananmens) in a structure that was better cemented before. Gaps can structure power quietly, as surely as loud protests can. Networks during reforms can often simply avoid higher levels of the state. They do their own things and co-opt low state agencies for their own purposes. They detach themselves from the hierarchy rather than challenge it. Ways of talking are habitual; these alter more slowly than ways in which people deal with concrete situations. Discourse and behavior can be separate.

Hinge leaders practically always avoid political articulation. A Chinese economist, for example, explains why PRC local managers evade laws rather than protesting them:

> Subordinates find they can benefit from hiding the information on the extra output obtainable from assigned resources; and for them, collusion becomes a better strategy than competition. [The] prohibition of organizations or groups independent of the state . . . requires inconspicuous and informal collusion, and this makes collective action emerge more slowly than it otherwise would. However, as time goes on, more groups of administrators and enterprise managers are able to collude. . . . They engage in rent-seeking activities, lobbying, and bargaining for the increase of resource allocation to their domains.[111]

These politics are not publicly articulated—they are secret—but nonetheless they are politics. They are a matter not of ineffective or hidden transcripts, but instead of mute behavior that leaves no verbal transcript but is nonetheless strong when many networks act on the basis of parallel local needs.

Most discussions of reforms do not address such quiet politics directly, although Richard Madsen does: "The interpretation of illicit memories is segmented. It takes place privately in relatively small groups shut off from communication with other segments of society, even those that might be sympathetic with the illicit interpretation. . . . Such means of communication constitute 'restricted codes,' accessible only to persons deeply familiar with the conventions of a particular culture and the habits of a particular social circle."[112] Actually, China has many such persons. They do not have to act with words, nor in public, nor together; but they have powerful public effects.

Most transcripts of consciousness are not hidden, they are overt—and if they were not, we would lack some evidence of them. Most are not defiant, but intentionally obedient even when they weaken hierarchy. Consciousness in any case is not the only factor behind action. Resources, not just notions, shape what people do. Such politics are very common in societies undergoing reforms. Hankiss, writing about Hungary, describes a "second society" that developed around the "second economy" and performed all the functions of the "first economy"—but unofficially and underground. Production, communications, socialization, political interactions between groups, and all other functions occurred in unopen forms, not just official ones.[113] This activity was hidden, but it was not just symbolic and certainly not weak.

Some theorists suggest that weak groups mainly wield two threats: to riot, or to ally with disaffected elites.[114] Insofar as political strength is defined to be measured as central, immediate, and expressive, this approach might be fine. But insofar as strength is local, long-term, or concrete (not just in the formal state, short-term, and symbolic), the power networks of the poor can constrain the political elite without open threats of expressive riots. The state may simply become less relevant to local situations. This is now the Chinese pattern, and it represents the greatest political challenge the Party regime there has ever faced. So much strength was not really expected from the people.

The most passionate expression of the impossibility of serious political change from the bottom comes, oddly, from Karl Marx. He described French peasant support in 1852 for the protofascist Louis Bonaparte with famous words that echo Chinese peasant contentment with local and central dictators: "Insofar as there is merely a local interconnection among these small peasants, and the identity of their interests begets no unity, no national union, and no political organization, they do not form a class." So, "they cannot represent themselves, they must be represented. Their representative must at the same time appear as their master, as an authority over them, as an unlimited governmental power that protects them against the other classes and sends them the rain and sunshine from above."[115] Never has tyranny been recounted so lyrically. But that is a clue to the problem: This explanation is based on ideals only. There is nothing substructural or situational in it whatever; it is all about consciousness alone. Change can occur from "small peasants," but not because they become so eloquent as Marx.

Peasants and ex-peasants may represent themselves inarticulately, not as an intellectual would, and the best bet is to assume they are conscious of their interests. Their collective actions, often concrete and nonsymbolic rather than matters of transcripts, can severely constrain high rulers. Individuals can have a collective political effect without intending to do so.[116] The problem with peasants is not that they have a false consciousness making them want to disserve their own interests, but merely that their many resources for political struggle sometimes act more slowly than those of the state.

Reducing an organization's resources, thus weakening it, can be a totally mute act. Exit does not require any explicit protest.[117] In many organizations, power is wielded by people who leave without voicing a word. The remaining members may be forced by this quiet act to do things they would not otherwise do, because they have fewer resources. So if political influence is defined by behavior, exit can be an act of public power. Staying out of the public purview and creating organizations that are officially sanctioned but not officially controlled is a very common stratagem of local leaders. When official actions involve traders heavily in politics, for example, business leaders seek new organizations linked to more malleable, often lower-level cadres. State rules have often politicized private firms; so businesses then develop suborganizations to use the state and to distance themselves from it.[118] A frequent reaction to state intervention is to avoid official bureaucrats entirely, rather than to participate in politics and create better public rules.

Intellectuals tend to overrate articulation. Most people are less interested in being able to say anything they want, especially after periods of revolutionary violence. Freedom of speech was important to urban Chinese by the early 1990s—but this mainly meant freedom of *private* speech. Intellectuals recalled how gossip during the Cultural Revolution, when told to find somebody to "struggle" against, had brought up trivial charges on the basis of minor verbal indiscretions about Mao or the Party, with results that were painful. People want to know they will not be attacked because of small talk that might nonchalantly disregard state leaders.[119] But many Chinese urban people frankly oppose full press freedom; when asked, they say they want the government to control not just pornography but also expression that could harm stability (*wending*). Civil society with articulation is not the main political aim of many who are relatively tongue-tied. But privacy, "freedom of the individual" in families and in local settings but not in public, is high among their demands for liberty.

Public speech is also overemphasized in debates between scholars who think China is becoming more pluralistic and those who suggest the nation's traditional authorities may prevent serious change. When can one say that a polity is becoming more diverse? The common answer has been to look for conflicts, openly articulated in state institutions, especially in legislatures and among bureaucratic agencies. If that is the test, China has scant pluralization. But that approach is very idealistic in two senses: First, by stressing conscious articulation, it neglects conflicts over resource arrays (for example, tax evasions) that can show real pluralization without spoken conflict. In China, this usually proceeds comfortably alongside vows of fealty to the state. Actors can be conscious of their infractions, forbearing to justify them publicly, while pluralization begins in a behavioral and realistic sense. The government does not mind "interest groups" (*liyi qunti*) so long as they are brought nominally into the official "system for social consultation" (*shehui xieshang duihua zhidu*).

The premise that political conflict must be articulated also neglects most pluralization between central and local state employees. A realist has to acknowledge that leaders in different jurisdictions may act against each other. They have often done so in reform China without losing their jobs. The official PRC bureaucracy is now so ungainly and multihinged, it makes little sense to seek Chinese politics in terms of a simple "state-society" cleavage. Pluralization exists within the state.

Yet another way in which articulation is detached from politics arises from the Chinese norm that some dissent is legitimate in groups presumed to be unimportant. Women, minority peoples, denizens of low-revenue places or firms, many who live outside large cities, and especially the young often can protest more safely, for a while at least, than older, urban, office-based Han men. This pattern is not unique to China. Symbolic inversions, Saturnalia, *Holi,* carnival, and other ritual rebellions are not generous grants from hierarchs. They legitimate articulation, but such expression is officially supposed in advance to be politically unserious and flaky. It may certify the low-power status of the merely ritual rebels. These traditions nonetheless reflect the interests of people who suffer abuses, and not just insults of a symbolic sort. Such rituals can have big political effects in the long run, especially when they do not satisfy the motives behind them. They serve the established elites, if they "let off steam" among people who are usually subordinate. They are politically safer for elites than are real rebellions.[120] But they show the lay of the political land, and they are not wholly innocuous to leaders. Scott, dealing with such symbols, does "not mean to imply that carnival or rituals of reversal cause revolt; they most certainly do not." Ritual rebellion says something without fully saying it yet. It shows that, even when a meaning is political and can provide means to shape behavior, articulation can be held separate from intention for a long time.

Youthful rebellion, for example, may become politically serious, as the Chinese government found in 1989. After the May 20 declaration of martial law in Beijing, a number of Shanghai university walls were graced with "Hang Li Peng" and "Hang Deng Xiaoping" graffiti. Students drew uncomplimentary cartoons of these notables, including recurrent sketches of Li Peng captioned "China's Hitler," and pictures of nooses.[121] This unusual time of bold expressions did not last long. Such expressions were sometimes presented, and more often read, as juvenile or naïve. By early May 1989, an elderly Shanghai tailor remarked to one of his clients that "ordinary people" (*lao bai xing*, the pre-Communist term) were not too concerned about the students and "all that."[122] Many Shanghai residents were sympathetic to some dissent, however, and sensed some of their own long-term interests in what the tiny intellectual minority was doing. Others, such as suburban entrepreneurs and immigrant workers, had less official fish to fry more quietly. Eventually, these all will affect the political structure of China along with intellectuals' ideals. Many inarticulate people in Shanghai at this time were pleased to have youths pointing out that the government could be better.

Publicly organized interests in China are all supposed to be parts of the state's apparatus. As Zhou Xueguang says, "If interests are independent of the state, they are often unorganized."[123] This slows the political effects of such interests—but does not stop them, because even the inarticulate know the state does not represent everybody. Ralf Dahrendorf describes "quasi-groups," including but not limited to classes, that have latent interests. These are large, quiet, unorganized bunches of people from which "conflict groups" (which have manifest interests and are easier to study) are recruited.[124] The interests of "quasi-groups," which appear often in reform China, are difficult but not impossible to know. Their concerns can be figured from circumstantial actions, more often than from statements by their members. These are not conflict groups, openly demanding power. Large, amorphous congeries of people emerge from geographical links, occupational similarities, institutional habits, and common ways of spending leisure. They arise from state and nonstate power networks in all sizes of collectivity, from patterns of action motivated by memories (including memories of conflicts they do not wish to repeat), from the human uses of new technologies, and from other sources. Open political articulation is not a requirement either for the political structuring of groups into networks or for their political power. China's main reform is that networks have become better articulated locally, but usually on the basis of new resources for politics, not on the basis of new political symbols.

Defining Rationality: Political Causation and Circumspect Evidence

Curiosity about major events should not require as much defense as it currently does in social science. Physicists waste little time arguing about method; instead, they "do physics" and find knowledge (*scientia*). Hypotheses are made and evidence is adduced. Concepts with which data seem inconsistent are discarded only *after* empirical research is done. Analysts have hunches and tastes, of course; but good method is not determined in advance. It comes ultimately from substantive conclusions that are sustained by observations.

Social scientists, by contrast, too often follow various metaphysics. The first question that many of them now ask about any study is not whether it tells them more about its ostensible subject. Instead, they first want to know whether its data are mainly about the contexts in which people acted—or alternatively, about the intentions or institutions of the actors. Most political scientists and practically all economists now prefer studies of the former sort; many anthropologists and historians prefer the latter. Both groups tend to insist that these two kinds of information, both of which are available about social phenomena, cannot easily be combined.

This leads in practice to the study of relatively small topics—or of large topics mainly by inference from research about, say, a specific village or a particular kind of market. Microthink is the trend of the time. Indeed, in atomic physics, molecular biology, or materials science it often proves fruitful. The premise that large phenomena merely sum many small phenomena is an interesting analytic idea. The present book uses that logic when trying to show how the personal interests of local Chinese leaders affected the content of national reform. But the premise that large phenomena shape smaller ones is also interesting. Questions about big congeries were usually the topics that inspired atomism in the first place. Why is the sun hot? How does life grow? What causes a revolution? What ends a revolution?

The search for reasons behind major events is basic to science. As we shall see below, causation is a dubious interest both among some scientists who want to talk about correlations in contexts only, and among some others who want to suggest that meaningful stories are always noncausal. A current mainstream view in political science, often called the rational-action approach, calls for thought experiments that show how individuals, whose preferences are assumed prior to research, react to their external situations. This approach is best for explaining small, immediate interactions, but it can try to make sense of large events by showing that they are a sum of what should be theoretically expected from many such reactions. To the extent that the motives for conduct, as suggested by the thought experiment (the model), are credible, the large event may be caused by smaller ones. But the word "cause" is seldom used so boldly—often it is avoided altogether—since even very strong correlations between predictions and observations do not prove causation fully. Causes are nonetheless implicit, even when speaking about them is hedged.

The present book explains many aspects of China's complex reforms as unintended consequences arising from individuals' reactions to contexts. It is not mostly about the nation as a whole, but is rather about its parts (especially local networks); and it is not mostly about ideals rather than contexts. This book's argument for local and circumstantial factors as causes of China's reforms is not held as a premise prior to research, however. Small-scale and contextual factors do not always explain everything best, even if they do quite well with China's reforms as documented in many parts of this book. The argument here is offered as a conclusion from many kinds of information gathered widely and circumspectly, not as an a priori research design to look at some kinds of evidence only.

The "methodological individualist" fad in political science is arguably just an ideology. The stress on individuals seems suspiciously liberal (very American, perhaps not currently very Chinese), moralizing against the power of hierarchic groups that impede creativity. Also, the claim that external situations determine ideas and political wills eventually, so that proper analysis should always look to contexts rather than intentions, could be characterized as smug about the future and dispassionately middle-class. The current author, if he were forced to choose, would surely prefer these biases for atomism and for contextualism as against their alternatives. But there is no need to make this choice. The premises are not science, not knowledge, only analytic methods that may aid findings. They provide useful tools for investigation. So do opposite emphases, on large collectives and on habitual norms.

There may be valid *psychological* reasons for social scientists to pay particular attention to individuals and to unintended contexts, but these are not logical reasons about the validity of arguments. Recent work in biopsychology suggests that humans tend to use certain means of cognition to perceive intentions. They use other specifiable means to perceive unintended facts. Evolution has not inclined our brains to think easily, without special training, about the interactions of objects that lack minds. We tend to be naturally better at thinking about our and other people's ideas than at contemplating other situations.[125] But this is psychology, not epistemology. It is no excuse for confining social science either to human meanings or to situational interactions only. Taking the latter approach might make researchers seem more specialist, less like ordinary mortals. But it would not be a convincing reason for scientists to throw out data about actors' intentions, which are useful for building knowledge, just because those were garnered on the basis of similarity between the researcher and the objects of research. Discarding such data would be as arbitrary as taking the opposite commitment, current among many anthropologists, that directly conveyed human meanings are all we can ever understand. The contextualist method may, for psychological reasons, add more to what most readers know, but that does not make it a way to know everything more surely.

There may, further, be valid *political* reasons for social scientists to pay particular attention to small-group and individual contexts, since governments stress large groups. But again, these reasons tell nothing about the validity of arguments. Leaders of state regimes, not just in China, have "bully pulpits" from which they propagate data about the large collectives they purport to lead. Often they use explicit or implicit sanctions to further a highly groupist viewpoint. So social scientists may add more to what most readers know if they instead offer information in individualist categories, which the most ardent suppliers of data, national elites, are unlikely to stress.

These two reasons are not silly. They explain why explanations that stress contextual and individual factors often seem more novel and interesting than explanations that stress intentions and large groups. Perhaps researchers can, in fact, spread knowledge most widely, if they hold informal biases against stressing ideal/habitual/cultural data and against stressing data about collectives. But the arguments for such biases are *psychological and political, not epistemological.* They concern the ways scholars and readers can most comfortably think; they do not concern any inherent superiority of the contextual or individual approaches, as compared to the cultural and collective ones. Nobody has found an epistemological "smoking gun" showing why either situational or individualist methods trump their opposites in the scientific search for knowledge. Considerable effort has been spent in this project, and several arguments aiming at that goal have been fired off, but none has surely struck its mark—apparently because none can do so.[126] Science is knowledge, not more, not less, and not just by etymology. People who want knowledge do not exclude data before examining them for whatever they can do to provide knowledge.

The irrationality of researchers, not the rationality of actors, is the main basis of the fad for "rational action" as an exclusive approach to social study. Local and concrete explanations actually do often add to previous knowledge more than explanations based on well-known intentions or large collectives. Individualist and situational narratives are often interesting—not because they can be better certified by any uniquely correct epistemology, but only because collective propaganda and researchers' familiarity with intentions previously obscured what the microcontextual approaches can show.

This book argues that local and concrete factors, not just large-collective and ideal factors, have been crucial causes of China's reforms. So this author is sorely tempted to jump on the bandwagon of the rational-action clique in academe, which sometimes forbears to disdain writers about exotic places if they stress concrete microfactors, even if they do not spell out the rules of a unified theoretic game. But I will join them gladly only after they see that scientists' blinders, not actors' rationality, is the basis of the interesting substantive results they sometimes can claim, and only after they stop ostracizing social scientists who study collective and intentional causes. All thoughtful area specialists, including those who study that really inscrutable country, the United States, are in the latter group. Above all, the rational-actionists might become aware that findings ultimately validate method, not vice versa. There is no way surely to know that any particular kinds of data offer the best account of an event until after the opposite kinds have been explored too.

This book's finding, after research, will be that contextual (rather than ideal) and local (rather than collective) factors are mainly responsible for China's reforms. It is meant to balance, not negate, what earlier writers have averred along other lines; and despite its compatibility with rational-action premises, the method here rejects these as assertions to be accepted in advance of empirical work. The four main parts of this book, shown in the table of contents, are generated by crossing the distinction between contextual and intentional evidence with the differences between small and collective actors.

Valid evidence for causation comes as norms, not just situations, and from collectives not just individuals, since each of those four categories implies a need to check its opposite. Maybe most readers who are interested in China rather than method can intuit, without need for further notes, the circumspect method whose genealogy in social science is presented below. They could move directly to more specific material in the next chapter. But since this approach needs a defense against narrower fads, that can be can be made most economically by means of a diagram. (See pages 58-67)

The diagram provides a way of showing the directions of change during reforms, while providing the opposite logical categories that need to be explored equally. The reader may ask: Why bother with all these abstractions? Why not just tell what happened? The answer is that, in order to tell what happened and to test whether the tale is relatively true (rather than a relatively arbitrary fiction), a researcher has to check out alternative stories systematically. An exhaustive field of types of hypothetical tales can be generated from the individual or collective traits of subject actors in hypotheses, and from the intended or unintended bases of predicated actions or traits. So any well-defined proposition immediately suggests three alternatives (or more, if time or space or other dimensions are added in a more complete treatment). What the abstract framework does is to test different accounts.

The main two dimensions suggested here generate four types of human motive. People may act because they individually feel the action is right irrespective of results, because of collective intended habits, because of external uncoordinated rewards to them, or because of coordinated powers they cannot control. Only the last of these types is a simple situation of authority, but it is a type that may be concurrent with any of the other three, which are respectively called charismatic-normative, traditional-coercive, or rational-utilitarian by theorists such as Weber or Etzioni. These three motives do not always involve authorities, and certainly not always the state. In respective order, an individual might act or pray for wholly personal reasons, or might act from a socialized "force of habit," or might trade in a horizontally structured market for private gain. These motives do not exclude each other, nor do they exclude concurrent political motives. Authorities, e.g. the state, often try to shape these reasons for action from outside, thus politicizing them. The reason why Weber's three authority types exhaust a field is that they classify the three other motives with which collective-external powers involve themselves.

Political reform in China, for example, can plausibly be explained because individuals believe charismatic leaders have insights on truth, because traditional-clientelist leaders can find ways of putting together reliable groups, or because individuals respond to new sets of external incentives rationally.[127] The involvement of authority is what makes these motives political; so the internal structure of state power in particular is a fourth source of reform. The four main parts of this book are, for these reasons, broadly suggested by the four quadrants on the diagram below. The two dimensions of the chart (along with the dimension of time, which is used to organize many subsections below) provide a way to ensure that factors which might cause reforms are covered comprehensively.

No activity, however, is wholly "in" any sector. Data presented in any part of this book are different from the analytic categories used to order their presentation. The aim here is to cast all four nets, to see what fish they catch. This research framework may seem elaborate—and to account for such a large political event, it must be very circumspect. The reforms are a major historical process, involving many state and nonstate political structures together. To explore a syndrome of this size, lasting for more than a quarter century already, the net for data must be cast widely.

Any statement involves a concrete nominative subject, to which an analytic predicate is attributed. Social descriptions involve people, so the concrete subject is some individual, or perhaps a small network, or a medium-sized or large structured group. This is often called the "level of analysis," although it is actually concrete rather than analytic. The subject is what the predicate purports to describe, and justifications of two main sorts—norms or contexts—are the main kinds usually adduced to validate attributions. These are, of course, not the only possible dimensions of analysis. Time is always important, too, and it interacts with these two dimensions, as they do with each other. Nonhuman factors are included in social science as they operate through people. When the predicate attributions are causal, they include a direct object, the effect.[128] Causal and noncausal descriptive predicates are otherwise very similar.[129]

The size of collectivity that is the subject in a social proposition cannot be left vague without making the proposal hard to test. So a continuous spectrum from small to large collectives is a natural way to categorize evidence about the concrete part of such a claim. This is a central dimension of social science. The other main range is analytic: the types of evidence to confirm predicates. These might be sorted in a number of ways—for example, by the time from which the evidence was taken or by its location in space—but the most usual sorting concerns an emphasis either on the motives of human action or on the context in which action occurs. Some predicates refer to habitual norms, and others refer to unintended situations. Unlike the concrete dimension, this is a dichotomous and analytic difference, not a spectrum.[130] It certainly does not exhaust all the types of things one might wish to say about a social subject; these two types of predicates do not even exclude each other (as sizes on the concrete dimension do). But this distinction between meanings and situations is the hardiest perennial, the main hang-up of epistemology, and a help in organizing information. A method is worth only so much as it lets us find. In this attempt to discover the bases of China's reforms, a circumspect approach is more promising than a narrow one.

Causal Circumspection About Norms and Situations

A cause is a condition that leads (by itself or with other similar factors) to the occurrence of another condition. Individualists, especially rational-actionists, tend to hold that "there is no collective entity underlying a social practice—no occult system of mores or traditions—that causally interacts with individuals." Despite this, "the reality of social customs, norms, mores, assumptions, worldviews, habits—practices, in short—is too compelling to be seriously doubted."[131] Rational-actionists, reluctantly affirming this much, join many humanists in conflating things that are different. Groups are not intentions, and separate persons are not situations.

Humanists, on one hand, sometimes complain that seeking causes is their anathema. Many anthropologists find social life so complex, they prefer to seek only typical symbols, customary options, among which people may freely choose. These cultural humanists stress the need to leave theoretically open all the alternatives that people can select, while at the same time seeking patterns in these alternatives, showing that their formal traits may echo each other in various fields (political styles, kinship structure, ways of handling wealth, and so forth). There is no need for consistency between the symbolic options—in fact, these choices are most useful to people when they are alternatives. They have survived as cultural elements for so long exactly because of their inconsistency, because of their flexibility for meeting varied problems in the past. Care in the project of understanding is taken by humanists as a higher goal than consistent clarity.

Many humanists suggest that positive social science, to which their rival "naturalists" aspire, is downright immoral. Some anthropologists practically claim it is illegitimate, an insulting slap in people's faces, to study anything unintended. Using natural-science methods for social subjects requires the analyst to construct testable hypotheses, including notions that the alien researcher created (and is thus sure to understand clearly).[132] But findings tainted by imported premises can support, and in Third World development projects have actually supported, coercive policies to manipulate people. The culturalists emphasize the problems with this pattern. And in the process, they neglect another need that their moral perspective should really require: There is no way to see how cultures change, or why people choose some options rather than others, without looking for causations. Not all predicates are causal, but some culturalists say they want to exclude causal predicates from interpretation. The results of action are nonetheless important to people. The purely aesthetic forms of postmodernism miss this meaning.[133]

A diametrically opposite complaint comes from "naturalists," e.g., "rational-actionists," most of whom doubt any interest in circumspection. Many of them say their only aim is to seek causes. They posit predicates about subjects, often neglecting the origins of their terms (which are cultural). Then they seek facts that test the extent to which these propositions are confirmed or rejected. These would-be natural scientists, who study social topics, want to downplay information that comes directly from their subjects when they are building their models, for the sake of explaining at least some things with stylized simple preferences. The aesthetic behind this is minimalist.

According to this line of thought, because social scientists hope for objectivity, they must throw out any analytic categories that smell of their objects of study. They must allow empirical research on external evidence of behavior only, positing preferences as theoretical premises that are so basic, there should be no need to depend on anybody to confirm them. Naturalists prefer to trade relevance for clarity; they tend to be satisfied with the most flimsy of hopes for real-world relevance, so long as the thinking remains "formal." (Their culturalist academic rivals do not, actually, have a formless method.) They prefer to sell vivid realism for logical neatness. Despite many efforts, nobody has found an a priori way to prove definitively that such a trade, in either direction, is always wise. Both unconstructed facts and constructed norms are usable evidence in explaining politics especially.

Each of these methodological positions seems zesty, providing the basis for much intellectual combat.[134] The arbitrary willfulness of both, however, becomes evident because strict adherents of either school find themselves unable—when dealing with any actual situation—fully to follow their own principles. Culturalists need objective evidence that conveys the subjective meanings of the people they study, and behavioralists need humanly significant categories with which to ask questions about objective effects. Both groups try to obscure these needs by developing learned reasons to ignore phenomena shown better from the opposite perspective.

Causal arguments are not satisfactorily handled by either of these two approaches. Dogmatic naturalists, especially rational-actionists, are oddly equivocal about causes. They want to stress that the only way to show a cause-and-effect relationship is to model a situation without reference to the (presumably) unscientific notions of the people being studied. Only professionals versed in naturalist techniques of modeling can, they say, even begin to suggest causes. Culturalists, in particular, cannot do so; this inability is claimed to be a fault of humanist interpretation, which naturalists say they can happily solve. But when these same naturalists are pressed to show any specific case of causation, they waffle. They stress that such proofs are strictly unavailable. Scientists should really talk about correlations, not causations. There is never any way to prove surely that a purported cause and effect do not both, together, result from some further factor that researchers have thus far missed.

The culturalists, stylishly retreating into whatever thatched hut or ivory tower is handiest, claim they were never interested in causes anyway, only in other kinds of predicates. Both these sets of claims are rife with inconsistencies. First, culturalists can and often actually do construct causal interpretations, because their subjects are very interested in causes. Second, the culturalists' good moralism about caring for people can be served only by their own knowledge of what causes benefit or harm. Third, naturalists ultimately have to agree that many of their concepts come, after all, from the actors being studied or from similar characters; even mathematical operations do not come from nowhere. Fourth, the idea of correlation is ultimately no more presentable than the idea of causation. These two links may differ from each other, but not even correlations can be shown absolutely, since there is no way to prove beyond a shadow of doubt that the instruments used to gather data did so with the full scope and accuracy intended by the experimenter.

It would hardly be difficult to deconstruct the academic career interests behind these debates, but the main concern here is China's reforms. It is legitimate to ask what "caused" them. It is legitimate to seek normative as well as situational factors in exploring such a causation. And it would be illegitimate to claim that any method has found a way to make hypotheses, mere sentences, as real as the things they treat. Intellectual hubris is evident in exclusionary claims about method. The case for circumspection is that it may offer a more convincing story about what happened, especially when the object of research is a complex syndrome.

The diagram below at least broadly shows how to relate two epistemological methods to each other. It is a research design, a checklist of alternative questions to ask. It may not strike some readers as such, because it relates methods rather than banning them. Ruling out approaches has acquired professional cachet, for reasons that do not bear much inspection. A passion for efficiency in allocating intellectual work has tended to overtake the need for mobilizing intellectual curiosity—without which nothing is found. It is not always best to treat with increasing precision decreasingly little of human interest. Many elegant models offer substantive insight into politics that have actually occurred, but many others do not.[135] It is odd that many social scientists—humanists and naturalists alike—advocate research designs that exclude whole types of plausible predicates prior to research.

Causal Circumspection About Sizes of Collectivity

Another, separate choice is between explaining politics in terms of large groups such as whole nations, or else in terms of small groups, especially individuals. Some say that because all groups are composed of separate people, all social action should be explained in terms of the reasons of individuals. Collective action, in this view, can be reduced to the preferences of individuals, which are treated as premises. This ideal is interesting, but it overlooks that individuals do not come out of thin air. It excludes curiosity about predicates that can be used to typify individuals' interests as conclusions rather than as premises. But of course, everyone knows that preferences grow where people do: in families and cultures. Individuals come from networks. Methodological communalism is as defensible theoretically as methodological individualism. It is arbitrary to throw out any perspective that can add to scientific knowledge.[136]

Careful positivists such as Daniel Little ask for "at least an approximate idea of the underlying mechanisms at the individual level, if we are to have a credible hypothesis about explanatory social regularities. . . . Whenever a social explanation is offered, . . . it must be possible in principle to indicate the mechanisms through which individual activity gives rise to this outcome."[137] Inductive circumspection, seeking such mechanisms, is part of the project of seeking causes, even though looking around is what many economizing positivists explicitly do not want to do. Group mechanisms are also relevant. Looking around for the causes of events (here, China's reforms) is a task that quickly shows the shortcomings of both the naturalist and humanist fads in social science. Either tendency to use methods as conclusions, rather than as research tools to find phenomena, turns science into metaphysics.

Dangers and Advantages in the Functionalist Legacy

The breadth of a circumspect approach may seem nearly megalomaniac. Its point is to cover as many analytic dimensions as possible for the purpose of testing them as merely analytic, excluding unimportant types of factors only after research has shown their unimportance, rather than beforehand. Intellectuals tend to think mere predicates are real or even influential, but the valid use of any term always implies the possibility of one or more alternatives that need seriously to be explored. Circumspection of the sort advocated here is more likely to cite things that might happen rather than requirements that must happen.[138] The circumspect approach uses inquiries based on logically opposite premises and types of data. In politics, it concerns conflict just as much as consensus, local power as much as the central state, influential winks as much as coercive laws, anybody's resources as much as anybody's values. True megalomaniacs prefer narrower approaches that promise keys to guide everything. The only way to exclude types of subjects or predicates a priori would be to show that they could apply nowhere.

Functions are semantically adjectival, claiming links between activities that are like traits of activities. Since the main aim of social science is to find such links, which may be either intended or unintended by the actors, it would seem difficult to get away from the idea of functions, even if a researcher chose not the use of the word. Sometimes functions harmonize with each other. Very often they conflict, especially when they serve different groups or networks. Data to validate claims about a network in which a function is thought to be "embedded" can be of several kinds. To propose an efficient cause function as a predicate, it would help to show that the attributed cause predated the effect. It also might help to show the cause and effect were physically connected or close to each other. Other criteria for credibility of the functional claim might be based on appropriate uses of each of the two main kinds of data that have interested social scientists: meanings and unintended facts.

The framework in the diagram below renews functionalism, but it avoids the inherent conservatism sometimes associated with that approach. It offers alternatives to the chance that consensual unity helps a system maintain itself over time; in fact, the left-hand side of the diagram is all about disunity. In China, the political system is in fact not maintaining itself very healthily. This framework provides enough ways to seek information about change. Criticism of the present book will surely allege that it overrates the potential for conflicts between large and small power networks, and perhaps also between values and behaviors. Implicit in this new functionalist approach is a need to take all such gaps seriously.[139]

Many rational-action theorists take the gaps between individuals with such cosmic and overweening seriousness, however, that they leap in a wobbly manner from the fact that concrete structures are composed of individuals to the conclusion that groups cannot cause anything. Bartholomew Sparrow corrects this: "Not only is organizational and institutional behavior the product of individual action, the reverse holds, as well: standard operating procedures, organizational routines, classifications, and framing may determine individual actions and, hence, aggregate outcomes."[140]

These dimensions can be kept in mind, but there is no possibility of separating everything neatly into four mailboxes. Institutions that are largely economic, for example, are not exclusively situational-individualist in what they do. Also, the terms written on the chart include many problems of viewpoint. "Extraction" is no more important when seen from the stance of the government than is garnering rents, avoiding taxes, or creating wealth in small groups. "Legitimation" need not be seen just as a matter for the official regime; the legitimation of other leaderships is also part of that topic. "Sanctions" are not just an instrument of the national collective, and they involve both carrots and sticks. "Steering," the main governmental function or pretense, includes the business of amending the procedures of rule, and nonstate actors also do some steering. This book is organized as a tour of the four broad sectors of action, but there is no way to confine institutions hermetically to one sort of analytic function alone. There is no way to deal, in a one-dimensional, discursive line of chapters, with a topic that inherently has multiple dimensions—the two on the chart, plus time and space at least. A touching nostalgia for specifying unique rather than multiple causes, insofar as possible, is still the hopeful enthusiasm of mainstream political science. More practical fields such as computer science and "no-fault" law have absorbed the reality of numerous correlated causes, but the study of politics is still dominated by efforts to find single "smoking guns." Analysts who are afraid of complexity may simply choose to skip questions about the causes of large historical syndromes. Others, who may like this book better, will not try to simplify answers to the point of triviality but will attempt to judge the interplay of causes for China's reforms.

The proof of any analytic pudding is in the eating. This book seeks evidence about small-collective local actors partly to balance the China field's usual concentration on national actors. Because previous literature in the China field has stressed normative causal factors, this book also goes out of its way to seek data about situational ones. No such emphasis makes sense, however, without a framework that allows the alternatives too.

Scope of the Book and Sources

Because the most striking recent changes in Chinese politics have been subnational, this book begins with local situations (especially management and taxes) in the first volume. The second begins with local norms (the politics of small groups' and individuals' ideas). Later chapters then focus on the politics of collective authority and steering. Categories such as those on the diagram below are abstract, and the chapter subjects are concrete, so there is no perfect correspondence between the two. Somewhat fewer pages are devoted to the collective focus than to individuals and small groups, because activities in concrete personal and family situations (which are largely economic) seem to have spurred many recent changes. Normative and collective factors have already received most attention in other scholarship that this book is designed to complement. There are inherently close connections between the four types of activities, so whichever of them is introduced later can be summarized more briefly. There is no need to reiterate the table of contents here, but its relation to the categories of data shown in the diagram should be evident.

This book deals with many aspects of China's reforms, but it does not deal with everything. The foreign aspects of reforms could well be covered at greater length. The emphasis here is domestic, even though international factors are not ignored. Three reasons may be offered for this bias. First, the two-volume book is long already. Second, the same author has already published an essay about Pudong and joint ventures at "New Shanghai."[141] The localist argument of that piece is consistent with this book. Third and most important, many previous writers have ably dealt with the effects of foreign investment and trade. This feature of reforms has been better analyzed in English than any other.[142] Influences from outside China are treated in the cultural chapters below, and the economic chapters include information on topics such as Shanghai's loss of foreign markets to other parts of China. But there is no need here to repeat previous findings about the great benefits of international economic exchange. This book aims to be more comprehensive than most, but no treatment of China's reforms can be definitive. A more important aim is to say a few new things.

This work is designed to complement others, especially those treating reforms as emanations from Beijing. It defines reforms in a somewhat heterodox way—as a syndrome of types of actions, rather than as anybody's wholly conscious plan—and this allows their complex causes to become more clear. The data are all offered as proof of partial, not exclusive, causation: Reforms came not just from the state. This hypothesis would be less interesting if many treatments of China's reforms did not imply the opposite. The aim here is to find the generators of reform, not to cover once again those endlessly intriguing characters at the top of the state, who have been given superb academic attention elsewhere.[143]

The coverage of this book in space and time should also be specified. The word "China's" in its title does not refer to the country taken as a whole. There is no claim here that reforms *throughout* the nation uniformly began in the same ways or at the same times as on the Shanghai delta. Even in areas where change in recent decades has been fastest, evidence suggests its causes have been somewhat diverse. For example, Guangdong also had quick reforms, but unlike the Shanghai delta it enjoyed major infusions of capital from Hong Kong. For some time in the early 1980s, Guangdong was the recipient of a "big guarantee" tax holiday from Beijing. On the Yangzi delta, taxes remained very high, and the overwhelming bulk of early new capital was raised locally. So reforms near Shanghai and Guangzhou have been partly different from each other. Another spatial treatment of reform is national: these changes partly arose from policies emanating from Beijing to all other parts of the country. The center is important, and it deserves the study it has been extensively given. But neither reform nor China is homogeneous. The reforms and reactions of about one hundred million people, in the Jiangnan area surrounding Shanghai, are important in themselves. If study of them throws new light on what has happened elsewhere, so much the better. Nobody should think that events in the other places can be understood without specific research on them.[144] The "embeddedness" of predicates in structures is not abstract; it is a prescription for work. Sinology on the cheap is no more convincing than social science on the cheap.

The time coverage here is set by the overall theme. Finding causes requires looking at early periods, not necessarily at late ones. The book does not need to cover data up to the very day the reader will see it. The emphasis here is on the period from the early 1970s to the mid-1990s, because that was the time when the bases of reforms were established. With great economic blossoming in the 1990s, this book's descriptions of mid-1980s tax and market problems in Shanghai may seem misleading to readers who are more familiar with the recent boom. In fact, the later quick development grew out of the earlier bottlenecks—which were largely its impetus. This is about the bud, not the blossom.

The most comprehensive sources for the study of Chinese politics are publications, but they often document local politics only by offering circumstantial evidence. Interviews have also been used here, and behavioral information from them has been crucial both for its own sake and for giving perspective to the documentary sources. The attitudes that frame data available from interviews can be deeply constrained by context (by reformist or conservative national phases, by the foreign origin of the interviewer, and by the fact that conservatives do not distinguish academic research from spying).[145] Publications remain indispensable, not only because other scholars can refer to them. Interviews are often said to help make sense of documents, but the opposite is more frequent. A statist-traditionalist bias in ways of speaking has been rational for most Chinese individuals, even while change in this habit has lagged behind the demonstrable rise of rational nonstatist behavior. Interviews can be and have been personally rewarding. Published reports cover more behavioral evidence, and they greatly aid the interpretation of interviews.

The concentration on Shanghai and its delta in this book is justified partly because of very extensive data from the lower Yangzi area. Other scholars have been studying Shanghai's development, but even more have worked on Beijing or Guangdong during reforms.[146] Shanghai is officially just a "locality" (*difang*). This word in Chinese covers a host of very different-sized places. Sichuan, a province of more than a hundred million souls (if independent, one of the most populous countries on earth) is in this odd statist language also just a "locality." Gushi, a small settlement on the edge of provincial Shanghai, is also a "locality." Government parlance distinguishes all these diverse places from "the center" (*zhongyang*) in Beijing. Official geography is as dubious as official chronology, and wordings in this book conform to neither.

Shanghai is frequently called a "province" in this book. Its official title, "directly ruled city," means little that formally differentiates it from other provinces.[147] These places are unique, but statist language does not capture their distinctiveness. Shanghai and its delta have been somewhat atypical of other Chinese regions throughout the reforms, especially as regards their timing. Everything in Beijing is affected by that city's status as the national capital; politics there is inherently governmental, under the shadows of ministries and the eaves of the Zhongnanhai compound of the Imperial Palace, where China's most famous leaders work. Beijing also has China's most dense concentration of intellectuals seeking official jobs. This mix creates an uneasy and often conservative approach to reforms. Late chapters in the second volume of this book include diverse criticisms of the Beijing mentality and intellectuals' love affair with statism. Such observations are not wholly Western; Chinese have also written in a similar vein.[148] Guangzhou, and many other Guangdong cities outside the provincial capital, such as Foshan or Shenzhen, are profoundly affected by Hong Kong. Fujian cities are similarly affected by Taiwan. Wuhan has been the largest modern conservative province capital, and Wuhan's recent tendencies toward statism have been well documented.[149] Cities in the most populous provinces, such as Henan, Sichuan and Shandong, seem to present further patterns—which need much further study. The northeast industrial belt or the northwest impoverished belt could be added to this list. Geographical differences in China, as in all other large countries, deeply affect the political meaning of any policies that may initially be conceived as central.

Ways of talking about reform in these sundry places throughout China have varied less than ways of making reform. Valid generalizations from one area can only suggest hypotheses about what may be happening elsewhere. In studying these links, it will be useful to look beyond the state, because the reforms are diverse. Their origins can be found in many places, including local networks of politics.

Appendix: Diagram of a Field of Functions and Activities

data = MEANINGS

INTENDED NORMS AND CUSTOMS

"Normative Referent" / Reversible Habits & Cognitive Values / Ideal Constraints

PEOPLE ARE TAKEN TO BE SIMILAR; so modern specialization cannot explain all their acts.
Scientific data are all "begotten" from people's ***memories***, like nonstop "constructions."
When the predicate is causal, actor(s) are free to choose an alternative cultural option.
Read action as a made-up fiction text **open to** inconsistent **twists of story at each point.**
INDUCTION, synthesizing observations about frequently echoed symbols, allows conclusions.
Functional predicates about structural subjects can be validated only if created by actors
"Identity"-based cultural action story can be understood *only because analyst shows empathy.*
Claims are "significant," colorful echo-metaphors, forms often seen, not surely replicable.
The resulting "vision" may be vividly grasped but also *MAY BE IDIOSYNCRATIC/HARD TO CONVEY.*
RESEARCHER CAN UNDERSTAND SYMBOLS, BECAUSE STUDENT IS LIKE PEOPLE STUDIED ~"HUMAN SCIENCE."
For "ideographic" knowledge of "controlling factors," subjective understanding, *Verstehen.*
"Voice" (by one or many) invokes "human organization" principles for "support-led security"

hypothesis predicates tested by normative data

(F. Nietzsche)	Ethic of Principles / Norms / *Sinn* / *Gemeinschaft*-	"Community"	(G. Hegel)
	L "Latent pattn-maint &tension managem't" **vs. members' apathy**	"Integration" **vs. war of all against all**	**I**
campaign cadre "foxes"	(truthful 'charisma' art, *voluntary org*) **"network" org'n (based on trust)**	(secure 'tradition,' courts and *police*) **clannish org'n (based on patronism)**	*traditionalist "lions"*
[practical] 'ideology' **for change** by a vanguard (reformism, "*fang*") political bargaining	***LEGITIMATIVE*** pol'cs Policy from inter-faction **struggle.**	***SANCTIONS*** politics Policymaking is by unified **command.**	'utopia' [pure ideology] **for stability** in a unit (conservatism, "*shou*") political bandwagoning
small group subjects FAMILIES, PARTIES INDIVIDUALS <—			—> **large group subjects WHOLE SET, NATION TOTAL COLLECTIVE**
data = SEPARATE			***data = TOGETHER***

small group subjects FAMILIES, PARTIES INDIVIDUALS <—			—> large group subjects WHOLE SET, NATION TOTAL COLLECTIVE
data = SEPARATE	"Adaptation" vs. [biological] extinction	"Goal-attainment" vs. absorption by another system	*data = TOGETHER*
CONFLICT ASSUMPTION (assume acts may compete) **conflict theories**	('rational' action, efficient *trades*) **market org'n** **(based on prices)**	(esp. high politics, e.g. *legislatures*) **org'n by hierarchy** **(based on authority)**	***HEGEMONY ASSUMPTION*** (assume functions bind) **systems theories**
"specular" *entrepreneur "foxes"*	***EXTRACTIVE*** politics Policy from inter- unit **competition.**	***STEERING*** politics Policy comes from gov't **"fluidity."**	*"technocratic"* *rentier "lions"*
(B. Russell)	A	G	(K. Marx)

Ethic of Results / Situations / *Evidenz* / *Gesellschaft*-"Society"

hypothesis predicates tested by situational data

"Exit" (by one or many) uses "technical organization" results for "growth-mediated security"
For "nomothetic" knowledge of laws about "conditioning factors," objective reason, *Vernunft*
RESEARCHER POSITS MODELS, THEN TESTS THE STATISTICAL EXTENT THEY APPLY ~ "NATURAL SCIENCE"
The resulting & uncertain knowledge is thus *ONLY AS VALID AS A PREMISE AT PROBABILITY.*
Claims found "significant" don't really make signs/send signals, but are partly true.
"Rational" (including collective) action tale leaves ***tastes/preferences unexplained.***
Functional predicates on structural subjects are tested only if clear to researcher.
DEDUCTION, analyzing a partial harmony of models with data, allows conclusions.
See behavior as mostly replicable despite intentions; **define clear fixed terms.**
Whenever a predicate is causal, such a model could completely miss other causes.
Models are "made," but scientific data are from discrete tests of ***environments.***
PEOPLE ARE TAKEN TO BE DIFFERENT, OFTEN COMPLEMENTARY, acting in contexts.

"Situational Referent" / Irreversible Habits / Concrete Constraints

UNINTENDED SITUATIONS

data = CONTEXTUAL INCIDENTS

NOTES AND SOURCES: This chart is a summary of two ways in which social scientists have arranged words about the actions of the people they study. All terms on this map are abstract. The reason to draw such a picture is to show how such notions relate to each other; the aim is to reduce the number of social science terms by showing that many can be brought down to just two dimensions. Another goal is to show that when an analyst uses any one category, an obligation is incurred to check out the possible relevance of its alternative (on the opposite side of the chart). This approach questions the common habit of scholars who restrict themselves with analytic forms rather than with empirical evidence.

The two axes are the whole story the chart has to tell. They generate four premises about data. These premises are: that data should be seen as separate or together, and that attributions to them should be based on constructed human meanings or on unintended incidental situations. The horizontal axis describes possible subjects of propositions; the vertical describes alternative kinds of backing to confirm the predicates in them.

The functions described on the chart are not quite the same as in classical functionalism. They can conflict with each other. They are "embedded" in institutional networks and are studied there. The table of contents of this book is based on these categories. This whole scheme tries to cover a great deal, and a reasonable first reaction to it would be to object that it is grandiose. But the terms on the diagram at least have the virtue of being all unoriginal. They might be skipped, without an attempt to organize them here, if many readers did not already have them in their heads as surely as other words of the language in which the book is written. Usages here stress politics, rather than other kinds of social bonds. Classical functionalists stressed social solidarity, but this expanded approach especially describes different kinds of leaders, who foster either unity or conflict (respectively, on the right or left sides of the chart) on the basis of either ideas or contexts (on the top or the bottom).

Every phrase on the diagram is paired with another, shown opposite. The horizontal axis (which might be associated with Mannheim or Pareto) shows sizes of social subjects in sentences, e.g., individuals, or families, or medium-size collectives, or national networks, or the global human community. This horizontal axis is concrete; and it is spectral, since the subjects of social propositions can come in any size along a continuum. The vertical axis (suggestive of Durkheim or others) shows, however, just two types of evidence for attributions (predicates). This vertical is analytic and dichotomous rather than concrete and spectral.

People who have read old classics and recent critiques in social science will readily link many of the phrases quoted on the diagram with particular authors, who are cited below. The chart includes some terms that were originally devised to describe "social functions" (which might more clearly be called "activities," because the word function need not require effectiveness). Especially in the middle of the chart, words are sometimes used with slightly different coverages than their originators had; but a claim here is that they can be used most consistently as presented above. This diagram is not quite so random as a Ouija board.

All activities, however general the phrases describing them may seem, can be read with special reference to political questions: How are these functions organized politically, if indeed they are organized at all? How do they constrain leadership types? By the same token, the view of politics here is behavioral; it covers all exercises of power, when any person or group acts only because another wishes. Such politics are not confined to the state, nor to any specific means by which the expectations of leaders are brought into the ken of followers. Both norms and situations may be involved in such communication.

No matter whether a predicate is causal or descriptive, the diagram's vertical dimension shows two opposite ways of trying to justify it. These normative and situational types of attributions are analytic and do not exclude each other. Any verbs or adjectives posited as norms do not disprove possible coexisting traits, posited as situations. Clear predicates are either normative or situational, but no one of them excludes the chance that different ones actually apply too.

The horizontal dimension, however, is concrete because there is a row of sizes of subjects (often oddly called "levels of analysis," though they are not analytic) to which predicates may be imputed. A sentence about one of them is not about any other. So unlike the two-part dimension on the vertical, items on this horizontal are exclusive as regards any specific statement. Attributing something to one size of collectivity is a different project from attributing it to another. Adequate accounts require research, checking several sizes of collectivity for both normative and situational traits, to see which combination of them renders most information about the query the researcher had.

Border lines on the map do no more than put the terms in clusters. None of the boxes are hermetic, and their most important aspects are the links between them. As the words "charisma," "tradition," and "rational" on the diagram suggest, Weber's three types of legitimate authority depend on connections at the boundaries between the most political, "steering" sector and the other three. (Talcott Parsons too hopefully called this political sector "goal attainment," although elites do not always achieve their goals.) "Charismatic" authority, eliciting "normative" compliance, links politics to "legitimative" activities—but only when people really believe in it. "Traditional" authority, eliciting "coercive" compliance, relates politics to integrative activities—to the incomplete degree a system may actually cohere. "Legal-rational" authority, calling for "utilitarian" compliance, links political steering to extractive activities—but only to the extent one group actually can collect from another.

Some terms, especially Parsons' phrases near the middle of the diagram, are inconsistent with the intent of the chart if they are read to imply more collective success in such activities than actually occurs. Here is a list of terms, though, and of prominent social scientists who used them:

"Function" implies some potentially comprehensible link—including (toward the left side of the diagram) one that might be described in terms of conflict or that almost completely fades into complexity. "Function" does not require, here, that subject actors or predicate data about their actions must cohere. This revises classical functionalism, as in Talcott Parsons, *The Social System* (Glencoe, IL: Free Press, 1951), although what Parsons said on this point seems to have varied from time to time. In any case, functions are not always fulfilled, but activities have results. Another departure from old functionalist categories is that the norms at the top of the map include habitual and ritual scripts, which are reflexive habits, not just immediate and conscious purposes.

"Embedded" functions cannot be fully separated from the structures and people that supply data to confirm them. The only reason for categorizing types of data, as on the vertical of this chart, is that scholars want to validate their propositions and need ways to show how facts relate to predicate attributions. See Mark Granovetter, "Economic Action and Social Structure: The Problem of Embeddedness," *American Journal of Sociology* 91 (November 1985), pp. 481–510. An even better reference is the revulsion that most ordinary people have toward abstract social science. They know that no category of method is good, until *after* it has proved itself. The aim of this exercise is not to prescribe any particular method, but to show that research is needed to double-check, with the alternative method, whatever a particular approach may find. The middle of the Ouija board suggests kinds of structures in which relevant functions may be found particularly embedded—but these structures are different from functions.

"Analytic" and "concrete" are explained in Marion J. Levy, Jr., "Structural-Functional Analysis," *International Encyclopaedia of the Social Sciences* (London: Macmillan, 1968), pp. 21–28, which notes that any relationship between topics chosen as a system and their external environment can be found only by "discovery." An analytic predicate is an ideal type, either a normative or a situational model, which does not bar the possible validity of others. But the other dimension describes concrete groups, often hastily called political "levels" (although this book finds high degrees of power in "lower," smaller, local networks). So the main point of the chart is that would-be political functions fall into four types—as individual-situational, collective-situational, collective-normative, or individual-normative. Just two dimensions can describe these four.

ON THE VERTICAL: INTENTIONS OR SITUATIONS

"Normative referent" and "situational referent" are sociological versions of the main hang-up in Western epistemology, the distinction between mind and matter, the process and object of thought. Near obsession with this difference is evident in thinkers from Plato or Aristotle to Descartes or Kant. This division is not surely absolute, according to others such as Dewey or Rorty; but the best way of escaping it is to recognize both the styles of social analysis it suggests. The two "referents" are in Talcott Parsons, *The Social System*; but similar ideas are in his more readable book, *The Structure of Social Action* (New York: McGraw-Hill, 1937). A circumspect functionalism can keep his words "norm" and "value" only with meanings that include semiconscious, ritual habits, as explained in the introductory chapter of Walter W. Powell and Paul J. DiMaggio, *The New Institutionalism in Organizational Analysis* (Chicago: University of Chicago Press, 1991). This retains functionalist categories while adapting them, including habits and institutions as norms.

"Human science" and "natural science" are terms that appear in many sources, e.g. H. Stuart Hughes, *Consciousness and Society* (New York: Vintage, 1961), pp. 309–11.

"Understanding" (*Verstehen*) as a means of social analysis was made famous by Max Weber. See *From Max Weber*, H.H. Gerth and C. Wright Mills, eds. (New York: Oxford University Press, 1958). These and Weber's authority types are interpreted in Reinhard Bendix, *Max Weber: An Intellectual Portrait* (Garden City, NY: Doubleday, 1960). The term "vision" in political science received its modern meaning from Sheldon S. Wolin, *Politics and Vision* (Boston: Little, Brown, 1960).

"Symbols" are central in many works by Clifford Geertz, especially "Deep Play: Notes on the Balinese Cockfight," in *The Interpretation of Cultures* (New York: Basic Books, 1973), pp. 412–53. Note the idea on p. 452 that a logically alternative kind of symbol, the quiet Brahmana ordination ceremony rather than the violent cockfight, is as "like Bali." Another symbol is an alternative, equally valid approach to understanding culture; and more, a systematically opposite one would serve this purpose.

Together with this detail in Geertz, note some hesitant admissions from the situationalist camp that "culture" can be seen as causal, at least after external incentive structures have been explored, e.g. on p. 136 of David Elkins and Richard Simeon, "A Cause in Search of its Effect, or What Does Political Culture Explain?" *Comparative Politics* 11 (January 1979), pp. 127–46.

"Voice" and "exit" are words specified for all social scientists by an economist, Albert Hirschman, in *Exit, Voice, and Loyalty* (Cambridge: Harvard University Press, 1970).

"Support-led security" and "growth-mediated security" are contrasted by the economist Amartya Sen, in J. Dreze and A. Sen, *Hunger and Public Action* (Oxford: Clarendon Press, 1989). Karl Polanyi's *The Great Transformation* (New York: Reinhardt, 1944) also suggests that collectivities' links to individuals and families are shaped in different time periods by alternating policies, which bring these same two results. A similar analysis, stressing the ways different elites vie to stabilize political agendas and to serve one or the other of these two goals, is E. E. Schattschneider, *The Semi-Sovereign People* (Hinsdale, IL: Dreyden Press, 1975).

An "ethic of principles" (or "ultimate ends") exercises basic values and identities. This principled rationality, *Wertrationalität*, is what psychologists and anthropologists try to understand; it is action that can be judged before the full results are known, depending on whether or not it follows precepts thought to be right. Weber contrasts this with an "ethic of results" (or "responsibility"), *Zweckrationalität*, which is action calculated to gain goals thought to be worthy and judged after-the-fact according to its success or failure in attaining them. (This is at least loosely akin to a distinction Machiavelli made, between *virtù* and *fortuna*.) *Sinn* is German for "meaning," which was contrasted to *Evidenz* by the most important nineteenth-century inventors of modern social science. *Gemeinschaft* and *Gesellschaft*, "community" and "society," are often cited in German not just because they look fancier that way, but because those words in common English have less specific meanings. In Chinese studies, identical notions have been called "human organization" and "technical organization" by Franz Schurmann in *Ideology and Organization in Communist China* (Berkeley: University of California Press, 1966). Durkheim's terms, respectively "mechanical" and "organic" solidarity, suggest so many counterintuitive implications they are omitted here; but the distinction is the same. The words "made" and "begotten," from the Nicene Creed, denote the logical difference between two kinds of creative acts, which can or cannot be abstracted from identity.

ON THE HORIZONTAL: SIZES OF ACTORS

"Ideology" for change by a small group acting as a vanguard, and "utopia" for stability, are ideas from Karl Mannheim, *Ideology and Utopia: An Introduction to the Sociology of Knowledge* (London: Routledge, 1936). Franz Schurmann, *Ideology and Organization*, brings these ideas into Chinese studies by mooting Maoist "practical ideology" for developmental "exploitation" and Liuist "pure ideology" for stable "control" (and he suggests the history of these functions in China by relating them respectively to the Ming's *lijia* and Qing's *baojia* systems). This distinction was personalized by Vilfredo Pareto, who distinguished "foxes" and "lions" (or in many recent Chinese studies, "reformers" and "conservatives.") Pareto typifies leaders who are especially adept at the reformist or conservative roles, and he shows the need in healthy elites for both kinds; see *The Rise and Fall of Elites* (New York: Arno Press, 1979). He also distinguishes four types of leaders, including "specular" foxes who gamble in practical affairs, and "rentier" lions who collect concrete rents. Pareto uses dimensions like those on the chart to describe "residues" or basic kinds of human motives—all presented from the viewpoint of the actor. The two the chart maps vertically he called "expressiveness, a tendency to symbolize," or "combination, a tendency to start adventures"; and horizontally, fox-like "sociability, a tendency to affiliate," or leonine "preservation, a tendency to consolidate." There is also some linkage between the horizontal dimension on this diagram and two aspects of democracy that Robert Dahl distinguishes: habitual contest about separate values and resources (by partial groups), and habitual participation together in a system (by everyone); see *Polyarchy* (New Haven: Yale University Press, 1971). Foxes do better in contests, but lions in mutual loyalty. An analysis of various analysts' usages, for which there is no space here, would show practical links between concepts that may at first seem different. Schurmann, however, uses lucid words for the four kinds of leaders who take these roles: "entrepreneurs" who are only most obvious in the economy, fox-like "cadres" who specialize in individual-normative mobilization, lion-like "traditional" leaders ("patrons" in many recent writings), and "technocratic" leaders.

"Conflict" is the theoretical theme of most works by Ralf Dahrendorf (e.g. "Out of Utopia: Toward a Reorientation of Sociological Analysis," *American Journal of Sociology* 64, pp. 115–27), or of many by Charles Tilly (e.g. *Big Structures, Large Processes, Huge Comparisons* [New York: Russell Sage Foundation, 1985]). In a different vein, Avery Goldstein distinguishes "bargaining" by actors who are in basic anarchy from "bandwagoning" by actors under hegemony; see *From Bandwagon to Balance-of-Power Politics: Structural Constraints and Politics in China, 1949–78* (Stanford: Stanford University Press, 1991).

"Hegemony" is a fixation of many writers, especially in international relations; but the classic is Antonio Gramsci, *Letters from Prison*, tr. Lynne Lawner (New York: Harper and Row, 1973).

THE MIDDLE: MAKING HYPOTHESES

Using four categories to describe all social activities, and without an emphasis on politics that is central here, Talcott Parsons referred to "adaptation," "goal attainment," "integration," and "latent pattern maintenance and tension management." Functionalists in their heyday felt familiar enough with these phrases to abbreviate them "AGIL." The four are repeated above only as overstatements. There is no guarantee of successful adaptation; state elites often cannot attain goals; not all tensions are neatly managed nor all patterns maintained (also, the word "latent" is confusing); and integration, as the whole left side of the chart implies, is incomplete. Parsons's categories actually implied partial disintegration, but he did not stress it. He was similarly circumspect on the vertical axis of the chart (because of tensions his German predecessors saw between subjective understanding, *Verstehen*, and objective reason, *Vernunft*). In one unguarded moment, Parsons called himself a "cultural determinist"; but more carefully, he wrote that a "cybernetic hierarchy" of "conditioning factors" with "high energy" might be as important as one of "controlling factors" with "high information." (See Parsons, *Societies: Evolutionary and Comparative Perspectives* [Englewood Cliffs, NJ: Prentice-Hall, 1966], p. 113 for the slip of pen; and for the hierarchies, Parsons, *The Evolution of Societies*, Jackson Toby, ed. [Englewood Cliffs, NJ: Prentice-Hall, 1977], p. 21.) It is quite possible, however, to borrow from Parsons only what is useful. See the arrangement of "subsystems" in Parsons and Neil J. Smelser, *Economy and Society* (Glencoe, IL: Free Press, 1956), p. 19. Parsons's proposal that activities might be analyzed under categories like the ones he offers can withstand his apparent pro-stability bias. His epistemology is not inherently conservative, even though he was. The divisions of this book on China—mainly about a political system that is breaking down—loosely follow these four categories, as the table of contents shows.

"Biological extinction," "absorption by another system," "war of all against all," and "members' apathy" are all ways in which systems can collapse. Avoiding them has been called "prerequisite," but they are a neat list of functional failures. See the classic article by Parsons's students, D. F. Aberle et al., "The Functional Prerequisites of a Society," *Ethics* 60, pp. 100–10.

Parallel categories, respectively "extraction," "legitimation," and "coercion" (clockwise on the diagram beginning at the southwest corner) are cited in Gabriel A. Almond and G. Bingham Powell, Jr., *Comparative Politics: A Developmental Approach* (Boston: Little Brown, 1966), and "steering" has been added by many authors to cover functions within governments. (This book about China refers to "sanctions" more than "coercion," because positive sanctions based on community ideals are part of that category.)

A kindred categorization describes regime types (respectively in the same clockwise order, but this time completing the circle: pluralist, syndicalist, monist, and corporatist). See Philippe Schmitter, "Still the Century of Corporatism?" in F. Pike and T. Stritch, eds., *The New Corporatism* (South Bend, IN: Notre Dame, 1974). Corporatist regimes, for example, specialize in solving collective/situational problems. This extension is complex, relying on a detailed look at the particular capabilities and shortcomings of each type as listed by Schmitter; so it is not included in the diagram. The very title of another Schmitter article (in which four words are italicized below) makes clear the relation between these notions and his: Wolfgang Streeck and Philippe Schmitter, "*Community*, *Market*, *State*—and *Associations*? The Prospective Contribution of Interest Governance to Social Order," in Streeck and Schmitter, eds., *Private Interest Government: Beyond Market and State* (Newbury Park, CA: Sage, 1985). For more, see the section below in Chapter 4.3 about Chinese choices of regime types.

A parallel set of categories has been used by students of policy-making, notably Graham Allison; or in the China field, by Kenneth Lieberthal and Michel Oksenberg, as well as

Murray Scot Tanner. In the same clockwise order from the southwest on this diagram these categories are: the "organizational [or bureaucratic] politics model" especially insofar as it relies on rationalized competition, the "leadership struggle [or 'power'] model," the "command model," and finally the "garbage can model"—which Tanner has re-christened with a more seemly name, the "fluidity model" (others have called this an "organized anarchy" model, since it asks about governmental goals, procedures, and participants). Many scholars are well-known for using one or another of these analytic approaches to good effect. Tanner's book on *The Politics of Lawmaking in Post-Mao China* has details. See also Michael Cohen et al., "A Garbage Can Model of Organizational Choice," *Administrative Science Quarterly* (March 1972), pp. 1–25.

International relations theorist James Roseneau has proposed four modes by which states adapt to their environments. His "acquiescent," "intransigent," "preservative," and "promotive" modes bear strong similarities to the diagram's four categories (clockwise from the southwest corner). There is no need to explain them here, but see Roseneau, *The Study of Political Adaptation* (London: Pinter, 1981)—and Carol Hamrin's application to China in Thomas Robinson and David Shambaugh, eds., *Chinese Foreign Policy: Theory and Practice* (Oxford: Clarendon Press, 1994), especially pp. 97–105. The aim here is only to suggest the very wide extent to which categories like these four have been used in the past, not to provide a bibliography of all such cases or to prove that academics' terms have much consistency. Just a bit more needs to be said about the top and bottom of the chart.

CONFIRMATIONS THAT THE TWO AXES ARE DIFFERENT

"Discipline" and "punishment" are the main categories in Michel Foucault, *Discipline and Punish: The Birth of the Prison* (New York: Pantheon, 1977). They could be slapped on this map ('discipline' on both the N and W sides, because it is both internalized and individual; and 'punishment' on both the S and E sides, because it is both external and collective), although such an option has been avoided here. The trouble is that group norms and individual situations—the alternative possibilities that existentialists prefer to neglect in favor of individual norms and collective situations—are also needed to explain some actions. Although Sheldon Wolin's idea of "vision" is suggested on the N side of the chart, he like Foucault tends to associate it also with the W side—with local groups and change, rather than with whole-group stability as most of the old functionalists (and others) would do. Many people tend, offhand, to guess values are collective and situations are individual. But the arrangement of Foucault's or Wolin's main ideas, above, is exactly the opposite. It highlights that the usual guess about linkage between the two axes on the diagram (S with W, and E with N) is arbitrary. Values can be individual, and situations can be collective. The main point of the chart is that efforts to conflate the contents on its horizontal and vertical will not last.

Epistemologists—though not particularly Russell, Nietzsche, Hegel, and Marx as mentioned on the chart—are the topic of Stephen Pepper, *World Hypotheses: A Study in Evidence* (Berkeley: University of California Press, 1970). Philosophers' preferences regarding data correlate with basic alternatives in social science. Russell stands as a representative for many positivists; and Nietzsche, for many existentialists. Hegel and Marx are mentioned (among others who might be) because their similarities and differences on the relevant issues are widely known. The choices above are meant to be contrastive, rather than to fix these epistemologists exactly. (Some analytic philosophers would say the word "data" on the chart should be "phenomena," but that is just a matter of definition.)

These two dimensions also structure some current disputes in political philosophy. On the horizontal, Robert Nozick, *Anarchy, State, and Utopia* (London: Blackwell,

1974), is an extreme individualist, while other liberals like John Rawls, *A Theory of Justice* (Cambridge: Harvard University Press, 1971), or especially Ronald Dworkin, *Taking Rights Seriously* (London: Duckworth, 1978), see a somewhat greater need to relate individuals to the collective contexts in which they were educated. Birth, nurture, and conversation are collective processes; they refine the liberal account. On the vertical, Ludwig Wittgenstein, *Tractatus Logico-Philosophicus* (London: Blackwell, 1973 reprint), underlies most economistic fads in social science. But see the different and more mature epistemology of later Wittgenstein, *Philosophical Investigations* (London: Blackwell, 1953), which develops a behavioral account of the influence of human definition on knowledge. This would be closer to the view that social data are human meanings, e.g. in Charles Taylor, *Philosophy and the Human Sciences* (Cambridge: Cambridge University Press, 1985). Circumspect approaches in comparative politics can help political philosophers with their main problems just now

CIRCUMSPECTION: ADVICE TO SEEK OPPOSITE CATEGORIES FOR TESTING

The aim here is to show convergence among writers on what is needed for an adequate explanation in social science, not to guarantee an absolutely nuanced representation of each previous use of the concepts cited above. If the authors mentioned could be gathered in a single room, they would not all agree on definitions. The chart nonetheless shows more unity in social science, along two dimensions, than many people realize.

The diagram suggests that writers' exclusivist preferences for certain kinds of data, even when these choices are useful for telling particular causal stories, do not work for all such stories. A choice for any position along either dimension is ephemeral, not a breakthrough. An insistence that a good social explanation must be translatable into the preferences or situations of individuals, because groups are all composed of persons, is just fine. But it is no more fine than an insistence that an adequate explanation should also be presentable in terms of the norms or situations of the collectivities that socialize people. Or on the vertical, above: A stress on the need to test propositions with evidence external to the minds that conceive them is entirely legitimate—but no more so than a stress on the need to understand that the terms of any such proposition come from human languages. No matter which bias is hailed, the alternative has actually been shown useful for accounting other kinds of causes or descriptions.

The chart is not, however, meant to suggest that only its dimensions are useful for explanation. Other kinds of conditions (e.g., historical time or geographic space) are needed to answer many questions. The individual-collective and norm-situation axes have structured much past social science, but the main point of the diagram is not a claim that any analyst trying to explain a social question must equally incorporate both normative and situational data, or both collective and individual data, in any specific account. This is an empirical question that cannot be decided prior to research. The proof of any analytic pudding is in the eating.

Many social scientists these days claim to know in advance which method will work best. They decry others who use data that do not match their epistemological preferences. But it does not forward the understanding of events to make such a claim metaphysically. The only way to substantiate it is to give answers to questions that people really have. Even *if*, for example, all normative and collective data could really be overwhelmed by situational and individual data for purposes of explanation, as many social scientists suggest, it does no good just to say so. The only convincing method of showing this would be to bring home the bacon and explain important issues from situational and individual data alone. Such tricks are often claimed but seldom turned.

For their part, culturalists sometimes imply that the unintended consequences of action cannot properly be studied, exactly because they are unintended. This also throws out data unnecessarily. The claim in this book is that because alternative categories imply each other, there is no basis to exclude any of them from a specific explanation until after the tale is diligently attempted also in terms of others. So the prudent tack is to scan them all first, in a circumspect style. All appearances to the contrary notwithstanding, social science is not a mess. Complementary approaches can hold it together.

Notes

1. Some social scientists, especially interpretive anthropologists such as Clifford Geertz, doubt the style of any search for causes. The partial validity (and substantial invalidity) of this point is discussed in Part 2, along with other theoretical aspects of this story about China's reforms.

2. See Frederick Teiwes's chapter about "The Establishment of the New Regime," in *The Politics of China, 1949–1989,* Roderick MacFarquhar, ed. (Cambridge: Cambridge University Press, 1993), which shows the very strong early-1950s consensus in the leadership that Mao made good decisions. Already by the end of that decade, the one-man model lost much of its applicability. Some scholars suggest this even for 1957–58; see David Bachman, *Bureaucracy, Economy, and Leadership in China: The Institutional Origins of the Great Leap Forward* (Cambridge: Cambridge University Press, 1991). Chinese politics changed more quickly than academic frameworks for studying them.

3. Lynn White, *Policies of Chaos: The Organizational Causes of Violence in China's Cultural Revolution* (Princeton: Princeton University Press, 1989) similarly discusses Mao's actions, especially the August 1966 temporary paralyzation of the police, as a necessary cause for the start of Cultural Revolution violence—though not a cause sufficient to explain its extent.

4. This premise is common but odd, since Westerners less regularly apply it to their own behavior. New works about China in the rational-action genre are starting to rectify a previous scholarly imbalance in this respect. The present book combines that approach with discussions of intended habits and large groups too. The aim is to avoid deciding, before testing data, which of them are important.

5. Hu Qiaomu's simple mnemonic notes that 1978 saw the reformist Third Plenum; 1979, the conservative arrest of Wei Jingsheng; 1980, the Gengshen electoral reforms; 1981, the conservative criticism of Bai Hua; . . . 1986, the December protests; 1987, the dismissal of reformer Hu Yaobang; and perhaps so forth. This scheme applies better to high-state politics than to local levels, and it requires a great deal of interpretation (for example, in 1979, it would stress the closing of "Democracy Wall" rather than the movement in early 1979 for democracy). Richard Baum has extended Hu's ten-year (1978–87) version as far as 1992–93. See Richard Baum, *Burying Mao: Chinese Politics in the Age of Deng Xiaoping* (Princeton: Princeton University Press, 1994), Table 1.1.

6. The verbal habit might be related to Buddhist notions about long-cycle *kalpas* or to Confucian notions about the dynastic cycle. A nine-year pattern, at least through 1949, 1958, 1967, 1976, and 1985, stirred more interest among a group of Chinese to whom it was proposed than it deserved. It is easier to give sustained evidence for the continuance of widespread interest in two opposing leaderships: by conservative "lions" and by reformist "foxes," to use Machiavelli's terms. See Niccolò Machiavelli, *The Prince,* tr. Luigi Ricci, intro. Christian Gauss (New York: Mentor, 1952), pp. 92–93 and passim. Or see Vilfredo Pareto, *The Rise and Fall of Elites,* intro. Hans Zetterberg (New York: Arno Press, 1979).

7. See Mark Granovetter, "Economic Action and Social Structure: The Problem of Embeddedness," *American Journal of Sociology* 91 (November 1985), pp. 481–510.

8. See Ruth Lane, "Concrete Theory: An Emerging Political Method," *American Political Science Review* 84:3 (September 1990), pp. 927–40, especially the quotation from Robert Bates on p. 931 (from *Markets and States in Tropical Africa,* pp. 120 and 129), which is expressed wholly in terms of concrete groups: "workers and owners" of "fledgling urban industries," state "elites," "farmers," "everyone"—whose interaction results from attributed "interests" of kinds that are described by dimensions of the sort indicated above.

9. A sometime example is Andrew G. Walder, *Communist Neo-Traditionalism: Work and Authority in Chinese Industry* (Berkeley: University of California Press, 1986).

10. Samuel P. Huntington, *Political Order in Changing Societies* (New Haven: Yale University Press, 1968), p. 345.

11. For example, see Michel Oksenberg and Bruce Dickson, "The Origins, Process, and Outcomes of Great Political Reform: A Framework for Analysis," in *Comparative Political Dynamics: Global Research Perspectives,* Dankwart Rustow and Kenneth Erickson, eds. (New York: Harper and Row, 1991), pp. 235–61. The word *great* in this title suggests an appreciation, which these authors definitely have, that other approaches are also possible.

12. Concepts are valid for inclusion in hypotheses when there is a possibility they can organize facts, not just when they are clear to the conceiver. See Ludwig Wittgenstein, *Philosophical Investigations* (New York: Macmillan, 1953). This book represents a major improvement in realism over that author's earlier work, the *Tractatus Logico-Philosophicus* (London: Routledge, 1974 [1922]), which has thus far had a much deeper and less fortunate effect on social science. Wittgenstein matured, but most social scientists have not yet done so. More on this is in the conclusion, below.

13. János Kornai, *The Socialist System* (Princeton: Princeton University Press, 1992), pp. 362, 387–92.

14. Harry Harding, *China's Second Revolution: Reform After Mao* (Washington: Brookings Institution, 1987), p. 39.

15. *RMRB,* June 13, 1987; italics added. This was translated and given to the author by his student Zhou Xiao, now a professor at the University of Hawaii.

16. See Harry Harding, *China's Second Revolution,* p. 92.

17. The methodological problems of trying to figure out leaders' policy positions are often ignored by journalists and policy analysts, especially in writings on China's foreign relations. Care in handling this issue became a famous virtue in the writings of Allen S. Whiting, especially *The Chinese Calculus of Deterrence* (Ann Arbor: University of Michigan Press, 1975).

18. The Soviet Union under Brezhnev offers many examples, as does China under Mao in his last half decade.

19. Harry Harding, *China's Second Revolution,* p. 272.

20. On the earlier case, see Stephen F. Cohen, *Rethinking the Soviet Experience: Politics and History Since 1917* (New York: Oxford University Press, 1985), esp. chap. 5.

21. *Shinian haojie.*

22. One might expect authors on Taiwan, for example, to be more critical; but when one of them moots alternative periodizations of PRC history, 1966–76 always appears as a single era. See Xu Guangtai in *Zhonggong zhengquan sishi nian de huigu yu zhanwang* (Recollections and Prospects on the Forty Years of CCP Power), Wu An-chia, ed. (Taipei: Guoji Guanxi Yanjiu Zhongxin, 1991), pp. 305–16.

23. Jiang Zemin et al., *Shanghai dangzheng jigou yange* (The Transformation of Shanghai's Party and Administration) (Shanghai: Shanghai Renmin Chuban She, 1988). p. 129, which is the summary section on the Cultural Revolution, completely omitted the years 1969–75; later detailed sections of the book give these years only negative, mechanical, and skimpy attention.

24. On continuing abuse of intellectuals in the 1970s, there are too many sources to cite in a single note. On continuing factional struggles, even at local levels, see especially Keith Forster, "The Politics of Destabilization and Confrontation: The Campaign Against Lin Biao and Confucius in Zhejiang Province, 1974," *China Quarterly* 107 (September 1986), pp. 433–62, and Wang Shaoguang, *Failure of Charisma: The Cultural Revolution in Wuhan* (Hong Kong: Oxford University Press, 1995), chaps. 10 and 11.

25. See Peter Nolan and Robert F. Ash, "China's Economy on the Eve of Reform," *China Quarterly* 144 (December 1995), especially Table 1, p. 982.

26. This is of course not just a trait of Chinese. But a recent conversation the author had with a Taiwanese concerning the tension between KMT guidance of democratization there and KMT fears of losing elections, made a similar point. He admitted that his fellow islanders did not have words to explain fully what they had unleashed on themselves—even though most of them really did want to unleash it. Only intellectuals tend to think that norms always precede situations. If it were so, intellectuals should always be leaders; but this would not be democratic. Words and situations interact.

27. Jiang Zemin et al., *Shanghai dangzheng jigou yange,* p. 134.

28. Hangzhou, for example, saw some clashes between labor factions in 1974 and 1975, which brought soldiers into factories as arbiters. Keith Forster, *Rebellion and Factionalism in a Chinese Province: Zhejiang 1966–76* (Armonk, NY: M. E. Sharpe, 1990), pp. 186–87, 216–17.

29. This graph, based on an index, is shown in Y. Y. Kueh, *Economic Planning and Local Mobilization in Post-Mao China* (London: SOAS Contemporary China Institute, 1985), Figure 3, p. 40.

30. Officials from the provinces were two-thirds of the 1969 CCP Central Committee (a higher portion than in other central committees), but they were also disproportionately military and had gone through more sifting for political loyalty than in other comparable meetings. The 1969 "Congress of Victors" represented political centralization within the provinces. For much more, see the account by Harry Harding, "The Chinese State in Crisis, 1966–69," in *The Politics of China,* Roderick MacFarquhar, ed., p. 229; and also MacFarquhar's own chapter, p. 255.

31. See Marc Blecher and Vivienne Shue, *Tethered Deer: Government and Economy in a Chinese County* (Stanford: Stanford University Press, 1996), of which an early draft contributed to this author's thinking about the early 1970s.

32. Light industries nationwide, from 1971 to 1975, reportedly received only one-tenth as much money as was put into heavy industries. Only in later reforms did more investment go to light industries—or at least, more was *reported* to go there. It is possible that the earlier statistics are incomplete on this, showing much light industrial investment as "agricultural." Zhou Shulian, "Changing the Pattern of China's Economy," in *China's Economic Reforms,* Wei Lin and Arnold Chao, eds. (Philadelphia: University of Pennsylvania Press, 1982), p. 49.

33. *Zhongguo xueshu jie dashi ji, 1919–1985* (Chronicle of Chinese Academic Circles, 1919–1985), Wang Yafu and Zhang Hengzhong, eds. (Shanghai: Shanghai Shehui Kexue Yuan Chuban She, 1988), pp. 266–69.

34. Lynn White, "Local Autonomy in China During the Cultural Revolution: The Theoretical Uses of an Atypical Case," *American Political Science Review* 70 (June 1976), pp. 479–91.

35. For details see "Towards Dominance of Technocrats and Leadership Stability: The Shanghai Leadership Change, 1976–1993," a currently usable but unattributable article this author was fortunate to see in manuscript. In the previous most important PRC purge of a top Shanghai leader, that of Rao Shushi in the mid-1950s, also very few other leaders were replaced. (The main exception was a suave police and intelligence agent named Yang Fang, whose reputation was never identical with Rao's in any case.) Factions certainly exist in Shanghai; but whenever a leader falls, most followers easily find niches elsewhere.

36. The 1964–71 periodization might also be applied to an analysis of direct army involvement in civilian education, which rose dramatically in 1964 and decreased similarly in the early 1970s. Perhaps it would apply to an analysis of the military budget, too.

Articles on these topics have apparently not yet been written for the 1963–64 change, although the present author's *Careers in Shanghai* (Berkeley: University of California Press, 1978) contains some relevant information. For the investment analysis, see Barry Naughton, "Industrial Policy During the Cultural Revolution: Military Preparation, Decentralization, and Leaps Forward," in *New Perspectives on the Cultural Revolution,* William Joseph, Christine Wong, and David Zweig, eds. (Cambridge: Harvard University Press, 1991), pp. 153–81. Economists Peter Nolan and Robert F. Ash, in "China's Economy on the Eve of Reforms," also show that official data show slower annual growth of the gross value of industrial output in 1970–76, only 8 percent, than in any other comparable period of PRC economic history—and this was mainly caused by a decline in heavy production, which was still overwhelmingly state-owned. The decline in national *reported* light industrial production for this period, though less than for heavy industry, may well result from a shift of factors to underreporting collectives.

37. Bonnie S. MacDougall, "Writers and Performers, Their Works, and Their Audiences in the First Three Decades," in *Popular Chinese Literature and Performing Arts in the People's Republic of China, 1949–1979,* Bonnie S. MacDougall, ed. (Berkeley: University of California Press, 1984), p. 292. MacDougall credits this distinction to the cultural officer of the Swedish Embassy in Beijing during the early 1970s, Anders Hansson. The closer one got to the scene, the more obvious was the need for a better periodization.

38. Anita Chan, "Dispelling Misconceptions About the Red Guard Movement: The Necessity to Re-Examine Cultural Revolution Factionalism and Periodization," *Journal of Contemporary China* 1:1 (1992), pp. 61–85.

39. Writing the history of the previous era was always a crucial function of Chinese imperial courts. The CCP's revolutionary dynasty takes this task to be needed even between reigns, and the job is naturally political.

40. Political scientist Kevin Lane, of Franklin and Marshall College, is engaged in research about Shaanxi. He shows that reforms have often been fiercely opposed by Shaanxi local leaders (even those in factions that disdained each other, and even when they could not express their views publicly) far into the 1980s and 1990s. Even in periods when central reformers touted change, local leaders in the Yan'an province proved to be strikingly antireformist.

41. Also see Thomas Weldon, *The Vocabulary of Politics* (Harmondsworth: Penguin, 1960).

42. See Timothy Mitchell, "The Limits of the State: Beyond Statist Approaches and Their Critics," *American Political Science Review* 85:1 (March 1991), p. 77.

43. This use of the word "power" differs from that by Lasswell and Kaplan, who call power "a special case of influence" because it threatens "severe deprivations for nonconformity with the policies intended." But large problems bedevil the projects of distinguishing degrees of "severe deprivation" and of restricting openly articulate (usually state) structures as the sources of powerful "policies." The earlier usages, along with the quotations from Lasswell and Kaplan, are best summarized in Gabriel A. Almond, "Introduction: A Functional Approach to Comparative Politics," *The Politics of the Developing Areas,* Gabriel A. Almond and James S. Coleman, eds. (Princeton: Princeton University Press, 1960), pp. 5–6.

44. Alfred Stepan, *The State and Society: Peru in Comparative Perspective* (Princeton: Princeton University Press, 1978), p. xii; also quoted in Theda Skocpol, "Bringing the State Back In: Current Research," in *Bringing the State Back In,* Peter B. Evans, Dietrich Rueschmeyer, and Theda Skocpol, eds. (Cambridge: Cambridge University Press, 1985), p. 7.

45. States in the "NICs" or "four little dragons" of South Korea, Taiwan, Hong Kong,

and Singapore are all authoritarian—but in each case, both the domestic and international situations keep the question of regime legitimacy permanently on the agenda in a way that was not usual in the PRC until 1989 (if ever). South Korea was wracked by a major civil war in 1946 and 1947, and specifiable families in several southern provinces such as Chŏlla and Cheju have been basically hostile to the capitalist and cosmopolitan government in Seoul; the military danger from the North is obvious. On Taiwan, the KMT government after a 1947 massacre in Taipei had a sure subethnic, mainlander constituency of only about 14 percent of the population, and only over many decades has economic and now political opportunity for the majority Taiwanese (and astute handling of the obvious security threat from the PRC) made the government less inherently shaky. In Hong Kong, the governor was in a racial minority of about 2 percent of the population; here, until 1997, the security threat was so overwhelming that the place was indefensible. Singapore is ethnically divided along several lines that could easily become violent; it is essentially a Chinese city surrounded by Malay-Islamic countries that have seen ethnic strife in the past. In all of these countries, the regime justified authoritarianism on grounds of long-standing, central domestic divisions and undeniable outside threats. The governments have been major actors, because people there agree their states could be overwhelmed if they were not. But in the PRC, the situation is entirely different: For long periods, the government has explicitly tried to stir up domestic divisions rather than to dampen them. The most populous state in the world (with the third-largest area) has some natural kinds of security that no small place can match. The type of authoritarianism could be more extractive, because its domestic basis and external environment were more stable. In the NIC cases, an autonomous state serves society better than it can in China during the reform decades. For state-centered treatments of Taiwan, see Lynn White, "The Political Effects of Resource Allocations in Taiwan and Mainland China," *Journal of the Developing Areas* 15 (October 1980), pp. 43–66; and Alice Amsden, "The State and Taiwan's Economic Development," in *Bringing the State Back In,* Peter B. Evans, Dietrich Rueschmeyer, and Theda Skocpol, eds., pp. 78–108.

46. Shanghai and Beijing surely suffered more extensive damage to bureaucratic staffs in the Cultural Revolution than any other places. Areas around Shanghai, in southern Jiangsu and northern Zhejiang, suffered less. Comparisons of the distribution of feisty specialists, if there were any way to research this topic properly, would tell much about China's political evolution.

47. This situation could change in the future, and scholars debate the coherence and incoherence of China's central state in the past. Analysts may, of course, define words however they wish. The aim of the text at this point is not to criticize previous usages but to suggest how the word might now be employed to highlight more political facts.

48. Wang Yu et al., *Da zhuanbian shiqi* (The Era of Great Transformation) (Shijiazhuang: Hebei Renmin Chuban She, 1987), p. 147.

49. Donnithorne's 1972 article—a seminal one for later debates in the China field—has the phrase "Since the Cultural Revolution" in a subtitle. The Cultural Revolution had actually ended. Donnithorne's contribution is in *China Quarterly* 52 (October–December 1972) pp. 605–19. See also Elizabeth Perry, "Rural Violence in Socialist China," *China Quarterly* 103 (September 1985), pp. 414–40; Vivienne Shue, *The Reach of the State* (Stanford: Stanford University Press, 1988); and Jean C. Oi, *State and Peasant in Contemporary China: The Political Economy of Village Government* (Berkeley: University of California Press, 1989). Andrew Walder's recent work concerns the "cleansing class ranks" campaign, which ended in 1971.

50. Helen F. Siu, *Agents and Victims in South China: Accomplices in Rural Revolution* (New Haven: Yale University Press, 1989).

51. This term is from works by Peter Katzenstein; see it used also in Kent E. Calder,

Strategic Capitalism: Private Business and Public Purpose in Japanese Industrial Finance (Princeton: Princeton University Press, 1993), p. 13.

52. This view is not new in studies of Shanghai. See, for example, Leung Yuen-sang, *The Shanghai Taotai: Linkage Man in a Changing Society, 1843–90* (Honolulu: University of Hawaii Press, 1990). The subtitle gives the thesis.

53. Joel S. Migdal, *Strong Societies and Weak States: State-Society Relations and State Capabilities in the Third World* (Princeton: Princeton University Press, 1988), p. 238.

54. See Martin Schoenhals, *The Paradox of Power in a People's Republic of China Middle School* (Armonk, NY: M.E. Sharpe, 1993).

55. This relates to the model of a central "selectocracy" and a local (though she seldom uses that word) consensus rule for decisions in Susan L. Shirk, *The Political Logic of Economic Reform in China* (Berkeley: University of California Press, 1993). See also Helen F. Siu, *Agents and Victims*. Franz Schurmann much earlier showed the importance in China of a distinction between continuous supervision (*jiandu*) and post-hoc inspection (*jiancha*), linking this with Durkheim's two types of integration (redubbed respectively "technical" and "human" organization) in the most creative book ever written about the PRC: *Ideology and Organization in Communist China* (Berkeley: University of California Press, 1966).

56. James G. March and Johan P. Olsen, in "The New Institutionalism: Organizational Factors in Political Life," *American Political Science Review* 78:3 (March 1984), p. 739, refer to work by the psychologist Daniel Kahneman. Neoclassical economists and other rational-choice theorists tend to presume individual people are black boxes, simple folk with simple preferences. Psychologists would all be out of work if that were true. So would other humanists. There is an accounting for tastes.

57. Wang Shaoguang, "The Rise of the Second Budget and the Decline of State Capacity in China," apparently unpublished paper, c. 1993, pp. 3–4, refers to Theda Skocpol, "Bringing the State Back In."

58. This book ordinarily uses the word "sanctions" rather than "coercion," to make clear that positive incentive sanctions can be included in the same category as negative coercion because they are both based on collective norms. A later part of this chapter classifies these four as combinations of individualist or large-group subjects with situational or normative predicates. Wang's terms are borrowed from Gabriel A. Almond and G. Bingham Powell Jr., *Comparative Politics: A Developmental Approach* (Boston: Little, Brown, 1966).

59. The main book on declining state capacity, about a country that has had no revolution, is Atul Kohli, *Democracy and Discontent: India's Growing Crisis of Governability* (Cambridge: Cambridge University Press, 1990).

60. Stephen D. Krasner, *Defending the National Interest* (Princeton: Princeton University Press, 1978), p. 56.

61. From 1952 to 1966, the first ratio was 40 percent, and the second was 59 percent. See Wang Shaoguang, "The Rise of the Second Budget," p. 43.

62. Dorothy J. Solinger, *China's Transition from Socialism: Statist Legacies and Market Reforms, 1980–1990* (Armonk, NY: M.E. Sharpe, 1993), p. 6.

63. The quotation is from Joel Migdal, *Strong Societies and Weak States,* p. 4. This notion of state capacity has been most often used by political scientists to help answer the question What can a government do to make its economy grow? But this just reflects the preference for data relevant to adaptive extraction; studies of capacity for ethnic integration, for example, can be developed in the same framework. See Peter A. Hall, *Governing the Economy: The Politics of State Intervention in Britain and France* (New York: Oxford University Press, 1986).

64. Theda Skocpol, "Bringing the State Back In," p. 21.

65. Ibid.

66. Lynn White, *Policies of Chaos.*

67. Dorothy J. Solinger, *China's Transition from Socialism,* pp. 3–4.

68. Ibid., pp. 143–44.

69. Barrett L. McCormick, *Political Reform in Post-Mao China: Democracy and Bureaucracy in a Leninist State* (Berkeley: University of California Press, 1990).

70. David M. Bachman, *Bureaucracy, Economy, and Leadership,* and other works.

71. Avery Goldstein, *From Bandwagon to Balance-of-Power Politics: Structural Constraints and Politics in China, 1949–1978* (Stanford: Stanford University Press, 1991).

72. See Timothy Mitchell, "The Limits of the State," p. 95, which can be used as a recent summary of these debates along with his non-Foucaultian critics in John Bendix, Bertel Ollman, Bartholomew Sparrow, and Timothy Mitchell, "Going Beyond the State," *American Political Science Review* 86:4 (December 1992), pp. 1007–20.

73. Timothy Mitchell, a student of Egypt, has put the Foucaultian case most strongly thus far; the quoted phrases are from "The Limits of the State," pp. 86 and 94. In studies of China, the historian Prasenjit Duara has contributed *Culture, Power, and the State: Rural North China, 1900–1942* (Stanford: Stanford University Press, 1988); our field will soon see related analyses in the work of political scientists such as Elizabeth Remick and Neil Diamant. These scholars are all young, and issues of evidence will ensure opposition to them in political science from Americanists especially. But because previous definitions of the state raise so many questions, their critiques will be heard. The approach of the present book is to value their search for habits that underlie power in any social institution while denying that such an approach should be applicable only to modern diversified societies and denying also that it need rest on metaphysical ways of handling evidence. Their future publications will surely show ways around these problems.

74. The distinction between concrete and analytic structures is made in Marion J. Levy Jr., "Structural-Functional Analysis," *International Encyclopaedia of the Social Sciences* (London: Macmillan, 1968), pp. 21–28.

75. This is a basic idea in Prasenjit Duara, *Culture, Power, and the State.*

76. Karl Polanyi, *The Great Transformation: The Social and Economic Origins of Our Time* (New York: Rinehart, 1944).

77. Kenneth Lieberthal and Michel Oksenberg, *Policymaking in China: Leaders, Structures, and Processes* (Princeton: Princeton University Press, 1988), p. 23.

78. Robert A. Dahl, *Modern Political Analysis* (Englewood Cliffs, NJ: Prentice-Hall, 1963), p. 40.

79. *Selected Works of Deng Xiaoping, 1975–1982* (Beijing: Foreign Languages Press, 1984), p. 114, speech of March 18, 1978.

80. *Jihui youxing shiwei fa jianghua* (Talking About the Law on Assemblies, Parades, and Demonstrations), Propaganda Office of the Judicial Department of the People's Republic of China, ed. (Beijing: Falü Chuban She, 1990), pp. 9–15.

81. Susan L. Shirk, *The Political Logic,* p. 124.

82. The *sibu* are *bu xuanchuan, bu fandui, bu zhichi,* and *bu zhizhi.* See Daniel Kelliher, *Peasant Power: The Era of Rural Reform, 1979–1989* (New Haven: Yale University Press, 1993), p. 79.

83. *Post,* May 16, 1989.

84. *Post,* February 12, 1990.

85. *Post,* January 10, 1994.

86. Hubert Dreyfus and Paul Rabinow, *Michel Foucault: Beyond Structuralism and Hermeneutics,* 2nd ed. (Chicago: University of Chicago Press, 1983); but the author first

saw this in Mayfair Mei-hui Yang, "The Art of Social Relationships and Exchange in China" (Ph.D. dissertation, Department of Anthropology, University of California, Berkeley, 1986), p. 321.

87. Frances Fox Piven and Richard A. Cloward, *Poor People's Movements* (New York: Vintage, 1979), p. 5.

88. Barrett L. McCormick, *Political Reform in Post-Mao China,* p. 23.

89. G. William Skinner, "Overseas Chinese Leadership: Paradigm for a Paradox," in Gehan Wijeyewardene, ed., *Leadership and Authority: A Symposium* (Singapore: University of Malaya Press, 1968). "Captain" is *kapitan,* the colonial Dutch for just this kind of leader.

90. Andrew G. Walder, *Communist Neo-Traditionalism,* p. 19.

91. Zhou Xueguang, "Unorganized Interests and Collective Action in Communist China," *American Sociological Review* 58 (February 1993), p. 57.

92. Marc Blecher and Vivienne Shue, *Tethered Deer,* pp. 44–45.

93. See Linda Chelan Li, "Provincial Discretion and National Power: Investment Policy in Guangdong and Shanghai, 1978–93" (ms., May 1996), and Jae Ho Chung, "Studies of Central-Provincial Relations in the People's Republic of China: A Mid-Term Appraisal," *China Quarterly* 142 (June 1995), pp. 487–508.

94. See Ding Xueliang, *The Decline of Communism in China: The Legitimacy Crisis, 1979–1989* (New York: Cambridge University Press, 1994).

95. The first quotation is from Grant Evans, *Lao Peasants Under Socialism* (New Haven: Yale University Press, 1990), p. 185; the second is in Michael Moerman, "A Thai Village Headman as a Synaptic Leader," in *Modern Thai Politics,* rev. ed., Clarke Neher, ed. (London: Schenkman, 1979), pp. 249–50.

96. Another critique of the stress on neotraditionalism is by Brantly Womack, "Transfigured Community: Neo-Traditionalism and Work Unit Socialism in China," *China Quarterly* 126 (June 1990), pp. 313–32. In Chinese studies, the classic article about factions—whose framework allows many of the considerations raised here—is Andrew J. Nathan, "A Factionalism Model for CCP Politics," *China Quarterly* 53 (January-March 1973), pp. 34–66. A major comparative analysis of factions is Ralph W. Nicholas, "Factions: A Comparative Analysis," in *Political Systems and the Distribution of Power,* Michael Banton, ed. (London: Tavistock, 1968), pp. 21–58.

97. Lynn White, *Policies of Chaos.*

98. See G. William Skinner, "Overseas Chinese Leadership," pp. 191–207.

99. In the Southeast Asian cases, this empowerment always included traditional court titles of nobility. Of course, these Southeast Asian situations differed in many ways from the setting of local leaders in China today. The ethnically divided patterns in traditional Manila, for example, are not identical with those in rural China. The point, however, is in the dual source of legitimacy for local leaders. The pattern that Skinner sets forth can be seen as very general.

100. Something like this paradigm has also been used in a book by a student of Skinner; see Helen Siu, *Agents and Victims.* The masculine pronoun is used here for hinge leaders only because in these traditional courts they apparently were always men.

101. Susan L. Shirk, *The Political Logic,* offers a rational-choice decision rule that is convincingly common in China: If all designated agents at any bureaucratic level can reach a consensus, then the decision (or information to negate it) is not referred upward in the formal system. Shirk in effect describes the political culture that prevents much vertical communication.

102. Many Western academics and governmentalists assume that the order that is easiest to footnote must be the real one, and much of the "cultural nexus of power" is in the minds of intellectuals. Duara is aware of this issue and provides extensive local

evidence on the situational ecologies of the places he studies.

103. The author's previous book, *Policies of Chaos,* employs a similar logic to explain another event (the start of violence in the Cultural Revolution). Campaigns, monitors, and labels are used there as adapted versions of charismatic, traditional, and legal-rational authority. All these saved costs and mobilized resources for Mao's state. But these administrative policy techniques to scare, oversee, and categorize people became, after spark causes of August 1966, the tools of individuals, networks, and groups that had previously been repressed by them. *Policies of Chaos* is organized somewhat like this book, with chapters about situational roles (largely of workers and managers) that alternate with chapters about normative activities (largely of residents and students). This book's topic is happier, but it is meant as a sequel.

104. James Scott, *Weapons of the Weak: Everyday Forms of Peasant Resistance* (New Haven: Yale University Press, 1985).

105. James C. Scott, *Domination and the Arts of Resistance: Hidden Transcripts* (New Haven: Yale University Press, 1990), p. 183. On the next page, Scott improves this implication by suggesting an analogy to the word "infrastructure." He says that infrapolitics "provides much of the cultural and structural underpinnings of the more visible political action on which our attention has generally been focussed." Being so, it is strong, not weak. A realistic recognition of the resources of the weak also makes them stronger in Scott's essay "Everyday Forms of Resistance," in *Everyday Forms of Peasant Resistance,* Forrest D. Colburn, ed. (Armonk, NY: M. E. Sharpe, 1989), pp. 3–30. On p. 4, Scott appropriately calls for more attention to "undeclared, disguised forms of autonomous resistance."

106. Liu Binyan's famous description of the interpersonal network of the corrupt cadre Wang Shouxin, in Bin county, Heilongjiang, suggests that many of the links she established were horizontal, although a "lovely curtain of fraternal loyalty, sincere gratitude, mutual concern, profound friendship, etc., etc. concealed relationships of out-and-out power brokerage. One side would invest a peach . . . and the other would answer with a plum." See "People or Monsters," in *People or Monsters,* Perry Link, ed. (Bloomington: Indiana University Press, 1983), p. 56.

107. "In the energy sphere, Li Peng and Kang Shien were the key actors in late 1985. The key energy ministries . . . depended on Li and Kang to be their voice among the 25 to 35 top policy makers, and those 25 to 35 in turn looked to Li and Kang as their key links to the energy bureaucracies." Kenneth Lieberthal and Michel Oksenberg, *Policymaking in China,* pp. 37–38.

108. This lancing critique of the PRC comes from a Marxist, Richard Smith, in "The Chinese Road to Capitalism," *New Left Review* 199 (May-June 1993), p. 78.

109. Victor Nee, "Peasant Entrepreneurship and the Politics of Regulation in China," in *Remaking the Economic Institutions of China and Eastern Europe,* V. Nee and D. Stark, eds. (Stanford: Stanford University Press, 1991), p. 173. Italics added to show the extent of the problem Nee addresses here.

110. A summary is in Huntington's article, "Political Development and Political Decay," in *Political System and Change,* Ikuô Kabashima and Lynn T. White III, eds. (Princeton: Princeton University Press, 1986), pp. 95–139, and pp. 8–10 for further analysis in the introduction by White and Kabashima.

111. Chen Kang, "Economic Reform and Collective Action in China," *China Report* 3 (May 1992), p. 3. This article explicitly uses logics from Mancur Olson.

112. Richard Madsen, "The Public Sphere: Civil Society and Moral Community," in *Modern China* 19:2 (April 1993), pp. 193–94.

113. Elemér Hankiss, *East European Alternatives* (Oxford: Clarendon Press, 1990), pp. 92ff.

114. See Frances Fox Piven and Richard A. Cloward, *Poor People's Movements.*

115. This famous passage is quoted from Karl Marx, "The Eighteenth Brumaire of Louis Bonaparte," in *The Marx-Engels Reader,* Robert C. Tucker, ed. (New York: Norton, 1972), pp. 515–16.

116. Thomas C. Schelling's insight about unintended effects in *Micromotives and Macrobehavior* (New York: Norton, 1978) would correct an overemphasis on "transcripts" as a basis of resistance.

117. Voice exerts influence by calling fellow members of an organized community back to its norms; exit, by reducing the situational resources of an unsatisfactory association. Exit can be powerful, even more surely than voice, when the organization's resources have no outside underwriter (just as voice exerts power more surely than exit in most voluntary organizations, for example). Albert Hirschman also suggests how voice may become mere ritual rebellion (a controversial example comes from a war protester kept inside Lyndon Johnson's administration), or exit may bring no result (as in the Nigerian railroads, which were safe as a line item on the state budget, no matter whether they provided service). Voice or exit can be powerful or not, depending on other characteristics of the organization that are specifiable. State-level organizations are included in this theory, and Hirschman has shown special interest in exit and voice among people dissatisfied with the German Democratic Republic. See *Exit, Voice, and Loyalty* (Cambridge: Harvard University Press, 1970).

118. France is the country where *dirigisime* got its name; see Ezra N. Suleiman, *Private Power and Centralization in France: The Notaires and the State* (Princeton: Princeton University Press, 1987).

119. This is partly based on the results of interviews of PRC university students in 1992 and 1993 by Solomon M. Karmel, now a professor but formerly a graduate student at Princeton University, who is publishing a paper with rich details of the views of young Chinese intellectuals about (and sometimes against) democracy.

120. James C. Scott, *Domination and the Arts of Resistance,* p. 168 and again on p. 178, follows Clifford Geertz and puts forward the opposite hypotheses; but symbols can have functions. The second quotation is on p. 181. See also Suzanne Langer, *Philosophy in a New Key: A Study in the Symbolism of Reason, Rite, and Art* (New York: Penguin, 1942). Also, social functions can serve nonelites.

121. Roy Forward, "Letter from Shanghai," and Shelley Warner, "Shanghai's Response to the Deluge," in *The Pro-Democracy Protests in China: Reports from the Provinces,* Jonathan Unger, ed. (Armonk, NY: M.E. Sharpe, 1991), pp. 194 and 222.

122. The client was a foreigner; see Joan Grant, *Worm-eaten Hinges: Tensions and Turmoil in Shanghai, 1988–89, Events Leading Up to Tiananmen Square* (Melbourne: Hyland House, 1991), p. 117.

123. Zhou Xueguang, "Unorganized Interests and Collective Action," p. 57.

124. Ralf Dahrendorf, *Class and Class Conflict in Industrial Society* (London: Routledge and Kegan Paul, 1959). The interpretations below use Dahrendorf's ideas but are not in full conformity with them. The author's thinking on this has been stimulated by comments from a professor who was a Princeton graduate student, Greg Felker.

125. See Alan Cromer, *Uncommon Sense: The Heretical Nature of Science* (New York: Oxford University Press, 1993).

126. This effort might be better explained in terms of academic politics and finance (in some cases, links between neoclassical economist-administrators and university donor–businesspeople) than in terms of anything epistemological. That would be a separate study.

127. Lynn White, in *Policies of Chaos,* associates these three motives for action with three typical institutions that were prominent in Mao's years: charismatic campaigns,

traditionalist monitoring of clients by bosses, and the rationality (at least for a socialist administration) of labeling groups to be benefited or shortchanged. As explanations of Cultural Revolution politics, these *institutions* did not exhaust a logically composed list of political motives, but the authority types they exemplified did so. Recent archival research by Elizabeth Perry and Shanghai labor historians has found superbly detailed archival data about workers' politics in particular. Concurrent use of the comparative literature on protest, however, has not thus far led to links between the motives for these actions, so that it is possible to refer back to the old campaigns/monitors/labels threesome in hopes for a more unified account of why the event happened. See Elizabeth Perry, *Shanghai on Strike: The Politics of Chinese Labor* (Boulder: Westview, 1996).

128. The type of predicate is what makes a claim causal, not the type of phenomena cited to confirm it. "The rain god makes people catch colds," to take an extreme example, is a causal proposition even though some of the data adduced for it will involve replicable customary meanings rather than replicable experiments about situations. If any predicate contains a direct object that is a purported effect, then the statement is causal no matter whether its validity is confirmed by conventional meanings (the power of the rain god, multiplication, and so forth) or by unintended situations (viruses, the temperature during the storm, and other circumstances for whose understanding human motives help not at all)—or, as usual, by a combination of the two.

129. This book uses the word "cause" in its conventional sense: something that makes something else happen. This allows multiple and partial causes, but it does not include the further restriction (often implied but seldom stated by rational-action theorists) that causes must be unintended by humans. Of course, if that is made by definition a necessary trait of a "cause," then human science explanations of events could never be causal. Perhaps we should expect rhetorical tricks from professionals. For a more commonsensical definition of "cause," the first source on which this author could lay his hands was the *New Collins Dictionary* (London: Collins, 1987), p. 154, where none of the nine proffered meanings implies that a cause must be unintended. Some of the example usages there (e.g., "to make common cause with" or "they fought for the miners' cause") positively reek of human intentions.

130. This discontinuity, like a cliff rather than a beach at the edge of an ocean, nonetheless comes in different heights. As Albert Hirschman has shown in *Exit, Voice,* the entry (or exit) costs of an organization tend to correlate with "loyalty" to it. Revolutionary change from partially tolerated to more ideal institutions becomes difficult if the transaction cost of that change is high. Evolution, e.g. in biology, is not always to "better" adaptation, since change is path dependent. See also Peter Passell, "Why the Best Doesn't Always Win," from *New York Times Magazine,* May 5, 1966, pp. 60–61.

131. Daniel Little kindly provided this to the author but is not responsible for it, because it was merely in draft for a review of a book by Stephen Turner.

132. The link between creating concepts and understanding them is proposed in Thomas Hobbes, *The Leviathan,* Everyman Edition (New York: E.P. Dutton Co., n.d.).

133. This book rejects wholly "skeptical" forms of interpretation, but it includes an "affirmative" version of the postmodern interest in the results of rhetoric (especially propaganda from the state). "Skeptical" postmodernism comes from theorists such as Jacques Derrida, who treats consciousness as if it were basically autonomous of any reality that can be perceived by more than one person. These theorists tend to keep discussion going because of radical doubt about the possibility of communication. But such narcissistic skeptics differ from "affirmative" postmodernists, who interpret the interests implicit in symbols and logics. A fatal deconstruction of "skeptical" postmodernism in social science is easy, since that view really reduces society to the analyst. But the "affirmatives" are not so lightly dismissed, because they leave the door open to conclu-

sions that can be understood between different people; and their deconstructions could be incisive. It is odd that most political scientists, of all people, have been so repelled by the obscurantist language of the skeptics that they have missed the political insights that affirmative postmodernism promises. They could well find political (e.g., American national) interests in "methodological individualism," but they could find much else too. The distinction between skeptics and affirmatives is presented in Pauline Marie Roseneau, *Post-modernism and the Social Sciences: Insights, Inroads, and Intrusions* (Princeton: Princeton University Press, 1992), esp. pp. 81–85 and 167–84.

134. A similar debate rages concerning the scientific basis of human consciousness. Some neuroscientists seek an "electrophysiological" or chemical basis of consciousness; others think that at least the brain's ability to change its wiring makes the problem more complex than science can soon handle; others from various fields hold that consciousness is an experience that even a successful physical theory of it could not comprehend. This debate may parallel the naturalist vs. humanist controversy in social science. A more obvious similarity between the two debates, however, is the tendency of partisans on both sides to speak as if they should mainly argue about methods rather than findings. When any kind of concept gives insights and furthers knowledge, it is scientific. Nobelist Francis Crick is mentor of the electrophysiological group; see John Horgan, "Can Science Explain Consciousness?" *Scientific American* 271:1 (July 1994), pp. 72–78.

135. See Ian Shapiro and Donald Green, *Pathologies of Rational Choice Theory: A Critique of Applications in Political Science* (New Haven: Yale University Press, 1994).

136. The reasons why professionals do this are social, not epistemological, but are beyond the scope of a book about China.

137. Daniel Little, *Varieties of Social Explanation: An Introduction to the Philosophy of Social Science* (Boulder: Westview, 1991), pp. 196 and 200.

138. The basis of such a view is presented in Laszlo Versenyi, *Socratic Humanism* (New Haven: Yale University Press, 1963), which interprets Plato in a naturalistic and economical way, especially relying on sections of the *Symposium* that define the good in terms of what is needed, what could fill a vacuum. This may unmask him more thoroughly than do usual references to the *Republic.*

139. Talcott Parsons's old functionalist framework remained inadequate in two ways that really must be pointed out here: First, in conceiving norms it emphasized discursive, conscious evaluation but neglected spontaneous, cultural habits of mind. Second, in conceiving individuals and small groups it overemphasized the extent to which they could be integrated into large collectivities but underplayed their independent (not just deviant) creative powers. So the old functionalism included both the norm-fact and collective-individual dimensions but did not take the less coherent side of either spectrum seriously enough. It assumed both more consistency among norms and more harmony in collectivities than actually exist. It tended to explain things by how they hold together more than by how they fall apart. It inclined to the presumption that continuity rather than change was the usual state. It often implied that deviation, rather than dullness, was the odd thing, deserving a special account. The value of any such premise can lie only in its research results. A new functionalism can include the possibilities of radically incompatible norms and conflicting groups. Words such as "norm" and "value" can be reread in light of research by anthropologists and psychologists who show the flexibility of consciousness. Words such as "society" and "polity" can be read in light of group conflicts and politicians' pretentiousness. Since it is the fad to put "neo-" before the names of old but remediable approaches in social science, and since the structural side of the matter has already been heralded by "neoinstitutionalists," the method here is neofunctionalist. This relies to some extent on cues from *The New Institutionalism in Organizational Analysis,* Walter W. Powell and Paul J. DiMaggio, eds. (Chicago: University of Chicago Press,

1991), but both refer mainly to works by Talcott Parsons, such as *The Social System* (Glencoe, IL: Free Press, 1951).

140. In John Bendix, Bertel Ollman, Bartholomew Sparrow, and Timothy Mitchell, "Going Beyond the State," p. 1012.

141. See Lynn White, "Joint Ventures in a New Shanghai at Pudong," in *Advances in Chinese Industrial Studies: Joint Ventures in the PRC,* Sally Stewart, ed. (Greenwich, CT: JAI Press, 1995), pp. 75–120. This is available in the U.S., was not just a working paper, and was meant to complement the present two volumes.

142. Many works in the footnotes of ibid. are germane. Special note should be taken of research on Pudong by Thomas B. Gold. On all of China, see Nicholas R. Lardy, *Foreign Trade and Economic Reform in China, 1978–1990* (Cambridge: Cambridge University Press, 1992), and Margaret M. Pearson, *Joint Ventures in the People's Republic of China: The Control of Foreign Direct Investment under Socialism* (Princeton: Princeton University Press, 1991).

143. Among the best books about China's reforms, including information about Beijing and elsewhere, are Richard Baum, *Burying Mao*, and Harry Harding, *China's Second Revolution.*

144. The most important notes this book lacks—because apparently the work has not yet been done—are to comprehensive treatments of recent decades around cities such as Chengdu (Sichuan) and Qingdao (Shandong). The Shanghai delta suggests many comparisons, but there are too few monographs with which to make them.

145. The author has tried to be careful in requesting help for this book from PRC citizens. He can report that no person who aided the project has to his knowledge been politically or legally inconvenienced. The PRC's current officials, including local ones, deserve some thanks for this situation—which is, for an academic, one of the most important reforms.

146. At the University of California at Berkeley, a group of eminent scholars (including Elizabeth Perry, Thomas Gold, Frederic Wakeman, Yeh Wen-hsin, and others) have found good support for work on Shanghai. Most of these researchers study periods before 1970; but Tom Gold has worked on Pudong development and several other recent Shanghai topics, and Elizabeth Perry has written very important studies of Shanghai workers both before and after 1949. Deborah Davis, of Yale, and Emily Honig, of Santa Cruz, have also done pioneering studies of various topics in Shanghai. Susan Whiting, of the University of Washington, has studied rural development nearby. The bibliography includes the names of several other scholars who are also working on Shanghai topics.

147. The title "autonomous region" for minority areas obscures that these are provinces too. The three "directly ruled cities" of Shanghai, Beijing, and Tianjin are *zhixia shi,* and the "autonomous regions" of Guangxi, Inner Mongolia, Ningxia, Tibet, and Xinjiang are *zizhi qu.* Many regulations are promulgated in a manner that suggests none of the thirty provinces are autonomous and all are directly ruled. Local resources and politicians affect this situation in practice. The titles, however, do not.

148. *"Pipan" Beijing ren?!* ("Criticize" Beijing Man?!), Luo Shuang et al., eds. (Beijing: Zhongguo Shehui Chuban She, 1994).

149. See Dorothy J. Solinger, *China's Transition from Socialism,* which is mostly but not exclusively based on data from Wuhan.

Part 1

Extraction: Local Entrepreneurs Reform the Political Economy—Prosperity Beyond the State

One has to have spent a long time in politics to understand the extent to which men push each other away from their own plans and how the destinies of the world unfold through the consequences, but often the contrary consequences, of the intentions which produce them, like a kite which flies by the opposing forces of the wind and the string.

—Alexis de Tocqueville[1]

Most people think of China's reforms as essentially economic, and rising wealth is the most obvious Chinese change in recent years. The continued prominence of the Communist Party leaves an impression that the PRC's social order and politics have been rather stagnant as the economy has bounded ahead. A general tendency of modern thought holds that change emerges mostly from concrete, material, economic factors. Reform China provides much evidence of this, as the pages below will show—but the reforms are not wholly economic; they are also cultural, integrative, governmental, and local. This first book in the two-volume set, concerning economic policies, begins with the popular view of reforms as essentially material, while questioning another popular view that they have all been directed from Beijing. The later three parts of the study test evidence that they were also partly caused by noneconomic factors.

Analysts find many ways to make their work easier and clearer while also making it less realistic. For example, the easiest course is to define reform as economic, and also as a top-down affair. Officials have an interest in providing data to justify that view of it; but this approach excludes, by *a priori* definition, most aspects of the syndrome that may be caused by medium-sized or small groups. Writers tend to avoid research on these aspects because of legalistic rather than behavioral definitions of power. But economic decentralization *is* political decentralization. Decisions by managers, buyers, and sellers have increasingly replaced those by state directors. Government as a function is embedded in many power networks. Unofficial "social" or "civil" networks become specifically political, like government, when they decide on resources or issue mandates. State elites are constrained, whenever they rely on local leaders to provide growth and employment.[2]

The CCP now depends on economic prosperity as its major claim to popular support. But quick economic growth produces losers and gainers. It can create political disequilibrium.[3] The most obvious economic loser during China's reforms, thus far, has been the state budget—for reasons that no part of the country illustrates better than Shanghai. The central government over many years has repeatedly issued proclamations about Shanghai's importance as the most crucial center of China's future modernization. But the state has depended so heavily on Shanghai revenues, growth there has been slower than that in other Chinese places. Smaller cities on the Shanghai delta have boomed heartily throughout the reform era, largely because their products have displaced Shanghai products on markets elsewhere. Although this pattern has created enormous problems for factories in the metropolis, it has hardly discomfited the many Shanghai families and local leaders who identify both with the city and with other parts of the delta.

Light industry dominated Shanghai's economy before 1949. That is the historical explanation for the city's later high-tax, low-growth syndrome. These consumer industries were tools to garner government revenues. The socialist state could decree prices, as planners gained control of markets throughout China during the 1950s: input prices low, and consumer product prices high. The difference, in profits, went to the state. When these light industries were nationalized, they became the government's main source of funds. Rates of tax and other extractions from Shanghai remained high until the mid-1980s, long after fiscal reforms had reduced the central tax burden elsewhere. Shanghai's most important product, from the state's point of view, has always been money. The change of the mid-1980s came not from liberal epiphanies among Beijing leaders. Instead, it came from the rise of cooperative and quasi-private factories in rural areas that the state could not control—and from socialist planners' consequent inability to deliver inputs to Shanghai light industries, or to sell their products in competition with rural industries.

This decline of government capacity began in the 1970s, although only late in that decade did it become evident. The slowly growing unavailability of materials and markets hindered Shanghai production. This metropolis was practically the only Chinese province to have a *lower* yearly growth rate in 1979–89, after reforms were announced, than in 1953–78.[4] The ballyhoo about reform in 1978 did not reduce central imposts on Shanghai nearly as much as on other places. More important, the continuing depreciation of Shanghai's capital stock was left basically uncompensated until after the mid-1980s. Taxes and controls are the reason for Shanghai's relatively poor 1979–89 performance. Both Jiangsu and Zhejiang grew at an average annual rate of 5.6 percent during the earlier 1953–78 period—but then respectively at 11.0 and 12.8 percent during the next decade. Shanghai, however, grew at 8.7 percent in the earlier period; but then its rate fell to 7.6 percent in the 1979–89 decade, which was a golden time for other places.

The main problem was not that fiscal extraction from Shanghai rose in real terms after 1978. The problem was that the impost rate did not decline after the city's capital infrastructure had already been milked dry. Shanghai industry was not permitted to recuperate from depreciation until the 1990s. Shanghai had much of the highest annual growth rate of local fiscal extraction in 1953–78 (rising 17.5 percent annually on average). Central budget-makers in that period became addicted to Shanghai money. In 1979–89, it was the only province to record a negative rate of fiscal growth (-0.1 percent).[5] With so little capital investment over the previous decades, the city's tax base had not been sustained.

This overview of extractive reforms would be incomplete without specifying what the PRC state in its revolutionary heyday had mainly taxed from rural areas. The state took grain from peasants to feed urban people. Well before 1978, this system had faltered—partly because the grain imposts could no longer be levied in customary amounts on an industrializing countryside, and partly because the population they fed in cities had exploded. If 1953 and 1978 are compared, the state's net take of grain rose 19 percent over that quarter century; but the number of urban people depending on this food rose 120 percent.[6] As the technology to grow grain changed, local networks of peasants established industries and devoted their work to newly profitable endeavors. The state structure had the capacity to control people when the urban population did not become large relative to the food supply for it, and when rural peasants stayed in agriculture so nationalized factories could prosper. Neither of these conditions applied by the 1970s. The result is called reforms.

Chapter 1.1

Rural Political Networks Beyond the State

Ordinary life for most people is regulated by the rules of work and the rewards of work which pattern each day and week and season. Once cast out of that routine, people are cast out of the regulatory framework that it imposes.

—Frances Piven and Richard Cloward[7]

. . . a pestilent, pernicious people . . . such as take oaths to the government but underhand labor its subversion. . . .

—Bishop Trelawny[8]

Reform politics on the rich Shanghai delta have especially benefited large rather than small organizations outside the official orbit. This pattern is not novel in developing countries. As Robert Bates points out, "Governments in Africa subsidize fertilizers, seeds, mechanical equipment, and credit" for large farmers—with the ostensible aim of increasing food production, and with the result of bolstering well-established, large-scale, and modern farmers rather than newcomers, small-scale, and traditional farmers.[9] The same thing has happened in China, because the government there too cannot control all the power networks on whose support it depends.

The most important rural subsidy to local cadres in Mao's time was the near-elimination of the price of land. Fields during the Maoist period were supplied to rural teams on the basis of institutions that evolved from the land reform of the 1950s. Nothing was paid for use of these plots, except taxes. The lease was rent-free, based on allocation. In exchange, cadres organized farmers to sell their products cheaply. But in rich parts of China, even more than in other parts of the developing world such as Africa, local organizations are traditionally well-developed, just as the central state is. Chinese rural leaders practically all thought of themselves as linked to the state; but objectively, they also had large, long-term conflicts of interest with the state. The most obvious in recent decades was whether they could garner more of the profits of processing rural materials. By the early 1970s, rural notables were better-placed to make gains in this tug-of-war over money from manufacturing.

Agriculture as the Root of the End of the Revolution

"Agriculture is the root" was a Maoist slogan that emphasized the importance to the revolutionary state of peasant support and tax grain. But China's reforms, which meant the end of revolution, also began in the countryside. On the Yangzi delta, by the early 1970s, two new conditions appeared: First, *the productivity of rural labor rose*, because field work had mechanized quickly at that time. Second, *the state could not take its previous high rake-off* from the profits of rural processing, because it had lost much of its monitoring ability through maltreatment of its own bureaucrats during the late 1960s, as well as much of its legitimacy among peasants because of the early-1960s famine. So local leaders conceived labor-management reasons to start new factories, and urban leaders could generally not prevent the rise of this new rural competition.

Field mechanization in the late 1960s and early 1970s offered technologies that could free large amounts of labor from land near Shanghai. Some local leaders established rural factories at this time, using raw materials that had previously gone to urban state industries that had been the central government's main tax base. More than any other event, this was the seed of China's reform and the end of the central revolutionary state that had been run in many crucial respects from Beijing. This industrial and "green revolution" of the late 1960s and early 1970s came from various kinds of agricultural extension: walking tractors and rice transplanting machines, new seeds for grains with shorter stalks that yielded more edible calories faster, especially when nourished by more inorganic fertilizer and more reliable water as supplied by canals during dry spells and by tube wells in soggy seasons. Shanghai's suburbs in 1965, for example, were only 17 percent machine-tilled. By 1972, this portion was already 76 percent (and by 1984, 89 percent).[10]

What did the ex-peasants, displaced from fields by these methods, do for incomes? Some local leaders set up factories, usually in brigade or team collectives, at first using local labor. Many techniques for making cement, bricks, pumps, bootlegged cigarettes, and other easily salable products did not require large amounts of capital or high technology. So in the early 1970s quick rural industrialization—not planned by the national government and disserving its interests—meant that state enterprises could no longer commandeer all the raw materials to which they had become accustomed at prices the state was willing to pay. Economic boom, inflation, bribes for procurement agents, government budget deficits, a drop of state control over migrants, and many other aspects of China's reforms followed agricultural mechanization and its main result, rural industry.

The Basis for Peasant Leaders' Tacit Autonomy

Technical extension in agriculture would not, by itself, have guaranteed that local leaders in peasant communities could found factories. Some could respond in this way by 1970–71, because the urban agencies with interests in preventing rural industrialization had decimated themselves in the Cultural Revolution. Also, many urban cadres, though greatly respected by rural leaders for their governmental status, had given much previous advice to farmers that had been egregiously bad. After some "penetration" of villages in the 1950s, the famine of 1959–61 encouraged local peasant leaders to make more of their own decisions, at least quietly.[11]

The post-Leap famine of 1959–61 was statistically the largest human disaster of the twentieth century; it killed more people than any other event. Estimates of above-normal mortality in China during this famine range from 17 to 30 million.[12] It was for that reason also a more important political occasion, for more Chinese, than was the Cultural Revolution—even though a scan of most publications does not suggest this. Scholars have written more about the Liberation of 1949, the administrative restructuring of 1958, the violent ideals from 1966, or the economic modernization from 1978 onward. These events all involved changes in ideology and at the top of the political system, where intellectuals tend to concentrate their attention. But 1960 (like the rise of early reforms about 1971) more deeply affected larger groups, mostly peasants. The famine tended to delegitimate the Party in areas where local CCP leaders followed orders from their official superiors.

The reform era is not the first in which local power networks completely re-shaped the most important state policies and indirectly determined which policy tendencies would prevail over time in the central government. The present author has written another book arguing that local reactions to earlier administrative policies caused the start of widespread violence in the Cultural Revolution. For the famine of 1959–61, too, the interests of local leaders also seem to have been causal. In the parts of China most affected by the famine, rural Party leaders had acquired interests in 1958 policies that a series of retrenching directives in May 1959 could not reverse. There is evidence that by early 1959 Mao Zedong was backpedaling on Leap policies, to the extent he could do so without further complicating his political embarrassment in Beijing then. Leap measures had already become odious to many peasants, and in the most populous provinces (Sichuan and Shandong) sharp mortality increases between 1958 and 1959 decelerated by 1960—apparently because local leaders saw a need for moderation to decrease the epidemic of deaths. But especially in Anhui and Henan, the Leap's decentralization was so agreeable to local leaders that they missed this chance. Local administrators in these places failed, for their own reasons, to follow the early-1959 central government signals for quiet retrenchment—with the result that the nationwide 1960 famine was most excruciating in those places. In provinces (including Jiangsu, Zhejiang, and Shanghai) where the 1959 rural administrators moderated the excesses of the Leap, the Party retained somewhat more widespread legitimacy over the next three decades than it did in places like Anhui and Henan that suffered real holocausts then.[13] Even in places where fewer had died, local peasant leaders heard informally about the disaster areas and had good reason to doubt the omniscience of high Party leaders on agriculture.

Rural leaders sought both new technologies and new systems for compensating agricultural labor. "Responsibility fields" (*zeren tian*) were introduced extensively as early as the post-Leap retrenchments of the 1960s. In secret, household contracting at some places was maintained straight through the Cultural Revolution, until it was publicly re-legitimated in the late 1970s.[14]

Three kinds of equipment, especially, saved agricultural labor. First, machines to pluck rice seedlings from nursery fields (*bayang ji*) became widely used around Shanghai and in coastal deltas further south from the late 1960s. The second major technology involved machines that transplanted these seedlings onto large paddies (*chayang ji*). Third, this same period also saw a major expansion of the number of hand tractors (*shoufu tuola ji*), which could be used both on nursery and large fields to aerate soil, or to pull a plowshare (*li*) or reaper (*shouge ji*). Also, the engines of light tractors could be hitched to pumps. With other attachments, they could haul trailers and perform many other tasks.[15]

The total wattage of all agricultural machinery in Shanghai's rural areas rose 19 percent *annually* between 1965 and 1978—a very high rate for a long period.[16] From 1979 to 1989, years that are usually conceived as central to reform, the annual increase was far lower—less than 3 percent. The relatively quick tenfold increase of electricity use for fields in suburban Shanghai saved a great deal of labor power.[17]

In 1965, the percentage of suburban Shanghai's cultivated area tilled by machine was only 17 percent; but by 1972, it was 76 percent; and by 1974, 89 percent. In 1965, few or no mechanical planters or harvesters had been used in these suburbs; but by 1974, the number of planting machines was almost 9,000; then by 1976, it was 27,000. The suburbs in 1974 also had over 1,000 harvesters, and almost 8,000 by 1976.[18] This very sharp increase of agricultural machinery in Shanghai's suburbs (and adjacent areas of the Yangzi delta) during the late 1960s and early 1970s was the basis for quick rural industrialization which became the driver of reforms. These machines freed labor, and they gave more local leaders means to seek new wealth and power. Old central policies for agricultural extension brought technological opportunities—and a higher portion of China's wealth—to rural power networks that later policies could not reverse, regardless of the effects of these changes on the state.[19]

Over time, the mechanization of agriculture also spread in other parts of China. The horsepower of all China's local irrigation machines doubled in the decade before 1973.[20] From 1971 to 1975, PRC local authorities completed 4.5 million small water conservancy projects.[21] Throughout the country, the number of machines in 1978 stood at the following percentages of those in 1970: pumps, 246 percent; motorized transplanting machines, 262 percent; large and middle-size tractors, 355 percent; walking tractors, 631 percent; and agricultural pick-up trucks, 914 percent.[22] This sharp growth in farm mechanization was a basic indirect cause of reforms in all of China, especially in the Shanghai delta where the rise was quick and early.

Agricultural mechanization was supported by new technical facilities in many rich parts of China, even though its most important support came from farmer leaders. By the mid-1970s, each of China's provinces had a research institute to study new seeds and new uses for agricultural machines. Shanghai and other South China provinces set up special programs to adapt machinery to water-covered paddies.[23] The Chongming County Agricultural Machines Research Institute began in 1971. By 1974, it was involved in 29 large projects; and in the winter of 1975–76, this institute devoted itself to improve the design of machines to take seedlings from nursery fields. The best aspects of seven different models were to be combined in a new device, to be ready for the spring harvest of 1976. This schedule was met.[24] Agricultural extension activities were reportedly opposed by radicals, who doubted that technical intellectuals could be of help, and who had their own agenda for rural areas. The radicals were wary of schemes that freed labor from agriculture without putting it into other uses of which they approved. The list of these alternative uses did not include making money.

Despite such high-placed political opposition during the early 1970s, agricultural extension continued—and not just at the relatively high county or township administrative levels. It required capital and support from villages. In 1975, in Shanghai's rural counties, more than half (51 percent) of all "means of production" already belonged to the lowest-level units, the production teams. Only 15 percent belonged to brigades, and 34 percent including some expensive factories were commune property. Radical quasi-mayor Zhang Chunqiao thought the communes' portion was too low and the team portion much too high.[25] But Zhang's views on this were not shared by the peasants over whom he just apparently ruled. He fulminated, correctly, that independent rural factories would weaken state socialism. Meanwhile, they continued to make money and raise local resources.

Chinese economists have suggested many reasons why the agricultural reforms raised output. Many of these are based in pre-1978 changes. In the crop cycle, there are diseconomies of scale except during "rush" periods such as transplanting and sowing, when all hands have traditionally helped in the fields.[26] State-paid cadres' attempts to organize the rural economy led to agricultural extension of seed-types, fertilizers, and irrigation that eventually proved fruitful. They also led to campaigns that too frequently ignored what more local leaders knew about their land. The compensation system for peasants under the Maoist system depressed labor incentives; a person who worked hard would not necessarily earn much. Especially after the benefits of agricultural extension in Mao's time had been spread, future growth in rural China depended on some decentralization of payments.[27] This change occurred in waves, often as indirect rather than direct effects of policies.

After 1970, structural changes in actual decision-reaching systems meant that the green revolution had political results, even though nobody talked about them as such. When top levels of the Party lost control of the countryside because of the early-1960s famine and the late-1960s violence, peasant leaders could go their own way. So by the early 1970s, the political shoe dropped. First it did so in many rich rural parts of Jiangnan, and perhaps in other prosperous areas, although not yet throughout the nation. The agrarian conditions for more wealth and power in medium-sized rural units had been growing for some time, and about 1971 the political conditions were also present. Reforms began slowly in other fields—ranging from foreign policy and military budgets to media technology and the 1973 reappearance of Deng Xiaoping—so much that it is no longer adequate to assert that "the reforms" began in 1978. Also, it would hide too much to claim that the Cultural Revolution ended in 1976.[28] The most important single reform—the localization of control over resources—began earlier, largely as an unintended side effect of earlier state measures for agricultural extension.

Ex–Field Hands Whom Local Leaders Could Gratify

The green revolution did not free a fixed number of potential field hands from the land; over several years, it freed a quickly rising number. Also, the spread of medical services in Mao's time, and the pre-1970s lack of attention to birth control, meant that the population rose. Field-area-per-farmer became smaller in absolute terms, both because there were more people and because encroachments from cities were already greater than newly reclaimed land. There was less area for each farmer to hoe. Arable land per head nationwide was 11.6 Chinese acres (*mu*) in 1952, but down to 6.3 *mu* by 1983.

This change was gradual, and its pressure on labor was compounded by other transformations. Over the same period, mechanization increasingly replaced manual farming. China's agriculture had 250,000 horsepower in 1952, but up to 2.5 billion in 1983—a growth of machine power, over three decades, of no less than 35 percent annually. Per field hand, this meant 0.14 horsepower in 1952, but 1.5 horsepower three decades later (an 8 percent annual growth).[29] The mutation began as exponential, and many inland provinces did not see it strongly until the 1980s.

In the Yangzi delta near Shanghai, population pressure on land became severe early. For example in Zhejiang, agricultural population rose to 34 million in 1982 from 18 million in 1949. While the rural labor force almost doubled over this time, the arable land decreased. There were 30 million *mu* of tillable land in 1952; but this figure dropped in absolute terms (to 28 million *mu*) in Zhejiang over the next three decades. Per-peasant arable land there between 1952 and 1982 dropped from 3.8 to 1.6 *mu*. "As a result, a huge amount of surplus labor power appeared."[30]

The whole wide Yangzi delta, by the late 1980s, contained over 800 people per square kilometer. This is a small fraction of the density in "rural" parts of Shanghai proper, but it is still high over a wide area. An economist rued that, "As industries and cities develop—big and middle-sized cities as well as small towns—they occupy more and more land. Arable land is decreasing." Tillable land per-capita in the Lake Tai area by the late 1980s was 1.2 *mu*, down from 2.2 *mu* in the 1950s.[31] Densities in different regions varied so much as to raise questions about the very meaning of words like "rural." Despite these variations in absolute levels of crowding for work, during Mao's years practically every delta place obtained far more people on less arable land.

Improvements in field technology caused food production to rise in rich areas. Rural surpluses were great. Each farmer (not including industrial workers) after maintaining him or herself, by 1974 in Suzhou for example, produced enough grain for one other person, edible oil for two, meat for three, and cotton for eight.[32] An interesting aspect of these statistics is that the industrial crop (cotton) was the main item in surplus, and apparently the fastest growing item. What Suzhou farmers did was to provide for inputs for the rural factories that created jobs for their newly industrial kin. The latter were no longer needed on the fields and could make more money as workers.

In rural Shanghai itself, population densities are even higher: roughly one person per *mu* of arable land, or 15,000 per km^2. The Shanghai delta in good years on good land could produce very high levels of output, for example, 18 tons of grain per hectare, in one crop of early rice, one crop of late rice, and another of winter barley or wheat. By the mid-1970s, such rates had been achieved in most of Shanghai. Just a few years before, in 1971, the average per-hectare production for the municipality was only 7.5 tons.[33]

Population was up, but production was up faster. The result was agricultural labor redundancy. As Fei Xiaotong roughly estimated, "If every laborer can manage four *mu* of land, one third of the population was [agricultural] surplus labor in the early 1970s."[34]

Triple-Cropping and the State's Implicit Bargain with Peasants

Radicals in the central state had a solution to this problem: more rice in triple-crop areas. This raised output per land unit, used labor extravagantly, discouraged rural competition to state industry, and facilitated taxation. In areas with sandy soil, where cotton tended to be the monoculture, growing much rice was unfeasible. But central state cadres mandated it wherever they could. Peasant leaders saw in it a large problem: harder work, for the extra output of taxable grain, than was required for similar returns in rural factories.

Agricultural involution is a long-term phenomenon that occurs when each unit of land can grow more only with increasingly intensive labor. The marginal return to labor approaches zero. Such a situation can persist for centuries; and state elites can be very content with it, especially if the crop is easy to measure and tax. This is the pattern that, after more gradual changes earlier, was broken on the Yangzi delta by the early 1970s, when many local political networks rejected more intensive triple-cropping involution, in favor of rural industrialization.

Throughout Jiangnan, a great deal of output growth had preceded this period. Historians studying agricultural change in the Yangzi delta, as far back as the Ming, have not found a long-term rise in productivity per person, despite the increases per unit of land. Returns to the state, which always claims its share as the ultimate rentier, certainly rose. Returns to tillers did not.[35] Commerce and traditional industry often flourished, so that even in the mid-1950s, some PRC historians claimed Jiangnan had not been just "feudal" but had long showed "incipient capitalism," because of technological changes and wage labor.[36] During the 1980s, these ideas came in for stringent criticism from other historians—not on grounds that the delta's economic structure was unchanging, but because of uncertainty about calling the direction of the change "capitalist." Central government socialists' fiscal and economic policies in recent years only furthered a process of agricultural intensification that had lasted for centuries. But agricultural extension policies in Mao's time boded an opposite change. The green revolution became a white one, from the viewpoint of a Communist government, because it let peasants pay their normal dues to officials while setting aside time for other uses from which they benefited more.

The state encourages multiple cropping regardless of labor efficiency. Peasants have only sometimes complied. Double cropping is an old practice; and as late as 1959 in Suzhou prefecture, for example, many fields were still single-cropped. The next dozen years saw very quick change. By 1971, three-quarters of all land in this large prefecture were triple-cropped. In rural Shanghai, triple cropping had been reported as a novelty in 1956, when a small part of Songjiang county managed to harvest two crops of rice and one of wheat. By 1965, still only 2 percent of arable land in Shanghai was triple-cropped. But by 1971, the change could scarcely have been more dramatic; the vast majority of grain fields in the suburbs were then triple-cropped. By 1974, of the two-thirds of Shanghai land used for grain, 83 percent produced three annual harvests.[37]

Triple cropping entails problems for the farmers who do it. If grain is harvested three rather than two times a year, total output value near Shanghai rises about 40 percent (rather than by 50 percent, because of shorter crop seasons and technical problems that decrease yields). But triple cropping raises income to the farmers by an average of only 16 percent—even though much more than 16 percent additional labor is applied.[38] Three harvests raise the need for fertilizers. Rice is apparently never attempted for all three crops on a single plot; but it is often planted for two, without time for fields to lay fallow. Rice-rice-wheat is a common pattern. Stalks are shorter in the "miracle" grain varieties which put more of the plant's available energy into making the fruit. Under one- or two-crop systems, longer stalks were usually left on the fields to rot and refertilize. Also, the demands of three crops on the fields may reduce soil quality. With the three season pattern, there is less time to grow clover, which can be fed to pigs for another means to enrich the fields.[39] Chemical fertilizers cost money, and the frequent regulation of water that triple-crop systems require is tedious. The yield is higher with three crops, but the work is hard.

Adding another crop tends to raise state grain tax revenues, and it also can increase peasant dissatisfaction with officialdom—unless the processes of planting, transplantation, fertilizer spreading, and harvesting are mechanized even more quickly. The specifics of this situation were not aired much in public until long after triple cropping had spread. Frank Leeming found that, "Shanghai and Suzhou . . . originated the powerful current of criticism of triple cropping which appeared in the winter of 1978–79."[40] The main trouble, from farmer leaders' viewpoint, was that maintaining the fecundity of triple-crop fields required great amounts of inorganic fertilizer, which cost money. These local leaders could accurately relay ordinary field workers' complaints that triple cropping led to overwork and illness. Triple-crop agriculture was better for the state than for land fertility or for farmers' incomes.

To the extent that the increased tasks of triple cropping could be mechanized quickly, this form of agriculture nonetheless could free more labor from the fields than two harvests without mechanization could do. It could also provide local leaders with more grain—with which to cement their own connections to higher state cadres and to their local constituents alike. Three harvests were scarcely feasible without machines and without the active consent and participation of farmers (who became more specialized, less like peasants, in this process). The only way for the government to get such consent, and additional grain from the third cropping, was to let rural leaders develop machine shops and other rural industries.

Radical statists in Mao's time, such as Zhang Chunqiao, were as conservative as Mencius on the need to have full public granaries. For them, this was essential to socialism. Mao himself made slogans about storing grain. To raise production, Mao called for the "complete mechanization" of all agricultural processes. But the unintended effect of this passion, given the technological possibilities of Chinese agriculture in rich areas like the Shanghai delta by c. 1970, was the need to mobilize more work from field hands—and soon this required an allowance for more decentralized rural industries. It eventually weakened the state sector.

Peasants in this situation concentrated not just on the possibility of more income through industry, but also on the fear of more work through triple cropping. Their attitudes have been informally reported in a peasant saying: "Better a little factory than a ton of grain to the *mu*."

The mechanization-industrialization course became politically more feasible than the agricultural mobilization course. By the start of the 1970s, rural industry was legitimated from the bottom long before the top fully approved it. This development was propelled by technological possibilities and potentials for labor in small communities, not by government intentions or long-term planning. Most workers gradually moved out of agriculture into factories. The ones who stayed on the land used more operating capital and equipment, becoming agricultural workers or farmers in more autonomous groups, no longer old-style peasants. Their economic diversification weakened a state of which they still spoke well. It benefited local power networks more than the central one.

Decollectivization

Most rural places were still officially supposed, in the Maoist state's ideal, to be "one crop producers" (*danyi shengchan zhe*). Monoculture had dangers for peasants, however, not just because it aided tax assessments but also for other reasons: Single crops were subject to plant epidemics. The opposite habit, mixing species, can be advantageous if the roots of some (e.g., beans) foster bacteria that fix nitrogen to be used by others. Mixed cropping lets the vegetables' roots take water and nutrients from different levels of the soil. It is beneficial, too, if some of the species notably help prevent erosion. Collectivized agriculture was plantation monoculture, foregoing these opportunities for the sake of easier marketing and taxation. China's reforms brought a greater range of crops, planted on more local and independent decisions.

The commune system ceased to work, long before it was formally abolished. Some local authorities "lent" (*jie*) land to farmers during the early 1970s, lest they be criticized politically for "contracting" (*bao*). Crop reports continued to underestimate actual yields, so as to leave a larger surplus for local distribution. Private plots were expanded without authorization by higher levels. Collectively owned trucks were used to haul individual households' goods to free markets. Brigade workshops repaired privately appropriated tools. Public storehouses protected households' grain. Peasants spent more time, especially in important agricultural seasons, on their own plots than on collective fields—and local leaders did not dock their work points. Families used their most active members in private work; they sent older or less energetic members to be symbolic representatives of the household in collective work projects.[41] In Sichuan, as near Shanghai, the process of rural reform began in the early 1970s—well before 1975, when Zhao Ziyang became the provincial First Secretary of that huge inland province, which was China's most populous. Sichuan's "decollectivization was driven from below—and occurred early—but was not ratified by local government until much later."[42]

Many parts of Jiangsu adopted "quota management" (*ding'e guanli*) for grain long before 1978.[43] Communes formally lasted in a few areas as late as the fall of 1983, but they had ceased to have most of their previous functions years before that, as townships took over from communes, and villages from brigades. Since most communes were officially "one-crop producers," mostly for rice, a good index of the reportable informal aspects of decollectivization is the portion of the other crops.

Subsidiary crops' gross real value practically doubled (up 91 percent) in the Shanghai suburbs during the short period 1978 to 1980. Main crops' value dropped then more than a fifth (down 21 percent). So in these two years alone, the value of reported main crops shifted from being 74 percent more than that of subsidiary crops to being 28 percent less.[44] Shanghai farmers changed what they grew, and they almost surely also raised the extent to which they *reported* their output of industrial "subsidiary" crops so as to avoid high rates of state extraction. Local networks gained more control of their own labor. In traditionally rice-growing parts of the delta, medium-level collective organization was very strong; and innovations in crops or accounting systems often met political resistance. Formal and public decollectivization generally began there in 1978, with a guarantee (*chengbao*) system under which the state made contracts with communes, and the communes did so with brigades. This open process often began earliest in jurisdictions on poor land, most of which in Shanghai is near the seacoast. To the east and south of the city, where the soil is still somewhat sandy and cotton had been the main crop, the advent of artificial fibers and new cotton growing techniques on the North China plain caused many farmers to switch into raising fish. Others moved into growing vegetables and other activities, not all agricultural. Local leaders in areas without much tax potential could experiment with decollectivization even before reforms were announced widely. Contracts between peasant households and production brigades for raising fish existed in East China, according to a report from a poor inland place, as early as 1969. These market exchanges presaged reforms and often violated radical policies during the Cultural Revolution. But they flourished, despite the radical politicians of that time, and often they were kept secret.[45]

China's vertical hierarchies for rural areas were mostly organized to tax and purchase (at low prices) traditional main commodities, especially grain. Therefore, agricultural entrepreneurs obtained higher profits by growing almost anything other than the officially designated main produce of the area. Institutional habits of taxing or requisitioning any increases in the traditional main products gave an incentive to use land, instead, for novel crops. A national paper admitted that, "As to new industries such as edible mushrooms, flowers, and plants, export of labor services, and so forth, which department should take charge of them as their 'anchor' has thus far not been known."[46] Local leaderships (often called "area" or "piece" leaderships, to distinguish them from vertical "string" leaderships[47]) had acquired an interest in supporting just these industries.

Nationally, grain production was four-fifths of total agricultural output in the 1950s, almost the same in the 1960s, but gradually down to three-fifths by the mid-1980s.[48] More specifically, the portion of grain in total agricultural output value for later years trended downward: in 1985, 63 percent; 1986, 62; 1987, 61; 1988, 56; 1989, 56; 1990, 58; and 1991, 57.[49] The reason was that farmers preferred to grow other crops.

When peasant leaders obeyed the state, they could fail as synaptic hinge chiefs, not serving their local constituencies well. A number of Sunan counties in the 1970s increased their grain output almost 100 percent.[50] But the costs of the new techniques that enabled so much more taxable rice rose 250 percent.[51] If low state-fixed grain prices were maintained, the increment of production was financially unsustainable. When forty workers as late as 1980 harvested vegetables for a whole afternoon, and sold the produce at state prices to Baoshan county, they received only 30 yuan—not enough to pay for the fertilizer they had used. The price of vegetables was so low that the head of a brigade said he "had no way of settling accounts" with his farmers.[52]

Officials' Opposition to Family Farms, Higher Grain Prices, and Household Contracting

Household contracting was still a natural option in the 1970s. Families had been the agricultural accounting units before 1949. Households remained crucial participants under the "mutual assistance teams" established in 1953, the "lower-level agricultural producers' cooperatives" in 1954–56, and even the "higher-level APC's" in 1956–57. The Great Leap Forward broke this pattern temporarily. But by 1961 at least, the need for grain during the famine caused cadres to let households work together under locally authorized contracts; this pattern involved over half the work teams in some provinces. Even under the communes, separate families generally had particular duties. So the publicized formal contracting by households after 1977 had many precedents. At no time were families unimportant on the rural scene.

Rural land contracting during the reforms rose not smoothly but in surges, and differently under different local leaders. Decollectivization in many parts of China was a top-down policy during the four years after 1982. As David Zweig makes clear, many Chinese peasants throughout the 1970s had scant sympathy with agrarian radicals' ideas about how they should organize farming.[53] Peasant leaders were at no time in full agreement even with each other, to judge from their actions. The articulation of nominal policy for family farms came from the high state and tended to be uniform, but decollectivization was sometimes opposed by local officials.[54] When they did not oppose it, its meaning was in any case deeply affected by the extensive industrialization of the rural economy after the 1960s.

At the start of the responsibility system, by 1978, peasants' enthusiasm to contract for new plots was high. In this early period, rural keenness for reform was so great that, "Anything decided at night would be acted upon by midnight." Decollectivization was not an idea from Beijing; it came from local farmers.[55] No less an authority than Deng Xiaoping attested to his astonishment at this crucial reform:

> Generally speaking, our rural reforms have proceeded very fast, and farmers have been enthusiastic. *What took us by surprise completely was the development of township and village industries. . . . This is not the achievement of our central government.* Every year, township and village industries achieved 20 percent growth. . . . This was not something I had thought about. Nor had the other comrades. This surprised us.[56]

By 1980, top leaders including Deng were unwilling and unable to countermand tens of thousands of local decisions that had, for example, already put 40 percent of Anhui production teams, 50 percent of Guizhou teams, and 60 percent of Gansu teams already under household contracts.[57] Although many foreign and Chinese writers have ascribed the very basic reform of rural decollectivization to wise new ideas from Beijing, that is not the main way it happened.

Later, as township enterprises boomed and peasants realized they could use their labor more profitably in industry than in fields, many leased plots were abandoned. This enthusiasm rose and fell depending on market demand for agricultural products. After the mid-1980s, when consumption demand rose quickly for meat and other sideline products, "Peasants again showed a renewed passion for land." In Zhejiang, for example, 1.1 m. *mu* (Chinese acres) were opened for new fruit orchards and fish breeding in one year. There was also an increase in specialization between different rural areas. Zhejiang's Hezhou prefecture, for example, grew more tangerines to supply its two new tangerine-processing factories. Zhoushan prefecture raised more shrimps, fish, and shellfish. In a classic market manner, "all products for which prices were liberalized were developed relatively early, at a quicker pace, and in greater varieties."[58]

As late as December 1978, the Third Plenum of the Eleventh Party Congress passed a resolution which specified that "contracting to households" was illegal.[59] If 1978 is taken as the crucial watershed toward reforms, this was a very odd way to begin them. The resolution was apparently a sop to conservatives, which more reform-minded leaders may have known would be unenforceable anyway. The ambiguous wording also had reformist aspects: it raised the authority of local work teams and suggested that agricultural commodity prices should rise by 25 percent; and it encouraged more sideline production and proposed opening more local markets. The plenum clearly showed its divisions. Local leaders followed the mandates they liked. Because they widely ignored others, it would be difficult to prove their activities were much affected by this broadly worded compromise document, despite its distinguished source and frequent citations to it. The same things might well have happened on the ground, if this ruling had never been issued. Local magnates who wanted substantive reform of agriculture had already begun it, and those who did not want it were still slow to start it. If any behavior was demonstrably affected by this high decree, it is mainly to be found in changes in the ways people spoke, not in what they did.

In spring of 1979, as Daniel Kelliher points out, "The top leadership in Beijing was against the experiment in family farming."[60] That did not stop the trend, however. High leaders had much to lose from it in the long run; but they apparently sensed that if they tried to stop it, they would face local disregard immediately. Friedman, Pickowicz, and Selden, writing about a place in North China quite different from the Shanghai delta, report a similar situation:[61]

> Villagers were not pawns permitting socialist kings to push them around. Local leaders tried to woo and win the resources controlled by higher-ups. Villagers and their allies and patrons among officials also tried, as they had for many generations under various regimes, to dodge, deflect, and blunt the impact of demands detrimental to local interests and values. Those negative impacts gradually eroded the new state's popular legitimacy.

This was the trend, yet at some times the state's position prevailed. So what were the conditions for peasant power? Kelliher proposes that peasants in reform China have exercised power under three conditions. First, their own preferences had at least to be presentable in terms of the state's main announced program at the time, economic modernization. Second, many had to act in unison, even though permanent interest groups or policy factions remained ideally taboo. Third, the state elite had to perceive that granting local demands would not threaten its secure tenure—at least not immediately. The gradual shift to recognize family farming met all these criteria.[62] The state in the reform era has sometimes won conflicts even with very large numbers of people. Over the long haul, however, these three criteria do not much constrain local power: First, the top elite's main program is subject to many interpretations; many different kinds of demands can be phrased in terms of modernization. Second, the CCP's confidential network for surveying mass views (instead of holding elections) can have a considerable hidden impact on state policy through mechanisms that open documents do not show; and even if protests, usually not reported in the press, are fairly small, they may confirm the surveys and soften up conservative state cadres. And third, local powers in China can fight what Mao called a protracted war. They are all over the map. If they lose ground once on a specific issue, they will be back again later. The state sometimes wins, but it is badly outnumbered. Its main strength often comes from the diversity of reformers and conservatives in localities, when for practical reasons they need to be coordinated. But if enough local leaders, for their own quiet reasons, keep acting together even with scant articulation for a long time, their powers tend to prevail.

State procurement price changes for grains and industrial crops are a very rough index of the relative powers of peasant and central networks. Peasant leaders can sometimes powerfully express discontent with these prices by defaulting on deliveries. They can shift rural labor to new activities. The prices were almost flat in the dozen years after 1966. State offices liked to keep their money and had nice-sounding arguments against the "economism" that would have been involved in giving peasants more for their work. Yet at the same time, the increasingly sophisticated technology of Chinese agriculture (more machines, more fertilizer, and more irrigation to go with better seeds) raised production costs especially in triple-crop areas like the Shanghai delta. To the extent that free, illegal, or nonstate markets were repressed, this combination of policies created rising grain production but stagnant prices. So peasants went into factories instead.[63]

A minority of ex-farmers went into commerce, rather than industry. During the early 1970s, peasants wanting to sell food in Shanghai had to do so themselves. Wholesale food transactions broke the law, unless the state conducted them. Peasants could not legally sell to a retailer. This was costly for them, and it reduced their incentive to grow and trade supplementary foods such as vegetables, even though many were able in practice to make illegal sales. By 1979, the law was changed; and the revival of retail agents made the food market more efficient.[64]

The state procurement price for grain was, in a large time frame, rather flat until 1984. There were slight increases in 1961, 1966, and 1978—but in size, these were overwhelmed by the 1985 increase, in which the grain price doubled. The *combined total* increases over the thirty-three years from 1951 to 1984 were only about two-thirds of the single-year 1984–85 increase. Table 1.1-1 does not, of course, report real scarcities or unofficial prices. These unreported indices probably rose faster, in many periods of reform including the early 1970s, than the state procurement prices. But the table shows the delayed effect of those scarcities on plans, especially in the striking rise of rates the state needed to pay for grain from 1984 to 1989, as well as the slight ebbing in 1990.

When seen in shorter time frames, state control over the grain price faltered slightly in 1979 and collapsed by 1985. Another change, however, came much earlier: In 1971–72, state procurement prices for economic crops rose somewhat, after a long period of stability since the end of the post-Leap depression. Rural factories were already, in the early 1970s, competing with the state sector for industrial crops. Mandated purchases of some main crops, notably cotton, in communes devoted to that product were still the order of the day. But especially for subsidiary industrial crops, there was price inflation. By 1978–79, delivery shortages to the state by rural industries made the non-grain materials prices jump again.

Decollectivization led to higher harvests, but demand for food soared even faster. The state doggedly tried to retain its "unified purchasing policy," which in

Table 1.1-1

Indices of State Procurement Prices for Grains and Industrial Crops
(1950 = 100)

	Grains	Industrial crops		Grains	Industrial crops
1951	118.3	118.4	1973	222.2	164.9
1952	121.4	113.0	1974	222.4	165.1
1953	137.1	112.9	1975	222.8	165.1
1954	137.1	119.3	1976	222.8	165.1
1955	137.3	120.0	1977	222.8	165.8
1956	139.9	122.6	1978	224.4	174.0
1957	141.4	126.4	1979	271.3	200.4
1958	145.1	127.9	1980	271.8	210.8
1959	147.0	129.9	1981	283.5	215.0
1960	151.7	133.8	1982	283.5	215.2
1961	191.9	140.6	1983	283.5	215.4
1962	192.4	145.0	***1984***	***282.4***	***212.8***
1963	190.9	152.9	***1985***	***522.2***	***277.3***
1964	189.2	152.6	1986	573.9	287.3
1965	190.9	152.8	1987	619.8	296.8
1966	220.8	152.0	1988	710.3	330.3
1967	221.1	154.9	1989	901.4	385.5
1968	221.1	154.9	1990	840.1	431.4
1969	221.1	154.9	1991	788.0	438.3
1970	221.1	154.9	1992	829.8	423.0
1971	222.0	161.4	***1993***	***968.4***	***476.2***
1972	222.2	164.2	***1994***	***1,419.5***	***687.7***

Source: Zhongguo tongji nianjian, 1991 (China Statistical Yearbook, 1991), State Statistical Bureau, ed. (Beijing: Zhongguo Tongji Chuban She, 1980–92), p. 257; and the 1992 edition, p. 263; and calculated from the 1995 edition, p. 247. Apparently shifts in accounting methods may have occurred in 1990–91. The mid-1980s (and the mid-1990s, but by that time the state contracted to buy less than before) showed quick increases.

Mao's time had allowed huge extractions from the countryside for industrial development. When the state price was good, peasants willingly sold; but the state had to use more and more price incentives, to obtain grain for its urban employees. During reforms, prices generally rose as the table shows. This quickly ruined official budgets. Government granaries sometimes could not hold all they had contracted to buy, and high inventories restrained price rises at least temporarily. Agricultural planning had been easier for the state when it could rely on its rural organizations more, and on price incentives less, to obtain rice for urban tables.

This problem extended to other foods, too. Peasants had one million more chickens in 1983 at Jiangsu's Haian county, than state purchasing agents had budget to buy. So the farmers strung most of these chickens on bicycles and took them to sell in Nanjing.[65] Most local leaders in such situations almost surely conceived themselves as socialists. But they needed free markets. State procurement requires state money; and with production soaring, the planners lacked enough funds to implement their plans. This was not a question of ideology; it was a question of payment.

When local cadres could not meet their obligations to the chiefs of farming networks, the latter were relieved of the need to reciprocate. Norms required that the administrative structure be conceived as a hierarchy—and practically no one ever spoke of it otherwise. What the higher leaders in this system needed was grain. The "lower" chiefs had decreasing interest in providing it. Peasants planted rapeseed in a large region of Zhejiang in 1983, according to one report, on nearly half their land. The profits were enough to buy grain for their required delivery to the state. This meant less food. So a law decreed that each team should put grain on four-fifths of the fields.[66] Laws of this sort pleased top state leaders in Beijing, who knew that urban state workers in politically important cities expected their usual rations. In practice, the state despite such laws soon had to pay much more, if it wished to buy grain.

By the mid-1980s, when necessary purchases at high fixed prices worsened the state budget deficit unacceptably, the government had to change its previous policy of buying mandatory grain amounts to a more flexible system of contracts.[67] Prices and shortages had risen so fast, the previous official system of an entitlement to the state had become an entitlement to the peasants—which the government could no longer afford. By the same token in 1985, the Planning Commission had to give up much of its previous presumption that it could restrain either grain or economic crop prices. Reforms continued after 1985; but the story of effective socialist price-setting for most commodities had already reached its end.

The local leaders of China's labor force responded to this new situation with great gusto. In the short time from 1984 to 1986, one-eighth of all China's laborers quit farming to "engage in industry and service trades in towns and urban areas."[68] Rural incomes rose sharply during those years—and over 80 percent of the new wages came from commercial businesses and services. Coastal areas led central and western parts of China in this development. Rural development of the densely populated "green city" in Shanghai's suburbs was especially fast.[69]

The Green City Shifts from Fields to Factories

Within Shanghai, ecological differences had long been important between less fertile cotton areas near the sea and more fertile places slightly inland that garnered heavy harvests of rice. Evidence from Chuansha county, a cotton area with sandy soil, shows a quick rise of the industrial portion of gross output as early as the first half of the 1970s. Here are industrial percentages in Chuansha's total product in various years, including crucial years of reform:[70]

1949	46%	1970	54%
52	53%	75	74%
62	52%	78	75%
65	51%	80	85%
		85	91%

These numbers show a rather flat curve of the industrial portion of product during the height of revolutionary centralization, through the 1960s. Local leaders were still responding at this time to municipal and central instructions to grow their main product (cotton), because the revolutionary appointment system was still strong and the technical means to industrialize were not yet available. But Chuansha has very strong traditions of nonstate political organization.[71] Local hinge leaders always had the option of responding more to their networks' local opportunities than to mandates from the state. After 1970, as the tables above show, there was sharp industrial acceleration. The portion of output from industry rose by 20 percentage points in half a decade. This rate was apparently exceeded only in the two years after 1978—when some previously hidden industrial activity was almost surely easier for local leaders to report, and when further reforms of the economic structure carried forward a momentum that had started early in the decade.

Chuansha comparisons with some other Shanghai counties show contrasts. Chuansha industry contributed 54 percent of product value in 1970, up in the next five years to 74 percent. But Songjiang county, a carbon-soil, traditionally rice-growing area of Shanghai, provides the data shown on a table below suggesting that Songjiang cadres obeyed government instructions to stress agriculture more faithfully than their peers in Chuansha. By 1970, even though Songjiang was richer, just 46 percent (rather than Chuansha's 54 percent) of its output was industrial. By 1975, the Songjiang figure was up to 61 percent; this was a fast increase, but not to Chuansha's 74 percent. Local leaders probably mediated this difference, and the different local cultures and agricultures concurrently help to account for it. Rural leaders responded diversely to the state's constant call for grain—and in effect, for slow local development.

Among the 25,000 production teams in rural Shanghai during these teams' last effective year (1978), the average distribution to rural workers was 230 yuan. Only about 1.2 percent of the teams were able to hand out more than 300 yuan; but at the low end, about 6 percent could not distribute more than 120 yuan. A focussed study of ten rich and ten poor Shanghai brigades found that, by 1978, there was a 71 percent difference in their per-capita incomes, and a 91 percent difference in their average fixed investment per worker. Why did the state's representatives allow the ten prosperous brigades to become rich? The answer seems evident in these places' ability to pay off higher levels by delivering more grain—either by growing it, or else by using collective industrial profits to buy it. The difference between rich and poor brigades as late as 1966 was not very great; in that year, the surveyed places that later enjoyed higher incomes delivered slightly less grain than the ones which later remained relatively poor: 556 *jin* per worker, rather than 580 *jin*. But by 1978, per-capita deliveries from the ten rich brigades in the survey had risen by more than three-quarters (to 980 *jin*), while the poor ones' deliveries had fallen by almost one-quarter (to 472 *jin*).[72] Local rural leaders in heavily controlled Shanghai did not all gain their economic autonomy free of change. They paid for it.

Along Shanghai's coasts, toward the Yangzi and to a lesser extent toward Hangzhou Bay, sedimentation has created land above sea level only over the last millennium or so. Agriculture near these shores produces less than do the fields further inland, because this coastal soil contains sand and salts and has a tendency to cake. Ploughing and irrigation are more difficult there. But coastal areas have advantages in a period of quick decentralizing industrial growth. Cotton, rather than grain, is the main crop; and demand for fiber was strong in rural Sunan mills. Especially when coastal collectives could avoid selling cotton through state channels, they made good profits.

Rural leaders' practical attitudes toward higher administrative levels varied by both place and personality; and they go far toward explaining different localities' economic stagnancy or growth during the early 1970s. Dengyi and Shanhuang brigades, both in Chuansha, had nearly identical net incomes in 1966. By 1978, Dengyi's income had doubled—while Shanhuang's had risen more than ten times. The ecological, resource, and market conditions facing the two brigades were similar. So the question becomes why subsidiary industries arose in one place but not the other. The answer seems clear: Shanhuang's local leaders were willing to run the early-1970s risks of nurturing the "sprouts of capitalism," while Dengyi's cadres avoided this political risk. The Shanhuang leadership encouraged peasants on their own time to raise more pigs, chickens, and milk cows. They supported the harvesting of grass from coastal commons and the founding of cottage industries, especially in embroideries. When situational factors gave similar opportunities to different leaders, they did not always react in the same way.

At inland Shanghai county, which has richer agricultural soil, a similar contrast has been documented between Xinlong and Yenong brigades. In the 1960s, these two places were broadly similar; but at the start of the 1970s, this pattern changed sharply. Surplus agricultural workers in Xinlong were encouraged by very local leaders to raise ducks, chickens, pigs, fish, and mushrooms, as well as to truck goods into central Shanghai. Yenong did none of these things extensively—with the result that by 1978, its nonagricultural workers produced 75 percent less value than those of Xinlong.[73]

Even in relatively conservative ex–rice-growing counties with large settlements such as Songjiang, the early 1970s rate of industrial growth was unprecedented. Its acceleration was not matched, over similarly long periods, until 1985. Table 1.1-2 shows this trend by 1970. From that year until 1975, the average rate of industrial growth was 21 percent (for rural industry, 37 percent). But over the same number of years beginning in 1978, it was lower, at 17 percent (for rural industry, 26 percent)—and then only 14 percent during the next year, 1984.[74] These reforms showed the common pattern: a boom in the early 1970s, a period of less change after 1976, then a resurgence after 1978, another reported slowing in 1984–85, another push in the late 1980s (and if the pattern were continued, another consolidation in 1989–90, followed by a further wave of growth thereafter). No aspect of this pattern after 1978 was lacking earlier in the 1970s. No aspect of it has yet disappeared.

The available data from Qingpu county, adjacent to Songjiang, are on the accompanying table and suggest only a somewhat lower rate of industrial growth there in the early 1970s, followed by the common deceleration in 1976–77, and then again an increase after 1978, with fluctuations in the rate continuing later. The Qingpu reports on grain are most interesting, because that county's production of staple food per capita generally decreased in most years after 1971 (despite some periods in which very high numbers were filed). Recurrent exhortations from high leaders that every county should grow more grain had no decisive effect. Weather naturally makes annual crops vary,[75] but a broader pattern is not hard to find. The 1987 tonnage of Qingpu grain was about the same as that grown a decade and a half earlier, in the early 1970s. The long-term trend for Shanghai rice production was stagnant and then negative.

Outside Shanghai on the delta, the rampant exodus of workers from fields was also impressive. Between 1983 and 1987, one-third of the peasants in Taixian county, Jiangsu, quit farming. They received less money if they stayed on the fields. In the urbanized county seat, the average 1983 personal income was 645 yuan; but the average Taixian farmer got only 287 yuan. By 1987, these wages for both categories had approximately doubled; so the difference between them was greater. Some farmers who had tilled rice specialized in animal husbandry or fish-raising. Many set up stores or found jobs in township industries. Others "became workers in small firms, often affiliated with larger enterprises in towns and cities."[76] The agricultural labor force of Wuxi county declined sharply, at an *annual* rate of 13 percent between 1978 and 1985.[77]

Many ex-farmers went into construction, living at their rural homes but going for day labor to building sites largely in urban areas. This pattern was encouraged by Shanghai's city administrators: "Experience shows that it is easier to cope with the inflow of rural people if they are involved in short-term projects. All in all, construction workers are easier to manage than those who open grocery stores or restaurants and stay on indefinitely."[78]

Men shifted from farm work more than women did. State pressure on rural areas to feed cities, together with opportunities for rural families to get income

Table 1.1-2

Songjiang County, Shanghai, 1965–1987

Population (in thousands), Gross Outputs of Industry, Agriculture, and Rural Industry (in million yuan), Budgetary Fiscal Revenues (in million yuan), and Changes in These, 1965–87 (some figures from the early 1970s are italicized)

Year	Pop.	Change	Indu	Change	Agricu	Change	Ru ind	Change	Budget fiscal revs.	Change
1965	380	5.3%	72	26.3%	75	–20.2%				
1966	395	3.9%	49	–31.9%	87	16.0%				
1967	396	0.3%	65	32.7%	89	2.3%			25	25.0%
1968	407	2.8%	66	1.5%	98	10.1%			29	16.0%
1969	415	2.0%	67	1.5%	114	16.3%	13		25	–13.8%
1970	421	1.4%	86	*28.4%*	106	–7.0%	17	30.8%	23	–8.0%
1971	424	*0.7%*	115	*33.7%*	118	11.3%	35	*105.9%*	31	*34.8%*
1972	425	*0.2%*	136	*18.3%*	133	12.7%	35	*0.0%*	36	*16.1%*
1973	430	*1.2%*	157	*15.4%*	136	2.3%	45	*28.6%*	44	*22.2%*
1974	435	*1.2%*	183	*16.6%*	149	9.6%	53	*17.8%*	51	*15.9%*
1975	439	*0.9%*	208	*13.7%*	134	–10.1%	75	*41.5%*	56	*9.8%*
1976	443	0.9%	226	8.7%	139	3.7%	83	10.7%	55	–1.8%
1977	450	1.6%	248	9.7%	123	–11.5%	98	18.1%	57	3.6%
1978	454	0.9%	272	9.7%	145	17.9%	115	17.3%	59	3.5%
1979	462	1.8%	333	22.4%	155	6.9%	150	30.4%	62	5.1%
1980	464	0.4%	382	14.7%	148	–4.5%	195	30.0%	79	27.4%
1981	473	1.9%	453	18.6%	215	45.3%	271	39.0%	80	1.3%
1982	479	1.3%	524	15.7%	260	20.9%	316	16.6%	83	3.8%
1983	481	0.4%	640	22.1%	225	–13.5%	384	21.5%	88	6.0%
1984	482	0.2%	730	14.1%	256	13.8%	443	15.4%	97	10.2%
1985	483	0.2%	1,004	37.5%	229	–10.5%	636	43.6%	111	14.4%
1986	486	0.6%	1,215	21.0%	259	13.1%	844	32.7%	133	19.8%
1987	492	1.2%	1,664	37.0%	303	17.0%	1,202	42.4%	162	21.8%

Source: Songjiang xian xianqing: Xiandai hua jincheng diaocha (The Current Situation in Songjiang County: An Investigation of the Modernization Process), Yao Xitang, ed., vol. 2 (Shanghai: no publisher but probably the Shanghai Academy of Social Sciences, n.d.) between pp. 6 and 4; a misprint caused two pages each to be labeled 4, 5, and 6. The outputs are gross values of production. "Rural Industry" is *xiangzhen gongye*. "Budget fiscal revenue" is caizheng shouru. Percentages are calculated with the help of Mr. Peng Dajin.

Table 1.1-3

Development in Qingpu County, Shanghai, 1970–1987
(growth percentages for sectors and population)

Year	Industry	Grain	Trade	Pop.
1970		–1	–2	1.9
1971	17	7	4	1.0
1972		9	18	1.0
1973	25	5	13	1.5
1974		3	8	0.5
1975	19	–6	9	0.5
1976	7	13	8	1.2
1977	11	–19	–6	1.7
1978	24	34	16	0.7
1979	23	9	23	1.0
1980	19	–22	17	0.5
1981	17	–1	4	1.4
1982	14	22	1	1.4
1983	19	–2	10	0.5
1984	23	9	20	0.2
1985	41	–23	26	0.2
1986	18	6	15	0.9
1987	36	5	22	0.0

Source: Calculated from *Qingpu xianzhi* (Qingpu County Gazeteer), Feng Xuewen et al., eds. (Shanghai: Shanghai Renmin Chuban She, 1990), grain, p. 206; gross value of industrial output, p. 271; retail trade, p. 360; population, p. 148.

from new industries, made rice paddy workers more often female. "Assisted by children and parents, a Taixian woman can on average manage 0.3 hectares of farm land. . . . But the question, 'Who should be growing crops,' is far less worrisome than the fact that men are not willing to do it."[79] The state harassed local peasants to grow grain. Local men largely got their wives and daughters to grow enough so that local leaders would not receive too much criticism from their bureaucratic superiors.

Some agricultural households contracted from local Sunan governments to produce quotas of crops that garnered high prices as farming "specialists," so that other families could work in factories. Dongfang township, Wuxi, from the fall of 1983 allocated 70 percent of its large tracts of "responsibility land" to just 85 families, a small minority in that town. Yongnan village, Yuqi township, in 1984 consolidated the land previously tilled by 327 families, reallocating it to merely ten families. "This greatly raised agricultural efficiency."[80]

The laborers of Changjiao village, Changshu, were 80 percent industrial by

1984. But somebody had to till the land—or supervise migrant workers from poorer parts of China to till it. Local notables contracted farming. They were still organized under presentably labeled units with good socialist names, always in accord with the statist language of the PRC. Sometimes the new plantations could change their unit designations from agricultural to industrial categories, even though both sectors were often administered together by closely interlocking village elites. As Fei Xiaotong writes,[81]

> Local leaders carried out a uniform management of agriculture and rural industry. Under this system, those who engaged in agricultural activity actually became members of rural industries. [Local 'industrial' offices] organized agriculture, rural factories, and sideline production too. In Wuxi county, 7,000 responsibility land families were managed by rural enterprises. There was an agricultural department in rural industrial offices. Peasants who wanted to do agricultural work had to apply for land from this department. They submitted the income from the land for which they took responsibility, but they could get wages from rural industry.

Members of the new rural proletariat, if they were not migrants, had better social security than their predecessor peasants. The tightness of organization in these areas would have pleased the ancestors of cadres who came from old leading families there.

In agricultural contracts, the legal parties on one side were often cooperatives. The other side was usually a household, rather than an individual. The text of an agricultural contract from the early 1980s specified that the local cooperative (*she*) provided land, water, seeds, fertilizer, and machines or animals. The family agreed "to arrange the contracting household's production tasks according to state plans." The household (*hu*) in theory could "not without permission buy and sell, transfer, or leave uncultivated, build houses, place graves, or plant bamboos or trees on contracted land." The household at least nominally undertook to "accept cadres' correct leadership and overall arrangement." The contracting family promised "to have children according to birth plans," as well as "to ensure timely completion of the sales task for agricultural products."[82] "Economic punishments" were prescribed for contract violation. Such clauses echoed Maoist rural arrangements, but these contracts in fact largely replaced commands.

A major benefit of contracting to households was that surplus from the land, above the agreed "sales task," could be sold at will. The language of planning nonetheless permeated contracts. As was typical of China's reforms generally, new agricultural practices were phrased in old symbols. The transactions cost of sudden changes in household sales patterns meant that the new system often resembled the old one more than classical economists have means to discover.[83] But incentives to produce rose, and essentially dependent peasants were reformed into potentially independent farmers. Collective decentralization was now the trend, even if the result was still far from pure capitalism.

Agricultural yields were maintained in many areas even as the majority of peasants left agriculture. Specialized farming families in a rural Zhejiang township by the mid-1980s were only 10 percent of the entire work force; nine-tenths of the adults there labored in factories.[84] Family farms flourished in East China, and plots that could not be tilled by "farmers preferring to work in township enterprises" were recontracted to households specialized in agriculture. In a Zhejiang county, only 3 percent of the rural families delivered one-third of the grain needed to meet the county's state quota.[85] One reason for sharp local increases of labor productivity in some areas was further use of field machinery. Another reason was exploitation of migrant field hands. Rural industrialization provided amounts of capital in the countryside that were unprecedented, and this affected not just factories but also agriculture. Ten Sunan townships in Wuxi, Changshu, and Wuxian counties set up "agricultural experiment zones" in 1988 to test the possibilities for greater mechanization and to "consolidate land holdings and attract more investment."[86] The remaining farmers were a smaller part of the population, and pre-industrial rural politics ended—but agriculture was still important as its methods were mechanized.

Some peasant families on the Shanghai delta opposed household contracting. Some had done well in agriculture through the late 1960s. Even in highly industrialized countries (ranging from France to Japan), nostalgia for old-style farming does not disappear and can shape politics. In China, production groups of about ten households, as well as production teams of about one hundred families, natural villages that were larger, and standard marketing communities that contained about 2,000 households *all* became more, not less, active because of industrialization. The units that lost most from reforms in the 1980s were larger than any of these, whose leaders were effectively below the purview of the central state.

Post-1984 Efforts to Revive State Agriculture

Suzhou peasants once had a slogan: "Better to plant cotton than rice, better melons than cotton, better sugar than melons; but best of all is to start a factory."[87] China's top leaders' interests became opposite to the interests of the rural majority, and the peasants prevailed. Local rural networks on the Shanghai delta planted less rice and sold their cotton, melons, and sugar increasingly to be processed in their own collective factories.

The budget crisis by 1985 made the state restructure agricultural procurement, trying to force peasants to plant unprofitable grain. These official efforts in the mid-1980s were temporarily effective, although they proved difficult to sustain. The changes were touted at the time as "reforms," but in fact they were reversals of previous unofficial reforms that had been created by peasants, not the state. Agriculture sagged in Shanghai's suburban counties during the 1980s. A peak in the number of small and hand-guided tractors was reached by 1984; but five years later, in 1989, the suburbs had 17 percent fewer of them. The number of larger tractors increased slightly. But the reduction of arable land and the transfer of labor into industries lowered the number of "walking tractors" used mostly for rice cultivation, and bureaucrats liked them more than peasants did.[88]

The fact that the state in many decrees exhorted and ordered peasants to grow more grain had scant relevance to what actually happened. Grain output in 1987–92 Shanghai varied no more than 6 percent between the high and low years in that period. The last year was the lowest.[89] Grain production always fluctuates with the weather; but except for this variance, the curve was essentially flat, not declining because of administrative pressure on production (or on reports of production). When buying new equipment, village leaders chose not to replace old tractors, but they put their capital to other uses.

East China peasants thus enjoyed a "double liberation," in both work and ownership. On one hand, they could shift from rural labor to industrial enterprises or to construction teams (*jianzhu dui*). They also accumulated extensive property in trucks, tractors, and houses. Long-term rental contracts raised their confidence that they had reacquired de facto ownership rights in land (even though technically they could only lease land).[90] Peasants therefore became even more difficult to monitor than they had been in Mao's time.

Government bureaus seldom received good data on what farmers were actually doing. Town-based officials were often reluctant to spend much time in peasant areas, especially poor places, throughout East China. For example, farmers in one part of Anhui, who diversified their economy during the early 1980s by developing freshwater oyster beds, were almost never visited by the commercial offices that in theory were supposed to help them. Local tax bureau cadres sometimes came, but revenue collectors seldom found it easy to obtain complete data on production.[91] Economic freedom could result simply from bureaucratic absence.

Rural leaders in both fields and factories were nonetheless somewhat constrained by higher officials, especially in matters of style and in the promises they were supposed to keep. Farmers and rural entrepreneurs seldom wrote the contracts they were supposed to follow.[92] They also did not advertise to visiting researchers (Chinese or foreign) the extent to which they sidestepped cadres' orders. Local leaders did not advertise the extent to which contracts were enforced to benefit local rather than central interests. Sometimes the government decreed peasant freedoms (e.g., to choose which crops to grow, or to sell surpluses over quota on free markets), while local leaders forced peasants to act otherwise. Local corporatism tended to strengthen midlevel leaders and reduce state power.[93]

Under the headline, "Farmers Ignore Administrative Orders and Do Their Own Thing," for example, the *China Daily* reported that a village in Zhejiang's Yuhang county massively evaded state plans to grow jute for state-owned mills. Official orders to plant jute were at least formally conveyed to peasants by township officials, but the farmers had strong economic disincentives to comply.

The annual monetary yield per hectare of jute was 900 yuan, but the same land planted in fruit or mulberry trees rendered 15,000 yuan. The peasants therefore grew jute on less than one-twentieth of the acreage where they were ordered to grow it. As a farmer said, "Now that we have the decision-making power over production, the township government has no power to order us about. If the jute price is raised high enough, we'll be willing to plant it."[94]

A town in Tongxiang county, Zhejiang, became "the kingdom of ducks" after one of its peasants found that the local environment was superb for breeding fowl. He earned 30,000 yuan a year by the late 1980s ("nearly ten times the income of the Zhejiang provincial governor," a PRC paper noted). Following suit, his fellow villagers soon all raised ducks. A majority of families in that village during 1989 earned 10,000 yuan a year. The boom also led to industrial diversification, because the village leaders founded a factory producing duck feed. As a local tycoon put it, "Believe me, we've really become masters of production. . . . That government officials have become our servants is a great change, brought about by reform."

Another local farmer-turned-duck-breeder suggested that alterations in the terms of trade between agriculture and industry had been long overdue. She expressed resentment at the expense of consumer durables, which in her view had become exorbitant in rural areas over many years: "Farmers are not demanding higher prices for farm products. What we demand is a rational price parity between manufactured goods and farm products. . . . We would not be happy if the government raised the prices of manufactured goods only, but not the prices of farm products. I am sure the price reform, which is enlisting the support of 800 million rural residents, will succeed."[95]

The most basic manufactured good that China's more diverse new agriculture required was inorganic fertilizer. The petrochemical industry provides much of this, and its production requires large capital investments, as well as inputs from limited places that state conservatives could still control. Burgeoning nonstate rural networks thus benefited some state bureaucracies. Farm input prices doubled in just two years, from 1986 to 1988.[96] This made rice-growing unprofitable, farmers claimed. When, by the 1980s, state planners could no longer restrain the inflation of fertilizer prices, peasants cited this as a reason to grow less grain. The betterment of agricultural technology, sponsored by the state, did in the state grain tax. Green revolution threatened what was left of the red one.

Central bureaucrats naturally wanted to tax rural profits to extract rents that might compensate the state's losses from newly flourishing nonstate networks. Taxes on profits from sales of nongrain agricultural products were therefore hit with an increment of 10 to 30 percent in early 1989.[97] Many such sales could be hidden, however. Because the government could not reliably monitor rural production for taxes, the main effect of the new impost was probably to increase the incentives for concealing grain sales.

Mechanized and chemicalized agriculture freed labor. But especially after triple cropping regularized somewhat higher output norms, available technologies could not further raise the output of grain. As Philip Huang has written, partly on the basis of data from conservative but industrializing Songjiang county, Shanghai: "To put it bluntly, marketized farming in the 1980s did no better in crop production than it did in the six centuries between 1350 and 1950, or than collective agriculture did in the preceding three decades." Total rural production and prosperity had sharply grown, but the big increase was industrial. It "came not from 'private' crop production and petty commerce that were given so much press, but rather from rural industry and new sidelines."[98] According to a 1993 sample, the odds that a laborer would have at least some nonfarm work were 30:1 in the area around Zhangjiagang, Jiangsu, near Shanghai.[99] Nonfarm jobs paid much more than work in paddy fields.

Unintended Effects of Local Industrialization

China's central leadership was broadly supportive of the general idea of rural prosperity. Beijing had long supported agricultural mechanization, evidently in the belief that both its rural and urban effects would be beneficial to the state as well as to the people. Government policies could be powerful in Mao's time and later, if they also met the interests of local leaderships. But major effects of agricultural extension had apparently not been foreseen in Beijing. The devil was in the details—especially the deleterious unintended consequences for state industries.

A study comparing the adoption of agricultural technology in two parts of Indonesia concluded that Javanese took to green revolution farming more easily than Ambonese—largely because the Javanese were more statist. They followed advice from Jakarta, which was based on solid new agronomy; and their crop yields duly rose. These central Java peasants trusted their local leaders better than those in Ambon, and their leaders also trusted the state better in Java.[100] The same attitude was present throughout much of the Shanghai delta. But it can lead eventually to an ironic result: industrialization, diversification, and thus pressure on the government to meet a greater variety of needs. Obedience to government could later raise problems for government.

How could peasants make reforms when their lineages, religious identities, and independent organizations had all been officially repressed? Much of the answer is that many rural leaders could evade campaigns for change, or could shape them to create structures benefiting themselves, without challenging government advertisements of official effectiveness. Daniel Kelliher has also noted the operation of inarticulate power, such as the present study discusses in many local networks: "Peasants with no plan, no communication, and often no knowledge of each other's action behaved as if [*sic*] acting in concert. Unanimity of action came from the sameness of circumstance."[101]

This influence is not random, not like Brownian motion, because it usually emerges as a reaction to technological opportunities or to official policies that had been used earlier to mobilize and save resources for the state.[102] Local resources and norms changed in parallel, responding to new economic possibilities and old administrative policies. Such changes can make powerful politics, even when the local policies they imply are "weak," mute, without any open articulation in civil society. China's ex-agriculturalists were able to make massive reforms, partly because many of their first changes were situational, not normative. The Chinese central elite has for centuries comprised intellectuals who proudly presume that ideas always shape situations more than vice-versa. Ex-peasant leaders might find in this presumption a beneficial bluff: They could retain good faith and credit with state hierarchy (and could maintain their own local hierarchies) by accepting the definition of politics as just a matter of ideas—all the while, taking resources that had previously been the state's.

The liberation of agricultural labor beginning in the early 1970s conjured reforms more surely than did 1978 pronouncements by CCP politicians in Beijing. If most high PRC leaders had been interested in Marxism as a means of political analysis, rather than merely as a language to legitimate their rule, they could have been interested in this transformation of rural China. Here is a case where Marx's ideas on the technological causes of political shifts apply quite well (as arguably they do not, in some other cases). Changes of "substructural" technology constrained China's government. They gave concrete wherewithal to local political networks that were still beyond the state's reach. New rural technologies freed people (or at least local leaders) in a classic Marxist way, although the Marxist state did not applaud its own withering.

The beneficiaries were mere peasants. Statist intellectuals noticed the process but did not soon take it seriously. A Communist reactionary, writing a book that became very well-known among PRC intellectuals in 1994, eulogized "the basic correctness of Mao's strategy of keeping peasants bound in poverty to the land [because of] the threat peasants have increasingly posed to China's social stability."[103] This conservative writer excoriated a reformist "provincial Party secretary" (Wan Li, though the book does not identify him) for maintaining that "China's peasants are simple and dutiful; their only demand is to eat their fill and have the freedom to farm." But according to the hardliner, "once the peasants have filled their stomachs they most certainly will continuously raise other demands. And these demands are no longer demands for a low level of existence. They have the desire to develop." They migrate to cities, violating laws and becoming a "powder keg," a "living volcano," that threatens national stability and Party rule.[104] Most data about reforms can be organized by such an analysis. But this Marxist/nationalist writer was unwilling to favor China's majority who wanted to better their lives, rather than a political elite who wanted to stay in power. Agricultural extension policies were not originally intended to end the revolution. In practice, they made most of China's localities more industrial and autonomous. Technical opportunities, first spread by agricultural extension programs, had not been designed to weaken the central state; but during early reforms, they did so powerfully.

Rural Industry: Replacing State Socialism with Local Socialism

Processing raw materials is almost always more profitable than extracting them. Silk-weaving, ceramics, and other industries have been prominent on the lower Yangzi for centuries. Electricity and internal combustion engines as early as the 1930s extensively provided more resources, security, and power for localities in the Shanghai delta. East China villages could make and sell goods, if competition from the metropolis did not drive their nonfarm products off the market.[105]

In the first two decades of the PRC, the state stressed the industrial growth of large inland cities. Shanghai, southern Jiangsu, and northern Zhejiang were taxed more heavily than most of China; and many of these revenues went north and west.[106] This investment strategy, pursued for two decades, ignored economic externalities on the delta that could have returned capital more quickly near Shanghai than in the places where it was sent. Taxes collectible on rural industries were much lower than on urban factories in Mao's time. But socialist planners during the revolutionary centralization of the 1950s and 1960s could still prevent the founding of most rural industries. They wanted to prevent competition for products from the large urban plants that provided most of Beijing's budget.

So after 1949, small industrial enterprises were sporadic in East China rural areas. Pressure to found such factories nonetheless became evident during the Great Leap Forward in 1958. In Jiangsu, the provincial government announced that every commune should open 15 to 25 small factories "within three to five years"—although the Leap's agricultural failure soon obviated many of these plans. The economic depression of the early 1960s led to a retrenchment campaign, during which the government closed about half of the rural plants (in 1961 in Jiangsu for example, reportedly over 5,000 of them). Not all such factories were closed, although many of the surviving firms remained small or underreported for a decade. Even when particular local industries did not outlive the post-Leap depression, peasants remembered their own ability to run them.[107]

The quick growth of Shanghai delta rural industries in the 1970s came partly from old local manufacturing and trading habits in East China, which resurfaced quickly in rural areas when state controls weakened there. As soon as local managers in rural parts of the Shanghai delta had the chance to diversify their production after 1970, because of new inputs or few monitors, they did so. When they could retain more money, they invested much of it in ways that kept future profits local. The output of Jiangsu rural industries rose speedily in terms of gross output, by more than three times between 1970 and 1975.[108] Industry's portion of rural Jiangsu output value was 13 percent in 1970—but up to 40 percent by 1976.[109]

Zhejiang's growth rates also accelerated very early in the reforms. The gross value of that province's industrial output increased each year in the half decade before 1974 at only three or four percentage points below the very high 17 percent yearly rate achieved in the five years following 1978. These early data are difficult to interpret, both because late 1960s political disruptions may have depressed industries in Zhejiang more than in most other places, and also because statistics on rural industrial output in the early 1970s may well be underreports. In any case, there was clearly a sag in the middle 1970s; Zhejiang gross industrial output in both 1974 and 1975 was lower than in 1973. It bounced up to an all-time high in 1977, and then expanded rapidly into the later 1980s.[110]

The factories responsible for most of this growth throughout the delta were not private; they were collective. They were precedented, because cooperatives run by villages and production brigades had grown during the early Great Leap Forward of 1958, even though they had been curbed during much of the 1960s.[111] The biggest economic change in the early 1970s was the rise of brigade and commune enterprises. These firms, which later became cooperatives run by townships, were not just precursors of China's reform. They were its industrial beginning.

Founding and Managing Early 1970s Rural Plants

Provincial data from very large areas such as Jiangsu or Zhejiang, as provided above, give an overview of reform in the very extensive region of China where it may have been earliest. Statistics from more local booming places on the Shanghai delta tell the tale more dramatically. Industry's portion of gross output value in rural Tangjiacun, in Qingcun commune, Fengxian county, Shanghai, was only 7 percent in 1970. Already by 1971 it was 11 percent, then up sharply to 22 percent in 1972, 44 percent in 1973, and a startling 59 percent in 1974. These figures on rural industry's contribution come from a place that a foreign (Japanese) anthropologist deems reasonably typical of the area. The percentages on Tangjiacun industrial growth are worth examining in tabular form, to show the early 1970s acceleration was not only steep but also constant until 1975 (when Zhang Chunqiao's last spurt of radical politics in Shanghai may well have forced underreporting). The industrial percentage of total product at Tangjiacun changed as follows:

1970	7	1975	57	1980	57	1985	79
71	11	76	52	81	69	86	81
72	22	77	48	82	65	87	80
73	44	78	35	83	74		
74	59	79	39	84	78		

By the same token, the portion of gross output value from agriculture in this place plummeted from 80 percent in 1970 to 16 percent in 1987. Industrial performance started reforms there.[112]

In many specific places, the change began with the founding of a particular industry or even a single factory. In 1972, a plastics plant and a silk filature were founded at the Shanghai rural commune that has been most circumspectly studied, Qingcun in Fengxian county. These were the first local industries in that area not directly involved in creating products such as fertilizer or household goods mostly used within the community. Although the town's enterprises in 1966 had employed about 400 workers, the number by 1971 was over 800, by 1972 over 1,000, and by 1978 over 1,700.[113]

These data do not count the rising employment, at the same time, of factories legitimated by lower administrative levels. Tangjiacun, within Qingcun, was only a village; but by 1970 it had a metalworking factory with 25 employees—a number that was ten times larger by 1980. By that latter year, after a decade of *de facto* reforms, the village also had further plants, and it employed 500 local industrial workers by 1985.[114] In later years, especially in the 1990s if this place is similar to other parts of the Shanghai suburbs, many of the added laborers were immigrants from inland provinces.

The same pattern can be found at many places throughout the delta. At Tangqiao commune, Suzhou prefecture, Jiangsu, the early 1970s was also a period of quick expansion. Some of Tangqiao's firms had been founded in the Great Leap Forward, but most were started in the first half of the 1970s. According to one report, Tangqiao's agriculture had reached the limits of its productivity under current technology at that time; so the only way for peasant leaders to raise their followers' incomes was to set up factories. Brigade-run enterprises of 1958 in Tangqiao commune were closed at least formally in 1962, but they resumed in 1970.[115] Because these businesses did not accord with the then-current radical policy of "learning from Dazhai," which stressed that rural places should "take grain as the key link" (*yi liang wei gang*), local Tangqiao authorities supporting such factories had to ignore many directives.[116] Some leading radicals opposed rural industries as peasant capitalism. In 1971, Tangqiao nonetheless set up its first power plant, along with a cardboard box factory, several metal shops, and an animal feed processing factory. In the next year, one of its rural production brigades set up a brick factory that proved to be very profitable; so by 1973, the value of that brigade's industrial product (240,000 yuan, with reported profits of 25,000 yuan) quickly made it the richest village in the commune.

Word of such success spreads quickly in a peasant society. By 1974, Tangqiao leaders could set up an industrial office; and a later analyst said these commune cadres "ran a certain political risk."[117] At first, many new plants in this commune were formally under the umbrella of a "comprehensive factory" (*zonghe chang*). By the end of 1976, this pretense of planned unity was no longer needed; the plants could split into separate administrations. By the next year, many villages in this commune found that the more they invested in agricultural production, the less total profit they made. Despite continuing campaigns under Hua Guofeng for agriculture to "study Dazhai," industrialization continued in many Jiangnan localities. State leaders did not bring this change; local leaders did so. The reported number of factories at Tangqiao doubled from 1976 to 1978.[118]

By the end of the decade, many of these rural plants switched to new managers. Local leaders who had established or reopened factories in the first part of the decade were replaced by new, more technically oriented cadres. Persons from families that had been rich before the revolution had long been active in the plants, but now they began to assume greater roles.[119] These new leaders sought much wider markets for local production; and by the beginning of 1982, Tangqiao factories sent a "comprehensive sales team" to tour more than ten provinces in search of buyers.[120] Also, the township established 90 "sales points" in various Chinese cities, including some that were not heavily served by producers of competing products. This was not private capitalism, and it showed collectives' abilities to seek markets. Tangqiao entrepreneurs raised the quality of management and products.

Nearly half of the plants in Tangqiao at the end of 1985 had been founded *before* the Third Plenum of 1978. Of those, one-third were established in the years 1970–72; and most of the others were post-Leap plants, reopened before 1978.[121] By the mid-1980s, more than half the workers in these particular factories were women. Practically no employees in village-run (*cunban*) factories had urban residence permits, and only 4 percent did so in plants that were township-run (*xiangban*). Many workers in rural industry (22 percent in the simpler village-run factories, and 14 percent in the more complex ones run at the higher rural level) were recent migrants from outside the township.[122]

Tangqiao might represent the overall experience just as well as ostensibly more comprehensive figures from Jiangsu as a whole—because reporting problems were reduced when they were published by careful Shanghai social scientists who obtained information directly from Tangqiao sources, after incentives either to show production or to avoid taxes had lessened. Data from both the province and the commune are on Table 1.1-4. The irregular pattern for all of Jiangsu may be a less accurate index of behavior than the steadier one for the single township that has been studied better. Tangqiao enjoyed a quantum leap of industrial growth in 1971, followed by basic maintenance of that pattern throughout the later reform years.

In Shanghai's suburbs, the pattern resembles Tangqiao even though radical administrators in the mid-1970s dampened both rural industries and rural reporting. Proximity to the metropolis nonetheless spurred quick diversification, as some urban institutions created links to nearby rural areas. At Qingpu county, Shanghai, from 1969 to 1973, the annual rate of gross industrial growth was 21 percent; whereas from 1979 to 1985, it was just one point higher (22 percent). New companies were being founded readily in those early years of reform: the number of factories in this suburban county rose 2.1 times from 1969 to 1973, but just 1.3 times over a later half decade, from 1978 to 1982.[123] Many of these were

Table 1.1-4

Rural Industrialization in Tangqiao, Sunan, 1967–1985, and in All of Jiangsu, 1970–1985 (gross yuan value of industrial product, percentage growths; rural industrial product in Jiangsu total gross output, and growths in that ratio)

	Tangqiao Commune/ Township (thou. yuan)	Tangqiao Product % Change	Jiangsu (r.i./total prod., %)	Jiangsu Product % Change
1967	146			
1968	169	16		
1969	210	24		
1970	391	81	7	
1971	1,038	165	8	14
1972	1,611	155	9	13
1973	2,380	148	10	11
1974	2,910	122	12	20
1975	3,736	128	16	33
1976	5,299	142	21	31
1977	10,031	189	31	48
1978	17,025	170	31	0
1979	24,788	146	33	6
1980	42,727	172	43	30
1981	61,099	143	44	2
1982	66,100	108	42	–5
1983	91,916	139	46	10
1984	129,630	141	49	7
1985	204,270	156	58	18

Sources: Rounded from figures in Xu Yuanming and Ye Ding, *Tangqiao gongye hua zhi lu* (The Way to Industrialization in Tangqiao) (Shanghai: Shanghai Shehui Kexue Yuan Chuban She, 1987), p. 61, and *Jiangsu xiangzhen gongye fazhan shi* (History of the Development of Jiangsu Rural Industry), Mo Yuanren, ed. (Nanjing: Nanjing Gongxue Yuan Chuban She, 1987), pp. 321–22 and 402.

connected to urban plants. Some factories had failed, and/or had deregistered themselves to avoid controls during the interruption of reforms surrounding 1976.

In Shanghai county's Shenzhuang commune by 1974, "household subsidiary production" accounted for 40 percent of the value of all output. Private plots, fish breeding, handicrafts, and short-distance transport all flourished, as did rural industry. Radicals criticized such growth not just because it was (as they rightly said) proto-capitalist, and not just because it diverted resources from state-owned enterprises, but also because it threatened deliveries of low-cost grain to cities. Communes on the delta managed to raise grain output in the mid-1970s, but the prosperity of small firms was shifting the interests of laborers away from rice paddies.

An unidentified "average" county in Suzhou prefecture in 1974 already had 46 percent of its rural workforce in industry. In Shanghai's Jinshan county by 1974, about half of all rural workers were reported as agriculturalists. Less than half may have actually spent most of their work hours in paddies, however, since there was political pressure to report as many peasants as possible. In the East is Red brigade, "Some cadres interested themselves more in production for cash than in the political line, encouraging diversification and economic crops at the expense of grain production; and some prosperous peasants neglected collective production in favor of private plots and free markets."[124]

A shift from state-owned to collective production also measures the same change. The portion of total nonstate output (from rural communes, brigades, and teams) in Jiangsu's Wuxi county rose very sharply after 1970: it was just 23 percent in that year; but by 1977, it was 64 percent.[125] State-managed companies' output portion fell correspondingly. The figures probably underreport the change, because the state tended to fix high prices for the products of its own factories, and because some collective-made goods were hidden to avoid taxes. This transformation predated the official 1978 onset of reforms. The booming ownership type was collective, not state nor private. The change was based on specifically new institutions: During 1974 in Wuxi county, 1,212 new rural factories were founded. Privatization of ownership was not crucial for the quick growth of rural factories; autonomous local management of formal collectives accounted for most of the change.

Nearly four-fifths of Wuxi county's 1,600 rural factories in 1974 were managed or authorized (the word *ban* had either meaning) by brigades. The output of such firms by 1977 exceeded that of the burgeoning industries in Wuxi City, even though the amount of capital investment in the rural area was much lower. The founding period for most of these companies was in the early 1970s. Wuxi county established many such firms in the early 1970s but then suffered a widespread slowing or temporary reversal of reforms in 1975–77, so that the number in 1978 was only 16 percent higher than in 1974.[126]

Most early rural plants were licensed at the brigade level, and to a lesser extent in communes. Production teams at first were still mainly confined to agriculture. So an index of the growth of decentralized industry in Wuxi county is the percentage of all rural output from brigades and communes (not from the state sector and teams). Between 1970 and 1977, this percentage in Wuxi soared from 23 to 64.[127]

The portions of industrial employment at the low village (*cun*) level, as distinct from that at the higher township/commune level, changed sharply during reforms at Tangjiacun, Fengxian county, Shanghai. The village-run factories' portion of local industrial workers was not linear but hump-shaped, rising but then falling: Local industrial workers hired by the village were 34 percent in 1971, up to 65 percent in 1979, then down to 43 percent in 1988. It is likely that non-local immigrants by then had already replaced many locals in the most

most difficult and low-paying jobs in village plants. The private portion of hiring in all three years was low, respectively rounding to 4, 0, and 5 percent.[128] So the push for rural industrialization began at the low-middle size of collectivity, brigades and townships.

Illegal Factories: Reformers vs. Radicals in the Early 1970s

As Fei Xiaotong has written plainly, at least some of the factories were secret:

> In the later stages of the Cultural Revolution [this refers to the early 1970s], many small enterprises emerged in Sunan. These enterprises established by local cadres were illegal [*sic*] at that time. They were "underground." Because of the Cultural Revolution, higher level cadres had no time to deal with such things; so more and more enterprises emerged. Peasants did not mind what the nature of ownership was. The only thing they did mind was to keep up their livelihood. . . . Capital came from collective accumulation; communes used a portion of their funds to develop [industrial] production after the income distribution. . . . The government did not give money or invest. . . . But this was the only way for peasants to make their living at that time.[129]

The North China Agricultural Conference and relative moderates in Beijing during the early 1970s condoned locally owned rural cooperative industries, but the radicals enforced regulations against them. Such ambiguity was typical of reforms—not just in the early 1970s. Serious socialists saw that rural factories' competition with state plants would threaten the Party's ability to plan the economy and finance the central budget. Many such factories were clandestine, but they were actively sponsored by local "state" cadres who undermined at least some of the mandates sent to them from very high levels of the state. They did not advertise their insubordination, of course. They could usually cite opposite mandates more to their liking. Splits between conservatives and reformers at the top allowed local cadres to keep low profiles, in order to make profits and employ local clients. As Fei says, "At the very beginning of these enterprises, they were not called village and town industries (*xiangzhen gongye*) but commune and production team enterprises (*shedui qiye*). . . . Actually, every commune and every village was an economic enterprise. . . . Big collectives were still managed by local governments, and for a long time there was no separation between enterprises and [local] governments."

Even at this time, there were also "small collectives," which were "established by individuals."[130] These businesses were an early-1970s form of enterprise that by the 1990s were often called "dependent firms" (*guahu*), because they relied for local protection on state cadres who had already separated their practice from the state.[131] Local officials acquired positive interests in local enterprises, even if they did not control them. Economic expansion in their jurisdiction gave them more bargaining chips with which to deal with their higher constituency.[132] These resources became important in politics. Local cadres had more wherewithal to grease palms at higher administrative levels, and resources determined cadres' power. Legitimacy from holding low-level state offices may have helped; but access to goods, ranging from fertilizer to factory capital, was increasingly important. As entrepreneurs without official status gained more of these resources, state cadres could no longer "capriciously order farmers around."[133]

An American delegation visiting rural Chinese industries in 1975 concluded that, "Much decision making in China has been decentralized to lower levels; and scientific and technical personnel from Peking, even if they were so inclined, cannot usually order factory and county revolutionary committees to divulge information that these revolutionary committees themselves, for whatever reason, are reluctant to give out."[134] This delegation visited several small plants on the Shanghai delta (in three Wuxi communes and the municipality's towns of Jiading and Malu). Their report found that, "The prime motive force for this extensive development lies within the counties and communes themselves. Provincial and central government planners sometimes provide financial aid and more frequently technical assistance, but it is the interests of the localities that drives the program forward."[135]

It may be unimportant whether state leaders in the early 1970s were divided, as they faced this independent industrial development. Some were clearly willing to wink at it. All high state cadres, including radicals, must have known about this new manufacturing, because China's leaders have many kinds of local information written in limited-circulation reports with great regularity. They could not and did not miss such a major trend. Radicals accurately said that it weakened the "dictatorship of the proletariat," as embodied by their state. State leaders at that time apparently had no unified will to prevent local power networks from expanding factories, and they were in any case almost surely unable to stop such an endemic development. In the specific mid-1970s years when top radicals had greater effective control at the center (and at court, personal factors such as Zhou Enlai's cancer and Deng Xiaoping's temporary eclipse were surely important), all they did was to slow the rate of rural industries' growth and the rate at which it was reported. About 1975, when radicals who most wanted to reverse nonstate industrialization had a political resurgence, the trend was interrupted but did not stop. The end of centralized revolution was evident in the 1970s.

Xu Jiatun was an important administrator in Jiangsu during the early 1970s. Since he was also the highest Party leader to leave China after June 4, 1989, his memoirs could be frank. Xu's language remained statist, the standard dialect that leaders and intellectuals use. But from the safety of a Buddhist monastery in California, Xu expressed pride in Jiangsu's progress during the early 1970s: "I tell you, we took a different road from the rest of the country. 'The planned economy was crucial, and the market economy was a supplement.' We had openly to support this, but in fact we had gone beyond it."[136]

Some high administrators were willing to condone local initiatives, Xu says, even if they were unwilling to be active for rural enterprise. There is scant contemporary evidence that province-level cadres went beyond the ambiguity Xu expressed two decades later. On occasion, they unambiguously opposed rural industries. After the Jiangsu Party committee ordered lower branches to "oppose capitalist tendencies more energetically" in 1975, peasants reacted by slaughtering team- and brigade-owned livestock and by diverting water to their own plots. In Jiangsu's Nanchang county and Zhejiang's Shaoxing county, there was "widespread sabotage."[137] There was much variance at the county level and more locally. Unified decisions about rural industrialization were difficult to enforce in an area so large as a province. Parallel opportunities for local networks differed among parts of China, and the whole Wu-dialect flatland provided a fertile context for new industries no matter what high politicians wanted. Xu observes that markets overtook plans early in Sunan. He and his colleagues had few effective bureaucratic helpers in the early 1970s, after the Cultural Revolution had cowed so many. He simply blinked at the change from a Nanjing office.

Shanghai's most powerful administrator, Zhang Chunqiao (one of the radical Gang of Four), was not willing to blink. Zhang fulminated often about "sprouts of capitalism in the countryside." His shrill complaints were widely deemed in the West at the time to be a mere mantra, representing what any devoted leftist would have said reflexively with or without evidence. Now it should be clear that Zhang knew what he was talking about. Nonetheless, partly because of the power of Shanghai's radicals, the suburbs did not develop as quickly as Sunan. Leaders of the Star brigade in Chengbei commune of Songjiang county, for example, were excoriated by radicals for having grown the least grain of any brigade in that commune during the decade before 1975. The fault reportedly lay in "capitalist" tendencies among local cadres—who introduced industries that took labor from the fields. The brigade officials were particularly criticized for claiming they had a shortage of workers.[138] In the radicals' view, they were assigning their workers to the wrong tasks: to factories rather than fields.

Not always did administrative superiors know what their nominal subordinates were actually doing. Steven Butler showed that the basis of rural autonomy was an avoidance of monitoring. The main issue was "at which level decision-making is made feasible by the nature of the problem at hand."[139] Away from Shanghai, for example in hilly regions at the edge of the delta and beyond, there is evidence of great autonomy at this time. In 1975, Changqi commune in Zhejiang "suffered from the capitalist faction's influence among the leading comrades." The pattern of labor leaving collective production in favor of "sideline" occupations (which include factories) was said to be widespread in 1975 throughout Zhejiang. A county of inland Anhui was said to be suffering at this time from capitalist "corruption of alarming proportions."[140] Wenzhou, in southern Zhejiang, took this trend to the extreme—and did so much earlier than public discussion of the singular "Wenzhou model" that later became an archetype of extreme reform. Private capitalism in that city and its isolated delta, which had been flourishing on an illegal basis for years before the spring of 1977, was the target of attacks in a government campaign that year against "capitalist forces." This hassle merely forced private firms underground on a temporary basis.[141]

Scant official support was available for most Jiangnan plants. Team or brigade factories, and in most cases even commune plants that could be more easily monitored, were seen by high cadres as crucially different from the enterprises hitched to the central socialist state. As one report put it, "Rural industry had no registration among the state's industrial departments, and no place in the state plan." So the government's economic committees, central or provincial, normally refused to guarantee the provision of credit, materials, machines, energy, or markets. On the other hand, these nonstate firms "had relatively complete freedom to do their businesses . . . they could adapt to suit changing circumstances and could survive." In contrast to state firms, they were highly competitive traders.[142]

The government was not quickly weakened by rural industrialization. Its response was reactive, sporadically acknowledging what had happened for the sake of eking some taxes out of a situation it could not control. Beijing found in the 1970s that important parts of rural China had "five small industries" (*wu xiao gongye*), producing steel, machines, chemical fertilizers, coal, and cement. These country factories inevitably vied with state firms selling the same commodities and needing similar materials to make them. The state plants produced more efficiently than the small ones, perhaps because they were on average much larger. There is nothing inherently "small" about steel, machines, chemicals, coal, or cement.[143] These companies remained small to avoid monitoring, imposts, and restrictions.

Rural enterprises in the early 1970s were started outside the "five small industries." Entrepreneurs established factories in other sectors, illegally if necessary.[144] In Jiangsu during 1970, a polyester fiber workshop created a cotton mill and developed new equipment for it.[145] Many parts of the China coast saw a "second economy" developing in this period.[146] The state budget was disserved by the emergence of all these new firms. They flourished not because of production efficiency, but because they could operate more flexibly in both upstream and downstream markets, seeking opportunistic benefits in either the socialist or proto-capitalist contexts. Beijing's non-consensus policy was to contain them by encouraging their formation under middle levels of administration, not low levels where state control was even more tenuous. As early as August, 1971, central decrees condoned the founding of some factories under prefectures or counties. At these middling-high levels of administration, larger imposts on economic activity could be expected than if the factories were established under communes, brigades, or teams. But for rural firms, the State Council already provided in 1971 that "60 percent of the profits made by newly established local industries at the county level could be kept at the county level."[147]

Several slogans helped to acclimatize cadres to rural industries. Cultural Revolution slogans that had been originally designed for urban purposes (to legitimize contract labor, or to send city youths to the countryside) could be adapted for the politics of rural industries. Such factories were alleged to create all-purpose proletarians who were "at once workers and peasants" (*yigong yinong*). These new plants made for the "integration of farm and factory" (*nonggong yiti hua*). Also, they were supposed to discourage urban immigration by allowing laxly employed people to "leave the soil but not the country" (*li tu buli xiang*). These people were said to be a national "reservoir" of surplus farm labor—but actually, rural factory workers had scant interest in ever returning to drudgery in paddies. Slogans put a patina of official legitimacy on a trend that was out of the state's control. They could not make the new pattern fully serve the central government.

Collectives during the early 1970s, which were numerous in Shanghai's rural suburbs, paid low taxes and few workers' benefits in comparison with state firms. They supplied less medical care, less housing, less time off, and lower wages—but still, they paid enough to attract labor. Many youths, who had been rusticated in the late 1960s, returned to Shanghai and could become politically active again if given nothing to do. The state had harmed most of these people by sending them to boondocks in 1968; so it had built the barrel over which it now found itself. By 1971, it sacrificed some control over local materials and product markets, in order to keep otherwise unemployed political youths (euphemistically called "social youths") off the streets by allowing collectives to hire them sometimes in the central city and very often in the suburbs.

The annual operating budget that collectives required per job, in this situation, was much closer to a subsistence rate than traditions in the state sector would allow.

> City and township collective enterprises . . . operated during the Cultural Revolution [this PRC commentator meant the early 1970s]. At that time, there were a lot of intellectual young people who could not find jobs in state firms. Collectives became an important place for them to work. . . . According to statistics of the Shanghai Handicraft Bureau, its collectives on average needed 2,278 yuan to arrange a job, but state firms took 10,049 yuan to do the same thing. . . . Street enterprises played an important role. Street firms had to collect financial resources and materials by themselves. They had to take charge of their own marketing. They also had independent accounts. They were not subordinate to any level of governments or to a trade system. They were established in order totally to resolve the employment problem for young people. After 1970, state enterprises, schools, and universities also established small enterprises in order to arrange employment for family members of their workers. . . . Small collectives got opportunities to survive and develop. Actually, they carried out a portion of the state ownership enterprises' functions. Shanghai street enterprises had an industrial output value more than 1 billion yuan. The figure was nearly three times that of 1966. . . . From 1971 to 1976, the average annual [*sic*] growth rate of state output was 5 percent, but that of collectives was 13 percent. . . . According to 1975 statistics, the profit rate per

> hundred yuan in state firms was 15 percent, but in collective enterprises, 44 percent.[148]

Collectives hired "social youth" and thus solved a short-term political problem for the state—while weakening state control of markets and creating larger difficulties for officials later.

Even when high-placed radicals opposed rural industries' prosperity, arguing for revolution over production, local leaders' support for nonstate factories did not vanish. Since rural industries were booming anyway, flexible Marxists gave it an ideological gloss. Marx had called, after all, for the release of productive forces that "slumber in the lap of social labor."[149] No serious advocate of the proletariat could long argue that China's countryside should remain poor. No Chinese could claim to be patriotic while standing foursquare against peasants increasing resources that arguably strengthened the nation. But radicals like Zhang Chunqiao saw that rural industry was a threat to state planning and to coordinated socialism. One reason why the PRC state of the early 1970s began to lose control of rural China is that its own leaders' goals were mixed. If the top politicians had been more unified, the long-term result would almost surely have been the same, but change toward it would have been slower. Hopes among the national leaders were sufficiently diverse that rural industrialization could not easily be repressed, despite its attack on the resources of the state.

The state was divided, in the early 1970s as in later eras of decentralizing reform, between "leftist" conservatives and nascent reformers. The radicals took portfolios more often in cultural and urban affairs than in the economic and rural fields.[150] An irony of the reform period, already evident in its early beginnings, was that rural prosperity created by new industrialists helped legitimate the CCP after its traumas in the famine and the Cultural Revolution of the 1960s. Communards might evade the government's imposts, hide data from tax collectors, and castigate cadres whose policies did not benefit them. Such actions could help legitimate the state by making it more tolerable locally. If rural people had not made themselves richer by foisting reforms on the Party-state beginning in the 1970s, the CCP would surely have enjoyed less legitimacy in the next two decades.

Different Rates of Rural Industrialization in Different Parts of China

Reforms came earlier to the Shanghai delta than to most other places in the country. This current study can make no claim that such changes were started by local leaders in the early 1970s throughout China. Some collateral evidence suggests that similar patterns may have occurred also in a few other regions.[151] They were not nationwide. Probably the Yangzi delta development of rural industry was, in general, about one decade faster than parallel changes in the country as a whole, although boondock areas held down the averages on any index by which rural reform might be measured. For example, Huayang commune/township, Songjiang, Shanghai, by 1976 had an industrial portion of total output already at 43 percent—a figure that China on average attained a decade later, in 1986.[152] Industrial growth in commune factories, and later in township and village plants, was uneven over both time and place. In Huayang, large increases in the portion of total output value from industry came in 1971–75 and in a single year, 1980, when reporting may have become more complete. The periods 1975–79 and 1981–83 showed somewhat less change.

Year	Huayang	China
1971	27%	7%
72	31	8
73	35	9
74	35	10
75	41	12
76	43	17
77	46	21
78	45	23
79	46	24
80	58	27
81	61	22
82	61	22
83	64	24
84		28
85		37
86		43

The flat region around Shanghai has strong traditions of rural entrepreneurship outside the state's span of control. Local leaders reshaped this heritage into new institutions by the 1970s. The dense network of canals was only the most obvious physical manifestation of a commercial culture the region had nurtured for centuries. The Shanghai delta's physical plant to support thousands of small medium-distance traders who lack capital is unexcelled anywhere. For state planners, this infrastructure for economic independence had represented a problem since the 1950s. Cadres responded by subsidizing canal tugboats, behind which long trains of otherwise free-lance freight barges (each with a family aboard) might be cheaply pulled—and thus monitored. But boat people sometimes dropped the tether. If they could get their own engines and avoid harassment from the water police (*shuijing*), they could sail off to make money on their own. The more general condition was an environment of cowed bureaucrats and local profits that actually emerged after the 1960s.[153] It was difficult for the regime to make Jiangnan trade socialist, because the endemic canals dispersed commerce away from central oversight.

Different Jiangnan rural towns have for centuries been somewhat specialized in manufactures, or marketing, or administration, or transport, or simply residence.[154] With this old diversification, early reforms in the delta were natural—even if the particular institutions that new local leaders used to implement them were not necessarily identical with pre-1949 structures. Private and individual trade was mostly prohibited in the 1971–1978 period, but collective and commune trade developed quickly throughout Jiangnan.[155] This pattern may have applied in some of the other parts of China that also experienced relatively early reforms. The highly efficient water transport system of southern Jiangsu and northern Zhejiang was not paralleled throughout China, but similar reforms apparently followed in reform-prone smaller deltas and plains that have similar infrastructures. These inherited contexts combined with local leadership choices to determine the intensity of reforms.

Sunan did far better in expanding rural industries than historically poorer and economically less diversified regions such as Subei (northern Jiangsu). By 1982, the gross product of rural industries per person in Wuxi, Sunan, was 714 yuan, the highest level in the province; and in the traditional Sunan administrative center of Suzhou, it was 537 yuan. But in northern Jiangsu's Xuzhou at the same time, this per-capita product was only 74 yuan; in Lianyungang, 68 yuan; and in Huaiyang, just 40 yuan. Even the provincial capital of Nanjing, which tended to have conservative leaders, recorded a level of just 143 yuan, far lower than Zhenjiang, Changzhou, or any other major city south of the river.[156]

If large provincial units are used for this comparison, Shanghai's high taxes and preponderance of state industries meant that the built-up parts of the metropolis did not do well. From 1982 to 1986, Jiangsu and Zhejiang grew much faster than Shanghai—at 17 and 21 percent annual industrial output increases, respectively, in comparison with Shanghai's 7.5 percent. Although Shanghai in 1982 still had 26 percent more industrial yield than Jiangsu, that province overtook the metropolis as China's largest industrial producer in mid-1985. Stagnancy in central Shanghai's state sector was clearly responsible for this difference. In 1982, industrial output from government firms had predominated in all three places: 58 percent in Zhejiang, 60 percent in Jiangsu, and 87 percent in Shanghai. But by the mid-1980s, state-owned enterprises created less than half the industrial product in both Jiangsu and Zhejiang, but still over 80 percent in Shanghai.[157]

From 1978 to 1984, the annual growth rate of rural enterprise output in Suzhou, Wuxi, and Changzhou, all in southern Jiangsu, was reported at 30 percent.[158] In the single year between 1984 and 1985, the amount of product made by rural industries under these Sunan jurisdictions reportedly rose by half. It contributed 70 percent of the value of all rural production in those places, and already one-third of all fiscal revenues.[159] These three prefectures by 1988 were producing 43 percent of the industrial output of Jiangsu—by then, the highest among China's provinces.[160] Rural industrialization hurt the state's economic monopolies and extractive capacities. So many top leaders actively tried, well into the 1980s though without much success, to close these country markets and factories operating with few plans or central taxes.[161] This rural boom localized the resource base for Chinese politics.

Enterprising Ex-Officials and Quasi-Official Entrepreneurs

Clearly local chiefs managed or legitimated many new factories. This leaves further questions: What administrative levels were most important for different kinds of industrial development? Were Party or state cadres more involved; or instead, was the boom led by unofficial local entrepreneurs, who may or may not have been in the same family lineages as cadres? Do the accurate answers to such questions vary over separate periods of reforms, over different sizes of networks, or in specific places? The last of these issues is important, because many data suggest that different patterns emerged over both time and space.

New factory managers on the Shanghai delta, especially during the early reform years, often had any of three backgrounds: in local government, in the local Party, or in local units of the military. Others, who were of sharply increasing importance during the 1980s, had previous careers as technicians or traders. Even if their qualifications for appointment were originally political, the market incentives surrounding them tended to make them business specialists rather than political generalists.

Peasant cadres and brigade Party secretaries composed the first generation of Sunan leaders in rural industries. Many were old and lacked much education. Village cadres in China have never been on state salaries. They are not civil servants. Even in the era of communes, only some high rural leaders were so—and these were often imposed on localities from the government. If village cadres tried to use methods of agricultural management to run modern firms, they could run into problems. Some reportedly admitted they were not up to the job. Dealing in new markets and selling products less standard than grain created needs for younger rural leaders. Some who took such roles after 1976 were ex-urban "intellectual youths," a second generation of local leaders who had lived for years in the rural places where they established new firms. Later a third generation of better-educated youths ran many Sunan rural companies. "In Maojiao township, Zhangjiagang, fourteen old leaders who were not good at enterprise management in rural enterprises were forced to retire in 1984, and nineteen young leaders were appointed as managers. Among them, twelve were technicians." These were said to have "great authority (*da quan*) to distribute profits, hire workers, and award or punish them."[162]

The most telling comparison is with urban directors, who adapted their managerial habits to the premise that higher-level state cadres would be able to aid their concrete operations: "Compared to managers in cities, rural executives are more powerful and independent. *Town leaders only involve themselves with rural businesses indirectly and in economic terms.* The government never interferes with the daily affairs of enterprises." For this independence, local government leaders naturally exact a price:[163]

> Many managers must have several thousand yuan as a mortgage, before they can be appointed or can apply to be managers. In Zhanjiang and Wuxi, plant directors must pay 10 percent of the planned enterprise [annual] profit before they can become formal managers. . . . If managers cannot complete their quotas, they have to pay for this incapability. On the other hand, the local governments give high awards to managers who show good performance. If they fulfill their plans, they may get salaries one to three times above the average wage of the workers.

Parvenu rural entrepreneurs in Shanghai's suburban Jiading by the 1990s reportedly tended to be young, partly educated, and well connected with local leaders. Some were themselves cadres in town government, although they openly expressed fears and resentments about potential antireform changes in state policies. They liked the status quo, in which they prospered.[164] Three keys to success, as these entrepreneurs identified them, might be summarized in alliterative English: "capital, courage, and connections."

A major reason why Shanghai delta enterprise managers often prefer remaining in the collective sector, instead of founding private firms, is that they like to deal with town leaders—who are often friends or kin—rather than with tax cadres from higher administrative levels. If their firms remain collective, rather than becoming legally private, they have better official cover against demands from more centralist government agents. Even if total bribes and imposts on an enterprise remained just as great under collective as under state ownership, the funds taken from collectives tended to remain local. Rural factory heads stood a greater chance of influencing the later use of such money, if more of it remained in town. Collective managers had to maintain very good relations with leaders in local governments.

Collectives therefore flourished better than formally private firms. For example in Jiangyin, near Wuxi, a private entrepreneur named Ren in the early 1980s opened an ironworks. Within two years, he was able to repay the 35,000 yuan loan with which he had started. Such prosperity, creating a new hinge leader on economic grounds, depends on local community support; so the private entrepreneur voluntarily paid the electricity, water, and ploughing bills of a hundred local households. But such prosperity—especially in a firm that had no socialist cover—also bred envy and costs: The town government approached this entrepreneur to pay a land-use tax that he had not expected. Then a fisherman, who claimed that the factory scared fish away from a nearby river, organized a gang of sixty boat people to smash windows and equipment in the factory. "Even though Mr. Ren had thousands of dollars, he could not get any help, because his factory was privately owned."[165] The entrepreneur, no longer able to do business, gave his whole plant to the local production team as a collective, retaining his position as manager. This allayed his problems in the immediate environment, but his troubles were not ended. When bureaucrats in a higher-level Wuxi company learned that he had given away his profitable plant, they were angry that he had offered it to the local team rather than to their own office. They sent tax collectors to inspect his books. Then they sued him—without success, because he had broken no laws. In this case, the court upheld his right to continue in business, as manager of a collective.

It was often crucial for profitability that local firms remain nominally collective, but the authority of their directors was as full as that of a private magnate. During the late 1970s, small rural state industries might be leased to their former managers or to ex-agricultural cadres. In order to maintain local budgets, the earlier state profits from such firms were replaced by other kinds of rents and taxes. Former managers or experienced team cadres were the main bidders for such leases. In some cases, the local leaders found ways in effect to give the factories to themselves. But as Jean Oi has written, "For the most part, team leaders had to exit the historical stage. . . . The post-1978 reforms robbed team leaders of most of their power, leaving them either as team leaders or as newly designated village small group leaders, with few duties."[166] Many resisted these changes, while others, if they had technical skills, prospered in the new era.

Scattered PRC evidence suggests that most rural industrialists by the 1980s had not been cadres. Local ex-officials could usually join new businesses—but they most often did so if their former posts were at low administrative levels. A large portion of ex-commune and ex-brigade cadres only assisted the new economy, without taking entrepreneurial risks, while ex-team officials more often participated in it directly. Some inland areas report more former high officials in new managements than coastal areas usually had. A large survey in an inland county found that 43 percent of the "specialized households" were headed by former team cadres, but a similar survey in coastal Fujian yielded a portion well below 5 percent. The power of local cadres was seldom so great as to scuttle peasant entrepreneurship. Many former local notables lost influence in this change. Some opposed the new development, while most accommodated it and extracted resources from it for themselves and their communities. A minority of cadres, especially those who had technical training, became entrepreneurs themselves.[167]

This evolution of local enterprise leadership, occurring early in Jiangnan, was later replicated elsewhere. In areas of North Jiangsu where the salt gabelle had traditionally made government the main entrepreneur, new rural industries ran into problems because local bureaucrats habitually stifled all businesses they could not control. Officials in July 1986 founded a company operating around Xuzhou and making products for export. This company had branches in many local towns and was thus called a "multi-village enterprise" (*duozhen qiye*).[168] Some "new" companies of this sort were apparently efforts by bureaucrats to restrict profitable cooperatives that had sprung up at lower levels in the early reform period. These were amalgamated, because high and mid-level administrators wanted to rationalize and maximize the revenues remitted to themselves.

This particular new joint company suffered "multi-faceted interventions" (*duofang chashou*) from higher cadres. They tended to hire their own friends to top jobs in the regional corporation that had nominal charge of former local collectives. The management form was familiar, derived from socialist "mother-in-law" corporations that supervised many factories in Mao's time and later. Higher bureaucrats in this Xuzhou conglomerate were accused of making personal loans from the corporate till. To counteract such tendencies—which finally bankrupted this company—the prefectural government established three regulations: that the individual factory managers should not suffer interference from the outside, that leaders should not hire their relatives, and that such a company could not borrow money without high-level authorization. This reportedly changed policy from "an interference mode to a service mode" (*ganyu xing wei fuwu xing*). The original leaders of the local plants remained in place and could operate under new rules that facilitated credit and technical improvements.

A 1990s survey of rural businesses found that a great majority called on relatives for capital loans. Most rural enterprises also hired different members of the same lineage in managerial posts. As an interviewee put it, "Relatives are reliable; one can relax with them." Another manager revealed his liking for hiring relatives: "That way, what I say goes." Over four-fifths of top staff, and nearly three-fifths of contractors, in a sample of 34 rural firms were "relatives or close contacts."[169]

Capital was an obvious need for new rural firms, but the new managers could obtain money. According to an estimate for China as a whole, the total amount of wealth that peasants had—in houses, tractors, animals, trucks, stored grains, monetary savings, and other assets—increased almost ten times between 1978 and 1985. The total in 1978 was calculated at about eighty billion yuan; and in 1985, seven hundred billion.[170] Some of this sharp increase may come from better reporting in later years, as the central state's ability to levy taxes decreased. Rural entrepreneurs, however, decreasingly needed state banks to raise seed money.

Rural Talent from Agriculture to Collective Factories, Rural Youths to Cities

The boom was industrial, and one category of local notables whose importance declined was those who would not switch from their traditional vocation in agriculture. The nationwide swell of rural industries was quick, but fluctuations in that growth line were an inverse mirror-image of the ups and downs in agricultural output.[171] When rural industry rose fastest in these years, agriculture often declined or rose most slowly. The hike of official grain purchase prices in 1978–79 was required, in effect, to buy peasant labor from rural factories for use in the fields instead. If grain prices had not gone up, state procurement would surely have deteriorated even more quickly (and city people would have had less to eat). The central government paid more, and went more deeply into debt, in hopes of keeping both its rural and urban constituencies.

The rise of rural industry took resources and personnel from agriculture. When rural factory output growth accelerated, as Table 1.1-5 suggests, agriculture's output usually decelerated. For the great majority of reform years from 1972 to 1985, either rural industry or else agriculture did better than the previous year—but not both. Also, in some years when rural industry grew fastest on a nationwide basis (1974–76, 1984–85), agriculture did least well. But in the mid-1980s and later, the rates of growth in rural industry were so high (and were reported fairly high even in years such as 1989–90, when central leaders were doing all they could to retard the industrial avalanche and to get more grain), this trade-off ceased to be normal. The industrial sector already dominated the rural economy by this time.

Few rural enterprises were directly run by villages or townships/brigades, even though these units in the mid-1980s licensed most of them. The companies merely had contracts with these administrative units. Reform managers were supposed to be appointed for fixed terms—and this was an apparent change from Mao's time, when managers' tenures began with no stated limit. Contracts were regularly renewable—they existed largely as symbolic ciphers for defunct planning—and no manager of a profitable rural firm was likely to be denied renewal so long as appropriate local payments were made. Workers in rural enterprises, especially those licensed at the village level or below, were practically never unionized. If they were local, many employees (and managers) received much of their compensation in the form of bonuses, so that the low wage scales of the previous plans ceased to restrict salaries.[172]

These changes gave local leaders in the countryside more power, while mid- and high-level rural bureaucrats became less influential. A very rough way to judge the changing clout of different kinds of leaders is to look at ownership categories. The proportion of output from collectives in China rose sharply *before* 1978. The second column of Table 1.1-6 gives some available nationwide figures on collectives. These may understate the rise of local units—and the fastest rise of the most local firms—because leaders on the spot had more incentives to hide rural production before 1978 than afterwards. The Shanghai delta experience, showing very quick growth of small rural industries at that time, gives only a somewhat early picture of what was apparently happening in other rich rural areas too. The trend in Jiangnan was very fast, but its direction was reflected in national averages even during the early 1970s.

A difficulty in interpreting such data is that the term "collective" covers such a wide variety of firms. The core problem is to judge the relative weight of collectives legitimated by towns and counties ("big collectives" as Fei Xiatong calls them), compared to *de facto* private "small collectives" that are nominally under village governments. This weighting changed over time. Township and village enterprises each accounted, in mid-reforms, for about half of the nonstate industrial output. A 1985 Wuxi county report put the higher-level township and

Table 1.1-5

Rural Industry or Rural Agriculture: The Trade-off (national growth rates, 1972–86, faster [f] or slower [s] than previous year)

	Faster or slower	
	Agricultural growth	Industrial growth
1972		
1973	f	s
1974	s	f
1975	s	f
1976	s	f
1977	s	s
1978	f	s
1979	s	f
1980	s	f
1981	f	s
1982	f	f
1983	s	f
1984	f	f
1985	s	f
1986	—	s
1987	f	f
1988	f	f
1989	s	s
1990	f	s
1991	s	f
1992	f	f

Source: Based on figures to 1986 calculated from *Zhongguo tongji nianjian, 1987* (China Statistical Yearbook, 1987), State Statistical Bureau, ed. (Beijing: Zhongguo Tongji Chuban She, 1987); and from 1987, from ibid., 1993 edition, p. 333. Many such results probably arise not just from real growth but also from accounting changes. Some growth of "agricultural" value in previous years came from industries licensed by low-level agricultural units; but by 1985 and later, much of this was more properly accounted as industrial. The actual figures are omitted here because of such problems. A trade-off between growth in the two rural sectors occurred in most reform years, especially early ones.

lower-level village licensees each at 48 percent. (The small remainder of the recorded total—which may well be less than the real total—was divided between production team enterprises, partnerships, and private enterprises that might also underreport.)[173] Villages (*cun*) have a low rank, but together they licensed about half of China's rural industry. Both large and small collectives were important, perhaps about equally so. Both types outpaced central, provincial, and prefectural state factories.

Table 1.1-6

Gross Value of PRC Industrial Output by Ownership Type (percentages)

	Collective	State owned	Other
1965	10	90	0
1970	12	88	0
1978	22	78	0
1979	22	78	0
1980	24	76	1
1981	25	75	1
1982	25	74	1
1983	26	73	1
1984	30	69	1
1985	32	65	3
1986	34	62	4
1987	35	60	6
1988	36	57	7
1989	36	56	8
1990	36	55	10
1991	36	53	11
1992	38	48	14
1993	38	43	19
1994	41	34	25

Source: The figures are rounded and approximate, and their meaning is not entirely consistent from one firm to the next, in part because there are many kinds of management within each of the three main categories: state, collective, and "other." This last refers mainly to private firms (49 percent of the total) at the end of 1949, to "joint" state-private ones in 1957, and to both joint jurisdiction and private firms by the mid-1980s and thereafter. See *Zhongguo tongji nianjian, 1991* (China Statistical Yearbook, 1991), State Statistical Bureau, ed. (Beijing: Zhongguo Tongji Chuban She, 1991), p. 396; but somewhat different figures—lower for the collective and private sectors—are in ibid., 1986, p. 273, ibid., 1988, p. 318 (see also p. 311), ibid., 1990, p. 413, and ibid, 1991, p. 391. Figures for 1991 come from ibid., p. 408; and for 1992–94 from calculations based on ibid., 1995, p. 377. The definitions and reporting apparently improved over time.

The Party became a decreasing presence in China's rural areas by late reforms. Many active young people, of the kinds that rural Party branches near Shanghai had often used for decades, could flock at least to medium-sized cities even during the early 1970s.[174] Demographic changes reduced rural recruitment to the Party. Total CCP membership reached 49 million by the end of 1990, when most members were apparently still in the countryside. But the absolute number of rural members was decreasing by mid-reforms at least. Government media complained of "a tendency toward senility in rural Party organizations."[175] Talented ex-peasants and rural youths could make better careers by staying out of the Party than by submitting themselves to its rules. The remaining agricultural peasants were now increasingly independent farmers, and they too wanted less regulation from above. Party members in the country became less useful than in the past. Top CCP leaders had certainly not planned this apathy to be part of reforms—even reformers among them spoke against it—but the distance between the Party and the peasants grew. The Leninist organization became even more urban than before, and in cities too it lost influence to other networks. Most important, the meaning of membership changed for many Communists. The CCP as a disciplined organization was increasingly separate from rural industry, the most dynamic part of China's economy.

Periodization Based on Behavioral Turning Points

A critic might suggest that the data above, showing quick nonstate rural reforms since the early 1970s, might prove nothing—because these began from such a "low base." Production from rural industries had indeed been rather minor before 1970, but the fast change after that is still highly relevant to periodization. Many local data series on tables in chapters from both volumes of this study show patterns of reform change after 1970, at least to the middle of the decade, that are similar to those in most periods after 1978. Often the series show decelerations in 1975–78. Many also show some slowing in the early 1980s, and again briefly in 1989–90.

National published data for industrial growth, especially in heavy industry, show a pattern that at first may seem different. The gross value of reported Chinese industrial output grew at an average annual rate of 12 percent from 1965 to 1970, but this dropped to 8 percent in 1970–76—and rose again to 14 percent in 1976–78.[176] Heavy industry accounted for most of this change, which at first might seem to show that the early 1970s were a period of recession, not a beginning of the reform boom. (Perhaps more surprisingly, these data also show a very respectable rate of industrial growth nationwide in the late 1960s.) But these data offer a record of industry that was nationwide, openly reporting, and state-owned—the very slowest sector to reform. Locally, at least in the Shanghai delta, many data show that industry was growing faster than in China generally. Also, the early 1970s were a period when many collective factories accelerated their production but also had great incentives to hide it; so the rates of change seem depressed. Also, the capture of factors by low-tax and underreporting firms caused shortages in the state sector—whose localization was a crucial aspect of reforms, not a counterindication of them.

The logical problems of discounting the significance of the early reforms after 1970, despite the initial low base of production from which many rural industries began, would be several: How low is "low"? When the level in a time series is practically zero, as it was for some of these series at the start of the 1970s, then a clear rise represents something to be explained. It may mark a watershed. If a higher initial value were required before any change could be deemed notable, then how much higher? By that reasoning, for many of the time series, the figures from 1984–85 (especially in fields where change slowed temporarily in the previous few years) would be as convincing a start for reforms as 1978. But to say the reforms began in 1985 would certainly neglect too many changes before then. In any case, the 1977–78 point does not hold up, for many behavioral time series taken together, as a more fundamental transition than the 1970–71 watershed. Near Shanghai, the standard periodization has defects.

The main reason for the usual emphasis on 1978 apparently relates to current interests of high leaders in Beijing. The standard periodization presumes reforms started from the wisdom of the central seers, notably the late Deng Xiaoping. Not only does this view deny him credit for his reform activities in 1973–75, it also overstates the power of the central government as China's revolution winds down. It prejudges the question of whether any origins of reform might be found outside Beijing.

The official periodization hides too much not only about reforms, but also about the Cultural Revolution. It suggests that the Cultural Revolution was a whole reasonably homogeneous decade of turmoil, from 1966 to 1976. Then after a brief hiatus hosted by Hua Guofeng, reforms are said to have begun under Deng Xiaoping in 1978. That view overwhelmingly structures scholarship, in the West and China alike, and even among researchers who realize that 1966–76 was not, actually, a uniform era. It makes no sense of many behavioral trends that are clearly relevant to reforms—not just in rural industry, but also in certain other fields.

The two volumes presenting this research do not claim, however, that the Cultural Revolution ended (or that reforms began) in all spheres of Chinese life simultaneously. Change came later and less surely for many intellectuals than for many others, e.g. most farmers. In normative fields of culture and political rhetoric, reform was slower and less decisive than in situational fields such as rural industry or international trade. The latter may seem less classy but are important. As the second volume of this work shows, some researchers have tended to neglect early 1970s changes even in arts and ideology. Even most intellectuals faced a somewhat different situation after 1970 than before, and this difference will be explored below. After that year, there was less chaos on the streets than in 1966–68, and there was less extensively organized coercion among most urban people than in the Cleaning Class Ranks Campaign of 1968–70, which was largely run by the army. It is time to begin writing about Chinese politics as if governmental and dissident intellectuals, despite their influence, were not the only participants.

No periodization can ever be perfect; yet in writing political history, the time periods chosen for analysis tend to frame whatever else is said. A periodization is only an idea, an analytic frame that does not exclude others. Whether China's sputtering pattern of reforms "actually" began in 1971 rather than 1978, the proposal that they did so can serve as a scope for seeing many aspects of Chinese politics that have often been obscured. It is hard to imagine any greater benefit that could come from a mere conceit.

The Inefficiency of Rural and Suburban Factories

Putting rural factories at the start and center of an account of the reform period explains much about this era's localization, inflation, corruption, and prosperity. An economist can rue village industries, despite their fast growth, because of their inefficiency.[177] Tax avoidances and beneficial prices, accorded by local regimes to local firms, can easily make small factories profitable—even if the available technologies and factor distributions make economies of scale better in larger plants. On the other hand, central planning of resources can also lead to waste. This was evident in the Cultural Revolution investment policy of 1964–71, which favored gigantic state factories inland.[178] During reforms, it may yet become more evident in the Three Gorges Dam project. Local hinge leaders are not by definition efficient users of capital—and neither is the central state.

Jiangsu industry's total factor productivity has been reported according to the official periodization of reforms. From 1953 to 1978, it showed a 2.1 percent reported annual decline; but in the next decade, the index grew 4.4 percent annually. But if shorter time periods are considered, the most startling results are a very sharp decline during the post–Great Leap depression, some rebound from this low-productivity era that continued into the Cultural Revolution, a rise in the early 1970s, a decline that began at least by 1975 for a couple of years, and then the re-starting of productivity reforms after 1977.[179]

State industries may be compared with collectives, during reforms, to assess their total factor efficiencies. The results are revealing: The decentralization of the Shanghai delta economy increased the efficiency of trade (and of the whole economy). The economic rise of local and autonomous authoritarian managers meant that quasi-private industries relentlessly exploited cheap factors, especially labor. New rural industries mobilized resources, often in a coercive manner, rather than in a civil way. They increased the economy's inputs, even more than they increased the outputs.

Sunan collective firms did not use resources with clearly greater efficiency than state firms.[180] The quasi-capitalist local economic leaders, running Sunan collectives, mobilized factors to raise production and make profits. But available evidence suggests that their new factories' input/output ratios were probably even worse, on average, than in the state sector. Total factor productivity in rural industries rose, but slowly because they used capital and labor at a great rate. They were no longer Maoists, but they had—now in local networks—communitarian resources and a great deal of exploitative power to make the economy grow. They took the same growth mechanism Mao's planners had used, and at least through the mid-reform years they merely miniaturized it. They were entrepreneurial petty tyrants, more than engineers or productivity experts.

Their firms nonetheless filled real market demands. Rural industries' products were generally priced lower than similar-quality items from the state sector. About half of China's cement and two-fifths of the nitrogenous fertilizer—both fast-expanding sectors—came from rural industries in the early 1970s.[181] Central authorities sometimes tried to close local factories that were objectively less efficient than state plants, but local authorities were usually able to prevent such closures.[182]

Because PRC state pricing traditionally overvalued manufactures and undervalued the products of agriculture, rural planners in every Chinese province had strong incentives to process all crops their areas could grow. They had scant incentive to develop bulk transport between jurisdictions, even though canal haulage was a major growth sector of several regional economies in East Asia (including the Shanghai delta before 1949). This pattern changed slowly in the reform era, both because more factory work was done in rural areas and because more bulk products were transported. By 1982, four-fifths of the wood products supplied to Shanghai came in finished or semi-finished form.[183] More processing fees went to the countryside. Cities, including the big metropolis, again became redistribution points.

Labor Exploitation in Nonstate Factories

Country managers during reforms could exploit labor; and they could avoid high tax-and-profit extractions—or at least they could make sure such funds were kept local, to be reinvested for their own interests. Local businesses hired more executive personnel. The number of rural managers-per-laborer rose. One source suggests that in 1982, there were as many rural factory managers as workers. This would have made the ratio 1.0, but then it reportedly soared to 3.4 by 1989.[184] These figures probably overstate the ratio by omitting contract and temporary laborers. However this may be, some rural managers worked hard, while many others had sinecures. The signal success of rural industry during this period, combined with a change in the managers-per-laborer ratio, suggests inefficiency both in rural plants and in the state factories with which they competed successfully. It also suggests that tyrannical local leaders were able to exploit unregistered labor more thoroughly than rosy pictures of this proto-capitalist growth have shown.

Local potentates could put more of their friends into jobs, as these trends continued into the 1990s. The number of migrant contract laborers, of whom half or more were unregistered and uncounted in many rural plants, expanded to provide factory footsoldiers for all these new industrial generals. A crucial advantage of rural manufacturing was low wages. In 1982, for example, rural firms already admitted hiring 35 percent of China's whole industrial work force, while they admitted making only 12 percent of the country's industrial product.[185] Part of this difference may lie in high planned prices for goods from the state sector, but it is also consistent with low wages and labor productivity in rural factories. Such factories contained a great many ex-farm workers, who would not have been there if employers had to pay more. This was a situation of "growth with unlimited supplies of labor."[186]

Migration and census data reflect this crucial reform, and they are the main basis of a later part of this volume. The reported part of Shanghai's population in the suburbs expanded from 41 percent in 1965 to 49 percent in 1978—when urban district boundaries were expanded by fiat at the expense of suburban counties.[187] Low rural wages were supported by the socialist tradition of residence controls, which reduced the markets on which peasants could offer their services, and by higher birth rates among commune members than among city people. The revolutionary regime through the 1960s was so solicitous of unionized urban proletarians, its policies created a situation in which its own state factories were easily underpriced by countryside labor. Revived rural organizations in the early 1970s used this person-power in areas where old entrepreneurial traditions still existed. The Cultural Revolution in cities and towns disabled the offices that might have prevented such a revival. The revolutionary regime was a necessary, though not sufficient, cause of its own demise.

Labor in Shanghai county, a suburb southwest of the main city, switched into local industry with extraordinary speed. By 1978, fully 24 percent of all nonurban workers there were already listed as employees of factories organized at either the village/*cun* or township/*xiang* levels, not even so high as the county level. Just two years later, in 1980, this portion (to the extent it could be reported) was up to 39 percent.[188]

Suburban township factories grew far more quickly than in-city ones. So despite the commute, urban "laborers were not reluctant to work there, even if they did not move their families to the suburbs. The state had to spend a lot of money to subsidize workers' transport costs." A Shanghai reporter went one afternoon to visit a large suburban factory and found that, "At 4 P.M., there were already ten big buses along the road in front of the plant. Workers stood in line, waiting to go back into Shanghai city." The daily trip required one and a half hours each way, and this single factory had to spend 400,000 yuan a year in wage supplements for transport (public bus fares were subsidized and low, but these vehicles were very crowded).[189] Such expenses were justified by the advantage of avoiding business in the more monitored city center, and by the quality of Shanghai urban workers for many technical tasks.

Many inland Shanghai delta localities started new industrial centers from scratch, inviting outside labor to do much of the work. Bixi, Changshu, in Sunan, began in the 1980s as "a small village of twenty families." Then Bixi somehow acquired the status of a township—on speculation, because previously it had been "a very narrow street with low houses." Four bridges were built across its canal, and beside them rose commercial buildings and twenty factories. By 1986, this small township had "attracted more than 5,000 people to come do work." Most were apparently migrants from further inland. The new township had cost more than 7 million yuan, of which the rural industries used 6 million.[190] Some rich business group from Bixi had apparently made money elsewhere and decided to invest it back home, where the communal rewards were great and the state could less easily take the profits.

Rural industry transformed the occupational structure of Sunan, as local and then migrant peasants became workers. At Shazhou, Suzhou prefecture, processing factories and field machine repair shops by the mid-1970s already employed thousands of people. This was a truly rural area at the time, and few migrants had yet come. More than 95 percent of Shazhou adults still spent at least some time in field work. By 1978, the area had 314 rural enterprises, mostly factories under agricultural units, in which 10 percent of these "peasants" worked full time and a larger number part-time. Change continued quickly in the next five years. By 1982 rural factories almost trebled in number and industrial workers became 39 percent of the Shazhou rural labor force.

In Wujing county, Changzhou, counting nonfield-hands in the booming house building trade and in transport as well as factory workers, the nonagricultural portion of the labor force by 1982 stood at 38 percent. In Wujing, there was one rural house-builder or transport worker for each two in factories. Fei Xiaotong concluded that by the early 1980s, "About one-third of the labor power in Sunan had turned to industry from agriculture within five years."[191] This conclusion may be based on figures that underreport part-time employment in rural industries during the mid-1970s, but the change to factories was by any account very sharp for millions of people in Jiangnan.

By 1984, in Nantong county that is north of the Yangzi but where a dialect of Shanghainese is spoken, more than one-third of the whole proletariat for both fields and factories was either working in collective firms or away from home (many in the nearby metropolis).[192] In 1985, three-quarters of the 16,600 workers in Tangqiao, Suzhou, were involved full-time at rural industry.[193] After the mid-1980s, these factories would have had to stop expanding if they had hired fewer outsiders. The supplies of local labor had become limited, even though the supplies of inland migrants were still copious.

Collective firms made seven of every eight new hires for regular jobs in Shanghai suburban towns during the 1980s. Regular jobs allegedly were 56 percent of all hires in these places, with "informal" temporary, contract, and seasonal jobs accounting for the remaining 44 percent—but this may well be an underreport. Of these impermanent jobs, seven-tenths were reportedly temporary, and three-tenths were contract. "Seasonal" employment was a separate category, whose omission from most accounts suggests further underestimation of informal hiring. In Shanghai suburban towns from 1980 to 1986, regular employment rose 45 percent. Academic surveyors ventured a guess that, during this time, the number of informal jobs rose at least 500 percent.[194]

For each new regular place in rural industry, there were about five new nonpermanent jobs. In Sunan during the 1980s, the rate of informal hiring by local collectives was very high. State factory managers in the suburbs had even greater financial incentives to hire temporary labor, since the national wage scales for unionized employees were expensive. Private entrepreneurs were few, but they had little more to lose by living up to their public reputations and exploiting labor. So managers in all ownership sectors increasingly hired contract workers, and nonstate managers could employ temporary labor most easily.

Maoist controls long prevented workers, as well as managers, from moving freely on job markets. State employees could find job-switching difficult, because the security bureau in the firm the employee was leaving was supposed to acquiesce by releasing the secret file (*dang'an*), giving the Party's evaluation of the worker. Rural or small firms, especially by the 1990s, could often ignore the norm to accept or keep such a file. Their business was more exclusively business; so these documents, as well as household registrations and other certificates, were decreasingly required for employment.

Less than half of the mid-1980s suburban workers in small industries had permanently registered households. Four Shanghai towns, varying in size and together credibly typical of the suburbs, provided evidence showing this. About one-third of these suburban workers (31 percent) labored daily in built-up areas but lived elsewhere nearby, presumably under ex-peasant landlords. One-fifth (21 percent) had lived in the Shanghai suburbs, practically all for more than a year, without any legal household registrations.[195]

Exploitation of workers in some Shanghai rural factories was brutal. A May 1989 survey found that two-thirds of the workers sampled in one Shanghai suburb were recruited from a distance. Factory heads and labor bosses drove them mercilessly, sometimes using open coercion—just as earlier in the century compradores, labor contractors, and secret society leaders had done. Local long-time suburban residents, by contrast, often went to downtown Shanghai if they had to do menial work. Fields were tended largely by the elderly. Many rural industries in this sample produced garments. Their "collective" managers, closely connected with local officials no longer under effective state control, were often interested exclusively in making more money.[196]

Reports of even more egregious exploitation usually come from East China areas further from the metropolis. Cangnan county, Zhejiang, surveyed 284 rural factories and found sweatshops containing about 500 child laborers between ten and sixteen years of age (with an average age of 13.6 years). Girls comprised 83 percent of the total, and almost all came from nearby villages. Just one-fifth of these children had finished the second grade of primary school. About one-third were illiterate. They worked generally from eight to eleven hours, on piece rates, earning 1.2 to 3 yuan per day. A report of these abuses stressed the effects of toxic chemicals on the health and mental development of the children, especially those in unventilated plastic shops using xylene, cycloketone, and banana oil solvents. Similar scandals were said to exist in many other rural factories that had not been surveyed.[197] Labor exploitation by local managers is a major aspect of the reforms, and many sources suggest a strong correlation between the informality of hiring and the formal lowliness of the administrative level licensing the employer.

Many adult workers voted with their feet to be "exploited" in this way. They moved to rural factories, away from fields, and they came great distances for this purpose. Their industrial wages were pittances, but the amounts were generally higher than compensation for work in paddies. Migrants to a locality did not immediately demand to be treated as well as locals. As Fei Xiaotong has reported, "Some rural enterprises employ more outside workers than local workers, but rural firms give low pay to outside workers. Not only the local laborers, but also the outside workers, do not think this is wrong or unreasonable."[198]

Rural Factories' Technology, Taxes, and Credit

The policy of top state leaders toward rural industry alternated. Conservative lions favored repression of these nonstate enterprises, while reformist foxes tended to favor benign neglect. These threads of state policy can be traced from the early 1970s for a quarter century or more. The contradiction between them—the fact that official decrees about rural factories alternated in basic intent—rendered each of the two strains impotent. Central politicians' attitudes toward rural industry might warrant more attention, if they were more clearly responsible for any consistent result.

A crucial question was the extent to which managers could take risks with money. How much capital, embodying either new or old technology, could new factory managers either keep within their firms, or else garner for local administrators whom they could influence? Many means for syphoning credit to firms were available: bank loans, tax holidays certified by various administrative levels, acquiescence to traditional rotating loan schemes or local equity sales, contributions of many kinds, direct allocations of public money to new firms, infrastructural investment to make them profitable, and other methods. In the opposite direction, money flowed through bribes, taxes, and profit remittances. The big difference between high and low administrative levels was not between these means, nor was it in the total amounts on offer. It was between the different extents to which credit went for risky but potentially rewarding ventures—or, instead, only for safe business as usual. Money regenerated itself quickly when put to uses that met demands. State corporate executives set an abysmal track record in this race, as compared with rural entrepreneurs. They had scant incentives to take any risks.

Some rural firms boosted production quickly even while their reported capital rose slowly. From 1978 to 1983, as Wuxi rural enterprises increased output by 24 percent per year, their net assets rose annually by only 7 percent. Sales revenues were used mainly to buy more inputs. Many rural places began with very little industry; but they boomed despite a lack of assets—or under a local policy not to report assets. Rural industrial output value in Wutang township, Changzhou, Jiangsu, was 88 million yuan in 1976 and reached 2.5 billion yuan in 1982, a 75 percent *annual* growth over those six years.[199]

Rural industry's share of gross output value in Sunan by 1985 was at least one-third of all industrial output value there. The portion in Wuxi was 34 percent; in Suzhou, also 34 percent; Changzhou, 22 percent; and Nantong, 30 percent—and these figures do not include village-run factories, which by then were expanding fastest in less urbanized flat parts of the delta. Industry by 1985 accounted for about 90 percent of all income in Sunan.

Most of the local hinge leaders who had taken risks and cut red tape to achieve this result were ostensibly part of the state, to which there is every indication they felt loyal. Their decisions for collectives nonetheless undermined the state sector. Local leaders in Suqian county, Jiangsu, helped peasants leave rice paddies by offering credit, materials, training, and licenses for work as tailors, carpenters, blacksmiths, nursery-school operators, small factory managers, and shopkeepers. Specialized ex-peasants were given permission to move from rural places into towns.[200]

Provincial leaders were forced to recognize this situation. They naturally wanted to take credit for the increased production and flourishing markets. In Shanghai, high taxes and state industries meant that high-level acquiescence to local industries was delayed about half a decade behind Jiangsu and Zhejiang. This delay was less serious for small plants licensed by villages than for larger firms—but it caused resentments among Shanghai rural entrepreneurs who saw their peers across the provincial border facing an easier regime. Taxes on Jiangsu collectives were reduced in 1979, apparently to stimulate their development and to improve reporting. The provincial government in Nanjing later announced that some new rural collective enterprises would be exempt from taxes for three years. Those contracted in 1981 would be tax-free for two years; and those that had already opened, for at least one year.[201] These allowances gave county and town governments leeway to extend yet more exemptions. The economic boom just across Shanghai's border was meteoric. Total gross 1985 production in Kunshan county, next to Shanghai, rose 51 percent in that single year.[202]

High reformers publicized some of the most successful plants on the delta, despite high conservatives' worry about their competition with state factories. The Haiyan Shirt Factory was endorsed as a model by the Zhejiang CCP Committee in March 1983, and plans were made to stop "controlling" such collectively owned enterprises in favor of "assisting" them. As a result, these firms produced 23 percent more gross output in the first ten months of 1984 than in the same period of the previous year, and 22 percent more profit.[203]

Collective firms by the mid-1980s practically eliminated state firms in some, but not all, of Shanghai's suburbs. In the Chongming county seat, fully 99 percent of all new hires in the mid-1980s went into collectives. But at Jinshanwei, an otherwise comparable town, collectives then offered only 15 percent of the new jobs, and the state sector still made up 85 percent. So local variation was great, and it depended in part on different decisions by local leaders.[204] On the whole, though, the collective rural industry was clearly the most dynamic part of China's economy by the mid-1980s. This was not good news for state firms, nor for the central budget.

Entrepreneurs reportedly often had to pay for medium-level political support. Their rising resources could finance this. Jiangsu in 1985 produced more than one-fifth of all gross output in China's rural industries. Zhejiang accounted for almost another tenth. Shanghai produced only 4 percent (and its two sister municipalities, Beijing and Tianjin, made just 2 percent each).[205] This meant, however, that Jiangsu, Zhejiang, and Shanghai rural industries together comprised one-third of the country's. In terms of tax receipts from these factories, the three contiguous East China provinces contributed 44 percent of the nation's total. This fiscal portion was more than their 33 percent of the national output. The difference between these rural industries' output and extraction, however, was less than for the same provinces' state sector.

Shanghai's role in the boom was not just slower and more hidden, but also more technical. The reasons will be covered more extensively in later chapters on urban management and "horizontal relations" between provinces. Places near the municipality's borders, whence many of its residents' families had come, benefited enormously from a combination of Shanghai technology and lower taxes. Fei Xiaotong wrote that,[206]

> . . . most rural industry in the four prefectures [of Jiangsu nearest Shanghai] developed economic and technical cooperation with Shanghai. . . . the economic development of Shanghai had a great impact on the rural industries and the whole surrounding area, playing the part of an economic center. Among the more than 2,000 rural factories in Wuxi, 709 were linked with major plants in large and medium-sized cities such as Shanghai . . . [This was] a new pattern of industrialization in China, where "big fish help small fish and small fish help shrimps."

By the mid-1980s, however, the big fish were becoming less official, the shrimps were nominally cooperatives but their managers were acting at least somewhat more like private entrepreneurs, and the stately shark got less food.

Within Shanghai, the main aim of centrally appointed municipal politicians had for decades been to raise money for the PRC state budget. Rural enterprises in Shanghai's suburban counties were caught in a bind, because they faced competition from similar firms elsewhere in the delta, while they also faced province-level administrators whose posts depended quite extensively on fiscal remittances to Beijing. Small Shanghai firms reportedly "worried" that high taxes were reducing their profits, especially in comparison with nearby Jiangsu firms. Detailed examples of the troubles of specific small businesses in Shanghai's Chuansha, Jiading, and Songjiang counties were adduced to show that costs other than labor and materials—especially for "administration" and taxes—were higher than in neighboring Suzhou and Wuxi. A newspaper article suggested that Shanghai's policies might be reformed to allow suburban industries quicker development through lower taxes now, so as to provide a larger tax base in the future. Such policies, the newspaper argued, had been followed successfully in Guangdong, Zhejiang, and Jiangsu.[207]

"Fake statistics" were inevitable in this situation. Localities of many sizes underreported their production, labor force, factor use, assets, profits, and other data. Quantitative lying was an embarrassment to the government, and not just for symbolic reasons. "Fake figures" were a problem that a State Statistical Bureau leader only much later could admit. "Under-reporting of profits and tax revenues" was publicly confessed, by the 1990s, as a major kind of "negative, corrupt behavior." As a Statistical Bureau cadre said, "Local officials know that others will judge the achievements of their political careers based on statistics." These reporting problems were "worst from coastal areas and township enterprises."[208]

This was all illegal, of course. It was a situation in which "nothing is allowed, but everything is possible"—and by 1996 it led to temporary government decrees against the publication of many kinds of economic data.[209] The accounts of the state were increasingly divorced from local realities. This problem had been important for decades, and it was finally reported by officials not because of epiphanies of honesty, but because wrong data had been used to support claims on the central state that it could not finance. The mid-1980s state, for example, was so strapped for money that officials had to announce that rural township governments were no longer part of the socialist family entitled to central support—even though they legally remained organs of the state.

The construction of Shanghai delta townships had been supported increasingly by rural industries. "The state did not provide much money." Shanghai suburbs at that time contained thirty-three county-level townships, but the municipal government disinherited these administrations. It could no longer control them, and it could no longer afford them. The municipal government's total investment in the suburbs during the Seventh Five-Year Plan was only 4 percent of its construction budget (less than 100 million yuan). Yet the infrastructure of these places could well have used attention. The road network, in particular, "had not formed yet."[210] The suburbs' portion of Shanghai people by the mid-1980s was ten times their portion of the state construction budget.

Local township and village governments by the mid-1980s provided almost half the credit for rural industries. In Wuxi county, they financed 44 percent; and the remainder was split almost equally between bank loans, notes, and a category that included depreciation funds, unpaid wages, private investment, and credits from other government agencies.[211] Bank loans were not crucial, and this is important because licensed banks were subject to some state control. In 1985, formal banks financed only 16 percent of a sample of Wuxi rural industries. Even if the sporadic central directives to restrict bank loans had been perfectly enforced, such crackdowns scarcely affected the credit lines of these rural firms.

Official decrees limiting loans to nonstate factories were recurrent during reforms, sometimes in public and sometimes in secret. But even the most severe of them, in the reaction of mid-1989, was abandoned by early 1990. The reasons for the ineffectualness of these decrees were many, but the most important was probably the hiding of money (and of whole companies) by rural entrepreneurs and local cadres. When they were allowed to apply for credit officially, e.g. at interest rates lower than their own informal finance sector offered, middle and high administrators could identify more of them. So in the first ten months of 1990, the Agricultural Bank of China announced it had loaned 110 billion yuan to rural industries, a "much larger" amount than in the whole of 1989.[212] Rural factories did a major inadvertent service for the government by giving jobs to laborers freed from the land. The growing resources of this sector helped the state immediately, while weakening it structurally.

Modern Rural Markets for Manufactured Goods

In the PRC's two revolutionary decades, the state not only became the main producer; state-coordinated organizations also formed the main market. During reforms, however, rural enterprises could not depend on sales to state agencies. Already by 1970, firms in Zhangjiagang, Jiangsu, sent only 15 percent of their output through state commerce departments, 35 percent through other contracts, and 51 percent to free markets. By 1978, the state purchased only 8 percent of these Zhangjiagang firms' production; and by 1988, only 3 percent. In that last year, 11 percent of the rural production in this South Jiangsu place was exported abroad, while 86 percent was sold under contracts to cooperatives or on domestic free markets.[213] The state no longer had any clout as a buyer. Markets were still made by power institutions, but no longer by the central one.[214]

Markets around Shanghai—offering local manufactures for sale nationally—were very active by 1971. In October of that year, industry in suburban Qingpu county was just beginning to grow quickly, but "twelve products from seven factories" were on sale to buyers who visited the county's Exhibition Hall for a trade fair. In the previous year, the county's CCP had been "restored at all levels," and the Fourth Qingpu County Party Congress was held in May 1971. Legal and police organs took longer to revive. By January 1974, the Qingpu County Court was restored; and in that same month centralized "military control was canceled" at the local public security bureau. Marketing requires police protection. By the spring of 1976, Qingpu's "agricultural" (now partly industrial) brigades all did their own accounting.215 Restored local governments, after the Cultural Revolution of the late 1960s, quickly became the protectors of nonstate industries.

Consumption, as well as production, became more rural during reforms. This reversed the trend of the 1950s and 1960s, which had been toward relatively more consumption in cities. From 1952 to 1978, a long period for which data are available, urban consumption rose at a rate well above 5 percent annually, while the rural figure crept up just 2 percent per year. During the half decade after 1978 by contrast, consumption rose 3 percent annually in cities, but 9 percent per year in the countryside.[216]

Housing booms in all economies augur more consumption. Fully 99 percent of residential buildings were one-storey in the best-surveyed Shanghai suburban village in 1975—but by 1987, this single-storey portion had plummeted to 31 percent. The remaining seven-tenths of residences then had staircases and at least two levels.[217] When families have more rooms in their houses, they buy things to put there. Residential construction in the PRC (as in Taiwan during its extremely fast economic growth) was a major spur to the whole economy, especially in the countryside where peasants often interpreted long-term lease contracts for paddy land as a convenient way to find building space.

Rural officials generally encouraged the new trade, and they taxed it as the central government had done. Commerce in China's countryside during reforms was often heavily restricted by county bureaucrats. Reforms increased rather than reduced local imposts on rural commerce. Counties have militia and trade bureaus. Both were reportedly used to keep out products with which county factories did not want to compete. Inspection cars ("*guan ka*") regularly patrolled rural roads, demanding local tolls from trucks.[218] Commercial drivers in such areas seldom resisted county tolls; they paid, received receipts, and were later reimbursed by their units. Their own property was seldom at risk; so there was scant reason to protest these levies or to point out their formal illegality. Imposts by local and by central coercive powers were nonetheless different, even though both kinds of regime were greedy: Traders could sometimes avoid the local governments that were most covetous, in favor of those that maximized revenues by charging lower rates.

Many rural industries still dealt with their previous upstream suppliers and downstream markets.[219] Many farmers still coordinated their field production in habitual ways.[220] But over time, more autonomous agents in rural China had options to switch to other methods and traders. Inertia and transaction costs disinclined people to bargain with new partners. Market contracts often echoed previous socialist plans. The option to change market partners nonetheless affected economic relationships, even when it was not taken. The move toward more liberal markets was slower, even in the richest parts of rural China, than most publicists and economists supposed; but over time, it was a trend.

"Models," and Wenzhou as an Excuse

Proto-capitalist modes were thought by government and dissident intellectuals to require a patina of theory. So several new economic "models" (*moshi*) emerged during reforms in East China. Most striking was the "Wenzhou model," identified with that large but isolated city on the Zhejiang coast. Wenzhou, despite its urban population of over half a million, was safely sequestered for economic experiments. No railway reached there, and during early reforms there was no regular air service. Partly because of extensive illicit contacts between Wenzhou boats and those from Taiwan, and especially because of the city's isolation, this was an apt place for daring tests of PRC capitalism. The late 1980s saw a spate of books by reformist intellectuals about Wenzhou.[221] About 80 percent of all Wenzhou capital was by the late 1980s private, rather than state or collective. Private Wenzhou banks loaned credit quite easily. Over 100,000 salespeople, scattered throughout China, launched strenuous marketing efforts on behalf of Wenzhou traders. Here was a highly distinctive and exploitative kind of urban PRC economy, but other kinds emerged too.

Models proliferated. Closer to Shanghai, the "Sunan model" of South Jiangsu was mainly distinguished by collective enterprises.[222] Aside from the Sunan, Wenzhou, and Gengche models in East China, the south had its "Zhujiang [Pearl River] model" around Guangzhou. Intellectuals in the north mooted a "Langfang model," a "Tianshui model" in the west, and a "Fuyang model" in the central part of the country. These were all named after the counties or prefectures in which various experiments took place.[223] Details of differences between them may be less important than intellectuals' charming premise that ex-peasants would willingly adopt whatever pattern wiser men decided was best for them. The rural actors were not making models, however; they were making money.

Some Chinese economists claimed by the early 1990s that northern Zhejiang and southern Jiangsu showed somewhat different models. In Sunan, industrial returns from collective enterprises were by then not accelerating at the previous brisk pace, reportedly because local governments gave wrong incentives to management, labor, and capital just as the previous system of state corporations had done. In northern Zhejiang, on the other hand, local governments more often limited themselves to protecting, rather than managing, collective enterprises. The result was more efficiency, according to this analysis. The post-socialist Wenzhou model legitimated higher levels of freedom in small collectivities throughout Zhejiang.

Its influence spread further north, too, into southern Jiangsu and Shanghai. Differences between the collectivist Sunan model and the privatist Wenzhou model have been somewhat overblown in both Chinese and Western sources. The main distinction relates to ownership form, but bosses of collectives were often at least as tyrannical as private owners. Autonomous practical managers, irrespective of ownership types, were more interested in low state imposts than were the government cadres they replaced. In Sunan, the new firms were mostly collectives, rather than state-owned. They were supposed to be linked to the state system more closely than private firms; and because central bureaucrats could neither run the government without money from the Shanghai delta nor prevent the rise of new industries there, they gradually found themselves agreeing to Sunan reforms.[224] In Wenzhou, which was smaller, poorer, and geographically isolated, more firms could become private. Wenzhou had a less promising tax base, and high politicians had larger fish to fry. As a Chinese economist put it, referring to the lower taxes in this secluded city, "The financial advantages of the Wenzhou model go a long way towards explaining the extremely lively state of manufacturing and commercial activity in many villages in the municipality."[225] But the same kind of difference was widespread; collectives on the Shanghai delta also paid a much lower portion of their earnings in central imposts than the old state industries there did. The Sunan and Wenzhou models have a practical similarity: more money remains local.

Chinese writers stressed distinctions between these models because Wenzhou presented such an obvious ideological problem. Reformers needed to defend the emerging pattern there against the accurate claim that it is not socialist. Market economists could previously argue that in a marginal area like Wenzhou a test of new economic forms served a national purpose without endangering the national budget. But this merely decorated the broader fact that local leaders in many coastal areas were now more solicitous of their own budgets. The Sunan version of the model is adapted to a relatively high-tax environment, whereas the Wenzhou version is adapted to an area from which Beijing never expected to extract much. The basic thrust of both the Wenzhou and Sunan models was more managerial and financial autonomy.

Wenzhou is just south of the Shanghai delta, and in Zhejiang whose main northern cities are part of it. Many links between these areas have also been substantive. When Jiangnan traders could not do their business on their own turf, within effective laws or at sufficiently low rates of official extraction, they sometimes made the trip to do it in Wenzhou. Some entrepreneurs in the Shanghai delta openly envied Wenzhou's loose regulations. By the spring of 1991, Zhejiang Governor Ge Hongsheng proudly asserted that his whole province (he did not distinguish Wenzhou from the northern part) could be different from others. As a reporter wrote, "So now, while the whole country is going all out to increase the efficiency of large state-owned enterprises, Zhejiang is studying how to increase the production and management level of its small and rural enterprises."[226]

The main issue was whether lower imposts could be extended to large collectives. In rural Wenzhou during 1985, among the "big labor-hiring households," with about fifty workers each, just one in twenty lost money. One-tenth of these private firms reported between 100,000 and 150,000 yuan of profits that year, and nearly half made between 30,000 and 100,000 yuan. The average private entrepreneur's income, reported in this survey, was about 50,000 yuan on an average output value of about 500,000 yuan—a profit rate of 10 percent. Party members were prominent in running these private firms, but non-Party people also participated. About two-thirds of the large firms had capital pooled among several households, although the remaining third were one-family shops.[227]

Wenzhou's penetration of far-flung markets was based on cheap labor and materials prices; but as a Chinese economist confessed,[228]

> The tax burden is light. This is mainly because the small, scattered, and independent nature of household industry makes it difficult for tax collection agencies to devise suitable methods of taxation. The majority of families engaged in household industries have not registered for tax purposes; and of those who have registered, many do not keep accounts; and even those that do, fail to keep them accurately. . . . According to statistics collected by the departments concerned, tax revenue of 1.26 million *yuan* should have been levied on household industry weaving plastics, located in Rui'an County's Shencheng District, on the basis of the value of production and marketing in 1984; but in fact, the value of taxation was only 0.6 million *yuan* [*48 percent of the legal taxes due*]. In Xianjiang Township, household industry producing shoes made of plastic and artificial leather should have paid taxes of 3.5 million *yuan* over a period of six years according to the value of its production, but only 0.26 billion [*just 7 percent of taxes due*] was received.

The ideological function of the Wenzhou model, especially its early sponsorship by Shanghai reformers and journalists, is a topic that appears in the next volume in the chapter on ideology. From a national perspective, the main role of the Wenzhou example was to make operations on the larger and wealthier Shanghai delta look almost anti-reformist. By comparison, Shanghai and Sunan seemed staid, loyal, and conservative. This record of normative obeisance arguably justified some practical reduction of the state burden on this most taxed part of China.

Suburban and Sunan Growth in Later Reforms

Rural industries were supposed to "go to the locality for three things" (*san jiu di*). Procurement, processing, and sales were all supposed to occur only in a collective's immediate vicinity. For processing, this norm was enforceable, because it met local interests. But once rural factories were established, they in practice obtained factors and sold products wherever they could profitably do so. The state's monopoly on trade was ended.[229]

This discomfited planners, who moved against the trend when the economic strain against state plants was high and when the political climate was conservative. For example, township enterprise production in all of South Jiangsu grew about 25 percent in the single year 1988. Credit to rural industries for 1989 was slated to drop to half the 1988 amount (from 14.7 billion yuan to 7.1 billion). The People's Bank raised interest on savings deposits from February 1, 1989, in an attempt to divert money from rural loans that the state could not control.[230] After the Tiananmen crackdown, reports indicated the growth rate in Sunan was reduced to 5 percent (although township enterprises still created about two-thirds of all industrial output there). Hardliners by August vowed to close 10 percent of

China's registered rural factories. But most workers in rural industries could not go back to till fields. As a spokesman for the Ministry of Agriculture's Rural Enterprise Bureau said, "The amount of land is limited; there is no land to which they can return."[231] The modesty of 10 percent, as a target for closures, suggests no confidence among conservatives that they could succeed easily in efforts to close rural industries. The number of ex-registered but operational firms probably rose in 1989. So the official credit crunch against rural industries in 1989 was one cause of decelerated rural growth then, although underreporting made the published figures dubious. The Ministry of Agriculture and its allies in Beijing reportedly opposed the hardline policy, which was reversed as ineffective, and as inflation dropped somewhat, during the next year.[232]

Centralists lost their rural agents to industrialization. "Basic level cadres" had already decreased in number by one-half in the 1978–84 period—and this was just the start of a hollowing out of government and Party offices throughout rural China. Although town and township officials during this early period rose by 9 percent, village/brigade cadres were down by 13 percent, and village/production team or small group cadres plummeted in number by 69 percent.[233] By the mid-1980s, there was "no assured source of funds" to pay rural cadres, and "some village cadres have not received pay for many years." At least one-tenth of the villages had "nobody to take responsibility for the work."[234] The portion of inactive local governments rose further in later years. A 1992 State Council report suggested that three-tenths of the Party's own previous rural organizations were defunct, and another six-tenths were "weak" and "disorganized," leaving just one-tenth strong. A 1994 survey suggested that three-quarters of the Party's organizations were in "a state of collapse." Three-tenths of village government offices by this time also had no resources with which to function.[235] Almost four-fifths of village leaders surveyed in a Jiangsu study indicated that a reason for their support of rural industry was to become more independent of higher state authorities.[236]

One reason for some high-level state support for rural industries, even during the post-Tiananmen conservative resurgence, was that they brought money to the villages. The central politicians were not of one mind; so bureaucrats favoring rural industries could fight hardliners who wanted to close them. The prowess of rural factories in earning foreign exchange gave them local power and national attention. A Zhejiang shoe manufacturer, the Seagull Foreign Trade Industry United Corporation, had been in late 1988 "by far the biggest foreign exchange earner" among rural Chinese enterprises. Its general manager waxed lyrical about the company, calling it "a little blade of grass that has grown out from between the stones" of overbearing administrators and rules. This factory made shoes from parts produced in household workshops. It sold shares and paid dividends, and it created seven-tenths of its township's total production.[237]

A national export fair was hosted by the Township Enterprise Administration of the Ministry of Agriculture in September 1989. During the first half of that year, township firms had exported 41 percent more than in the same period of the previous year; and their foreign earnings were already U.S. $3.8 billion. They employed at least 24 percent of the rural labor force nationwide (on the very brave assumption that the published statistics are complete). Their gross industrial output value was reported at 21 percent of the country's total in the first half of 1989.[238]

The technological sophistication of rural industries was also on a sharp upswing. In southern Jiangsu, a computer factory run by "peasants" was advanced enough to make components for missile-launching systems.[239] Software writing is a decentralized and experimental activity in many countries; and Jiangnan had its "little green men" by the 1980s. The functional equivalents of their "garages" were often suburban. Technical flexibility and high standards justified mid- or high-level support for some firms that otherwise might have been closed because they competed with state companies.

The reported annual growth rate of Jiangsu rural companies in the last months of 1989 was only 2.4 percent; but by August 1990, it jumped back up to 8 percent.[240] This bumpy progress could be continued, because rural industries were increasingly able to procure support from higher levels of the state administration that their advocates were able to penetrate. The Ministry of Agriculture strayed into industry, and into industrial finance, because ex-peasants did. In 1990, it recognized the existence of rural stock markets—and the need to begin regulating them—with a set of "Temporary Provisions on Farmers' Cooperative Enterprises Held in Shares." These rules insisted that rural firms selling equities to the public must be called "collectives." The peasant shareholders could resell their interests at will, however; so from a financial viewpoint, this situation was hard to distinguish from that of a private corporation garnering capital on a market. The law imposed "administrative fees" and requirements that firms should pay normal taxes as well as retirement and welfare benefits. The main restrictive provision was that not more than 20 percent of net profits could be distributed as dividends, and 60 percent had to be reinvested. But local managers could find ways to redescribe their budgets and lessen such strictures if necessary.[241] The regulation of capital markets for rural industries may have stabilized them somewhat. To the extent that it required registration of new ventures, it also created opportunities for bureaucrats to use new legal requirements corruptly. In any case, ministerial agents began regulating these markets many years after they had begun.

As Fei Xiaotong said, "Sunan's today will be other places' tomorrow."[242] This was already to some extent happening nationally by the 1990s. An estimated 1,600,000 farmers in 1991 alone were "newly released from the land this year, as a result of continued growth in the country's rural enterprises." Jobs for them could reasonably be expected, as rural industries continued in some years of the early 1990s to grow at rates that may well have been one-fifth or more annually, if all the reporting were accurate. Rural manufacturing was by that time not only the fastest-growing sector, it was already large in absolute terms. By the end of 1990, rural industries accounted for 25 percent of China's total GNP and 60 percent of its rural production. Ninety million people were registered as employed in rural industries, and the real number may have been much higher.[243] Two years later, at the start of 1993, the number of rural employees was reported over 105 million.[244] The 1990 figure implies that rural industries employed 87 percent as many people as state industries; and the 1993 figure implies these two sectors were about equal in employment.[245]

Conclusion: Rural Industry as the Impetus of Political Reform

What can explain the very high sustained growth rates in reform China? Incentives from market reforms alone—which are still somewhat limited and often joined traders that already had earlier particularistic bonds—may not explain the spectacular long-term growth rates in industry that approach 20 percent annually. They may not explain the respectable simultaneous growth of agriculture that often exceeds 5 percent, or for the whole economy over 10 percent. Local entrepreneurialism may be a basic cause both of the booming markets and of the production growth.[246] This factor is local and political, more than it is economic.

Rural industries were the most presentable outcome of this entrepreneurialism, and their resources created new local power. They sprang from a green revolution, and they have quietly changed China's political structure. These firms were often inefficient. Their internal decision structures were certainly undemocratic. They were exploitative and uncivil in every sense. But many of them flourished, and they outstripped the state sector because they were relatively free of central control and taxation. Local Party leaders' loss of face in the famine and then the Cultural Revolution might be redeemed through growth in local communities. This required a weakening of the state as run by leaders in Beijing; so the reform syndrome was generally foisted on China's most famous leaders by myriad ex-farmer leaders whose names are not publicly known. When the powerful lack enough resources to stay where they are, as Pareto suggested, the elite changes. This is now happening in China, as the centralist revolutionaries have already done all they can for most people.

Notes

1. *Alexis de Tocqueville on Democracy, Revolution, and Society*, John Stone and Stephen Mennell, eds. (Chicago: University of Chicago Press, 1980), p. 261.

2. See Charles Lindblom, *Democracy and Market System* (Oslo: Norwegian University Press, 1988); and Mark Granovetter, "Economic Action and Social Structure: The Problem of Embeddedness," *American Journal of Sociology* 91 (November 1985), pp. 481–510.

3. Mancur Olson, Jr., "Rapid Growth as a Destabilizing Force," *Journal of Economic History* 23:4 (December 1963): pp. 529–52.

4. The only province with a lower rate of "national income" growth was arid Qinghai. See *Quanguo ge sheng zizhi qu zhixia shi lishi tongji ziliao huibian, 1949–1989* (Historical Statistics Collection on Provinces, Autonomous Regions, and Municipalities Throughout the Country, 1949–1989) (Beijing: Zhongguo Tongji Chuban She, 1990), p. 47.

5. Ibid., p. 51.

6. Daniel Kelliher, *Peasant Power: The Era of Rural Reform, 1979–1989* (New Haven: Yale University Press, 1993), p. 51.

7. Frances Fox Piven and Richard A. Cloward, *Poor People's Movements* (New York: Vintage, 1979), p. 11.

8. Quoted in James C. Scott, *Domination and the Arts of Resistance: Hidden Transcripts* (New Haven: Yale University Press, 1990), p. 190.

9. Robert H. Bates, *Markets and States in Tropical Africa: The Political Basis of Agricultural Policies* (Berkeley: University of California Press, 1981), p. 50.

10. *Chūgoku no toshika to nōson kensetsu* (Chinese Urbanization and Rural Construction), Kojima Reeitsu, ed. (Tokyo: Ryūkei Shosha, 1978), pp. 293–94 and p. 299.

11. See Yang Dali, "Making Reform: Leadership, Societal Initiative, and Institutional Change in China" (Princeton University, Politics Department, Ph.D. Dissertation, 1992), now revised as *Calamity and Reform in China* (Stanford: Stanford University Press, 1996).

12. For the estimates, see J. Dreze and A. Sen, *Hunger and Public Action* (Oxford: Clarendon Press, 1989), Table 11.2.

13. Yang Dali, *Calamity and Reform*, chap. 3.

14. The most specific evidence comes from Anhui. Yang Dali, "Making Reform," p. 185, cites Ou Yuanfang, *Anhui baogan daohu yanjiu* (A Study of Anhui Household Contracting) (Hefei: Anhui Renmin Chuban She, 1982).

15. The widespread introduction of hand tractors was important not just in rice-growing areas, but also on the North China plain that during most of the year grows wheat, alternating with peanuts, rice, and other crops. *WHB*, December 19, 1977.

16. The source, like too many others published in China, faithfully avoids offering statistics for any years between 1966 and 1976, precisely as if that period did not exist. The 19 percent annual increase is calculated from *Shanghai shi nongye jixie hua fazhan zhanlue yanjiu* (Studies on Strategy for Developing Agricultural Mechanization in Shanghai Municipality), Xie Zifen, ed. (Shanghai: Shanghai Kexue Puji Chuban She, 1991), p. 104.

17. Marion J. Levy, Jr., has suggested that a good summary index of modernization is the ratio of animal to machine power. Scholars who do not subscribe to modernization theory might still be interested in such a dramatic increase of mechanical power as occurred in Shanghai suburbs after 1965.

18. Also, markets in agricultural products boomed during this time. The marketed tonnage of pork from Shanghai's suburbs, for example, rose 84 percent between 1965 and 1973. See a book by the most distinguished non-Chinese team working on such issues: *Chūgoku no toshika*, pp. 293–94 and p. 299.

19. No such basic set of technological changes had occurred on the Yangzi delta since the Song, when new "Champa" *indica* rice varieties had arrived there. About the same time, new higher-yield annual cotton seeds had also been found. The sharp increase of rice and cotton in the Song created radically improved sources of food and clothing. See references to work by Kang Chao, *The Development of Cotton Textile Production in China*, and Francis Bray, *The Rice Economies*, in Stephen L. Morgan, "City-Town Enterprises in the Lower Changjiang (Yangtze) River Basin" (M.A. Dissertation in Asian Studies, University of Hong Kong, 1987), pp. 22–23. More broadly, see Philip C. C. Huang, *The Peasant Family and Rural Development in the Yangzi Delta, 1350–1988* (Stanford: Stanford University Press, 1990).

20. See Xiao Zhenmei, *Xian jieduan zhi dalu nongjing biange* (The Transformation of the Mainland's Rural Economy at the Present Stage) (Taibei: Juliu Tushu Gongsi, 1988), p. 126.

21. Bo Fengcheng, *Zhonggong nongye xiandai hua zhengce zhi fenxi* (An Analysis of CCP Rural Modernization Policy) (Taipei: National Chengchi University M.A. Thesis, 1978; written under the direction of Agricultural Economics Prof. Lee Teng-hui, later President of the ROC), p. 30.

22. Calculated from absolute numbers of these machines, which are in *Dangdai Zhongguo de nongye jixie hua* (Agricultural Mechanization in Contemporary China), Wu Shaowen, ed. (Beijing: Zhongguo Shehui Kexue Yuan, 1991), p. 53.

23. *WHB*, June 10, 1976.

24. The spring harvest at this time was called the "three-snatch" (*sanqiang*); radicals emphasized the traditional fact that all able hands—now including some urban people—should work in the fields to bring in the ripe grain and transplant the seedlings quickly. For more on the politics of the traditional rice cycle, see Lynn White, "Agricultural and Industrial Values in China," in R. Wilson, S. Greenblatt, and A. Wilson, eds., *Value Change in Chinese Society* (New York: Praeger, 1979), pp. 141–54. WHB, December 19, 1977.

25. Zhang Chunqiao in *Hongqi* (Red Flag), No. 4 (April), 1975, 3–12, cited in Jurgen Domes, *Socialism in the Chinese Countryside* (London: C. Hurst, 1980), p. 84.

26. See Lynn White, "Agricultural and Industrial".

27. See Nicholas R. Lardy, *Agriculture in China's Modern Economic Development* (Cambridge: Cambridge University Press, 1983), and Peter Nolan and Suzanne Paine, "Towards an Appraisal of the Impact of Rural Reform in China, 1978–1985," in Ashwani Saith, ed., *The Re-emergence of the Chinese Peasantry: Aspects of Rural Decollectivization* (London: Croom Helm, 1987), pp. 82–83.

28. The late-reform political uses, for the Chinese government, of a 1976 ending date for the Cultural Revolution are discussed in Anita Chan, "Dispelling Misconceptions about the Red Guard Movement: The Necessity to Re-Examine Cultural Revolution Factionalism and Periodization," *Journal of Contemporary China* 1:1 (1992), pp. 61–85. Another essay highly compatible with the argument here is Sebastian Heilmann, *Turning Away from the Cultural Revolution: Political Grass-Roots Activism in the Mid-Seventies* (Stockholm: Center for Pacific Asia Studies Occasional Paper 28, September 1996).

29. The increase of non-human sources of power is taken as a leading index of modernization by Marion J. Levy, Jr., *Modernization and the Structure of Societies* (Princeton: Princeton University Press, 1966). See also *Zhongguo renkou qianyi* (Population Shifts in China), Tian Fang and Ling Fatong, eds. (Beijing: Zhishi Chuban She, 1987), pp. 23–32.

30. *Zhongguo renkou*, pp. 248–59.

31. Yao Shihuang, *Jin sanjiao de tansuo* (Search for the Golden Delta) (Chongqing: Chongqing Chuban She, 1988), pp. 10–12.

32. *RMRB*, September 17, 1975, quoted in Frank Leeming, *Rural China Today* (London: Longman, 1985), p. 106.

33. Frank Leeming, *Rural China*, pp. 104–6.

34. Fei Xiaotong and Luo Yanxian, *Xiangzhen jingji bijiao moshi* (Comparative Models of the Village and Town Economy) (Chongqing: Chongqing Chuban She, 1988), pp. 40–45.

35. Philip C. C. Huang, "The Paradigmatic Crisis in Chinese Studies: Paradoxes in Social and Economic History," *Modern China* 17:3 (July 1991), p. 311.

36. Historian Li Bozhong wrote about cropping patterns and fertilizer, and historian

Wu Chengming claimed to have found "sprouts of capitalism" near Shanghai by the Ming at least. One of Li's titles suggests the story, '"Mulberries Take Over Rice Fields': The Intensification of Agricultural Production in Jiangnan during the Ming and Qing." This is cited in Philip C. C. Huang, "The Paradigmatic Crisis," p. 301.

37. This calculation did not even try to estimate the price effects of the marketed third-crop grain. Materials compiled by the Shanghai Revolutionary Committee, reported in Frank Leeming, *Rural China*, pp. 110–12.

38. Materials compiled by the Shanghai Revolutionary Committee, reported in Frank Leeming, *Rural China*, pp. 110–13.

39. See Lynn White, "Agricultural and Industrial," pp. 141–54, for some discussion of the social effects of crop cycles.

40. Frank Leeming, *Rural China*, pp. 112–13.

41. From Domes, *Socialism*, pp. 91–92.

42. Chris Bramall, "Origins of the Agricultural 'Miracle': Some Evidence from Sichuan," *China Quarterly* 143 (September 1995), pp. 732 and 753.

43. Yang Dali, "Making Reform," p. 185, cites *RMRB*, June 24, 1978. There are many similar reports from other provinces, ranging from Guangdong to Gansu.

44. Calculated from output figures, in 1970 prices, from *Shanghai shi nongye,* p. 102.

45. *Gaige mianlin zhidu chuangxin* (The Reforms are Faced with System Innovation), Development Research Institute, ed. (Shanghai: Sanlian Shudian, 1988), p. 285.

46. *FBIS*, December 1, 1987, p. 17, quoting *RMRB* of November 24.

47. For more on the old distinction between "vertical" or "string" (*tiaotiao*) and "horizontal" or "piece" (*kuaikuai*) leaderships, see the classic by Franz Schurmann, *Ideology and Organization in Communist China* (Berkeley: University of California Press, 1966).

48. The portion of grain in all agricultural output was 80 percent in the 1950s, 75 to 80 percent in the 1960s, but just slightly more than 60 percent in the 1980s, according to *Zhongguo renkou*, pp. 23–32.

49. *ZGTJNJ92*, p. 329.

50. The term "Sunan" is used in these volumes to denote the counties that by the mid-1980s were put under the jurisdictions of Changzhou, Wuxi, Suzhou, and Nantong cities, i.e. southern Jiangsu. The term "Jiangnan" also includes the other parts of the Shanghai Economic Zone in its small version, proposed in April 1983, i.e. counties under the Zhejiang cities of Jiaxing, Huzhou, Hangzhou, Shaoxing, Ningbo, and Zhoushan prefecture (an archipelago), as well as Shanghai municipality.

51. Daniel Kelliher, *Peasant Power*, p. 120.

52. *JFRB*, September 6, 1980.

53. See, for example, David Zweig, *Agrarian Radicalism in China, 1968–81* (Cambridge: Harvard University Press, 1989).

54. The irony that the policy was supposed to be "applied in accord with local conditions (*yin di zhi yi*) is mentioned in Jonathan Unger, "The Decollectivization of the Chinese Countryside: A Survey of Twenty-eight Villages," *Pacific Affairs* 58:4 (Winter 1985–86), pp. 585–606.

55. The most comprehensive treatment is Kate Xiao Zhou, *How the Farmers Changed China* (Boulder: Westview, 1996).

56. *RMRB*, June 13, 1987. Emphasis added.

57. Solomon M. Karmel, "The Neo-Authoritarian Contradiction: Trials of Developmentalist Dictatorships and the Retreat of the State in Mainland China" (Princeton University, Politics Department, Ph.D. Dissertation, 1995), p. 25, quoting a speech of Gu Zhong, published by the Beijing Economics Association.

58. *FBIS*, December 1, 1987, pp. 17–18, quoting *RMRB* of November 24.

59. "Contracting to households" is *baochan dao hu*. Work by Kate Xiao Zhou, then a Ph.D. student in Politics at Princeton, referred to the text of this resolution in Yang Jianwen et al., *Dangdai Zhongguo jingji sixiang* (Economic Thought in Contemporary China), (Shanghai: Sanlian Shudian, 1991), pp. 395–412.

60. Daniel Kelliher, *Peasant Power*, p. 63.

61. Edward Friedman, Paul G. Pickowicz, and Mark Selden, *Chinese Village, Socialist State* (New Haven: Yale University Press, 1991), p. xv.

62. Adapted and slightly altered from Daniel Kelliher, *Peasant Power*, chap. 6.

63. See Yang Dali, "Making Reform," chap. 4.

64. *WHB*, December 21, 1979.

65. Prof. Kate Xiao Zhou cites this material from *RMRB*, January 5, 1984.

66. Jean C. Oi, *State and Peasant in Contemporary China: The Political Economy of Village Government* (Berkeley: University of California Press, 1989), p. 211.

67. These contracts generally contained clauses about natural disasters, floods or droughts, which reduced peasants' obligations—and about state obligations, especially the interest to be paid if official warehouses were too full to take grain on the agreed dates. Jean C. Oi, *State and Peasant*, p. 174.

68. *FBIS*, December 29, 1987, p. 41, reporting radio of December 28.

69. For more on the practically urban green countryside around Shanghai, see Lynn White, "Shanghai-Suburb Relations," in Christopher Howe, ed., *Shanghai: Revolution and Development in an Asian Metropolis* (Cambridge: Cambridge University Press, 1980), pp. 240–68.

70. The *Chuansha xian zhi* (Chuansha County Gazetteer), Zhu Hongbo, ed. (Shanghai: Shanghai Renmin Chuban She, 1990), p. 251, is somewhat unusual in that it gives a bit of information for the early 1970s. The table includes all recent years for which these were published. Similar gazetteers were briefly scanned for Shanghai's Baoshan, Chongming, Fengxian, Jiading, Jinshan, Qingpu, and Songjiang counties too; but except as reported elsewhere in the text, to a surprising extent most of them avoid offering much behavioral information about the first half of the 1970s.

71. The Green Gang leader of the Republican period, Tu Yuesheng, was a Chuansha native. As part of the second volume of *Unstately Power* will report, evidence of shamanism during the mid-1980s remains strong there. Chuansha farmers included many Roman Catholics. When most of the county was re-named Pudong, local construction teams (and the networks behind them) proved very effective in assuring they received much of the building work. The CCP was not alone in its ability to mobilize Chuansha people's loyalties. More on the variation of local cultures, notably Chuansha particularism, is in the chapter about religion, below. This is a theme that could not be developed from research on just one functional subject.

72. Frank Leeming, *Rural China*, p. 108.

73. Materials compiled by the Shanghai Revolutionary Committee, reported in Frank Leeming, *Rural China*, p. 109.

74. The last column of the table shows changes in the reported county budget that are intriguing but difficult to interpret—partly because of a need to know much more about Songjiang extrabudgetary funds in those years. The odd and irregular pattern of change is as follows: initially high but steadily decreasing rates of reported budgets, 1971–76; low rates thereafter until c. 1983, but with one very high year (1982, probably because of a reporting campaign); then moderate and more slowly increasing rates of extraction to 1987. Songjiang is not a minor or officially neglected place; it is a very considerable city containing many kinds of state and other industries. It is thus also an interesting tax base,

and the available data may show as much about reporting as about anything economic or fiscal.

75. Comparisons of agricultural data from different Shanghai counties generally show increases or decreases of output in synchronization among them for most years—but not for all (e.g., 1981 or 1987). These local irregularities would require more research to explain. The avoidance of growing grain, however, was a broad trend during the reform years.

76. This one-third was surveyed at 32 percent. *CD*, January 24, 1989.

77. William A. Byrd and Lin Qingsong, eds., *China's Rural Industry: Structure, Development, and Reform* (Washington: World Bank, 1990), p. 395.

78. *CD*, January 24, 1989.

79. *CD*, January 24, 1989.

80. Fei Xiaotong and Luo Yanxian, *Xiangzhen jingji*, pp. 67–74.

81. Fei Xiaotong and Luo Yanxian, *Xiangzhen jingji*, pp. 67–74.

82. A sample contract text is in Peter Nolan and Suzanne Paine, "Towards an Appraisal," pp. 99–101.

83. A parallel argument for industry can be found in Dorothy J. Solinger, "Urban Reform and Relational Contracting in Post-Mao China," in Richard Baum, ed., *Reform and Reaction in Post-Mao China: The Road to Tiananmen* (New York: Routledge, 1991), pp. 104–23.

84. Yao Shihuang, *Jin sanjiao*, pp. 140–44.

85. *FBIS*, March 11, 1988, p. 36, reporting radio of March 10.

86. *FBIS*, February 2, 1988, p. 36, reporting radio of January 31.

87. Quoted in Frank Leeming, *Rural China*, p. 119.

88. The 1984 number was reported exactly at 32,972; and in 1989, only 27,473 tractors. *Shanghai shi nongye*, p. 104.

89. Calculated from *ZGTJNJ* (in years noted below), finding a low in 1992 and a high in 1991 by inspecting the following pages, always in the edition of the next year: for 1987, p. 250; 1988, p. 202; 1989, p. 367; 1990, p. 350; 1991, p. 362; and 1992, p. 368.

90. See *Gaige mianlin*, p. 4.

91. *Gaige mianlin*, p. 250.

92. See Philip Huang, *The Peasant Family*, pp. 206–7, 233–34.

93. See Jean C. Oi, *State and Peasant*.

94. *CD*, January 16, 1989.

95. *CD*, January 16, 1989.

96. Guilhem Fabre, "The Chinese Mirror of Transition," *Communist Economies and Economic Transformation* 4:2 (1992), pp. 262–63.

97. *CD*, April 12, 1989.

98. Philip Huang, *The Peasant Family*, pp. 17–18.

99. The survey covered ten counties in as many provinces, and the chances of nonfarm work in this southern Jiangsu place was higher than in any of the other locations. See William L. Parish, Xiaoye Zhe, and Fang Li, "Nonfarm Work and Marketization of the Chinese Countryside," *China Quarterly* 143 (September 1995), p. 718.

100. See Jacques Bertrand, *Compliance, Resistance, and Trust: Peasants and the State in Indonesia* (Princeton University, Politics Department, Ph.D. Dissertation, 1995), chap. 5.

101. Daniel Kelliher, *Peasant Power*, pp. 30–31.

102. Lynn White, *Policies of Chaos*, offers these organizational policies in three categories, linked to Weber's three forms of authority: charismatic campaigns, patronist moni-

toring, and categorical labeling so that bureaucrats could easily know whom to serve and whom to ignore.

103. These are the words of Joseph Fewsmith, in his review of the pseudonymous "Leninger" (Luoyiningeer), *Disan zhi yanjing kan Zhongguo* (Looking at China Through a Third Eye), tr. Wang Shan [also a pseudonym, because the book was written in Chinese, not German, and needed no translation], (Taiyuan: Shansi Publishing House, 1994), in *Journal of Contemporary China* 7 (Fall 1994), p. 101.

104. Ibid.

105. Prof. Cui Zhiyuan has referred me to a section in Fei Xiaotong's 1948 book *Xiangtu Chongjian* (Rural Reconstruction) entitled "Electricity and Internal Combustion Engines Enable the Decentralization of Modern Industrial Production."

106. One of the China field's most important debates, between Nicholas Lardy and Audrey Donnithorne, is assessed in this book's later section on taxes—which concludes that Mao's state succeeded in sending extensive resources inland, even though state budgets failed to cover an exceptionally great deal of income on the Shanghai delta.

107. See Liu Dinghan, ed., *Dangdai Zhongguo de Jiangsu* (Jiangsu in Today's China) (Beijing: Zhongguo Shehui Kexue Chuban She, 1989), p. 106.

108. Calculated from a table in *Jiangsu xiangzhen gongye fazhan shi* (History of the Development of Jiangsu Rural Industry), Mo Yuanren, ed. (Nanjing: Nanjing Gongxue Yuan Chuban She, 1987), p. 140. Interestingly, the rise in rural industrial output from Jiangsu commune-run factories was higher (262 percent) than that from brigade-run factories (172 percent).

109. This portion was 7 percent in 1965. The early-1970s increase was overwhelmingly in Sunan, and that change would be even more dramatic if it had been reported for South Jiangsu alone. See *Xin Zhongguo gongye jingji shi* (A History of New China's Industrial Economy), Wang Haibo, ed. (Beijing: Jingji Guanli Chuban She, 1986), p. 364.

110. The pattern in Zhejiang agriculture is broadly similar though less sharp and affected by flooding in some years, notably 1975. Tensions between Zhejiang and originally non-local cadres (many from Shandong) probably account for some of the actual variations in both agriculture and industry, as well as in the extent to which their outputs were reported. See data in *Zhejiang tongji nianjian, 1989* (Zhejiang Statistical Yearbook, 1989) (Beijing: Zhongguo Tongji Chuban She, 1989), p. 22.

111. Xu Yuanming and Ye Ding, *Tangqiao gongye hua zhi lu* (The Way to Industrialization in Tangqiao) (Shanghai: Shanghai Shehui Kexue Yuan Chuban She, 1987), p. 38, offers a table showing the number of teams, their gross outputs, and their profits.

112. Ishida does not stress this interpretation, although his data suggest it. See Ishida Hiroshi, *Chūgoku nōson keizai no kiso kōzō: Shanhai kinkō nōson no kōgyōka to kindaika no ayumi* (Rural China in Transition: Experiences of Rural Shanghai toward Industrialization and Modernization) (Kyōto: Kōyō shobō, 1991), p. 149.

113. Ishida Hiroshi, *Chūgoku nōson*, pp. 121 and 132.

114. After that, Tangjiacun's carpentry and barrel industries failed for financial reasons, however. So the number of employees in its own factories decreased to 425 by 1987. Ibid, pp. 138–39, provides information about just a single place. But the wealth of circumstantial evidence in Ishida's book raises confidence that Tangjiacun is not a "Potemkin" village. The author of the current book realizes that not all readers are dying to know exactly how many barrel makers Tangjiacun had in 1987. But the issue is larger: Local reporting from a relatively independent source may provide more accurate suggestions, even about large situations, than ostensibly comprehensive reporting from sources that have official or other unacademic interests. Ishida provides a useful check, because he could monitor the consistency of many different kinds of data.

115. Xu Yuanming and Ye Ding, *Tangqiao gongye*, p. 10, says that Party members at Tangqiao took the initiative to spur the development of these new and reopened factories.

116. Central and provincial politicians disagreed among themselves, at this time, about the appropriate kinds and extent of rural industrialization. Radical "policy winds" were nonetheless recurrent, fiercely opposing rural entrepreneurship—especially in East China where Shanghai head Zhang Chunqiao was the main radical spokesman. The interpretation above substantially agrees with the best treatment of these ideological trends: David Zweig, *Agrarian Radicalism*. See also Xu Yuanming and Ye Ding, *Tangqiao gongye*, pp. 10–13.

117. The cadres were said to "*mao yiding zhengzhi fengxian*." Xu Yuanming and Ye Ding, *Tangqiao gongye*, p. 13.

118. For more, see Xu Yuanming and Ye Ding, *Tangqiao gongye*, pp. 15–17.

119. Ibid. This phenomenon is also noted for poorer areas and for agriculture by Jonathan Unger, " 'Rich Man, Poor Man': The Making of New Classes in the Countryside," in *China's Quiet Revolution: New Interactions Between State and Society*, David S. G. Goodman and Beverley Hooper, eds. (New York: St. Martin's, 1994), pp. 43–63.

120. The references to this *zonghe tuixiao duiwu* team and the *xiaoshou dian* sales points are at ibid., p. 25.

121. Based on calculations from a complete list of all Tangqiao factories in Xu Yuanming and Ye Ding, *Tangqiao gongye*, pp. 139–43. These pages include detailed information on each plant's number of employees, fixed capital, liquid capital, and 1985 production.

122. Calculated from figures in ibid., p. 68. These may well be underestimates, however, because they may ignore temporary and contract workers, many of whom are usually migrants.

123. The number of factories is in either case large enough for a good sample: 1969–83, 346 to 732 factories; 1978–82, 598 to 796. Since the 1978 number is lower than the 1983 one, the text above suggests the conclusion about business failures and deregistrations. See *Qingpu xian zhi* (Qingpu County Gazetteer), Feng Xuewen et al., eds. (Shanghai: Shanghai Renmin Chuban She, 1990), pp. 270–71.

124. Frank Leeming, *Rural China*, pp. 104–5.

125. Ibid., p. 115.

126. For the data, see ibid.

127. Ibid.

128. The township (*xiang*; earlier, commune) accounted for 62 percent of industrial employment in 1970, a low of 35 percent in 1978, and then back up to 45 percent in 1988. Ishida Hiroshi, *Chūgoku nōson*, p. 151.

129. Fei Xiaotong and Luo Yanxian, *Xiangzhen jingji*, pp. 5–9.

130. Ibid., pp. 1–4.

131. For more on *guahu*, see Kate Xiao Zhou and Lynn White, "Quiet Politics and Rural Enterprise in Reform China," *The Journal of the Developing Areas* 29 (July 1995), pp. 461–90.

132. David Zweig, "Urbanizing Rural China: Bureaucratic Authority and Local Autonomy" (ms.).

133. Scott Rozelle, "Decision-making in China's Rural Economy: The Linkages between Village Leaders and Farm Households," *China Quarterly* 137 (March 1994), pp. 123–24.

134. Dwight Perkins et al., *Rural Small-Scale Industry in the People's Republic of China* (Berkeley: University of California Press, 1977), p. 2.

135. Dwight Perkins, et al. *Rural Small-Scale*, p. 252.

136. Xu Jiatun in *Shijie ribao* (World Daily), May 6, 1993.

137. Jiangxi Provincial Broadcasting Station, November 25, 1975, and Zhejiang Provincial Broadcasting Station, November 16, 1975; in Jürgen Domes, *Socialism*, p. 90.

138. *WHB*, December 4, 1975.

139. Steven Butler, *Agricultural Mechanization in China: The Administrative Impact* (New York: East Asian Institute, Columbia University, 1978), p. 45.

140. *Zhejiang ribao*, October 8, 1975, Anhui Provincial Broadcasting Station, August 23, 1975, and Zhejiang Provincial Broadcasting Station, October 6, 1975; from Jürgen Domes, *Socialism*, p. 88.

141. Zheng Yongnian reports this from the Municipal Government of Wenzhou, *Wenzhou shiqu geti gongshang yehu qingkuang diaocha* (Investigation of Private Industrial and Commercial Enterprises in Wenzhou), 1984.

142. *Xin Zhongguo gongye*, pp. 361–63.

143. Christine Wong, Thomas Rawski, and other economists have assessed the comparative efficiency of various kinds of plants nicely. Small plants—even economically successful ones—often turn out to be technically inefficient. Like the socialist enterprises they tend to replace, they mobilize resources better than they coordinate resources. A major advantage of the state sector in the 1970s and beyond was its ability to acquire capital openly. For example, see a striking comparison, by product rather than ownership type, that shows the importance of this advantage in Rawski's *Economic Growth and Employment in China* (New York: Oxford University Press, 1979), p. 47 and passim.

144. Samuel Ho, *Rural China in Transition: Non-agricultural Development in Rural Jiangsu, 1978–90* (New York: Oxford University Press, 1994), p. 18.

145. Audrey Donnithorne, "China's Cellular Economy: Some Trends Since the Cultural Revolution," *China Quarterly* 52 (October-December 1972), p. 607.

146. John P. Burns, "Rural Guangdong's Second Economy," *China Quarterly* 88 (December 1981), pp. 629–44.

147. Prefectures (*diqu*) are areas comprising several counties (*xian*). *Xin Zhongguo gongye*, pp. 356–58.

148. *Xin Zhongguo gongye* , pp. 359–61.

149. See Karl Marx and Frederick Engels, *Manifesto of the Communist Party* (Beijing: Foreign Languages Press, 1970), p. 37.

150. This pattern was also evident before the Cultural Revolution. On the political-administrative separation, under Shanghai Mayor Ke Qingshi in the early and middle 1960s, of cultural czars like Yao Wenyuan and Zhang Chunqiao from economic czars like Cao Diqiu and Chen Pixian, see Lynn White, "Leadership in Shanghai, 1955–69," in Robert A. Scalapino, ed., *Elites in the People's Republic of China* (Seattle: University of Washington Press, 1972), e.g. p. 346, and Lynn White, *Policies of Chaos*, e.g. p. 224.

151. Preliminary data from Wenzhou, for example, are offered in the text above. More research needs to be done to compare local, statist, or non-PRC causes of reform in the deltas of the following rivers: the Min (Fuzhou), the Jiulong (Xiamen and other cities), the Han (Shantou and Chaozhou), and especially the Zhu and its tributaries (Guangzhou and many other cities—near Hong Kong). Specific comparisons also need to be made for many other places, including parts of Shandong and the very rich Chengdu plain far inland. There is no way to be sure of what happened in these areas on the basis of data from Beijing (or Shanghai) alone. It is necessary actually to look there. Several other books like the present one need to be written. Several scholars have done such work, including Ezra Vogel on Guangdong where reforms were quick and Dorothy Solinger on Hubei where they seem to have been slow.

152. Percentages are rounded from the source. See Philip C. C. Huang, *The Peasant Family*, p. 355.

153. A notable portion of the boat people in the Shanghai suburbs, especially in Qingpu county but also elsewhere, came from families that were Roman Catholic before 1949. For more on their partial maintenance of ideological autonomy from the CCP during the 1970s, and on the economic correlates, see the chapter below concerning religion. One of the theses of these two volumes is that reforms in different areas are interconnected.

154. Fei Xiaotong, *Small Towns in China: Functions, Problems, and Prospects* (Beijing: New World Press, 1986).

155. An economist in the Chinese Academy of Social Sciences emphasized the early importance in Jiangnan of distinctions between "private" (*siying*) enterprises that may hire outside workers, "individual" (*geti*) units that rely on one household, and "joint" (*lianhe*) firms that combine several households. Such phrases were reportedly used earlier in common parlance than in official documents. These types were all contrasted with collective (*jiti*) and state-run (*guoying*) firms. Not just in the early 1970s, but also later, the collective sector has been the largest fast-growth one. But so many collectives are so plainly under the leadership of one or two top cadres, they are operationally hard to distinguish from private enterprises.

156. *Jiangsu xiangzhen*, p. 448.

157. *FEER*, December 11, 1986, pp. 82–83.

158. Some of this increase almost surely represents more complete reporting from rural factories that before 1978 had to hide their output—or even their existence—both for political reasons and to avoid central imposts. But see Fei Xiaotong and Luo Yanxian, *Xiangzhen jingji*, pp. 46–48.

159. As immediately above, part of the increase may result from more complete reporting. But there can be no doubt these industries grew very quickly at this time. *Hengxiang jingji lianhe de xin fazhan* (The New Development of Horizontal Economic Links), Shanghai Economics Association, ed. (Shanghai: Shanghai Shehui Kexue Yuan Chuban She, 1987), p. 96.

160. *Post*, August 29, 1988.

161. See David Zweig, "Rural Industry: Constraining the Leading Growth Sector in China's Economy," in U. S. Congress, Joint Economic Committee, *China's Economic Dilemmas in the 1990s: The Problems of Reforms, Modernization, and Interdependence* (Washington: Government Printing Office, 1991), pp. 418–36. Reprinted with index, by M.E. Sharpe, Armonk, NY, 1992.

162. Zhang Xingduan in *LW* 2 (January 1988), p. 26.

163. Ibid., p. 27. Emphasis added. The meaning of "economic" here is unclear.

164. See Lu Feiyun, "Zhuanye chengbao zhe—Yige xin jieceng de quqi" (Specialized Contractors—The Origins of a New Stratum), *Shehui* (Society) 3, Shanghai, 1990, pp. 30–31.

165. *Post*, February 11, 1989.

166. Jean C. Oi, *State and Peasant*, p. 185.

167. Victor Nee, "Peasant Entrepreneurship and the Politics of Regulation in China," in V. Nee and D. Stark, eds., *Remaking the Economic Institutions of China and Eastern Europe* (Stanford: Stanford University Press, 1991), pp. 185–86.

168. *Jingji xinwen bao*, January 26, 1989.

169. Solomon M. Karmel, "The Neo-Authoritarian Contradiction: Trials of Developmentalist Dictatorships and the Retreat of the State in Mainland China," pp. 72–74, quoting 1992 work by Wang Manchuan.

170. *Gaige mianlin*, pp. 4 and 9.

171. Yang Dali, "Making Reform," p. 156.

172. Peter Nolan, "Petty Commodity Production in a Socialist Economy: Chinese Rural Development Post-Mao," *Market Forces in China: Competition & Small Business, The Wenzhou Debate*, Peter Nolan and Dong Fureng, eds. (London: Zed Books, 1990), p. 12.

173. Wuxi is a modern city with many large companies. The chance that the portion of village-run industry there would be overreported is very low. William A. Byrd and Lin Qingsong, eds., *China's Rural*, p. 68. Among the four counties surveyed by the World Bank, the ownership structure in Jieshou, Jiangxi, was most different from that of Wuxi, Jiangsu. This relatively poor Jiangxi county borders Fujian province, and demonstration effects are suggested by the fact that private enterprise contributed about one-third of the nonstate output there.

174. See further information, in the migration section of this volume, showing a very sharp early-1970s immigration to cities having between 500,000 and 1,000,000 people (though not to larger cities yet). Many youths who had been sent out of Shanghai after 1968, for example, were able to return to medium-sized Shanghai delta cities in the early 1970s (before they flowed back to the metropolis after 1978). Many rural young people who had been born in the countryside also joined this urban immigration. For a Taiwan comparison, which shows youths' leaving the countryside for Taipei and Kaohsiung, see Bernard Gallin, *Hsin Hsing, Taiwan: A Chinese Village in Change* (Berkeley: University of California Press, 1966).

175. *CD*, October 10, 1990.

176. See Peter Nolan and Robert F. Ash, "China's Economy on the Eve of Reform," *China Quarterly* 144 (December 1995), pp. 981–82.

177. Christine Wong, "Fiscal Reform and Local Industrialization," *Modern China* 18:2 (April 1992), pp. 197–227.

178. Barry Naughton, "Industrial Policy during the Cultural Revolution," in W. Joseph et al., eds., *New Perspectives on the Cultural Revolution* (Cambridge: Harvard University Press, 1991), pp. 153–81, provides investment data from state construction budgets that justify both an earlier starting date (1964) and an earlier ending date than are usual in descriptions of the Cultural Revolution. In some parts of China, notably Shanghai, the earlier starting date also makes sense in terms of certain kinds of data from cultural spheres, although the 1964–66 sequence of events is at least as unique as any other.

179. This and the next two paragraphs interpret material found by Penelope B. Prime, "Industry's Response to Market Liberalization in China: Evidence from Jiangsu Province," *Economic Development and Cultural Change* 41:1 (1992), pp. 37–40.

180. The calculation is complex, for reasons involving intermediate inputs. In one way of making the test, state industries raise factor productivity more than collective industries; using another test, the opposite is true. The conclusions are interpreted from data in Penelope B. Prime, ibid.

181. Peter Nolan, "Petty Commodity," p. 11.

182. Most of this story has been told by Christine Wong, "The Economics of Shortage and Problems of Reform in Chinese Industry," *Journal of Comparative Economics* (1986), pp. 363–87.

183. *Shanghai jingji, neibu ben: 1949–1982* (Shanghai Economy, Internal Volume: 1949–1982), Shanghai Academy of Social Sciences, ed. (Shanghai: Shanghai Shehui Kexue Yuan Chuban She, 1984), p. 683.

184. See sources cited in Yang Dali, "Making Reform," p. 258.

185. This 12 percent (by value) may be underreported, but the qualitative point here

still stands. See Y. Y. Kueh, *Economic Planning and Local Mobilization in Post-Mao China* (London: SOAS Contemporary China Institute, 1985), p. 56.

186. See the classic by Arthur Lewis, "Economic Development with Unlimited Supplies of Labour," *The Manchester School of Economic and Social Studies* (1954), pp. 139–91.

187. Calculated from figures in *SHTJNJ88*, p. 77. This table gives numbers for other years without noting changes of administrative boundaries that affect these data. A jurisdictional change in 1983 also seems to have affected the figures somewhat. (The earlier large changes c. 1959 predate the comparison in the text.)

188. *Xian de jingji yu jiaoyu de diaocha* (Survey of County Economies and Education), Task Force for Research on China's Rural Education, ed. (Beijing: Jiaoyu Kexue Chuban She, 1989), p. 127.

189. Yao Shihuang, *Jin sanjiao*, pp. 105–132.

190. Yao Shihuang, *Jin sanjiao*, pp. 105–132.

191. Fei Xiaotong and Luo Yanxian, *Xiangzhen jingji*, pp. 48–50.

192. Stephan Feuchtwang, "Basic Social Security in the Countryside," in Ashwani Saith, ed., *The Re-emergence of the Chinese Peasantry: Aspects of Rural Decollectivization* (London: Croom Helm, 1987), p. 192.

193. Xu Yuanming and Ye Ding, *Tangqiao gongye*, p. 5.

194. *Fei zhengshi zhigong* includes *linshi gong, hetong gong,* and *jijie gong.* Sometimes texts also mention workers who are part-time or periodic (*zhouqi*). But no statistics at all have been given on seasonal or part-time informal labor—even by an expert team of Fudan and East China Normal University surveyors—apparently because the local managers just would not tell academics about this. We have here a principle like Heisenberg's: to gather such information, a coercive (police, labor federation, tax) authority would be needed; but it is precisely to keep these data from such agencies that local managers are secretive. Gathering the facts affects their content. On regular workers, however, more can be known. The portion of them hired by suburban collectives was 77.6 percent; with only 12.5 percent employed by state plants, and 10 percent by private firms, in this extensive 1986 survey of four Shanghai *zhen*. *Zhongguo yanhai diqu xiao chengzhen fazhan yu renkou qianyi* (Migration and the Development of Small Cities and Towns on the China Coast) Liu Zheng, et al., eds. (Beijing: Zhongguo Caizheng Jingji Chuban She, 1989), p. 187.

195. Only 48 percent were registered as permanent. The three towns (*zhen*) in this fascinating study were Jinshanwei, a designated "satellite city" (*weixing cheng*) of Shanghai in Jinshan county (near Hangzhou Bay, and south of the county seat, which is called Zhujing); Chengqiao, the county seat and the largest town on Chongming Island; and Luodian, a *zhen* under Baoshan county, whose c. 10,000 population in the mid-1980s was one-third the size of Chengqiao and one-fifth that of Jinshanwei, and three times that of the smallest *zhen* studied: Zhuiqiao, in southern Shanghai county about halfway between the metropolis and its major suburb Minhang, *Zhongguo yanhai diqu*, pp. 178–81.

196. This startling report on exploitation is Hua Daming, "Xiangban chang dui nonggong de guofen bodu ying yinqi zhuyi" (The Overexploitation of Workers by Township-run Factories Calls for Attention), *Shehui* (Society) 2, Shanghai, 1990, pp. 12–13.

197. Victor Nee, "Peasant Entrepreneurship," pp. 198–99.

198. Fei Xiaotong and Luo Yanxian, *Xiangzhen jingji*, pp. 77–81.

199. Village industries often grew even faster than township ones, though the reported data on this lower level (where the government has no offices) are less reliable. Fei Xiaotong and Luo Yanxian, *Xiangzhen jingji*, pp. 40–45.

200. Sidney Goldstein and Alice Goldstein, "Population Movement, Labor Force Absorption, and Urbanization in China," *Annals of the American Academy of Political and Social Science* 476 (1984), pp. 99–100.

201. Liu Dinghan, ed., *Dangdai Zhongguo*, p. 605. Thanks goes to Zheng Yongnian for this reference.

202. *Hengxiang jingji*, p. 143.

203. *FBIS*, December 21, 1984, p. 5, reporting radio of December 17.

204. *Zhongguo yanhai diqu* , p. 1.

205. The greater need to hide rural output to evade Shanghai's high taxes may make this 4 percent a slight underestimate. The current books avoid tenths-of-percents. They describe especially uncertain portions as rough fractions, so as not to pretend more accuracy than the data collection system likely offers. See William A. Byrd and Lin Qingsong, eds., *China's Rural*, p. 256. Hebei produced 10 percent; Shandong, 9 percent; and Guangdong (if the figures are complete) a surprisingly low 7 percent. Each of the other provinces had a lower figure.

206. Fei wrote this in 1986. See Chris Bramall, "The Wenzhou 'Miracle': An Assessment," *Market Forces in China: Competition & Small Business, The Wenzhou Debate*, Peter Nolan and Dong Fureng, eds., pp. 54–55.

207. *SHGYJJB*, February 15, 1988.

208. *EE,* March 2, 1994.

209. See Seth Faison's article in the *New York Times*, January 21, 1996, p. 4.

210. Yao Shihuang, *Jin sanjiao*, pp. 105–32.

211. William A. Byrd and Lin Qingsong, eds., *China's Rural*, p. 223.

212. *CD*, November 9, 1990.

213. Zhangjiagang Bureau of Rural Industries, *Zhangjiagang shi xiangzhen gongye zhi* (Gazetteer of Zhangjiagang Rural Industries) (Shanghai: Shanghai Renmin Chuban She, 1990), p. 80, as referred to the author by Zheng Yongnian.

214. This refers to, but expands on, Karl Polanyi, *The Great Transformation* (New York: Rinehart, 1944). Many of Polanyi's historical examples postdate revolutions, especially the English one. Police and fiscal centralization is a precedent to the modern transformation, which power networks outside the state can also support. This is a point that E.E. Schattschneider can be seen as adding to Polanyi, though their basic categories are very similar.

215. *Qingpu xian zhi*, pp. 42–45.

216. The source says urban purchases rose four times in 1952–78, but just 58 percent in the countryside; and in 1978–83, the total rises were respectively 17 and 51 percent. The annual rates have been calculated from *Zhongguo renkou*, pp. 23–32. There is no adjustment for inflation, but the main comparison above is between urban and rural consumption, not between the two periods. Compounding over the long 1952–78 period means the urban 5.48 annual rate created big results.

217. These data are from Tangjiacun, Fengxian county, Shanghai—a place whose typicality has been checked by a non-official academic. See Ishida Hiroshi, *Chūgoku nōson*, p. 192.

218. The similarities to "likin" taxes in imperial times are evident. A Chinese interviewee reported taking a 1988 pleasure trip on back roads from Shanghai to Suzhou (by train or fast road, the journey takes only an hour)—and being stopped four times for "tolls." The impositions on trucks, and especially in less prosperous areas of more inland provinces such as Anhui, are reportedly far more frequent.

219. An analogous situation for large state companies is described with reference to Oliver Williamson's ideas in Dorothy J. Solinger, "Urban Reform," pp. 104–23.

220. Thomas B. Gold, "Still on the Collective Road: Limited Reform in a North China Village" (1987 manuscript).

221. A small sampling: Yuan Enzhen et al., *Wenzhou moshi yu fuyu zhi lu* (The Wenzhou Model and Way to Affluence) (Shanghai: Shanghai Shehui Kexue Yuan Chuban She, 1987); *Wenzhou qiye daquan, 1986* (Compendium of Wenzhou Enterprises, 1986), Wang Wence, ed. (Wenzhou: Wenzhou Shi Qiye Guanli Xiehui and Wenzhou Shi Gongye Pucha Bangong Shi, 1986); *Wenzhou moshi de lilun tansuo* (Theoretical Exploration of the Wenzhou Model), Lin Bai et al., eds. (Nanning: Guangxi Renmin Chuban She, 1987); and *Wenzhou shiyan qu* (The Wenzhou Experimental Zone), Pan Shangeng, ed. (Beijing: Nengyuan Chuban She, 1988).

222. Xu Yuanming and Ye Ding, *Tangqiao gongye*, p. 3, describes the Wenzhou and Sunan models, as well as a Gengche model (about which it offers no details).

223. *FBIS*, December 21, 1987, p. 21, reporting *RMRB* of December 5.

224. This issue has been crucial in Chinese politics since the "Nanking Decade" of 1927–37, when the militarist constituency of the Guomindang was in constant tension with its Shanghai capitalist constituency. See Parks M. Coble, Jr., *The Shanghai Capitalist Class and the Nationalist Government, 1927–37* (Cambridge: Harvard University Council on East Asian Studies and Harvard University Press, 1986).

225. Dong Fureng, "The Wenzhou Model for Developing the Rural Commodity Economy," *Market Forces in China*, Peter Nolan and Dong Fureng, eds., p. 84.

226. *CD*, June 22, 1991.

227. Calculated from Chen Ruiming, "A Preliminary Analysis of the 'Big Labor-Hiring Households' in Rural Wenzhou," *Market Forces in China*, Peter Nolan and Dong Fureng, eds., p. 141.

228. Li Shi, "The Growth of Household Industry in Rural Wenzhou," *Market Forces in China*, pp. 115–16. In the original, county is *xian*, district is *qu*, and township is *xiang*.

229. Cf. Louis Putterman, "Institutional Boundaries, Structural Change, and Economic Reform in China," *Modern China* 18:1 (January 1992), pp. 3–13.

230. *Asian Wall Street Journal*, January 23, 1989.

231. *Post*, August 11, 1989.

232. Interview with an officer at the U.S. Consulate-General in Shanghai, June 1991.

233. Chen Kaiguo, *Zhongguo nongcun da qushi* (Trends in Rural China) (Hefei: Anhui Renmin Chuban She, 1989), as cited to the author by his student and friend, Mr. Wang Xu.

234. Quoted from a deputy governor of Zhejiang by Tyrene White, "Political Reform and Rural Government," in Deborah Davis and Ezra Vogel, eds., *Chinese Society on the Eve of Tiananmen: The Impact of Reform* (Cambridge: Harvard University Press, 1990), p. 49.

235. This all-China report is based on information from Pei Minxin in a paper, "Creeping Democratization in China?"

236. Mr. Wang Xu referred me to this in Scott Rozelle and Richard Boisvert, "Quantifying Chinese Village Leaders' Multiple Objectives," *Journal of Comparative Economics* 18 (1994), pp. 25–45.

237. *CD*, March 10, 1988.

238. *CD*, August 2, 1989.

239. *FBIS*, December 21, 1987, p. 21, reporting *RMRB* of December 5.

240. *CD*, September 26, 1990.

241. Edward J. Epstein, "China's Legal Reforms," in Kuan Hsin-chi and Maurice

Brosseau, eds., *China Review* (Hong Kong: Chinese University Press, 1991), p. 9.8.

242. Fei Xiaotong and Luo Yanxian, *Xiangzhen jingji*, pp. 1–4.

243. *CD*, April 12, 1991.

244. *ZGTJNJ93*, p. 395.

245. For 1990 the data are better; see *ZGTJNJ91*, p. 201, for the denominator.

246. For more suggestions along this line, see a paper by the author's former student Dr. Roger Cliff, "Technical Progress and the Development of China's Steel Industry Under Mao."

Chapter 1.2

Business Management Beyond the State

The natural strength of the people in a large community,
in proportion to the artificial strength of the government,
is greater than in a small.

—Alexander Hamilton

The preceding chapter, which is about farms and rural industry, shows that a local cause of Chinese reforms near Shanghai can be found in agricultural extension before the 1970s. In the more diversified and modern environment of cities—where the state had much heavier fiscal interests—the situation was more complex. Part of the difference, with which this book will deal in later chapters, was normative: Campaigns from the mid-1950s to the late 1960s affected the morale of entrepreneurs in Chinese cities; thus China's urban industrial reforms cannot be ascribed wholly to concrete causes. Another part, which is the business of this chapter, was situational. The rural boom created a new and unanticipated context for urban state industries' markets both to buy raw materials and to sell products. Adapting to this new external situation became the main job of managers.

Urban shortages of factors for state industries emerged slowly in the 1970s, before inflation during reforms became very evident. Labor unrest and management difficulties were already rife by 1975, when a State Planning Commission document declared its managers "in chaos because of raw materials shortages, low productivity, and rising costs."[1] These problems cumulated for a decade at least, and by the mid-1980s they forced major structural changes.

The Raw Materials Crisis as the Origin of Urban Industrial Reforms

"In the beginning of the 1970s," as a PRC publication explains, "the country's economic life had 'three breakouts' [*sange tupo*]."[2] The number of state noncadre workers reached 50 million, wage expenses for them became more than 30 billion yuan, and the state's grain sales volume reached 80 billion kg. All three of these "breakouts" were unintended, all can be dated from the early 1970s, and each caused major problems for the state while creating the basis for China's economic boom.

Only three million newly designated workers were supposed to be added in 1970 and 1971, according to official PRC plans; actually, ten million were hired. Under the state budget, total wage expenses in 1971 were supposed to be limited to 29.6 billion yuan, but 30.2 billion yuan were in fact paid. Grain sales volume was supposed to be only 79 billion kg, but the actual volume was 86 billion kg, and the state was the buyer of last resort, at prices it was politically loath to lower no matter whether it had spare funds.

Official budget crunches and unintended results of previous policies, more than any new official liking for markets, combined by 1971 to force government responses to these problems. Many aspects of this early 1970s pattern strongly resemble the state's difficulties during later reforms. Six million of the ten million unauthorized hirings in 1970–71 were of workers "from the countryside," apparently a combination of peasants who became temporary workers and youths who refused to stay in rustication. This caused a corresponding rural problem: "On one hand, agricultural labor was decreased quickly because so many people left rural areas, hindering rural economic development; on the other, crop supply tension rose quickly because so many urban workers were hired in such a short time." There was in most areas, at that time, no grain shortage; this "crop supply tension" resulted from a lack of official money to buy food from peasants for workers, causing resentment in both groups.

Beijing tried then (as later) to solve its problems by decree: "Premier Zhou Enlai discovered the 'three breakouts' problem first." At a national economic planning conference held from November 16, 1971, to February 12, 1972, he pointed out big dangers to the state's budget implicit in these growing trends. "However, his ideas could not be implemented"; so the "three breakouts" continued, strengthening local power networks at the state's expense. Through the end of 1972, the number of workers reached 56 million (beyond then-current plans by another 2 million). The total state wage bill was then 34 billion yuan, up 4 billion yuan from 1971. Crop sales volume reached 93 billion kg, up more than 4 billion kg over 1971—although in 1972 the grain the state could purchase was only 79 billion kg.[3]

Classic patterns of later reforms were already obvious: The Party launched sporadic efforts to slow its loss of control over urban hiring. At the same time, it tried to spur grain production and pay as little as possible for procurement, so that its worker constituency might face low prices and be content with low wages. Local power networks had sporadic successes in just the opposite directions: hiring more cheap workers from rural areas, paying favored employees more, and refusing to produce rural grain until the state was willing to pay for the work in fields. This last problem was acute in the early 1970s, when new rice technologies, which allowed greater total yields through triple-cropping, pressed the marginal benefit of production to peasants even lower than before—often below zero.

Neither side in this prolonged war could ever obtain total victory. The government had some successes. But various local power networks' victories unsteadily became more frequent or fiscally important, on an upward ratchetlike zigzag rather than a smooth trajectory, from 1970 onward. This reversed an earlier, opposite trend during the 1950s, in which the state had penetrated many urban and rural networks.

The Start of the Factors Crisis

China's largest metropolis prospers on manufacturing and trade, not extraction. Shanghai has, for example, the dubious distinction of being practically the only province-level unit in China never to have produced any coal.[4] As data from many cities in East Asia have shown, local primary production is not a prerequisite for big economic success, even in industry, if materials can be brought from elsewhere.

Before 1949, Shanghai industrialists were famed for their sharpness in trade and finance as well as management. But after the Transition to Socialism retired many old businessmen, who were replaced by new cohorts (including many demobilized Red Army soldiers), the functions of managers changed. The government's plan—and the bureaucrats who administered it in offices that were now more often physically distant from factories or shops—were responsible for obtaining raw materials, for getting credit, and for wholesale marketing.

Economic planning had meant political control. The mobility of factors in China's economy had been sharply regulated by state efforts, in Mao's time, to guide not just commodities but also people. The reforms meant inconsistent or weak central restraints on land use, on rural work point systems, on loan requirements, and on the criteria for business licenses, urban household registrations, and the accompanying allocations of food, housing, education, or jobs—even marriage or birth certificates. These changes together have allowed economic factors, as well as people, to seek more profitable uses. For the CCP, workers were the crucial Shanghai people to be guided. Low prices for their food and shelter, and low prices for raw materials in the state factories where they worked, were prerequisite to workers' political and fiscal support of the state.

Shanghai materials prices had for many years been kept low—like the prices of rent and food. This situation led economists to call the city a "price basin" (*jiage pendi*). Officially, prices were of three kinds: fixed (*dingjia*), negotiated (*yijia*), and floating (*fujia*). The legal prices of commodities that could still be controlled were often set on a "cost plus" basis. The costs at a major producing location for any good would be added to other expenses (such as transport). As reforms progressed, and especially after 1984, price competition raised efficiency, and cost-plus calculations to fix prices became less effective, especially if the calculations were influenced politically to set prices high and protect inefficient procedures. But for early reforms or for commodity markets where socialist norms continued, the price at one place in China, usually the largest center of production, remained the baseline. Shanghai was for many manufactures the major producer. Transport within the city was cheap. This became an accounting rationale for an essentially political policy: low prices in proletarian Shanghai.

Cheap prices hindered the supply of goods in the metropolis, however. As a newspaper pointed out, "Water flows to a low place, and commodities go to a high [price] place."[5] Shanghai materials purchasing departments were said to be "poor" and to lack cash. Actually, they were poor only because Shanghai bore China's highest state extraction rate, while burgeoning rural industrialists could pay more for inputs that otherwise would have come to the city.

Shanghai's *urban* industry grew more slowly in the early 1970s than in the late 1960s. From 1966 to 1970, Shanghai's national income grew at a rate of 14.0 percent annually (not much below the halcyon 1963–65 annual growth rate of 18.0 percent). Political disruptions of businesses in 1966–70 did not slow Shanghai's growth as much as might have been expected. But from 1971 to 1975, this city's annual growth of urban industry was only 6.3 percent. The reasons for the slowdown were almost surely multiple. Fiscal imposts on urban factories rose during the early 1970s. Capital for army-related projects, which the Gang of Four (the number of whom were from Shanghai) had installed in the city during the late 1960s, decreased in the 1970s. Perhaps the high tide of the Cultural Revolution had inspired some workers' enthusiasm, which later atrophied. But the main reason for the slowdown was that Shanghai's urban factories were struck with a raw materials shortage because of booming rural industries elsewhere in East China.[6] Early reforms meant faster economic expansion for most of China, but not for central Shanghai.

State control lasted longest over markets for goods that are physically bulky per unit of value. Planning lasted in particular for materials that could be extracted only at specific locations, or that could be produced only with capital-intensive technologies from bulk materials (e.g., coal at major seams, or inorganic fertilizers from petrochemical factories). For small but valuable goods, those extracted in many places, and those that can be made with little capital, official control was hard to maintain.

Central state politicians encouraged production that they could tax. Hua Guofeng's economic program of 1978 was somewhat like the Great Leap Forward, calling for support from central planners, heavy industries, and probably many in the army and Party who saw continued honor to Mao as a source of stability for continued imposts that supported their networks. But Hua did not win for long in central politics. He and many of his followers had not suffered during the Cultural Revolution. These lions were able to mobilize less support within the Party than Deng Xiaoping's coalition of foxes.

Locally, practical problems accumulated to confirm the view that China needed new, expert managers to replace the demobilized generalists who had dominated the state sector for a quarter century. Already before 1979, the Shanghai Production Materials Service Company could not "freely manage" its trade. So it established a new market in many inputs (as well as some finished goods).[7] By the end of that year, over a thousand sellers and buyers from all parts of China exchanged commodities worth more than 300,000 yuan *each day,* at this market. Yet the socialist idea had been that such markets, in which prices were bargained for major commodities, should be unnecessary.

The Shanghai Handicrafts Bureau, desperate for inputs, had to negotiate for long-term "compensation trade" agreements beginning in 1979. In that year and the next, it signed ten such agreements with enterprises in Jiangsu, Zhejiang, Jiangxi, Hunan, and Guangxi. Its first treaties, which set the pattern, were settled with the Hangzhou Light Industrial Bureau and with the Zhenjiang Prefecture Building Materials Bureau. Under a large group of such contracts, Shanghai bartered 9.8 million yuan worth of machinery (not handicrafts) in exchange for raw materials. The inland areas promised to send Shanghai (within the periods of years that the contracts specified) 6,000 tons metric tons of paper, 1,000 tons of thick paper, 100 tons of glue, 6,000 tons of cement, and 1,000 sets of wooden furniture.[8]

Already by 1980, allocation through normal city plans could provide only 30 percent of the local demand for most construction materials—roof beams, bricks, steel rods, and glass.[9] Inland leaders did not always deliver the inputs they had promised, because they could make more money by processing these locally. Between 1980 and 1982, there was a 60 percent decrease in the quantity of goods available in Shanghai's raw materials free markets.[10]

Management in the Factors Crisis

The official periodization of PRC history (like the view that economic expansion was a post-1978 event) conflicts with data on Shanghai's economic growth. Shanghai's national income from 1966 to 1978 increased by an annual rate of 10.2 percent. But in the years from 1979 to 1982, its growth decelerated to 7.0 percent.[11] In particular, growth in Shanghai heavy industrial production decelerated from 10.0 percent annually between 1966 and 1978 to 2.6 percent annually between 1979 and 1982. These changes were not the reforms that many writers came to know and love.

Firms producing consumer goods—which garnered more money for the central bureaucracy from rural markets throughout China—did better than Shanghai's heavy industry in the late 1970s and 1980s. But their performance was still not as good, relative to that of domestic competitors, as in previous years. Light industrial production was greatly stressed in this era, and its rate of expansion, at 7.0 percent annually in the period 1966–78, rose to 8.5 percent annually between 1978 and 1982. The latter period saw a clear decline in Shanghai's capital-intensive industries and an expansion in the businesses that gathered revenues most widely for Beijing coffers. After 1982, when inputs became scarce, light industries suffered too.

The Mid-1980s Watershed

The first and main reason for Shanghai's mid-1980s economic emergency was the raw materials shortage. By the second quarter of 1984, actual deliveries to Shanghai of inland iron, lumber, fuel, ferrous ores, coal, water, and chemicals suffered sharp drops—by at least 30 percent below plan for all of these vital materials, and for some of them by 50 percent below plan. Industrial energy shortages were especially severe and could halt factories in a startling manner. Shanghai paid 545 million yuan for industrial fuels in 1984. But by 1985, the city's cost for energy rose "wildly," to about 1 billion yuan—even though at least 30 percent less was supplied despite the doubling of payments.[12] Especially in fields where finished product prices were inflexible, the losses from higher costs of major inputs in 1985, compared to the previous year, were enormous. They were estimated at 730 million yuan of lost profits in the steel industry alone. The inputs crisis was so tightly bound with many other management problems, it makes sense to list them together, even though most of the others will also be mentioned in later chapters.

Shanghai managers could no longer get essentially free credit. This was a second problem—or at least a second excuse for any other. Managers could not solve the mid-1980s input shortages by their previous usual method, which was to obtain loans and offer higher payments for materials. Thus they tended (very politely, so as not to discomfit their essential suppliers with accusations) to describe much of the problem in terms of a restricted money supply. For "lack of funds," the Shanghai Dyeing Factory had a stoppage in 1986 that lasted twenty-five days. Textile factories in all Shanghai together suffered losses that were too severe to publish. Actually, funds could have been arranged on an inflationary basis—and to some extent, this happened so that high-priced inputs could be bought.

Bureaucratic companies had become unused to completing jobs quickly, and this third problem implied costs. Oversupplies of materials and indolence with time had been established as necessary lubricants in the economy for decades—so managers' reaction to basic shortages was delayed. For example, construction activity in the mid-1980s, as before, disrupted firms adjacent to building sites for much longer periods than were necessary; but now more space was needed. Building had suffered such a low priority for the three previous decades in

Shanghai, state construction companies lost the knack of conjuring structures out of the ground quickly, like mushrooms—as happens with great regularity in Hong Kong, Taipei, or Singapore (or Shanghai by the 1990s). Construction companies were official and paid no sanctions for being disruptively slow. Because of building and because of less reliable coal supplies, whole districts of Shanghai city periodically suffered "stopped electricity, stopped water, and stopped gas" (*ting dian, ting shui, ting qi*). In the first quarter of 1986 alone, losses for this reason in the metropolis were estimated at 71,560,000 yuan.[13]

A fourth difficulty was that real labor compensation declined, despite all the best proletarian intentions to keep it stable—and incentives for labor productivity demonstrably declined along with real pay. State cadres lacked money to give their workers, especially in contrast to the paymasters of collectives. Slogans, medals, and administrative orders could no longer replace hard cash. The year-end bonuses (*nianzhong jiang*) and material incentives of 1985 were less in Shanghai than in other cities—and labor productivity statistics at the beginning of 1986 showed a decrease.[14]

A fifth reason was that managers were disheartened because their economic environment left them no way to do their jobs well. Some simply resigned, to take more technical or limited-liability posts that offered a chance of success on the job. Like "guerrilla warriors," according to *Shanghai Economic Research,* they changed their positions as frequently as possible. They deemed it foolhardy to take blame for enterprise failures they knew they had no means of correcting. This pattern sped the decline of Shanghai's previously famous tradition of bold, risk-taking entrepreneurs. A theoretician might have expected the opposite result from reforms. General managerships of state companies in Shanghai, as distinct from more specialized expert posts, could not in this era attract talented incumbents. Propaganda about the need to increase the authority of managers, and even the explicit and extensive propaganda about the need to decrease the power of Party officials in factories, could not compensate for a lack of money, energy, and raw materials. The transition period, with both fixed and free prices, did not reverse the decline of Shanghai managerial culture that Maoists had begun earlier. On the contrary, the reforms ironically at first made this slippage worse.

A sixth reason for the mid-1980s crisis in Shanghai was that officials politically had to blame each other for structural faults caused by the traditionally high tax regime and bad national planning. Scapegoats were needed for production losses. Inspection commissioners and tax collectors tended to blame the managers of firms. If a factory head had successfully reformed a plant so that its production rose, its input shortages soon became more severe than in a lackadaisical plant that needed fewer materials. The successful manager was all the more likely to become a target of criticism. As a commentator pointed out, fruitless infighting severely harmed the "activism" of factory managers.

Because Shanghai was such an "important economic center," i.e. such a big taxpayer, the central government's ideas about it were exceptionally conservative. Although suggestions had often been made to cut costs by reducing the number of supervising "administrative companies," there had been practically no action on this.[15] The article that listed these problems proposed ways to solve them. First, it recommended a "management responsibility system" under which factory CCP committees would defer to managers on most decisions. Second, it advocated that firms should be accountable, assuming "economic responsibility" for profits and losses on which "there is no roof above and no floor below."[16] Third, it recommended macroeconomic policies to avoid restricting enterprises that could be profitable but lost money only because of irrational state pricing; the "one knife cuts" uniform policies in lending institutions might be replaced by different policies for factories that faced different external prices during the reform period. Fourth, this article called for serious reform of governmental supervising organs, not just a reshuffling of personnel into offices with new names but old styles, "changing the hot water but not the medicine."[17] In particular, supervising bureaus (*ju*) were asked to loosen their controls over subordinate companies (*gongsi*). Fifth, hiring and personnel were recommended under factory managers, even though that change would reduce the powers of Party committees.

A 1985 draft of the Enterprise Law, which got as far as the National People's Congress Standing Committee, mentioned no role at all for firms' Party committees. Some legislators argued that it was "not advisable" for government laws to define the role of the CCP. Also, this draft did not reconfirm local trade unions' leadership of workers' congresses.[18] More traditionalist laws were later passed, but these drafts show that reformers were prepared to go very far in restructuring management.

Many other policies were also mooted: Sales of shares could be allowed, labor could be authorized to move between jobs more easily, salaries and retirements could involve more incentives. The habit of discussing many policies, but then shelving them—could be reversed. The article listing all these difficulties averred that Jiangsu and Zhejiang had adopted more reform policies than Shanghai. They had accordingly progressed faster. (The main reason, which lay in Shanghai's even higher tax rates, was not mentioned.) Cures for the managerial "Shanghai sickness"—which was really in large part a central government sickness—might also involve expanding the responsibility of factory directors, increasing firms' freedom to hire contract labor, and lowering the power over factories of nonproductive supervisory bureaus.[19] Each of these policies threatened to reduce state imposts in the short term or to reduce the power of established cadres. Many such measures had to be adopted, but slowly because of political resistance from state economic bureaucrats.

"Wars" for Raw Materials

The inputs crisis cumulated over several years, and traditionally high inventories delayed its effect. Reforms by 1980 had already led to a "tea war," however, because many tea cooperatives in East China during the 1970s began processing local leaves rather than delivering them to state plants. Government economists still wrote plans for commodities such as tea leaves, but rural managers did not follow them. A business cycle, linked to the Paretan elite cycle of alternation between reformers and hard-liners, emerged in areas such as Shanghai where rural reforms were far advanced.

Shanghai's light industrial production increased by 10 percent yearly from 1979 to 1981, and this was the main reason for a concurrent annual rise of 2.3 percent in the city's industrial profits and taxes. But in the first ten months of 1982, the rate of growth in light industry halved. Textiles were especially hard hit, and in that year the production of cloth decreased by 3 percent. Profits and taxes went down by more than 10 percent. Many other parts of the country had "caught up" with Shanghai.[20] More important, they had caught on to the fact that the state could not easily punish all of them even for gross violations of materials delivery plans. The official explanation for the change in Shanghai was different, putting a positive spin on the same facts: Technical improvements in other provinces had created the basis for sharp competition with Shanghai products. Although the city won 49 percent of the first prizes in product fairs during 1980, in the next year it won only 41 percent, and in 1982, only 37 percent. The inland infrastructure for change had been accumulating for many years. The good news was that a partial collapse of central delivery plans had already inspired diversification in, and transfers of Shanghai technology to, other parts of Jiangnan.

Factory Materials Price Rises and Delivery Shortfall Amounts

The bad news was that Shanghai's own urban economy could no longer obtain its habitual supply of inputs. The number of Shanghai products under mandatory production quotas had to be allowed to drop in the mid-1980s, from 150 kinds of commodities in 1984 to only 37 types in 1987.[21] During the same period, the number of products for which city agencies required mandatory sales to each other also went down, from 53 to 23. The number of raw materials that were distributed on a mandatory basis under city plans likewise decreased, from 19 to 13. Even then, not all the mandates were fulfilled. Planners largely went out of business in the mid-1980s.

"Developing the commodity economy without commodities is a major vexation for many enterprises in Shanghai."[22] The gallows humor of the two irreverent journalists who wrote this was justified by facts. A 1985 survey of a large number of major Shanghai commodities showed that state plans could supply all needed raw materials for only 27 percent of them. The manufacturers of these could "still" garner "a certain profit." For another 18 percent, rising input costs meant profits lower than the plans foresaw, as well as "difficulties" in obtaining needed raw materials. For fully 55 percent of the surveyed products, factories could no longer process their more expensive inputs without losing money.[23]

Raw materials prices before the 1980s were generally low and stable, even when there were shortages. The unintended reforms made them high and volatile. The portion of all Shanghai factory inputs to be allocated by plan plummeted from about 70 percent to about 20 percent in the mid-1980s crisis—not because planners wished this drop, but simply because they could not deliver the goods.[24]

Shanghai's textile industry reported having to fight "big wars" to get rabbit hair, wool, ramie, silk cocoons, and cotton.[25] The whole of Jiangnan, in 1986–87, delivered fewer silk cocoons to Shanghai than before, because Jiangsu and Zhejiang were setting up more of their own local mills. Planners were unable to maintain quality standards, even for mandated quantities that were delivered. When the mulberry areas delivered cocoons, they sent some that had not been inspected, in which the worms were still alive. The water content of such cocoons is higher, so they are heavier—and the quota is by weight. But the worms are still spinning inside, and they contain less silk. Jiangsu and Zhejiang cocoon sellers in the mid-1980s paid more attention to the batches sent to new factories in their own provinces, perhaps because these plants were better situated to complain when deliveries were bad.

Silk is a quintessential Jiangnan product, but the government's centralized companies paid farmers little for cocoons and woven silk, while charging much higher prices to foreign buyers. Peasants in East China found ways around this and engaged in "wild and erratic price rises by illegal silk traders, especially in Jiangsu and Zhejiang."[26] Although export demand for Chinese silk reportedly remained higher than supply, the government's desire to control and extract from this market disrupted the flow of goods. The rise of inland plants raised national demand for materials. China's total raw silk production by 1988 could meet only 70 percent of all the new and old factories' total needs.[27]

Xinjiang and Mongolia did not deliver as much wool to Shanghai as they had previously done. Apparently to ensure wool supplies, Mayor Jiang Zemin himself in April 1986 led a Shanghai trade group to Inner Mongolia. A return delegation came to Shanghai in late 1987, visiting several firms including the Shanghai Leather Shoes Factory, which uses Mongolian hides, and discussing "several projects to develop raw and semi-finished materials industries."[28] But in the few years after 1984, when the prices of many commodities were allowed to float, the system of markets-by-arrangement tended to break down.

The central government's ability to supply Shanghai with raw materials decreased significantly after the mid-1980s reform, when the prices of more inputs were allowed to float and the local guarantee system was expanded in many provinces. Of all the resources for steel making distributed under the state plan in various years of the 1980s, as Table 1.2–1 shows, the percentage Shanghai obtained from state plans dropped dramatically. There were especially sharp decreases in 1985 and 1987.

During the first half of 1986, as one analysis put it, the "Shanghai disease"

Table 1.2-1

Percentage of Raw Materials for Steel Making in Shanghai Allocated by State Plans

Year	Percent
1981	86
1982	78
1983	73
1984	75
1985	58
1986	54
1987	34

Note and source: Shanghai jingji nianjian, 1988 (Shanghai Economic Yearbook, 1988), Xiao Jun et al., eds. (Shanghai: Shanghai Renmin Chuban She, 1988), p. 84. "Raw materials for steel making" are *gangcai ziyuan*.

brought a depression to local processing industries. The growth of the city's production during that time was lower than during the same period of 1985, and much lower than all of China's. In industry, the national growth rate during the first five months of 1986 was 4.8 percent; in Shanghai, it was only 1.8 percent, all of which was attributable to large factories in Baoshan and Jinshan alone. During some of these months, Shanghai's total industrial growth was negative.[29]

Domestic sales of Shanghai's industrial products took a significant drop in some months of 1986. Clothing sales went down 3 to 4 percent.[30] Also, the portion of industrial income in the local government's budget plunged. This local recession affected collective industries more than state-owned ones, if the reporting on the state firms was complete. The causes of such disasters were many, and the results could be justified in reformist terms. Reforms were the short-term cause of most of them.

Fulfillment of delivery obligations under the "responsibility system" had been massively "impeded." The quality of products in sixty-one companies was declared below par, and twenty-seven of these were given "red light" warnings.[31] In a survey of many industrial finished products, 36 percent were substandard. But the biggest change from the previous pattern in Shanghai was the shortfall of materials deliveries.

Shanghai factories had to find more of their own materials, especially if their tax contributions were relatively unimportant to the government. Plants under the city's Handicrafts Bureau by 1983 already had to find 43 percent of their nonferrous metals and 60 percent of their steel.[32] By 1985, the citywide situation—counting all state corporations—was as shown in Table 1.2–2.

Table 1.2-2

Shortages of Materials in Shanghai, 1985

	Requirements (millions of metric tons)	Planned allocation %	Shortage %
Cement	3.50	51	49
Steel	2.43	60	40
Lumber	1.50	60	40
Ferrous metals	0.21	69	31
Chemical inputs	3.04	76	24

Note and Source: The cement allocation includes both central and local planned deliveries; apparently the other materials were all centrally regulated. Tabulated from narrative material in *Shanghai jingji* (Shanghai Economy), January 1985, p. 3; percentages are calculated. "Requirements" may be somewhat overstated by managers, but the degrees of shortage reported in the mid-1980s represent something about an economic problem then or about more open expression then, ot both.

Table 1.2-3

Sources of Shanghai National Income

	1980 percentage	1986 percentage
Gov't (central & local)	76	58
Enterprises	9	18
Individuals	16	24
Total	c. 100	100

Note and Source: Note that "Shanghai national income" (*guomin shouru*) does not include the output of a few large plants that are in the city but are completely managed by central ministries. The portions allocated to individuals seem low in this report; not all the reasons for this are clear, but the trends of change mean more than the reported figures. Xu Zhenliang, "Shanghai caizheng shouru 'huapo' de xiankuang, chengyin ji qi duice" (The "Slide" of Shanghai's Financial Income: Situation, Reasons, and Countermeasures), in *Caijing yanjiu* (Financial and Economic Studies), March 1988, p. 21.

Both individuals and local enterprises increased their share of Shanghai's income, at the expense of government, during the 1980–86 period covered by Table 1.2–3. This was the crucial midpoint of reforms in which change was fastest. State profits and taxes for each 100 yuan of fixed capital in Shanghai's state industrial sector declined from 81 to 45 yuan.[33]

By 1985, many managers' lives in Shanghai became difficult for the first time in years. No longer did external bureaucracies "distribute" materials and credit to them; no longer could they ignore whether their products were sold. The cost of negotiating with superiors had, before reforms, been lower than the cost of fending independently. The hard world of upstream and downstream markets appealed to economists, reforming politicians, and intellectuals cheering from the sidelines. For Shanghai managers, calling for efficiency was less important than providing raw materials. Beijing leaders had allowed other provinces to have a more gradual adjustment to markets. Shanghai still had relatively high tax burdens, and few sizeable autonomous enterprises could operate openly in the metropolis even as late as 1988.

The cost per 100 yuan of industrial output that Shanghai had to pay in 1987 remained fairly high, at 76 yuan for all factors.[34] Centrally mandated prices, which had been enforced essentially by police power, had mostly ended.[35] These mandates ultimately required state coercion for enforcement, and their defeat must be traced to similarly effective and coercive networks that were local. As the PRC anthropologist Fei Xiaotong admitted, "Managers in rural enterprises use some unsuitable methods to get what they need." He offered a reason: "This may be necessary because we have not yet established a market from which they can meet demand."[36]

An estimated 590 million yuan of additional funds were needed in Shanghai's fifteen main municipal bureaus for materials, industry, and commerce during 1986, because of the inflation of input prices during the twelve-month period.[37] This increment of costs for inflation alone was about 10 percent of total expenditures in Shanghai in 1986.[38]

The situation thereafter became worse. By 1988, state and market prices for factors diverged so much that, for example, a metric ton of aluminum officially cost 4,800 yuan, but the market price (at which it could actually be obtained) was 12,000 yuan. Timber planks of a standard width at the state price were supposed to cost 90 yuan per square meter, but the actual and market price was 500 yuan. A ton of coal was still planned to cost 50 yuan, but it could not be had ordinarily for less than 110 yuan.[39]

Local jurisdictions outside Shanghai have sometimes required "export licenses" for their materials. Authorities in Inner Mongolia held on to their cashmere for local weaving: "Unless you sack us, you can't have it!" A Zhejiang local planning committee attempted to prevent Jiangsu mills from buying raw silk so that it could be processed in the places it was grown. Similarly, some jurisdictions inhibited imports of manufactured goods. Shanghai bicycles could sometimes be wholesaled only on the condition, imposed by inland authorities, that the purchaser also buy a quantity of local goods. Tractors from Changzhou, in Jiangsu near Shanghai, could not be registered for licenses in some places, where gasoline could thus not legally be bought for them.[40] Shanghai delta managers had to find better means of dealing with inland places, whether or not such agreements served state interests.

Shanghai Investment Inland

There is nothing unusual about cosmopolitan centers financing raw materials extraction for their own industries. At the height of China's revolution this practice was nationalized, so the central government largely paid for major projects such as the mid-1950s heavy industries that started production in 1958 or the Great Third Front inland investments of 1964–71. Vertical integration in Shanghai firms by the mid-1970s remained extensive, especially in heavy industries.

Of all firms managed in the city under the First Ministry of Machine Building during 1976 above the district level, 80 percent ran subsidiaries that extracted their raw materials. Some were praised for being "large and complete" (*da er quan*). Others were medium-sized or small—but just as "complete" in terms of their vertical integration. A ministry survey found that two-thirds of these companies made the capital goods they used. Under Mao, Shanghai managers had developed the habit of trying to leave nothing to chance.[41] The rise of markets, with chancy fluctuations, began to knock this comfortable but inefficient system into the brave new world of competition.

Materials shortages would surely have caused more Shanghai investments to migrate inland during the 1970s if the city's provincial politicians appointed from Beijing had not been committed to keeping Shanghai's central remittances much higher than those of anywhere else in the country. Fiscal "slippages," which were delayed in Shanghai until the 1980s, partly reflected socialist planners' realization that the metropolitan economy had to strengthen its sources of supply. By 1982–83, Shanghai invested heavily in the extractive industries of Sichuan, Shanxi, Shaanxi, and Anhui. Municipal planners had long wanted to do this, to ensure Shanghai's raw materials supplies, but central planners had always preferred to veto such initiatives in favor of investing directly through their own ministries. The reason why Shanghai was able to make such investments by the 1980s was the center's budget deficit.[42]

A major agency for garnering raw materials from other parts of China was the Shanghai Joint Development Corporation (Shanghai Lianhe Fazhan Gongsi), which was established in 1984. Three years later, it had set up twenty-seven materials production enterprises in other provinces. Many of these brought metals and construction materials to Shanghai, and investments were made with places as far afield as Qinghai and Ningxia to bring materials such as aluminum. Connections with inland areas were run through state corporations, which became more independent as mere mandates could no longer deliver supplies. By the end of 1985, Shanghai textile industries had established almost 1,100 joint projects in the ten suburban counties. Only 5 percent were "joint enterprises," but 50 percent were "cooperative processing points."[43] These were like traditional companies for out-contracting (*waibao*). Together they contributed only 8 percent of Shanghai's textile output, but they both dispersed technology to the counties and gave urban plants surer supplies of cotton.

Inland investment in factories whose products came through the city consumed over a billion yuan of Shanghai capital in 1987 alone. Metropolitan companies in many fields had no alternative to investing elsewhere.[44] A 1988 report said that Shanghai had forty "production materials trade centers" in other provinces.[45] Shanghai was not alone in competing for materials from rural networks increasingly unwilling to part with them at low prices or without side benefits. Other cities did the same thing. When a thermal power plant was needed in Nanjing, local banks successfully issued bonds to finance it, on condition that the bondholders would enjoy priority in buying the plant's electricity after it was built.[46] Vertical ties often remained almost as strong as in the planned economy, but in reforms more of them were arranged directly between localities and fewer benefited the central state.

Shanghai in 1987 started 88 new projects in other provinces to obtain raw materials. The total number of major subsidiaries for this purpose was reported at 667, and total Shanghai investment there was 1.05 billion yuan. Under the contracts for these projects, Shanghai was scheduled to obtain 68 kinds of raw materials with a total value of 3.5 billion yuan.[47] These estimates assumed the prices could be fixed into the future.

Sometimes inland places took money from Shanghai firms to raise raw materials production—but later kept the inputs to process themselves. The central state was unable to prevent this practice, even in its most profitable industry, which is tobacco. The Shanghai Cigarette Company helped finance production in a Henan tobacco-growing area that was to send all its crop to the metropolis. The quality of shipments turned out to be low. When the leaves were graded, Shanghai assessors deemed one-quarter of them unfit to use. The Shanghai company refused to buy the bad leaves. But in the reform period, inputs markets were seller's markets. The Henan suppliers, apparently threatening to send their whole crop to new cigarette companies elsewhere, succeeded in raising the price the Shanghai company had to pay for the good leaves, to cover their losses from the non-sale of the bad ones.[48]

A Shanghai aluminum processing company in 1986 similarly invested 6.7 million yuan in a far-western Qinghai company, which signed a contract guaranteeing the Shanghai investor 7.8 percent of the aluminum production at a set price as part of its dividend. By 1988, however, this Shanghai-Qinghai cooperation had failed. The inland mine delivered only three-fifths of the agreed amount, and the Shanghai buyer had to pay a higher price.[49] A 1988 journal reported that Shanghai had put 920 million yuan into 599 materials supply projects of other provinces in order to obtain various kinds of inputs from there.[50] Many of these ventures succeeded, but others did not.

The Paper Crunch as an Example

Before 1987, one ton of newsprint in Shanghai had cost 900 yuan; by late 1988, it cost 3,400 yuan. At least one supplementary publication of the *Liberation*

Daily was temporarily suspended in November 1988 solely because there was no paper on which to print it.[51] The *Wenhui News* in early 1987 had a supply of paper on hand that would last seven months, but by the worst period of 1988, this had been reduced to a supply for just two days.

Editors commented that the situation was very "tense" (*jinzhang*). Distinguished journalists, in high Party posts, were not just worried about the paper shortage; they were apoplectic about it. They faced a real possibility that their editions would fail to appear merely for lack of paper. Journalists are normally an articulate lot, and this situation sent them through the roof. No shortage has been better reported in Shanghai than the lack of newsprint. In May 1988, a metric ton of paper was supposed to cost 1,550 yuan at the state-fixed price. But paper mills in southern China were then charging 200 yuan more than that price to their distributors. And to Shanghai journals, newsprint was unavailable below 2,500 yuan per ton.[52] The market was also volatile because paper in different localities had very different prices. Northern paper (mostly from the northeast) cost 1,550 yuan; in the south (where the main producers were Guangdong, Fujian, and Jiangxi) it cost 1,750 yuan; and the market price in Shanghai and many other cities was 2,500 yuan.

A paper supplier in Fujian province demanded foreign exchange for providing newsprint—which came from Chinese, not foreign, trees. Under state plans, convertible currency was supposed to be used normally under close supervision only to purchase imports, but this Fujian paper company got what it asked.[53] Nonetheless, most of the price increases were not just the result of paper mills' greed. Wood and labor costs had risen sharply, especially in South China. The price there of a ton of lumber for paper in early 1988 was about 400 yuan—between two and three times the 1985 price. Even at the 1988 prices for newsprint, mills made low profits or could claim to suffer losses. Absorption of labor in more lucrative industries, combined with a long-term ecological decline in supplies of wood and sharp rises in prices for paper-processing chemicals, lay behind this inflation. The only reason why paper prices had remained low until the mid-1980s was that planners had been able to commandeer all these factors, essentially by police methods, without any serious attention to scarcity values. This system had served the profits of Shanghai state industries until it collapsed.[54] The one side of the coin was higher prices; the other was lower coercive capacity in the central state as compared to local networks.

During the first third of 1988, all of China produced 28 percent less newsprint than in the same period in the previous year. Yields in Guangdong, Fujian, and Jiangxi were all down, and some mills closed for lack of wood. The estimated 1988 demand for paper nationwide was 600,000 metric tons, but the rate of production was only 450,000 (one-quarter less).[55] China's average per-capita consumption of newsprint at this time was only 0.48 kg (as compared to a world average then of 6 kg, including an average of about 20 kg in developed countries). None of China's public newspapers, and reportedly only a few of the limited-circulation media, bear any resemblance to the heft of the *New York Times;* so Shanghai editors opined they were not demanding too much in asking for budgets to finance their newsprint.

Some Chinese industries are spendthrift with resources, but others including journalism, are abstemious. Aside from Shanghai's *Liberation Daily,* only three other eight-page newspapers were published in China in the late 1980s: the *People's Daily,* the *Bright Daily,* and the *Tianjin Daily.* Circulation of the *Liberation Daily* reached a peak in the early 1980s, standing at 9.3 million in 1984. But by 1987, this figure had dropped to 8.5 million; it fell to 8 million by the next year. Part of the reason was a price increase needed to buy enough newsprint.

The main official response to the paper shortage was a plea for recycling. The Shanghai Paper Company in 1989 "had to buy 140,000 tons of pulp from China and abroad . . . and also made use of 230,000 tons of waste paper as raw material for pulp." In a recent previous year, the company had obtained 83,000 tons of pulp from the state, but by 1989 this amount was down to 17,000 tons.[56] Waste paper became the main source of raw material for these Shanghai factories. An apologist claimed that buyers from outside the city "stole" scraps before these could reach the city's mills:

> Paper factories are waiting for materials, and many have to close. Most paper recycling stations in Shanghai were established by educated youths, private households, welfare organizations, or street offices. But recently, paper businessmen from Jiangsu and Zhejiang came to Shanghai with huge amounts of money to buy waste from these paper recycling units. They pay in cash, at a high price. Their business is very smooth. They collect waste paper during the day but transport it out of Shanghai at night for sale to local paper factories in Jiangsu or Zhejiang.[57]

The chief editor of *Wenhui News* in 1988 said his journal should really be eight pages, not just four. The only reason for its size was a simple lack of paper. Importing from sources such as Canada or Alaska, which sold to Japanese publishers, was out of the question. *Wenhui bao* is one of China's most distinguished newspapers, read by educated people in many cities throughout the country, but it earned practically no foreign exchange. The editor frankly hoped that Chinese relations with Russia (then still Soviet) might improve, but his reason was totally apolitical. He was interested in any means to get paper. Russian suppliers had some, and he had to find a way around PRC foreign exchange controls. The largest forests on the horizon were in Siberia, where it was possible to barter.

In-Kind Exchanges: Meeting Shortages Without the Politics of Inflation

"Compensation trade" (*buchang maoyi*) was the elegant official name for barter. This method was extensively used in interprovincial trade in scarce goods. For example, by the mid-1980s, Shanghai was sending bicycles and washing machines to Jilin in China's northeast, in exchange for paper pulp.[58] Barter arose because factories needed raw materials that the plan no longer supplied, but it also arose for a second reason: Consumer durables in the 1980s were often priced by state regulations at rates lower than they could actually fetch from consumers—now including many rich peasants and rural industrialists. The price fixers did not keep up with the boom, and they feared the reaction of urban state employees if they let the retail costs of consumer durables soar along with demand from nouveaux riches in rural areas that were politically less sensitive than cities. When factories traded manufactures in kind directly for inputs, they could maintain their production and employment.

The main political danger was urban inflation, and with barter there are no monetary prices. The breakdown of planning encouraged economic expansion through barter—a method that by the mid-1980s could further postpone the effects of shortages on prices, even after coercive means to hide those effects had failed. So the government developed a major official interest in legitimating barter trade. Nonmonetized exchange had purely cosmetic attractions for many state agencies. Apparently some cadres thought this method of exchange was very socialist, a way to avoid the cash nexus.

Exchanges in kind rather than money were also given cachet by their use in China's international trade companies, for which they lessened the need to obtain official approvals to spend hard currencies. But compensation trade mainly grew within China, whenever buyers needed goods and had the physical wherewithal to obtain them. This system seemed natural because ration quotas (along with money) had long been required to obtain goods. It seemed necessary after allocations by fiat were no longer effective to get commodities delivered.

Barter arrangements became so common that state agencies published broad, suggested rates of exchange for them—even though most such trades were not actually planned. For example, one metric ton of steel was supposed to be exchanged for 16 to 25 tons of cement, or 2 to 5 cubic meters of lumber, or 2 to 3 tons of pig iron, or 1.6 to 3 tons of iron salvage, or one-quarter to one-third ton of copper.[59] Similar barter exchange rates were also officially published for aluminum, rubber, fertilizers, and East Wind brand trucks, all-terrain vehicles, and cars produced by the joint enterprise with Volkswagen. These rates were indicative only; they left margins for bargaining. These quasi-prices confirmed that planners should still have a say, even after planning had signally collapsed. Each province regularly published lists of materials it had for exchange, as well as lists of materials that it needed. "Adjustment meetings" (*tiaoji hui*) were convened in many jurisdictions to circulate the lists and conclude barter deals.

One of the logical difficulties of such a system is that the bits of information necessary to make it work multiply geometrically as the number and variety of products expand to resemble those needed in the real world. For 1987, the State Statistical Bureau at the central level published a matrix of nonmonetary prices to be used in barter. This valued just 10 industrial goods in terms of just 21 agricultural products. Even if issues of product qualities, seasons, and transport values are ignored, the exercise already implied an array of 210 barter "prices" (compared to only 31 prices that would have been needed if money had been used).[60] The amount of information that must be processed soars if barter is the mode of trade in a diversified economy.

Money, as an institution, has many well-known drawbacks. The spectacle of a major modern government trying to run part of an economy without money, however, soon suggests that on the whole money is not a bad idea.[61] The value of this invention is that it concisely summarizes a complex situation.[62] Compensation trade became especially unwieldy when it involved the transfer of nontangible assets, such as technology or services. Shanghai was relatively rich in these.

The city's main items for barter were consumer durables, however, and it engaged in extensive in-kind trade. By 1987, about 15 million yuan worth of bicycles, refrigerators, and cars that Shanghai sent to various inland places were in partial exchange for 330 million yuan worth of raw materials. The city government mainly wanted to reduce the prices of rural inputs that came from areas it could no longer control, while keeping the prices of processed goods from state factories high.

To some extent, this relationship can be summarized in industry-agriculture terms of trade. These moved during midreforms in a direction more favorable to agriculture and less favorable to industries. These terms can be quantified by choosing a single year (e.g., 1987) and then showing the higher rate of inflation in prices of agricultural versus industrial goods compared to various earlier years. Specifically, the 1987 purchase prices of agricultural subsidiary products were 130 percent above those of 1965, 122 percent since 1970, 99 percent since 1978, 52 percent since 1980, and 19 percent since 1985.[63] On the other hand, 1987 rural retail prices of industrial products were only 12 percent over those of 1965, 18 percent over 1970, 20 percent over 1978, 19 percent over 1980, and just 8 percent over 1985 levels. So the price rise had been greater for agricultural than for industrial goods.

Shanghai in each of these years was at the extreme low end, among all provinces, for the cheapness of the agricultural raw materials it was able to buy.[64] It had China's lowest provincial index of prices for purchases of agricultural subsidiary products. This situation arose because of continuing state subsidies to keep those prices low—perhaps not to benefit the city, but to maximize that part of the government's fiscal revenue that depended on Shanghai's imports of cheap farm-produced industrial materials.

Shanghai also had the highest provincial ratio in each of these years for the value of the industrial goods it produced divided by the value of the agricultural goods it purchased. The terms of trade were such that the real 1987 value of agricultural raw materials in 1965 prices that Shanghai bought per yuan of its industrial sales in those prices was only .65 yuan; for 1970 prices, .69 yuan; for

1978, .76 yuan; for 1980, .95 yuan; and for 1985 prices, 1.19 yuan. So only by the mid-1980s did the terms of trade turn against Shanghai state-owned industries. But when they did so, the change was sharp. The planning system, which had used the city's light industries as an instrument of the state budget, mostly broke down then.

Beijing and Tianjin, the other two province-level units that are most similar to Shanghai, were near the national average (usually below it) for all these years in the value of agricultural raw materials that they bought per unit of value of their industrial product. But Shanghai was always highest in the country, until the mid-1980s reforms decentralized trade patterns.

Imports and New Sales Channels

A *Liberation Daily* columnist pointed out in 1988 that Shanghai's economic troubles could not be blamed solely on a lack of materials. If the city could raise the prices of its own products, it would have enough money to buy inputs. Or if the city could dispose of its own products by barter, the problem would also be solved.[65] But national plans constrained retail product prices, which were relatively easy to monitor, for years longer than they constrained factor prices, which were harder to check.

Protectionist plans also constrained factor imports from abroad. During Shanghai's historical period of fastest growth, ending in 1937, the city had taken materials from anyplace in the world where the price and quality were best. This was a distant unpleasant memory for patriotic socialist planners, but rural industrialization had reduced their domestic supplies within China. So in 1984 and 1985, shortages were so great that Shanghai spent about half of its local foreign exchange reserves to import raw materials.

Local bankers had a proposal to relieve this hemorrhaging of reserves: More credit for Shanghai loans would have allowed factories to pay for domestic materials (and would have encouraged China's producers to create more of them), so that fewer raw imports would be needed.[66] But to avoid inflation, this would have required real subsidies from Beijing. The central government was more in the habit of taking money from Shanghai than giving to it. When raw materials became often unavailable to Shanghai firms from previous domestic sources at sufficiently low prices, many sought them from abroad, even though the rules mandating firms to balance their foreign exchange inflow and outflow militated against this.

The rules against buying foreign products bent under pressure from the mid-1980s factors crisis. Ninety-four percent of Shanghai's 1986 imports were "means of production," mostly raw materials. In 1987, this figure rose to 98 percent. That year, the total cost was US $1.79 billion, of which $1.75 billion went for "physical materials." Over nine tenths of the total went to expendable raw inputs, not to capital (including machines, software, and licenses) that could embody new technology. Only $85 million went to capital—just 5 percent of the total foreign exchange cost.[67] Progress in using foreign exchange to develop new technologies in Shanghai was less than it would have been if the need for raw materials had not been urgent.

The shortages also led to new institutions, especially brokerage firms, which sought buyers, markets, and "stable sources of materials" throughout China and around the globe. By early 1988, Shanghai's Taicang Road was one of many streets on which middlemen conducted such trade.[68] The central city's most reliable suppliers were its closest ones, in the suburbs. In August 1987, the Shanghai Materials Bureau organized "development companies" that served as brokers or intermediaries for finding inputs.[69] It also set up "materials trading centers," as well as a center for foreign sellers of industrial materials. The bureau's Party school established training courses for managers in suburban counties to help them establish companies that could provide more agricultural products to the city. Shanghai's ten counties supplied to the inner city about one-quarter more, by value, in 1987 as in the previous year.

During the late 1980s, "exchange fairs" offered another way for Shanghai firms to obtain raw materials. In 1987, for example, such a meeting drew together the "production materials service companies" from practically all of China's other provinces; in three days, the value of trade was more than 1 billion yuan.[70] These relatively free markets in factors helped, but they did not solve all problems.

The Shanghai Electric Cable Factory in mid-1988 was daily losing 400,000 yuan because of a shortage of copper. Part of the staff was laid off for three months. The average cut in their bonuses and "floating wages" was 30 percent.[71] Inflation and rising tastes for consumption, however, meant these employees were "unwilling" to become unemployed. Of this factory's total estimated copper requirement for the second half of 1988, the state plan was scheduled to provide only 22 percent—and the planners could not "guarantee" even half of this small portion. Shanghai factory managers often overestimated their needs as a bargaining ploy, but by mid-1988, this ruse had been carried very far. It would almost surely have been more profitable to hold copper in inventory than to process it. During the previous year, the price of copper had risen 86 percent.[72]

The manager of this factory offered large bonuses for any of his employees who could line up more copper. The profits and taxes that the cable plant was able to remit in 1986 and 1987 were 200 million yuan; but the value of the factory's total product in the first half of 1988 was 178 million. The manager of this cable plant had a problem beyond his control and raised questions in public about whether it should not be possible to expand the powers of large and medium enterprises that lacked raw materials so that at least some of them might become parts of a "special factory system" (*techang zhi*), authorized to import raw materials so that they could "struggle to have rice to eat" (*zheng fan chi*).

In light industries' spending, more than four-fifths of the inflation at this time came from rising materials costs.[73] In thirty-one light industrial firms in the middle of 1988, production costs went up 14 percent over those of the previous year. In some product lines, the inflation that year was over 50 percent. Labor costs were relatively stable, although expenditures to subsidize workers' food rose. Managers openly admitted that public discussion of future housing reforms (involving higher rents) scared them. Whatever the economic merits of this idea, they had no spare money to pay for it.

The main flow of factors was still out of Shanghai, because prices remained low there for the items that could still be bought. The factory that made prize-winning White Cat washing powder, mostly sold in Shanghai, began to lose money in the mid-1980s because raw materials costs were up, but the manager could not raise the product price. The right to approve any inflation, even in the price of washing powder, was in Beijing, not Shanghai. Fully ten months of intensive negotiations and frequent travel to Beijing were needed, in order to get a small price rise of 0.40 yuan per box.[74] Buying agents from other areas quickly discovered they could send delegations to Shanghai to purchase the city's products at low cost. Low-price rules, enforced in Shanghai to prevent wage inflation for heavily taxed state firms there, were simply ignored elsewhere.

So trade was fueled by official attempts to keep Shanghai's consumer prices lower than those in other places. This trade had several aspects: First, it tended to boost the volume of goods that Shanghai reported sending inland. Between 1986 and 1987, the outflow of all products from Shanghai to other provinces increased 64 percent. Shipments to Guangdong (especially Shenzhen) and Fujian were very great, because prices were highest there. For example, Shanghai's Phoenix and Everlasting bicycles could be sold in Shenzhen for 350 yuan—double the Shanghai retail price. Garment prices were also several times higher in Guangdong. Trade between Shanghai and other parts of the PRC during reforms actually flowed in both directions. The combination of relatively high Shanghai wages (at least among employees in the state-owned system) and high profits from volume in shops selling commodities imported from elsewhere meant that the portion of goods sold in Shanghai but produced elsewhere also rose sharply. Part of the increase was caused by state-fixed price differences between different places in China.

A second aspect of the trade increase was that an outflow of many Shanghai goods created shortages in the city's own markets. Speculative profits from official price differentials were enormous. If goods could be bought at official low prices in the city but then be sold to eager buyers there or elsewhere on a free market, the trader could become enormously rich. A popular saying was "If you want to make money, run to Shanghai."[75] In order to slow the loss of goods so that Shanghai's own demand could be met, the municipality set up inspection stations at its borders.

Domestic exports from Shanghai of grain, cigarettes, pork, and sugar in bulk were illegalized. These items were all supposed to be kept less expensive in the city than inland. Inspection stations proliferated; on one road leading out of the city, a truck would have to pass through seventeen of them. But the incentives to smuggle were great. For example, during April 1988, the price of rice was 0.15 yuan per Chinese pound (*jin*) in Shanghai; but next door in Jiangsu, it was twice as much. Sporadically the state admitted it could no longer effectively control prices; so it had to authorize inflation in 1988. During the first three months of that year, the prices of more than three hundred products in the city were "adjusted," all upward, on average more than 20 percent. Some rose by half. Included were the prices of soap, salt, shoes, raincoats, thermoses, and many other staples and items for daily use.[76]

Very basic consumer goods (especially staple foods, housing, and transport) were the main items still under state pricing. Capital and raw materials markets, where enterprises had to deal, became more free than those in which ordinary urban residents had to deal. State pricing in 1978 had applied to 188 agricultural products—but by 1988, the number was reduced to just three. Among consumer durables, 392 were subject to fixed prices in 1978—but by 1988, only 46 were controlled. Among capital goods by 1988, 80 percent (by total value) were priced by the market.[77] The reason for continued price controls for basic food, housing, and transport was political and evident: The government wanted to avoid wage increases and urban unrest.

Shortages of other consumer goods became rife. A city leader averred that Shanghai people often "heard about raising production but did not see much buying." The mayor himself complained that "Shanghai people can't buy Shanghai products." Rules mandating low prices in the city gave companies great incentives to sell elsewhere. A 1988 newspaper admitted that fixed rates for Shanghai products outside the city were at least 15 percent higher than in the city—and for illegal trade, the difference was greater. Shanghai's contribution to China was not just money, but also goods. This was true of consumer products, and it was even more true of "industrial enterprise commodities" sold to units elsewhere. Exports from Shanghai of these items rose 60 percent between 1986 and 1987 alone, not because of much higher production but because Shanghai factories lacked the money to buy.[78]

Shanghai, which trades widely throughout the nation, has many east-west streets named after Chinese cities and north-south streets bearing the names of provinces. A 1988 article, alluding to this pattern (which is not unique to Shanghai), said it was particularly appropriate there. The metropolis was still economically central to China as a whole.[79] Four-fifths of Shanghai's raw materials in the mid-1980s came from other provinces, and Shanghai was a "locomotive" and "processing factory" for the whole country.[80] Also, as the article reported, for every 10 yuan of production in Shanghai, the state in 1988 still received 8 yuan in profits and taxes. This report is like many others from the city, even though they may overestimate the high imposts there. One-sixth of the total revenue of the Chinese government still came from Shanghai. Local people could rightfully argue that their city was trying to be loyally Chinese, not separate from the rest of the country.[81]

Non-Shanghai Interests Among Shanghai Managers

When Shanghai firms did not receive from inland places the materials for which they had contracted, this may in some cases not have been a crucial worry to factory managers. Shanghai cadres sometimes had personal connections with inland places that benefited from such arrangements. If the high bureaucracy cared for Shanghai firms only as tax farms, managers might have little compunction about taking a similar view. By the middle and late 1980s, they could get permission from embarrassed procurement officials in municipal bureaus to sign almost any deal with inland places that promised materials—whether or not that locality would actually deliver. When these bargains in practice only worked to the advantage of other East China places where the managers had personal ties, these cadres might more willingly bear the problems for their plants back in the city. They were not, under earlier socialist planning norms, supposed to be ultimately responsible for lining up their factory inputs anyway.

That approach could not, however, solve Shanghai's problems. Also, some entrepreneurs in the municipality were not closely associated with other places in Jiangnan (or with other places that might help them, or that they could help). Managers in Shanghai's suburban counties were often in this position if they needed raw materials from outside their own jurisdictions. No effective legal means were available to compel jurisdictions outside Shanghai to send "compensating" materials on time. Contracts specified delivery dates, but there was no real sanction against defaulters who failed to meet these schedules. In the suburbs, five Shanghai counties had signed compensation trade contracts outside the municipality for 400,000 tons of cement by June 1986, but only 36,000 tons actually came—less than one-tenth of the total due. Three counties had signed compensation trade agreements for steel products, but their factories received only 14 percent of the steel for which they had paid.[82] Inland suppliers usually claimed this was merely delay, not default; in actuality, they found buyers able to pay higher prices elsewhere. They could put off fulfillment of their contracts indefinitely, and this was hard to distinguish from not fulfilling them at all. If high Shanghai politicians had major interests in Beijing, and evidence from their career paths suggests many of them did, then local Shanghai factory managers who served places elsewhere in Jiangnan did nothing unprecedented.

Hepatitis as a Spur to Reform in 1988

Random external shocks could help stimulate institutional change, and this happened in Shanghai with a major outbreak of hepatitis A at the beginning of 1988. The reformers in this case were a batch of contaminated clams. The medical aspects of this epidemic are treated in a later chapter, and they are noteworthy because the hepatitis spread quickly. The important point now is the effect on industry. Shanghai's total output was 17 percent less in February than in January.[83]

It had been clear to central politicians for some time that Shanghai's function as their most reliable tax base had suffered "slippage" (*huapo*). The hepatitis epidemic in Shanghai certainly solved no problems, but by exacerbating them, it led to lower tax remittances and more public discussion of Shanghai's future. At about the time of this event, the Cabinet (also called the State Council) in practice enforced a new approach to raw material shortages. Rather than trying to restore whole plans, it set priorities. In effect, the plan was to be followed for those priorities, many of which involved activities remitting profits to Beijing ministries. For other activities, the plan could be underfulfilled.

First, "key factories" were identified, as were the main materials they lacked—and the State Council proclaimed the state plan should hold as regards these particular factories and supplies. Second, special priority was to be given to all electrical products. Third, the Council issued the norm that materials departments ought to stress coordinating rationed supplies for the production of specialized products. Fourth, the Council advocated free trade for other products. The most basic inputs (27 of them) were to fall under "mandatory planned management."[84] Another larger set of products (496 of them) was handled under "indicative planning," which in fact did not involve much planning at all but legitimated free trade, horizontal and dubiously enforceable purchase contracts, or else markets that could be entered by designated traders only.

The State Cabinet's policy was in principle clear, because it distinguished different classes of commodities that were or were not subject to free trade. But it was in practice very difficult to enforce, because products on different lists were used together as inputs to production. Many of the twenty-seven full-plan materials were inputs to the making of downstream products that were less controlled. Inland authorities often set up factories to make unplanned products, and the planned materials often had low set prices, so that high authorities had big troubles ensuring their supply to Shanghai. Instead, low-priced factors tended to be processed in the administrative districts that extracted them. By making highly varied rules for large groups of different products, the State Council in practice gave traders greater leeway to do as they wished.

Factory managers had every interest in avoiding the task of negotiating for raw materials in these volatile markets. Bureaucrats in the corporations that "supervised" factories nonetheless pressed plant managers to take charge of purchasing and selling, because such operations had become risky. These supervisors' own jobs, however, had been ultimately justified by such work. Central ministry officials managed to shift some of the risk to city ones, but factory managers had no reason to take such responsibility until they were given the financial freedom to pay market prices. Shanghai's tax burden obviated that chance.

By 1988, 30 to 40 percent of all Shanghai's industrial materials in many fields were still supposed to come through the central government, often through municipal bureaus (*ju*) and large municipal holding companies (*gongsi*). These "higher-level" (*shangji*) offices often needed to scramble on free markets for inputs that central authorities had failed to deliver.[85] When remittance of funds to Beijing decreased, as it did temporarily because of hepatitis in 1988, managers could buy more on factor markets.

At the high tide of socialism in Shanghai's economy, at least 70 percent of all raw materials for the city's industries were allocated through the state. Already by 1988, the portion had been reversed from the start of that decade: Shanghai local agents had to find 70 percent of all inputs themselves. This problem affected not only major materials such as steel and lumber, but even dried potatoes, leather, and industrial salt.[86] Central policies had created an environment in which managers did not want to solve this problem for their firms. The environment of high taxes and many rules had temporarily destroyed Shanghai's once-famous entrepreneurialism.

In the second half of 1988, partly because of obvious materials and hepatitis problems during the first half, the central authorities mustered more raw materials for Shanghai—and the city's industrial economy responded, with a better growth rate than in most Chinese provinces. Partly for this reason, and because many revenues had been "hidden" in budgets below the province level in Shanghai, the city fathers slightly overfulfilled their revenue quota in 1988, as if to make up for the bad first half.[87]

Factory Closures, Industry Subsidies, and Bankruptcies

The hepatitis epidemic temporarily brought a standstill at some factories, and it raised the politically unpresentable question of whether long-term difficulties should bring closures. But almost no state factories were shut down. Managers' autonomy and factory independence are not necessarily good for reform at the local level, according to the usual microeconomic logic, unless bad management carries the threat of bankruptcy. If cadres' failure merely leads to state bailouts and subsidies—and taxes to pay for them—that is not evidence of reform but of bad planning.

Many failures in particular firms were not caused by especially bad management, but by changes in the prices of their inputs or products. By the late 1980s and the start of the 1990s, the state, operating through its corporations, attempted to do on reform markets what it had failed to do by planning. *Larger subsidies went to support factor prices for whole nationalized industries in trouble than to bail out individual plants.* State enterprises lost about 20 billion yuan in 1990, but the government's price-support subsidies were perhaps five times that amount.[88] Even though this policy could not solve the overall problem of irrational prices, it would have been more reasonable if the state had been able to afford it.

Bankruptcy laws in China began mostly as an ideological critique by reformers against inefficient management in state enterprises. Practically everyone agreed there was much mismanagement. But the stress on bankruptcy laws for individual firms (even though these laws were opposed by political conservatives) missed the larger point: The state no longer had the capacity to maintain both its political and fiscal bases in big cities. The central system as a whole, constructed in the Maoist manner, was nearing bankruptcy. Its supplies and markets were increasingly dominated by many smaller political networks. State leaders lacked the resources to do things they deemed essential.

A national Enterprise Bankruptcy Law, which could not address the problem at the state level, was adopted in 1986, albeit "for trial use" only. It had in 1987 still "not been extensively implemented." It was not supposed to be "enforced" until November 1988.[89] When enterprise deficits arose, firms took "full responsibility for their profits but cannot assume full responsibility for their losses. Rather than going bankrupt, they demand loans from banks through the government. . . . Even when these enterprises are fined and ordered to repay the bank loans they have borrowed at a higher interest rate, they will still ask for more bank loans, because they know that they will not suffer losses themselves."[90] Local laws were adopted with different definitions of bankruptcy and with varying provisions about the types of firms to which they might apply. In short, bankruptcy laws were not written for state firms.

Private and collective companies could and often did fall on hard times because of rampant inflation. Because such firms were not line items on the state budget, and no wage assurances had been implied by high officials to workers, these could go bankrupt. They were not part of the regime's system; no government credit would be available to save them. So even though this point was not stressed to visiting economists, local bankruptcy laws were not implemented in ways that might violate the state's particularist norms.

Many companies outside the state system did go bankrupt. The Shanghai Collective Enterprises Administration held an auction in 1988 to sell collapsed firms to the highest bidder. Individuals were not allowed to bid; only collectives, state enterprises, and joint ventures could do so. The director of the Collective Enterprises Administration promised that successful bidders could make all decisions regarding both production and management in their newly acquired firms.[91] Newspapers duly heralded that Shanghai had procedures for bankruptcy. They did not herald that debt-heavy corporations in the state sector were effectively exempt from this danger.

Amalgamation of healthy firms with sick ones was permitted in low-tax jurisdictions—but not in Shanghai, lest remittances to Beijing be reduced. Profitable state enterprises were allowed to buy money-losing ones in some Chinese cities, including Beijing and Shenyang but not Shanghai, during 1988.[92] Buyout mergers encouraged investment in the bankrupt subsidiaries, to put them back in the black. But this practice reduced total profits—and fiscal revenues—at least in the short or medium term. The greatest virtue of this spreading of losses among state firms was political: All the managers and workers could keep their jobs. In Shanghai, however, pressure on the city government to maintain its usual tax remittances prevented such comfortable mergers. Structural changes aiming at better management occurred elsewhere, but not in the metropolis whose long-term efficiency Beijing politicians never considered more important than its current remittances.

State enterprises resisted reforms. Their managers' incentives were not much changed by the shift in the main target quota they were supposed to deliver: output or profits. The shortages of materials and capital, the scarce information on how to resolve these shortages, the "soft budget constraint," the lack of quality and design standardization, and the widespread reliance on collective rather than individual responsibility for performance—all these factors remained substantially unchanged in many state plants well into the 1980s.[93] The lack of serious management reform, despite high politicians' speeches calling for it, was especially striking in some cities (such as Wuhan and the region around it). Where the change was greatest, in smaller cities farther south, the dependence of many managers' careers on their economic performance remained weak in the state sector. Shanghai and its delta was a middling case, with more serious management reform than in the area around Wuhan but less than in the delta around Guangzhou. Promotions of better-educated company heads began to change this pattern, but structural changes in the incentives they faced came more slowly because state plants were mutually linked, and because often the economically rational solution (bankruptcy) was politically dangerous.

Brownouts and temporary blackouts had been known in Shanghai for years, but state factories could sometimes avoid them. These brought frequent reminders of the reality of shortages, although few state plants formally closed. In the first half of 1988, Shanghai's electricity supplies were irregular. The voltage was often not up to par, and there was overloading because of a shortage of lines.[94] Low voltage affected 352 factories for over a quarter of the days in the first six months of the year, and overloading was sometimes at a level that was a fire hazard.

By the end of 1988, electricity supplies were publicly reported to be at 94 percent of the planned amounts. Shanghai sent coal-buying teams to Shanxi, Inner Mongolia, Henan and other mining provinces. Because the shortage could not be reduced, energy-consuming factories had to lessen their work hours. The city "moved step by step to a five-day week"—even though plans did not yet call for that particular modernization.[95]

Coal, the main energy source, is a bulk resource that the government could control relatively well. The state had a monopoly of the rail system and a near monopoly of mining. So rural industries outside the state system were especially hard hit by coal shortages. But sometimes they could trade or bribe their way into finding supplies. They sometimes had more money relative to state managers, and they usually had strong political support in their localities.

The *Economic Daily* at the end of October 1988 reported that China had "thirty million workers with nothing to do. . . . More than 400,000 enterprises across the country are operating at a loss, and three-quarters of them should be closed." This PRC newspaper estimated that the government would have to spend half its industrial profits, or about 40 billion yuan, "to subsidize ailing state-owned enterprises this year."[96] It seemed clear to everyone that this situation could not last long. Yet the political cycle in 1989 headed into a deeply conservative mood, and practically all state factories continued to limp along. The state could not afford to lose the acquiescence of its workers in 1989.

Energy shortages idled "about 15 percent" of Shanghai's production in the early part of that year, when "many factories are running only four or five days a week because of the power shortage."[97] A local economist pointed out that services and light industries consumed less energy than heavy industries. Energy-expensive plants had been imposed on Shanghai at Baoshan and Wujing, whose large steel and chemical complexes were directly under central management and taxation. The huge Baoshan Steel Plant, for example, benefited the central government and perhaps a few top Shanghai leaders, but not most of the city's people. The coal shortage was most obvious to residents, since it affected people both at work and at home. Other materials shortfalls continuing into the late 1980s had consequences that were delayed.

Factories using chemicals in Shanghai suffered such severe shortages of inputs by the end of the decade, their managers and workers cooperated in unprecedented ways to keep the plants in operation. Wujing Chemical Factory, Chenyuan Chemical Factory, Pudong Chemical Factory, and other very large plants were by some reports in danger of closing. Because these factories provided downstream supplies to drug, textile, and other light industrial companies, the danger to Shanghai's economy was great. For example, chemical factories needing industrial salt to make alkalis had been promised 38,000 metric tons in January 1989; apparently they had expected to purchase more on the open market, up to their total requirement then of 50,000 tons. But as a newspaper reported on its front page, "not a single ton has reached Shanghai."[98] The central government said that factories could use reserve warehoused salt—but by this time, little was available.

Shanghai's Chemical Industries Bureau sent buyers urgently, "like sparks," to the salt-producing areas of Tianjin, Shandong, and Jiangsu. Problems emerged at each of these places. In Shandong, a cold spell was said to have frozen canals, so that all barge transport of salt had to be stopped. In Jiangsu, the port facilities were said to be inadequate. In Tianjin, a structural reform of the relevant company had divided it into two parts, so that salt would no longer be provided from there as in the past. The most important reason for this problem, however, was that inland places had established their own chemical factories which needed all their salt.

The Shanghai Solvents Factory had in store only a three-day supply of industrial alcohol and some other materials that it required for production. Because of a nationwide shortage of kerosene, which is used to make urea, the Wujing Chemical Factory—apparently Shanghai's largest producer of this fertilizer—

was forced to suspend its production entirely in early 1989. Shanghai factories had no funds to move into new fields. They had simply to close old lines. The upshot was that the city government was "urgently asking for help" from central departments—whose budgets were still addicted to their accustomed fixes of Shanghai profits and taxes. But their power to keep Shanghai factories in the black had disappeared.

Central hard-liners' basic policy was to force closures of nonstate plants. A late-1989 campaign against nonstate industries was presented as an effort against inflation—and indeed, raw materials price hikes created problems for state industries. But the regime failed to redirect the material flows back into the state sector. By October 1989, Shanghai's industrial production was down 6 percent below the same month in the previous year. Its light industries' output was down by 8 percent (and heavy industry by 4 percent, a loss only half as much for the heavy sector facing less nonstate domestic competition). This was blamed on a "slack market." But the market for nonstate industries' products was not slack. As a cadre of the Shanghai First Commerce Bureau said, "We must find a way out." The city government vowed "immediate measures to salvage some of the major enterprises in trouble."[99] This proposal was very expensive, however; and the underlying problems were long-term, not temporary.

Rural companies, which were supposed to trade with the Shanghai state sector at terms set by the state, now could effectively avoid doing so. They made more money by trading with each other. In its fight against them, the conservative government had to blink first. It lacked power to enforce its policy of effective economic centralization, and the costs of that policy were unsustainable. It became evident that rural entrepreneurs, using their own resources and power networks, could together outlast the state.

The political lions' show of force reached the countryside. When police investigated restaurants in a Jiangsu county, they found that over three-quarters of the state-owned eateries exceeded their planned profits. For this success, they had been fined![100] They had reportedly paid their taxes due, but local conservative leaders did not like the disruptions their growth brought. Surplus production and remittances could elicit praise from reformers, but the concomitant surplus profit used resources and weakened plans.

Controlling rich suburban and rural collectives was beyond the central state's capacity, despite the consequent economic losses to official coffers and political threats of renewed unrest among urban workers. A tacit battle, lasting for most of the late 1980s, was waged between central and local power networks over this control. Its effect on China's future will probably be as great as that of the well-known events at Tiananmen, where nonintellectual rural entrepreneurs—the regime's most constant and dangerous opponents—were nowhere to be seen.

By 1990, Shanghai municipality was spending over half its municipal budget on price subsidies.[101] The conservative trend continued, but the regime had to pay a larger portion of its resources to support its political-economic system. The

Ministry of Materials and Equipment by the end of 1990 "decided" to change from being "the official distributor of supplies" into merely a "market broker."[102] That transformation had in fact already occurred, generally without benefit of state policy. The ministry announced in 1990 that it would do in its field the only thing it still had the capacity to do. Reality was declared official.

Chinese cotton production dropped between 1991 and 1993 from 6.5 million tons to just 4 million tons. This was awful news for the Shanghai industry employing more workers than any other. The cotton price had been low, and people in producing areas had never been organized in such a tight "Chinese" hierarchy as those in areas growing grain; they readily used their land and labor for industry. So the price of cotton more than doubled quickly in the mid-1990s, and textile factories closed. One official claimed in 1994 that "about 90 percent of the textile factories in Shanghai have recently shut down." This was an overestimate; but the real situation was officially underreported, and for textile workers it was bad news. Many lost their jobs or were "sent down from posts" (*xiagang*), receiving only a fraction of their former salaries as a kind of delayed severance pay.[103]

Half of China's state enterprises by the mid-1990s were running deficits, and another third would have been in the red except for hidden subsidies. Urban inflation was rampant, "as high as 40 percent."[104] Industrial strikes were rising because state firms had no money for millions of their workers. Shanghai was the last test for the strength of Chen Yun's "birdcage" hopes for market socialism. Chen, who for decades had been a major CCP economic guru, espoused a policy of using the market and command economies together. Since all developed industrial nations have both strong markets and much regulation, his idea had theoretical appeal to all but the truest believers in capitalism or socialism.

Chen thought market socialism would work in China if crucial limits on the market allowed state cadres to set the prices of major commodities. So he likened the free market to a bird, which could be kept in a cage large enough so that it could live, but also small enough so that it would not fly out of control. Shanghai had been Chen's best cage. The socialist market economy had worked—but only so long as the state was strong enough to keep free traders from dealing in major goods. The question became political, not economic: Could the state, as the revolution wound down, continue to direct behavior among local leaders? During the 1980s, that question was answered decisively in the negative.

Taxes and Local Powers

Financial extraction from Shanghai has been extraordinarily heavy. This continued through the end of the 1980s at least. Severe erosion of the socialist tax base by rural industries in the early 1980s made the central bureaucracy, for a while at least, try to extract even more from Shanghai. Throughout China, there has been pervasive fragmentation between different sectors and jurisdictions. Some parts of the country bear very high rates of tax, while others are greatly subsidized.[105]

This pattern gives lightly taxed jurisdictions incentives to break away from heavily taxed centers. All local governments hide their funds and act as independent units whenever possible. Extractions and subsidies have been heavy, subject to changing political arrangements, and sharply uneven.

Shanghai Budget and Extra-Budget Burdens Through Mid-Reform

The extraordinary importance of Shanghai in China's financial system, at least until the mid-1980s, is quickly apparent from figures such as are presented in Table 1.2-4. By no means has all of Shanghai's revenue gone to the central government. But the portion of total local revenues that went to Beijing during the whole period from 1949 to 1984 was 87 percent, with only 13 percent remaining in the local till.[106] In Mao's time, from 1950 to 1976, Shanghai sent thirteen times more revenue to the central government than the amount it received for the city budget. Nearly a decade later, in 1984, it still had to give more than 85 percent of its revenue to Beijing.[107] Beijing's announcement of reforms did not change its need or greed for Shanghai money. From 1980 to 1984—well after reforms were supposed to be the norm—Shanghai reportedly retained, to cover local spending, only 12 percent of its revenues. In Guangdong, the comparable figure at the same time was 82 percent.[108] Not only were Shanghai's amounts of extraction very much higher than in any other province on a per-person basis—even very much higher than the most similar other such unit in China, Tianjin—but so were the total lack of spending per unit of revenue and the portion of revenues sent to the central treasury.

How Great Were the Subsidies to Shanghai from State Price Fixing?

This analysis cannot be considered complete, even through the midreform period covered in the table, because Shanghai industrial materials prices have for many years been kept low—like the prices of rent and food (though not of most consumer durables). There is no full budgetary record of these implicit subsidies to cities. How large were they? Did they compensate Shanghai for extraordinarily high taxation? Many low prices for factors and high prices for products are matters of law, not economics. Police enforcement of plans *as* law—i.e., state coercion—was the bulwark of this structure. Exact statistics have not been found on the actual or implicit state subsidies for cheap raw materials delivered to Shanghai, or on high Shanghai product prices, because part of such subsidies never appear on budgets. They are based on nonmonetary coercion.

Can we make an estimate of the value of nonmonetized subsidies? Any conclusions from the data above would depend on some sense of the financial effects of police power over Shanghai's inputs and outputs markets. Maybe a few of these subsidies are already included in the statistics for budgetary and extrabudgetary spending; to the extent they are, the analysis has covered them. But we cannot assume that all, or even most, such subsidies are in budgetary and extrabudgetary spending on any market.

What has been the difference between actual prices charged to Shanghai for factors and to other places for Shanghai products, on one hand, and their scarcity prices, on the other? According to Ministry of Agriculture estimates (referring specifically to 1978 but stated broadly enough to apply in many years before the 1980s), the prices of all China's rural retail sales averaged 15 to 20 percent, on a weighted basis, above their scarcity values. The selling prices of all products from rural areas averaged 25 to 30 percent less than their real values.[109]

On this basis, it is possible to make a rough estimate of the effect of state-mandated prices in subsidizing Shanghai by lowering the cost of its factors and raising the cost of its products. This amount may then be compared with Shanghai's high tax and profit burdens to see how much it compensated the city for them. At least two assumptions are needed: First, the calculation cannot be considered exact; the aim here (as with the logic on Shanghai's suspiciously low capital-output ratio, below) is only to gather a broad sense of the economic realities as a prerequisite for political analysis. Second, we assume that Shanghai did not very quickly suffer higher prices (although it did suffer shortages) in the four years after 1979, when the state raised rural procurement prices, because the extra money to farmers came directly from the central government budget rather than from Shanghai, and the greater productivity of rural areas aided sales of Shanghai products there. It is possible, for the sake of this crude estimation, to say that Shanghai faced a price structure in 1983 that was still similar to that in 1978 (even though this structure became more problematic for the city by the middle of the 1980s).

The calculation is as follows: Shanghai's net 1983 purchases from other areas of Chinese rural subsidiary products—the country's inputs to city industries—were worth 2.4 billion yuan; so their scarcity-price value can be estimated at 3.3 billion yuan. The difference (the implicit 1983 subsidy to Shanghai from cheap factors) was thus about 0.9 billion yuan.[110] In the downstream direction, Shanghai's net domestic sales of high-price manufactures in 1983 was worth 10.0 billion yuan nominally, or 8.5 billion yuan at scarcity prices, for an implicit subsidy to Shanghai of 1.5 billion yuan from sales.[111] The sum of these factors and sales subsidies was thus about 2.4 billion yuan (a bit below that, using more decimals than this figuring justifies). This is not a trivial amount, but it is *very* much less than the 1983 revenue burden on Shanghai, counting both budgetary and extrabudgetary sources, of 19.9 billion yuan.[112] The implicit subsidy lessened the direct burden by one-tenth or a bit more—in any case, not by an overwhelming amount.

In other words, benefits to Shanghai through state pricing scarcely began to counterbalance the direct central extractions from there. Subsidies, especially hidden or implicit ones, for Shanghai have been large. The main fact here is not that the subsidies were low, but that the direct exactions were enormous. These taxes were so

Table 1.2–4

State Extraction, by Province

	Ratio of state expenditures to revenues (%)				State revenues minus expenditures, per capita (in yuan)			
	1982	1983	1984	1985	1982	1983	1984	1985
Shanghai	23	27	36	39	1,349	1,218	1,142	1,253
Tianjin	68	70	67	7[illegible]	234	215	265	288
Beijing	54	69	74	74	375	237	232	264
Liaoning	62	69	72	79	134	100	107	98
Jiangsu	60	61	68	70	66	72	67	71
Zhejiang	66	65	72	7[illegible]	51	58	52	68
Shandong	79	79	84	82	21	25	20	28
WHOLE PRC	79	82	89	90	29	25	18	20
Hubei	79	79	84	89	25	27	23	18
Hebei	86	83	92	93	15	21	11	11
Guangdong	101	103	98	95	–2	–3	3	10
Hunan	86	88	93	99	13	11	7	2
Henan	102	89	95	101	–1	8	4	–1
Sichuan	91	95	98	102	6	4	2	–2
Anhui	83	89	98	104	12	8	2	–4
Jiangxi	113	112	124	115	–9	–9	–21	–17
Fujian	104	128	113	112	–4	–27	–15	–19
Guangxi	111	114	128	120	–8	–11	–21	–21
Yunnan	106	114	122	113	–6	–15	–27	–21
Guizhou	138	144	150	125	–21	–23	–35	–23
Heilong'g	127	114	121	111	–34	–21	–36	–24

(continued)

Table 1.2-4 *(continued)*

Shaanxi	117	121	133	122	–13	–20	–35	–27
Shanxi	100	98	102	115	0	4	–4	–31
Gansu	109	118	132	123	–11	–20	–41	–35
Jilin	117	109	117	121	–22	–13	–31	–47
In. Mong.	178	171	200	170	–76	–77	–124	–109
Ningxia	180	200	200	200	–76	–97	–141	–135
Xinjiang	192	173	183	211	–36	–59	–101	–142
Qinghai	225	200	217	200	–170	–80	–144	–207
Tibet	4,600	2,800	5,900	1,800	–520	–610	–560	–520

Notes and Sources: This and similar tables are aimed to undergird a political analysis, and the relative positions of provinces (especially Shanghai) is more certain than the exactitude of the numbers. The tale is in the gradients, not the econometrics. Note especially the Shanghai, Jiangsu, and Zhejiang levels; the subsidies for Western provinces, especially Tibet; and the "whole PRC" figures, which suggest that large quantities of money went into funds that are not even recorded as extrabudgetary.

The table is in order by 1985 revenues minus expenditures per person. Computed from raw data in *Zhongguo caizheng tongji, 1950–1985* (Chinese Fiscal Statistics, 1950–1985), Comprehensive Planning Office of the PRC Ministry of Finance, ed. (Beijing: Zhongguo Caizheng Jingji Chuban She, 1987), pp. 54 and 144 for the budgetary and extra revenues, and pp. 92 and 145 for the budgetary and extra expenditures. Many, but probably not all, subsidies for cheap raw materials that were delivered to Shanghai are included in the statistics for budgetary and extrabudgetary spending. A complete list of the line items that make up these categories of spending is not public—even though Chinese economists say that the government keeps unpublished figures on the reasons why it has run such big deficits, and subsidies rank very high among these reasons.

great, credible reports suggest that Shanghai managers not only had more incentives to hide money than did cadres anywhere else in China, but also that they actually did so in great amounts, which government collectors have on a confidential basis tried to estimate.[113] The policy of hiding accurate books "under the rice bin" and concocting false ones for tax collectors is hardly an innovation for East Asian (or other) entrepreneurs. Linda Chelan Li's nice attempt to compute the excess of actual Shanghai investment over Beijing budgets for that purpose shows that excess at 195 percent of plan in 1988, 135 percent in 1991, and 145 percent in 1992.[114] Shanghai's high portion of "improper accounts" for tax collection was second among all China's provinces in the early 1990s (Guangdong took gold, quite literally, in this unofficial race).[115] Despite Shanghai's probable distinction as a foremost center of fake, misleading, and incomplete accounts in all China, this city has also been the site of major extraction. Shanghai economists call their place China's "pocket" (*koudai*), because the government always reaches into it for money.

This odd honor for the city grew out of its history. As China's preeminent light industrial center at the middle of the century, Shanghai provided a major means for the PRC government to garner money. State-owned industries in the metropolis bought raw materials at low state-mandated prices, processed them at low wages, and sold consumer products at high state-fixed prices largely to inland areas. The profits redounded largely to Beijing coffers. The metropolis acted like a sponge, soaking up rural resources for the national budget.[116]

Fiscal Fragmentation with Uneven Remittances

Much of the debate about the extent of extraction turns on the completeness of reported budgets. Scholars following Nicholas Lardy, who show that Shanghai at least through Mao's period (and in fact until the mid-1980s) was milked of funds, do not claim that the published data are absolutely complete; but they stress that the available figures show such overwhelming taxation as to suggest central state efficacy. This net extraction greatly exceeded the predictable flows of funds to inland projects in the course of development, such as occur to some extent in all industrializing countries. Other scholars, following Audrey Donnithorne, stress that China's compartmentalized economy gives many incentives to hide money, so that the official figures are too incomplete to use for any major purpose. In any case, these data do not cover the implicit subsidy to Shanghai that comes from state-fixed low raw materials prices and high product prices. Actually, these two viewpoints, though published as different, are quite compatible with each other in both logic and practice.

Researchers of China used to argue that data about fiscal fragmentation there conflicted with regional data about very heavy central remittances. One of the most fruitful debates among sinologues moots the extent to which China has been fiscally centralized or fragmented, integrated or compartmentalized. Donnithorne's classic *China's Economic System* showed how unsystematically "cellular" the PRC economy has long been. But Lardy responded with provincial budget data seeming to have an opposite implication: China's coastal areas were taxed heavily, by a centralized bureaucracy in Beijing, to support inland provinces.[117] After these two were published, many other scholars refined the terms of their original debate. Two contributions told the sequels: Thomas Lyons stressed the importance of Donnithorne's insight that China's economy was surprisingly unintegrated.[118] Barry Naughton, a student of Lardy's, found that over the whole 1965–71 period, the central government was strong enough to concentrate fully *two-thirds* of its industrial investment budget in inland Great Third Front projects, which were extremely slow to return the capital they absorbed.[119] Much of this money came from Shanghai.

Scholarly writings in this debate among economists soon became the most precise genre in a broader academic literature that had begun much earlier, during the early 1960s, in an effort to explain the Great Leap Forward. Schurmann, Townsend, and Skinner conceived the Leap not just in terms of its ideology, but also as an attempt at organization.[120] Its egalitarian and activist norms could then be analyzed in terms of their functions, not as abstract philosophies or inconsequential dogmas. Such studies of the Leap affected—and improved—research on contemporary China in later years. The economists were exploring the linked fiscal and investment aspects of this organizational view of China. Their arguments were quantitative, of course, but the conclusions were all about central and local organization—and they seemed to contradict one another. Shanghai, as the preeminent taxpayer, was at the center of the economists' discussion. Another look at the situation, however, suggests that it is possible simultaneously to find that the published budgets were grossly incomplete, that Shanghai was very heavily taxed, that the economy remained cellular, and that most of the relevant politics was between central and local leaders within the city.

The Case of the Missing Money: A Capital-Output Ratio Clue

Is Shanghai's growth consistent with its scant capitalization in published budgets? Do the reported investment figures imply a capital-output ratio for the city's industry that is credible, or instead one that is too low to sustain the reports of its industrial product, which are more surely complete? The argument that follows tries to test, at least loosely, for omissions from the budget data. The conclusion will be that Shanghai's industrial growth over the long term must have used far more capital than the published budgets show.

Field, Lardy, and Emerson estimated that Shanghai's 1957 gross value of industrial output (GVIO) was 11,402 million yuan.[121] The 1957 investment in the city was 372 million yuan, of which we could estimate 250 million was industrial.[122] If so, the 1957 ratio of industrial investment over gross industrial product in Shanghai must have been very roughly 0.02. Of course this does not include old investment, nor was all of this capital immediately productive; but if we consider a much longer time—say, twenty years—the problems of old capital and time lags become insignificant. Over that time, a rough but safely overestimated 1949–73 ratio of industrial capital to gross industrial output may be obtained after dividing the 0.02 investment rate by the pace of industrial expansion in Shanghai over this long period.[123] What was that latter rate? According to one calculation, the ratio of capital to gross output in Shanghai's industry over this long time was below 0.2.[124]

Gross output, however, double-counts values added whenever they are exchanged in semifinished goods between firms. A standard estimate of the extent of such double counting would put the sum of industrial values added (industrial GDP) at about 40 percent of gross industrial output. This adjustment raises the 0.2 figure, above, to 0.5—still too low to believe as a capital-output ratio in a large industrial economy. A further adjustment, for which data on which to base even a rough estimate have not been found, would account for the fact that an unusually high part of Shanghai's capital stock was old. Even this would not double the 0.5.

Arthur Lewis notes a "remarkable agreement" among economists: "First, that in the industrial countries the ratio of the value of capital to the value of output seems to be pretty constant at the margin, when capital-intensive and capital-sparse industries are taken together; and second, that this marginal ratio lies between 3 to 1 and 4 to 1, when the value of land and other natural resources is excluded from capital and the value of external assets from both capital and income."[125] A ratio for industry might go somewhat below 3.0. But 0.5—or several times that figure, as the case in Shanghai probably was—would be remarkable, to the point of impossible, for a very big industrial city over a period of decades.

The published data about investment seem to be very incomplete. All the economists whose estimates are used here agree that the available investment data, especially if they exclude extrabudgetary investment, do not cover all the change in Shanghai's capital stock. Enterprises illegally divert working capital to fixed investment, and Shanghai's entrepreneurs use their pools of skilled labor and their ability to acquire extra raw materials to produce capital goods within their own repair facilities and workshops. Also, increased productivity with the nearly constant average wages in Shanghai could have raised state industry profits, and thus state revenue, faster than output. In addition, some allowance can be made for variations in capital-output ratios among different places and sectors. China as a whole may have a modestly smaller ratio than do most countries, and Shanghai probably has the lowest ratio in the country (if anybody had the figures to calculate it, which is unlikely because revealed money becomes taxed money). It is probable that part of the reason for the big shortfall in reported capital for Shanghai is the hiding of funds by managers there.[126] Even Shanghai's industry was not efficient enough to reproduce resources quite as fast as the budgets imply.

How Much Should Shanghai Pay?

Was such a high tax on Shanghai justifiable in economic terms? The reasoning above and the picture of heavy exaction that it paints (with wide margins for uncertainties) would still not be sufficient to prove that Shanghai's burden was excessive in any economic sense, even though this kind of reasoning is already sufficient to raise many political questions. Some movement of capital from urban centers to hinterlands may be natural in the course of development. Economically, the rub in the high-tax policy is this: Extraction from areas such as Shanghai, which can regenerate capital more quickly than other places, may become so severe that overall growth—even the long-term growth of poor areas to which the taxes are sent—becomes slower than it would be if a less draconian tax were imposed on rich areas. But the main neoclassical economic model that might tell how much tax Shanghai would have paid, assuming an aim of maximum long-term growth regardless of final allocations by sectors, is not well adapted to testing the national efficiency of the actual tax, even though it shows the Chinese government has a patriotic case to answer when imposing such high and nonuniform extractions.

Shanghai's relatively good transport location, skilled labor force, wide variety of preexisting industries, and other advantages allow many new investments there to return capital used for them more quickly than do the same new investments elsewhere in China. On the other hand, scattering resources all over the country may widen the range of places where future investments reproduce speedily; for example, such dispersal encourages the basic training of modern labor in boondocks, and it provides more semifinished products and transport for later ventures there. This situation varies by industry, but in general, for most lines of work, Shanghai's advantages are far more favorable than in most other PRC locations. A policy of widely dispersed investments, such as China before the mid-1980s used more than other developing countries, might slow the growth of GNP in the short term but could allow faster growth later, because of expanding infrastructure, trained labor, and a wide spread of markets. The danger is that such a communitarian long-term policy could drain rich areas so badly, the benefit could be overwhelmed by the costs of not recouping capital quickly.

What is the best balance between Chinese coastal investment, which generally leads to spurts of growth in rich areas soon, and inland investment, which results in more widespread growth later? Some neoclassical Western economists use a "turnpike" metaphor to describe the growth-efficient way to put capital in sectors (which here are geographic):

> Take *any* initial capital structure [a matrix with sectoral dimensions, e.g., by place and industry] and *any* desired terminal structure. . . . The corresponding optimal capital program will be describable as follows: The system first invests so as to alter its capital structure toward [growth-efficient] proportions. . . . When it has

> come close to these proportions, it spends most of the programming period performing steady growth at the maximal rate. . . . Then it bends away . . . and invests in such a way as to alter the capital structure to the desired terminal proportions. . . . It is exactly like a turnpike paralleled by a network of minor roads. There is a fastest route between any two points. . . . The best intermediate capital configuration is one which will grow most rapidly; even if it is not the desired one, it is temporarily optimal.[127]

This model shows in abstract the problem faced by many high Communists whose behavior clearly shows they wanted to tax Shanghai and to develop other places. Even if this set of allocative values is right in some absolute sense, too much burden on Shanghai could slow long-term growth nationally (even inland alone) by forgoing too many profits from coastal areas that regenerate money quickly. This point was not Shanghai mayor Chen Yi's when in the 1950s he plainly said, "We must evacuate the population of the city systematically and transfer factories to the interior whenever possible."[128]

During reforms, and occasionally before then, some state leaders showed an understanding that unlimited taxes on rich places might disserve the country.[129] But the evidence suggests they did not act on this insight. To serve other values (and inland political constituencies), China in the last four decades has seldom stressed growth efficiency. Shanghai has paid obviously, under this policy. A more important question is how much China as a whole paid in lost overall growth. Much of the money went for disastrously unprofitable military industries in the Great Third Front (*da san xian*). Some of these inland investments never produced anything. The Third Front did not cease to exist when China's reforms began. In 1988, this program was still run by a State Council organ called the Third Front Enterprises Management Office (Sanxian Qiye Guanli Bangong Shi). Such projects had long been associated with the People's Liberation Army, and there were strong political reasons not to end them.

Budgets record inflows and outflows, and only the size of extractions and expenditures in various places allows general statements about transfers. By no means, however, did all of the money taxed from Shanghai, Jiangsu, and Zhejiang go to poor inland places. In absolute terms by the early 1980s, coastal Liaoning, Guangdong, and Shandong were also important recipients. The sources of most Shanghai remittances were in the central part of the city; suburban industries had lower tax rates. Provincial capitals as a group, prominently including Hangzhou and even Guangzhou in the far south, had higher remittance rates than other large cities that were not capitals.

Beijing was in a special category—and the difference between Shanghai's and Beijing's fiscal treatments has been sharply understated in published data such as those in Table 1.2–4. A much higher portion of Beijing spending never appears in geographically organized budgets or extrabudgetary reports, but instead is in the funds of ministries and other functional units. These build a great deal of infrastructure, e.g. housing, that is nominally not Beijing's. As late as

1984, Shanghai delivered profits and taxes of 16 billion yuan, compared with Beijing's 4.56 billion yuan (only 29 percent as much revenue). But Shanghai's reported expenditures that year were only 2.77 billion yuan, compared with Beijing's of 2.71 billion yuan (98 percent as much).[130] And these figures underreport the difference. This "capital" fully deserves the pun as a name. Two decades before Shanghai's construction boom in the 1990s, Beijing already had many new streets and buildings, a subway system, and much better maintenance.

Most expenditure afforded to Shanghai before 1988 went toward maintaining its role as a tax base. Light industries came in for some renovation in 1979; this was a timely move to raise more revenue, because rural markets for Shanghai consumer products had flourished throughout the 1970s. This stress on light industries was also consistent with some decentralization of fiscal powers to the city—and at first, this was derogation to the top Shanghai municipal officers, who are appointed by the central state and fully part of it, not to Jiangnan managers at the factory level. So Shanghai participated in the national wave of "management by dividing fiscal levels." An announced aim was to change a situation in which Shanghai had been "unified too much and administered to death."[131]

The high tax/profit-extraction rate affected all aspects of Shanghai's politics and economy—as well as the lack of complete reporting there and the extraordinary care of central politicians to include among their number the satraps sent to head the municipal government. Provincial wealth correlated with high rates of extraction, but also with high status for the province head, with low rates of expenditure through official budgets, and with high rates of hiding capital. There is also a correlation between the provincial rankings on Table 1.2-5 and those on Table 1.2–4, showing degrees of taxation by place. Shanghai is not unique in having depended to a great extent on nonplan spending. It is the extreme example of a genre of such places, including the provinces of Jiangsu and Zhejiang that are largely on the Yangzi/Shanghai delta. Having paid so much regular taxes and profits, these places had less to remit through other means. High extraction from rich places gives very strong reasons for extrabudgetary accounting there.

Finally, provinces such as Shanghai that report little reliance on extrabudgetary revenues nonetheless depend to a greater extent on nonplan spending. Bank accounts are easier to conceal than construction sites. But also, having paid so much regular tax and profit, less may be extractable by other means; and having so little to spend in the regular plans, Shanghai runs into more unexpected, less fully authorized costs. Shanghai's reliance on nonbudget spending does not, however, mean that it has more to spend on per-capita, per-product, or any other standard basis; in these terms, the metropolis still has least.

Comparisons with Other Cities

Comparisons of Shanghai with other provinces that are mostly countryside may be inappropriate for some purposes. More than two-thirds of Shanghai's popula-

Table 1.2–5

Shanghai's Relative Non-use of Budgeting

	Budgetary revenues as a percentage of extrabudgetary revenues				Budgetary expenditures as apercentage of extrabudgetary expenditures				Index (sum of percents)
	1982	1983	1984	1985	1982	1983	1984	1985	
Shanghai	**25**	**29**	**33**	**37**	**66**	**54**	**57**	**75**	**376**
Jiangsu	**46**	**51**	**64**	**63**	**74**	**86**	**81**	**102**	**567**
Liaoning	58	74	79	101	67	71	65	73	588
Beijing	57	75	83	88	74	71	77	83	608
Tianjin	44	46	50	63	138	100	91	96	628
Shandong	50	75	78	78	97	84	93	106	661
Zhejiang	**57**	**55**	**60**	**60**	**100**	**110**	**116**	**128**	**686**
WHOLE PRC	62	70	74	76	111	113	116	129	751
Hubei	58	58	60	70	125	127	123	138	759
Hebei	78	81	82	84	113	108	124	120	790
Hunan	70	76	76	82	110	125	125	133	797
Guangdong	76	89	74	66	100	119	130	156	810
Sichuan	76	83	89	95	119	109	123	121	815
Anhui	64	73	79	80	131	143	133	155	858
Henan	45	53	56	55	158	158	176	185	886
Shanxi	95	104	115	116	117	100	103	138	888
Shaanxi	64	87	100	85	170	127	135	165	933
Fujian	93	108	88	72	133	129	140	182	945

(continued)

Table 1.2-5 *(continued)*

Heilong'g	141	132	111	97	117	115	109	125	947
Jiangxi	100	86	93	95	125	142	157	165	963
Gansu	92	100	92	94	108	160	175	171	992
Yunnan	100	106	105	93	127	150	163	168	1,012
Jilin	142	150	173	141	100	100	92	121	1,019
Guangxi	108	100	107	100	131	146	164	167	1,023
Guizhou	129	78	82	80	175	229	233	240	1,246
In. Mongol.	260	200	188	173	167	177	207	200	1,572
Xinjiang	200	150	157	138	188	271	230	264	1,598
Ningxia	150	150	200	133	200	233	300	250	1,616
Qinghai	300	150	200	250	200	233	225	250	1,808

Notes and Sources: This table very roughly measures the extent to which different provinces rely on budgets to manage state revenues and expenditures, as compared to extrabudgetary funds and expenditures. The sums in the right-hand column may serve as a rough index of the differences between provinces in this respect. Budgetary subsidies to border areas are evident near the bottom of the chart (though the available figures for Tibet, an ethnically separatist area where the government spends very freely to enure control, are excluded as incomparable with the other statistics). Provincial wealth correlates with non-reliance on budgets, and this may be caused by the central bureaucracy's eagerness to subsidize prices in the most important tax bases. Computed from raw data in *Zhongguo caizheng tongji, 1950–1985* (Chinese Fiscal Statistics, 1950–1985), Comprehensive Planning Office of the PRC Ministry of Finance, ed. (Beijing: Zhongguo Caizheng Jingji Chuban She, 1987), pp. 54 and 144 for the budgetary and extra revenues, and pp. 92 and 145 for the budgetary and extra expenditures.

tion (roughly as much as in Tianjin and Beijing) is urban, and a considerable portion works in industries. Shanghai's fiscal situation must be compared with cities, first in East China, and then in China as a whole. Statistics have been found for such comparisons, and they are revealing, even though they do not cover the part of revenues and expenditures that is extrabudgetary.

Shanghai was not the only city on the delta or in East China to have a high official extraction rate. Compared with other parts of the country, extraction minus expenditure in Shanghai's nearby provinces and cities was also heavy. But from 1981 to 1985, the ratio of revenues to spending in these places dropped sharply. Table 1.2–6 shows the change both over time and between the major cities in this most important part of fiscal China.

Commodities produced in Shanghai also brought the state a windfall of sales tax. In the mid-1980s, the average sales tax on Shanghai goods was 21 percent, much higher than the similar imposts on goods from nearby Jiangnan cities (for Wuxi and Suzhou, only 13 and 12 percent respectively).[132] Even formally uniform national taxes—when they existed, though they have never supplied most central revenues—tended to raise Shanghai costs more than those of most other places.

A progressive profits tax introduced in 1984 used varied rates by industry and by location, for example, but the gist of the change was that Shanghai ended up paying one-quarter of the whole country's money that was produced by the progressive aspect of the tax. This could have resulted from several factors (larger plants in Shanghai, better management, or less ability to hide profits from the tax collectors, for example). It nonetheless added to the city's fiscal burden. Of the 1,411 Shanghai local enterprises that had to turn in taxes on profits above the minimum bracket, 72 percent had to remit one-fifth of their profits or more, and 39 percent had to remit three-tenths or more.[133]

National comparisons can also show how Shanghai budgetary extraction compares with that in cities outside the East China area. Since the Tang era, the Yangzi delta has been a center of production, whereas official consumption and politics were mainly elsewhere, especially in the north. Even in modern times, e.g., during the Republican period, Shanghai delta capitalists were in considerable tension with military politicians, whose main relation with them was one of taxation.[134] This pattern did not change for many years, even after China's reforms were announced.

Postentrepreneurialism, and Exactions Other Than Money

The tax regime centralized Shanghai under the state in Mao's time in many nonmonetary ways too. The metropolis not only gave more money to the PRC budget than other places; it also gave more technicians, had fewer and smaller nonstate institutions (including collective and private enterprises), and operated in general under notoriously tighter rules. Most important, the heavy tax regime

Table 1.2–6

Budgetary Revenues Over Budgetary Expenditures and Budgetary Revenues Minus Expenditures Per Person for Major Cities Near Shanghai
(percentages, and yuan per capita)

	Budgetary revenues as a percentage of budgetary expenditures					Budgetary revenues minus expenditures per capita, 1984 (in yuan)
	1981	1982	1983	1984	1985	
Shanghai	1,054	880	808	582	432	11,073
Weighted avg.	*936*	*803*	*558*	*470*	*370*	*363*
Hangzhou	536	563	470	n/a	323	322
Wuxi	1,058	840	569	505	523	282
Suzhou	930	585	420	363	391	212
Changzhou	1,085	810	436	372	404	193
Nanjing	515	510	366	312	296	171
Ningbo	845	1,016	428	360	264	137
Huzhou	552	561	342	244	277	67
Nantong	1,068	752	279	241	273	56
Yangzhou	517	351	161	155	175	20
Lianyungang	340	309	165	124	146	13
Wenzhou	n/a	n/a	138	109	126	4

Notes and Sources: The second, italicized row is a weighted average for all these cities, and its decrease shows a lessening of extraction rates over time (although these figures would be very slightly altered if the three cells of unavailable data could be added). Yangzhou and Lianyungang, from which per-capita extraction was low, are in northern Jiangsu; and southern Zhejiang's Wenzhou, the least taxed city, has been a center of quasi-capitalist experiments. The order of the table is by budgetary revenues minus expenditures per capita (extrabudgetary figures were not available); even though a full account of it would include the effects of fixed prices, the degree of extraction from Shanghai is evident. If the cities are, instead, put in order by the ratio of budgetary revenues over expenditures, Shanghai does not top the list in all years (though it does so in 1983 and 1984); but Shanghai and Sunan cities show considerably heavier budgetary extraction rates than the others. Computed from raw figures in *Zhongguo caizheng tongji, 1950–1985* (Chinese Fiscal Statistics, 1950–1985), Comprehensive Planning Office of the PRC Ministry of Finance, ed. (Beijing: Zhongguo Caizheng Jingji Chuban She, 1987), p. 57, and *Zhongguo chengshi tongji nianjian, 1985* (Statistical Yearbook of Chinese Cities, 1985), State Statistical Bureau, ed. (Beijing: Zhongguo Tongji Xinxi Zixun Fuwu Zhongxin and Xin Shijie Chuban She, 1985), p. 37.

drained the spirit of enterprise. As a local editor put it, "Shanghai was the 'golden milk-cow' of the planned economy. As long as the state fed and protected it, Shanghai continued to give the most milk. But . . . the city learned to rely on the state and lost its ability to organize its own markets and sources of raw materials."[135] The long-term economic cost for all China, not just Shanghai, of this loss of managerial will is difficult to estimate, but it may have been very great. Nonmonetary extractions from the city are basically inseparable from the direct imposts.

Technical talent and machines were systematically removed from Shanghai, just as funds were.[136] When the northeast needed good laborers in its electrical, chemical, rubber, and machine industries, a technical recruiting team got them from Shanghai.[137] When a new automobile factory was constructed in Manchuria, over ten thousand Shanghai engineers and workers went there to help build it.[138] In the first decade of the PRC, a campaign forced many Shanghai firms to leave the city entirely—though often to nearby places. Sixteen newly "joint state-private" stencil factories were ordered to shift from Shanghai to Hangzhou.[139] Other firms went farther, to Lanzhou, Urumqi, or Xining.[140] All told, 196 factories and 168 stores left the city for twenty different provinces in one year alone.[141] This pattern continued long after it began in the 1950s, and it affected institutions and physical plant as well as personnel.[142]

Private enterprises in Shanghai have been even more restricted by heavy taxes than in other places. Private firms in the city have to pay an 84 percent "accumulation tax" (*leijin shui*).[143] In Jiangsu, there is only a 20 percent income tax (*suode shui*) and a 5 percent business tax (*yingye shui*) on profits. By 1988, Shanghai private entrepreneurs were demanding that the municipal government pass a law to protect them. Many kinds of taxes and license fees were, they complained, more onerous than in other places. The relatively great difficulty of renting space in Shanghai also meant that the city's reforms outside the state sector were, in comparison with those in other Chinese cities, at least as constrained as were reforms in the state-owned major revenue factories. Central Shanghai's private and collective sectors as a portion of the economy remained small by all measures much longer than in other places. The manager of a small metal-punching factory in Shanghai's Jiading county figured that if he moved his plant just a few kilometers across the border into Jiangsu, his profits would rise by 50,000 to 60,000 yuan each year.[144]

Shanghai private managers reported that the taxation they faced was "heavy and diverse," and that excessive levies were the main cause of scant development in the city's private sector. For example, the Coral Knitting Factory in the first quarter of 1988 had a gross revenue of 317,000 yuan, and it had profits of 36,000 yuan. But the private manager reported that his firm, after all its taxes, could retain only 4,000 yuan—so that his effective tax rate was 89 percent.[145] Levies this high, of which there are many reports, may lead an analyst to assume books must have been cooked, and almost surely they were. Otherwise, a business under such conditions would have scant incentive to exist. The pressure to hide money in this system amounts to a control, because it threatens managers with being found in illegality. The main unevenness is that Shanghai businesses are more restricted and less in charge of their own fates than are firms in other places.

Competition for Shanghai from Cities Nearby and Inland

Shanghai has sometimes been compared to a "big boat" (*da chuan*)—not liable to rock, but also difficult to turn. This pattern has been hard to hide from foreign investors, although it is even more prevalent in domestic capital allocations. For example, throughout China including Shanghai, overseas investors are supposed to enjoy a choice of "three capital" (*san zi*) arrangements: foreign investment and management, joint investment with Chinese management, or joint investment with joint management. But in Shanghai, interpretations of these rules have been more restrictive than elsewhere.[146] Chapter 1.3 will explore these restrictions in more detail. With regard to Shanghai and other PRC entrepreneurs too, no matter whether private or collective, bureaucratic rules in the taxpaying metropolis were by all accounts more stifling than elsewhere.

The Chinese government announced many innovations of industrial rules during the reforms, to let companies explore new products and management forms. But Shanghai, because its main product was revenue, very seldom benefited from allowances for such experiments. For example, during early 1988 sixteen cities—including Changzhou, Guangzhou, Nanjing, and Ningbo but not Shanghai—were chosen to "trailblaze" in a new wave of PRC urban reforms. Among the many areas to be explored were "experimentation in the reduction of tax rates . . . creating an external environment of fair competition for various types of enterprises."[147] Stock shares could be sold by factories in these cities to encourage more efficiency among large state enterprises—even though the dividends directly reduced state revenues in the short run. Bankruptcy laws were not just to be passed; they were actually to be implemented, allowing strong enterprises to buy weak ones. More short-term money markets were to be approved, and "the wage system of enterprises was to be separated from the wage system of [state] institutions." Such changes would have benefited Shanghai too—even open discussion of them, if implementation was very ragged, could allow more flexibility in the ossified economic structures of many cities. But the central budget makers and their satraps in Shanghai forced any such changes to be clandestine in the large industries of their most important tax base.

The metropolis acquired a reputation as a "house that follows the law" (*shoufa hu*). Mayor Zhu Rongji said in September 1988 that Shanghai people are very "law-abiding" (*guiju*).[148] Whether this was a compliment or a snicker, it was by many accounts generally true. A disgruntled columnist said Shanghai was always overly "law-abiding, following the straight and narrow" (*xungui daoju*). The only things that could be done were those that appeared on official documents with red letterheads (*hongtou wenjian*).[149] Shanghai economists have often made the argument that big cities in general, and their own city in particular, have long been heavily "controlled."[150] These reins include strenuous birth controls, restrictions on the availability and use of land, rationing of nonindustrial energy consumption, and many other restrictions. High tax and profit extraction may be the most obvious form of economic control, but it is integrally related to all the others. What the tax shows is not injustice to Shanghai, and certainly not ordinary poverty there, but an uneven pattern of control that worked against the city more sharply than the politicians who enforced it have wished to make public.

Why Such High Rates of Extraction in Shanghai?

Shanghai's imposts have been high, but many of the reasons still need to be explored. Various causes might be adduced for the phenomenon: (1) the city's history as a light industrial center surely contributed to it, since light industry makes consumer goods that provide a means for the government to tap resources in China's largest market, which is rural; (2) Shanghai's role as a base for radical politicians during the Cultural Revolution may have contributed to later tax discrimination (whether justified or not); and (3) there may be further grounds for such discrimination, perhaps based in subethnic tensions between northern Jiangsu (Subei) people in the city government and the majority from southern Jiangsu or northern Zhejiang (here called Jiangnan), or based on other factors that affect periodic central government negotiations about provincial tax rates.[151] These various hypotheses to explain the high taxes are worth exploring, even before a look at their economic effects.

Did Naturally Taxable Industries Bring High Extraction?

Shanghai's traditional economic forte, light industry, meant that the city's economy would—and did—come under more stringent Beijing control than any other province-level unit in China. During the 1950s, the Chinese government raised money mainly because of two "scissors gaps" (a term from Soviet 1920s debates, but in Chinese *jiandao cha*). The first developed because the state set industrial prices high and agricultural prices low. It mandated sales prices for both sectors; and because it owned the factories, it reaped the profit on the difference, which peasants paid. The second came about because the state set light industrial prices high, but heavy industrial prices low. Because light industries sell mainly to consumers (both rural and urban), whereas heavy industries sell mainly to state-owned units, the government budget benefited, and all Chinese people paid.

Shanghai had a great deal of light industry in 1949 and was able to develop the consumer goods sector further during the next decade, so the government was able to process many low-priced agricultural inputs and sell the products dearly. The stricter its control of factory costs, the more profits it could realize.

The Transition to Socialism and the Great Leap Forward were also opportunities for Shanghai to develop heavy industries. Despite their expense and lack of ability to absorb much labor, heavy industries might have diversified the city's potential for independence—contrary to the interests of fiscal, though not heavy industrial, bureaucracies in Beijing—if those big factories in Shanghai had been locally run. But most of them, until the mid-1980s or in some cases longer, remained central fiefdoms. They did not hire so many workers as light industries, but they fostered a conservative, unionized, central-associated, mostly male workforce in Shanghai that was a local support of the municipal leaders who were appointed by Beijing to ensure a flow of taxes especially from light industries.

For three decades, from the mid-1950s to the mid-1980s, this structure became established. After 1984, however, the state could no longer hide its inability to provide low-priced inputs, especially for the industries producing consumer goods. As light industrial costs rose, the "scissors gap" between light and heavy industry became less important. So a long-term basis was created for more fiscal independence of the city—but in the short term, Shanghai industrial costs rose. The metropolis faced competition from rich but lower-tax Chinese areas. Its efficiency (as measured by indices of total product over cost) declined sharply. Although the natural taxability of some industries was important in Shanghai's historical evolution as a center mainly for revenues in the 1950s, by the late 1980s materials price inflation had cut the state's possible profits from this way of using the metropolis. Bureaucratic inertia in both Beijing and Shanghai tended to slow the fall of Shanghai's tax rates. Not until the middle and late 1980s did central cadres begin to change their intended habits about taxes, because of a new situation: the tax base of many quick-growth industries, selling to the newly wealthy rural population, had already developed inland, outside Shanghai.

Did Resentment at Shanghai's Cultural Revolution Role Bring Taxes?

To what extent is Shanghai's history during rule by the Gang of Four responsible for its later burden? Especially in the late 1960s, many other provinces' production of consumer goods suffered more than Shanghai's.[152] In 1969, for example, the metropolis's growth rate was relatively high. This was an era in which "the whole country protected Shanghai," at least for the purpose of assuring its raw materials supplies.[153]

Table 1.2-7

Shanghai's Budgetary Expenditures and Revenues Through the Early Reforms (average annual percentage increases)

	1953–57	1958–65	1966–78	1979–82	1953–82
Local revenues	24	41	7.9	–0.3	17.4
Local expenditures	4.8	12.3	10.4	–6.2	7.6

Note and Source: Separate figures for years in the early 1970s were, unfortunately, not offered in the source. *Shanghai jingji, neibu ben: 1949–1982* (Shanghai Economy, Internal Volume: 1949–1982), Shanghai Academy of Social Sciences, ed. (Shanghai: Shanghai Shehui Kexue Yuan Chuban She, 1984), p. 993.

Table 1.2-7 shows that in the whole 1953–82 period, Shanghai's budgetary revenues rose at the phenomenal rate of 17.4 percent annually. Expenditures also rose annually, but by just 7.6 percent. The only period in which the yearly increase of expenditures is greater than that of revenues was 1966–78. That pattern would not reappear until the late 1980s. The increase of discrimination against nonstate elements in Shanghai was somewhat slowed in the early 1970s, but spending always remained far less than revenues. The amount of money extracted from Shanghai has been much greater than the amount spent there in all periods of PRC history before the 1990s.

Shanghai's infrastructural investment was three times higher between 1977 and 1982 than between 1966 and 1976, but this mainly reflects its low level during the earlier period.[154] Radical rule in Shanghai poured money into military and heavy industrial plants, not into basic improvements, urban services, or the beginning of production in new industries with new technology. Shanghai's history of fiscal treatment in the late 1960s was somewhat less extractive than in other years, but the expenditure pattern was similar to that of other periods there since the 1950s: spending was not much, and in projects that benefited central interests rather than the city's people or their economic prospects. The radicals were central satraps, too.

The figures in Table 1.2-8 show a relatively fast rise in taxation during the time that Shanghai radical politicians held power in Beijing—but also a peaking of the percentage of local revenue from local taxes (not necessarily for local uses) toward the end of that time, about 1975. The radicals put some money into Shanghai, but they also extracted fast-increasing amounts for uses in national politics that undoubtedly benefited them. Although Shanghai expenditures, as a portion of local revenues, rose notably during the Cultural Revolution, they also

Table 1.2-8

Shanghai Revenues (contrasts with Tianjin, Guangdong, and Guangzhou)

		Sources						
	Revenues (billions of yuan)	Central units' revenue %	Shanghai units' revenue %	Loans and bonds %	Shanghai spending as a % of Shanghai revenue	Tianjin spending as a % of Tianjin revenue	Guangdong spending as a % of Guangdong revenue	Guangzhou spending as a % of Guangzhou revenue
1952	2	87	7	6	11	28	46	
1957	5	90	9	1	8	20	45	
1962	6	28	71	1	6	25	46	
1965	8	24	74	1	9	26	47	
1970	11	12	86	1	11	23	52	
1975	15	7	91	1	18	27	50	
1978	19	11	88	1	14	37	70	
1979	19	10	88	1	14	40	81	
1980	20	12	87	1	10	36	73	
1981	20	15	84	1	9	35	69	
1982	20	16	82	1	10	53	76	
1983	20	23	75	1	11	52	81	
1984	22	24	75	1	14	47	97	
1985	26	30	69	1	17	56	96	
1986	26	30	68	1	23	64	109	51

(continued)

Table 1.2–8 *(continued)*

1987	24	30	68	2	22	56	97	49
1988	26	38	60	2	25	78	107	47
1989	30	44	55	1	25	84	103	53
1990	28	40	58	1	27	90	115	66

Notes and Sources: See *Shanghai tongji nianjian, 1988* (Shanghai Statistical Yearbook, 1988), Li Mouhuan et al., eds. (Shanghai: Shanghai Shi Tongji Ju, 1988) [*SHTJNJ88*], p. 65, and *SHTJNJ91*, p. 53, from which the yuan figures are rounded to the nearest billion and most of the percentages are calculated. Another table, in *Shanghai Statistical Yearbook: 1988 Concise Edition*, Municipal Statistical Bureau of Shanghai, ed. (Beijing: China Statistical Publishing House, 1988), p. 25, provides the basis for calculating the last Shanghai column. This gives the ratio of total Shanghai budgetary expenditure in total Shanghai revenue. For the time series from which the relatively high Tianjin expenditure/revenue ratios were calculated, see *Tianjin tongji nianjian, 1986* (Tianjin Statistical Yearbook, 1986), Tianjin Statistical Bureau, ed. (Beijing: Zhongguo Tongji Chuban She, 1986) [*TJTJNJ86*], pp. 333–34; *TJTJNJ88*, p. 237; and *TJTJNJ91*, p. 267. For raw data that were the basis of the Guangdong figures, see *Guangdong sheng tongji nianjian, 1986* (Guangdong Province Statistical Yearbook, 1986), Guangdong Province Statistical Bureau, ed. (Beijing: Zhongguo Tongji Chuban She, 1986) [*GDTJNJ86*], p. 299; *GDTJNJ87*, p. 367; and *GDTJNJ91*, p. 340. See also *Guangzhou tongji nianjian, 1991* (Guangzhou Statistical Yearbook, 1991), Guangzhou City Statistical Bureau, ed. (Beijing: Zhongguo Tongji Chuban She, 1991), pp. 24–25. The sums of the third, fourth, and fifth columns, all percentages, do not necessarily add to 100 because of rounding.

did so in the Chinese place most like Shanghai (Tianjin)—from a much higher base level. The partial lessening of pressure on Shanghai's finances at that time cannot be taken as a peculiarity of radical rule there, since it applies elsewhere too.

Under the radicals' tax regime, the Shanghai city government was given a great many firms to run without even nominal supervision from cadres in Beijing. The rise of extraction (especially for an era when prices were stable) was very sharp at this time. After 1976, this acceleration of total taxes did not reverse; on the contrary, it continued at least through 1978.

The reforms in less tightly controlled places, especially those in Jiangnan outside central Shanghai, reduced those areas' contributions to the central budget. So after 1975, until the 1990s, an even lower portion than before of the central budget could be afforded for infrastructure in the metropolis. Thus the ratio of Shanghai local spending to revenue began a period of decline that lasted at least until 1981. (These changes are presented in the sixth column of Table 1.2–8, along with comparative figures from Tianjin, Guangzhou, and Guangdong that show very much higher rates of local spending to local revenue for all periods—and in the Tianjin case, a 1975–81 pattern that contrasts sharply with that in Shanghai.) Only by 1984–85, when the state planning system collapsed, did this spending/revenues ratio begin a rise. The reason was not just that Shanghai units desperately needed capital after so many years of uncompensated depreciation. Evidence from behavior and reasonable premises about interests also suggest the central state could then no longer effectively prevent some Shanghai firms from keeping more funds.

A corollary, presented in the table's third column, was that the government had to rely increasingly on revenue from firms that were at least nominally under the central state. During the whole period from 1975 to 1990, this portion rose from 7 percent to 40 percent. Total extraction also rose in the later parts of this period. But except in 1989, a special year, the increases were by that time not much different from the rate of inflation. In the 1990s, they slowed further.

Change in the national structure of funding was sharp by the mid-1980s—and this is made clearest if the situation then is compared with much earlier times. The documented portion of the state budget spent by central ministries in Beijing decreased from about 70 percent in the 1950s, down to 60 percent in the 1960s, and further down to an average of about 50 percent in the first seven years of the 1980s. In the period 1981 to 1985, the portion of the total state budget transferred to individuals, especially as wages and bonuses, exceeded three-fifths. Also, the portion of national income in the hands of local governments, enterprises, functional agencies, and service units—but outside their budgets—increased sharply, from 13.5 percent in 1979 to 21.4 percent in 1986.[155] Even though the extrabudgetary total income of these nominally subordinate units was reported to be only half as large as the state budget, the increments in absolute value by the mid-1980s were similar, as was also the case between the PRC budget and extrabudgets.

Shanghai in late reforms badly needed infrastructure, but central conservatives wanted to keep enough money going into operating capital and quick-return projects, which produced more tax revenues. The response of Shanghai local leaders, far more independent by 1989, was to invest in infrastructure with large loans whose repayment would require later investment in factories. As the director of the Shanghai Planning Commission himself explained, "The [investment limit] 'cage' was really too small. . . . Now the infrastructural projects were already in progress, we could only cut the industrial projects. But in this way, we would have cut our ability to pay back the loans for infrastructural projects."[156]

In 1990, when President Yang Shangkun visited Shanghai, some locals there "complained to him about the plight of Shanghai and mocked that they wondered whether it was the center's policy to see the decline of Shanghai. Yang reassured Shanghai leaders that the center was determined to assist Shanghai," and he claimed that Deng Xiaoping (also then in town) had the same view.[157] In fact, they were so grateful for the city's relative quiescence in 1989, they had little choice. April 1990 and March 1992 saw new central concessions of powers to the city. These surely spurred Shanghai's major revival in the early 1990s, but a broad political view of the situation is that Beijing at this time had no other option. Political safety for the regime lay, more clearly than before, in lower rates of extraction from this metropolis.

Did Shanghai/Jiangnan Disdain of Subei Politicians Bring the Unevenness?

Simple political discrimination against Shanghai is, among these hypothesized reasons for the high taxes, one of the most plausible and understandable—but all the evidence for it is circumstantial. A full outline of East China's political economy must take account of the continuing power of politicians who were associated with General Chen Yi's Third Field Army, which took this whole area for the PRC in 1949 and established all major administrations there. This topic may not seem to concern taxes, but since the main state policy at Shanghai was taxation, the means to implement it locally deserve to be discussed. Cadres from relatively impoverished parts of East China were very important in this organization, and many of them from areas such as northern Jiangsu had been given no reason for special fondness toward Shanghai. Jiangnan people have on occasion openly disdained them, and it should hardly be surprising that they resent this opinion.

Shanghai-Jiangnan people were not dominant at the very top level of the city's politics from the mid-1970s to the 1990s, even though they have always staffed most managerial posts and are a majority in the population. But in 1989, Zhu Rongji from Hunan was promoted to the mayoralty and for a period was as popular in Shanghai as anyone in the heated atmosphere of that year could have expected. By the 1990s, the change to subtler satraps, more in tune with Jiangnan entrepreneurs, was permanent.[158] But for more than a decade of reforms before that, leaders from Subei and other traditionally less well-to-do parts of the country dominated two extraordinarily different types of activity in Shanghai: they led the city's Party, and they picked the city's garbage.[159]

Jiangnan people in Shanghai freely report they disdain some habits of the approximately one-quarter of their city's population that hails from Subei and is disproportionately employed in lowly occupations such as sanitary maintenance, stevedoring, and construction. Subei people are thought to wear garish clothes, eat too much garlic, and have a bumpkin culture. This pattern of discrimination has given the local government, often led at the top by Communists from Subei who were educated in Shanghai, a very understandable bent toward affirmative action, as well as a nonlocalist view of Shanghai's proper role in China's whole polity and economy.

Among later mayors of Shanghai, the most important 1980s politician was Jiang Zemin, originally from Yangzhou, an elegant city that he, at least, considers Subei. Jiang is a person whom surprisingly many Shanghai local leaders rather openly report disliking despite his suaveness and very high political position (by the 1990s, head of the CCP). But Jiang was reported by some interviewees to be essentially a tax collector in Shanghai. During his earlier period as minister of electronic industries, Shanghai had often been on the short list of places for approval of investments in computers—just the sort of industry the metropolis needed then. However, Jiang had presided over a series of decisions that sent high-tech projects to Beijing and elsewhere, rather than to Shanghai. In May 1989, Jiang personally ordered the closing of the most important reformist newspaper in the city, the *World Economic Herald.* When he was elevated to the general secretaryship of the CCP in the next month, he acquired a very high-profile role in a national government whose most obvious traits were its willingness to use state coercion and its large budget deficit. Interviewees in the metropolis, referring to their top local leaders over several decades in general, opined often that such politicians "speak Pekingese but not Shanghainese." They did not think their city had been well represented in the nation as a whole.

Subei cadres have also been a dominant group in another administration of great importance to Shanghai: the top of the Party in Jiangsu.[160] For that large province they have been able to garner lower tax rates. Leaders in Nanjing have understandably hoped to control the parts of their domain that reproduce capital most quickly, i.e. Sunan. There is no evidence that they were anything but happy to see Shanghai taxed. The metropolis is Jiangsu's main economic competitor, if seen as separate, and it was long deemed all but officially as a place that needed to live down its history as a "parasitic consumption city."

Although Subei cadres in Nanjing had scant love lost on Shanghai, Wu-dialect-speaking Sunan leaders in Jiangsu's booming southern cities such as Suzhou and Wuxi have long enjoyed extensive personal contacts in Shanghai. They also enjoyed, however, the rather favorable economic climate Nanjing arranged for them—in fact, they were the biggest beneficiaries of this situation. Shanghai businessmen, for their part, often had family links in Sunan. They could find some value in the structure that emerged, even though they knew it slowed the growth of Shanghai.

Cellular Negotiation vs. Overall Planning: Jiangsu, Shanghai, and Beijing

The complex cellular *and* extractive pattern meant that decisions were made with more regard to maintaining local exemptions than to maximizing overall or long-term growth. Jiangsu, for example, has been more successful in this political negotiating than has Shanghai, partly because the newness and geographical dispersion of Sunan rural industries have made extraction more difficult for high officials, partly because Jiangsu economic politicians have been more assiduous or successful in obtaining good central rules for their area, and partly because constraining rules have been ignored or changed more readily in that province. Jiangsu overtook Shanghai in the mid-1980s as China's most productive industrial province.

Less than a month after the Gang of Four was arrested, Jiangsu was designated an "experimental province" for fiscal reforms. Beijing set a yearly ratio of Jiangsu revenues that would be handed over to the central budget. In 1977, this amount was 58 percent of the local fiscal intake; from 1978 to 1980, it was 57 percent. Under this four-year guarantee, Jiangsu could keep the remainder.[161] Like Guangdong or Fujian—but unlike neighboring Shanghai—Jiangsu was allowed to prosper. No habit of uniform treatment underlay decisions in China as a whole. The cellular structure meant that each different compartment had an individualized regime. Taxes were haggled, year by year and place by place.

Some of the payments, even in late reforms, have been traditional and in kind, not in money. At least twenty provinces have agreed to give the central government first claim on negotiated amounts of specific classes of produce. In the case of Shanghai, light industrial products as a group are among those on which central ministries had options to buy. These were "appropriated commodities" (*diaobo shangpin*). They were not purchased by Beijing, but were sent there much as tribute was once shipped on the Grand Canal to the northern capital. Shanghai's tributes included a number of consumer durables, such as refrigerators and color TV sets. Money for the budget in Beijing, however, is in practice the most important contribution from the metropolis. A Shanghai economist averred that the process for determining this whole structure of taxes, prices, profits, and production has been guided not by economic principles but by political ones. He chided the State Planning Commission for being, in practice though not in name, a "State Negotiating Commission."[162]

Similar bargaining takes place periodically in Beijing at national economic conferences that decide various provinces' share of the central budget. Inland and poorer provinces are more autonomously represented than is Shanghai, whose top leaders got their jobs precisely because they made big promises of remittances on those occasions. Bureaucratic offices of the central government tend to support the idea that Shanghai should make large contributions, since it has always done so. The history of such haggling may be traced over many periods, even the early 1970s, and good information on it is available for the 1980s.

City, District, and Factory Taxes After 1970

In 1970, Shanghai sent 88 percent of its fiscal income to the central government. In 1971, a new revenue system was introduced, and this early decentralizing reform followed the slogan "Fixed receipts and fixed expenditures, with both receipts and expenditures guaranteed."[163] Fiscal powers were "sent down," and the managements of many enterprises were localized. The fiscal principle of the Fourth Five-Year Plan was that "upward remittances would be guaranteed, and the surplus would be retained, as determined each year."[164] These national rules of the early 1970s are very like ones advocated in the post-1978 reforms. But these procedures for setting Shanghai's tax rates did not, of course, guarantee they would be low.

Shanghai's 1971 fiscal target of 10.882 billion yuan was overfulfilled slightly. The local expenditure target, however, was only 9 percent the size of the revenue quota for that year.[165] This was underspent by one-twentieth of the target. Such high taxation and low spending meant that all of Shanghai for 1971 had a paltry 426 million yuan to keep—at least, only that much was reported. This was less than 4 percent of actual revenues. The low retention (some of which could later be contributed to the national budget), when supplemented with the central government's actual total expenditure in Shanghai, totaled just one-eighth as much as the city's intake of all official money.

In 1972, the plan was changed in a way that further disadvantaged Shanghai: Each province-level unit, including the metropolis, was required to send half of any collected surplus over a set amount (a standard 100 million yuan) to the central government—regardless of the province's economic size. The 1972 fiscal target for Shanghai was 11.893 billion yuan; in that year, the actual collections were only 57 million above that. But in 1973, the target went up to 12.404 billion, and excess collections were 369 million (of which most was therefore sent to Beijing). From 1971 to 1973, the money that Shanghai could retain was reportedly less than 12 percent of what it forwarded to the national government.[166]

For 1974 and 1975, the extraction rules became much more severe. Central authorities declared that Shanghai could retain only 1.1 percent of its targeted fiscal revenues, plus 30 percent of collections above that. The combined quota for these years was 27.332 billion yuan, and actual collections were 3 percent less than that. The city thus could retain less than 300 million yuan—a far smaller sum than in 1973. This pressure on Shanghai during 1974–75 was exercised through raising the city's fiscal target beyond what was actually collectable. Shanghai's own expenditures had to come from a set, small percentage of the base amount. Post-1978 reform tax policies for the metropolis bear a much stronger resemblance, in both procedures and results, to patterns of the early 1970s than either does to the draconian policies of 1975.

In 1976, the tax system was changed yet again, in a way whose only clarity was its reflection of conflicting top policies at that time. The new formulae for figuring taxes were complex enough to incorporate all the diverse extractive and incentive principles in various earlier years. Local receipts and expenditures were supposed to be fixed, but also "linked." Shanghai's economy performed anemically in that year, notably in heavy industries,[167] so profits were reduced. The upshot was that in 1976, Shanghai's fiscal quota was lowered to 13.840 billion yuan, of which only 95 percent was collected. At the same time, the central government reduced Shanghai's authorization to spend as much as had been originally planned.[168] The habit of each province bargaining for its tax rate, with no national standard on how much any place should pay, was completely normal by this time.

In a pathbreaking move of 1979, the state decided to "divide the stoves from which people eat" (*fenzao chifan*), so that the center disclaimed a right it was slowly losing anyway: It could no longer take funds arbitrarily from provinces.[169] But this meant that supervising companies, far above the factory or store level where production and services actually take place, became fully responsible for any losses in the units below them—and for subsidizing them when they could not break even.

The annual economic conference in Beijing, which became a regular institution in the 1980s, includes the leaders of provinces, along with representatives of central ministries that need money. The centrally appointed leaders of Shanghai attend, of course—and are duly honored for the great sums they volunteer their city to pay. Even Shanghai people, who know that Shanghai's tax from this process has been far too great, have real pride that their city has made such a large contribution to China. During this period, the central budget was beginning to develop big deficits, largely because farmers now had to be paid real money to supply the state's urban constituencies. Beijing was compelled in some cases explicitly to "borrow" from provincial governments, especially Shanghai. These funds were never returned.

In February 1980, a financial guarantee system was mooted in the State Council for all parts of the country.[170] To maintain some predictability in the central government's revenues, however, this system was not implemented nationwide on an immediate basis—and as before, even where it was implemented, the rates for each place were negotiated separately. What actually happened over the next several years can be schematized in a chart that shows the kind of system that determined each province's revenue retention or subsidy, as well as the various coefficients involved. Table 1.2–9, presenting this information for all of China's provinces in the early 1980s, is arranged in approximate ascending

Table 1.2-9

Provincial Revenue Retention and Subsidy Rules, 1980–1983 (summary of central government agreements with each locality, percentages, and millions of yuan)

	1980			1981			1982			1983		
	Way (1)	% (2)	Local subsidy (3)	Way (1)	% (2)	Local subsidy (3)	Way (1)	% (2)	Local subsidy (3)	Way (1)	% (2)	Local subsidy (3)
Shanghai	Z	8.6%f		Z	8.46%		Z	10.51%		Z	n/a	
Tianjin	Z	30.6%f		Z	31.07%		Z	34.92%		Z	n/a	
Beijing	Z	28.1%f		Z	26.95%		Z	35.49%		Z	n/a	
Liaoning	B	30.1%f		B	30.0%		B	30.0%		B	34.2%	
Jiangsu	B	39.0%f		B	37.0%		B	38.0%		B	35.7%	
Shandong	H	10.0%s		B	48.9%		B	48.9%		B	51.5%	
Zhejiang	H	13.0%s		H	13.0%		B	56.0%		B	51.8%	
Hebei	H	27.2%s		H	27.2%		B	67.5%		B	63.5%	
Hubei	H	44.7%s		H	44.7%		B	69.0%		G	63.8%	
Hunan	H	42.0%s		H	42.0%		B	75.0%		G	70.3%	
Anhui	H	58.1%s		H	58.1%		B	77.0%		B	76.15%	
Henan	H	75.4%s		H	75.4%		B	82.0%		G	77.8%	
Sichuan	H	72.0%s		H	72.0%		B	85.0%		B	83.7%	
Shaanxi	H	88.1%s		H	88.1%		B	100%		B	100%	
Shanxi	H	57.9%s		H	57.9%		H	75.4%		G	82.6%	
Guangdong	D			D			D			D		
Fujian	D		150	D		150	D		150	D		63
Jiangxi	H		138	H		138	H		138	H		150
Gansu	H	53.2%s		H	53.2%		B	80.0%		H		169

(continued)

Table 1.2-9 *(continued)*

Jilin	H	300	H	300	H	300	H	234
Guangxi	H	297	H	327	H	359	H	308
Ningxia	H	300	H	330	H	363	H	355
Qinghai	H	402	H	442	H	486	H	452
Yunnan	H	330	H	477	H	525	H	448
Tibet	H	496	H	546	H	601	H	581
Guizhou	H	526	H	578	H	636	H	597
Heilong'g	H	887	H	887	H	887	H	900
Xinjiang	H	895	H	984	H	1,083	H	1,121
In. Mong.	H	1,168	H	1,285	H	1,414	H	1,387
(Total Subsidies):		5,889		6,444		6,941		6,765

Source: Tian Yinong, Zhu Fulin, and Xiang Huaicheng, *Zhongguo caizheng guanli tizhi de gaige* (The Structural Reform of Chinese Fiscal Management) (Beijing: Jingji Kexue Chuban She, 1985), pp. 88–89.

Notes and abbreviations: Blank cells in the graph indicate no transfer of money; numbers indicate provincial governments' funds, coming either from retention on the specified bases or from central subsidies. The table has been put in approximate declining order of extraction, based on a revision of the other table on extraction by province; the list in the source is regional. Each tax regime involves three elements:

(1) Way: method (*banfa*) of figuring local retention

Z = *zong'e fencheng*, percentage part of total revenues is retained by the local government, to be renegotiated each year (in these years, for the three "directly ruled cities" only, with Shanghai having much the lowest retention rate)

H = *huafen shouzhi*, percentage or amount of specific line items of state revenues and budget is retained by the locality, to be renegotiated each year

B = *bili baogan*, guarantee to locality of a variable percentage of local tax revenues only, for several years running

D = *da baogan*, a "big guarantee" that the province is free of central taxes, for several years running (in these years, only for Guangdong and for Fujian with a subsidy also)

G = *guding bili zong'e fencheng*, a fixed percentage of total revenues goes to the locality, for several years running

(2) Local %: division ratios (*fencheng bili*)

f = *fencheng bili*, the locally retained percentage of all local revenues, or

s = *gongshang shuiliu*, the locally retained percentage of industrial and commercial taxes

(3) Subsidy: fixed amounts of subsidy (*butie ding'e*), for some places

order by the portions of extraction that each tax regime implied over the whole period. The rates of impost decreased in later years, but the types of arrangements remained similar. The pattern is motley, and only in the early 1990s did some leaders, such as Zhu Rongji, seriously propose a uniform tax law to replace it.

Shanghai has been subject to several different fiscal rules, of which the most important lasted from 1976 straight through to the mid-1980s materials crisis. Under the 1976 system, the center set both a revenue target and a local spending target for Shanghai (in that year 1.6 billion yuan, with another small amount, 0.15 billion yuan, retained for discretionary use by the city). All other tax collections up to the mandatory revenue target went to Beijing—as well as 70 percent of any above the revenue target, though, as the most recent close analyst of this situation has written, "in practice the target was so high that it was very difficult to overachieve."[171]

By 1985, the "slippage" of earlier years had already shown that the structure had to be changed. So the 1976 fiscal reform was reformed yet again. Shanghai was assured of 23.2 percent of its local revenue that year—a portion that was scheduled to apply for the next six years, although in fact it did not. This percentage was still low, but the center did not budget it in detail. Thus 1985 remissions were 77 percent of Shanghai revenue, rather than 88 percent as in 1980–84. This was still too high to make the city competitive, as events soon showed. There is an uncharitable way to put this: Either the Beijing-appointed Shanghai municipal leaders in 1985 made faulty economic predictions, or else they acted more on the basis of their own careers than of the interests they ostensibly represented.

A third fiscal reform was needed already by 1988, because the period 1986–88, climaxed at the end by the hepatitis epidemic, had seen more revenue "slippage." The tinkering continued: from a low percentage of retention back to a low absolute amount of retention (as in 1976). The weight of the burden, figured either way, was the main issue, but this discourse on methods obfuscated it with some success. The city fathers agreed to a "contract," committing Shanghai to remit 10.5 billion yuan each year from 1988 to 1990, retaining the rest. This was better than the previous tax regime, but still much the heaviest for any Chinese province. The two "slippages" of 1981–83 and 1986–88 were the main generators of fiscal reform in Shanghai.

Although Shanghai came out worse than any other province in terms of each set of extraction rules, it at least could extend a more uniform system over its own subordinate areas. By 1985, the portion of their own revenue that districts could keep was raised; in particular, they could retain almost a quarter (23 percent on average) of the profits realized from district-managed firms. Five-year remittance contracts were signed with the city in 1988 by district and county governments. Budgeting for local governments was not zero-base; it explicitly assumed "the basic figures for last year's receipts and expenditures."[172] But receipts were rising fast, and local expenditures were largely off budgets.

Sometimes when the central state was strapped for funds, it solved the problem by neglecting the payment of bills rather than by trying to raise more money. The most public example during the early and mid-1980s came in the form of unexpected deductions from the salary checks of state workers. Payroll deduction schemes were instituted extensively by 1983–84 for the mandatory purchase of state bonds.[173] The rates of this confiscation were not extremely high (about 20 yuan per year for people with moderate incomes, and somewhat more for anyone who was relatively affluent). Such bonds had five-year maturities, with no option of early redemption. By 1986, speculators in Shanghai were purchasing the bonds at discounts of about 20 percent. So shortly thereafter, the People's Bank of China began redeeming them at face value. This may have been necessary to keep a potential or partial Ponzi scheme credible, although investment information on these bonds was scanty.[174] It was difficult for bond holders to get their funds, partly because bank hours were restricted. The wage bonds made clear, however, that state imposts could be placed in an unexpected way on individuals (even if, for practical reasons, they were administered through banks). Reforms did not eliminate direct extractions of this sort.

By 1987, a full fiscal guarantee system was extended to districts by the city (just as the central government also extended it then to Shanghai as a whole). The slogans governing this fiscal decentralization were nearly the same between districts and municipality as they were between the provinces and Beijing: definite amounts of payment, linking income to expenditures, sharing the total sum, and fixing the system for three or five years.[175]

Localization at lower administrative levels, however, brought more practical autonomy than localization at the province-municipality level, whose top rungs were generally staffed by very loyal centrists. The relation of Shanghai's top leadership to the center was substantively different from the relation of district chiefs to them; further down in this very large formal system, the heads of scattered offices had a good deal of independence. By 1988 (in the middle of the hepatitis A epidemic), Shanghai laid down rules by which tax receipts would be divided between the city and its urban districts or counties. An expenditure base was set for each of these subordinate units, and the district or county could keep that amount. Revenues above that were divided. For five years, the districts and counties could retain 70 percent, giving the city 30 percent; for the next three years, the division was equal. This plan was called "guarantee the base, divide the increment, and set [this plan] for five years."[176]

The heavy tax load on rural units in or near Shanghai was obvious in a 1989 report about the seven counties throughout China that in the previous year had state revenues of more than 300,000 yuan. *All* of these counties were in Jiangnan (three near Wuxi, one near Hangzhou, plus three counties of Shanghai).[177] Such statistics might suggest that the Shanghai delta is the only rich part of China, though it is not. It is just the richest part that pays very high taxes.

There was more uniform treatment between Shanghai's districts, apparently, than between China's provinces. The basic productive units in any economy, however, are enterprises, and a look at these shows big differences between firms in the same fields but different places. These compete with each other not just for markets, but also for inputs. Variation in their tax treatment directly affects their ability to compete. Many local industrial yearbooks that have been published in China during the reforms stress detailed data, institutional as well as statistical, about particular sectors and factories. In 1983, for example, the Shanghai Flour Factory had production per unit of capital at about the same rate as was separately reported from a similar "keypoint" flour factory in Guangzhou. But the Shanghai mill paid about half again as much state profits and taxes per unit of capital. In another case, data for the Shanghai Cigarette Factory, when compared with those from all other keypoint cigarette factories (in Changde, Kunming, Qingdao, and Wuhan), show that while the 1983 return of profits and taxes per yuan of fixed capital averaged 60 percent higher in Shanghai, and of operating capital a sharp 288 percent higher, the Shanghai return per yuan of sales revenue was 11 percent less.[178]

Shanghai factory managers customarily hide more funds (especially liquid nonfixed capital) than do managers elsewhere, and they also customarily have to pay higher rates of tax and profit. The greater rates of impost give Shanghai cadres greater incentives to obfuscate the ways they handle their factories' money. What firms—or provinces—do is determined by a highly political combination of secrecy and bargaining. Premises about extensive information or standard procedures cannot explain the observable pattern. Every tax in China, at least into the 1990s, is a particular arrangement.

Depreciation and Livelihood Problems as Results of Heavy Taxes

Shanghai investment was only 2 percent of the national total over the first three decades of the PRC.[179] It is therefore unsurprising that Shanghai's capital stock became very aged by the end of this period. It remained so even half a dozen years later. The city's industrial equipment was antiquated, and sectors that paid higher imposts did not necessarily receive higher capitalization. From 1949 to 1978, investment in Shanghai's light industry was only 4.3 percent of the city's total industrial investment. Even this small amount could not be freely used by factory managers; it came in the form of funds assigned for particular purposes, and these line items were not easily fungible to other uses.[180] Some kinds of light industry were more subject to stable taxation than were others.

Shanghai's cotton textile industry, in particular, was a "tree for shaking off money."[181] Profits from Shanghai cloth production accounted for 30 percent of the national total in 1979—and textiles also provided a very large 39 percent of the city's total industrial profits. But in the thirty years after 1949, the state invested only 500 million yuan in Shanghai textile plants. Eighty percent of the cloth factory premises in 1980 dated from before 1937. One-ninth of the city's textile plant space was officially classified as too dangerous for use (though people kept working there). Some of these factories leaked rain, and occasionally their roofs would collapse in storms. Facilities for Shanghai textile workers—the great majority of whom were women—were notoriously inadequate. One plant had five hundred women workers, and for all of them it provided a single toilet of ten square meters.[182] This kind of scandal was reported in the Shanghai press, but not much was done to relieve it.

Even by 1987, one-third of the machines under the Shanghai Textile Bureau still dated from the 1930s or 1940s—though the percentage of such aged machinery was slightly smaller there than in other light industries. The relative ease of state control over bulk cotton inputs for textiles had, over the decades, made them especially lucrative sources of taxes. In the woolen industry, however, the portion of pre-1950 machines was four-fifths.[183] Differences of this sort, as interviewees confirm, also correlated with varying degrees of freedom given to plant managers. High-tax-yield production was controlled and supported by the state, whose personnel resources apparently did not allow the same intensity of control over low-tax-yield production.[184]

Equipment in the country as a whole was less old than in Shanghai. By 1985, one-third of the machines used nationally in large and medium plants had been made during the previous five years, and 77 percent had been produced in the 1970s or 1980s. Less than one-quarter predated 1970.[185] Although these portions show some general reluctance by PRC planners to retire old machines anywhere, Shanghai was forced to make do with ancient capital much longer than most other cities.

What capital Shanghai did receive was often of more evident use to Beijing bureaucracies than to Shanghai people. Huge amounts were poured into just a few large blueprints, even as the reforms progressed. The most famous example was the Baoshan Steel Mill, in Wusong north of the city center. Local and national debate raged during the late 1970s on this financially and ecologically dubious project. In June 1979, the State Finance and Economic Commission discussed the Baoshan Steel Mill, and some mistakes of planning were admitted. But "because construction had already been decided," there were calls for the whole Party to unify behind it.[186] Baoshan continued the Stalinist investment strategy for China's biggest city.[187]

High-technology development in this metropolis was seen by hard-liners as a threat to tax collection. Local housing maintenance costs might (if the government had paid any substantial amount of them before the 1990s) have been another threat to total extraction. The central bureaucracy's abstemious attitude toward Shanghai hurt not only the productive infrastructure, but also the livelihoods of its people. Fiscal imposts affect people's lives, not just bureaucratic budgets. Good housing is the most obvious of the shortages caused by high taxation. Various parts of Shanghai and different specific families varied considerably in the amount of space they had. Suburban peasants had much more space in which to live than did dwellers of the built-up city—and farmers near the edge of the metropolis in late reforms leased living space to immigrants without legal household registrations, often at high rents.

The severe, long-term deficit of Shanghai housing was inseparable from a similar deficit of public transport. Most new housing was far away from workplaces in the city. Planners resisted the idea that people should live where they wished, instead of in satellites far from town. High taxes correlated with many other kinds of urban inconvenience, too. General spending for maintenance of the city was budgeted as low as possible: 3 percent of local government spending from 1957 to 1965, up to 6.3 percent by 1981 because the need for upkeep was so obvious in many places by then.[188] The results were evident in all kinds of urban infrastructure—of which a few more, besides housing and transport, should be mentioned to put the effects of the high taxes into perspective.[189] In comparison to the other sixteen largest PRC cities, on a per-capita basis in 1985, Shanghai had fewer hospital beds, university places, or consumer service units.[190]

Only 50 percent of telephone calls got through to their recipients in mid-1980s Shanghai, even with redialing. It was commonly known that during business hours, numbers with some exchange prefixes were effectively unavailable; the caller would hear signals indicating that the system was busy. Of switchboards, lines, and equipment, three-tenths were thirty or more years old.[191] This situation improved somewhat toward the end of the decade, because the government correctly sensed that business investors would not come if they could not make phone calls. But in 1987, Beijing had 7.0 telephones for each hundred people in the urban districts, whereas Shanghai had 4.8 phones.[192]

The 1986–90 Five-Year Plan was mostly earmarked for big projects such as Shanghai's port expansion, sewage plants, and (because the need was so obvious) some new housing. Roads, parks, and schools had lower priority.[193] The reforms, in other words, did not lessen the pressure of taxes on people's daily lives. A city official summed it up: "The average Shanghainese is not happy. He works hard to contribute one out of every six yuan the country spends, but he cannot even get a decent place to live."[194]

The State Budget Crisis of the 1980s

The budget deficit of the PRC rose by 50 billion yuan from 1979 to 1986.[195] Although Shanghai total state profits in 1979 were 9.5 percent higher than those of 1978, enterprise revenues were up only 1.8 percent. In the next year, local state enterprise profits rose only 2.9 percent—and Shanghai firms' income actually decreased 1.9 percent. By 1981, because of rules allowing more profit retention and because product prices fell somewhat, total enterprise revenues were down 4.7 percent. So 1981–83 saw Shanghai's first "fiscal slippage" (*caizheng huapo*), a term that came into official discourse only in the middle 1980s, especially during the second "slippage" after 1986. Competition from other provinces meant reductions of state profit remittances from Shanghai.[196]

Within a very few years, this "slippage" worsened quickly from the viewpoint of the state. In 1981, the realized profits and taxes for each unit of fixed capital were 3.4 times the national average; but by 1983, they were down to 3.1 times. If the same comparison is made in terms of all capital funds, the decrease is from 3.1 times to 2.8 times.[197] Technical improvements in other provinces also created sharp competition for Shanghai products. Whereas the city had won 49 percent of the first prizes in product fairs during 1980, by the next year it won only 41 percent, and in 1982 only 37 percent. The city could still sell products, but its relative inability to reinvest profits, rather than sending them to the central treasury, was one of the factors that eroded this tradition of making China's best products.

Rural prosperity also created much larger markets, and this benefited Shanghai firms as well as their competitors in other places. By the early 1980s, even though Shanghai's total shipments of industrial goods did not rise quickly, the city sent out increasing quantities of high-quality consumer durables. Washing machine sales in 1982, for example, went up by 116 percent; bicycles rose 36 percent; tape recorders, 33 percent; and sewing machines, 26 percent.[198] These figures, combined with stagnant total sales, imply that domestic sales of some other major commodities (apparently including textiles and tractors, and perhaps machines generally) decreased in value during this time. Other Chinese places now produced these, and Shanghai lost market share in them.

In 1983, Shanghai produced 13 percent of China's light industrial products—a portion that had gradually decreased from over 20 percent in the 1950s—but it was still generating 18 percent of the whole country's taxes and profits. It sent most of these products (more than three-fifths) to be sold in other provinces, and another portion went abroad.[199] This had been the city's strength for most of a century—but now other areas were strong in it too. Because the inertia of the plan still required taxes of Shanghai, the city was still denied the opportunity to move into new fields.

The Tax Effects of Inland Competition

Economists at the Shanghai Academy of Social Sciences have tried to calculate the decline of revenues (profits and taxes) in Shanghai state industries that can be attributed to the rising raw materials prices in the period from 1985 to 1987. This effect was estimated by a ratio that, if high, would show a greater negative effect on remittances for each loss of Shanghai enterprise income due to rising prices. The numerator was the factories' income reduction because of materials price rises. The denominator was the decrement of actually remitted taxes and profits in various years, discounted by the city's growth rate, plus the factories' income rise due to the inflation of Shanghai's product prices. This term was a rough index of the results of the government's inability to control prices on Shanghai's ability to pay remittances.[200] Putting actual figures into it suggested that 75 percent of the reduction in Shanghai state industry's ability to deliver profits, during 1986 and 1987 as compared with 1985, was related to price changes.

The same calculation can also be performed sectorially, to show that materials price rises accounted for 97 percent of the revenues "lost" in metals other than steel, 77 percent in steel, 73 percent in ordinary machines, 69 percent in rubber, 40 percent in plastics, 14 percent in electronics and telecommunications, and 11 percent in precision machinery.[201] So the high-technology industries, using few inputs other than skilled labor, fared much better in Shanghai's mid-1980s crisis environment than did the state's old tax producers.

In other words, the materials crisis—ironically—forced a new structure in Shanghai's economy that the bureaucracy did not plan. This crucial reform was unintended, to the extent it happened. Perhaps the state bureaucrats were not especially interested in having Shanghai as an important center for silicon electronics; many of their specific decisions on computer and other investments in the 1980s suggest their greater interest in Beijing or Xi'an, and Wuxi was also finding money. But the materials crisis meant that Shanghai made much of this change anyway; so electronics emerged as a good taxpaying industry. The collapse of inefficient state industries and the rise of new firms were usually as unintended (and in these cases, as good) as most other reforms. Their basis was not a new epiphany in Beijing.

State Profits: Comparisons Over Cities, Sectors, and Time

Inland competition also forced management reorganization. It might at first seem odd that the profits of Shanghai's centrally managed firms rose sharply after 1980, while those of locally managed firms declined. These effects are accounting mirages, caused by ownership changes, and the reasons seem to be two: After 1980, the central government took over several large factories that had previously been run by the municipality (notably the Jinshan Chemical Plant and several Shanghai shipyards). The first part of the 1980s also saw the establishment of a number of central corporations, including new national companies for chemicals and ships. These assumed control of such industries and absorbed their profits.

The second reason concerns profits from banks. Many of these, notably the People's Bank, were central enterprises. Like all other central firms, they remitted profits directly through their ministry. But before reforms, bank profits were low because interest rates were low, and so banks sent little profit to the central treasury. As interest rates rose during the reform, banks in Shanghai supplied more to Beijing.

Most state-owned industries, however, are locally managed. Table 1.2–10 shows how they fared in the largest Chinese cities (in the total number of officially designated cities, called *shi,* which was about three hundred in this period). The position of Shanghai becomes very evident on this table, as does the sharpness of change in the mid-1980s.

Table 1.2–10 suggests that until 1984 Shanghai realized profits and taxes at a much higher rate than any other large city in China, but then a sharp decline began. Shanghai also paid a somewhat greater portion of this realized money to the state at both central and local levels.[202] The technical problems associated with proper interpretation of these published figures are many, and there would be no excuse at all to reprint the data if there were not a very sharp gradient of difference in Shanghai over just a few years in the mid-1980s, or if there were not an even sharper gradient between Shanghai and all the other cities.[203]

In 1984 and previous years, Shanghai paid a great deal of its realized "profits and taxes" into Beijing coffers. For the next three years, profits and taxes were realized at a lower rate—and the rates of payment from these funds into all government budgets declined.[204] This reduction of Shanghai's tax burden was offset, however, because the government no longer so fully guaranteed Shanghai factories raw material input supplies or the prices at which they might be purchased. This policy of putting more factory inputs on the market aimed to raise economic efficiency—and eventually it would do so—but the transition period was inevitably painful for Shanghai.

The reduction of this city's extraordinary remittances by 1987, when the state did far less to guarantee factor prices, is implied by these figures. But capital per unit of product value in Shanghai has been less than elsewhere, and the extraction remained heavy. These statistics, based on fixed and circulating capital, may be more useful than comparative statistics based on gross value of output, because the latter index includes double-counted products, and the degree of vertical integration has been relatively high in Shanghai.

The term "profits and taxes," used on the table and elsewhere, refers to money that goes into a considerable variety of uses: remittance to the central budget (for units that are centrally managed) and to the municipal budget (for others, though much of the local budget is later remitted to Beijing). Also included are welfare funds and "production development funds," as well as other percentages of income retained in factories—but such legally retained monies were small in Shanghai before the mid-1980s. The main use of this table on profits and taxes is to show changing profitability per unit of capital in Shanghai over time, and to show differences between Shanghai and other places.[205] The substantive conclusions are clear: This city's reported profitability and taxes plummeted in the mid-1980s.

The unexpectedly low tax/profit payments of cities with a population of between one million and two million (eleven cities in 1984) arises from the fact that most are provincial capitals: Nanjing, Xi'an, Chengdu, Changchun, Taiyuan, Lanzhou, and Ji'nan are all in this group.[206] The next-largest cities, with populations between half a million and a million (thirty-one of them in 1984 and a few more in later years because of population increases), tend to be industrial and to pay more heavily than the provincial capitals mentioned above. Variations in the rates of realized profits and taxes in years such as

Table 1.2-10

Profits and Taxes Realized from State-Owned Local Industries Per 100 Yuan of Capital (in yuan)

	1983	1984	1985	1986	1987
Shanghai (1)					
urban districts		73	63	42	34
with rural suburbs		63			
Beijing (2)					
urban districts		36	36	31	29
with rural suburbs		35			
Tianjin (3)					
urban districts		33	35	32	29
with rural suburbs		33			
Shenyang (4)					
urban districts		22	23	22	19
with rural suburbs		27			
Wuhan (5)					
urban districts		21	26	23	26
with rural suburbs		21			
Guangzhou (6)					
urban districts		37	39	32	31
with rural suburbs		35			
Haerbin (7)					
urban districts		16	17	15	15
with rural suburbs		16			
Chongqing (8)					
urban districts		22	24	16	18
Averages for urban districts only:					
8 largest cities (cities with 1984 pop. 2,000,000)	39	38	39	31	28
Cities with pop. 1,000,000–2,000,000	25	28	30	26	24
Cities with pop. 500,000–1,000,000	34	27	25	21	21
Cities with pop. 200,000–500,000	22	19	19	18	18
Cities with pop. 100,000–200,000	18	20	20	18	17
All cities	26	27	27	23	22
All China	21	21			

(continued)

Table 1.2-10 *(continued)*

Notes and Sources: See notes to the text for caveats about this table, which should be read not for its exact quantities but for the dramatic gradients it suggests both spatially and temporally in the mid-1980s. Such slopes can be conjectured more than proven on the basis of the available data. Some figures, which have been rounded, are in *Zhongguo chengshi tongji nianjian, 1985* (Statistical Yearbook of Chinese Cities, 1985), State Statistical Bureau, ed. (Beijing: Zhongguo Tongji Xinxi Zixun Fuwu Zhongxin and Xin Shijie Chuban She, 1985), pp. 146–52, and *Zhongguo tongji nianjian, 1985* (China Statistical Yearbook, 1985), State Statistical Bureau, ed. (Beijing: Zhongguo Tongji Chuban She, 1985), pp. 53–77, for 1984; *China: Urban Statistics, 1986*, State Statistical Bureau, PRC, comp. (Hong Kong: Longman, 1987), pp. 290–93 and almost identical figures for a slightly different indicator in *Zhongguo chengshi jingji shehui nianjian, 1986* (Economic and Social Yearbook of China's Cities, 1986), Zhongguo Chengshi Jingji Shehui Nianjian Lishi Hui, ed. (Beijing: Zhongguo Chengshi Jingji Shehui Chuban She, 1986), pp. 44–51, for 1985; *Zhongguo chengshi tongji nianjian, 1987* (as above), pp. 155–62, for 1986; and *Zhongguo chengshi tongji nianjian, 1988* (as above), pp. 185–93, for 1987. Additional relevant sources (but reporting the situation somewhat differently) are *Zhongguo gongye jingji tongji ziliao, 1987* (Statistical Materials on China's Industrial Economy, 1987), Guojia Tongji Ju, Gongye Jiaotong Wuzi Tongji Si, ed. (Beijing: Zhongguo Tongji Chuban She, 1987), p. 129, on 1985–86; and *Shanghai tongji nianjian, 1988* (Shanghai Statistical Yearbook, 1988), Li Mouhuan et al., eds. (Shanghai: Shanghai Shi Tongji Ju, 1988), p. 66, on 1987. The 1983 figures are available for the indicated lines in *Zhongguo shehui zhuyi chengshi jingji xue* (Chinese Socialist Urban Economics), Zhu Linxing, ed. (Shanghai: Shanghai Shehui Kexue Chuban She, 1986), p. 41.

1985, according to interviewees, come largely from a mixed pattern of extensive borrowing by different cities to pay their unequal burdens—and many such loans were repaid irregularly, or later than scheduled. The main collateral seems to have been the symbolic prestige of local politicians, on which it was difficult for banks to foreclose. The rate at which locally run state factories retained profits rose sharply, from 5 percent in 1979 to 16 percent in 1984, and then to 34 percent in 1987.[207] This would have been more meaningful if there had been during these years more substantial profits to retain. But the situation of crisis changed the norms of politics; the state treasury learned it could not expect so much as in the past from these locally managed government firms.

Another aspect of this table, or of any other that deals comprehensively with all of China, is the immense differentiation by geography. In 1985, the national income per person in counties of the Yangzi delta was 1,174 yuan—well over twice the all-China average of 529 yuan. The realized profits and taxes per 100 yuan from all industrial enterprises in the delta was 50 yuan in 1985, compared to only 21 for the whole country. But there were many differences between localities, as the table suggests.

Shanghai's own value added per unit of capital was almost five times higher than that of the poorest and least-taxed places in the delta, according to Table

Table 1.2-11

Income and Realized Profits and Taxes Per 100 Yuan of Capital in Cities That Govern All Jiangnan Rural Counties, 1985
(in yuan; in order by profits and taxes)

	National income	Profits and taxes
Shanghai	2,539	63*
Huzhou	622	50*
Hangzhou	905	46*
Ningbo	788	38*
Wuxi	1,094	36
Jiaxing	706	34*
Shaoxing	510	33*
Changzhou	888	32
Suzhou	883	32
Nantong	520	28

Source: Shanghai jingji qu fazhan zhanlue chutan (Preliminary Research on the Development Strategy of the Shanghai Economic Zone), *World Economic Herald* and Shanghai Economic Zone Research Society, eds. (Shanghai: Wuxi Branch of Shanghai Eighth People's Printers, 1986), pp. 30–31.

*Shanghai and Zhejiang cities are marked with an asterisk; Jiangsu cities are not.

1.2–11. Nantong and Shaoxing were, however, the only places in this area below the national average of output per unit of capital. (The reasons almost surely lie in outdated textile equipment at Nantong, which was not renovated because of lack of funds in earlier years, and in the numerous traditional handicraft industries of Shaoxing, which despite their fame were very low on planners' priority lists.) Only a loose correlation existed between a place's capital productivity or wealth, on one hand, and the rate at which it was extracted, on the other. Jiangsu was more successful than Zhejiang or Shanghai at avoiding taxes on its current production.

Many light industrial centers elsewhere in the delta also had heavy fiscal burdens. A deputy director of the Hangzhou Planning Commission, for example, said in 1985 that his city could keep too little of the money it earned. This burden increased during the early 1980s, when Guangdong, Fujian, and other places were being more lightly taxed. In 1984, Hangzhou paid 38 percent more than in 1980. The portion of this money sent into central budgets remained nearly the same in both years for Zhejiang's capital (at a high level, 86 percent). By 1985, Hangzhou could keep an even lower portion of what it collected.[208]

From 1982 to 1986, both Jiangsu and Zhejiang grew much faster than Shanghai—with 17 percent and 21 percent annual industrial output increases, respectively, compared to Shanghai's 7.5 percent. In 1982, Shanghai still had 26 percent more industrial yield than Jiangsu, but the province overtook the city as China's largest industrial producer by mid-1985 (and in later years, other provinces further afield may take this place). The stagnancy of the state sector, more prominent in Shanghai because of that city's role in China's fiscal system, was largely responsible for this midreform difference between Shanghai and Jiangsu.

In 1982, the state-owned sector had dominated in all three places: 58 percent in Zhejiang, 60 percent in Jiangsu, and 87 percent in Shanghai. But by the mid-1980s, state-owned enterprises generated less than half the industrial product of both Jiangsu and Zhejiang, though still over 80 percent in Shanghai.[209] More analysis by ownership sectors will follow in the next chapter, but the relative rise of nonstate firms in the adjacent provinces had major revenue effects on the still-dominant state firms in Shanghai.

Tax collection in other parts of East China by early 1989 involved less direct participation by tax offices than during previous years. In a Subei city, for example, an earlier policy of active inspections, "going to doors to receive taxes," was replaced by a stress on propaganda, "paying imposts by going to the [tax office] door."[210] This meant that inspectors visited business premises less often. Education of company managers was supposed to raise compliance instead. Tax evasion was still, of course, illegal. Within one week after a sporadic campaign to publicize the punishments meted out to a hundred private firms that had evaded taxes, the tax office received a windfall of payments. But the number of rural China's firms and the independence of their managers were increasing quickly. The previous, more intrusive methods of tax collection were reformed, at least in politically favored parts of the country.

New, somewhat more standardized national taxes were introduced during the reforms—and this was a trend Shanghai managers would surely have welcomed more if the new rules did not usually raise the imposts on them. The "replacement of profits by taxes" could be less important to managers than the amount they had to pay of both added together. This remained high in Shanghai for much longer than elsewhere.

Causes of "Slippage" in Shanghai Taxes During the 1980s

The decline of Shanghai local revenues per yuan of gross product from 1978 to 1987 was more than 40 percent.[211] *Three-quarters of this decline came in the period 1984–87,* the years when Shanghai profits and taxes were plummeting even faster than those of the nation as a whole.[212] And the rate of the dive accelerated in 1987 particularly: Shanghai's fiscal revenues fell by 550 million yuan in 1986, but then by another 1,110 million in 1987.[213] This phenomenon caused great consternation among the military, industrial, and other state bureaucrats whose budgets it cut.

During the 1980s, Shanghai's government revenues—both those collected as part of the local budget and those forwarded to Beijing—dropped precipitously.

Table 1.2-12

Shanghai Revenues Decline

	Shanghai local gov't revenues (millions of yuan)	All Shanghai revenues as part of nat'l revenues (percent)	All Shanghai revenues as part of Shanghai nat'l income (percent)	Shanghai local revenues as part of Shanghai nat'l income (percent)
1980	17.5	18.3	70.4	61.9
1981	17.4	18.8	70.3	60.0
1982	16.8	17.9	68.0	56.9
1983	15.6	16.4	67.3	51.5
1984	16.4	15.1	63.2	48.1
1985	18.4	14.4	64.4	45.0
1986	17.9	12.0	60.6	42.2
1987	16.5			

Source: Collated from several tables in Xu Zhenliang "Shanghai caizheng shouru 'huapo' de xiankuang, chengyin ji qi duice" (The "Slide" of Shanghai's Financial Income: Situation, Reasons, and Countermeasures), in *Caijing yanjiu* (Financial and Economic Research), March 1988, pp. 18–19.

Table 1.2–12 shows the extent of these changes during the years when they were sharpest. Groups smaller than the huge national or municipal bureaucracies were controlling more resources. But some very large state factories that are managed directly and completely from Beijing, such as the Baoshan Steel Plant and Jinshan Chemical Factory, are not included in figures such as the ones above. Because of them, state revenues from Shanghai on average still increased 2.3 percent per year from 1980 to 1986. The greater freedom from tax of Shanghai's medium and small enterprises was nonetheless a big change: enough to create bigger government deficits in the 1980s.

By 1987, the "slippage" of fiscal revenues in Shanghai industry was partly attributed to poor management—but blaming factory managers was difficult in this case. The main cause lay in rural materials markets, which were more efficient than planned "markets." These markets, serving new industries in rich parts of the countryside, tended to draw off primary produce, because they offered higher prices. Factory raw materials accounted for 80 percent of all industrial costs in Shanghai's low-capital environment. These price rises took a big toll on factory profits.[214]

When Shanghai revenue was "lost" to local bureaucrats, it went to other parties inside and outside the metropolis. It did not disappear just because state organizations failed to collect it. Of the reduction in Shanghai revenues during

1987, calculations show that 57 percent was "shifted" from Shanghai to other provinces or central agencies. Also, Shanghai at this time "reduced and adjusted" many taxes and raised depreciation allowances, so another 37 percent of the total revenues lost to local state offices were kept by enterprises within the city. Yet another 7 percent went to active and retired workers.[215] The revenue slippage shocked high officials, since it meant they did not receive their usual money. But others received it in less official settings, and in terms of economic efficiency, this change was almost surely positive. Shanghai was still saddled with many old rules and cadres, and denying them resources was arguably a patriotic policy.

Taxes Under "Moderate" and "Hard-line" Politicians

All planners agreed that Shanghai had to move into new fields, but the bureaucracy was slow to finance such change. Many people thought that the government was in danger of "killing the chicken that lays the egg" (*sha ji qu luan*). But mere consciousness of the faults of that policy proved less important than institutional habits. For example, Shanghai's electronic equipment industry progressed less quickly than plans projected. One local economist slightly overstated the case, saying that "nothing has happened" and that Beijing politicians wanted only to exhaust Shanghai as a source of revenue. He said the government was willing to gamble with Shanghai's money to the last penny.[216]

Central government financiers had become so dependent on Shanghai revenues, they got themselves into the position of having to control all important economic initiatives in Shanghai, whether they wished to do so or not. Well into the 1980s institutionalized tax habits set the city's economic course at least as much as any policy makers, intention, or ideology did. As it became increasingly clear in the 1980s that Shanghai could not fulfill its earlier role in China's fiscal system, top cadres in Beijing were impelled by the resource squeeze—whose exigencies tended to overwhelm any policy preferences they had—to suggest basic change in Shanghai. Various high politicians of different stripes did this, even if they could not easily act on their ideas. In late 1987, Party head Zhao Ziyang and Vice Premier Yao Yilin made an inspection tour of Shanghai, apparently with a view to finding out what could be done about maintaining the city's declining contribution to Beijing.

The weeks after that visit were a turning point in official rhetoric about Shanghai, though much of the sequel was compelled by circumstances irrespective of wordings. The State Council in December approved a "Report on Deepening Reform, Opening Wider to the Outside World, and Accelerating the Development of an Export-Oriented Economy in Shanghai." This called for an "all-encompassing financial contract system," more exports to raise foreign exchange for the purchase of better technology and needed materials, and a fixed-amount fiscal contribution from Shanghai for five years.[217]

Zhao Ziyang stressed that Shanghai's contribution to China should be measured in terms of its production—clearly implying that the city's tax and profit remittance was no longer to be seen as the main aim. He said, "Shanghai's position is such that if Shanghai doesn't progress, then the whole country will have difficulty progressing."[218] Zhao was also in favor of putting rural areas under the administrative guidance of their central market cities; for Shanghai, the largest metropolis in China, that might have meant a very large hinterland. It is easy to see how such notions would have an appeal in Shanghai. But Zhao was not the only kind of politician in China, as mid-1989 made very clear.

Conservatives, seeking to modernize rather than destroy the Party patronage system that still ruled most areas, were represented in Shanghai by the municipal government—even though the cosmopolitan style of its leaders concealed that relationship. Jiang Zemin's plan for the Shanghai economy, as expressed in an early 1988 speech, was a study in flexible contradictions. On one hand, he said Shanghai should "learn humbly from the advanced experience of Guangdong Province in deepening reform." On the other, "being the largest economic center in our country, Shanghai most prominently reflects the planned economy."[219] The answer, according to Jiang, was contracts: "fixing basic quotas, guaranteeing fulfillment of these quotas, sharing surpluses, and making up for shortages." To prevent the case-by-case, year-by-year habit from obviating these incentives, the contracts, "once signed, should remain unchanged for five years." And they should allow institutions to raise money from "their own operations to support themselves." To the extent these freedoms were allowed, they meant less central revenues. They changed China's money politics.

The High-Tax Regime, Illegalities, and Quiet Politics

When traders are independent of the state, then government action on markets may involve them in politics. For example, in France, where *dirigisime* got its name, state rules have often politicized private firms.[220] But Shanghai managers in firms of any size have been so tied to the state for so long, it became more likely by the end of the 1980s that small entrepreneurs in new firms would be most affected by official efforts to control them. And their reaction to state intervention would often be to avoid the official bureaucrats rather than to participate in politics in hopes of creating better public rules. Like "weak" individual actors in other contexts (such as markets), they used secrecy as a major weapon in politics, and that was collectively strong enough to be public.[221] The CCP has discouraged the articulation of managers' views in Shanghai, and managers respond to China's sporadic periods of political thaw more slowly than do other intellectuals.[222] Now, however, factory heads have to deal with rural suppliers who have collectivist ethics of a more local kind. The power of planners over them has become less strong.

Midlevel and lower economic leaders by the end of the decade were more active, if no more articulate. Transfers of industrial raw materials soared throughout China. When these transactions were still illegal, many of the arrested criminals had previously worked in the factories from which they hijacked materials. They were familiar with easy ways to obtain these, and undoubtedly some of them acted for on-the-job officials. Others were explicitly identified as buyers from rural industries, and their business was booming: "The more they steal, the more bold they become."[223] Managers and workers in Shanghai were eager to cooperate with such traders—because the alternative was to close up shop. Factory heads often faced a choice between breaking the law and firing their workers, and it is unsurprising that in the interests of their collectives the ex-statist option usually seemed best to them.

Attempts to Recentralize Control of Funds and Taxes

Under the national guarantee (*baogan*) system that was announced in 1988, Shanghai was to send 10.3 billion yuan annually to the center for the three years 1988–90. But highly public plans involving province-level actors were no more stable than local contracts under the PRC's cellular and case-by-case norms. Because of factory input and hepatitis problems, the central authorities apparently mustered more raw materials for Shanghai in 1988—and the city's industrial economy responded with a better growth rate that year. So the "guarantee" was simply changed. Shanghai's actual remittances that year were 10.5 billion yuan (200 million more than had earlier been projected). Jiang Zemin, as the chief local politician, apparently gained credit for this overfulfillment of the city's 1988 revenue guarantee. But the difference between Shanghai and other provinces remained huge; Guangdong, for example, that year remitted much less than that province's production would warrant if treated uniformly: only 0.42 billion yuan.[224]

There was still great concern in Beijing about the large central government deficit. In particular, official economists warned that the fiscal reform policy of "dividing the stoves from which people eat," despite its benefits for local budgets, meant that the central administration ran out of money. As a Beijing writer pointed out, China's central budgetary revenue fell below the level that was usual in Western countries, where national governments generally get 60 to 70 percent of all taxes. The income of workers, new money in the hands of local cooperatives and private firms, and extrabudgetary money by the late 1980s comprised three-quarters of China's national income—up from two-thirds only a few years before. The writer suggested that Beijing should collect more money even if it also established a "system of dividing taxes," under which more centrally collected funds would be sent to local governments.[225]

Beijing views, however, meant less by the late 1980s than they once had. Top

PRC leaders kept sending down dicta, and many of these were received and merely filed in the most dynamic sectors of China's economy. The State Council approved rules, for example, restricting the size and use of managers' discretionary funds. It decreed that managers' funds in 1988 should be reduced 20 percent below 1987 levels—but in the first seven months of 1988, actual expenditures for such funds *rose* 20 percent instead.[226] And this was not a minor line item. The total of discretionary funds for these months was greater than the sum of money for all urban construction and education—almost 37 billion yuan throughout the country.

Debate About Imposts in Shanghai and Elsewhere

In this multinorm period of 1988–89, central government writers raised in public the issue of whether Shanghai had been fairly treated. Two reporters for a Beijing journal criticized Shanghai people's view that a "cosmic imbalance" was at the heart of the city's problems. They said Shanghai's people too often felt the state should "protect" that city because it paid so much in taxes. This attitude led to laziness, they claimed, and it meant Shanghai enterprises became like flowers in a hothouse, unable to withstand the winds of competition.[227] Such views might well be expected from Beijing, but they ignored that central policies had built this hothouse by imposing an environment of heavy taxes and rules, so that Shanghai's once-famous entrepreneurialism had at least temporarily disappeared. The conclusion from the plan's collapse was implicit: Shanghai's people should "break out of the circle of 'not asking anyone for anything.' "[228]

During the thaw that ended in June 1989, published articles could raise questions about whether Shanghai was receiving a fair deal under reforms. The city had often been praised officially as the "elder brother" among Chinese localities, because of its contribution to central coffers: "Shanghai is the big brother; he cares for the family before himself." Eldest brothers in Chinese tradition have a special responsibility for parents—which a favorite metaphor always likens to government. The elder brother is specifically obliged to provide money first, and this duty could later be divided among the younger brothers, i.e., the other provinces. But now, according to a 1988 article, the reforms altered this pattern by creating enormous changes throughout China's inland areas.[229]

This article opined that if the policies accorded to Guangdong (allowance for massive importing and exporting, and low-tax responsibility contracts at all levels) were also applied to Shanghai, the East China metropolis could catch up with Guangdong in about three years. But the author who made this estimate also said the bias implicit in Shanghai's high rate of taxation was inevitable. If China's biggest city were allowed to participate fully in international markets, and if it failed in the fierce competition there, the effect on national revenues would be too disastrous for China. Therefore experimental policies for importing, exporting, leasing, financing, and personnel reforms, such as were variously allowed in other places (Guangdong, Chongqing,

Wuhan, and Shenyang were all cited), could not be implemented in Shanghai until they were sure to work. Cities with smaller taxpaying roles could practically be in some other China, according to this view. But for national reasons, Shanghai could not.[230]

Shanghai's *World Economic Herald* carried detailed descriptions of the generous rules allowed for Guangdong, but not for Shanghai, during the 1980s. These rules allowed fixed and predictable tax levies; they let local cadres take charge of balancing the local budget over extended periods, without running local deficits by sending high remittances to Beijing. Some rules extended the loose laws of Shenzhen and Guangdong's other special zones, in effect, throughout the whole province.[231] The paper did not need to mention the contrast with Shanghai to make its reformist and localist point.

Shanghai's own CCP newspaper was also not too reticent to report, in mid-1988, that the metropolis could retain only one-third as much money in absolute terms as Beijing (and half as much as Tianjin) despite its greater production.[232] Official sources recognized "differences between the southern coastal regions adjacent to Hong Kong and Macau, on one hand, and the northern coastal regions, on the other; between old industrial bases and newly arising cities."[233] To raise this issue, however, even in defense of the central government's uneven taxes, was to answer questions about justice that clearly were on people's minds.

Conclusion on Economic Efficiency and Fairness

Albert Hirschman presents a model of the conditions under which groups may postpone their frustration when they see other groups advancing more quickly. He refers mainly to classes, as in Brazil, that long remain poor. He likens their situation to that of a line of drivers stopped in a two-lane tunnel. When the other lane (e.g., a middle class) begins to move, they may be happy even if they remain stuck, because advance of the other group could forebode motion for themselves.[234] This "tunnel effect" may illustrate why Shanghai people were slow to become irate about their taxes, even when they knew that other places enjoyed much lower rates of extraction. They may have considered this a good omen for their own futures, as next in line for prosperity. As the 1990s showed, they would have been right. By June 1989, their patience had been stretched very thin. The central government reacted by taking less from the city. The reasons were partly economic; more crucially, they were political. The hard-line regime after June 1989 could not afford to lose its wavering constituencies in Shanghai, so it had to supply them.

A month after Tiananmen, Finance Minister Wang Bingqian admitted that Beijing's program of "austerity" to cut government expenditures was not working: "Not only has there been a failure of bringing down outlays which were supposed to have been cut . . . rather, those expenditures have been increased from last year." In the first five months of 1989, "taxes paid by state firms" were 38 percent less than in the same months of the previous year. Administrative expenses in the first five months of 1989 had been scheduled to rise only 2.5 percent; in fact, they rose 24 percent. Government spending as a whole had gone up 16 percent, revenues only 8 percent.[235]

Wang did not suggest any dramatic solutions, but an *Economic Daily* editorial of the same era suggested more money should be put into coal, oil, and steel—industries the state could most easily tax because of the technologies and materials they use. This proposal would not accomplish what the mid-1989 hard-line government most needed to do if its conservatives wished to update the socialist system that had been deeply eroded over several years in the mid-1980s. It would not destroy the dynamic rural industries that gave China most of its growth during the reforms. By the 1990s, few really wanted socialism.

Fair conclusions about Shanghai taxes can be several, despite the complexity of the situation and real uncertainties that arise from it. In economic terms over many years, the extraction has surely been too high for China's maximum long-term growth, and probably for most mixed tastes that would give any weight to the value of economic expansion. In patriotic terms, the economic result in Shanghai and in places where most of the extracted money went (as compared with those the government neglected) is a severe indictment of past state leaders. In political terms, they will never be held accountable. Many who created the fiscal structure that lasted through the 1980s are retired or dead. A possible lapse of patience on the part of Shanghai people—if controls over expression in the city do not remain tighter than in other Chinese cities, or if workers hear about more strikes despite standing orders that journalists not report them—could bring increased frustration that the end of the "tunnel" is not in sight. But state allowances for Shanghai development in the early 1990s were the regime's necessary reaction to its political quandary. The result, finally, was a reform toward prosperity and fairness.

Notes

1. Roderick MacFarquhar, "The Succession to Mao and the End of Maoism," in *The Politics of China, 1949–1989,* Roderick MacFarquhar, ed. (Cambridge: Cambridge University Press, 1993), pp. 293–94.

2. *Xin Zhongguo gongye jingji shi* (A History of New China's Industrial Economy), Wang Haibo, ed. (Beijing: Jingji Guanli Chuban She, 1986); the quotations and the figures are from pp. 337–38. This source, which covers the next two paragraphs, also, mentions that at the end of 1970, the total number of state workers was 53.18 million.

3. *Xin Zhongguo gongye,* pp. 337–38.

4. *Zhongguo gongye de fazhan, 1949–1984* (China's Industrial Development, 1949–1984), Guojia Tongji Ju, Gongye Jiaotong Wuzi Tongji Si, ed. (Beijing: Zhongguo Tongji Chuban She, 1985), p. 53; the only other such unit is Tianjin.

5. "*Shui wang dichu liu, huo wang kaochu zou.*" *JFRB,* May 15, 1988.

6. There was an increase in Shanghai's annual growth of national income during

1976–80 and 1981–85 (in both eras, it averaged 8.4 percent). But because Shanghai remained extensively under the thumb of Beijing fiscal officials, its 1966–75 average annual growth of national income, at 10.2 percent, was slower than its 1976–85 growth, at 8.4 percent. Figures are from *SHTJNJ88,* p. 52.

7. *WHB,* December 20, 1979.

8. *WHB,* June 11, 1980.

9. *JFRB,* September 6, 1980.

10. *Dangdai Zhongguo de jingji tizhi gaige* (Reform of the Economic System in Contemporary China), Zhou Taihe et al., eds. (Beijing: Zhongguo Shehui Kexue Chuban She, 1984), p. 559.

11. The city is not a nation, but its "national income" (*guomin shouru*) is supposed to approach its "gross national product"—and either of these is a better summary measure for growth performance than is the more commonly available "gross value of output" (*zongchan zhi,* which is a sum of values of firms' output rather than of their values added). The latter statistic involves extensive double counting. Any of these data, however, would show the situation highlighted in the text above. It is not well known simply because the official periodization has prevented open publication of numbers for the years that show it. These data are directly from *Shanghai jingji, neibu ben: 1949–1982* (Shanghai Economy, Internal Volume: 1949–1982), Shanghai Academy of Social Sciences, ed. (Shanghai: Shanghai Shehui Kexue Yuan Chuban She, 1984), p. 991.

12. *SHJJYJ,* January 1987, p. 60.

13. Ibid. for the data here and in the earlier paragraph.

14. The factual details are in ibid. The source also offered a further reason for the mid-1980s decline, namely the high statistical bases of production in the early 1980s; but this seemed primarily a political apology for presenting the main brief on other reasons, which unlike previous performance was subject to change by new policies.

15. These companies were called *xingzheng xing gongsi.* The list of reasons and the quoted phrases are in *SHJJYJ,* January 1987, p. 60.

16. *Shang bu feng ding, xia bu bao di.* Ibid.

17. *Huan tang, bu huan yao.* Ibid.

18. Murray Scot Tanner, *The Politics of Lawmaking in Post-Mao China: Institutions, Processes, and Democratic Prospects* (ms.).

19. Ibid.

20. "*Ganle shanglai,*" in *Jingji shichang yanjiu* (Economic Market Research), January 1983, p. 1.

21. *Shanghai jingji nianjian, 1988* (Shanghai Economic Yearbook, 1988), Xiao Jun et al., eds. (Shanghai: Shanghai Renmin Chuban She, 1988), p. 90.

22. *FBIS,* November 26, 1986, p. 3, reporting radio of November 20.

23. *SHJJ,* January 1985.

24. The exact time period was not specified. *JFRB,* May 15, 1988.

25. These "wars" were called the *tumao dazhan, yangmao dazhan, zhuma dazhan, canjian dazhan,* and *mianhua dazhan.* *RMRB,* August 16, 1988, also computed a loss during these years in the silk industry, both in tonnage and in yuan, because of sub-specification cocoon deliveries.

26. *CD,* November 2, 1988.

27. *RMRB,* August 16, 1988.

28. *FBIS,* December 7, 1987, p. 39, reporting radio of December 4.

29. The disease was called the "*Shanghai bing.*" Although the article claimed this was a low tide in a cycle, and that actually Shanghai had recently been more stable (*pingwen*) than other places, part of the reason was that other places were progressing much faster. *SHJJYJ,* January 1987, p. 60.

30. Ibid.

31. This meaning of "*hong deng*" contrasted starkly with an enthusiasm the phrase was once supposed to elicit, e.g. in the title of Jiang Qing's model opera "The Red Lantern" (*Hong deng ji*). Thus passes worldly glory. *SHJJYJ,* January 1987, p. 60.

32. *SHJJ,* January 1985, p. 3.

33. See the same source as for the table. Valuation of fixed capital presents many institutional problems that have kept most of the author's calculations on that basis out of this book. But the change reported here is sharp enough that, if understood as a trend rather than exact, it is significant.

34. The comparable figures in a group of cities were: Shanghai, 76 yuan; Chongqing, 68; Xi'an, 67; Shenyang, 66; Haerbin, 63; Tianjin, 62; Beijing, 59; Nanjing, 56; Guangzhou, 53; Dalian, 53; Qingdao, 49; and Wuxi, 32. Figures were not available for Wuhan or Suzhou, even though they were generally included in the survey *SHGYJJB,* August 19, 1988.

35. See the next section, about taxes, for a calculation of the monetary value of coercive mandates for low input and high output prices in Shanghai.

36. Fei Xiaotong and Luo Yanxian, *Xiangzhen jingji bijiao moshi* (Comparative Models of Rural Economy) (Chongqing: Chongqing Chuban She, 1988), pp. 51–55.

37. Although *SHJJ,* January 1987, p. 24, is not entirely explicit on how this 590 million yuan was calculated, it apparently was the additional money that was actually spent in 1986 simply because of the materials' inflation.

38. See *SHTJNJ93,* p. 55, where total local expenditures of the state in 1986 are recorded at almost exactly ten times this 590 million.

39. These figures were supplied to the author by Zhou Xiao, on the basis of work by Hu Heli, "The Estimation of Rent-Seeking in China, 1988," *Journal of Comparative Economic and Social Systems* 5 (1989), pp. 10–15.

40. The particular Zhejiang local effort failed. These examples are in Huang Weixin, *Economic Integration as a Development Device: The Case of the EC and China* (Saarbrücken: Nijmegen Studies in Development, Breitenbach Verlag, 1992), pp. 53–54. Changzhou was able to export tractors abroad, however; the current author saw many of them in Nepal.

41. Cao Linzhang, Gu Guangqing, and Li Jianhua, *Shanghai shengchan ziliao suoyu zhi jiegou yanjiu* (Studies of Shanghai Production and Ownership Structure) (Shanghai: Shanghai Shehui Kexue Yuan Chuban She, 1987), p. 146.

42. Interview with a Shanghai economist.

43. There were only 84 *lianban qiye,* but 861 *xiezuo jiagong dian. Hengxiang jingji lianhe de xin fazhan* (The New Development of Horizontal Economic Links), Shanghai Economics Association, ed. (Shanghai: Shanghai Shehui Kexue Yuan Chuban She, 1987), p. 132.

44. *Shanghai jingji nianjian, 1988,* pp. 140–41.

45. These were *shengchan wuzi maoyi zhongxin*; see *LW* 47 (1988), p. 12.

46. *FBIS,* November 14, 1986, p. 1, reporting radio of November 11.

47. *Shanghai jingji nianjian, 1988,* p. 139.

48. *Shanghai qiye* (Shanghai Enterprise), February 1985, p. 43.

49. Linda Li, "Central-Provincial Relations in the People's Republic of China, Nature and Configurations" (PhD. dissertation, School of Oriental and African Studies, 1994), chap. 7, p. 8, quotes Tu Jimo in *Shanghai jihua jingji tansuo* (Discussions on Shanghai's Planned Economy) 1 (1990), p. 29.

50. *LW* 47 (1988), p. 12.

51. This was the *Shanghai yebao;* interview at the *Liberation Daily* office, one week after the suspension occurred. It was then unclear when or whether this publication could resume.

52. *JFRB,* May 25, 1988.

53. This and other unreferenced data in the text come from 1988 interviews.

54. For much more information on similar cases, see Lynn White, *Shanghai Shanghaied? Uneven Taxes in Reform China* (Hong Kong: Centre of Asian Studies, University of Hong Kong, 1989).

55. The amount was 88,000 tons in the first quarter of 1988.

56. *SF,* March 19, 1990.

57. *XMWB,* April 2, 1989.

58. *LW,* 47 (1988), p. 12.

59. *JFRB,* April 13, 1988.

60. The full matrix would be printed here, and would be very instructive for readers in capitalist countries who are not used to contemplating the implications of trying to run a diversified economy without the aid of money—but the author respects the patience of the typesetter. Did you really want to know that in 1987 (neglecting season, location, quality, or more subtle considerations such as the greed or personal connections of traders) 100 kg of Chinese tung oil should trade for 595.74 bars of soap or 1,096.08 packs of matches? For this and very much more, see a published table that represents the tip of an iceberg of thousands of local and seasonal "compensation trade" rate schedules, in *Zhongguo wujia tongji nianjian, 1988* (Statistical Yearbook of Chinese Prices, 1988), Urban Society and Economy Survey Group, ed. (Beijing: Zhongguo Tongji Chuban She, 1988), pp. 114–15.

61. The invention of money in China is first evidenced in the Shang.

62. A price is the most classic example of a social fact on "the situational referent," diagrammed in the introduction of this book. It is not "constructed" by either the supplier or demander, but by their interaction as different while complementary. They act as context to each other. The price is strictly unintended by either; the buyer probably wanted it lower, while the provider wanted it higher. Yet when people are not giving to each other (as they often do), they can trade. One of the difficulties of a narrowly hermeneutic view of social science is that it would unnecessarily limit the study of situational facts, such as prices, which do acquire meanings for people.

63. These estimates are based on prices of the base year. See *Zhongguo wujia,* pp. 108–12.

64. This index does not include grain and other foods, which were also subsidized to mesh with low wage costs in Shanghai's state-owned enterprises. The figures are in ibid.

65. *JFRB,* May 30, 1988.

66. The amount spent was the equivalent of U.S. $6 million. *SHJJ,* January 1987, p. 24, was written by a staff member of the Hongkou Branch of the Industrial and Commercial Bank of China.

67. *Shanghai jingji nianjian, 1988,* p. 121.

68. *CD*, February 29, 1988.

69. These development companies, designed for trading rather than extraction, were *kaifa gongsi;* brokers were *jingji ren;* intermediaries, *zhongjie.* The trading centers were called *wuzi maoyi zhongxin. SHJJ,* February 1988, p. 21.

70. The exchange fairs were *jiaoyi hui,* and the service companies were *shengchan ziliao fuwu gongsi. Shanghai jingji nianjian, 1988,* p. 33.

71. Floating wages were called *fudong gongzi,* though most Chinese socialists advocate fixed basic wages for unionized employees. *SHGYJJB,* July 28, 1988.

72. Calculated from *SHGYJJB,* July 28, 1988, which gives raw figures.

73. *SHGYJJB,* July 25, 1988.

74. *JFRB,* April 18, 1988.

75. This makes a tiny poem: "*Yao fa cai, pao Shanghai.*" *JFRB,* April 18, 1988.

76. A comparison was made with the "oil crisis" in *JFRB,* April 18, 1988.

77. *SHJJDB,* August 22, 1988.

78. These commodities were called *gongye qiye shangpin. JJRB,* January 18, 1988.

79. This pattern largely predated 1949; but after Liberation, as streets that had foreign names were given Chinese ones, the habit was continued. Bubbling Well Road became Nanjing Road W.; Avenue Joffre, another major commercial street, became Huaihai Road C.; Avenue Edward VII became Yan'an Road S.; Route des Soeurs, Ruijin Road 1; Rue du Consulat, Jinling Road E.; Route Cardinal Mercier, Maoming Road S.; Avenue Pétain, Hengshan Road; and Lincoln Avenue, Tianshan Road. Shanghai, the "other China," is linked more than nominally to the rest of the country.

80. *ZGQNB,* September 20, 1988.

81. See a somewhat different emphasis in Marie-Claire Bergère's essay, " 'The Other China': Shanghai from 1919 to 1949," in *Shanghai: Revolution and Development in an Asian Metropolis,* Christopher Howe, ed. (Cambridge: Cambridge University Press, 1981), pp. 1–34.

82. It is unclear whether the contracts provided for damages in case of late delivery or default. The five counties needing cement were Baoshan, Fengxian, Jinshan, Qingpu, and Songjiang; the three needing steel were Baoshan, Fengxian, and Songjiang. *Hengxiang jingji,* pp. 207–8.

83. *FBIS,* March 7, 1988, p. 76, reporting radio of March 4.

84. This "mandatory planned management" was called *zhiling xing jihua guanli.* "Indicative planning" translates as *zhidao xing jihua.* The materials departments were called *wuzhi bu,* and the most important of these was the municipal bureau, the wuzhi ju. *SHGYJJB,* July 21, 1988.

85. Interview with an economist at the Shanghai Academy of Social Sciences.

86. The percentages above are of commodities by value; but various sources estimate the percentage the state still delivered in 1988 differently, between one-fifth and one-third. See *JFRB,* May 15, 1988; *ZGQNB,* September 20, 1988; and *LW* 47 (1988), p. 12.

87. This information comes from interviews with a highly knowledgeable source in Hong Kong. A few relevant statistical data are available on a limited-circulation basis, and the author was unusually asked not to quote them; but *SHTJNJ93,* p. 55, shows a 1988 increase in Shanghai fiscal revenues, after decreases during the previous two years.

88. See *FEER,* March 21, 1991.

89. The first city allowing a bankruptcy was Shenzhen. See Edward J. Epstein, "China's Legal Reforms," in *China Review,* Kuan Hsin-chi and Maurice Brosseau, eds. (Hong Kong: Chinese University Press, 1991), pp. 9.24–9.25.

90. *FBIS,* December 29, 1987, p. 45, reporting *RMRB* of December 15.

91. *CD,* March 11, 1988.

92. *CD,* February 29, 1988.

93. The best description of the problem is in Dorothy J. Solinger, *China's Transition from Socialism: Statist Legacies and Market Reforms, 1980–1990* (Armonk, NY: M.E. Sharpe, 1993), chaps. 4 and 5.

94. *SHGYJJB,* July 25, 1988.

95. *XMWB,* December 8, 1988; the percentage was calculated.

96. *CD,* October 31, 1988.

97. *CD,* March 13, 1989.

98. The phrasing was harsh: "*dan yidun ye meiyou di Hu.*" *SHGYJJB,* February 2, 1989, also supplies information for the next two text paragraphs.

99. *SF,* November 13, 1989.

100. *Jiangsu fazhi bao,* January 21, 1989.

101. The portion was 53 percent. Another report suggests that 16 percent of municipal revenue was spent on subsidies in 1985, but this may be for food alone. See Linda Li, "Central-Provincial Relations," chap. 6, p. 19.

102. *CD,* December 4, 1990.

103. This is based on *Cankao xiaoxi* (Reference News), May 27, 1994, and on reports from a good friend of the author.

104. This report came from the PRC-run Hong Kong China News Agency, reproduced in *Post,* April 23, 1994.

105. The word "tax" has two uses in this research: Occasionally it may be contrasted with "profit" (in China, mostly from state-owned industries). But the usual meaning will be the plain one, in China referring to all state exactions, including state profits. There would be more reason for purism in using this word if "profit" did not mean a host of different things in various kinds of PRC units and contexts. Below, readers will find more about the reform policy of "replacing profits with taxes." But this slogan hardly illegitimates treatment of their aggregate, which at least until the mid-1980s was tax, merely administered in various ways.

106. *Shanghai caizheng yanjiu* (Shanghai Financial Research), February 1985, p. 10.

107. *FEER,* December 12, 1985, p. 28.

108. Linda Li, "Central-Provincial Relations," using the statistical yearbooks, chap. 4, p. 24.

109. This estimate, based on official sources, surely reflects the conclusions of limited-circulation (unavailable) reports. "Scarcity value" is a term that could have several definitions; we can trust that the renowned economist Ma Hong used a viable one. The amount of retail products sold in rural areas was 81 billion yuan, and all rural products garnered 46 billion that year. The government's total 1978 revenue from police effects on prices may therefore have been very roughly 25 billion yuan, or about one-fifth of the value of all these exchanges (127 billion yuan). Calculated from *Zhongguo jingji jiegou wenti yanjiu* (Studies on Issues of Chinese Economic Structure), Ma Hong and Sun Shangqing, eds. (Beijing: Renmin Chuban She, 1981), pp. 126–27.

110. The agricultural subsidiary products sold to Shanghai were worth 2.776 billion yuan, but this should be reduced by the 0.408 billion yuan worth of such goods that left the city. The real price is found as the quotient of that difference divided by 0.725 (unity minus the average of 25 and 30 percent). Ibid.; also Tao Yongkuan et al., *Dali fazhan disan chanye* (Vigorously Develop Tertiary Industry) (Shanghai: Shanghai Shehui Kexue Yuan Chuban She, 1986), p. 72.

111. The numbers are: 11.979 billion yuan total 1983 Shanghai industrial domestic exports, minus 2.008 billion yuan similar imports, making a net of 9.971 billion yuan, divided by 1.175 (unity plus the average of 15 and 20 percent), to render a real value of 8.486 billion yuan, which exceeds the nominal value by 1.485 billion yuan, viz. the implicit subsidy. *Zhongguo jingji*, pp. 126–27; and Tao Yongkuan et al., *Dali fazhan,* p. 72.

112. The main point in this calculation does not depend on the precise figures (which can also be made using 1978, 1980, and 1984 figures in the sources). By no means did the revenues from implicit subsidies all stay in Shanghai; they were included in profits, mostly from state-owned industries, and the bulk of them were remitted into the central budget in any case. The 1983 revenue figure is a sum of 15.4 billion yuan budgetary and 4.5 billion yuan extrabudgetary monies; see *Zhongguo caizheng tongji, 1950–1985* (Chinese Fiscal Statistics, 1950–1985), Comprehensive Planning Office of the PRC Ministry of Finance, ed. (Beijing: Zhongguo Caizheng Jingji Chuban She, 1987), pp. 54 and 144.

113. From a discussion with a very well-informed economist, not in Shanghai, who referred to reports on this subject that he understandably was unable to show the author.

114. Linda Chelan Li, "Provincial Discretion and National Power: Investment Policy in Guangdong and Shanghai, 1978–93" (manuscript of May 1996), chap. 1, p. 7.

115. Linda Chelan Li, "Provincial Discretion," chap. 6, p. 35.

116. Audrey Donnithorne has used this metaphor of the sponge.

117. The classic briefs in this case are Audrey Donnithorne's "Comment: Centralization and Decentralization in China's Fiscal Management," *China Quarterly* 66 (June 1976), pp. 328–39, and Nicholas R. Lardy's immediately following "Comment." Donnithorne's previous works "China's Cellular Economy: Some Economic Trends Since the Cultural Revolution," *China Quarterly,* 52 (October-December 1972), pp. 605–12, and *China's Economic System* (New York: Praeger, 1967) are the main background. Lardy also published *Economic Growth and Distribution in China* (Cambridge: Cambridge University Press, 1978).

118. See Thomas P. Lyons, *Economic Integration and Planning in Maoist China* (New York: Columbia University Press, 1987).

119. Barry Naughton, "The Third Front: Defence Industrialization in the Chinese Interior," *China Quarterly* 115 (September 1988), pp. 351–86.

120. Franz Schurmann, *Ideology and Organization in Communist China* (Berkeley: University of California Press, 1966), James R. Townsend, *Political Participation in Communist China* (Berkeley: University of California Press, 1967); and G. William Skinner, "Marketing and Social Structure in Rural China," *Journal of Asian Studies* 24:1–3 (November 1964–May 1965), pp. 3–43, 195–228, 363–99.

121. Robert Michael Field, Nicholas R. Lardy, and John Philip Emerson, *Provincial Industrial Output in the People's Republic of China: 1949–75* (Washington: U.S. Department of Commerce, Bureau of Economic Analysis, 1976), pp. 11, 20–30; also U.S. National Foreign Assessment Center, *China: Gross Value of Industrial Output, 1965–77* (Washington: National Foreign Assessment Center, 1978), p. 5. For an earlier estimate in different prices, see Robert Michael Field, Nicholas R. Lardy, and John Philip Emerson, *A Reconstruction of the Gross Value of Industrial Output by Province in the People's Republic of China: 1949–73* (Washington: U.S. Department of Commerce, 1975), Table 2, p. 9. The much later Chinese *SHTJNJ86,* p. 44, says the 1957 industrial output figure was 11,851 million yuan—so the 1975 estimate published in Washington is not very far away from the 1987 one published in China. Considering the climate of scarce data in which Field, Lardy, and Emerson then worked, that was an accomplishment.

122. Not all of the investment went to industry—housing, roads, and agriculture claimed shares—but most of it, maybe 250 million yuan as an estimate, was industrial. Counting all of it as industrial would not much alter the conclusions below. See Lardy, "Centralization and Decentralization of China's Fiscal Management," *China Quarterly* 61 (March 1975), p. 40. In a personal communication to this author, Nick Lardy agreed that the very rough estimate of 250 million yuan might be reasonable.

123. This 1957 rate of investment does not generally underestimate Shanghai's industrial investment for the whole Maoist period. Within the First Five-Year Plan, 1957 was almost surely the highest year for Shanghai investment; 1953–57 capitalization in Shanghai was reportedly a greater portion at least of local revenue (7.25 percent) than in the whole 1949–73 period (6.7 percent). See Lardy, "Economic Planning in China: Central-Provincial Fiscal Relations," in U.S. Congress, Joint Economic Committee, *China: A Reassessment of the Economy* (Washington: Government Printing Office, 1975), p. 112.

124. Statistics from Field, Lardy, and Emerson, *A Reconstruction,* imply that Shanghai's portion of China's total GVIO declined only slightly over about two decades (from 19 percent in 1952 to 16.5 percent in 1971). Michael Field, "Civilian Industrial Production in the PRC: 1949–74," in U.S. Congress, Joint Economic Committee, *China: A Reassessment*, p. 149, reports China's industrial economy was, over this term, expanding at about 13 percent per annum; so Shanghai's industry must have grown almost as fast, since its portion of the country's total was fairly stable. More recent information could be used for this estimate, but the data previously published are as appropriate for the

argument, are substantially the same, and show the ability of outside economists to make good estimates even with figures from the late Mao period.

125. W. Arthur Lewis, *The Theory of Economic Growth* (Homewood IL: Irwin, 1955), p. 201.

126. Some ideas in this paragraph are from Nicholas Lardy, who generously commented in a personal communication on an earlier version of this argument. Audrey Donnithorne has also offered ideas on it, and I am grateful to both. The present chapter argues that Lardy's stress on coastal taxation and Donnithorne's stress on "cellularity" are accurate—and entirely compatible with each other.

127. Robert Dorfman, Paul A. Samuelson, and Robert Solow, *Linear Programming and Economic Analysis* (New York: McGraw-Hill, 1958), pp. 330–31 and generally chap. 12. Economists ordinarily use this "turnpike model" to analyze sectors defined by savings and consumption—but its beauty is that it can apply to any sectoralization.

128. Quoted in Rhoads Murphey, *Shanghai: Key to Modern China* (Cambridge: Harvard University Press, 1953), pp. 27–28. See also Janet Salaff, "The Urban Communes and Anti-City Experiment in Communist China," *China Quarterly* 29 (January–March 1967), esp. pp. 83–84.

129. The most famous example is Mao Zedong's speech on "The Ten Great Relationships," of which the best English version is in *Chairman Mao Talks to the People,* Stuart R. Schram, ed. (New York: Pantheon, 1974).

130. Calculated from *FEER,* December 11, 1986, p. 82.

131. "*Tongde tai duo, guande tai si.*" The new fiscal system was called "*caizheng guanli fenji.*" Jiang Zemin et al., *SHGYJJB*, (The Transformation of Shanghai's Party and Administration) (Shanghai: Shanghai Renmin Chuban She, 1988), p. 143.

132. This is calculated by dividing the data on sales-tax creation per worker by the figures on revenue creation per worker in *SHGYJJB* (Shanghai Industrial Economy), August 19, 1988. The rates were: Beijing, 22 percent; Shanghai and Wuhan, 21 percent; Dalian, 20 percent; Tianjin, 19 percent; Guangzhou, 18 percent; Qingdao, 17 percent; Chongqing, 15 percent; Haerbin and Xi'an, 14 percent; Wuxi, 13 percent; and Suzhou at only 12 percent. The amount of variation seems extremely high for this kind of index. The sales tax is not all paid, of course, in the places where these goods are produced.

133. Cao Linzhang, Gu Guangqing, and Li Jianhua, *Shanghai shengchan,* p. 222; for some additional information, see also *Shuiwu gongzuo shouce* (Tax Work Handbook), Zou Yunfang, ed. (Beijing: Nengyuan Chuban She, 1987), p. 119 and other pages.

134. See Parks M. Coble Jr., *The Shanghai Capitalists and the Nationalist Government, 1927–1937* (Cambridge: Harvard University Press, 1980).

135. Zhu Xingqing, an editor at the quasi-dissident *World Economic Herald* with whom this author also conversed, is quoted in *FEER,* December 11, 1986, p. 83.

136. See Nicholas R. Lardy, "Comment," p. 349.

137. *LDB,* April 26, 1950.

138. *NCNA,* August 31, 1953.

139. *NCNA,* January 14, 1956.

140. *NCNA,* February 15 and May 30, 1956; *JFRB,* June 4, 1956.

141. *XWRB,* January 19, 1957. This article implies that the average moved factory had thirty employees, and the average moved store had eleven.

142. There is no space here for an extended report on this topic, but additional information may be found in Lynn White, "The Road to Urumqi: Approved Institutions in Search of Attainable Goals in Pre-1968 Rustication from Shanghai," *China Quarterly* 79 (October 1979), pp. 481–510.

143. The basis of this "accumulation tax" is not fully explained in the source. *SHJJ,* April 1988, p. 26.

144. Based on interviews in Shanghai, as well as on sources in notes 143 and 145.

145. *SJJJDB,* August 29, 1988.

146. More discussion of these problems is in Lynn T. White III, "Joint Ventures in a New Shanghai at Pudong," Sally Stewart, ed., *Advances in Chinese Industrial Studies: Joint Ventures in the PRC* (Greenwich, CT: JAI Press, 1995), pp. 75–120.

147. *FBIS,* February 1, 1988, pp. 35–36, reporting radio of January 18.

148. This word could also be translated as "obedient." *ZGQNB,* September 20, 1988.

149. This kind of company is called a *taozhai gongsi. JFRB,* May 9, 1988.

150. The extent of this "*kongzhi*" is stressed in *Zhongguo shehui zhuyi chengshi jingji xue* (Chinese Socialist Urban Economics), Zhu Linxing, ed. (Shanghai: Shanghai Shehui Kexue Chuban She, 1986), p. 41.

151. For more about these negotiations, see Michel Oksenberg and James Tong, "The Evolution of Central-Provincial Fiscal Relations in China, 1971–1984: The Formal System," *China Quarterly* 125 (March 1991), pp. 1–32.

152. Jiangsu, however, did notably well in this period. See Penelope B. Prime, "Central-Provincial Investment and Finance: The Cultural Revolution and its Legacy in Jiangsu Province," in *New Perspectives on the Cultural Revolution,* William Joseph, Christine Wong, and David Zweig, eds. (Cambridge: Harvard University Press, 1991).

153. Interview with a Shanghai economist, who used the phrase "*quanguo baohu Shanghai.*"

154. *Shanghai jingji, neibu ben: 1949–1982,* p. 798.

155. This statistic is called the "*difang, bumen, qiye he shiye danwei zhangwo de yusuan wai zijin.*" Ibid., p. 14, also says its average rate of increase from 1979 to 1985 was 22.4 percent.

156. Chen Xianglin's speech to a 1989 NPC meeting is quoted in Linda Li, "Central-Provincial Relations," chap. 6, p. 27.

157. Quoted from interviews by Linda Li, "Central-Provincial Relations," chap. 6, p. 11.

158. Zhang Chunqiao, Shanghai's administrative head during the Cultural Revolution and protoreforms, was (like many of his municipal colleagues then) thoroughly Jiangnan; but his entrepreneurialism was of a radical sort. The text above applies to the period after his demise, when politicians from elsewhere took the very high Shanghai-central jobs.

159. These paragraphs, and a further section on the implications of Subei staffing of Shanghai's most dusty and menial jobs in chapter 2.5, depend on the author's research and especially on the pathbreaking work of Emily Honig, *Creating Chinese Ethnicity: Subei People in Shanghai, 1850–1980* (New Haven: Yale University Press, 1992).

160. This could also be said, almost surely, of the Nanjing Military District. Less information has thus far been found about the backgrounds of the main leaders there. Industries under their administration are important in Shanghai's economy.

161. *Zhonghua renmin gonghe guo jingji dashi ji, 1949–1980* (Chronicle of Economic Events in the PRC, 1949–1980), Fang Weizhong et al., eds. (Beijing: Zhongguo Shehui Kexue Chuban She, 1984), p. 571.

162. "*Guojia tanpan weiyuan hui*" was the sarcastic phrase used by this economist (who has since departed China).

163. "*Dingshou dingzhi, shouzhi baogan*" sounds strikingly like slogans of the mid-1980s, although it comes from 1970 (in a plan first implemented in the next year). So does the slogan in the next sentence, about "*xiafang caiquan.*" See *Shanghai jingji, neibu ben: 1949–1982,* p. 891.

164. Ibid., "*baozheng shangjiao, jieyu liuyong, yinian yiding.*"

165. Ibid. quotes the expenditure target at 961 billion yuan. The rate of overfulfillment of the 1971 revenue target was 3 percent. Even this limited-circulation source does not give such detailed figures on reform years—maybe because the Shanghai economists

who wrote it were especially upset by the exorbitant tax rates during the early 1970s protoreforms.

166. Ibid.

167. Ibid., p. 30, presents graphs to suggest this.

168. After 1977, a series of small taxes on real estate, licenses, and many other items were introduced to raise more local revenues. But the bulk of the state's revenues, at all levels, continued to come from profits and taxes on its companies. Ibid., p. 892.

169. *SHJJDB,* July 25, 1988. The difficulty of keeping stoves together for a household is a full symbol of modernization in Margery Wolf, *The House of Lim* (Boston: Beacon, 1972).

170. *Zhonghua renmin gonghe guo jingji dashi ji,* p. 645.

171. See Linda Li, "Central-Provincial Relations," chap. 4, p. 23. For facts in the next paragraph, see pp. 25–27.

172. *JFRB,* April 1, 1988.

173. This material comes mainly from interviews in Shanghai.

174. Charles Ponzi, a Bostonian, in 1919 paid back old investors with "interest" money he received from new ones. "Ponzi schemes" work, without any productive investment, so long as public credibility in them continues to escalate. Then they can collapse spectacularly.

175. *SHJJNJ88,* pp. 100–2. The slogans referred respectively to *ziding jishu, shouzhi guagou, zong'e fencheng,* and *yiding sannian.*

176. "*Jishu baogan, zengshou fencheng, yiding wunian.*" *JFRB,* February 4, 1988.

177. In order by amount of payment: Wuxi county (Jiangsu), Chuansha county (Shanghai), Jiading county (Shanghai), Changshu [county-level] city (Jiangsu), Xiaoshan city (Zhejiang), Jiangyang city (Jiangsu), and Nanhui county (Shanghai); *XMWB,* January 24, 1989. China at this time had more than two thousand counties in all, plus two hundred odd county-level cities; but the seven that paid the highest taxes were all close to Shanghai.

178. Calculated from tables in *Zhongguo gongye de fazhan, 1949–1984,* pp. 160 and 163 (where an average is taken of the rates from the four non-Shanghai cigarette plants, because their composite rate is not available). This author intends that a future research project will be on the Chinese and international politics of nicotine addiction, which is for biological reasons a very reliable supplier of revenues.

179. *Zhongguo shehui zhuyi chengshi jingji xue,* p. 89.

180. *WHB,* December 4, 1979.

181. "*Yao qian shu.*" *WHB,* August 10, 1980.

182. Ibid.

183. *Hengxiang jingji,* p. 131.

184. For further arguments on the importance of CCP personnel scarcity on all Chinese politics, see Lynn White, *Policies of Chaos: The Organizational Causes of Violence in China's Cultural Revolution* (Princeton: Princeton University Press, 1989).

185. *CD,* February 1, 1988.

186. *Zhonghua renmin gonghe guo jingji dashi ji,* p. 625.

187. The city's second largest capital construction project was the Shanghai Shidong No. 2 Power Plant (like Baoshan, also in Wusong). It was built with funds raised by the Huaneng International Power Development Company and the Shanghai government. *FBIS,* February 2, 1988, p. 36, reporting radio of January 30.

188. *Shanghai jingji, neibu ben,* p. 913.

189. Chapter 2.5 contains more material on the effects of the high-tax regime on Shanghai individuals.

190. Reginald Yin-wang Kwok, "Metropolitan Development in China: A Struggle Between Contradictions," *Habitat International* 12:4 (1988), pp. 201–2.

191. Tao Yongkuan et al., *Dali fazhan,* p. 59.

192. Calculated from *Zhongguo chengshi tongji nianjian, 1988* (Statistical Yearbook of Chinese Cities, 1988), State Statistical Bureau, ed. (Beijing: Zhongguo Tongji Xinxi Zixun Fuwu Zhongxin and Xin Shijie Chuban She, 1988), pp. 23–25 for the population figures and pp. 239–41 for the telephones.

193. See *FEER,* December 12, 1985, p. 30.

194. Ibid., p. 28.

195. *Caijing yanjiu* (Financial and Economic Research), May 1988, p. 15.

196. *Shanghai jingji, neibu ben,* p. 889.

197. These figures also show that Shanghai was rich in comparison with all of China, and of course that is true. But the meaning of the statistics in terms of people's lives, rather than in terms of state-fixed valuations for capital and products, is not easy to determine. *Shanghai shehui xiankuang he qushi, 1980–1983* (Situations and Trends in Shanghai Society, 1980–1983), Zheng Gongliang et al., eds. (Shanghai: Huadong Shifan Daxue Chuban She, 1988), p. 203.

198. *Shanghai jingji, neibu ben,* p. 562.

199. *Shijie xin jishu geming yu Shanghai de duice* (The Global Revolution in New Technology and Shanghai's Policies in Response), Shanghai Economic Research Center and Shanghai Science and Technology Committee, eds. (Shanghai: Shanghai Shehui Kexue Yuan Chuban She, 1986), p. 194.

200. The economists (not identified by name) would not have put the issue in this fashion, at least not in print. There are a number of premises that might be questioned in this model, but it is an interesting approach to the problem. A topic that may deserve more exploration is the loss of remittance caused by the cases in which Shanghai industries could not buy materials at all. On the other hand, nonprice effects on profitability (including effects of bad management) could affect remittances. This is not a perfect model, but the fact that it was proposed in this form is notable. *SHJJ,* April 1988, pp. 26–27.

201. Ordinary machines are *yiban jixie,* while precision machines are *jingmi jixie. SHJJ,* April 1988, p. 28.

202. A group of administrative centers with relatively high rates of payment from realized profits and taxes shown on this table is the group of cities (thirty-one of them in 1984) with population between 500,000 and 1,000,000. That group, including many provincial capitals, paid out about 85 percent of its realized state income, whereas the other three types of cities (below the largest) could retain 5 or 6 percentage points more, e.g. in 1984. This may have been a transient phenomenon, because reform was sometimes (before 1989) better supported both at the top level and in hard-to-control small places than at middle levels.

203. These figures, which are not described in all sources in exactly the same manner, require many technical notes—and even then, more extensive interviews with Shanghai auditors who were actually engaged in mid-1980s state extraction assessments might give a less incomplete picture. A full interpretation would partly depend on any changes during this period in methods of evaluating fixed assets, and on changes in handling extrabudgetary funds, to determine how much of the very sharp gradient over time in the Shanghai figures, and of the difference between Shanghai and other places, was real and how much was a result of altered reporting practices. But some things are known, for example about the denominator term underlying this table. "Capital" (*zijin*) includes both fixed and circulating capital, is calculated at year's end, and has two parts: quota circulating capital (*ding'e liudong zijin,* administered by banks) and fixed capital net value (*guding zichan jingzhi,* based on original prices minus yearly depreciations after purchase). See *Tianjin tongji nianjian, 1987* (Tianjin Statistical Yearbook, 1987), Tianjin Statistical Bureau, ed. (Beijing: Zhongguo Tongji Chuban She, 1987), pp. 120 and 352, for especially clear

definitions. "Circulating capital" comprises these five elements: reserve capital (*chubei zijin*), which is the value of materials yet to be processed; production capital (*shengchan zijin*), referring to those in process; finished product capital (*chengpin zijin*), for those yet to be sold, overstocked inventory (*chaochu jiya wuzi*), in warehouses and not necessarily ever sold (sometimes a large item); and losses of circulating assets to be disposed of (*dai chuli liudong zichan sunshi*); see *Shanghai shi 1985 nian gongye pucha ziliao* (Materials from the 1985 Industrial Survey of Shanghai), Gu Delun et al., eds. (Shanghai: Zhongguo Tongji Chuban She, 1988), pp. 723–24. Before 1985 in Shanghai, and before 1978 in all parts of China, the central government could claim 100 percent of local industrial taxes (although some of these might flow back to the paying province in subsidies and investments), according to a Chinese economist highly knowledgeable on such subjects in 1988. The numerator term "profits and taxes" (*lishui*) is difficult to translate concisely into English, because "profits" normally include items that are costs of incentives to labor: welfare funds (*fuli jin*), bonus funds (*jiangjin*), and production development funds (*shengchan fazhan jin*—which are often used not for investment but for incidental administrative and sales costs, since most investment can be financed by administrative allocations or easy bank loans).

204. Interviews confirm this, as does Xu Zhenliang, "Shanghai caizheng shouru 'huapo' de xiankuang, chengyin ji qi duice" (The "Slide" of Shanghai's Financial Income: Situation, Reasons, and Countermeasures), in *Caijing yanjiu* (Financial and Economic Research), March 1988, pp. 18–23.

205. Some municipalities—notably Shanghai—show a relatively great amount of industry in their subordinate counties. Reports for 1984 were published separately for the built-up urban districts and for whole cities; the urban areas' ratios are larger than those of the whole municipalities. Suburbs have lower remittance rates per unit of capital. Shanghai's suburbs nonetheless had industries realizing revenues more effectively than the suburbs of other cities.

206. The very low burden of one capital reported on the table, Haerbin, reflects the fact that the oil center of Daqing is in the same province, Heilongjiang; so local officials can pay from oil revenues—and may also have military backing to keep their total burden low.

207. *Shanghai: Gaige, kaifang, yu fazhan, 1979–87* (Shanghai: Reforms, Opening, and Development, 1979–87), Shanghai Statistical Bureau, ed. (Shanghai: Sanlian Shudian, 1988), p. 44.

208. Calculated from *Shanghai jingji qu fazhan zhanlue chutan* (Preliminary Research on the Development Strategy of the Shanghai Economic Zone), *World Economic Herald* and Shanghai Economic Zone Research Society, eds. (Wuxi Branch of Eighth People's Printers, 1986), p. 266.

209. *FEER,* December 11, 1986, pp. 82–83.

210. *Shangmen shoushui* was thus replaced by *nashui shangmen.* See *Jiangsu fazhi bao* January 21, 1989.

211. *SHJJ,* February 1988, p. 5.

212. In 1984, Shanghai had 30 yuan of realized profits and taxes per 100 yuan of capital, but in 1987 this was down to 21 yuan. The estimate in the text is calculated from *Zhongguo chengshi tongji nianjian, 1985* (Statistical Yearbook of Chinese Cities, 1985), State Statistical Bureau, ed. (Beijing: Zhongguo Tongji Xinxi Zixun Fuwu Zhongxin and Xin Shijie Chuban She, 1985), pp. 146–52, and ibid. for 1988, pp. 185–93.

213. *JJRB,* August 15, 1988.

214. *Shanghai jingji nianjian, 1988,* p. 23.

215. The exact figures, computed by the Shanghai Finance Bureau apparently to mollify critics of its tax collection efforts, were 56.5 percent to other provinces and the center, 36.7 percent to the city's firms, and 6.8 percent to individuals—which accounts for 100 percent of the "loss." *SHJJ,* February 1988, p. 5.

216. This was expressed in Chinese form, on analogy to an old saying, "If you don't go to the Yellow River, you can't die yet" ("*Bu dao Huanghe xing, busi*"); for the government, "If it doesn't take the last fen . . ." ("*Bu ba zuihou yifen qian . . .*").

217. *FBIS,* March 4, 1988, p. 9, reporting radio of the same day.

218. *Shanghai jingji qu fazhan zhanlue chutan,* p. 14.

219. *FBIS,* February 1, 1988, pp. 40–41, reporting radio of January 23.

220. Ezra N. Suleiman, *Private Power and Centralization in France: The Notaires and the State* (Princeton: Princeton University Press, 1987).

221. For comparative perspectives on this phenomenon, see James C. Scott, *Weapons of the Weak: Everyday Forms of Peasant Protest* (New Haven: Yale University Press, 1985); an application to large-scale politics is Lynn White, *Policies of Chaos,* p. 308.

222. For more, see Lynn White, "Leadership and Participation: The Case of Shanghai's Managers," in *Citizens and Groups in Contemporary China,* Victor C. Falkenheim, ed. (Ann Arbor: Center for Chinese Studies, University of Michigan, 1986), pp. 189–211.

223. *Yue tou, yue dan da.* Ibid.

224. Based on conversations with Shanghai economists. Much more work can be done with figures for both output and taxes from Guangdong and other places, toward a better comparison of the provincial burdens. But the raw remittance figures in the text give some picture.

225. This proposed system was a "*fenshui zhi.*" *Caizheng* (Finance), March 1988, p. 36.

226. *JFRB,* August 19, 1988.

227. *LW* (1988), p. 12.

228. Ibid.

229. "*Shanghai shi da ge, xian gu jia, hou gu ji.*" "*Jiao gei fumu, zai fen gei xiongdi,*" according to *ZGQNB*, September 20, 1988.

230. Ibid. The author of this article was a Mr. Wang An—apparently not the famous Shanghainese-Massachusetts computer magnate of the same name.

231. *SHJJDB,* August 22, 1988.

232. *JFRB,* May 15, 1988.

233. *FBIS,* March 11, 1988, p. 33, reporting *RMRB* of March 9.

234. See Albert Hirschman, "Changing Tolerance for Income Inequality in the Course of Economic Development," *World Development* 1:12 (1973), pp. 24–36.

235. *Post,* July 8, 1989.

Chapter 1.3

Business Incentives Beyond the State

We have just two principles. One is satisfying demand.
The other is making money.

—Hu Yanchou, President of Shanghai Cable TV[1]

For urban industry, the main content of the Chinese revolution was state management. After that, reforms to specialize business power networks began very slowly. They strained against all explicit norms, so that the change was often more real than acknowledged. In the 1950s, the earlier socialist change had also not occurred suddenly. The Party in the first half of that decade lacked enough personnel even to make a pretense of control in an industrial economy as complex as Shanghai's. But as the new order was established, most formally with the Transition to Socialism in 1956, the pecking order of companies by ownership types became more than a mantra: "First the state [firms], later the collective, last the private" (*xian guojia, hou jiti, zai geren*).

Ownership, such as these phrases describe, can imply several different kinds of rights that are not coequal but are mutually dependent.[2] They are also a function of the law as it is actually enforced. The state—or whatever other coercive network is effective—has a role over marketed commodities, since it establishes rules for selling or contracting assets. That right of regulating markets is not ordinarily conceived as a matter of ownership, but it can limit what happens to commodities in a way that is practically indistinguishable from ownership rights. A second kind of ownership is the right to forswear control of an asset, e.g. to sell it; and this kind is usually conceived as the main one. A third category of ownership rights involves other management decisions. A fourth category is the right to income from property. There is a priority order among ownership rights because some (e.g. the right to sell) foreclose options for others. Theorized linkages between the different kinds—especially those typified by selling, managing, and receiving income—make for constant debates about the efficiency and justice of various ownership regimes.

The Chinese top leaders, as regards property "owned by the whole people," became unable during reforms to prevent limited alienation of some of their previous ownership rights. The Chinese state as a whole has always been too unwieldy to engage in detailed management of all business, or even of all sizeable businesses. During the peak of the revolution, its leaders nonetheless attempted this. In 1965 nationally, over ten thousand firms, producing 47 percent of all state-factory industrial output, were supposed to be run (as regards their main functions) directly by central ministries. This situation did not last long, even on a nominal basis. So in the early 1970s, practically all nonmilitary central enterprises were switched to provincial control. They were still "state firms"—provinces and counties in China are state agencies, and at that time so were communes. They were still "owned by the whole people," but run in different respects by a great mixture of administrative levels. Already by 1971, only 142 firms producing just 8 percent of China's output were designated in public as wholly central.[3] One result of this change was that depreciation funds from large factories were, in most areas, now sent to local governments.

These early 1970s decentralizations were mostly changes of management, not of legal ownership. For years, formal sales of "state property" were prevented; they remained rare throughout the decades covered by this book until the 1990s. Top leaders hoped that state corporations or local bureaucrats would manage assets to assure a good income flow into central networks. Because of the continuing normative importance of state institutions for local Chinese leaders, these hopes were fulfilled—especially in Shanghai—until the contextual basis for them in socialist planning mostly collapsed. Even then, the development of collective and private property came overwhelmingly through economic growth in those sectors, rather than through sales from the state.

Ownership, Corruption, and Entrepreneurship

Because the Cultural Revolution incapacitated most central ministries, much localization of control over property during the early 1970s occurred by default. The State Planning Commission (SPC) had expired by 1969, and Zhou Enlai set up a temporary group to fill the void—but expert administrators were still demoralized, so that few plans would have been enforceable in any case. A "Little State Planning Commission" of fifty people tried to do the job of the previous SPC with its thousand experts.[4] All the industrial ministries, the People's Bank, and the Ministry of Finance were similarly decimated. Socialism is a difficult proposition for a state without planners.

Central coordination was nonetheless more important for Shanghai, and to a lesser extent for the flat areas around the city, than for most other Chinese places. Beijing depended on the main appointees in each province, who were part of the unified state even though they could assume some advocacy roles for their regions. They met periodically in the capital, and by the early 1970s—as during later reforms—their conferences replaced the pretense of planning that had been fashionable until the mid-1960s. Although central ministries still had important roles in several large Shanghai industries, economic work conferences and politicians' meetings set the pattern in the early 1970s and later. Beijing offices became largely secretarial, following the decisions of conclaves of top politicians and their satraps elsewhere.

Dissident economists in Shanghai privately referred to the State Planning Commission as a mere "negotiating commission" (*tanpan weiyuan hui*). Every year, from the 1970s at least, there has been an economic meeting in Beijing among provincial leaders, whose main object is to figure out how the central government's budget will be met. Poor inland provinces with strong guerrilla heritages, along with the defense and heavy industrial offices of the capital's bureaucracy that need money, tended to dominate these gatherings during early reforms. The meetings were reportedly cordial, and everyone regularly agreed that Shanghai was making a large contribution to China. But until the mid-1980s, it was not the task of the Shanghai representatives to lower their city's assessment; rather, it was their main task to tell how the city would pay.

"Mother-in-Law" Supervising Corporations

Politicians have long been deemed superior to businesspeople in China. The late-Qing statesman Li Hongzhang advocated that "officials supervise and commercial people manage."[5] Li knew the government was often needed to set up new industries, and this linked firms to the state regardless of legal property arrangements. Li began to adapt the traditional state view of hierarchy's efficacy to modern industrial problems.

By the 1950s, state corporations, each of which grouped many firms in the same trade, were organized under Shanghai municipal bureaus. At that time, the Party had enough power among workers and patriots to force nationalization on capitalists. Only cooperative businesspeople made profits. But there were still not enough Communist managers to replace the capitalists. So in the mid-1950s the CCP distributed its few trusted accountants (and many demobilized soldiers wanting civilian sinecures) into corporations that "supervised" factories but were often located in offices physically far away from production sites or stores.

Within whole industries, Shanghai's 1950s structure for running the economy was divided into two levels: "government business management departments" and "civilian business associations."[6] Government organs were supposed to take care of middle- and long-term plans, including investment, credit, quality inspections, and any technical renovations. Local firms and civilian associations, at lower administrative levels, were supposed only to "assist and consult with" their supervisory agencies, rather than making basic plans. This structure lasted until the mid-1960s; but with the Cultural Revolution and then the lapses of materials deliveries, the upper level was weakened.

This top-heavy management system became a major object of reform. In Shanghai, it changed slowly because of its fiscal role, but the new market context affected the system's several layers differently. At the municipal level, a few offices reported directly to the mayor, with responsibility for large sectors such as commerce, light industry, or finance. The second level within the city consisted of municipal bureaus with somewhat more specific functional areas such as grain, housing, or textiles. Only at the third level—corporations—did managers' accountability for numerical quotas become public and definite. In industry, these large corporations managed many subordinate factories. In commerce, there was also commonly an intervening layer of urban district corporations (*qu gongsi*) or central stores (*zhongxin dian*). Reforming economists wished to amalgamate the submayoral offices and the municipal bureaus in some fields, and to merge the corporations with the bureaus in other trades. They wanted to extend authority with accountability as far down in the system as possible.

The practical meanings of ownership are best captured in terms of specific functions in specific agencies. But under socialism, despite conservatives' hopes for planning, the structure of control over Shanghai's production was often difficult for anyone to determine. Similar firms, using similar materials to produce similar goods, were often coordinated neither by single-price markets nor by a unified management. Machine-building enterprises, for example, were fragmented in Shanghai among more than ten municipal bureaus in the mid-1980s. Food processing companies were distributed among more than eight bureaus. Construction and metallurgy were scattered among another eight (owing obedience also to five districts and nine counties). Packaging businesses were led by twenty-two "systems."[7]

From the viewpoint of most local politics, e.g. for factory-level managers, the practical content of socialism was the existence of a municipal corporation. Especially as reforms weakened the role of planning, these came increasingly to resemble nonmanagerial holding companies. They were colloquially called "mothers-in-law" (*popo*), since factory managers had the traditionally uneasy place of a new bride, married into the socialist clan but having low status in it. For most firms, the "mother-in-law" was a municipal bureau or state company, which was formally in charge of many factories or stores. This bossy relative was usually in a head office geographically separate from the component firms. Managers were notoriously hemmed in by their "supervising agencies" (*zhuguan*).

This structure, which had been imposed by effective state control of many raw material and product markets during the 1950s, provided a kind of relief to

Shanghai managers decades later, when that control collapsed because of new rural industries. The task of finding inputs and markets was not supposed to be the managers' worry. This was the job of the supervising corporations. Shanghai's most knowledgeable economic cadres at the store or factory level acquired, during reforms, strong interests in being able to forswear responsibility for precisely the problems that became most urgent: difficulties with upstream supplies and downstream markets. The officials in supervising corporations, to whom managers could refer such problems under socialist norms that had been fostered for many years, were often at a sufficiently high level to withstand criticism. This management structure paid taxes for a long while, it employed some lucky workers, and it preserved bureaucratic jobs. It did very little, however, to advance Shanghai's economy.

Property rights (*chanquan*) are normally devolved, during reforms, from supervising companies to subordinate units. But in some cases, this meant that no unit became clearly responsible for the property. Special policies (*teshu zhengce*) sustained many inefficient firms. One Shanghai economist recommended that badly managed enterprises should be allowed to go bankrupt. Then they could be put up for public auction so that any government agency, social organization, enterprise, or even individual who had the money to buy might do so.[8] The usual allocation system for capital was purely administrative.

"Managers' responsibility" is a two-edged sword. A reformist Party secretary in one East China plant put the problem neatly: The prereform style of "separating authority from responsibility" meant that CCP policy makers could not be blamed for their mistakes—and factory managers (who were very often blamed for bad results) could not make policy. This official advocated a new "managers' responsibility system."[9] In 1984, he called a meeting of all his plant's employees to announce that henceforth the manager would have full power over all five major areas: policies, production, administration, guidance, and even personnel. But such a situation, here in a joint venture, was rare. This case is mainly an example of how the "opening" to foreign investment provided demonstration effects for domestic Chinese companies. In most firms, "managers' responsibility" was at least partly a matter of maintaining factory Party cadres' ability to keep their links to clients safe from dangers, in a time of volatile budgets and economic unrest. The ambiguity of this slogan reflects tensions that are entirely typical of reforms.

Ironic Equilibrium: Efficient Managers' Incentives to Desist

The degrees of freedom that factory managers could exercise varied sharply by industry. Among all light industries and handicrafts (except textiles), 60 percent of the managers by the mid-1980s had free legal rein to "adjust" their planned quotas. But in metallurgy, where supplies were also tight but where the consumers were often powerful bureaucracies, none of the plant managers had this power. In machines and construction, only 15 percent had it; in chemicals, 17 percent; and in instruments, just 25 percent. Among Shanghai's light industries, the only one whose managers remained heavily constrained was the oldest and largest—textiles—which was also most important for raising central revenues. Only 11 percent of textile factory managers could "adjust" their quotas; cloth plants were like heavy industries, not like other light industries, in their limited degree of management freedom. High rates of managerial freedom correlated by industry with relatively low tax rates.[10]

Plans did not die; they just faded away. Factory managers complained that the rules distinguishing "mandatory" from "indicative" plans were increasingly vague and changeable. If a plant was successful in making more than its quota of products, this excess would soon be included in the mandatory amount. The "indicative plan" was really not a plan at all, but a temporary mandate for materials purchasing in hopes of surplus production. As the director of the Shanghai Third Steel Mill said, his mandatory plan quota was already so high that any flexibility to produce surpluses on the "indicative plan" was "empty talk."[11] His factory usually ran at full capacity. His supervising bureau raised the mandatory amount whenever there was a chance they could get more products—at the price they set—within the fixed plan. This steel mill had a right freely to sell above-quota products, but the "mother-in-law" constantly adjusted the quota to make sure there never were any.

A second criticism was that although the effective production quotas were mandatory, upstream units' targets for raw materials supplies were often merely indicative. Mixing the two kinds of plan meant no plan at all. Factor costs could increase so fast and inputs could become so scarce during reforms, basic quotas were hard to produce. A third complaint from factory-level managers was that the mandatory plans often quickly changed, to tax and channel any products that the market temporarily made profitable. But if supplies were plenty, e.g. if finished goods were likely to be hard to sell, the supervising agencies would classify them as part of the "indicative plan."[12]

The grant to managers of powers to sell above-quota products therefore became a recipe for endemic local conflict between them and higher-level units that had long handled their procurement and merchandising. If a factory made marketable "hot products" (*rexiao shangpin*), the supervising companies could confiscate them by declaring them within the mandatory quota. During the 1980s, large corporations increasingly needed these "hot products" to barter for scarce raw materials. Managers' rights to sell over-quota surpluses became inconsequential.

Well-known Shanghai brands, including many that became "hot products," tended to be made in companies that were therefore increasingly controlled as shortages worsened. The more enterprising a factory manager was—the more innovative, stylish, marketable, and profitable the products became—the less benefit that same manager would be allowed to retain.

This ironic equilibrium, under which the success of internal reforms in efficient units brought greater pressures to make them fail, was surprisingly widespread in Shanghai's economy during the 1980s. The head of a plant that made one of the city's famous brands of toothpaste said that he had been driven to advertise his lesser-known lines, rather than his more profitable wares, so as to keep some of his managerial powers. This syndrome, brought on by reforms in a context of ever less successful state efforts to restore fiscal control, was the opposite of a profit incentive. As another Shanghai factory manager put it, "A gold brand or a silver brand is nothing, compared to a so-so brand of freedom."[13]

Macroeconomic Management with Multiple Pricing

The government had its problems, too. CCP leaders wanted to placate potentially restless urban workers while keeping wage budgets low in state firms. Maintaining urban consumers' purchasing power was the crux of the official interest in preventing inflation. Since the state-fixed prices of many basic urban goods (food, housing, energy, transport) would have to float upward if they were to approach levels that reflected their scarcity, these commodities had to be subsidized. The prices of materials used to produce them were also rising. Party conservatives saw problems of political management whose solutions were often in tension with the issues faced by factory managers.

Their favored solution was to arrange low prices for crucial constituencies, notably for urban state workers. They often set up systems that benefited groups other than the people they had intended. For example, the Shanghai Blanket Factory in 1985 could legally sell its blankets for only 72 yuan each (making a mere 3 yuan profit) in Shanghai's "price basin." The price of very similar blankets from Yinchuan in Ningxia was not controlled, however, and these blankets fetched 120 yuan on free markets nationwide, establishing a normal price. Illegal private traders smuggled blankets out of Shanghai to other provinces. As the manager of the Shanghai Blanket Factory sarcastically put it, "This is the state giving a cash subsidy so that the [smuggling] private entrepreneurs get rich."[14] Multiple pricing that attempted political management led to distortions.

Another problem of unintentional effects from political management arose because of the shift, during reforms, of the way factories got new credit. Under the traditional prereform system of "unified receipts and unified expenditures," practically all the money a company made was sent to higher levels that represented the state; any money a factory needed was appropriated from there.[15] By the mid-1980s, however, these hand-outs of funds had to be replaced by loans, because central agencies were short of money. Factory managers realized that any new profitable activities they undertook on the basis of borrowed money would be classified into their "mandatory" sales quotas. They had no incentive to take out these loans, even to implement good money-making ideas, because they would later be unable to repay them. Shanghai's capital equipment was obsolescent in many industries, and even highly conservative politicians could see that

Shanghai should move out of many traditional fields into new industries that would require massive infusions of capital for higher technology. But the inertia of bureaucratic interests—built into the structural separation of supervising and operating managements and their differing abilities to control income flows from "state" property—tended to stymie policies for growth.

Obsolete equipment, holding back productivity over the long term, could not be replaced in many Shanghai industries because of short-term efforts to control inflation. The Yangzi Lumber Mill in Shanghai, for example, had many pre-1937 machines. Its manager looked into the rationality of new investment. Even using a very long depreciation period of twenty-six years, he figured that his total annual "development fund" (the official source for renovation money) was one-third of what would have been necessary to pay the interest on the capital improvement his factory needed. His proposal would only have replaced worn-out equipment; if he opted to go further, bringing in newer lumber technology, the bill would have been much higher. This manager did not take out a loan to counterbalance depreciation. He thought his supervisors, in offices away from the factory, would over time keep the development fund low, whether or not his production improved because of investments from it.[16]

Managers' costs during reforms were raised by expenses for "social responsibility" to their employees, some of which might have been borne by the municipal budget if less money were remitted further upward. Costs for housing construction, food subsidies, pensions in lieu of social security, child care, and many other items rose quickly in the 1980s. Factories were increasingly hard pressed to find money for all this. A Shanghai economist complained that insufficient incentives were given to managers for use of their funds to raise their technological levels or the long-term profitability of their plants.[17] It is debatable whether these costs should have been municipal or corporate. They were underfunded, especially as the city's budget was constrained to maintain its remittance flow while its revenues were slipping. But some managers appropriated their scarce production development funds for welfare or bonus use. Since using money for major technological improvements would only bring more interference, exactions, and demands from their supervisors, factory managers preferred to keep a low profile and build up personal support among their subordinate clients. A way for Shanghai managers to serve enterprise efficiency and personal constituencies at the same time was to use money for joint enterprises in other parts of the delta, where tax rates were lower and "mothers-in-law" were farther away.

Supervisory companies could claim "autonomy" as easily as basic-level factories could. The meanings of autonomy in these two contexts were often opposite. Some basic-level factory heads even claimed that the taxing corporations were mainly interested in debilitating their subordinate firms. With too much dramatic flourish, a Shanghai factory head used bitter metaphors: "The method by which supervising agencies control firms now is that 'live fish eat dead fish'; 'only be afraid of a live business, not of a dead one'; 'only be afraid of a rich enterprise, not a poor one.' "[18]

Official chops were still needed from supervising agencies for many decisions at the factory level. The "vetoes" (*foujue quan*) that these chops represented were, one factory manager said, increasing rather than decreasing in the 1980s. Much-publicized intentions among top reformers to reduce them were said to be ineffective. The "factory managers' responsibility system" was supposed largely to have replaced Party cadres' authority, but in practice many firms did not follow this new rule. "If factory managers make a decision, but if the Party committee disagrees, it cannot be carried out."[19] The pattern was implicitly compared to the feudal custom by which a weak emperor had to "hang a curtain and listen to policy" from behind it.[20]

The obstacles to more efficient decentralization in Shanghai's management were many. Clear laws protecting factories and their managers were still absent in the late 1980s, and it was easy to return to premarket norms when market incentives infringed the powers of high cadres. The reforms were opposed by real interests in politically powerful supervising corporations. The management culture that state policies had sponsored for many years severely discouraged enterprise within the urban state system, which was reformed or replaced mostly because of competition elsewhere.

Types of Ownership

China officially has three ownership systems—by the state (theoretically representing "all the people," called the *quanmin suoyou zhi*), by collectives (*jiti suoyou zhi*), and by private persons (*geti suoyou zhi*). These can also be used in any combination to create a diverse fourth "joint" (*lianhe*) category. But dissident reformers joke that in fact China has just one major ownership system: by supervising departments (and they call this the *bumen suoyou zhi,* using a very unofficial name for it). These are the "mother-in-law" agencies described earlier, no matter whether they are in government offices or state corporations.

The Chinese state in effect slowly recognized, in the course of reforms, that it did not control many lower-level units of its administrative hierarchy, and that many "state" cadres were not solely beholden to the state. Official definitions of economic ownership categories acknowledged this situation. Government offices reported statistics from four types of owners, of which three require little explanation here. The issue of "state cadres" who act outside the official apparatus arises most clearly in the large and important third category, the collectives.

1. State-owned enterprises are nominally nationalized, though often managed by provincial or other jurisdictions.[21]
2. Private enterprises are fully owned and operated by individuals.
3. Collective enterprises are extremely diverse. They are first officially subdi-

vided into two types, urban and rural. Each of these is said to contain three subtypes: Within the urban category, some collectives are founded and controlled by state enterprises as satellites. These in practice are mainly designed to minimize remittance imposts and to hire more staff than the planned personnel rosters of state enterprises allow. A second type of urban collective is supposed to be controlled by local governments, whether at the city, district, or street levels (*shi, qu,* or *jiedao*). But ownership in these cases is very ambiguous: It is not even nominally vested in the state, since these are collectives. It is supposed to be socialist at the local level, monitored by local leaders who should have concurrent official posts but somehow should avoid using official power to help the firms. The third type covers true collectives, formed by individuals cooperating with each other who find they can succeed best by not formally designating their firm as "private." Rural collectives also come in three types. First are the firms authorized by local governments that are not state enterprises; such companies created the "Sunan model," which has provided the main dynamism of reform in the Shanghai delta and is the most important category on this list. A second type is founded by local community organizations that are not technically part of the state, such as "united front" groups. A third sort comprises rural collectives run by groups of citizens.[22]

4. A residual "other" category includes all kinds of firms that are joint (state-with-collective, collective-with-private, state-with-foreign, collective-with-foreign, and so forth). Among such firms, the degree of coordination by high state levels varies a great deal, from considerable planning to very occasional regulation.

These official categories make clear that "the state" has no very clear boundary vis-à-vis more-local power networks, that many managements that are formally parts of the state are also largely autonomous from the central government, and that many combinations of authority by group size and officialness have been recognized in China. Furthermore, legal categories and actual practices are not in perfect harmony. Some local managers have reasons to wield less influence than the state allocates them, while others by intention or by circumstance wield more.

Reform meant a rise of collective ownership, not just private ownership. In central Shanghai, even this change was delayed. It began almost covertly, in the suburbs and in urban lanes, because conservatives' control of zoning prevented new businesses from acquiring quarters on main streets. Collective firms grew nonetheless, partly because the quality of service in the state sector was often abysmal. At Shanghai, consumers took particular pride in their consciousness about quality.[23] To sum up: Ownership change in central Shanghai was very slow. It was mostly toward the collective, not the private, form into the mid-1990s at least. It arose first in market niches and in geographical corners that the state had neglected.

Collectives' Dominance over Ownership Change in Shanghai

Collective industries for many years played second fiddle to state-owned industries. Their wages were on average lower. They were subject to almost as much official planning (although in theory, workers in collectives were supposed to have rights to make production decisions). Pensions in collective industries were usually less generous, although current bonuses were in some cases better. The average size of these companies, as measured either by output or by employees, was less large than the average for state-owned firms. Some conservative Party officials clearly felt that collectives were not quite legitimate, not advanced historically—merely a transitional form of management, to be replaced later by state plants.

By 1980, the existence of discrimination against collective industries was in effect admitted officially, and they were declared essential.[24] More stress was laid on the need to have more specialized collectives, and explicit calls were published to oppose discrimination against them. Collectives were declared, in Marxist terms, to be historically as legitimate and prospectively as long-lasting as state industries—and reformers duly noted that Marx foresaw the withering away of the state. Although workers' administrative rights over purchasing and marketing decisions were not stressed, the theory underlying them was published.

Shanghai collectives became especially important in retailing perishable goods, which required more care than state employees could usually muster. Collectives in the early 1980s sold 63 percent of subsidiary food products by value, and 35 percent of other nongrain foods—but only 4 percent of staple grains (which were usually rationed). State-owned shops at this time still controlled over 90 percent of sales volume in department, stationery, and clothing stores—and state shops had higher portions of these markets in Shanghai than in most Chinese cities. In any service that required care, however, collectives could thrive in competition with state firms. Among restaurants and other eateries in Shanghai, 84 percent of the firms by 1983, and already 51 percent of the sales volume, were collective.[25] Industry remained overwhelmingly state-owned, and private firms were still few and small.

State industry remained far more important in Shanghai than in nearby and comparable places, even well into the reform period. The growth rate of collective industry in the metropolis and in Zhejiang, as Table 1.3–1 shows, was slower than in Guangdong and in Jiangsu.

Of Shanghai's GNP in 1978, the state sector produced 84 percent; in 1985, 72 percent; and in 1989, 63 percent. Similar calculations for Guangzhou, a provincial capital, indicate a 1989 public sector share of GNP almost identical to that in Shanghai. But a much lower share, 36 percent, was state-sector in the large Guangdong city of Foshan, which is not a provincial capital. By the same criteria, the 1989 state share of product in Suzhou was 31 percent; in Ningbo, 30 percent.[26] Even between the first two years of the 1990s, when the portion of

Table 1.3-1

Shanghai and Other Provinces' Industrial Output Growth by Ownership Type, 1980 and 1990
(percentages of gross value, and ***decade increase percentages***)

	1980		1990			
	State-owned	Collective	State-owned		Collective	
Shanghai portion	87	12	64		21	
1980–90 % increase				***41***		***247***
Jiangsu portion	57	33	34		40	
1980–90 % increase				***129***		***440***
Zhejiang portion	56	43	31		60	
1980–90 % increase				***212***		***690***
Guangdong portion	63	28	35		27	
1980–90 % increase				***237***		***494***
All China portion	76	24	55		36	
1980–90 % increase				***136***		***396***

Sources: Shanghai growth figures have not been found in these sectors for 1981–85. But see *Quanguo ge sheng zizhi qu zhixia shi lishi tongji ziliao huibian, 1949–1989* (Historical Statistics Collection on Provinces, Autonomous Regions, and Municipalities Throughout the Country, 1949–1989) (Beijing: Zhongguo Tongji Chuban She, 1990), p. 387; *Zhejiang tongji nianjian, 1991*(Zhejiang Provincial Yearbook, 1991), Zhejiang Statistics Bureau, ed. (Beijing: Zhongguo Tongji Chuban She, 1991), pp. 155–56; *Jiangsu tongji nianjian 1991* (Jiangsu Statistical Yearbook, 1991), Jiangsu Statistical Bureau, ed. (Nanjing: Zhongguo Tongji Chuban She, 1991), pp. 122 and 124; *Zhongguo tongji nianjian, 1991* (China Statistical Yearbook, 1991), State Statistical Bureau, ed. (Beijing: Zhongguo Tongji Chuban She, 1991), p. 396; *Shanghai tongji nianjian, 1991* (Shanghai Statistical Yearbook, 1991), Li Mouhuan et al., eds. (Shanghai: Shanghai Shi Tongji Ju, 1991), p. 153; *Guangdong tongji nianjian, 1991 s(Guangdong Statistical Yearbook, 1991),* Guangdong Province Statistics Bureau, ed. (Beijing: Zhongguo Tongji Chubanshe, 1991), pp. 96–97; and the *Far Eastern Economic Review*, December 18, 1986, p. 107.

gross output in state plants decreased in Zhejiang from 31 percent to 29 percent, in Jiangsu from 34 percent to 33 percent, and in China as a whole from 55 percent to 53 percent, the portion of state production actually rose in Shanghai by a slight amount, to 65 percent.[27]

China's state-owned sector did not give way precipitously to the private sector during the first dozen years of reforms. Some Western journalists and economists (who were joined by PRC planners wanting to hoodwink foreign investors) fostered a widespread prescriptive impression to the contrary, but it was false at least through the mid-1990s and insofar as collectives could not be

Table 1.3-2

Ownership Sector Change in Shanghai by GNP, 1978–1984
[Cheng Xiaonong's estimates for Shanghai in brackets]
(Tianjin data in parentheses) (percentages)

		State-owned (*guoying*)		Collective (*jiti*)		Other (private and joint/mixed)	
1978	[84][1]	87[2]	(76)[3]	12[2]	(22)[3]	1[2]	(2)[3]
1979		86		13		1	
1980		85	(75)	14	(23)	2	(2)
1981		83		14		3	
1982		81	(72)	16	(26)	3	(3)
1983		80	(71)	17	(26)	3	(3)
1984		78	(70)	19	(23)	3	(7)
1985	[72]		(68)		(26)		(6)
1986			(65)		(22)		(13)
1989	[63]						

Notes and Sources: This became, especially after the mid-1980s, a topic for which the interpretation of statistics was difficult. Some formidable technical problems are reviewed in Cheng Xiaonong, "The Structure of Economic Growth in China: An Approach to Measuring the Contribution of the Public and Non-Public Sectors, and Some Estimations" (unpublished paper, Princeton University, 1993); and Cao Linzhang, Gu Guangqing, and Li Jianhua, *Shanghai shengchan ziliao suoyu zhi jiegou yanjiu* (Studies of Shanghai Production and Ownership Structure) (Shanghai: Shanghai Shehui Kexue Yuan Chuban She, 1987), rounded from p. 214. This is based on national income (*guomin shouru*), including all goods and services. The Tianjin figures come from *Tianjin tongji nianjian, 1986* (Tianjin Statistical Yearbook, 1986), Tianjin Statistical Bureau, ed. (Beijing: Zhongguo Tongji Chuban She, 1986), p. 89. Guangdong statistical yearbooks for 1986 and 1987 do not seem to offer data analyzed by ownership sector. More appropriate comparisons would be with other cities, but many urban yearbooks also do not emphasize this topic. Some of the data are from *Tianjin tongji nianjian* (Tianjin Statistical Yearbook), Tianjin Statistical Bureau and Liang Zhaoxin, ed. (Beijing: Zhongguo Tongji Chuban She), for 1984, p. 4; 1985, p. 5; and 1987, p. 49.

[1]Cheng Xiaonong's estimates for Shanghai, in percentages (in brackets).

[2]Shanghai sources' data, in percentages, non-parenthetical.

[3]Tianjin data, in percentages (in parentheses).

considered actually private. Table 1.3–2 shows that although the share of China's GNP decreased in Shanghai (and for comparison, in Tianjin) between 1978 and 1989, the private sector remained small. More of the new production was in collectives. This table aims to include all functional sectors, not just industry, and it deals with the middle stages of reform. More private ownership will almost surely arise later, but at least into the 1990s in large cities, the relative decline of state firms was mainly accompanied by a growth not of private enterprises, but of collectives.

These changes in large cities, which are important for the central budget, contrasted with reforms in other parts of the country. In most of China, especially outside cities, the collective, quasi-private, local–state-licensed and local-controlled sector grew sharply. Regular state firms in 1978 still made more than three-quarters of China's industrial product, but by 1992, their reported share of manufactures had dropped to about half the total. In China as a whole, if agriculture and services are counted along with industry, only about one-quarter of the economy's 1992 output value was in the state sector.[28]

Wenzhou is the only sizeable city in the Wu-dialect region that offers a sharp contrast to Shanghai, because by 1986 in that very unusual Zhejiang place, only 17 percent of gross industrial output came from state factories; 53 percent came from collectives; and 30 percent from private factories. In Wenzhou commerce, interestingly, the state and private sectors' lag behind collectives was less than in manufacturing: 28 percent of goods were sold in 1986 through state-owned stores, 35 percent through collectives or cooperatives, and 37 percent through private shops.[29] But Wenzhou is an extreme case, for reasons to be detailed below, and it is not a provincial capital.

Shanghai's position was at the other end of the tax-and-control spectrum. It was not completely off the charts, because most other cities' industries in 1988 were still about three-quarters nationalized—though in other cities, the portion from the collective sector averaged about twice Shanghai's. In China's officially designated "cities," 77 percent of factory output by value in 1988 was state, 21 percent was collective, and the private sector was still a minor residual at 2 percent.[30]

Collective and private industries together made only 2 percent of Shanghai's industrial output by the late 1980s—much less than in most other Chinese cities. Collective enterprises in Shanghai, more than in other places, have also been far more tightly restricted as regards the authority of their managers. Some urban Shanghai collectives were hard to distinguish from state firms, mainly because the extraction regimes have been similar to those of state plants. In Guangdong under reforms, the term "cadre" (*ganbu*) has generally referred to state enterprise officials only. But in urban Shanghai, collectives' leaders were also called "cadres." They paid enough taxes to earn the title.

Shuffling Nameplates

The 1956 Transition to Socialism is important for management reforms, because it is what they reversed. This early socialism had been, for factories and especially for stores, largely a matter of renaming previously private enterprises as branches of state corporations. Active state management mainly affected large industries, such as textiles. There the centralizing regime could induce capitalist owners to part with their factories, because at that time the state could influence materials flows, and the market environment had traditionally limited profit margins. This process of the mid-1950s created a more monopolistic structure, in which the government could soon make big manufacturing profits. Many commercial firms, especially family-run shops, were only slowly merged in a way that gave managerial meaning to their new status as branches of large socialist corporations. Their prices and some supplies were partly fixed by the state; but the regime had too few personnel to monitor them all, and the rake-off from doing so was less than in major industries using bulk inputs.

State leaders tried to internalize or "take over" any activities that made profits. They tried to externalize, turning over to other levels or managements, any activities that led to losses. Higher administrative levels have often simply assumed control of factories that had earlier been managed locally, or else sloughed off others that had been managed centrally, depending on their profitability. The tradition of continued tinkering with nameplates thus became well established in China even after the 1950s. It involved a stress on functions and factories from which the state (at any level) could make money, perhaps because it could control inputs or because large amounts of capital were required. High state leaders often ignored any market where production and sales, to the extent these could be monitored, did not allow high extraction of profits and taxes.

When the central state took over plants "owned by all the people" that had previously been administered locally, the expenditures of the jurisdiction whose revenues had been raided did not necessarily fall. In later budget negotiations, the loss was often made up by political fiat, reallocating funds.[31] Central conservatives (whose army and heavy industrial ministries needed Shanghai money) tended to argue against such reallocations, however, and instead often demanded a further restructuring of functions between administrative levels, usually accompanied by a changing of company names.

Socialist conservatives argued for large and centrally managed plants, claiming these would be sure successes because of high political support for them. Shanghai's output growth between 1980 and 1988, for example, was far below the national average. Conservatives explained this by blaming the 1986 abolition of sixty-eight large corporations. "According to this answer, all Shanghai needs is to return to the large-scale [state corporation] economy."[32] Most economists, however, knew that the roots of the problem lay instead in factor markets and in the long-term depreciation of Shanghai's capital stock, which local companies could not correct unless they could retain more of their own profits. Reshuffling the nameplates on major factories would not reverse such basic deterioration. Lower imposts on the city would do that. National politicians tended to propose organizational fiddling, and local reformers tended to suggest lower taxes.[33]

The statist tradition was that each Beijing office should treat "the country as a single chessboard," maximizing revenues wherever possible.[34] The Seventh Five-Year Plan allowed the Ministry of Electronics Industries, for example, to retain profits from its companies. But officials in that ministry sent these funds all over China; money was not retained in the place where it originated. This did not encourage economic efficiency. When chronic inefficiency became impossible to hide in the management of state-owned firms, the normal response of high bureaucrats outside the fiscal system was to approve enterprise mergers (*qiye jianping*).

Basically different kinds of leaders might agree on managerial mergers, even if they disagreed about much else. Party conservatives had a traditional liking for large firms, which the army and heavy industrial ministries had long managed. They could point out that Cultural Revolution radicals had briefly criticized Liuist "trusts," which therefore had afterward to be deemed good. Marxist reformers, on the other hand, could see how *zaibatsu*- or *chaebol*-like coordination had raised the international competitiveness of Japan or South Korea, and similar conglomerates exist in Hong Kong and Taiwan. So politically different leaders might agree, in principle, on the value of mergers. They often put off knottier questions of what kinds of merger they meant. By August 1988, new marriages of more than four hundred state-owned firms, in about half of China's provinces, had already been officially blessed. High reformers sponsored the idea that "the best win and the weak are defeated," i.e., merged.[35] They spoke for the survival of the fittest—as measured by criteria that were odd, however, because profits were seldom based on scarcity prices and unfit managers often merely became part of larger enterprises. This spread losses and saved jobs.

Acquiring companies could assume control of their new subsidiaries in exchange for assuming their debts. A second method was that the buying company could pay a higher administrative level for the assets and any liquid cash of the failed business. A third and more gradual method was called "first guarantee, then merge," which meant that the takeover company would assume contractual obligations to meet product, profit, tax, and other quotas of the merged company; it bought the subsidiary by paying the latter's financial obligations. Finally, high state decisions could simply mandate "uncompensated transfers." In theory all state enterprises were property of "the whole people." High politicians in Beijing might understand this to mean, in practice, themselves. Late-1988 sources claimed that the fourth, basically coerced kind of transfer had changed in style during reforms, that it met the "mutual interests" of both parties, and that allegedly the taken-over company opted for it. Many mergers involved at least some financial transfers.

Fourteen Shanghai towel factories, for example, were merged "with compensation" under the Shanghai Dalei Clothing Factory in the mid-1980s. Within ten months, because some women employees who had apparently been laid off could resume their jobs after the merger, the total budget for wages went up by half.[36] The Machiavellian-Paretan lions in China had an economic principle to match their distaste for mobility: the retention of jobs. This was different from the principle of maximizing profit, but it served political stability by maintaining the "face" of bureaucrats, even when their companies were failing. The conservatives' aim was to maintain at least some support for the regime among urban workers.

What is the relation between ownership types, on one hand, and local politics, on the other? Evidence suggests that ownership by socialist agencies abets the statist pattern, and formally private or autonomous collective ownership helps the market. The result for income stratification may be either egalitarian or incentive, depending on who legally holds the relevant property. Collective, avowedly local-state ownership was predominant on the Shanghai delta, as compared with other parts of the China coast, through the 1980s when the autonomy of many of these collectives gradually rose.

Those who stress the prevalence of local corporatism and those who stress market power are both able to find valid data for their different emphases by looking at different Chinese places or periods. One reason is that labor demand varies. The general economic boom eroded corporatist power by encouraging migration to areas such as the Shanghai delta, where local labor cannot fill all the job opportunities created in the very quick economic expansion. Local corporations there follow the same pattern that the CCP used in large cities in Mao's time: Favored local workers get plum posts, and temporary migrant workers receive less good jobs at lower wages. This pattern strengthens the boundaries of corporations only temporarily. Units wanting completely to exclude outsiders tend to lose market share and disappear.[37]

Residual Planning and Managerial Freedoms

The purpose of planning was always to maintain a relatively stable elite, whether by use of the state to encourage the legitimacy that comes from market growth or to distribute resources directly. The Chinese government's main problem, as the factor crisis loomed and the business cycle became more obvious, was to maintain productive structures in which relatively loyal local leaders had jobs. From 1978 to 1980, for example, the Shanghai government hesitated to approve the construction of new hotels, including the Hongqiao Hotel and the Huating Sheraton. At the beginning of the next decade, however, after construction had begun on major hotels in Beijing, Guangzhou, and Nanjing, Shanghai's authorities reversed this policy and approved many projects. They could not keep pace with rising demand. In the autumn travel season in 1983, the shortage was so great that some international tourists were shipped off to Suzhou and other nearby cities, because there was no room for them in Shanghai. Their stay in the city was usually shortened, and time was added onto their itineraries at other places.

By the 1980s, in an effort to compensate, planners approved a great deal of new construction. At that time, policies against overbuilding and inflation led to the cancellation of several plans.[38] A similar pattern (hesitation in the early 1980s, approvals amid shortages in the middle of the decade, and constriction again as 1990 approached) was evident in decisions by many kinds of units. At Fudan University, a group of alumni in the late 1970s offered loans to build a hotel, which would then have been profitable because guest housing was short in that part of town. The university's authorities urged deliberateness and went forward with the project only after several other hotels in the area had already been started. Profitable projects that might have brought foreign exchange tended to reduce planners' autonomy and were resisted by some officials.

The mid-1980s factor crisis saw an end to effective planning, but not an end to the writing of plans. On the contrary, at the beginning of 1985, the national State Council ratified an outline for Shanghai's economic development. The city government published a more specific, detailed economic strategy document. These were followed by an urban plan for spatial development, a seventh five-year economic plan for Shanghai growth, a five-year "social development plan," and even a "cultural development strategy."[39] Technical committees at various administrative levels, using advice from universities and the Shanghai Social Sciences Academy, also drew up local plans for each district and county. The language in these documents overwhelmingly suggested that all serious initiatives for change begin at the top of the governmental system. Then any impetus for serious reform was supposed to work its way down through formal administrative levels. But a look at mid-1980s actual behavior in East China, which was deeply affected by the power of local collectives, offers a very different picture. Many aspects of the new plans were indirectly driven by the recent florescence of activity that had escaped plans by thriving in every niche the high planners could not control.

Reform growth did not add much real value to the state treasury. Conservative efforts to discipline the economy—and tax it more—were sporadic both before and after the Tiananmen disaster. Two months earlier, on April 4, 1989, a Shanghai office "for rectifying and readjusting the economy" declared that 22 percent of all firms in the urban area would be closed. Almost three-fourths of the companies slated for closure were commercial, but only a minority had been established by Party and government organs. Decrees specified that "existing companies run by the Party and government organs have to separate themselves from these agencies."[40] Like the attempt to close companies, rather than merely force them underground, this may have been mere preaching. Managers not wishing to close their businesses could turn, of course, to local Party leaders for protection against the closure decrees—which in any case did not last long.

Very few threats to managers' tenure accompanied mergers of state corporations in Shanghai. Nothing in China even distantly resembles the Treuhandanstalt, the postunification government office in Germany that took over ex-state factories and sold them in a massive liquidation. The Chinese Party-state did not plan on its withering away. It was weakened, especially in its industrial branches, by forces outside those it could still control. The late reforms still saw plans, however. The 1991–95 Five-Year Plan aimed at "revitalizing existing industrial undertakings, instead of investing in new projects."[41]

National leaders looked broadly for advice on planning. They found national sources with impeccably Chinese characteristics in old classics. Thus a group of PRC business sages showed a link between old intellectualism and modern socialism by hosting a conference to study "how the *Book of Changes* helps economic planning."[42] The plan needed help from all quarters at that point. Old military strategists and councilors to princes, notably Sun Zi, offered precepts that managers proposed to use. Adherents of these oracles had to admit that Chinese classics were mostly elitist and often opposed business. These scriptures, despite their virtues, also contained "dross to be rejected, such as a general tendency to discard democracy and look down on commerce."[43] No rural industrialists came to the conference, apparently because they were too busy dispensing their new money from trade.

Contracts and Particularist Management

The contract system for state-owned industries implied that the government would become like a stockholder—originally with 100 percent of the shares. So supervisors and factory managers alike needed to justify their and their clients' jobs. For creating sinecures, contracts served as plans had. Some reforms challenged institutional and career interests, but others avoided upsetting bureaucracies. Proposals for decentralization that allowed cadres in localities and offices to maintain their vested interests were generally easy to adopt. These can be called "particularistic contracting."[44] But "standardization reforms," redistributing rights or money, drew bureaucratic fire from any agencies they disadvantaged. Even if such reforms were advocated from the top of the system, they were not necessarily implemented.

Local Business Leaders' Incentives Against Reform

A random survey of 100 Shanghai state factories in 1985 showed that 77 percent still lacked the authority to "adjust" their plans. The idea behind contracts was that local hinge managers would have to agree more explicitly to their conditions of doing business. Reforms had been announced, but sixth-tenths of the surveyed factories lacked any right to sell their own products. Nearly three-quarters could not adjust their prices—even of products over the plan quota. Over four-fifths still did not purchase their own materials.[45] All the surveyed companies also lacked the right to set their employees' basic wages (although this was less important, because they could set bonuses). In other words, most *external* management powers, involving the firms' relations with markets, had been legally authorized but had not been realized. Such changes were supposed to be a major part of the industrial reform proclaimed from central reformers in Beijing.

Managers understandably avoided these tasks in fast-changing markets. Their rights to adjust *internal* aspects of their firms expanded more quickly, because this was in their own interest. For example, 66 percent of the surveyed firms could freely allocate their own liquid capital, and three-quarters could decide how to use any excess fixed capital. Also, 73 percent could set their own internal organization charts without consulting higher levels. Almost two-thirds assumed the authority to decide issues concerning their own workers (except for basic wage rates, which in any case they could supplement with other emoluments). In addition, practically all (98 percent) of the firms had the right to promote at least some of their employees.

With respect to one kind of external power—namely, the right to set up joint projects with other jurisdictions or offices—81 percent of the managers said they could act on their own. This was the main external authority that the hinge leaders really wanted, considering the sum of pressures on them, because most others in the mid-1980s implied more costs than benefits. So Shanghai companies became generally free to associate with each other and with firms in other places.[46] Because partners elsewhere usually had less restrictive rules on market operations, these "horizontal" connections were a crucial aspect of reform as it was actually implemented in Shanghai.

Yet this fell far short of the full vision of central state reformers in the mid-1980s, whose initiatives were then stymied not so much by central conservatives as by *collectively* more powerful sets of local urban managers. These local hinge leaders in business did not need to articulate their position, nor to organize politically for it. All they needed to do was to act on it in parallel with each other, choosing selectively from central mandates without any need openly to oppose anything from on high.

Adoption of the contract system without adoption of ownership reform would have meant that a "mother-in-law" supervising agency or corporation could sign a contract on behalf of its subsidiary factory. Contracts could thus bind factories more tightly to socialist trusts. When contracts first replaced plans, they often temporarily strengthened ex-planners. But these higher-level agencies often had little sense of what was possible and what was not in terms of new productive operations. Also, a factory or store often had more than one supervising "mother-in-law." If its different higher-level governmental agencies signed contradictory contracts on its behalf, the manager was still supposed to deliver.[47] Without much enforcement or sanction, however, such contracts meant little. In the long term, managers' authority rose.

"Because contracting gave every organization the opportunity to retain its privileges through bargaining," as Susan Shirk says, "it was easier for contracting to win a consensus of bureaucratic support than for inherently redistributive policies such as tax or price reform to do so."[48] Sometimes this bargaining resulted in terms that were good for the hinge leaders of small collectivities—as was usually the case in rural areas. But it could also have the opposite result. Enterprise freedom could, for example, shift the risks previously borne by bureau-level planners to factory directors instead. As a Shanghai manager complained, "When supply becomes short on the market, all products are purchased [by the supervising bureau] and plants are not permitted to sell by themselves. When the market slumps, plants are ordered to sell their products by themselves."[49]

Control could tighten during reforms, and the leader of any network was at a disadvantage if leaders of larger networks had accurate information about local activities. This was as important as whether such power was exercised through plans or contracts. Before 1986, for example, the Shanghai No. 10 Iron and Steel Corporation could use its own scrap steel and leftovers—and it "organized surplus labor" to make washers. These were "warmly welcomed in the United States and Canada. However [in 1986], these scraps are allocated in a unified way by the higher-level units. The equipment which produces washers has had to suspend operations and wait for the arrival of scrap." If the mother-in-law office had not bothered about the scrap or the washers, the factory could have earned more foreign exchange.

Plans were often used for quota production, and contracts for surplus. This combination could be devastating for any urban manager who did not underreport the surplus. "Production plans show the quota is raised at each level. While the ministry draws up its plan, the municipality and bureau have drawn up their own plans to increase production. As a result, enterprises have no products in excess of production targets and, accordingly, nothing to sell."[50]

Contract Terms

In late 1986, only 18 percent of Shanghai's total output value was reportedly still under the mandatory plan. But almost 100 percent of the main products were subject to some plans in crucial industries, including metals and textiles. "In some departments, even products in excess of production targets are also incorporated into the 'mandatory plan.' " When the plan did not suit them, bureau-level cadres were able in practice to ignore it. Factory managers at "Shanghai's cotton textile plants all complain that, although the State Council has plainly stipulated that cotton yarn is a product under the 'guidance plan,' the departments concerned simply deprive them of the right given by the State Council to sell products in excess of production targets."[51] Bureau cadres were more beholden to deliver profits upward than to deliver the raw materials with which the profits could be made. As one of the bureau cadres said, "We have had to lay down 'hard and fast rules' for yarn-producing enterprises. Otherwise, who is going to shoulder the responsibility to fulfill the output and output value plans issued by Shanghai Municipality and the Ministry of Textile Industries?"[52]

This tightening of control reversed grants of freedom that had been made earlier. As the director of the No. 19 Factory of the Shanghai Cotton Textile Corporation put it,

> Over the past two years [1985–86], our plant has used the right to establish coordinative relations with fraternal provinces and cities. We have helped supply each other's needs and invigorated our enterprise. Now that the [Textile] bu-

> reau has taken away this minor right, how can we supply each other's needs and maintain coordinative relations? If a commodity [cotton] is in great demand, then it is more important to give enterprises the power of decision to handle this commodity, and encourage enterprises to raise production by establishing more domestic ties.[53]

The best revenge of local managers, faced with pressures from leaders in their supervising corporations, was to try to hold the "mothers-in-law" responsible for finding inputs and selling products. Even in fairly late reforms, few state managers wanted to depend on these external markets, but they had no choice. This conflict persisted intensively through 1988 and later. If the costs of inputs were high, or if the materials were simply unavailable, this was not supposed to be the problem of plant managers. It is unsurprising they were reluctant to shoulder it. The officials to whom they could refer the problem were at a sufficiently high political level to keep their jobs even without really performing them. This system (like others in many countries) was built to preserve careers, not just to get business going.

As one economist said of Shanghai factory managers in the 1980s, "They can't break with the higher level (*libukai shangji*)."[54] They had strong disincentives to break this tie; it was a bond of conflict but also of dependence. So "guaranteed management contracts" in early 1988 still governed the relations between 92 percent of Shanghai's state-owned firms and their supervising corporations.[55] The guarantees of the basic-level factories and stores were of three sorts: to remit a quantity of profits, to protect technical quality, and (for some firms) to guarantee specified amounts of foreign exchange from export sales. The first guarantee—to remit money upward—was the most onerous, applying to all state firms.

Different kinds of contracts were required of different companies. The main contract proviso was about remittances. Many (38 percent of the enterprises) guaranteed a basic set quota of profits to higher levels, as well as a fraction of any profits above that. Another 37 percent signed contracts that guaranteed the fixed remittance only—but it was often, in Shanghai, very high. A further 25 percent were asked to promise during the first year a fixed amount (perhaps not very high, in view of the materials shortages), but then increasing amounts of remittance for several years afterward.[56] The time periods of these contracts varied, but many were for three or five years. In practice, midreform contracts in the state sector were like socialist plans, because their frequent violations merely punctuated their constant renegotiation.

Incentives of Managers

When plans or contracts existed, even state-appointed managers did not necessarily follow them. In an attitude survey of enterprise cadres in the early 1980s, barely half of the respondents (52 percent) claimed to put the state plan above other considerations in making their decisions. Fully 27 percent admitted openly they would put their own firms' interests above those of the state plan. Another 21 percent said they would pay prime attention to their customers' needs. Attitude polls are notoriously difficult to relate to behavior, but the open expression of willingness to violate the plan—by 46 percent of the managers who were asked this question directly—measures the extent of management reform.[57]

In this same group of businesspeople, 60 percent had been appointed solely by higher-level cadres; 31 percent had received their posts only after a period of "fermentation" and discussion at basic levels. (The other 9 percent got their jobs by other methods, including election.)[58] Once they were in their posts, no matter how they had been chosen, they seem to have put the interests of their local communities foremost.

Managers cared for the communities within their firms, and they often could adapt plans. When use of the "guarantee system" (*chengbao zhi*) was surveyed in October 1987 among Shanghai firms, 78 percent of the respondents reported they were using the one-man management system or leasing their factories. The person who took responsibility for production, in 85 percent of the cases, was a member of the previous leading group in the factory. In only 10 percent of the cases did the new manager come from outside. From the viewpoint of managers, an advantage of the contract system was that their own salaries in most cases doubled.[59]

The new structure was supposed to destroy the "mother-in-law/daughter-in-law" relationship (*poxi guanxi*) between supervising corporations and basic-level firms. It did not mean that the managers of factories were under less pressure, but the main problems no longer came from their stately patrons. Their political relations with superiors may have become less important, but they had to worry more about where raw materials were available, where products might be sold, and what the prices would be. Worry about "management operations" (*jingying yunxing*) tended to replace worry about pleasing supervisors.

An important effect of the guarantee system was the creation of more flexible factor markets for labor, capital, and other inputs. Because the prices on these markets were often higher than for firms operating with socialist allocations, the latter often could not make the purchases they expected. Free markets acted like vortex whirlwinds, pulling in managers who did not originally want to deal on them.[60]

Contract systems were supposed to be implemented, by early 1988, for 1,700 large and medium-sized Shanghai state firms—more than had subscribed to them before. The official making the announcement implied they had been too slow to switch from planning. He "criticized state-owned enterprises in Shanghai, which form the main source of the city's revenue, for failing to adapt themselves to the planned commodity economy now being developed in China."[61] In the previous year, only 465 companies had adopted the contract system. The reason for factory managers' resistance is not hard to find: Since 1984 at least, managers had been given no reason to think the contracts would be honored. They were often unenforceable in courts. Factory-level managers had scant incentive to take a burden of responsibility from the state's materials and marketing cadres. Contracts were often merely a means to decentralize the scapegoats for planning's collapse.

The main kind of incentive that eventually inspired factory managers to accept such responsibility was monetary: iron-clad state assurances of lower tax extractions over a long period, to allow investment that could make Shanghai firms more efficient. This was exactly what conservative politicians did not, at first, want to offer. The greater management autonomy that factory directors within Shanghai were given under the contract responsibility system was not initially worth the expected costs of defaults on contracts. Bargaining for full decentralization—of money, not just management—was a procedure that extended over several years in the middle and late 1980s. Urban Shanghai's economic hinge leaders gradually had to receive more funds, not just more risk.

The decline of state capacity to supply inputs by either plan or contract, and the increased pressure on factory managers to take this burden, made conservatives of local leaders who otherwise might have taken risks. Shanghai managers were "obedient" in an ambiguous way that is typical of restorations (and sometimes comic, as the next part of this book will argue). Shanghai was reportedly "law-abiding, following the straight and narrow" (*xungui daoju*). Every transaction had to be justified by papers with red letterheads (*hongtou wenjian*).[62] Shanghai managers came up with many innovations they could not follow. This was a standing joke in administrative circles. At a national conference, a spokesman from another province listed flexible management procedures that his own units elsewhere employed with great success. He drew chuckles when he said those ideas "all came from Shanghai."[63]

New enterprises had difficulty in getting repayments of bad debts owed to them. So researchers at the Shanghai Academy of Social Sciences established a company to specialize in debt collection. Although this sort of firm was entirely legal, municipal officials conveyed the government's opinion that it should not be established. Apparently the slow debtors were mainly state corporations. One of the proffered reasons was that lawyers could better handle such work. A second reason was that no such company had been established before; Shanghai was better at coming up with management ideas than at carrying through on them.

Warehoused Waste

The arbitrary nature of many prereform plans can be highlighted by the fact that socialist managers received credit for products never sold. The advent of contracts did not immediately change this situation, because sales were not on consignment and state buyers were not supposed to refuse their assigned purchases. Production "for the warehouse" (*na sklad* among Russians, who knew it well) was commonplace in most of China, where it was euphemistically called "surplus saved products" (*chaochu chanpin*). State factories got quota credit for profits on all output, whether or not it was ever used by consumers. For many years, China's amounts of "surplus saved products" were very large. In 1979, for example, warehouses contained 60 billion yuan worth of electrical products and 20 million metric tons of steel items.[64] This waste in Shanghai was not as severe as elsewhere, partly because many Shanghai products proved salable eventually, partly because godown (warehouse) space was scarce in the big city, and mostly because stringent finances encouraged companies to find prices at which the products can be cleared. Reformers in Shanghai sought to impose a special tax on the value of "surplus saved products," because Shanghai goods tend to sell more reliably than goods from elsewhere. But large portions of the state's production throughout China were never sold. Since the switch away from state plans practically never involved on-consignment contracts, the new institutions did not automatically erode the production of commodities for which there was no demand. Market competition and booming prosperity, rather than new legalisms, brought this result.

The amounts of warehoused waste were not publicized, except anecdotally. In 1986, 70 million wristwatches were made in China, but only 40 million were sold (and few were exported). Yet producers did not get the market message, because in the first three months of 1987, 30 percent more watches were made than in the same period of the previous year. China's bicycle industry reportedly made one-tenth more bicycles in 1986 than in 1985, but sales then were only 53 percent of production. A Ministry of Commerce survey of 650 products concluded that "at least 25 percent are virtually unsalable."[65] Textiles and clothes, black-and-white TV sets, refrigerators, and bicycles were prominent among the "surplus saved products," made solely for shelves. Unusable goods, sent directly to warehouses, reportedly accounted for 12 percent of China's total GNP as late as 1991.[66]

Decentralist Commerce

Trade reformed faster than industry. It had never been most profitable for the Party-state to devote scarce loyal personnel to exchange rather than processing, where taxes and profits were higher. But pre-1956 store owners could often claim compensation for mistreatment in the Anti-Rightist or Cultural Revolution eras.[67] Retail stores that had previously been closed might reopen by 1982. Outlets for consumer goods, foods, tobacco, hardwares, and apparel had been merged or terminated in 1956 and later years. Often their buildings had become warehouses or had been converted from commercial to factory use. But in the early 1980s, the city government realized a need for more stores, to spur the consumer economy. It held meetings for retail trade groups, and apparently some of the employees were able to open their old enterprises again as part of the state sector.[68]

State mercantile firms grew in number. From 1978 to 1988, state commercial enterprises in China tripled (from 103,000 to 327,000). Industrial state enterprises scarcely rose in number (from 84,000 to 90,000).[69] Many of the state trading firms were, like the vast majority of collectives, quasi-private in practice. Commercial reform was also sharp because resource allocation offices in many ministries and places including Shanghai had in-house outlets (*menshi bu*) that increasingly enjoyed great autonomy on markets.

Legal Decrees and Hesitant Managers

Decentralization of management within the state sector for both industry and commerce was implemented either by the "contract responsibility system" (*chengbao ziren zhi*) or the "lease system" (*zulin zhi*). The formal difference between these two was that contractors paid a portion of reported profits, whereas lessors paid a fixed remittance. In practice, however, a more important difference was that contracts could be made with workers. If part of a factory constantly lost money, and if better-motivated labor might solve the problem, the management could strike a bargain with its workers: They could be given permission to take over their workshop (or part of the production process), nurse it back to profitability, and then share the profits at a prearranged rate with the original firm.[70] In Shanghai by 1990, the criteria for granting contracts had become less restrictive than before, especially in retail and service trades that could create new jobs.

The "responsibility system" was not introduced throughout Shanghai—but selected industrial bureaus tried it experimentally, as Table 1.3–3 suggests, even in the early 1980s. The experiment was common in plants for which the state had most difficulty maintaining supplies of inputs. The table reports a rise of contracting only in those sectors, not in the city's whole economy.

Neoclassical economists might hold their applause at the quick rise in these figures, to 100 percent of products covered already by 1982. The relevant industrial bureaus were networks of leaders and workers. The aim of the organization was not just to maximize profits, but to ensure jobs and a lifestyle that had grown up over decades. If contracts were defaulted on, in the hectic raw materials markets of the early 1980s, the parties were unlikely to press each other hard. At this time, bankruptcy was not yet even a theoretical option.

The Party organization in Mao's time had nonetheless guided management. By the mid-1980s, there was agreement among top reform leaders to let managers manage, but this was more a matter of words than incentives. The debate climaxed during discussions of an "Enterprise Law." Reformers proposed a "general rule that the organizations of the Communist Party of China in enterprises should support factory directors exercising their power in accord with laws and regulations." This kind of wording got as far as the draft of the Enterprise Law. Conservatives objected strongly.

The result was an ambiguous compromise, which assured that local actors rather than any uniform national law would set the primacy of either Party secretaries or else manager-technicians. The law held that "the organizations of

Table 1.3-3

Quick Rise of the Economic Responsibility System, 1979–82, in Some Shanghai Industries (number and percent of factories in this system among firms under eleven Shanghai industrial bureaus)

	No. of factories	% of factories	% of output
1979	711	36	58
1980	1,242	66	82
1981	1,389	75	87
1982	1,839	100	100

Note and source: The "economic responsibility system" means use of the principle that profit should be replaced with taxes and that a factory should be responsible for its own profits and losses. *Dangdai Zhongguo de jingji tizhi gaige* (Reform of the Economic System in Contemporary China), Zhou Taihe et al., eds. (Beijing: Zhongguo Shehui Kexue Chuban She, 1984), p. 554.

the CCP in enterprises guarantee and supervise the implementation of Party and state policies in the enterprises."[71] This wording retained Party primacy as a symbol, and the CCP organization was still supposed to have a monitoring, information-gathering role. The extent to which it would still help manage firms was left uncertain. What happened in local companies depended largely on the personalities and resources of particular leaders there.

Hinge leaders could become effective local reformers, if they wished, because of their authoritarian control over people they hired. Local leaders who looked like "reformers" from the vantage point of higher administrative levels were therefore often uncivil and unconsultative within their own bailiwicks. When reforms were seriously attempted without this condition, e.g. at Beijing's mandate, the result was sometimes a disaster for midlevel authorities. For example, selling stock shares to workers in a company was considered a reform. China's first such sales occurred during 1986 at Nanchang, Jiangxi, then in the outer periphery of the Shanghai Economic Zone. This reform was tried in a low-tax-revenue sector, among vegetable shops. So 135 state-owned and collective groceries sold shares. Most of the shops soon thereafter elected new managers! Reportedly the new worker-stockholders did not believe the old leaders would reap sufficient profits for them.[72] This liberal experiment in worker management was rare, because it meant that bureaucrats lost their jobs.

More usually, reformer managers ruled their underlings with a style of command that even the Chinese state could seldom muster in public. The best examples come from rural enterprises in rich areas of Jiangsu and Zhejiang, which employed transients from poorer inland areas to do hard work. For the sake of efficiency, many heads of enterprises also liked to hire managerial talent from elsewhere, because locals found it difficult to make some kinds of tough economic decisions. As pressures on such firms increased,

> more and more rural enterprises are trying to break away from traditional community interference. They seek independent decision-making power and personnel management. As suppliers of the initial investment, communities frequently tax these enterprises heavily for short-sighted welfare purposes. They claim the right to send more than enough hands to the work force and even managerial staff. These superfluous workers, most of whom are the beneficiaries of nepotism, do not have to work hard but enjoy greater job security than their colleagues [including many contract workers from other areas]. . . . Successful entrepreneurs have devised ways to prevent this from happening.[73]

In Zhejiang, the manager of a large rural enterprise said that he "only hired people from outside the community as his chief assistants. 'I've got a system that somewhat resembles the so-called guest official system of the Warring States period. . . .' Only the guest officials have the much-needed coldheartedness to turn down a whole batch of products—no locals would do this, because they know the factory is making money for themselves and their parents down in the village." He hired these managerial visitors only for short terms and "when the contracts expire and the job is done, I pay them at least five times the amount I pay others and let them go."[74]

Centralized state capitalism during Mao's revolution had been able to muster such control only by political campaigns. Now rural industrialists were doing this regularly. Reformers sometimes proposed that these uncivil methods be imported to the state sector so that it could compete. Wuxi city leaders proposed publicly that "state-owned enterprises above the county level must learn from rural industries."[75] In 1986, Wuxi's industrial growth in state-owned firms was only 0.6 percent, but in rural industries it was 26 percent. In Changzhou, city officials claimed that "an important factor for economic development was to adopt rural industrial management in state firms," urging cadres to take more personal risks and responsibilities.

On the other hand, the local origin of township managers—especially heads of collectives—was the main reason why these hinge leaders could not just get by economically, but had to succeed. No other place would give them comparable careers. As a news correspondent wrote,

> I once visited a manager in a township factory, and he told me, "It is not easy to be a manager. [We] have several hundred thousand yuan and more than a hundred people, but everybody is a neighbor. Money [for investment] was collected by all of them. If the factory isn't profitable, what can I do? Managers in the state companies can go someplace else to continue their careers after they fail to manage their factories well. They do not have responsibility for their mistakes. But I am a native person here; so where could I go?" This pressure forces them to raise their enterprises' competitive strength in markets.

Also, these local managers' friends in local reformed governments trusted them better than had previous bureaucrats, who had been more beholden to higher levels of the state. The same reporter interviewed officials, too:

> A vice director of the Shaoxing County Rural Industry Bureau told me his unit had only thirteen cadres. They were in charge of 2,680 enterprises. He said, "We cannot be like mothers-in-law (*popo*)," like cadres in state-owned enterprises, and try to manage everything. "We just do three main jobs: upholding broad policy directions, analyzing markets, and encouraging larger enterprises' development." But as far as production, supply, and marketing go, the enterprises have full freedom.[76]

Even the great tax-paying metropolis was affected by the fad for rural management styles. This inevitably meant even more hiding of financial information relevant to taxes. In early 1987, Shanghai industrial bureaus were supposed to implement "indirect management" over subordinate firms.[77] This was to be brought about by "putting" power away from supervising bureaus, by "shifting" social services to local governments, by "turning" from administrative organs to professional associations, and by "reforming" so that economic levers and laws would guide managements (rather than administrators doing so). The rearrangement externalized from companies costs that had been borne by their budgets, but it also externalized from the state most responsibility for materials and sales. The new structure was more decentralized, and in the long run it empowered local leaders. In the short run, they had to pay heavily for it in new expenses on markets where state budgets could no longer pay enough.

There was more circulation among Shanghai firms by the mid-1980s. Among large and medium-sized companies, 19 percent changed their charters in 1987. Three-fifths of these amendments altered their "scope of management," i.e., the products or fields in which they operated.[78] In addition, 6 percent of the firms closed in 1987; of these, two-fifths were industrial and slightly over half were suburban.[79] Among the rural closures, three-quarters were industrial; within urban districts, 82 percent were in services. Some were shut down because of legal violations, including 409 in the relatively poor and industrial Nanshi district alone.

A late-reform survey of the autonomy of enterprises in Shanghai claimed that two-thirds had "complete" autonomy to manage production, while the remaining third had "partial" autonomy. In hiring decisions, as regards both executives and nonmanagers, 70 percent of the firms surveyed were deemed at least to have "partial" autonomy, and another 17 percent to have full powers. Still, only 58 percent had even "partial" autonomy in a matter more relevant to state revenues: the setting of their product prices. Another 29 percent of firms had no say in these prices. About half still had no say in the politically sensitive matter of dismissing workers. Union and CCP bosses tried to keep the authority to hire.[80] The autonomy of managers in Shanghai was increasing but constrained.

Property, Land, and Leasing

Real estate was a kind of property whose ownership and control by bureaucrats was especially important in a dense city. For almost forty years, Shanghai in effect had no land market. The only reason why the state gave up any land was to raise money to make up its deficits. For socialist ideological reasons, land was not formally sold. Instead, transferrable "land use rights" were auctioned—and the minimum reserve prices were high. "More land in suburban and urban Shanghai [was] leased out for a maximum term of fifty years," after an "initial experiment" to see what price it could fetch. State banks in Shanghai promised mortgage loans for construction projects on specified categories of land. Payment by foreigners was in hard currency. During reforms, a neoclassical argument for this market became apt: "At present, the efficiency of land use in China is very low, because enterprises can occupy state-owned land for as long as they like and at no cost."[81]

Conservatives tended to hope, however, that all profitably used land in the post-Mao era would be considered merely on loan from the government. This norm grew from various confiscations in the 1950s, but it had never been fully regularized in legal or administrative terms. So by the end of 1987, the state planned a full-scale cadastral survey of the whole country. New "land certificates" (*tudi zheng*) were to be issued in three kinds: "Certificates for Using State-owned Land," "Certificates for Using Collective-owned Land and Land for Construction," and "Certificates of Collective Land Ownership."[82] The aim was to normalize nationalizations of land from long-past campaigns that had used institutional violence. But for reformers, the same process also would codify guarantees to local leaders who managed land.

The State Constitution of 1982 provided that "land in cities belongs to the state." Particularism affected city planning and investment in offices at Shanghai. One aim of the late-1984 urban reforms for Shanghai was to bring a "rational distribution of tall buildings in the urban areas."[83] In practice, "rational" meant that each district would receive some tall buildings. This political rather than economic rationality meant that new buildings were put up in Shanghai on a surprisingly even basis in the 1980s. Each urban district received some, and the pattern of new construction was unlike that of most central cities. Only during later reforms did more new skyscrapers go in the middle of town and in Pudong.

Rural and Suburban Land

Socialist land had been treated as a free good. The "labor theory of value" priced undeveloped land as worthless, and reform implied a radical upward revaluation of land prices. This process affected Shanghai's near suburbs most dramatically. From 1981 to 1985, the social gross output value of Meilong township, Shanghai county, grew 28 percent annually. The source of greatest growth was construction. Each year in this period, Meilong industry grew at 26 percent, transport at 19 percent, agriculture at 14 percent—and building construction at a phenomenal 55 percent annually on average, for the five years. The housing boom was a major engine of growth, and it required land.

Rural residences have, both traditionally and legally even in the PRC's most radical eras, been private property. When a farm family built a house on public or collective land, therefore, it also presumed effective ownership of the tract on which the new structure stood. Neighbors might object, and since house-raising is still a matter for neighborhood cooperation, the locality had zoning powers. But the high state had little leverage to prevent farmers from confiscating land by building on it. An official agency reported that 95 percent of the houses built by cadres were on land that had been illegally occupied.[84] Local officials, many of whom did this themselves, were hard pressed to prevent other farmers from doing it. This popular means to obtain free land spread quickly. Since cultivating land did not customarily imply ownership, while residing on it at least implied possession, China's rural construction boom arose not just from farmers' desire to have better houses, but also from their desire to lay claims on land.

When peasants became rich, most built houses. This became "a universal phenomenon," as an inland newspaper reported: "peasants mistake their rights over contracted land for ownership rights and build houses on their responsibility fields."[85] Peasants tore up this aspect of their contracts in such numbers, the state could do nothing about it and local cadres apparently did not wish to. There is much evidence that peasants strongly wanted official recognition of longer-term rights. They often took the situation into their own hands, if their local cadres supported them, by squatting on land and using it as they wished.

Land contracting from collectives led to subcontracting that was like renting. No matter to what use subtenants put the land (whether agricultural, industrial, or residential), they were ordinarily expected to pay the state grain procurement quota for that turf, plus a premium that was the unofficial or local-official rent. This devolution of ownership did not mean, in the reform era, that families necessarily worked their plots separately. Cooperative work had often been individually arranged even before 1949, and the collectivized production teams of the early 1950s (and their successors under communes) had accustomed many families to this mode of work. By the 1980s, they could still arrange this. In the Shanghai delta, the number of farm families decreased as a portion of the rural population. Some hired outside labor at exploitive wages. Some were also willing to cooperate with their friends, either as they had in Mao's time or in other combinations they preferred.[86]

Near cities, ex-peasants built new residential space for themselves, leasing their previous housing space to renters and to companies for functions such as storage. Warehouses in suburban Shanghai became profitable. Old buildings were converted into transient rental housing or into godowns. Data on residences are less available than on storage, perhaps because the renters often lacked

Shanghai household registrations. "With economic development and increasing exchange from foreign countries, goods on the Shanghai market increased dramatically. A lot of goods need to be kept in warehouses . . . . So Meilong created storage space by making use of empty houses."[87] The annual growth rate for stockroom space in Meilong over the sixth five-year plan was 291 percent, and income from warehousing in this town increased 245 percent annually.

Urban Land Auctions

Shanghai private real estate was sold for the first time in decades at a fair organized by the Shanghai Real Estate Society in November 1986. Two thousand suites, averaging a very large 50 square meters in size, were sold for between 520 and 550 yuan per square meter in the city, and interestingly for more than four-fifths as much in nearby suburbs.[88] People with state jobs, living in low-rent apartments, had no incentive to pay such prices. Newly rich industrialists, often ex-peasants, or overseas Chinese arranging Shanghai residence registrations for relatives might pay these high rates.

Commercial and industrial land was also auctioned at a premium. To eliminate "unpaid utilization of land for unlimited periods," the city at the beginning of 1988 opened auctions for public bidding on rights to use land for twenty to fifty years. These rights could be inherited, and the ownership of buildings put on the land could be transferred.[89]

Shanghai's first auction of a whole building after 1949 was held in 1988. Only two structures were for sale, but 108 bidders registered, of which 63 were state-owned agencies and 45 were "self-employed people." The more expensive property went for 130,000 yuan, to a company in suburban Nanhui for a new retail shop. The other, for 89,000 yuan, was sold to a suburban company that made switchgears in suburban Chuansha.[90]

Use rights to commercial space owned by state enterprises in need of money could also be leased. State department stores, needing to pay their staffs, rented counters to collective and private firms. This converted many department stores into malls, or groups of boutiques. Large state stores by the 1990s often garnered more than half their revenues from rents, not from profits on sales. The boutiques might be called "dependent firms" (*guahu*), but their independence was what kept the state staffs paid. These smaller firms were more able than the state stores to obtain commodities for which consumers would pay high prices.

Leasing and renting, though they may allow efficient resource allocation, can also become means for local networks to gain at the expense of the state. Almost anything can be leased. A Shanghai sports shop, for example, "rented" its bank account to a rural construction team from Jiangsu that had no license to make transactions. The state-owned shop wrote receipts, issued cheques, and in other ways served as the financial department of the illegal construction company. In the northern city of Baoding, a survey of over a hundred firms found that at least

15 percent were engaged in various illegal forms of renting.[91] Even in straitlaced Shanghai, many collective "dependent firms" operated by renting some legitimacy from august state firms that needed their money.

Agencies for leasing expanded wildly in Shanghai during the 1980s.[92] By the start of 1987, the city already had 570 specialized companies for renting—and six months later, it had over 1,400. Many were based on old cooperatives, though some new co-ops and private enterprises also entered the field, and a few new leasing companies were registered as state enterprises. The 1986 average reported monthly income of employees in leasing companies was about 150 yuan (more than state employees generally received). The reforms' uncertainty was nowhere more evident than in the kind of ownership they encouraged: the most temporary kind, which is rental.

"As long as the system of public ownership remains, politics and production will never be separated," an urban economic thinker wrote in 1987.[93] Conservatives prefered to conduct economic reform by leasing state property, but thoroughgoing reformers wanted the state to start selling its economic interests.

Competition and Corruption

As Mark Granovetter writes, "The anonymous market of neoclassical models is virtually nonexistent in economic life, and transactions of all kinds are rife . . . with social connections."[94] These connections often involve transactions among people in communal groups who see themselves as similar, or who conform to norms sent down by leaders.

Markets require costly attention from both buyers and sellers; when they change, they require even more attention. An increase of market competition toward the turn of the decade into the 1990s meant that vendors of items such as grain and oil would "skimp on the pounds and be short in the ounces" (*duanjin queliang*). Complaints reached police and newspapers about shortchanging in retail sales of rice, cooking oil, and salt.[95] Competition assumes disunity among actors, and efficiency is not its sole result.

The most obvious beneficiaries of communitarian state efforts to restrain prices, during the reform era, were illegal smugglers and speculators. They bought materials at low state prices and then sold illegally at higher market prices. They made handsome profits, from which the state received nothing. A Shanghai brand-name bicycle that could be sold for a maximum of 200 yuan in the city fetched between 300 and 400 yuan elsewhere. The price at which Shanghai cigarettes could sell in the city legally was only half the retail price elsewhere. Shanghai also produced color TV sets, whose market was supposed to be limited by ration coupons. The black-market price of the paper tickets alone (500 to 600 yuan each) was an increment to the official price that reflected high demand.[96] The price of black-market ration coupons for consumer durables rose sharply in the late 1980s. If a buyer of any commodity had to pay extra money to get the coupon—but then later sold the product to a further buyer—the resale price included the cost of the coupon plus a rent for the risk of being caught.[97]

If state companies could have received the difference over factory-fixed prices that illegal sales of ration tickets brought, then these firms could have remitted more money to the state in profits and taxes. But the government often disallowed this kind of policy. The requisite price hikes would have involved socialist cadres more obviously in the inflation. Such changes would have allowed Shanghai to establish more flexible "horizontal relations" with other areas. Keeping state-fixed prices low prevented such patterns from emerging. Low state prices were a major cause of corruption in Shanghai. Their distortion of retail markets, where the illegal profit on each individual trade was relatively petty, legitimated the norm that state prices were not serious. This allowed much larger illegal profits on wholesale trades. Low state prices were supposed to symbolize Communist stability. They ideally represented the care of the state for the interests of the whole people. Reforms gave smaller groups and networks higher profiles.

Although by 1987–88 the city had established limited (albeit still high) revenue guarantees to the state and a local "right to allocate finances," it still did not have a "right to float prices" or a "right to allocate products." A local economist suggested that Shanghai ask the central government for such powers.[98] To adopt such a proposal, however, would have led to lower remittances for the central state. The conservatives resisted this, because it threatened the finance of their national structure. They were acting on their preferences and interests, perhaps not intending corruption but nonetheless generating it.

Individual Corruption Amid Chaotic Prices

Corruption is of several kinds, depending on the size of network that legitimates it. It can be defined as an improper, dirty use of power—but the effective concept of corruption has changed over time in the PRC according to the sizes of networks with which people most closely identified.[99] As the revolution gained strength, especially in the 1950s, large and centrally organized groups became the referents for setting the criteria of what was dirty and what was clean. But then during the drawdown of centralization, especially in the 1980s, smaller networks more often served that role of setting criteria for corruption. Any claim of corrupt behavior implies networks of two sizes: the one that is said to have acted improperly (which is often smaller or individual), and the one that sets criteria for the judgment.

A straightforward but uncommon type of corruption is theft by an individual for his or her own sake. Embezzlement for strictly personal gain was severely punished during China's reforms. A Shanghai newspaperman who had risen to the deputy directorship of the *Guangming Daily*'s Shanghai office embezzled 43,000 yuan over a period of four years by claiming reimbursements for "labor service fees" under false names, by forging receipts, and by otherwise pretending expenses that his unit had not paid.[100] The head of the finance office in a chemical fertilizer factory in Changzhou, over the border in Jiangsu, was sentenced to death for listing false construction expenditures, forging receipts for them, and apparently pocketing the money himself.[101]

Police reports do not formally distinguish individual thefts from nonplan and noncontract trades in commodities the state leaders feel they should control. Informally, however, extractions that benefited local networks had local political support. Each jurisdiction was most eager to prosecute criminals from other places. By 1988, more than half of Shanghai's indicted criminals came from other provinces, many of which traded such goods. Some were ordinary robbers, of whom 70 to 80 percent in Shanghai hailed from elsewhere.[102] But collective "gangs" were prominent, and some of these were in effect procurement agencies for inland places. For example, a "Huaiyin Clique" was for many years active in "robbing materials" from factories and stores in Zhabei district. The Zhabei Public Security Bureau in 1988 arrested members of the "Huaiyin Clique" and "Baoying Clique" (whose names both derive from cities in northern Jiangsu), because they were engaged in massive "thefts," i.e. unplanned purchases, of metals.[103]

Because Shanghai prices were low, practically all of the illegal trade consisted of exports from the city. Police would patrol Shanghai's borders in an effort to prevent such leakage, but the hemorrhage was massive. Three-quarters of all daily-use products (*riyong pin*) bought by Shanghai wholesalers in 1982 were sent out of the city. This comprised about 30 percent of all such products in China.[104] By no means was all of this trade legal, and the profits on the illegal portion must have been munificent.

Corruption Through Resales in Large and Small Networks

It would be odd to assume that morality could be based on one size of human network with no reference to others. The state, which passes laws and has helped educate most people, tends to define corruption as violating the norms of the nation, a very large group. Liberal economists, on the other hand, either avoid talking about corruption or point to inefficiencies as the messes to be cleaned up. Many ordinary people, including most Chinese, stress the importance of middle-sized groups. Even local guarantee contracts were mostly "based on blood and locale."[105]

State and collective managers were responsible for most corruption—on behalf of their whole firms. Because most real prices rose over state-enforced prices during reforms, the golden path to wealth was through illegal reselling (*daomai*). Better profits could be made by speculating than by managing well. Government agencies, such as state banks, engaged in this endemic reform practice freely, although when the benefited network was large or official, speculation was not deemed corrupt. For example, the state for a long time tried to enforce a legal monopoly on the purchase of foreign currencies, which in various ways it bought cheaply and sold dearly, taking the profit. When individuals speculated—for example, by scalping tickets at the Shanghai railroad station—police tried to arrest them.[106] The most important actors on speculative markets were state enterprises and large collectives, which had the most extensive funds to use for this purpose.

A major type of "speculation" involved state agencies "selling to big houses" (*mai dahu*), mainly nonstate stores, rather than to state-owned retail agencies that had purchase contracts. The Shanghai Poultry Egg Company in April of 1987, for example, sold 32 percent of its produce to secondary wholesalers, who resold the eggs at a price considerably higher than that fixed for state-owned shops.[107] The state system and its rake-off were simply bypassed. This was a common local form of detour to avoid higher or more enforceable profit or tax revenue collections in the state sector.

Another type of speculation involved selling low-quality commodities as if they were good. This problem arose especially with bulk items such as fertilizers and chemical products, which can be adulterated with other substances. Cheating raised profits, and many practices of this sort could be justified as if they were good reforms in enterprise management to establish new horizontal sales relations.[108] Officials or their relatives might serve as middlemen in arranging materials purchases for large state factories, charging an illegal commission for this service. These middlemen, who could pocket large amounts of money in resale transactions, were called *guan dao ye* (literally, "official supply grandfathers"). When a Shanghai cable factory could not obtain enough copper to continue operations, for example, the managers informally consulted with workers to "gather opinions" on whether they should break the law and use an "official supply grandfather." He charged a personal commission of 2,000 yuan for every metric ton of copper for which he could arrange delivery. There was consensus in the factory that the deal should be made.[109]

It was frequently difficult to distinguish where normal business operations ended and corruption began. When managers were making money for their groups, they could often deny such a difference. Cotton-purchasing cadres in Jiangsu in 1988, for example, bought at low state prices—and resold at several levels of wholesale trade—until the price paid by the factory that finally did the spinning was two or three times the official price.[110] Such practices violated rules handed down by the State Council. They were commonplace anyway.

More than a thousand small boats leave Shanghai every day carrying industrial goods, according to the Public Security Bureau. Many were engaged in illegal trade. From 1979 to 1987, Shanghai's Water Police handled a great number of commercial cases, mostly of people whose household registrations were outside Shanghai.[111] Corruption was totally "embedded" in both the physical and normative structures where it flourished. The delta's canal system, and the separate communities of boat people who plied its waterways, were facts the state could not feasibly change.

Small agriculturalists, if they did not reform to become small industrialists, could be disaffected from state officials because of resale corruption. The economy of Shanghai's suburbs was very prosperous by 1981, for example, and the pancake-flat terrain made bicycles useful for suburban farmers. Demand was much greater than supply, largely because Shanghai factories were obligated by plans (and encouraged by low official prices in the whole municipality, including the suburbs) to send bicycles for sale elsewhere. Ration coupons, rather than price, were the main means of allocation. Thirty percent of suburban bicycle coupons in the early 1980s were allotted to towns, with the remaining 70 percent to ex-commune administrations. But the town "cadres took some," and "'cooperators' retained some." There was a leakage of 40 percent of the total. Less than one-third of Shanghai's rural bicycle coupons remained for peasants.[112] This kind of corruption affected many consumer products. It did not endear state officials to farmers who really earned money but could not buy goods.

Corruption by wholesalers was the most lucrative kind. In May 1989, police cracked "the most serious bribery ever to occur in Zhejiang province," in which "the criminals used their administrative power or influence to obtain bribes by selling raw silk to Hong Kong businessmen through illegal channels." The scale of this illegal operation was enormous; it reportedly extended throughout the province. The problem arose because the state takes an especially large markup over costs when selling silk. Yet growing mulberry trees and raising worms is a dispersed activity, difficult to monitor. Revenues to central state agencies "should have reached about 5 billion Hong Kong dollars for silk exported to Hong Kong [from Zhejiang] in 1988, but the actual income was only 2 billion Hong Kong dollars." The report railed against the sales commissions that forty-seven illegal traders made. It did not mention that much more—this amount plus the HK $3 billion differential that was caused by the high official price—would have been the state's sales commission.

The government procurator waxed lyrical about "solving" this case, comparing its complexities to the "silk thread the worms make when spinning cocoons, which is almost endless." But he recovered only 300,000 yuan, plus HK $29,000.[113] With the sales price of Zhejiang silk still very high, and production of the basic material still very scattered, this was not so much an issue for courts as for monitors. Zhejiang province is large, and the end of this "almost endless" thread was likelier to be found in scarcity-price markets than in courts, although that structure would also have reduced central revenues.

Correlates and Estimates of Corruption

Corruption was most feasible and profitable in rural and suburban areas from which most high state cadres were absent. Reform China, like other countries after spates of violent centralization (e.g., the United States after 1865), reported kinds of corruption that correlate strongly with economic growth. The amounts of materials and money involved in illegal exchanges were immense. They were reported especially in periods of Party conservative rule. From January through

July, 1989, police in Jiangsu handled 2.2 times as many corruption cases as in the previous year. Most of these involved sales that violated laws. In the first two years of a Jiangsu rural enterprise supply company, it illegally sold "large amounts of iron, wool, and other products." A single oil company in Zhenjiang city illegally sold about 2,000 metric tons of petroleum in these few months.[114] More famous examples of corruption in reform China occurred further south, notably in Hainan, but the Shanghai delta contributed to the record.

There was decreasing agreement, as reforms progressed, about the proper definition of corruption. "Some leading cadres resist the fight against corruption and view running a clean government as inconsistent with economic construction and a hindrance to production."[115] The purely economic and direct costs of corruption in China became immense during the late 1980s. Partly because of changing definitions and partly because of price changes, these costs probably decreased somewhat during the next decade.[116] By 1988, according to economists in the Chinese Academy of Social Sciences who made a heroic attempt to estimate part of these costs, endemic shortages meant that total "negotiated" money transfers for capital goods were about 200 billion or 300 billion yuan more than the theoretical costs at "fixed" prices. Of this increment, the experts estimated that 20 percent (40 billion to 60 billion yuan) went for commissions to the negotiators, i.e., for corruption.[117] That amount approximates the total spent that year on urban housing investment, for example, or on agricultural price subsidies.

This was only the cost of corruption in capital goods markets, however. For other services and commodities, a Chinese estimator has figured the 1988 excess of market over planned costs at 356 billion yuan, of which over 100 billion was "excess interest" that had to be paid to banks over the official rates, before they would make loans. A French analyst, assessing this drain a bit higher and taking all corrupt rents together, estimates that 10 percent of China's national income in 1988 may have gone to graft. These activities led Guilhem Fabre to write about the development of a "casino state."[118]

Decentralization, Corruption, and Efficiency

The two main facts about reform China's economy are its quick growth and its inefficient management. How could a regime that largely fostered sinecure jobs, "wrong" prices, chaotic decentralization, and uneven taxes enjoy such spectacular prosperity? The answer may lie in decentralization. That pattern aided entrepreneurship, even if it also meant odd allocation. In Shanghai, economic decentralization finally was a clear trend by the late 1980s and early 1990s. Shanghai industries had long been more vertically integrated (performing even more processes in-house, rather than going on the market for them) than firms in other large Chinese cities, as Table 1.3–4 suggests. These figures are an index constructed from two indices of production, one of which is designed to measure only the value added by the firm (the cost of inputs and factors is deducted), while the other counts the total value whenever a product leaves the firm. The first is the numerator; the second, the denominator. When the index falls, so approximately does in-house vertical integration. This ratio in Shanghai dropped from 1978 to 1990 (and from lower bases, it also fell in the comparable cities of Tianjin and Guangzhou), showing increased use of upstream and downstream markets.

But decentralization can sometimes work against increased allocative efficiency. Local agencies can have as much desire to interfere with the market as do national ones, if they gain from such interference.

Entrepreneurial spirit was heightened by competition not just between individuals and small groups, but also between different levels of collectivity. Small networks responded to the vacuum after the state's search for rents lost steam. Reform in China's rich coastal deltas occurred in all five categories that Joseph Schumpeter, the main economist of entrepreneurship, listed as engines of fundamental change: China's rural-coastal innovators created new commodities and old ones in better quality. They introduced new techniques of production. They penetrated new markets. They sourced new factors and semifinished products. They organized their industries in new ways.[119] Realizing any one of these five criteria would be enough, by Schumpeter's standards, to qualify a reform as a seed of change, rather than just a continuation of the previous economic structure. Schumpeter's entrepreneur is like Weber's charismatic leader: the main sign of life on an otherwise dull bureaucratic or market scene.

Urban managers of local state firms (if not of "mother-in-law" corporations) knew perfectly well that their system was inefficient. To deal with the market, they expressed willingness to shoulder risks if they had autonomy. Interesting results came from a survey of businesspeople in China during a relatively liberal period of reforms, asking the question "If you had the chance of being either a senior executive of a large [presumably state] corporation or the owner-manager of a smaller firm, assuming equal financial rewards, which would you have chosen?" Among government factory managers, not just cooperative and private bosses, there was a clear preference against being a cog in a large state bureaucracy. Most admitted they would prefer to be owner-managers of small firms.[120]

Official use of the term "entrepreneur," which was widespread by the mid-1980s, suggested a manager willing to take risks and make decisions. A group of economists nonetheless pointed out, very classically, that entrepreneurship means nothing without free markets in labor and capital.[121] Otherwise, there is no sure way to show whether economic risk taking has been socially beneficial. According to these analysts, China was burdened by a simplistic psychology, looking down on entrepreneurs and considering them unimportant. These economists stressed the cultural rather than policy causes of a decline in entrepreneurial creativity. They blamed age-old Chinese traditions of seeking "moderation," as well as anti-individualist and anticommercial mores. They described Chinese culture as one that had condoned only egalitarian levels of wealth and thus had

Table 1.3-4

Declining Vertical and Rising Horizontal Integration in PRC Urban Economies (ratio of values added to gross trade, x 100)

	Shanghai	Tianjin	Guangzhou
1978	41	38	37
1979	41	38	40
1980	40	38	
1981	40	37	
1982	39	35	
1983	39	35	
1984	39	35	
1985	39	35	38
1986	36	35	36
1987	35	34	35
1988	34	31	35
1989	31	28	33
1990	30	27	33
1991	30	27	33
1992	29		

Notes and sources: These figures were all calculated by dividing national income (*guomin shouru*) by gross value of social product (*shehui zongchan zhi*). As the value of transactions between different companies (which mostly remain state-owned in these cities) rises, the denominator rises; so the index goes down. The numerator at least roughly measures a sum of values added, whereas the denominator double- or multiple-counts the values of trades between units, so that a decline in the ratio correlates with a decline of vertical, and a rise of horizontal, economic integration. (National income is used, rather than the theoretically more appropriate gross domestic product, because of a lack of GDP figures for many years and places in China and because it is sufficient to show trends.) See *Shanghai tongji nianjian, 1983* (Shanghai Statistical Yearbook, 1983), Shanghai Statistical Bureau, ed. (Shanghai: Shanghai Shi Tongji Ju, 1984), p. 43; ibid., 1988 edition, p. 20; ibid., 1991 edition, pp. 38 and 43; ibid., 1992 edition, pp. 37 and 42; and ibid., 1993 edition, pp. 44 and 39; also *Tianjin tongji nianjian, 1987* (Tianjin Statistical Yearbook, 1987), Tianjin Statistical Bureau, ed. (Beijing: Zhongguo Tongji Chuban She, 1987), pp. 48 and 50; ibid., 1988 edition, pp. 38–39; ibid., 1991 edition, pp. 148 and 150; and ibid., 1992 edition, pp. 115 and 117; also *Guangzhou tongji nianjian, 1988* (Guangzhou Statistical Yearbook, 1988), Guangzhou Municipal Statistics Bureau, ed. (Beijing: Zhongguo Tongji Chuban She, 1988), p. 4; ibid., 1991 edition, pp. 15 and 17; and ibid., 1992 edition, pp. 23 and 25. *Quanguo ge sheng zizhi qu zhixia shi lishi tongji ziliao huibian, 1949–1989* (Historical Statistics Collection on Provinces, Autonomous Regions, and Municipalities Throughout the Country, 1949–1989), State Statistical Bureau, ed. (Beijing: Zhongguo Tongji Chuban She, 1990), pp. 93 and 96, has data on Tianjin. The calculations were not made in the sources, and the index is rough but revealing. The extent of continuing vertical integration in a city such as Guangzhou (a capital, not fully like other parts of Guangdong) is somewhat unexpected.

discouraged the search for profits. They did not stress that intellectuals, more than any other Chinese group, had been the specific sustainers of these habits, the policy makers who had separated prices from values.

Neoclassical economic theory holds that if ownership rights of each commodity (including money) are clear, so that owners will not trade a good except at its unique scarcity price, then factors will be allocated to maximize production. This "Pareto efficiency" among factors at any particular time does not, however, guarantee the fastest rate of economic growth. That kind of progress over an extended period is not the same as a static efficient allocation of factors at any particular moment. As Schumpeter wrote, "A system—any system, economic or other—that at every point of time fully utilizes its possibilities to the best advantage may yet in the long run be inferior to a system that does so at no given point of time, because the latter's failure to do so may be a condition for the level or speed of long-run performance."[122] Markets, on which decisions are governed by price competition, distribute money to traders. But price competition alone does not guarantee new technologies, better modes of economic organization, or entrepreneurial zeal in finding new kinds of materials, new markets, and new products. Efficient markets do not ensure maximal growth.

In this light, some of the most obvious characteristics of China's economy—the fuzziness of ownership rights, the frequent use of multiple state and nonstate prices, even the diversion of money to corrupt officials—might help rather than hinder long-term growth. These habits could do so, even if they somewhat reduced the efficiency of factor allocation at any given time, *if* they were linked to establishing firms that made new goods, seeking new places to sell them, finding new finances, and inspiring better managerial and productive techniques.

There is nothing wrong with neoclassical factor efficiency. It may contribute to growth rates, but reform China suggests it does not refer to the main generators of growth. The mainstream model in economics has been notoriously unable to predict any long-term economic change. In the Far East, the Philippines as late as 1959 had per-capita income and (apparently) factor efficiency higher than in Taiwan; yet as subsequent decades showed, Taiwan had more of something else that the Philippines lacked. The entrepreneurship Schumpeter stresses, and a political regime to support it, is a convincing summary of that element in light of Chinese experience. During the PRC reforms, the pattern of unclear ownership, multiple pricing, and rampant corruption did not prevent the economy from growing quickly. Economic theory has not yet sorted all these matters, especially for predictions over any time span longer than a few years. The economies of many countries have boomed in periods of "wrong" prices, oligopoly, corruption, and experimentation with mixed forms of ownership. If managers seek opportunities and take risks, as many are now doing in reform China, then these problems, which most economists emphasize, do not preclude fast growth. A historical overview suggests that some inefficiencies may correlate with quick development.

Credit, Savings, and Depreciation

Bad allocation of capital was, in the view of some Shanghai economists, the central fault that reforms must correct. Investment in the Jinshan Chemical Plant, for example, was said to have been decided on completely noneconomic grounds by Mao Zedong himself. Even in the 1980s, a widespread presumption that high politicos knew what they were doing when they made investment choices was, in this view, China's main economic difficulty. In a talk at Fudan University, one economist said that many past, wasteful projects had been identifiable with particular political leaders, such as Gang of Four members Wang Hongwen, Jiang Qing, and Zhang Chunqiao. In a mood that was just partly jocular, he also averred that Shanghai's then-current (1987) fifteen largest projects could well be identified with Jiang Zemin.[123] He did not go so far as to call these wasteful too.

The political habit of allowing high cadres, who often lack economic expertise, decide everything without sufficiently good advice could in this view be reformed only if producers made production choices. This economist also called for contract relations between different administrative levels.[124] Yet another, more political view of Shanghai's problems, insofar as they relate to capital, would stress not that the allocation of capital was inefficient, but instead that the *amount* was insufficient because too much for years had been taxed away to Beijing.

Investment in Shanghai was only 2 percent of the national total over the first three decades of the PRC.[125] Yet Shanghai was objectively not a bad place in which to recoup capital. A comparison of the economic returns from fourteen Chinese cities showed that Shanghai got notably better-than-average results in 1987, using its liquid capital. Its industry could obtain a full return on cash within 84 days—a result that compares very favorably to the least efficient surveyed user of such money, Haerbin (which took 160 days), or to the capital, Beijing (which took 110 days). The nearby Jiangnan cities of Wuxi and Suzhou were, like Shanghai, quick to return money (taking 97 and 95 days to achieve this, respectively).[126] State predations on Shanghai's infrastructure were severe until the early 1990s, as the previous chapter showed. Financial credit for Shanghai nonetheless came through various domestic institutions that can be examined in turn: the state's budget and quasi-budgets, the banking system, and public sales of stocks and bonds.

Budgets and Extrabudgetary Investments

Budgets can serve as rough indices of political centralization. Inland capital construction investment peaked about 1970 (after smaller rises in the 1950s and a steep rise in between 1964 and 1966). After the precipitous decline of inland investment from 1971 to 1975, there was a slight rise for the next two years, and then after 1978 a less sharp continuation of the earlier (reform) decline into the mid-1980s at least.[127] This index vividly shows the rise and fall of the centralized power created by China's revolution. There can be much doubt about the completeness of data or about the economic wisdom of the inland investments, but the ability to make them until 1971 certainly represented a central state capacity before then.

A parallel index of the decline of budgetary power in the central state is the rise of new capital that came through other sources. From 1972 to 1977, the growth of "extrabudgetary" investment nationally averaged about 10 percent per year—*five times* as fast as the growth of the more centrally controlled investment budget. Also, the year-to-year rise of nonbudgetary investment at this time was more stable than that of budgeted investment.[128] Research by Vivienne Shue and Marc Blecher from a county in Hebei suggests broadly similar trends there—and a need to look beyond published budgets and extrabudgets before claiming anything like an adequate account of local money flows in China.[129]

The documented portion of the state budget allocated nationally from the central ministries in Beijing decreased from about 70 percent in the 1950s to 60 percent in the 1960s, and further down to an average of about 50 percent in the first seven years of the 1980s. For the period 1981–85, the portion of the state budget transferred to individuals, especially as wages and bonuses, exceeded three-fifths.

Also, the portion of national income in the hands of local governments, enterprises, functional agencies, and service units—but *outside* their state budgets—increased sharply, from less than 14 percent in 1979 to 22 percent in 1986.[130] The *reported* extrabudgetary income of these subordinate units was half as large as the state budget, and the increment in these funds by the mid-1980s was similar. Furthermore, some local credits were reported in neither the budgets nor the extrabudgets.

In Shanghai, the sources of capital for state-sector construction investment changed radically over time. Between 1953 and 1978, almost three-quarters (72 percent) of funds for basic construction came to Shanghai from the state budget; but between 1979 and 1987, this portion plummeted to 22 percent.[131] Rural industries' power over factor prices, and the consequent need to use more of the state's money to pay operating expenses, easily accounts for this drop in capital funds. Because the inflation in factor markets was hidden by state pricing and appointment systems in the early 1970s, and because unreported reserves of credit (as of every other factor) were large in the planned economy, the trend of Shanghai's published budget matches the standard periodization of reforms from 1978 better than many other indices do.

As an old industrial center, Shanghai was richly supplied with institutions for supplying nonstate capital. Between 1976 and 1980, the reported portion of the city's total investment outside the state budget was only 31 percent; but between 1981 and 1985, this rose to 80 percent.[132] In China as a whole, the state had to be more generous. Alternative funders were less available. During 1986 in all of China, a lower portion than in Shanghai (62 percent) of construction capital reportedly came from sources outside the state budget.[133] Much is murky about the ways in which enterprises and governments obtained finances in reform China, because the potential sources were many and some of them were hidden.

Depreciation

Not all new capital goes into new economic activity; some is needed to offset wear and tear. Depreciation is both financial and physical. The capital infrastructure Shanghai possessed, to support China's highest rate of tax remittances, had already severely deteriorated by the time of reforms. In 1980, four-fifths of Shanghai's textile factory premises dated from before 1937. In the whole three decades after 1949, the state invested a niggardly 500 million yuan in Shanghai's textile plants (a total, over thirty years, of about one-quarter of the profits of just a *single* year from this local industry). About 70 percent of the workers in these factories were female. One plant, with five hundred women workers, provided a single toilet area for all of them. Many textile factories leaked in the rain. Several suffered roof collapses in storms.[134]

Shanghai's *budgeted* industrial depreciation rates from 1956 to 1980 overall averaged 4.2 percent per year, but much of the money was not used for the purpose its label implied.[135] Just three-tenths of this designated depreciation money could actually be retained by enterprises in most of these years. A full 70 percent went directly into government funds. For city-managed firms, 40 percent was remitted to supervising bureaus of the municipal government, and 30 percent of these depreciation allowances went into central coffers in Beijing. This was another form of tax.

Some depreciation allowance money since the late 1960s went, however, into the extrabudgetary funds of companies that actually had the equipment whose wear and tear the funds were supposed to balance. Various depreciation rates were used in different industries and locations, and all of them were very low. In 1970, the central government allowed a 0.5 percent general increase in depreciation allowances. This small increment may seem trivial, but since the allowance depended on the value of all fixed assets in a firm—and since the amount of such assets doubled in China between 1970 and 1978—this small change of rate alone brought 12 billion yuan more extrabudgetary funds to enterprises in those years.[136] This amounted to a considerable reform toward decentralized finances in the early 1970s.

The general rate for depreciation in 1978 was 3.7 percent; this rose to 4.1 percent in 1981, 4.2 percent in 1983, 4.7 percent in 1984, and 5.3 percent in 1985 and later.[137] These percentage changes may seem small, but they imply large transfers of money because the basis of the calculation was all fixed capital. With the first of these changes, the central state laid claim to half of the depreciation funds but decreed that the companies (rather than local governments) could retain somewhat more of the remainder. The deal for Shanghai may have been different than for most other areas, but the local portion rose in the early 1980s. By the middle of that decade, the central government gave up its share entirely in most areas—and all depreciation funds were supposed to stay in firms.

Depreciation rates had risen by successive decrees of the State Council.[138] But the 1980s plans were slow to be carried out—for an unexpected reason. An outsider might suppose that factory managers would have welcomed any increase in their depreciation allowances. They did not, because depreciation funds were counted as a cost of production. So those amounts were not as available for local managers to use so easily as were bonus, welfare, and production development funds, which counted as part of profits (not costs). Profit components were subject to less effective higher-level monitoring than were depreciation allowances, whose increase did little for managers' autonomy.[139]

In 1984, the average depreciation rate was allowed to rise slightly, to a level above 5 percent. But the price of capital goods rose much faster in this decade, so that companies could buy less for their wear-and-tear money. For example, a 40,000–yuan automobile that a firm might buy in 1980 cost 140,000 yuan in 1988. Also, depreciation funds in Shanghai were often used for purposes other than replacing equipment.

In the early 1980s, two-fifths of the machines used in the city reportedly dated from before 1949. The quality of products suffered because of such antique tools. Outdated capital fixtures were largely responsible for Shanghai's low growth rates from 1981 to 1983. At the start of that decade, Shanghai's Light Industrial Bureau noted that 70 percent of its factory space had been constructed before 1949, and 3.3 percent of the space was officially considered "dangerous."[140] From 1949 to 1978, investment in Shanghai's light industries had been only 4 percent of the city's total industrial investment. Even this small amount could not be freely used by factory managers, because it came in line-item funds that were not easily fungible to other uses.[141] The Shanghai factories that produced consumer goods had an interest in extending their operations. At the start of the 1980s, they called for renovation to improve their "small, old, dispersed" facilities, promising sharp increases of output if the government would give them capital.[142] Beijing responded only in the second half of the decade, and only because its urban political and tax bases were threatened by rural industries. To do their jobs, Shanghai managers had long since developed the norm of operating partly with credit whose flows were not reported in a full or unified way.

Equipment in the country as a whole was less old than in Shanghai. By 1985, 77 percent of the machines used nationally in large and medium plants had been produced during the 1970s or 1980s. Less than one-quarter predated 1970.[143] These portions show a broad reluctance by planners to retire old machines. National depreciation rates were "so low that much equipment has a standard life expectancy of twenty-five years."[144] In the early 1980s nationally, more than 25 percent of all capital was operating beyond its scheduled service life—and the percentage in Shanghai was much higher.

High depreciation rates raise managers' nominal costs (*chengben*) and thus lower their nominal profits. Bonus funds are their most flexible general means of establishing links with their workers. Managers' dislike of high depreciation rates was purely a result of the accounting system. The mid-1980s "contract system" further decreased factory managers' interests in high depreciation allowances, because the contracts generally fixed absolute quotas for output and fiscal remittances, leaving bonus funds as the remainder to be reduced on a yuan-for-yuan basis by any increased depreciation.

State Investment in Heavy Industry and Profit Retention

Fifty-seven percent of Shanghai's total basic construction investment from 1950 to 1985 went into heavy industry, but only 8 percent went into light industry.[145] Only 9 percent went for public infrastructure. The reform pattern remained very statist and conservative in built-up Shanghai long after the 1978 announcement of reforms. Economists had written countless academic articles showing that overinvestment in heavy industry was one of China's biggest problems—yet it continued.

Reformist foxes in Beijing, such as Hu Yaobang, Zhao Ziyang, and Deng Xiaoping at this time, apparently wanted more money for light industries. They failed to get it, not just because of central conservatives but also because of local conservative lions in Shanghai. The central state for decades had entrenched bureaucrats in that city who would remit taxes at all costs. The whole governmental institution of the city was designed for that, and it could not be changed overnight. So state investment is not one of the fields in which metropolitan Shanghai reforms began in the early 1970s. Nor did they begin in 1978. Investment reforms in this city were delayed until the mid-1980s. In capital-intensive heavy industries, where central bureaucrats could control the technology and bulk inputs, they followed their own policies rather than those of central reformers.

There was nonetheless a very uneven pattern of state investment into Shanghai. As Table 1.3–5 shows, investment rose in the early 1970s and was erratic in the late 1970s and early 1980s, rising later. This report includes funds from both central and local state organs, but it does not include "self-generated" (*zichou*) and certain other investment money. In 1984 and later, the rate of change in investment was generally positive for political reasons. But by that time, the state budget was less important for total investment.

In China as a whole, the government became just one of the capitalists. Its budget financed decreasing portions of investment in state enterprises: more than 60 percent before 1980, but only 35 percent by 1984, and 21 percent by 1987.[146] Managers had to spend more money for raw materials. In 1978, 58 percent of their "accumulation fund" outside of operating expenses went for fixed capital, but this part of their nonliquid account rose to 74 percent by 1982.[147] The portion of planned credits dropped from 42 to 27 percent. A cursory glance at this change

Table 1.3-5

State Investment in Shanghai

	Millions of yuan		Millions of yuan
1950	16	1970	521
1951	52	1971	507
1952	141	1972	379
1953	213	1973	551
1954	177	1974	919
1955	241	1975	1,757
1956	267	1976	1,015
1957	330	1977	594
1958	851	1978	1,139
1959	876	1979	1,755
1960	714	1980	1,222
1961	240	1981	1,008
1962	169	1982	733
1963	260	1983	693
1964	348	1984	978
1956	283	1985	1,186
1966	169	1986	1,435
1967	91	1987	1,830
1968	196	1988	2,179
1969	409	1989	2,344
		1990	2,441

Notes and sources: Shanghai tongji nianjian, 1983 (Shanghai Statistical Yearbook, 1983), Shanghai Statistical Bureau, ed. (Shanghai: Shanghai Shi Tongji Ju, 1984), p. 206; *Shanghai tongji nianjian, 1986* (as above), p. 243; *Shanghai tongji nianjian, 1988* (as above), p. 246; and *Shanghai tongji nianjian, 1989* (as above), p. 278. Later data were found in the same source by Peng Dajin, but these may not be exactly comparable because of slight changes in the way state investment was calculated in 1990. The figures after 1980 may also not be exactly comparable with earlier ones, because foreign loans and some additional domestic borrowing are included. Furthermore, figures in different yearbooks do not exactly match, but they are close. In cases of discrepancy, the later edition has been used.

might leave the impression that managers were more constrained for money during the reforms than before. But such was not the case, because the reduction of plan credit was compensated by a sharp increase in the amount of companies' "own capital" (*ziyou zijin*) outside the budget plan. Supervising bureaucrats, after the reforms began, had less extensive control over managers' capital.

Central budget makers let factories keep more of their profits in the country as a whole than in Shanghai. Profit retention in state-owned enterprises rose sharply in China after 1978. It had to do so because of market pressure; some state industries were now in competition with nonstate companies that often reinvested profits. All Chinese state enterprises retained an average of only 4 percent of their profits in 1978, according to one source; but in each successive year thereafter, this portion rose to 11, 19, 21, 27, 33, and 35 percent, reaching 39 percent by 1985.[148] Loan repayments, deducted before profits were calculated, amounted to another 13 percent since the loaned money stayed within firms. In 1986, the national average retention of profits went up further, to 42 percent (or 58 percent before the pretax loan repayments).[149]

Even in Shanghai, the rate at which locally run state factories retained their profits rose sharply, from 5 percent in 1979 to 16 percent in 1984, and then to 34 percent in 1987.[150] The cloud on this silver lining, of course, was that they needed the money to pay new, higher materials prices. Also, rates of retention outside the state sector, and especially outside Shanghai city, were much higher. This is just another way of speaking about factor price inflation, since much of the money went to bid the prices of inputs up closer to their scarcity values.

Many collectives retained more than most state firms. A large Wuxi collective by 1978–79 was able to keep 71 percent of its after-tax profits. This was more than was admitted for any other collective in a sample of data gathered nationwide. The other East China collectives in this fairly small sample reportedly kept less, down to about 30 percent, but the high retention of the most advantaged collectives represents a sharp change from the previous pattern on the Yangzi delta.[151] From collectives, more of the remitted money remained under local leaders' control. For state companies, especially in Shanghai, new capital for technological improvement was scarce both before and after the onset of contract reforms. By the mid-1980s, the main source of such funds became bank loans.

Banks

From 1953 to 1978, only 28 percent of new Shanghai capital came from bank loans and "self-generated" sources; but by the 1979–87 period, this figure soared to 74 percent.[152] Financial reform began about 1979, not just because central politicians had a reformist change of heart then, but specifically because that was the year when the factors crisis began to become obvious not just in shortages but also in prices that had to be paid with money.

Standard criteria for bank loans suggested that at least 30 percent of the capital for renovation in an existing firm should come out of the company's own money. This might be financed either from the three-fifths of depreciation funds that the enterprise could keep, or else from the four-fifths of profits that fed its "development fund." Bank loans also required feasibility studies (sometimes even environmental studies) by the late 1980s, but negotiations and pulling strings remained the

Table 1.3-6

Interest Rates on Different Shanghai Bank Loans
(annual percentages, compounded monthly, in 1982)

	Interest rate
Industrial/commercial borrowers	
For liquid cash	6.0
Short- or mid-term construction/repairs:	
One-year loan or less	4.2
One-year to 3 years	4.8
More than 3, up to 5 years maximum	5.4
Surcharge on interest for late repayments	+20%
Surcharge on interest rate for overdraft	+50%
Agricultural borrowers	
State farm production loans	4.8
State farm equipment loans	4.2
Township (commune or brigade) production	4.8
Township equipment loans	3.6
Sub-township loans for seeds or agronomy	4.8
Sub-township loans for equipment	3.6
Farm machines, planned-item loans	0.0
Loans for downpayment to buy farm equipment	4.8
Loans to individual farmers	4.8 to 5.0

Notes and sources: Administration of these rates was not supposed to discriminate between state-owned, collective, and private clients, except as noted. See *Shanghai jingji, neibu ben: 1949–1982* (Shanghai Economy, Internal Volume: 1949–1982), Shanghai Academy of Social Sciences, ed. (Shanghai: Shanghai Shehui Kexue Yuan Chuban She, 1984), p. 924.

fundamental requirement. Loans were not a whit less political than budget allocations. But when loans were approved, the interest rates were low.

A more efficient money market in China meant higher interest rates. In 1978, the interest on one-year time deposits was 3.24 percent; by 1985, this had more than doubled to 6.84 percent. For working capital loans, rates of about 5 percent in the late 1970s rose to about 8 percent in 1985.[153]

Rates on loans were different depending on the identity of the borrower. The economic profitability of a project was in principle a secondary consideration to the borrower's identity. The state, while still in its planning mode, attempted to encourage specific kinds of economic activity (and to discourage others) by charging different rates of interest on loans to different categories of borrowers. Table 1.3–6 shows the rates prevailing in Shanghai during 1982. Loans to industrial and commercial firms required relatively high interest. "Agricultural" borrowers could not have paid such high rates—but many of them by 1982 were actually engaged in industry. Except for farm machines and small equipment, the rates they paid were not concessionary. By the mid-1980s, the picture changed sharply, because of higher inflation and because the sources of credit became more diverse.

Deposits and Loans

Going into the 1980s, Shanghai bank deposits at nominal value were 9.8 times their 1952 value—but bank loans had risen much faster, by 46 times between 1952 and 1980. It had become much easier for banks to risk money. Industrial loans were up 70 times; commercial loans, 36 times. Savings deposits were only 22 percent of total deposits, because the bulk of funds (apparently still under enterprise plans) were held in accounts not bearing interest. Shanghai industry was financed by direct allocations more commonly than was commerce, which relied more on loans; the early 1980s ratio of outstanding commercial to industrial loans was 1.27 to 1.[154]

Official plants received generous credit. The state sector was provided with loans and capital—especially in Shanghai because state plants there had great fiscal importance, but also on a nationwide basis, as Table 1.3–7 shows. The portion of fixed capital investment in Shanghai's state sector, as compared with its collective and private sectors, was practically identical in 1978 and 1990. It ranged between 80 and 90 percent of all such investment during those dozen years, despite or because of the state sector's growing problems then. State companies' credit was not so much to maintain production as to maintain state-sector jobs, for both workers and local officials.

Local Credit

Banking in China provides clear instances in which local administration overwhelmed central policy. Five lines of change were evident in reform banks, and each of them can be explained in these terms. First, revenue extraction became less a function of banks than previously. The People's Bank of China was supplemented by others, often with names denoting sectors, which had fewer fiscal monitoring roles. Banks, like other economic units, were supposed to become more independent of "the government." They became more autonomous from Beijing—but not necessarily from local officials, whose pet projects needed loans and drove the changes in banks at least as obviously as any directives from the top.

Second, interest rates rose, for both deposits and loans. Since China's state firms had previously hoarded credit lines (and many other resources) and faced "soft budget constraints," the higher interest rates often raised their efficiency in using funds at the company level. This rationalization of the price of money also put the

Table 1.3-7

Composition of Fixed Capital Investment (percentages of reported public, collective, and private capital)

	National			Shanghai			Guangdong		
Year	Pub.	Col.	Pri.	Pub.	Col.	Pri.	Pub.	Col.	Pri.
1978				85.4%	11.5%	3.2%	73.6%	3.1%	23.3%
1979				90.2%	6.8%	3.0%	70.9%	3.4%	25.7%
1980				88.6%	7.9%	3.5%	67.2%	4.4%	28.4%
1981	69.5%	12.0%	18.5%	82.4%	9.9%	7.6%	57.3%	10.6%	32.1%
1982	68.7%	14.2%	17.1%	86.4%	7.2%	6.5%	61.1%	13.6%	25.3%
1983	66.6%	10.9%	22.5%	85.6%	8.2%	6.2%	63.0%	13.4%	23.5%
1984	64.7%	13.0%	22.3%	82.1%	9.7%	8.2%	61.9%	14.0%	24.2%
1985	66.1%	12.9%	21.0%	80.9%	8.8%	10.3%	71.0%	13.1%	15.9%
1986	65.5%	13.0%	21.5%	83.3%	9.5%	7.1%	72.0%	12.5%	15.5%
1987	63.1%	15.0%	21.9%	82.9%	10.0%	7.1%	69.3%	14.5%	16.2%
1988	61.4%	15.8%	22.7%	81.0%	11.8%	7.2%	70.0%	15.7%	14.3%
1989	61.3%	13.8%	24.9%	83.3%	9.8%	7.0%	67.4%	17.7%	15.0%
1990	65.6%	11.9%	22.5%	84.7%	8.1%	7.3%	70.5%	15.8%	13.7%
1991	65.9%	12.7%	21.5%	80.5%	10.8%	9.5%	71.7%	14.9%	13.4%

Sources: Calculated from *Zhongguo tongji nianjian, 1991*, p. 143; ibid. for 1988, p. 559; and ibid. for 1992, p. 145; *Shanghai tongji nianjian 1991*, p. 260; ibid. for 1989, p. 271; and ibid. for 1992, p. 280; and *Guangdong tongji nianjian, 1991*, p. 191; and ibid. for 1992, p. 230.

rates closer to what private local lenders charged. State banks were no longer an exclusive source of funds at the going rates, because the going rates went up.

Third, reform banks were supposed to make profits. This meant local bank managers could sometimes claim rights to reallocate credit to potentially performing loans and to deny money to those they deemed likely to default. No matter whether these new bank powers were used to make profits or instead to make political connections, there was a relative rise in the authority of locals. The insistence on profits in banking also led to new procedures by which banks were supposed to attract even more savings than before from companies and people in their areas. Altogether, the impulse to profits justified in China's banks a massive decentralization.

Fourth, fixed investment capital had once been centrally planned, but during reforms this control eroded. Profitable new factories, especially in suburbs and rural areas, meant many loan recipients could pay extremely high returns. Two-track prices also meant that (for reasons unrelated to efficiency) some firms became extremely lucrative, while others, including many reliable borrowers before the reforms, became loss centers. All these changes, some spurred by new technological opportunities and some impelled by uneven norms during the transition from socialism, undermined the state's ability to plan capital. In the new procedures for capital finance, local interests became prime. Reform banks channeled large amounts of credit from surplus to deficit units. Either to save jobs or to start projects, the power of local boosters became at least as important in money management as were any coherent policies from the central bank. All these overlapping changes in China's banking system may have raised microeconomic efficiency within some firms and local areas. They even more surely led to a practical end of macroeconomic controls—and to more inflation.[155]

The time sequence of these changes in various places was no more uniform than the principles or actors behind them. But the long-term trend was clearly localist. Central banking policies were largely reactive to political and technological opportunities for loans after the late-1960s, and then to the inflationary results of earlier reactions that had justified loans because of those opportunities. This was policy, but it was situational, not ideal. Over time, it bore no resemblance to a coherent macroeconomic plan. There was a macropolitical plan, run mainly by and for leaders at the local level and aiming to strengthen them.

Personnel, Rural Credit, and Jobs

The heads of Party groups in Chinese banks are attached to—and their careers are largely dependent on—the CCP committees in their localities, not the Party leadership in the central bank. Formally, appointments also go through higher-level Party heads in the same functional system (*xitong*). But in practice, when banks contravene the wishes of local politicos, their managers suffer. They are not always hurt if they merely violate national rules. For this reason, China has often lacked a truly central bank.

Managers with political friends have obtained loans easily from bank directors during most periods since the Great Leap Forward. Although the government keeps Shanghai enterprises on a tight rein, to ensure delivery of taxes and state profits, it does not gather full information from firms about their loans. Such data are mainly handled through banks, and the amount of money sent to particular enterprises is a less important issue in practice (periodic Beijing statements to the contrary notwithstanding) than is the perennial difficulty of bank managers who should stay within the local loan quota but are pressed by politicos to exceed it.

Loans have often been the only means of ensuring remittances, which are a hard constraint for many firms and places in Shanghai. All else—output, efficiency, profit—was long secondary to remittances. For that reason, when enterprises could not meet their revenue quotas, they simply took out loans. This was often a matter of "the state" going in debt to itself. The practice nonetheless preserved appearances and jobs. Once it was normalized for paying taxes, it extended to other purposes, and bank representatives could seldom resist advice from local officials to give loans.[156]

"Soft budget constraints" are widespread in many kinds of economy—and they may actually aid, not hinder, economic growth if easy credit inspires entrepreneurs to make experiments with new techniques, markets, and products. In most capitalist countries, for example, the state encourages banks to loan out more funds than they have on deposit (e.g., through fractional reserve requirements). This policy may forebode runs on banks, crises in savings institutions, recessions, even depressions—but it also lowers interest rates and thus provides a countervailing public benefit: fast growth at most times.[157]

So companies needing funds could obtain bank loans after state plans no longer appropriated much money. Total loans for fixed assets soared in the 1980s throughout China, from 8 billion yuan in 1981 to 225 billion yuan in 1990 (on average up 45 percent yearly). Banks' lending, as a portion of all fixed-asset investment over the same period, rose from 9 percent in 1981 to 50 percent in 1990. In particular, lending by state banks to urban collectives and individuals rose throughout China from 8 billion yuan in 1980 to 83 billion yuan in 1990 (an average rise of 26 percent annually). Between the same years, loans from state banks to rural collectives rose from 18 billion yuan to 104 billion yuan (up 19 percent yearly).

Rural credit cooperatives led this enormous increase of lending. Data from local credit co-ops that reported their activities suggest that their loans soared from 8 billion yuan in 1980 to at least 141 billion yuan in 1990 (rising on average by one-third each year over the whole decade).[158] If more local, less formal revolving credit schemes were fully accounted too, this trend would be sharper. All these statistics were affected by inflation—and were major causes of it. Credit became available to entrepreneurs during reforms in unprecedented amounts, and the sources were by no means restricted to banks the state could control. Having a strict credit policy would have meant either defaulting on revenues or declaring bankruptcy. These are precisely the two things that socialist managers in China by tradition were never supposed to do. Taxes were paid, except in the periods of "slippage." Above all, money-losing state companies were kept afloat, at least until the mid-1990s.

The Mid-1980s Reform of Banks

This practice arranged situations to meet statist norms. An unintended consequence was credit expansion and thus sporadic efforts to control inflation and the money supply. In 1979, the People's Bank of China received top-level orders to stress its role as a central bank and fight rising prices. This was a fairly early example of the effort in Beijing to restore control over China's booming economy, but it was certainly not the last such attempt. Exhortations to and by the bank, aiming to control credit, became a recurring hallmark of reforms from then into the 1990s.

The People's Bank had previously been China's most active lender. It remained so well into the 1980s, partly because it had offices all over the country—in fact, more branches than any other bank in the world. The needs of the time required local lending, but with guidance from a central bank as in other diversified economies. These two functions did not mesh perfectly together. The People's Bank's mandate was increasingly to supervise and lend to other banks. Many loans were then supposed to be made by revamped or new banks, to which the People's Bank was gradually to hive off this function. Foreign trade, for example, was the old Bank of China's special area. The People's Bank was complemented in other sectors by China's Agricultural Bank, the Industrial and Commercial Bank, the People's Construction Bank, the People's Insurance Company, the International Trust and Investment Company, and the Communications Bank centered in Shanghai.

The Bank of Industry and Commerce was mainly responsible for short-term loans. The People's Construction Bank supplied fixed capital, and the Agricultural Bank worked in the suburbs. The People's Bank of China accepted many deposits and acted not only as the central bank, but also as the supervising corporation in the field of finance. But reforms eroded the People's Bank's previous near monopoly of finance, just as they eroded other "mother-in-law" companies.

This system, in which the banks were not supposed to compete because they were divided by function, changed during reforms—and the change was unplanned and abrupt, because credit became urgently needed to buy scarce materials. In August 1986, the several separate banks were given broader mandates. By October, the local Communications Bank could conduct almost any legal transaction. The other banks followed suit in later months, so they began to vie with each other.[159] Among these, the Agricultural Bank became pivotal because its loans mainly went to rural industry, the fastest-growing large sector of the economy.

Shanghai's banking reforms were conservative until the mid-1980s, but the previous financial order collapsed in 1986. That year saw the initial rebirth of Shanghai's stock exchange. An interbank short-term credit market was also established. The large banks became more autonomous from each other. A "swap" center for trading foreign credit was created; this was to help joint ventures meet their legal obligation not to run hard-currency deficits (and unavoidably, it aided transactions in convertible currency for other purposes too). Finally, a new kind of bank—not owned by the state, and essentially regional in East China rather than nationwide—was approved in the form of Shanghai's renovated Bank of Communications.[160] Each of these five steps was important, and each deserves separate attention.

The interbank market began as a conclave of about forty bank officers, meeting each Thursday morning near central Shanghai's waterfront, the Bund, starting in August 1986. Such a market was unusual in the PRC, because it allowed exchanges of short-term credit between different organizations and regions without authorization from any planner. When this interbank market began, probably one-third of all goods and services in China's economy were already traded at prices that responded strongly to demand. So this new financial institution, which allowed traders in need of supplies to get money more easily, may well have been inflationary; it supported an economy that had higher prices. It also raised the growth rate and efficiency of many other markets. As an official of the People's Bank of China said, "The vertical allocation of funds is incompatible with horizontal economic integration. . . . [But] there has been no fundamental change in the actual practice of banks indiscriminately providing funds to enterprises. . . The economic regulations and control measures have no teeth."[161] The interbank market swept many such rules aside. In practice, it meant that credit was no longer the province of planners.

On the other hand, the previous system had dammed parts of the money supply in specific places, so that wealth could not easily be used. A Shanghai banker complained, "There had been no movement of funds among the specialized banking systems, no flow between Shanghai and other places, nor even within the network of offices and branches of a single system in one place."[162] So each place and system had hoarded credit, just as each unit also hoarded all other supplies. Even though the interbank loans pressed prices upward, they were prerequisite to creating a unified money supply that could later be controlled.

They also bailed out many state enterprises that became bankrupt by the mid-1980s. One year earlier, when strict constraints had been imposed on short-term credit, many firms had been unable to roll over or extend their loans—and thus they defaulted. They could not pay their suppliers, many of which also defaulted. By December 1985, it was estimated that state firms' unpaid bills in China exceeded ten billion yuan; two months later, that amount was reported to be "out of control."[163] Horizontal credit markets alleviated this problem somewhat. Financial planning could not be maintained when other kinds had been forgone.

Along with the interbank lending by 1986, Shanghai also revived local banks that inevitably took some loan business from the central bank.[164] Money flowed more easily in the mid-1980s, because enterprises needed more funds to pay for factors. During the first six months of 1986, loans to Shanghai firms soared by 15 percent.[165] In this same period, gross output rose only 2 percent. Comparisons may be made for this period with other parts of East China:

	Rise of loans (%)	Rise of output (%)
Shanghai	15	2
Jiangsu	16	9
Zhejiang	36	11
Jiangxi	56	11

Loans were harder to procure in Shanghai than in most other East China areas, and more of them apparently went to buy raw materials. After Shanghai's "short-term funds market" opened at the end of August 1986, in the first fifty days 900 million yuan flowed there "horizontally" from other Chinese banks. This was as much as three-tenths of the *whole year's* planned credit in the city.[166] It represented a short-term increase in the speed at which Shanghai received credit, from this additional source alone, of two or three times the planned rate. The money was needed to pay for raw materials.

Local Banks

The Bank of Communications resurrected the name of an institution first established in 1908, but inactive after 1954. In its new form, it was conceived as a joint stock company. Although "the state" at the national level then purchased half the stock, the other half was sold to local governments, official and collective enterprises, and individuals (who were limited to 5 percent of the total shares). Dividends were paid based on profits.[167] The reestablished Bank of Communications in 1986 was accorded wide powers to accept enterprise deposits and make both long- and short-term loans. Its interest rates could float within a range set for each term. It could help issue bonds, finance international trade, and loan foreign exchange. This Shanghai institution was the PRC's closest equivalent to retail "one-stop banking."[168]

Shanghai also established the first nonstate (*minjian,* "among the people") urban financial institutions of the reform era. In August 1986, the local Aijian Credit and Investment Company was founded. That December, two local credit cooperatives in the downtown part of Shanghai were also openly registered. In the same month, controls over foreign exchange were relaxed, and the Shanghai branch of the Agricultural Bank and also the Shanghai Insurance Investment Company were authorized to act independently of the national corporations that had previously supervised them.

The municipal branch of the People's Bank of China was authorized in 1986 to make financial decisions independently of the bank's headquarters in Beijing. Previously, all provincial branches of the People's Bank had "allocation and distribution relations" with the headquarters, but these were reformed into mere "loan links." The headquarters and Shanghai branch of the bank were enjoined to lend each other money as needed—at interest—but in other respects the central bank could not tell the branch what to do.[169] For administrative and appointment purposes, the People's Bank was still centralized, but not (at least in 1986–87) for loan decisions.

Banking followed technicians and trade "horizontally" out of Shanghai to other parts of Jiangnan. Shanghai's Bank of Communications in 1988 had eight sub-branches in Jiangsu and Zhejiang (as well as eight provincial branches in the metropolis, those provinces, and Guangdong, Hubei, Liaoning, Shandong, and Sichuan). It also then planned fifteen more sub-branches in various provinces, so as to become "a real commercial bank."[170] All major cities on the Shanghai delta diversified their banking facilities in 1986 and established other credit institutions to take business from rural cooperatives. Wuxi opened its money market in late 1986, specializing in interbank loans. Within a year, this exchange was handling more than 10 billion yuan and was China's largest money market.[171]

In 1988, the People's Bank of China headquarters in Beijing (which acts as China's central bank) approved 186 new banks in Shanghai—a rise of about 15 percent in one year.[172] The Bank of China issued Great Wall credit cards, whose accounts were all in the national currency (*renminbi*). By 1987, it joined with MasterCard International to convert these into Great Wall MasterCards.[173] The state's central bank diversified its services to compete with other institutions.

New bank offices showed some division of labor. A quarter of the People's Bank new sub-branches were specialized in accepting savings, one-eighth were credit unions, and about three-eighths were "business offices" (*yingye suo*), mainly for deposits and loans of companies. Six of the new governing banks, including the local Communications Bank, became independent of control by the Shanghai branch of the People's Bank. The six independent banks were even designated "nongovernmental" (*minjian*), not run by the state.[174] The Party, of course, had cells in them, but these became more autonomous because the Party itself was not perfectly unified despite the elegance of its organization chart. Banking requires expertise; Party technocrats might survive in this field, but Party generalists could not last in it.

The six banks increased the number of their branches in 1988, and they were largely designed to encourage savings. The new offices of all banks specialized for savings rose sharply in that year alone. Efforts to restrain bank loans were mostly ineffective during the mid-1980s, partly because the number of banks and managers rose. In 1986, fully 26 percent more bank credit was approved than in

1985. In 1987, the rate of increase decelerated only slightly, to 19 percent.[175] The total of money in circulation nationally was 23 percent more in 1986 than the previous year, and in 1987 again 19 percent more.[176]

When Moody's Investors' Service in mid-1996 lowered its credit ratings for major PRC banks, the issue was "exactly what the government would be responsible for and what would be considered the liabilities of quasi-privatized banks" in case of bankruptcy.[177] The foreign accountants could not tell whether these banks were really state-owned or instead should be judged by the rules for private firms. Were their debts sovereign? Chinese officials protested hotly, but apparently they too did not know the answer to this question.

Savings as the Basis of Credit

Bank loans during the 1980s were supposed to depend on deposits. Some provinces, for example relatively poor ones that received net subsidies from the central treasury, practically always had a "surplus of deposits" (*cuncha*)—but had fewer actually profitable projects than did richer areas, including Shanghai, which had a "surplus of loans" (*daicha*). Early in the decade, banks that had credit they could not use sent representatives to Shanghai, where they found borrowers. Telex was used to transfer this money quickly. Even before an interbank market could open, the need for it was evident in other behavior. Like many other aspects of Shanghai's change in this period, it was an unintended result of the high rate of fiscal extraction.

In an attempt to control this credit, the central government allocated to banks in some places, including Shanghai, an estimated "gap between deposits and loans" (*cundai cha*). This was supposed, in 1987, to be the sole determinant of allowable loans. From an economic viewpoint, it was ideally a less inflationary institution than the previous system of politicians negotiating a total allowable amount of credit (*xindai zong'e*). This latter system was still used in most parts of China. But in either case, bankers inland were accused of pressing enterprises to take unneeded loans. In view of the economic boom and materials prices, these charges against loan officers apparently show little more than central inability to control them. The different systems used in different jurisdictions made little difference, because banks could now lend anywhere in the country. This created competition among them to use up their loanable quotas on profit-making projects.

From January to June 1987, Shanghai borrowed 100 million yuan from banks in Guangdong. Credit in the reform period remained cheap. "Self-gathered" (*zichou*) funds came from any sources other than the government and its main banks—for example, from local bonds, foreign investors, other enterprises, or the employees of the borrowing firms with or without their consent. In late 1988, Beijing again launched major efforts to stem the flood of credit (and inflation) this system had brought.

To attract deposits (and as noted earlier, to grant loans), interest rates varied with the identity of the bank's client. Individuals received better rates than "units," espe-

Table 1.3-8

Interest Offered to Different Shanghai Bank Depositors
(annual percentages, compounded monthly, 1982)

	Savings deposits	Time deposits					
		6 mo.	1 yr.	2 yr.	3 yr.	5 yr.	8 yr.
Units							
Firms on plan	1.5						
Extra-plan, and offices	1.5		3.0	3.6	4.2		
Persons							
PRC citizens	2.4	3.6	4.8		5.7	6.6	7.5
Overseas Chinese	2.4	3.6	6.0	6.9			

Notes and sources: Interest was apparently not normally available for the categories left blank above—and the lack of interest or low interest for enterprise time deposits must have saved the state's banks a great deal on interest payments. See *Shanghai jingji, neibu ben: 1949–1982* (Shanghai Economy, Internal Volume: 1949–1982), Shanghai Academy of Social Sciences, ed. (Shanghai: Shanghai Shehui Kexue Yuan Chuban She, 1984), p. 924.

cially if they were less vulnerable to alternative state controls. Overseas Chinese, even if resident in Shanghai, received more attractive interest on savings than did ordinary residents—presumably because they could keep their money abroad if the return there were higher. This situation is presented in Table 1.3–8.

These rates are hardly spectacular, but quick prosperity meant that disposable incomes rose quickly in Jiangnan, and so did savings. Although bank accounts became larger, other deposits went into local nonstate institutions, especially informal loans. The relation of consumption to disposable income probably reflects savings at least as well as deposits do at this time. Shanghai consumed less of its disposable income in the mid-1980s than any other province of China. Savings were relatively high in Shanghai. The specific quantities mean less on Table 1.3-9 than the order of provinces that did or did not consume the income they made. Jiangsu and Zhejiang are not far from Shanghai on the list.

Savings deposits in Shanghai by late 1986 were at an all-time high, averaging 760 yuan per person.[178] At the edge of the city, Meilong township residents' income in the sixth five-year plan rose 21 percent each year (insofar as it was reported). They did not easily spend such a quick windfall. Throughout these five years, their bank deposits grew *annually* at 39 percent.[179]

The story was similar elsewhere on the delta. Per-capita savings in Wuxi county rose almost ten times between 1978 and 1984. This was almost twice the

Table 1.3-9

Consumption and Disposable Income, by Province
(million yuan and percentages, 1985, for most provinces)

	Consumption/ disposable income	Disposable income	Consumption
Shanghai	*46%*	*304.34*	*139.51*
Beijing	49%	212.20	103.70
Tianjin	50%	139.90	69.63
Shanxi	56%	187.20	105.10
Zhejiang	*59%*	*345.48*	*203.00*
Yunnan	59%	196.83	115.45
Jiangsu	*62%*	*507.50*	*313.48*
Shaanxi	62%	192.30	119.64
Shandong	63%	501.65	317.29
Hebei	65%	328.32	214.57
Guangdong	65%	522.40	337.27
Liaoning	66%	370.54	244.91
Hubei	68%	325.22	221.10
Heilongjiang	68%	271.38	184.49
Henan	68%	370.89	251.36
Anhui	69%	276.25	190.87
Inner Mongolia	69%	147.69	101.36
Jilin	70%	187.35	130.23
Fujian	71%	176.39	124.76
Sichuan	72%	511.95	370.65
Jiangxi	73%	190.55	139.64
Hunan	74%	305.50	226.23
Guangxi	74%	179.74	133.39
Guizhou	75%	122.99	92.13

Note and source: Calculated from *Zhongguo tongji nianjian, 1987* (Statistical Yearbook of China, 1987) (Beijing: Zhongguo Tongji Chuban She, 1987), pp. 40 and 60. Some heavily subsidized "autonomous regions" in western China have been omitted.

(reported) output increase of the county's rural industries.[180] Compensation to savers may have increased more sharply than production, or savings from nonindustrial activities may have been large, or more probably some of the industrial output was unreported. Very rapid expansion of the informal service sector was also a factor in this loss of macroeconomic control.

Even within the metropolis, there was quick income growth. An economist at a Shanghai bank in 1987 admitted that people were reluctant to deposit money,

Table 1.3-10

Private Deposits of Shanghai Residents in Banks
(millions of yuan and portions, year-end)

	Shanghai savings	Shanghai GNP	Rural deposits: Rural savings	Rural deposits: % Rural	Savings/ GNP
1970	1,047	15,667	53	5	7
1975	1,466	20,412	100	7	7
1978	1,818	27,281	126	7	7
1980	3,020	31,189	256	8	10
1982	3,794	33,707	526	14	11
1984	5,610	39,085	597	11	14
1986	9,095	49,083	1,026	11	19
1988	14,121	64,830	1,547	11	22
1989	19,347	69,654	2,054	11	28
1990	22,305	74,467	2,522	11	30
1991	32,822	85,771	3,781	12	38
1992	41,309	106,594	4,509	11	39

Notes and sources: Percentages calculated from figures in *Shanghai tongji nianjian* (Shanghai Statistical Yearbook), Shanghai Shi Tongji Ju, ed. (Beijing: Zhongguo Tongji Chuban She), 1990 edition, pp. 34 and 403; 1991 edition, pp. 34 and 419; 1992 edition, pp. 33 and 455; and 1993 edition, pp. 37 and 397; as well as *Shanghai Statistical Yearbook, 1989 Concise Edition*, Municipal Statistical Bureau of Shanghai, ed. (Beijing: China Statistical Publishing House, 1989), pp. 16 and 172. Economists, concerned about the inflationary effect if many creditors withdrew their savings suddenly, urged the government to encourage gradual withdrawals by the 1990s. The problem was to find new things that people could buy, using the money without causing inflation that could damage people's livelihoods. In Shanghai's state economy, people have trouble making money, but they also have trouble spending it. High-quality consumer goods are few, and planners wish to limit the markets in other commodities (notably stocks and land). The table reports deposits by residents and non-state collectives.

because the interest rate lagged behind inflation.[181] As Table 1.3–10 shows, Shanghai bank deposits rose quickly in the 1980s, from one-tenth to three-tenths of product value. The areas with the quickest growth of all, the rural suburbs, had a lower bank deposit rate—but probably not a lower savings rate. The portion of rural deposits peaked in 1982 and was stable after the factors inflation hit industrial goods prices most heavily. Suburban people were loaning money most profitably to each other, not through state institutions.

High monetized savings became common in many rural areas. From 1981 through 1987, individual deposits skyrocketed throughout the country, showing an average *annual* increase of 34 percent. A newspaper noted, "The increase in savings deposits, however, would be bigger if prices were not rising so fast." It pointed out that "when there are no other means to maintain the value of money, such as buying gold and foreign currency, people have to deposit their money in the bank because more would be lost if they kept cash in hand. In other words, people are somewhat forced to put their money in the bank. Saving is also being forced by a shortage of goods that people want to buy, such as color television sets and high-quality bicycles."[182]

Zhejiang residents' cash in banks was 7 times, by 1987, the amount of deposits in 1980.[183] Zhejiang's total value of output increased to 3.8 times the earlier amount (not accounting for inflation) between these same years—a respectable rise, but not as quick as the sevenfold increase of deposits. The growth of reported gross industrial output value was 4.2 times over this same period. Because of probable underreporting and changed career incentives for local cadre-entrepreneurs, some of these figures may be understated, but the bank deposits are almost surely accounted best. Credit expansion in late-1980s Jiangsu was "very active." State banks could not coordinate most of this activity.

Deposits in the ordinary banking system of Jiangsu nonetheless declined in the late 1980s. People with spare money used it instead for direct loans to specialized and private enterprises, as well as to small factories run by villages.[184] These private loans garnered higher interest than banks would pay. They were most common in economically developed rural areas of Jiangsu, especially its southern part. "Loans among the people" (*minjian daikuan*) were acknowledged to have positive economic effects, raising the free circulation of funds, mobilizing idle money, and developing the commodity economy. Private loans also lessened pressures on state banks for credit.

On the other hand, the newspaper noted four major disadvantages of such private loans, from the viewpoint of the state system. First, the supply of savings for state banks declined, because the amount of these loans (whose total was unpublished and apparently unknown) was large by 1989. Second, the existence of private loans reduced the possibilities of state control over money use. Private creditors reportedly "wasted" funds (although it was not mentioned that the state sometimes did this too). Third, official banks were affected because of upward pressure on interest rates and the absorption of personnel in this informal banking system. Illegalities there often went unchecked, and especially for "loans based on personal relations" (*renqing daikuan*—a phenomenon that was frequent, though less published, in the official banks too). Fourth, the private financial system was deemed bad for economic stability.[185] The rural industrialization it financed absorbed raw materials and led to breaches of contract in the state system.

A Jiangsu official thus called for laws restricting the amount, above official interest rates, that private lenders could charge. He also called for stricter policing of all loan procedures. By 1988, when the northern Jiangsu economy began to boom, Xuzhou city had a shortfall of nearly one-third of the amount of capital that the standard plan ratio indicated should have been available for its level of production.[186] The area had a "hunger and thirst for capital," and local credit institutions were said to suffer from "bank anemia."[187] Because the "state fiscal measures were tight," the local government vowed to raise more money from ordinary citizens. This gave the economy more credit immediately, and the government less power eventually.

Within Shanghai by late August 1988, the metropolis suffered a run on banks because depositors wanted their money to buy goods before price hikes they expected. A local official said that banks throughout the city had been "plagued by long lines" of people withdrawing their money. Some were investing in silver and gold as a hedge against inflation.[188] People put their wealth in whatever financial instruments they deemed safest or profitable, and these were often local. The central bank could not reimpose macroeconomic control on this situation, in which unregulated arrangements had become common. In early 1989, the People's Bank imposed on its own branches a new rule that set a ceiling on loans regardless of deposits.[189] But it no longer tried to impose this rule on other banks, each of which could face the Party's financial politicians directly.

Was inflation the inevitable concomitant of postrevolutionary decentralization? Probably not. Periods of quick economic growth during the rundown of centralization in other countries have also sometimes been inflationary. Comparisons show, however, that the more reliable regularity is the increase of savings. Postrevolutionary France had sharply increasing deposits in savings banks. Although the usable statistics begin only in 1835, they show an extremely quick rise of deposits (16 percent annually, nearly 600 percent total) over the next dozen years to 1847.[190] New savings—mostly uncontrolled by the state—expanded smartly after the revolutionary violence and wars ended. But they did not stoke so much inflation as in China.

Much of China's savings occurred within nonfinancial institutions such as stores or factories. Reforms encouraged units to have "small treasuries" (*xiao jinku*) that were often secret and often not small. Materials shortages gave managers both a reason and an excuse to stow money wherever they could. The rise of materials prices meant that companies had to keep bigger reserves against insolvency. In a sample of Shanghai light industrial firms, the requirements for cash on hand rose almost one-quarter during the year before mid-1988.[191]

Private saving and lending boomed, and they easily went underground if the state bank tried to stop them. In Zhejiang, illegal private banks were established in public and operated openly. When high officials discovered that some private loans carried annual interest rates of more than 40 percent, they decreed guidelines for lower rates. Then they had to admit these policies had only meant that "free loan activities have become more hidden."[192]

Bonds

New nonstate enterprises created a great deal of money that sought investment instruments. Bond and stock markets were nothing new in Shanghai, even though socialist conservatives and Western journalists alike professed to be shocked by them. Aside from the prerevolutionary equities exchanges, Shanghai's bond markets had been very active in the 1950s before they were closed. Beginning at low levels during early reforms, and then nationally in 1981, the state issued large tranches of treasury bonds (*guoku zhai*). As budget deficits worsened during the late 1980s, and as opportunities for profitable investments expanded, many local governments issued bonds to raise money. There was practically no regulation of these markets until a 1987 State Council decree, which was supplemented by more rules in 1989 and 1990—but these were superseded by later rules and sometimes violated.[193]

Not just good rates of interest on bonds, but also other perquisites for bondholders, let firms garner significant funds in the mid-1980s through bond sales. When the Shanghai Petrochemical Works wanted to establish a new ethylene plant in the mid-1980s, for example, it launched a bond issue. Interest of 12 percent was offered to individual buyers—well above the 7.44 percent then for some residents' savings accounts. Enterprises that bought the bonds got less (only 8 percent, which still was more than the 3.66 percent on government one-year paper for them). Most interesting was an alternative scheme for corporate buyers: they could buy bonds that paid only 4.2 percent but included options to purchase the plant's products once it got into operation. On that basis, which was highly attractive in Shanghai at a time of materials shortage, the first tranche of bonds was quickly oversubscribed.[194]

Because of Shanghai's old reputation as a market, the city could also attract money from prosperous entrepreneurs throughout the country who wanted to buy bonds. The city's Construction Bank announced that bonds for a new plant, carrying 12 percent interest, would be sold on November 25, 1986. The queue began forming at midnight on the previous day, and the line was a thousand people long when the bank opened the next morning. Some investors "came especially to Shanghai from other parts of the country, to buy the bonds."[195]

Regulatory Relations and Rural Markets

Commercial paper, under which one company gives credit to another at interest, was legally phased out after 1949. Such loans "resurfaced in Shanghai after 1981," even without the benefit of laws to enforce repayment. Not until 1988 did the municipal government pass a regulation to make this kind of contract binding. Then, "the new law will only apply to those commercial papers signed, issued, negotiated, and paid in Shanghai, including drafts, cheques, and cashier's cheques."[196] In this and other areas, Party conservatives were slow to give legal recognition to a routine that reduced their ability to monitor the economy. These practices developed anyway, without any regulation. Institutions that grew without the state's blessing, if they were not hidden but also not politically dissident, tended at first to be haughtily ignored by state intellectuals. These institutions were not official and not intentionally political, so how could they be important?

Regulation was thus delayed for some time after the trading of commercial paper began. By October 1988, Shanghai was only the second PRC city to make systematic rules governing the negotiation of bills, checks, and promissory notes. This was a local law. Despite its clear reliance on the Chinese text of provisions from a previous statute on Taiwan, where capitalism is rampant, these rules did not cause a quick acceleration of exchanges in corporate paper.[197] Even before regulation, this practice had already been growing rapidly. It then expanded into some personal checking.

Previous socialist regulations were loosened at this time. PRC treasury bonds, such as had been sold in the 1950s, could be freely traded under the law only in 1988. Before that time, prudent and legal investors were obliged to wait for the expiry dates before realizing any money. Shanghai for years had eight official exchange centers—but as was usual for state agencies, they charged very high commissions. "Why should I trade in there?" one bondholder reportedly asked after the monopoly ended. Unofficial brokers, on the street outside the state agencies, started to do the same business for less commission.[198]

Rural money markets remained mostly illegal. That detail did not keep them from flourishing. Like other unregulated capital markets, they were subject to very sharp fluctuations. The Wenzhou money market, for example, crashed in early 1989. Local people called it a "second Cultural Revolution." More than a hundred thousand individuals reportedly suffered losses.

> Unregistered financial societies are built on family networks. Members borrow money from each other for working capital and sometimes apparently for speculation. . . . Some of these money societies have grown so large that they have exceeded the boundaries of family and clan relations. Participants have no way to know the credit situation until, all of a sudden, the society goes broke. . . . In the development of township enterprises and the management of rural money, the role of local authorities is minimal.[199]

According to this report, 95 percent of the funds needed by Wenzhou rural and private enterprises came from local sources rather than the state banking system.

Wild financial schemes proliferated in many rural parts of East China at this time, even though Wenzhou was extreme, partly because the returns on capital could be so high. The oddest examples come from Wenzhou, but they test the limits of what could happen more moderately elsewhere too. A furniture factory there found a bold and enterprising method to boost immediate sales: It offered a 12 percent rebate on the cost of its products after five years, or the entire money back after sixteen years. To guarantee its own payment, it put 15 percent of its annual profits in a local credit cooperative that offered interest and acted as guarantor. Furniture sales doubled each month during the first ten months of this scheme.[200]

Another side of the Wenzhou story is that unofficial capital flows could be more safely reported there than elsewhere. They sharply reduced the business of the state's banks. As a Chinese economist says:

> . . . Non-governmental lending has developed, including both direct lending between peasants and indirect forms of credit. There are not only various "associations" (*hui*), but also a few old-style private banks (*qianzhuang*). Due to excess demand relative to supply, as well as on account of speculation and profiteering by some people, the rate of interest on loans among the people is very high. The volume of deposits taken by the Agricultural Bank and the cooperatives has been affected [this is always the state dialect's word for 'reduced'] by the high interest rate on loans among the people.[201]

Stocks

The Shanghai Stock Market is worth a book and many articles—and they are being written.[202] Shares were first sold in Shanghai in 1882, and the local stock exchange grew along with the capitalist economy, until closure in the early 1950s. Business ownership sales were then regulated under socialist laws, not until 1978 but until the mid-1980s. In the quarter century before 1984, no shares of any company were legally bought or sold in Shanghai. By that year, rules still forbade enterprises from selling more than 15 percent of their worth to any individual, or even to any collective.[203] Supervisory socialist corporations were line items on official budgets. No matter how dismally their planners performed, they were the effective owners of the stores and factories below them; and they had scant incentive to recommend selling stock.

During China's postrevolutionary reforms, the "shares system" (*gufen zhi*) was instituted late, in January 1985, and it expanded very slowly.[204] In that year, Shanghai Feile Acoustics was the first PRC company to sell stock. The Shanghai Stock Market was relegitimated in September 1986. On its board, nearly fifteen thousand of the city's enterprises soon sold bonds, although only twenty firms sold shares at this stage.[205]

A suitably intellectual-statist justification for stock markets came from a very unexpected field: birth planning. Population policy depends on financial markets, because parents have children partly for support in old age, which pensions also provide. Bond and equity exchanges are supposed to preserve wealth for old people's social security. A relatively trustworthy mechanism in which savings can earn interest is crucial. Reforming foxes argued, though conservative lions disbelieved, that good socialist planning of population size would require stock markets.

Reopening the Shanghai Stock Market was a media event, on which news was leaked in phases. The scope of the market's operation was extended on several occasions in the late 1980s, and each was reported as a revolution. First came a government announcement that this archetypal symbol of capitalism might again raise its head in Shanghai. Bonds were then traded. The market slowly listed a very few stocks. Each "opening" of the market has been a cause for fanfare in the style of a striptease. Party conservatives braved the advent of this most risqué market, but they made sure that nonstate reformers were lured to pay for every step. Here was evidence, from the Chinese city with the most sordid financial history, to convince capitalist investors throughout the world that the Communist coverings of reform would be no bar to progress.

Investment Fever and Categories of Shares

Shareholding boomed in Shanghai during 1987, when several large state enterprises, especially the Shanghai Vacuum Electrical Appliance Co., raised capital by selling a good deal of stock. About a year later, the city had nine enterprises issuing shares. By late 1988, only eleven Shanghai firms sold stocks, but more than 350,000 people in the city owned equities. Shanghai Yanzhong sold its whole first tranche, at a face value of 4.5 million yuan, in a mere six hours.

Shanghai Vacuum soon came to dominate Shanghai's nascent stock market because of the amount it offered to the public. Its manager said the purpose was to separate ownership from management, so as to reduce administrative interference in economic decisions. Shanghai Feile Acoustics Company sold stock mostly to its own workers, of whom 77 percent purchased shares, with the aim of raising their interest in their jobs.[206]

The State Council decreed in 1987 that no state-owned firm could issue stock on its own. Exceptions soon proliferated, however. At various times (e.g. February 1992, with Deng Xiaoping's "southern tour"), these restrictions were at least temporarily lifted. No enterprises were sold off fully. The state, as represented by the original supervising corporation, retained many shares. Others were sold to "legal persons," which were often other state agencies. Cadres who had run the selling corporation earlier could still muster a controlling majority of shares. A price was imputed for state shares—but then the People's Bank of China often charged four or five times that much to unofficial buyers. Administrative control was ensured for Party conservatives on a continuing basis, while outside money could be raised for reform.

The categories of shares were four: state (*guojia*), legal persons (*faren*), individuals (*geti*), and foreigners. The "legal persons" were collective or state organizations; in practice, they were often companies with which the firm had long enjoyed commercial relations. When companies were "sharized" (*gufen hua*), the manager usually became the new chief executive officer. The Party secretary was often dubbed chair of the board.[207] Capitalist gestures were made and new money was mobilized, but no further real change was necessary. Shanghai firms that went public in this controlled way were often in financial straits. Some could not pay much in taxes. Even when no other change was made, however, the managers sometimes did a better job after the ownership change.

This effect was most pronounced among joint ventures, which used shares involving specific overseas owners. A striking example was the Shanghai Construction Machinery Factory, into which a Hong Kong company put "cash only"—and enough of that to buy only a "small" percentage of the firm. None of the managers was changed. The "form and functions of the Party organization were left unaltered." The Party secretary still participated in management decisions, especially on personnel. The firm's tax on profits was not reduced at all. Although a consultant's survey showed that two hundred of the nine hundred employees really should have been fired, to improve the plant's efficiency, only two workers were let go. The Hong Kong partners were not represented at the plant on a permanent basis. They visited just once a year, to ask questions, make sure the accounts were accurate, and take their share of the profits.

Yet *Liberation Daily,* the local Party newspaper, reported a beneficial "joint venture effect," even at this plant where outside participation was very casual. The small nonstate ownership meant that "superior-subordinate relations between the company and the government were weakened, inspections and appraisals were reduced, and the organizational setup was determined independently." Purchases no longer had to be approved by higher levels. Wage bonuses were no longer taxed through the company, but through an individual income tax. Nonstate partners meant that the government no longer guaranteed the company's materials or its markets—but the firm could now seek both upstream purchases and downstream sales on its own. It could bargain freely on prices for these. The outside capital was far less important than the firm's ability, for these reasons, to accumulate new money (partly by keeping wages low). The symbolic value of being a joint enterprise lessened "ownership by the state" and strengthened local managers at the expense of supervisory cadres. So the ownership change made habits more efficient, even when nothing else changed. Efficiency rose, if only to ensure that the investors would get the rate of return they expected.[208]

Firms often sold shares at the low, first-issue price to important officials. General "stock market fever" in Shanghai normally ensured that the value would rise after public offering. This was common—and legal, though a skeptic might call it a form of corruption.

A maximum of one-quarter of the shares of any Chinese company may be offered for public sale, under rules prevalent in the early 1990s. No individual may own more than one-twentieth. The pressure for disclosure of financial information is therefore not great. Official stockholders are always the majority. When Chinese state firms were approved by the government for listing on stock markets, some legal conditions had to be met. Fewer than half of the shares could be sold publicly: "A" shares to domestic PRC buyers, or "B" or "H" shares internationally. Majority ownership had to remain with the state. Also, firms with shares listed overseas had to establish a "surplus reserve fund" to support pensions if the company went bankrupt. The PRC would not approve firms suffering huge losses to be listed abroad, lest Chinese investments in general acquire a bad reputation. A "welfare fund" was also legally required. An official holding company would be established to exercise the state's majority vote in the "privatized" firm to manage these two funds, and to make sure that no management decisions threatened political instability among the workers.[209]

The 1990s Stock Markets

By December 1990, no securities law had yet attained sufficient political consensus within the government to be passed. But reformers were eager to encourage foreign investors and to soak up domestic personal savings, then estimated at more than U.S. $200 billion. Six weeks after the market reopened in its late 1990 form, only eight stocks and twenty-two bonds were listed. One of these (Shanghai Vacuum) accounted for 84 percent of the capitalization.[210] After that, the market somewhat diversified.

Socialist conservatives have nonetheless been unwilling to see very many large state plants go on the auction block. Although their sale could raise funds while also improving management, this source of credit was reformed very slowly because of ideology and socialist jobs. In the future, and especially for new companies, local money could nonetheless become important for Shanghai's economy, as it was even for foreign-associated companies before 1949.

A more extensive stock market opened in 1990 in renovated rooms of the Pujiang Hotel near the Bund. The main aim was to sell state securities, but a few other stocks (already being traded less formally) were also listed. The "transaction hall" was equipped with modern computers, several dozen small rooms for bargaining, and electronic transmission of prices "to 47 transaction centers and service spots scattered around the city to keep a consistent quotation both in and outside the securities exchange."[211]

The Jing'an Stock Index has fluctuated wildly. It more than doubled, for example, between May and November of 1992, but then fell from a peak of 1,400 to 300. It soared back up to 1,500 in March 1993, then down to 1,000 two months later.[212] Riding this roller coaster, China had three thousand joint stock companies nationwide by 1994, although only four hundred were listed on the Shanghai Stock Exchange (and five hundred in Shenzhen, but only eight on the more seriously licensed Hong Kong exchange).[213] Regulators abroad needed many kinds of information before approving wider listings. These were data that Chinese state managers had long deemed confidential "business secrets." If they were fully revealed, tax extraction would rise. Stocks in PRC state enterprises performed abysmally in the mid-1990s. The most solid of these "red chips" were surveyed by the Hang Seng China Enterprise Index, which fell by two-thirds from the fourth quarter of 1993 to the fourth quarter of 1995.[214]

The uncertainties of evaluating enterprises did not dampen many Chinese investors' enthusiasm for less formal, decentralized stock offerings. Despite a lack of laws to protect folk transactions, peasants created their own local stock markets. Cooperative finance was a long-standing tradition among rural leaders, even if the PRC government charged high prices to countenance it in large-scale industry. As a Chinese source reported in English:

> A peasant service agency has been set up for selling shares in Yishan District, Tielong County [Zhejiang], where peasants joined the agency by purchasing shares and electing a board of directors which takes care of routine matters. In the Pingyang Woolen Mill, workers join the mill by purchasing shares, with each worker investing 500 yuan .... The mill has issued 300 shares altogether, and 70 percent of factory profits are shared out. The emergence of a general share market is inevitable and is wholly necessary to allow the growth of individual enterprises or large labor-hiring households, at least in the short term.[215]

Fully 29 percent of all PRC shareholders in early 1994 lived in Shanghai, Jiangsu, or Zhejiang.[216] Jiangnan investors took to securities markets with great gusto. Stocks will once again become a major form of finance in the Shanghai area.

The Boom or Bust Cycle

Business cycles have been a pattern in China, as elsewhere, for many years even under socialism. Seven business cycles were identifiable from midcentury to the mid-1990s, with an average length of 4.6 years. The frequency of the cycle seems to have increased during the 1980s and 1990s, with a trough showing 4 percent national GNP growth in 1981, a high of 15 percent in 1984; then another relative low of 8 percent in 1986, up to 11 percent in 1988; then down again to 4 percent by 1991, but soaring to 13 percent in 1992.[217]

Government conservatives were interested in the cycle because of inflation, not growth. Their structures were running out of money to operate as prices rose. The main event that focused attention on the business cycle was the mid-1980s structural reaction to the factors crisis. The economic restructuring of 1985 caused increases of China's money supply by about one-quarter in that year and again in the next two, and reported inflation rates of 8.8 percent, 6 percent, and 7.2 percent in those years.

China's money supply was thus badly out of control by late 1987, when the "social commodity purchasing power" reached 690 billion yuan (one-fifth more than in 1986). Public demand for consumer durables was intense. Officials were aghast at this market expansion. As one official complained, "Although all this can stimulate industrial development for a short time . . . it cannot sustain development for a long time because of the absence of a solid base."[218] This wide extension of social credit was not just an economic phenomenon; it also hurt many bureaucrats' power.

As a conservative analysis admitted, "Many departments in the national economy are still ill-adapted to such a high industrial growth rate. Thus, there are shortages and strains. For example, as a result of the present heavy pressures on railroad transportation, there is an overstocking of coal and phosphate ores in southwest China, of coal and raw salt in northwest China, and of timber and corn in northeast China." The main recommendation was to "check the growth in social demand."[219] Without reversing the reforms' prosperity, it was unclear how this could be done.

By 1988, planners called for a reduction of China's money supply by almost one-third. The lions wanted slower growth, even if that meant less trade. The Bank of China planned to "self-supply" its own credit by collections on old loans and by increased deposits. The bank garnered by self-supply 38 percent of the capital it used in 1987, as compared to 31 percent in 1986. The plan was to raise this portion to 60 percent in 1988.[220] "Self-supply" largely meant enforcing loan contracts, rather than letting loans go unpaid.

But by this time, many companies had joined unregulated credit cooperatives in extraplan lending. Managers' discretionary funds were supposed to be restricted in both amount and use by State Council proclamation. For example, the Cabinet decreed that managers' funds in 1988 should be reduced 20 percent below the 1987 levels—but in the first seven months of 1988, actual expenditures for such funds *rose* 20 percent instead.[221] The total for discretionary funds in those months was greater than the sum of money for all urban construction and education—almost 37 billion yuan throughout the country. Dinners paid for by managers of publicly owned firms reportedly contributed between 60 and 70 percent of the total income of all large and medium size restaurants in China. To get raw materials, it was necessary to wine and dine cadres who could deliver them. Another major cost, typically from managers' funds, was the import of "company" cars. A third use of such money was to purchase items for employees, such as luggage, overcoats, even food. But there was no effective way to check local managers' uses of these funds, so state leaders were mainly eager to reduce their amounts. Decrees to this effect were made—with uncertain results, because managers for many years had been well trained in methods of hiding money.

On October 1, 1988, new "provisional regulations on cash administration" banned monetary transactions by state firms and agencies, including military units, except through monitored bank accounts.[222] Ceiling amounts were set for cash on hand. "Account transfer certificates" were required to prove that expenditures conformed to plans. Such rules might have related the profitability of firms more closely to efficiency and less to speculation—but they could not be enforced. Local state organizations spent 20 percent more in the first seven months of 1988 than in the same period of the previous year, despite central orders to lower their budgets. Bans on new purchases were circumvented. As a government official explained, "They get the garage to write a receipt for car repairs equal to the cost of a new car. A copying machine is billed [vaguely] as 'electrical items.' Who cares? It's the state's money."[223] There was now a great deal more such money, and nominal cadres of the state were mostly supporting their local structures instead.

Coastal regions' recovery from the 1987–89 credit austerity was much quicker than the recovery of inland China. In the first half of 1990, Jiangsu was among the coastal provinces to register industrial growth of about 5 percent "while the overall economy [including the coast] just crept along with a 2.3 percent growth."[224] By the end of the 1980s, it was explicit that credit for farming was to be less tightly restricted than industrial credit.[225] The growth of rural industries was explicitly supposed to be slowed, and peasants were to be helped to go back to fields. This proposal seemed most convincing to urban bureaucrats. The Agricultural Bank was supposed to support only field (as distinct from rural industrial) production "with all its strength." But it was very unclear how such money, given to rural units at low levels after so much administrative decentralization, could be kept from its most profitable uses, which were industrial.

Forty percent of China's state-sector plants were officially reported to be running in the red by 1991, up from 34 percent in 1990.[226] The 1991 Chinese economy was growing (real GNP was 7 percent higher than in 1990), but the healthy firms were generally nonstate. The government could not openly abandon its local structures, which in any case had enough influence to ensure that local banks would keep socialist firms from collapse if they supported local interests. The economic boom kept this system afloat while eroding its foundations. Central Party conservatives and reformers alike had no choice but to let China's new local economic systems prosper out of control, because the demand they generated was apparently crucial for keeping many state investments profitable and preventing recession.

The 1992 reformist resurgence made news with Deng Xiaoping's "southern tour," but it was linked to political interests extending far beyond the top leaders of the state. Changes at that time benefited Beijing less than they benefited other parts of China's polity. So local leaders could gladly speak of them in the conventional and legitimate way, as benefits bestowed by high officials and especially the preeminent leader. Specifically, tax rates on local enterprises were lowered, municipal bureaucrats referred fewer investment decisions to ministries in Beijing, and restrictions on the Shanghai stock exchange and financial institutions were somewhat reduced.

Jiangsu retail prices at the beginning of 1993 continued to suffer nearly double-digit inflation. In cities, the annualized rate was over 12 percent then. The reason was not hard to find; at the end of 1992, China's currency in circulation was once again a quarter (27 percent) above the amount one year earlier.[227] In mid-1993, Acting Premier Zhu Rongji fired the head of China's central bank, took the job himself, and declared war on the expansion of credit. Many in Shanghai expressed less concern. Especially with the Pudong plans prospering and with some reversal of the discrimination Shanghai had long suffered, the local mood was expansionist. "'No one here is worried at all,' said a Chinese lawyer based among the chain-link fences and dusty construction sites that cover Pudong. 'We have 35 office buildings over 20 stories tall, expected to come on line in the next three years.'"[228]

Beijing showed predictable concern about this inflation and overheating. Whatever the top leaders' reasons, their warnings may prove on economic grounds to have been correct. The size of the economic danger was difficult to judge, partly because official interests could inspire overrreporting of the problem. Central government conservatives were nostalgic to restore a structure in which they controlled credit, using funds as in the past on pet projects (the Three Gorges Dam was the most obvious current example). Conservatives only sometimes weighed carefully the economic value of such investments, as compared with alternative uses of money, or the speed with which they would regenerate capital. This was the macroeconomic threat from the conservatives, most likely to show up as inefficiency rather than inflation.

On the other hand, the opposite macroeconomic threat from reformers was also great. Many serious Chinese economists were concerned to limit the quick expansion of the money supply that the PRC experienced in the early 1990s—which was largely used for the pet projects of local cadres rather than those of central leaders. If no controls on credit succeeded, Chinese consumer and investor confidence, prices, and output could go through sharp gyrations. By 1993, many Party cadres at many levels realized that the lack of macroeconomic control (no matter whether it came in the conservative or reform versions) could become a threat to China's political stability.

The mechanism by which such a crisis might occur is classic: Businesses that used credit, e.g. to expand capacity expecting higher demand, could quickly find their expectations were wrong. Then they could not pay debts. Their creditors, in turn mostly debtors to other units, would likewise default, furthering the syndrome and lowering demand. The extent to which early-1990s credit expansion in China was justified by future demand was a question on which data were inherently not yet available. A common guess among intellectuals was that the boom in China's economy could lead to a recession. Even if this was later followed by another expansion, the temporary fall-off of performance could hurt the regime's legitimacy—just as economic success was its main strength after Tiananmen.

It is far easier to predict this pattern when macroeconomic controls are weak, however, than to predict the dates when such things actually occur. The roller-coaster economy may or may not be the most practicable way to make China grow. Its influence on the politics of the world's largest socialist state was easier to predict. Some business cycles were evident as reforms deregulated many economic activities. But a sharp recession, such as China's macroeconomy may have been breeding by the mid-1990s, could create violent politics, not just volatile economic indices.

This cloud may have a silver lining: There may be no other means except a sharp recession to achieve thorough economic restructuring of inefficient state industries. If the central government would find it politically too dangerous, because of labor unrest, to close money-losing plants, perhaps it is in most Chinese people's eventual interest that a recession force this instead.

A second but very different possibility is that the much-discussed recession may not occur. Most econometricians do not claim to have tools to measure, even in rough terms, the extent or longevity of pent-up demand in a decentralizing economy like China's. The massive, uncontrolled credit expansions could eventually prove to have been justified. Even these markets may be as rational as some economic theorists like to claim all markets are. It is difficult to prove sustained irrationality, even in a sharply fluctuating market, until a time too late for policy to do much good. If that turns out to be the case in reform China, the ominous recession could at least be much delayed.[229] No really good framework for knowing these things yet has any consensus; so top CCP politicians, who were risk-averse about danger, sporadically decreed credit crunches. Local leaders who wanted money for local projects sporadically got around them.

Notes

1. *Asian Wall Street Journal,* December 2, 1993. The reference came through the courtesy of Prof. Jan Prybyla.

2. In mid-1996, Prof. Jean C. Oi convened a conference in Hong Kong that brought together new research by many young and active scholars concerning ownership rights in China. Their papers will almost surely appear together in book form.

3. Much of the military economy is included here, although the exact percentage in the text above is not certain. See Barry Naughton, "Industrial Policy During the Cultural Revolution: Military Preparation, Decentralization, and Leaps Forward," in *New Perspectives on the Cultural Revolution,* William Joseph, Christine Wong, and David Zweig, eds. (Cambridge: Harvard University Press, 1991), p. 166.

4. Peter N. S. Lee, *Industrial Management and Economic Reform in China, 1949–1984* (Hong Kong: Oxford University Press, 1987), p. 104.

5. The famous slogan is "*guandu shangban.*" For historical analysis of this in light of current Shanghai problems, see Hong Ze et al., *Shanghai yanjiu luncong: Di yi ji* (Papers on Studies of Shanghai: First Set) (Shanghai: Shanghai Shehui Kexue Yuan Chuban She, 1988), pp. 164–65.

6. These were *zhengfu hangye guanli bumen* and *minjian hangye xiehui.* Li Pan, Li Douheng, and Chu Zhongxin et al., *Gaige yu kaifang xin wenti yanjiu* (Studies of New Questions in Reform and Opening) (Shanghai: Shanghai Shehui Kexue Yuan Chuban She, 1987), pp. 52–53.

7. Ibid., p. 51.

8. *SHJJDB,* August 1, 1988.

9. *Jingli fuze zhi.* Zhang Shanmin, Li Xin, Wu Zhangnan et al., *Zou xiang chenggong* (Marching to Accomplishments) (Shanghai: Shanghai Shehui Kexue Yuan Chuban She, 1988), p. 107.

10. *SHJJYJ,* September 1985, p. 23.

11. On the difference between *zhiling xing jihua* and merely *zhidao xing jihua,* see ibid.

12. These higher-level units are generically called *gongxiao bumen* or *shangye bumen.* See ibid., p. 24.

13. "*Jinpai, yinpai bu ru zapai ziyou.*" In ibid.

14. "*Zhe shi guojia tiele chaopiao, rang geti hu facai.*" Ibid., p. 25.

15. Ibid. This system was called *tongshou, tongzhi.*

16. Ibid.

17. This responsibility is called *shehui fudan*. Some of the specific factory funds mentioned in the text were called the *zaofang zijin, gongren tuixiu jin, zhurou jiage butie,* and *ying you er tuo fei*. Ibid., p. 25.

18. Ibid.

19. The factory managers' responsibility system is called the *changzhang fuze zhi*. Ibid., p. 26. See Franz Schurmann, *Ideology and Organization in Communist China* (Berkeley: University of California Press, 1966) on the "single manager system" (*yizhang zhi*) of the 1950s, adopted then from a Soviet ideal.

20. "*Chuilian tingzheng,*" in *SHJJYJ,* September 1985, p. 25, suggests an analogy between factory Party committees and the Dowager Empress, Ci Xi, the most widely detested figure in modern Chinese history.

21. State ownership is not a simple concept, because major management roles (including various supply and marketing roles) can be transferred between central, provincial, and other levels. These issues are not raised in the text above, in order to allow a focus on ambiguities in the word "collective" instead; but they are classically discussed in Audrey Donnithorne, *China's Economic System* (New York: Praeger, 1967), and Barry Richman, *Industrial Society in Communist China* (New York: Random House, 1969). Christine Wong and others have written more recently about this.

22. Cheng Xiaonong, "The Structure of Economic Growth in China: An Approach to Measuring the Contribution of the Public and Non-Public Sectors, and Some Estimations" (unpublished paper, Princeton University, 1993), pp. 1–2.

23. This is superbly documented by Thomas B. Gold, in "Urban Private Business and Social Change," in *Chinese Society on the Eve of Tiananmen: The Impact of Reform,* Deborah Davis and Ezra Vogel, eds. (Cambridge: Harvard University Press, 1990), pp. 157–78.

24. See Liu Gang et al., *Shanghai chengshi jiti suoyou zhi gongye yanjiu* (Studies of Shanghai's Urban Collective Industries) (Shanghai: Shanghai Renmin Chuban She, 1980), especially pp. 97ff.

25. *Shanghai shehui xiankuang he qushi, 1980–1983* (Situations and Trends in Shanghai Society, 1980–1983), Zheng Gongliang et al., eds. (Shanghai: Huadong Shifan Daxue Chuban She, 1988), pp. 79–80.

26. Cheng Xiaonong, an economic sociologist who studied at Princeton University and who knows a great deal about the structure of PRC production, has made these calculations. Data published openly in China about output by ownership sector are not recent (after 1986, these tables were apparently shifted into classified *neibu* statistical yearbooks, whose existence is confirmed for Shanghai but which were not available for this study). In any case, even the published PRC data that are sometimes cited here in raw form need further testing for several reasons. First, although GNP figures are now reported in Chinese statistical yearbooks, these numbers are not sums based on sectoral surveys, as per the international standard method for calculating GNP. Instead, they are generally just figured from social gross output value (*shehui zongchan zhi*) at central and provincial levels according to a mathematical formula decreed by the State Statistical Bureau. GNP, used elsewhere in this book, refers only to such numbers; but Cheng Xiaonong has attempted to circumvent this problem in his calculations. Second, the quasi-private nature of many collective enterprises, combined with the relative clarity of the definition of state firms proper, makes estimates of state sector size more meaningful than estimates for the private, collective, or residual sectors. Third, although relatively straightforward means exist to figure outputs by ownership category in agriculture, industry, and construction, the tertiary service sector (divided for statistical reporting into transportation, trade, and services) presents more difficulties. Much more on approaches to solving

these econometric difficulties is in ibid. The data cited for the cities are in Cheng Xiaonong, "The Structure of Economic Growth in China," on pp. 10, 13, and 16, respectively.

27. Interestingly, there was also a reported 1990–91 rise in the portion of Guangdong gross industrial output from state plants, albeit from a lower base than in Shanghai (from 35 to 37 percent). This is all based on the sources for Table 1.3–1 and on the 1992 editions of the same yearbooks on the following pages: Shanghai, p. 109; Zhejiang, p. 146; Jiangsu, p. 135; Guangdong, p. 184; and China, p. 408.

28. *The Economist,* "When China Wakes: A Survey of China" (November 28– December 4, 1992).

29. Chen Benlin et al., *Gaige kaifang shenzhou jubian* (Great Change in the Sacred Land [China] During Reform and Opening) (Shanghai: Jiaotong Daxue Chuban She, 1984), p. 34.

30. In Guangdong, 66 percent was state and 28 percent collective in 1988. In Jiangsu, 59 percent was state and 37 percent collective. Calculated from raw figures in *Zhongguo chengshi tongji nianjian, 1988* (Statistical Yearbook of Chinese Cities, 1988), State Statistical Bureau, ed. (Beijing: Zhongguo Tongji Xinxi Zixun Fuwu Zhongxin, 1988), pp. 158–64 for the state sector figures, pp. 167–73 for the collectives, and pp. 176–82 for the private firms.

31. A very nice example, not from Shanghai, is in Vivienne Shue, "Beyond the Budget: Finance Organization and Reform in a Chinese County," *Modern China* 10:2 (April 1984), p. 165.

32. *CNA* 1409 (May 1, 1990), p. 3.

33. National reformers, such as Zhao Ziyang, tended to adopt the coastal viewpoint on these matters. Many local conservatives were either Beijing appointees or trade union officials whose followers worked in state plants.

34. "*Quanguo yipan qi*" was a slogan in the title of a famous *Red Flag* article by Shanghai's radical centralist mayor Ke Qingshi, an associate of both Mao Zedong and Lin Biao, who died just before he could lead the Cultural Revolution in Shanghai.

35. "*Yousheng, lietai.*" *SHGYJJB,* August 4, 1988.

36. See *SHGYJJB,* August 4, 1988.

37. A debate flourishes between scholars such as Jean Oi, who stress that corporatist leaders stymie the market's ability to allocate resources and income, and other scholars such as Victor Nee, who stress the market's ability to do that. Other researchers mediate this dispute by focusing on the background conditions, in William L. Parish, Xiaoye Zhe, and Fang Li, "Nonfarm Work and Marketization of the Chinese Countryside," *China Quarterly* 143 (September 1995), p. 698; and for part of the next paragraph, p. 709.

38. Yan Tingchang, Cai Beihua, Xu Zhihe et al., *Shanghai lüyou ye de jintian he mingtian* (Shanghai Tourism Today and Tomorrow) (Shanghai: Shanghai Shehui Kexue Yuan Chuban She, 1987), p. 74.

39. The State Council's plan was entitled *Guanyu Shanghai jingji fazhan zhanlue de huibao tigang.* The documents mentioned next above were called the *Shanghai jingji fazhan zhanlue,* the *Shanghai shi chengshi zongti guihua,* and the *Shanghai shi wenhua fazhan zhanlue.* See the lecture by Shanghai County Party Secretary Shang Yafei, in *Yige chengjiao xiangcun de jintian he mingtian*: *Shanghai shi Shanghai xian Meilong xiang jingji fazhan zongti guihua yanjiu* (A Suburban Village Today and Tomorrow: Comprehensive Plan for the Economic Development of Meilong Town, Shanghai County, Shanghai), Ling Yaochu and Zhang Zhaoan, eds. (Shanghai: Shanghai Shehui Kexue Chuban She, 1988), pp. 1–6. For much more about Shanghai's urban development plan, approved on October 13, 1986, see *JFRB,* November 6, 1986.

40. The total number of enterprises in Shanghai at that time was reported as 5,288. *XMWB,* April 19, 1989.

41. *CD,* September 18, 1990.

42. Compare the ideas of another sometime modernist, the Dalai Lama, about social choice by his main oracle (on matters as important as whether, when, and by what exact route to leave Lhasa), in Tenzin Gyasto, *Freedom in Exile: The Autobiography of the Dalai Lama* (New York: Harper Collins, 1990).

43. Some businesspeople in Hong Kong think the Zhou dynasty strategist Sun Zi offers particularly valuable pointers on how to deal with commercial competitors. A society named after Sun, including both Chinese and Western entrepreneurs, has met in China to discuss the business relevance of his precepts. See also *CD,* December 17, 1990.

44. Susan L. Shirk, *The Political Logic of Economic Reform in China* (Berkeley: University of California Press, 1993).

45. The numerical portions reported above were respectively 61 percent, 72 percent, and 83 percent. The technique of this survey, involving a mix of large and small state firms in proportion to their outputs, was relatively sophisticated. *SHJJYJ,* September 1985, p. 23.

46. The exact Chinese romanization of these ten different managerial powers, presented in the same order as above, is worth noting because it shows the official way of differentiating the different kinds of acts managers can take: *zizhu tiaozheng quan, zixiao chanpin fanwei er wu chanpin zixiao quan, chao jihua shengchan chanpin wu jiage fudong quan, zixing xuangou quan, zixuan gongzi xingshi zijin shiyong quan, duoyu xianzhi guding zichan chuzhi quan, jigou shezhi quan, renshi laodong guanli quan, bufen zhigong jinji quan, kua bumen kua diqu xuandian lianying quan.* See *SHJJYJ,* September 1985, p. 23.

47. *Asian Wall Street Journal,* January 31, 1989.

48. Susan L. Shirk, *The Political Logic,* p. 281.

49. *FBIS,* November 26, 1986, p. 4, reporting radio of November 20. This is the source of the next quotation in the text also.

50. Ibid.

51. *FBIS,* November 26, 1986, p. 3, reporting radio of November 20.

52. *FBIS,* November 26, 1986, p. 4, reporting radio of November 20.

53. Ibid.

54. Interview with an economist at the Shanghai Academy of Social Sciences.

55. The contracts were *chengbao jingying hetong. JFRB,* April 1, 1988.

56. The three methods were respectively called *shangjiao lirun jishu baogan/cengzhang fencheng, shangjiao lirun ding'e baogan,* and *shangjiao lirun diceng baogan.*

57. Wang Yu et al., *Da zhuanbian shiqi* (The Era of Great Transformation) (Shijiazhuang: Hebei Renmin Chuban She, 1987), p. 155.

58. Ibid., p. 156.

59. *JJRB,* January 22, 1988.

60. Ibid.

61. *CD,* January 30, 1988.

62. This kind of company is called a *taozhai gongsi. JFRB,* May 9, 1988.

63. Ibid.

64. Interview with a knowledgeable economist in Shanghai, who had seen these figures in print. In the next text sentence, a "godown" is standard China coast English for a warehouse.

65. Huang Weixin, *Economic Integration as a Development Device: The Case of the EC and China* (Saarbrücken: Nijmegen Studies in Development, Breitenbach Verlag, 1992), pp. 127–28.

66. *The Economist,* November 30, 1991; *FEER,* August 23, 1990.

67. See the 1957 complaints, during the Hundred Flowers, of nonintellectual small businesspeople who had nationalized their firms but then were abandoned by Party bureaucrats who had promised supplies and capital to them before their acceptance of the 1956 Transition to Socialism. Lynn White, "Leadership in Shanghai, 1955–69," in *Elites in the People's Republic of China,* Robert A. Scalapino, ed. (Seattle: University of Washington Press, 1972), pp. 302–77.

68. *XMWB,* January 5, 1982.

69. Guilhem Fabre, "The Chinese Mirror of Transition," *Communist Economies and Economic Transformation* 4:2 (1992), p. 262.

70. Edward J. Epstein, "China's Legal Reforms," in *China Review,* Kuan Hsin-chi and Maurice Brosseau, eds. (Hong Kong: Chinese University Press, 1991), p. 9.10.

71. *CD,* March 13, 1988.

72. *FBIS,* November 14, 1986, p. 3, reporting radio of November 8.

73. *CD,* March 1, 1989.

74. Ibid.

75. Yao Shihuang, *Jin sanjiao de tansuo* (Search for the Golden Delta) (Chongqing: Chongqing Chuban She, 1988), pp. 140–44.

76. Ibid., pp. 145–54.

77. *Jianjie guanli* was summed up in the four characters "*fang, yi, zhuan, gai.*" *JFRB,* March 19, 1987.

78. The charters of some large firms already allowed flexibility in this respect; "scope of management" is *jingying fanwei. SHJJ,* April 1988, p. 63.

79. These *xieye* firms were, however, 38 percent fewer in 1987 than in 1986. Clearly the government was trying to prohibit closures. Ibid.

80. Quoted from *JJYJ,* 4 (1988), in Huang Weixin, *Economic Integration,* p. 81.

81. *CD,* March 16, 1988.

82. *Tudi zheng* is colloquial for *tudi fangchan suoyou zheng. FBIS,* December 29, 1987, p. 40, reporting radio of December 24.

83. *FBIS,* December 17, 1984, p. 2, reporting radio of December 15.

84. This phenomenon was rural, not urban. Nine-tenths of the land was occupied illegally. Kate Xiao Zhou cites an article by Ma Gujun in *Dangdai* (The Present Generation) 5 (1991). The suggestion about house-raising is based less on reports of rural America before the present century than on observations by the author in various parts of South China during 1994.

85. From *Hubei ribao,* October 25, 1981, in Daniel Kelliher, *Peasant Power: The Era of Rural Reform, 1979–1989* (New Haven: Yale University Press, 1993), p. 179.

86. The current author has thus far been unable to obtain enough data from rural areas of the Shanghai delta about the lineage relations of sibs that continued to cooperate in farming, or about possible demands for part of the land they knew had been tilled by their ancestors.

87. See *Yige chengjiao xiangcun,* pp. 9–11.

88. *FBIS,* November 3, 1986, p. 4, reporting radio of November 3.

89. *FBIS,* December 29, 1987, p. 50, reporting radio of December 22.

90. *FBIS,* March 9, 1988, pp. 61–62, reporting radio of March 8.

91. Reported by Kate Xiao Zhou, on the basis of a 1985 article by Cai Fuyuan in *Minzhu yu falü* (Democracy and Law).

92. These rental enterprises were *zuling qiye,* and in Maoist terms they were not "productive" despite their good effects on efficiency. *Tansuo yu zhengming* (Investigation and Debate), March 1988, p. 51.

93. Zhang Gang is quoted in Edward J. Epstein, "China's Legal Reforms," p. 9.4.

94. Victor Nee, "Peasant Entrepreneurship and the Politics of Regulation in China," in *Remaking the Economic Institutions of China and Eastern Europe,* V. Nee and D.

Stark, eds. (Stanford: Stanford University Press, 1991), p. 171.

95. The portions of whittling on sale weights ranged up to 18 percent in some cases, but for the most part they were about 3 or 4 percent. *Shanghai fazhi bao,* January 30, 1989.

96. *JFRB,* May 30, 1988.

97. Printed avowal that there was an illegal market in coupons can be found in many sources, including *Shanghai fazhi bao.* Coupons from many parts of China (including Shanghai) were on sale in Macau as collectibles in the mid-1990s.

98. These three rights, respectively, were called *chanpin fenpei quan, jiage fudong quan,* and *caizheng fenpei quan. JFRB,* May 30, 1988.

99. An ebb and flow in definitions of corruption may be traced in terms of kinds of purported uncleanliness, e.g., physical dirt, political disloyalty, foreign impurity, sharp business, or bribed government. On opposite trends of these criteria in two Chinese eras, including European historical comparisons on usury as corrupt, see Lynn White, "Changing Concepts of Corruption in Communist China: Early 1950s vs. Early 1980s," in *Changes and Continuities in Chinese Communism: The Economy, Society, and Technology,* Yu-ming Shaw, ed. (Boulder: Westview, 1988), pp. 316–53.

100. *FBIS,* March 16, 1988, p. 19, reporting radio of March 15.

101. *FBIS,* March 14, 1988, p. 38, reporting radio of March 14.

102. *XMWB,* December 7, 1988, includes in the crucial sentence the vague qualifier "sometimes"—but this was apparently a matter of courtesy to other jurisdictions, and possibly to northern Jiangsu in particular, rather than a statistical matter.

103. *LDB,* March 19, 1989.

104. *Shanghai jingji, neibu ben: 1949–1982* (Shanghai Economy, Internal Volume: 1949–1982), Shanghai Academy of Social Sciences, ed. (Shanghai: Shanghai Shehui Kexue Yuan Chuban She, 1984), p. 545.

105. Dorothy Solinger, "China's Transients and the State: A Form of Civil Society?" *Politics and Society* 21:1 (March 1993), pp. 91–122.

106. During the summers of 1987 and 1988, the author heard much about such arrests both in public media and informal conversations.

107. *LW* 33 (1987), p. 33.

108. *LW* 5 (1987), p. 12.

109. Interview with an economist in Shanghai.

110. *RMRB,* August 16, 1988.

111. *LDB,* March 19, 1989.

112. *JFRB,* August 8, 1981.

113. *SF,* May 29, 1989.

114. *Xianggang jingji yuekan* (Hong Kong Economic Monthly), August 4, 1989.

115. Margaret Y. K. Woo, "Legal Reforms in the Aftermath of Tiananmen Square," *Review of Socialist Law* (1991), p. 58.

116. On such definitions, see Lynn White, "Changing Concepts of Corruption."

117. Guilhem Fabre, "The Chinese Mirror," p. 262.

118. Ibid., pp. 262–64.

119. A reference to Schumpeter is made by a PRC economist, Li Shi, in "The Growth of Household Industry in Rural Wenzhou," in *Market Forces in China: Competition & Small Business, The Wenzhou Debate,* Peter Nolan and Dong Fureng, eds. (London: Zed Books, 1990), p. 112.

120. Victor Chi-leung Chui, *Chinese Perception of Organization and Authority* (Hong Kong: M.B.A. dissertation, Department of Management Sciences, University of Hong Kong, 1987), p. 34.

121. *Xiandai qiye jia* (Contemporary Entrepreneur), September 1987, pp. 15–16.

122. Quoted from Schumpeter in Cui Zhiyuan, "Epilogue: A Schumpeterian Perspective and Beyond," in *China: A Reformable System?* Gan Yang and Cui Zhiyuan, eds., ms. p. 11, from which many ideas in this paragraph are drawn.

123. *Fudan feng* (Fudan Breeze) 1 (Shanghai) (March 27, 1988), pp. 16–17 (article by Chen Shenshen).

124. See a series of *SHJJDB* articles by Chen Shenshen on July 18, July 25, August 1, and August 8, 1988.

125. *Zhongguo shehui zhuyi chengshi jingji xue* (Chinese Socialist Urban Economics), Zhu Linxing, ed. (Shanghai: Shanghai Shehui Kexue Chuban She, 1986), p. 89.

126. Shanghai was only somewhat above average among the surveyed cities in the production it could obtain from each yuan of fixed assets: in 1987, this was 1.72 yuan of gross output. The Jiangnan cities of Wuxi and Suzhou, however, did better on this score than *any* other surveyed places, producing 2.40 and 2.60 yuan respectively. Jiangnan as a whole returned capital better than most other Chinese regions. *SHGYJJB,* August 19, 1988.

127. See this graphed in Barry Naughton, "Industrial Policy," p. 162.

128. Nonbudgetary investment rose at an even faster rate from 1977 to 1983, although the ratio of its increase to that of budgeted investment in the later period is lower. See ibid., p. 174.

129. See the recently published and very sophisticated treatment of these matters in Marc Blecher and Vivienne Shue, *Tethered Deer: Government and Economy in a Chinese County* (Stanford: Stanford University Press, 1996).

130. This statistic is called the *difang, bumen, qiye he shiye danwei zhangwo de yusuan wai zijin. Caijing yanjiu* (Financial and Economic Research), May 1988, p. 14, says its average rate of increase from 1979 to 1985 was 22.4 percent and would report the 22 percent, above, as 21.4 percent (but 22.0 percent comes from calculations on data in the later *ZGTJNJ88,* pp. 51 and 764). It is reassuring, not the opposite, when different PRC sources give or imply only trivially different statistics.

131. In Shanghai from 1950 to 1983, according to another source, more than half (54 percent) of the money appropriated for basic construction came from the state budget. But during the last five of these years, from 1979 to 1983, the state's allocation dropped to less than one-third. *Shanghai caizheng yanjiu* (Shanghai Finance Research), February 1985, p. 10. The main text above is based on *Shanghai: Gaige, kaifang, yu fazhan, 1979–87* (Shanghai: Reforms, Opening, and Development, 1979–87), Shanghai Statistical Bureau, ed. (Shanghai: Sanlian Shudian, 1988), p. 44.

132. *SHTJNJ87,* p. 233. This was 81 percent in 1985, and 79 percent in 1986.

133. *ZGTJNJ87,* p. 474. In the previous year, the national figure was 61 percent. These numbers were authoritatively published in a year when reporting may have been less biased than usual, but the author would encourage the reader to use them for trends and comparisons, more than as sure statements about absolute levels.

134. By 1982, total profits from Shanghai textiles were 2.303 billion yuan (25 percent of national profits in this industry, although the 13 billion yuan of total Shanghai output was less than 18 percent of the nation's). See *Shanghai jingji, neibu ben,* pp. 151–56; *WHB,* August 10, 1980.

135. This paragraph is based on information from a Shanghai economist.

136. Michel Oksenberg and James Tong, "The Evolution of Central-Provincial Fiscal Relations in China, 1971–1984: The Formal System," *China Quarterly* 125 (March 1991), pp. 1–32.

137. From Wang Shaoguang, "The Rise of the Second Budget and the Decline of State Capacity in China," unpublished paper, p. 31.

138. The State Council raised depreciation in various categories by one percentage point on February 6; see *Zhonghua renmin gonghe guo jingji guanli dashi ji* (Chronicle of

PRC Economic Management), *Dangdai Zhongguo jingji guanli* Editorial Dept., ed. (Beijing: Zhongguo Jingji Chuban She, 1986), p. 494.

139. This has been confirmed by completely separate sources in Shanghai and Shenzhen.

140. The bureau's total amount of such space was 3.2 square meters. *WHB,* December 4, 1979.

141. Ibid.

142. *Xiao, jiu, san. WHB,* December 4, 1979.

143. *CD,* February 1, 1988.

144. Richard Conroy, "Technology and Economic Development," in *Reforming the Revolution: China in Transition,* Robert Benewick and Paul Wingrove, eds. (Basingstoke: Macmillan, 1988), p. 130.

145. Seventy-seven percent of all Shanghai investment over this long period was classed as "productive," and the remainder covered all investment in "nonproductive" commercial and service firms, housing, offices, schools, banks, and much else (including transport and all utilities). Another 8 percent went into transport and communications. See *SHTJNJ86,* p. 250.

146. Zheng Yongnian has compiled this conclusion from several issues of *ZGTJNJ.*

147. The accumulation fund is called the *jilei jijin. Shanghai caizheng yanjiu*, February, 1985, p. 10.

148. *Dangdai Zhongguo de guding zichan guanli* (Fixed Asset Investments and Management in Contemporary China), Zhou Daojiong, ed. (Beijing: Zhongguo Shehui Kexue Chuban She, 1989). All percentages are rounded from the original.

149. *Caijing yanjiu,* May 1988, p. 14, thus implies that pretax loan repayments rose from 13 percent in 1985 to 16 percent in 1986.

150. *Shanghai: Gaige,* p. 44.

151. Y.Y. Kueh, *Economic Planning and Local Mobilization in Post-Mao China* (London: SOAS Contemporary China Institute, 1985), p. 16.

152. This increase of "self-generated" or "self-sought" (*zichou*) funds was general throughout the country—and an obvious index of increased localism. See *Shanghai: Gaige,* p. 44.

153. These figures were supplied to the author by Zheng Yongnian.

154. The total of Shanghai deposits at the start of the 1980s was 10.1 billion yuan, and savings deposits were 2.29 billion yuan. Savings deposits rose 9.4 times since 1952. The total of end-1979 credit was 16.45 billion yuan, of which 7.22 billion were industrial loans and 9.17 billion were commercial. *Shanghai jingji, neibu ben,* p. 921.

155. This summary is based loosely on William Byrd, *China's Financial System: The Changing Role of Banks* (Boulder: Westview, 1983), but with more emphasis than Byrd gives to the broad organizational rather than high leadership sources of policy.

156. This is based on several interview reports, including one concerning a nationwide 1988 meeting of bank managers in Beijing. Together, they asked that local politicians no longer pressure them to exceed authorized loan quotas. But the efficacy of a declaration on this point, without real means of enforcement against either the local politicians or bank managers who might violate the rule, was subject to great doubt among several interviewees.

157. See Cui Zhiyuan, "Epilogue: A Schumpeterian Perspective."

158. This is 33.2 percent annually. Zheng Yongnian garnered the raw figures from various issues of *ZGTJNJ.* The average annual percentage rises are calculated. Bank loan figures are not adjusted for inflation.

159. *JFRB,* February 27, 1987.

160. *FEER,* January 10, 1985, p. 51.

161. *FEER,* December 11, 1986, p. 86.

162. Ibid., December 11, 1986, p. 87.

163. Ibid.

164. Harry Harding, *China's Second Revolution: Reform After Mao* (Washington: Brookings, 1987), p. 123, refers to Vigor Fung, "Peking Loosens the Reins on a Multi-service Bank," *Asian Wall Street Journal Weekly,* November 24, 1986.

165. There were 15 percent increases in both Shanghai and all China during this period. *SHJJ,* January 1987, p. 23.

166. Ibid., p. 26.

167. *FEER,* December 11, 1986, p. 94.

168. Ibid.

169. The first kind of relations was *diaopo yu fenpei guanxi;* the second kind were only *jiedai guanxi. JFRB,* February 1, 1987.

170. The quotation is from the bank's president, in *CD,* March 10, 1988.

171. *NCNA,* November 28, 1987.

172. Computed from *Shanghai Statistical Yearbook, 1989 Concise Edition,* Municipal Statistical Bureau of Shanghai, ed. (Beijing: China Statistical Publishing House, 1989), p. 25, and *LDB,* January 31, 1989.

173. *CD,* December 21, 1987.

174. *Minjian* is translated by the *Shiyong Han-Ying cidian* (Practical Chinese-English Dictionary) (Nanjing: Jiangsu Renmin Chuban She, 1983), p. 708, as "nongovernmental." This word is related to *minban* (run by the people), used since the 1950s to describe some schools and other institutions that did not receive official money.

175. *SJJDB,* February 8, 1988.

176. Ibid.

177. *FEER,* August 1, 1996.

178. *FBIS,* November 13, 1986, p. 1, reporting radio of November 12.

179. *Yige chengjiao xiangcun,* pp. 9–11.

180. Calculated from *China's Rural Industry: Structure, Development, and Reform,* William A. Byrd and Lin Qingsong, eds. (Washington: World Bank, 1990), p. 136. Per-capita savings in 1978 were 16.6 yuan, and the increase was 9.3 times. The industrial output was 426 million yuan, and the increase was 5.1 times.

181. *Post,* August 15, 1988.

182. *CD,* December 17, 1987.

183. Calculated from statistics provided by Zheng Yongnian.

184. The three kinds of recipients were specified in the article as *geti hu, zhuanye hu,* and *cunzhen ban de xiao gongchang. Jiangsu fazhi bao,* January 24, 1989.

185. Ibid.

186. By the end of the 1980s, a consortium of three organizations centered in northern Jiangsu was publishing a weekly paper called the *Jingji xinwen bao* (Economic News Report). The consortium members' names show new economic ventures in Subei: the Economic Opening Liaison Group of the Huaihai Economic District (Huaihai Jingji Qu, Jingji Kaifa Lianhe Hui), the Xuzhou City People's Government, and the Jiangsu-Shandong-Jiangxi-Anhui Adjacent Districts News Cooperative (Su-Lu-Gan-Wan Jierang Diqu Xinwen Gongzuo Xiezuo Hui).

187. This "hunger" was called a "*zijin jike zheng,*" and the "anemia" was a "*yinhang pinxue zheng*"; see *Jingji xinwen bao,* January 26, 1989.

188. *Post,* September 1, 1988.

189. *CD,* January 25, 1989.

190. There was a sharp temporary decrease in French savings deposits in 1848; but by 1850 the total climbed smartly again until 1870, which saw another merely temporary

spate of withdrawals. Calculated from B. R. Mitchell, *European Historical Statistics, 1750–1975,* 2nd rev. ed. (London: Macmillan, 1980), p. 507.

191. *SHGYJJB,* July 25, 1988.

192. Daniel Kelliher, *Peasant Power,* pp. 194–95.

193. This is based partly on interview work by Solomon M. Karmel, then a graduate student at Princeton University, in "Capitalism with Chinese Characteristics," (ms. paper, 1994).

194. *FEER,* December 11, 1986, p. 83.

195. *FBIS,* November 28, 1986, p. 2, reporting radio of November 26.

196. *CD,* June 22, 1988.

197. The first such city was Shenzhen. See Edward J. Epstein, "China's Legal Reforms," p. 9.17.

198. *Post,* May 30, 1988.

199. *CD,* March 1, 1989.

200. *JJRB,* September 26, 1988, reporting on the Wenzhou Dongfang Furniture Factory. The *monthly* interest given by the co-op was a high 1.5 percent; this is about 20 percent per year.

201. Dong Fureng, "The Wenzhou Model for Developing the Rural Commodity Economy," *Market Forces in China,* p. 95.

202. Ellen Hertz has researched the market for her dissertation in anthropology at the University of California, Berkeley. Many others have worked on this subject, including Bridget Williams and others in Hong Kong. See also Solomon M. Karmel, "Capitalism with Chinese Characteristics."

203. Wu Yantao et al., *Shanghai de gupiao he zhaijuan* (Shanghai Shares and Bonds) (Shanghai: Shanghai Shehui Kexue Yuan Chuban She, 1988), p. 4, suggests that the rules for collectives were even more stringent than for individuals—perhaps because some of the latter were overseas Chinese.

204. *RMRB,* September 12, 1988.

205. Charles F. James in *The China Traveller,* December 1987, p. 3.

206. *CD,* October 10, 1988.

207. This section relies partly on information from Ellen Hertz, who is not responsible for any misinterpretations that may have been made in the text above.

208. Cf. *JFRB,* December 2, 1991, tr. in *Inside Mainland China* 14:2 (February 1992), pp. 55–59.

209. Bridget Williams, untitled ms., Hong Kong, July 1994, p. 6.

210. Miron Mushkat and Adrian Faure, *Shanghai—Promise and Performance: Economic and Stock Market Review* (Hong Kong: Baring Securities, 1991), p. 1.

211. *CD,* July 31, 1990.

212. See Solomon M. Karmel, "Capitalism with Chinese Characteristics."

213. Bridget Williams, untitled ms., July 1994, p. 7.

214. See graph in the *New York Times* business section, December 27, 1995, p. 1.

215. Li Shi, "The Growth of Household Industry," p. 123. In the original, "county" is *xian,* "district" is *qu,* and "township" is *xiang.*

216. The portion from Guangdong was 17 percent, and from Beijing, 6 percent. (Shanghai alone was 16 percent.) Over half of the investors were enterprise cadres, technicians, or professionals—and a third were "others," apparently including entrepreneurs. Two-thirds had less than 30,000 yuan invested in stocks. See *EE,* March 8, 1994.

217. See Hiroyuki Imai, "China's Business Cycles," *China Business Review,* January–February 1994, pp. 14–16.

218. *FBIS,* December 10, 1987, p. 16, reporting a journal of November 25.

219. Ibid.

220. This applies to loans affecting the foreign sector, but the same principles were attempted for purely domestic credit at this time also. "Self-supply" is *zichou. FBIS,* February 8, 1988, pp. 24–25, reporting radio of February 3.

221. *JFRB,* August 19, 1988.

222. Marlowe Hood, "Crackdown Ordered on Money Abuses," *Post,* September 14, 1988.

223. Reuters, *Post,* September 19, 1988.

224. *CD,* August 27, 1990.

225. See *Jingji xinwen bao,* January 26, 1989, which gives an example from Linyi, Shandong, of this credit situation that was then typical of East China rural areas.

226. *The Economist,* November 30, 1991, p. 23, and *FEER,* August 30, 1990, p. 35.

227. *Social Science Information Monthly* (*Sheke xinxi*), April 10, 1993.

228. Reuters, July 17, 1993.

229. The author has been told by a non-China economist that there are no adequate models to forecast this kind of situation well, even irrespective of any problems about the accuracy of current PRC data that might be used in them.

Chapter 1.4

Business Outreach Beyond the State

The taylor does not attempt to mend his own shoes, but buys them of the shoemaker. The shoemaker does not attempt to make his own clothes, but employs a taylor.

—Adam Smith, 1776

Shanghai's high taxes and credit crunch harmed efforts to develop new technology and embody it in equipment. So the city lost markets to other Chinese areas that had lower taxes and newer equipment. During 1980, in all of Shanghai's industry, 50 percent of the machines dated from the 1930s and 1940s, 35 percent were produced in the 1950s and 1960s, and only 15 percent were made in the 1970s.[1] A limited-circulation book was published on the antiquation of Shanghai's industries.[2] The modern sectors of Shanghai's economy (electronics, lasers, biological engineering, new materials, optical fibers, and robotics) altogether in 1980 still did not make as much as 5 percent of the city's product value.[3]

Local Technical Innovation to Market Quality Products

There are ways of measuring the extent to which technology (as distinct from material supplies and labor inputs) raises output quality and production. Shanghai was fourteenth among Chinese provinces—rather than first, as its pre-1949 history would have suggested—in the portion of its 1964–82 industrial growth attributable to technology. In this long period, the contribution of technology to Shanghai's development was calculated at only 10 percent; in the 1970s, it was only 13 percent. A lack of capital, which could embody new techniques, explains this sad past performance, which slowly improved during reforms. Of Shanghai's economic growth in 1982, over one-third (35 percent) was already estimated to depend on new technology.[4]

This situation did not change quickly. Fairly little capital equipment was added in the early 1980s, and by 1986 the proportion of Shanghai industrial machinery that was twenty, thirty, or even fifty years old was virtually unchanged from 1980.[5] Continued high tax remittances before the mid-1980s crisis prevented much investment then.

High Tech or High Taxes?

Simon and Rehn, despite their "cautious optimism" for Shanghai's potential role in semiconductors after the mid-1980s, frankly reported the problems of developing computers there:

> One can better appreciate the relationship between the central government in Beijing and Shanghai by looking at the competition between the two entities. After the electronics industry in Shanghai had exhibited its technological and economic strengths, the Fourth Ministry of Machine Building (MEI) . . . tried to acquire control of a number of Shanghai's key electronics enterprises and place them under its administration. The municipality refused to accede to what in reality constituted a grab for resources by the MEI. . . . It was only after Shanghai's computer industry almost collapsed in the early 1980s that measures to reform the system were discussed and introduced. . . . While the importance of electronics was generally recognized, the notion of taking high technology as the core of Shanghai's development was not well received by a large number of influential individuals, many of whom were concerned about the future status of so-called traditional industries in Shanghai.[6]

In this field Shanghai's rival, which had a great deal of central support, was the Zhongguan Cun area in Beijing.[7] In late 1985, when the government had decided to designate one location as "a special site for mainframe computer development," Shanghai was on the short list of places—but Beijing was chosen.[8] As late as 1989, Shanghai's own "Silicon Valley" was still announcing the list of areas (microelectronics, information technology, optical fibers, lasers, bioengineering, aviation, and materials science) in which it hoped for investment—without indicating that much money had actually come.[9]

Economists in the municipal planning commission by the mid-1980s were openly protesting that Shanghai had too many "traditional industries," with dull managers using old equipment to make unstylish products. These economists estimated that 98.6 percent of Shanghai's industrial output came from such "traditional industries." To prove this, they offered definitions of international standards for quality in many commodity lines, specified for each decade since the 1950s. They then rated the portion of Shanghai's output that met these criteria. Even in the late 1950s, Shanghai products did reasonably well by these standards. The general decline was not across the board; for example, products from plants under the local Electrical Machines Bureau rose sharply in quality between the 1950s and 1960s (prior to declines in the next two decades). That pattern applied to other bureaus also, but an overall decline was found for practically all of the bureaus between the 1960s and 1980s.[10]

Well into the 1980s, profitable Shanghai companies had to pay such high taxes that they had no money for technical improvement. The eleven industrial bureaus of Shanghai in 1982 paid 90 percent of their realized profits and taxes to the state, retaining only 10 percent.[11] Within this tenth, only 4 percent of the total went into the "production development fund."[12] In the early 1980s, Beijing planners practically forbade the development or renovation of Shanghai industries.

The feeling was reciprocated. Some Shanghai economists called for a withdrawal of textile factories and other light industries from the city.[13] These factories' importance as revenue earners for the central government was so great, the state was doing all it could to prevent the city from developing in any manner that might absorb energy from what was officially taken as Shanghai's main task: the sending of tribute. Central politicians' actions (despite their avowals) were generally consistent with the following rule: New civilian technologies in Shanghai were discouraged, because they would use capital. Shanghai modernization—especially in semiconductors, the cutting-edge technology—progressed slowly. Local plans projected much faster development than was actually financed.

The central government's favoritism to Beijing in research investment was egregious. The northern capital in 1983 received 20 percent of all China's investment for research (more than twice as much as the next-highest province, Sichuan with 9 percent), and Shanghai received only 7 percent despite its technical resources. The number of engineers in Shanghai during that year was almost exactly the same as in Beijing, but the national allocation for research was considerably less than half as much.[14]

The Talent Pool for Innovation

Technical talent had been drained from Shanghai for decades, just as funds were, although the remaining engineers were still many. By 1983, only 8.5 percent of the city's employees in state units were technicians or scientists, as compared with 12.5 percent in Beijing, 12.2 in Nanjing, or 10.5 in Shenyang.[15] Especially in some industries, such as textiles, factories throughout the country were extensively staffed by technicians who originally hailed from Shanghai; they had been assigned there throughout the Maoist period. As these statistics show, the brain drain from the metropolis continued for many years after the reforms began.

The problem was not that the remaining workforce in Shanghai was badly educated, but that the portion of the city's technicians had been reduced by send-downs. Levels of education among Shanghai's workers were not high. Only 1.4 percent of industrial employees below 35 years of age had any higher education. Of all the people employed in Shanghai industry during reforms, almost two-thirds were less than 35 years old; and two-thirds of this group lacked even junior high school educations.[16] The portion of Shanghai's whole population in 1983 that had university degrees was 0.66 percent—as compared with 0.95 in Beijing, 0.94 in Wuhan, 0.94 in Taiyuan, 0.93 in Nanjing, and 0.86 in Xi'an.[17] The contribution of Shanghai's universities toward graduating new staff for the city's economy largely took place after 1979, because so many previous graduates had been sent elsewhere. From that year until 1986, the city's tertiary institutions graduated 165,000 students, or 43 percent of Shanghai's total since Liberation.[18] The number of university students in Shanghai, on a per-capita basis, doubled from 1978 to 1986.[19]

At the upper secondary level, schools had been able to nurture more local talent that stayed in the city. By 1982 in Shanghai, 24 percent of the population had attended high school (as compared with only 7 percent in the PRC as a whole). Of Shanghai's state employees, 40 percent had attended high school (compared with 20 percent in the country at large).[20] Among Shanghai people of senior high school age, 55 percent in 1982 were actually attending school. Twelve percent of university-age people were students.[21] Primary and junior high schools were probably more important to Shanghai's overall development than were the higher levels of education, if only because these schools affected more of the workforce.

The Capital Pool for Innovation

From 1949 to 1978, investment in new technology for Shanghai was low, averaging less than 240 million yuan per year. In 1983, 40 percent of Shanghai's total investment came from enterprises' "self-sought funds."[22] The increase of internal investment was a new trend, but it took off only in the mid-1980s. Until that time at least, the high taxes created a regime of "closure and guardedness" that kept Shanghai manufacturing old products only. Shanghai marketers were positively encouraged to rest on their city's past laurels, because any other policy would have lowered tax revenues by requiring investment to improve product quality. Overconfidence about sales of the city's products was reported as a belief that "if foreigners don't want it, the domestic market will; and if Shanghai doesn't want it, other places will."[23]

This attitude might have been sound, except that new technologies were quickly being developed in other parts of East China, which could retain funds to improve their products. Top-quality refrigerators, for example, had long been a Shanghai specialty. But by 1979, the prosperous Zhejiang city of Jiaxing (on the railroad line between Shanghai and Hangzhou) was making refrigerators for the many parts of China where energy supplies are erratic. As Shanghai journalists reported, these Jiaxing coolers could be adapted to kerosene, gas, steam, or even solar power, and they were free of noise and vibration. These were classy, innovative, marketable products such as Shanghai had once sold, when it had money to invest in making them.[24]

Shanghai's Loss of Inland and International Markets

From 1978 to 1983, Shanghai's exports of industrial products to other parts of China were essentially stagnant, rising scarcely at all, because of competition from growing industries elsewhere. The values of these domestic industrial exports in yuan were: 1978, 11 billion; 1980, 11 billion; 1982, 11 billion; 1983, 12 billion. Because of inflation, this was a real decrease. Unsold goods in Shanghai's warehouses rose 7 percent in 1982 alone.[25]

These marketing problems became obvious after reforms were announced, but their basis had been cumulating for years. Shanghai taxes were so high that companies had no spare capital to finance production of newer, popular, marketable products. As an official in the Shanghai Clock Company complained:

> It certainly isn't that we don't want to make new styles and products, but we are suffocated by pressure on production amounts and values. In wristwatches, for example, our ability to produce the internal mechanisms is great; but the watch lenses, faces, and pointers have gotten short shrift. The Watch Lens Plant cannot fill its production targets in time. How are we to make our products elegant?[26]

Wenhui News alleged that even in Tianjin these "suffocating" pressures were not so great. Shanghai made women's watches that were less stylish than Tianjin watches "for little girls."

In textiles, the industry that for decades churned large amounts of money to and through Shanghai, the city lost most of its market to inland producers. Although Shanghai spun 37 percent of China's cotton yarn in 1952, it spun only 12 percent by 1983.[27] Shanghai in 1985 sold 38 percent of all apparel in China, but by 1986 this portion declined to 28 percent, and by 1988 it plummeted to 17 percent. In household electric appliances, Shanghai sold 35 percent in 1986, but only 22 percent in the first half of 1988.[28] These reductions were not necessarily bad in themselves. They reflect development inland and on the Shanghai delta. The problem was that the metropolis could not greatly raise its output of more sophisticated items as it turned over more clothing and household goods production to inland places.

Jiujiang, Anhui, was one of the Yangzi cities that developed a booming textile industry in successful competition with Shanghai. The total industrial product of Jiujiang rose about 18 percent per year in much of the 1980s. The municipal government there wanted to allow factories flexibility to use different raw materials for their products. In textiles, for example, some local factories converted quickly from cotton to mixed fibers. Jiujiang local authorities also hoped that rural industries—which already by 1988 contributed 27 percent of the prefecture's industrial product—would also prosper further.[29] This kind of change was natural. The only surprise was that Shanghai, whose products these factories displaced, did not develop in more modern fields to replace its lost markets in textiles.

Shanghai delta factories, similar to those inside the city, often made products of superior quality. In 1980, for example, five Wuxi printed fabric plants developed a program of "studying Shanghai and raising levels."[30] But by 1983, various measures of economic efficiency and product quality showed their output was better than that of factories in the metropolis. By 1984, these Wuxi factories were delivering more profits and taxes per worker and per unit of capital. They enjoyed better access to factor markets and newer equipment than similar Shanghai plants, and their technical staffs were as expert. The reasons for Wuxi's prowess lay not just in better infrastructure, but also in more responsiveness to market demand for new styles—and in lower taxes.

Demand from other parts of the country for Shanghai brand-name products remained strong. But the city's factories, partly because of problems with material supplies and high taxes, could not raise production of its best products fast enough to meet this demand. Even if factories could make these commodities, they often could not sell them at the best price. Many goods were planned to be kept for the city's own consumers—to allay workers' concerns during inflation in a politically sensitive metropolis. Firms in this situation could disperse licenses to use their brand names and technologies in factories that paid lower taxes in other provinces. So "Shanghai" products were decreasingly from Shanghai. In tennis shoes, Shanghai firms established more than forty joint factories with Jiangsu, Zhejiang, Anhui, Jiangxi, Shandong, Guangdong, and Henan companies. So "Shanghai" shoes, but not really from that metropolis, were widely sold in those places.

The Forever brand of bicycles, for example, had become famous because a Shanghai company once made them very well. But by the mid-1980s, many Forever bikes were produced in Jiangsu. Markets there and in other provinces often found the Jiangsu Forever bikes cheaper and more available. Many rival inland companies were bettering Shanghai bicycle makers by the mid-1980s and 1990s. Parts of Forever (*Yongjiu*) and Phoenix (*Fenghuang*) bicycles were made in places as close as Suzhou and Nantong, in Jiangsu, or as far away as Urumqi, Xinjiang. This kind of cooperation in 1984 increased the number of bicycles with these brand names by more than 900,000, so that 30 percent of the bikes and parts with these names were made outside Shanghai. Sales fell. Referring to these two Shanghai brands, a reporter quipped, "'Forever' may not stay on the market forever. 'Phoenix' may have to rise from the ashes soon."[31]

The main competition came not just from ordinary inland plants, but from inland-foreign joint ventures making bicycles with international brand names. "They have used new materials and have developed new products. Some of them have turned out world-famous brand bikes. But Shanghai bicycle producers still stick to their old products without making much effort to develop new ones." Shanghai's attempts to set up cooperation with inland plants often led to losses for

Table 1.4-1

Declining Shanghai Share of China's Exports

Year	Shanghai share as % of PRC value	Year	Shanghai share as % of PRC value
1970	38	1986	12
1975	31	1987	11
1978	30	1988	10
1980	24	1989	10
1981	17	1990	9
1982	16	1991	8
1983	16	1992	8
1984	14	1993	8
1985	12	1994	7

Notes and sources: Calculations are made from raw data quoted in American dollars, since 1970 just for the listed years, in *Shanghai tongji nianjian, 1993* (Shanghai Statistical Yearbook, 1993), Shanghai Statistical Bureau, ed. (Beijing: Zhongguo Tongji Chuban She, 1993), p. 300. These are divided into the national export figures in *Zhongguo tongji nianjian, 1993* (China Statistical Yearbook, 1993), State Statistical Bureau, ed. (Beijing: Zhongguo Tongji Chuban She, 1993), p. 633. For late years, this is calculated from data and exchange rates in the all-China yearbook, 1995, p. 537, and in the Shanghai yearbook, 1995, p. 101. A larger portion of China's exports passes from inland factories through Shanghai's docks, but this table covers commodities last processed in Shanghai only.

the city, even though companies earned profits. Shanghai's bicycle factories set up joint firms, for example, with counterparts in Suzhou and Nantong nearby in the delta (as well as with Hefei, Anhui), greatly increasing the output of Shanghai brand-name bikes. Profits in these joint firms were reportedly good.[32] But for these brands, "ordinary customers cannot tell which bike is made in Shanghai and which is not. This has . . . made people reluctant to buy."

So the Shanghai Light Industries Bureau vowed to inspect inland products with Shanghai names randomly. It threatened to "take action against the leading manufacturer as well as the associated factory" if the vehicles were substandard or if they were not marked with the place where they were made. Measures of this sort, however, did little more than make a profit on Shanghai's past reputation for product quality. Actual production of many of these commodities, during the 1980s, moved inland.[33]

These problems were evident not just on the China market, but also in international markets. Shanghai's export prowess fell because Beijing wanted the capital that could have allowed the creation of better products there. Shanghai had less potential to develop competitive products. As Table 1.4-1 shows, the city's portion of all PRC exports dropped drastically (albeit from a high percentage of the national total). This change was quick throughout the 1970s, and it continued also during later reforms. Inland companies taking Shanghai's domestic and international markets for traditional goods would have been no problem—in fact, the trend toward this was predictable and natural—if state leaders' expectations of Shanghai had left the city free to diversify in appropriate new fields.

At the county level, many Jiangsu and Zhejiang county-level administrations by 1990 had created joint ventures with Shanghai foreign trade corporations in various commodity lines. The aim was to promote exports using Shanghai commercial expertise and products from factories elsewhere on the delta. Over four-fifths of all the counties that joined such ventures with Shanghai traders were in Jiangsu or Zhejiang, and about that portion of Shanghai's total exports came from these provinces. This required Shanghai experts to arrange the paperwork—but not necessarily Shanghai's port to do the shipping. That city's share of China's national exports plummeted in the 1980s and 1990s, as the table shows. Even more striking, Shanghai's *re*-exports as a portion of China's total exports fell from 10 percent in 1980 to a mere 3 percent in 1991.[34]

State Plans for Shanghai's Development

Central investments at Shanghai stressed heavy industries. A "steel-eating" pattern persisted in the metropolis, and especially in a ring around the old built-up area, until state budget deficits forced its end. This was a classic Stalinist development strategy, and at Shanghai its flagship was the Baoshan Steel Mill. Baoshan had a larger scale than any of its predecessors, but official early reforms did not change prereform understandings of how Shanghai's economy should grow. Machine building and iron remained the central vision. Shanghai's consumption of steel rose 74 times in the three decades from 1949 to 1979—and energy consumption rose 24 times (closely parallel to the rise of manufacturing output value).[35] By the 1980s, Shanghai could not sustain this pattern for several reasons.

First, Shanghai mines no coal or iron ore. It has none in the ground. Leaders of inland provinces that have mines wanted more profits not just from weight reduction but also from refining and further processing. Some had the political clout in Beijing to obtain the capital for new factories. A second, related reason was that some central reformers, as distinct from revenue collectors, hoped Shanghai could upgrade its technology rather than relying as extensively as in the past on metals and manufacturing, so that China might hope to compete on world markets. But they provided practically no money for Shanghai to obtain this new technology. Third, the old metals industries are egregious polluters. Less densely populated parts of the country could present valid environmental reasons in Beijing to take such tasks over from Shanghai.

When the central government determined during the mid-1970s that China needed a large new steel mill and that foreign help was necessary to build it, a survey was launched on the suitability of several locations. Shanghai was chosen from a short list of four places (including Dalian in the northeast, perhaps because much of the prospective capital was Japanese).[36] Some sources say that the central economic politician Chen Yun strongly argued to put it in Shanghai.[37] Planning for a project of this size almost surely had to begin years before March 1978, when ground was broken for this vast new steel factory.

Baoshan, a suburb north of central Shanghai on the Yangzi, was the selected site. The huge plant built there has encountered numerous difficulties, partly because its port is shallow. Its profits have been low and at least sometimes negative. This gigantic factory's linkages with other aspects of Shanghai have also been problematic: Steel plants are inherently polluting, and Baoshan is no exception. They absorb vast amounts of capital and land, but they employ relatively few workers. The Baoshan Steel Factory contributes all its profits to the central government in Beijing, not to Shanghai. It confirms the vertical pattern of economic organization in Shanghai, and it strains against efforts to make the municipal economy more efficient by marshaling Shanghai's resources for horizontal market contracts rather than administrative fiats. This Baoshan project also bears a moot relation to the idea (important in plans only since 1983, long after the decision to locate in Baoshan was made) that Shanghai should develop new Chinese industries, especially in electronics, and should not try to do what inland places could soon or already do better.

The Baoshan plant absorbs many Shanghai resources. In return, it provides at least a few benefits for the surrounding area. The steel plant supplies metal for the Satana cars made in a joint enterprise with Volkswagen of Germany, as well as for Shanghai's shipbuilding industry. The second-largest project in Shanghai was the Jinshan Chemical Factory. This also fed downstream industries that made bulky products. Electronics and other "new industries" in 1984 still contributed only 5 percent of Shanghai's gross industrial output value. Metals, chemicals, textiles, and other engineering industries, when combined with building materials, food, lumber processing, and energy—mostly heavy industries—together contributed 95 percent.[38]

Heavy industrial investments at Shanghai were rationalized in terms of the notion that modern light industries—especially electronics and robotics—would mesh with them later. The problems of pollution and distance from mines, however, were so cogent that professionals were sometimes allowed to publish about the virtues of alternative strategies, which nonetheless received slow funding, for the development of more services and light industries instead.

Shanghai Electronics

Econometric calculations suggested that a program emphasizing Shanghai's development of bioengineering and other high-technology industries—and a use of electronics in particular to raise efficiency in more traditional sectors—was superior to two alternatives: a plan to raise manufacturing output along traditional lines, or a plan to stress low-tech light and textile industries. The superiority of the high-tech plan lay in better profit rates, expected competition from inland places in older industrial lines, and less pollution in a very crowded city. Economists studied whether Shanghai's main economic targets should be set in terms of total output, an across-the-board efficiency goal in each sector, or a special emphasis on service industries. They figured that the last of these strategies was best.[39] These academics called on Shanghai to supply more "software" to China—more know-how, information, and technology—and less "hardware."

Shanghai's nascent electronics industry had been largely created in the early 1960s, when some textile factories switched into this new field. Southern Jiangsu's electronics firms also grew largely from converted Shanghai textile plants, which had been moved to that area by administrative fiats in the first decade of the PRC. Two-thirds to three-quarters of the workers in these plants were female. After these beginnings, until the late 1980s, discussion about Shanghai's possibilities in electronics were not matched by much investment in the field. Shanghai's relatively dirty water and air were reasons presented against electronics investment in the metropolis (although the alternative of continued heavy industrial investment made them dirtier).

Money for this purpose went to many other places, notably Xi'an and Beijing, after 1981 when Jiang Zemin was minister of electronic industries (although later, in 1985, he became mayor of Shanghai). The place whose computer industry grew fastest, with less help from Beijing than other places had, was Wuxi. This Sunan city, less than two hours by train from Shanghai, could tap the talents of Shanghai engineers while providing lower taxes and more managerial freedom for electronic development. As a Shanghai economist put it, the strategy was to "use Shanghai people's heads to develop Wuxi people's wealth."[40] Others in the metropolis had more affection for Wuxi. The No. 742 Electronics Factory in Wuxi became, by the late 1980s, one of China's foremost producers of desktop computers. As Santa Clara became "Silicon Valley" and Cambridge became "Silicon Fen," Wuxi could claim to be "Silicon Paddy."

Wuxi has bred new industries, notably electronics, without losing its position in traditional industries such as textiles and silk. By 1987, the gross value of industrial output in Wuxi city exceeded 26 billion yuan. Surrounding Wuxi county had the highest output of all China's two thousand counties.[41] What accounted for this success? There were lower taxes in Wuxi than in Shanghai, but this does not tell the whole story, because Shanghai's taxes were off the usual scale and Wuxi, like other delta cities, paid at higher rates than most places. Inland products could compete with Wuxi's in many commodity lines.

A crucial reason for the quick prosperity in Wuxi seems to be the speed with which local entrepreneurs built industries based on new technologies while keeping profits from their old markets too. Another reason was the ability of the collective sector there to avoid buying from or selling to the state sector at unfavorable terms. The Sunan agricultural boom, which meant peasants could purchase more of what Wuxi made, also underlay this success for all delta cities. The ones whose local networks could hide most from the central revenue collectors were almost surely among those that did best.

Shanghai's production of computers was for a long time not as notable as Beijing's or even Chengdu's. Instead, Shanghai had been forced to specialize in TV sets, tape recorders, and radios—none of which were based on recent technology. These items, designated for East China production by planners in Beijing, brought revenues to the government but little potential for expansion to Shanghai. They had some prospects for export; but problems of quality and sharp international competition were deterrents in some markets. China's labor costs in late 1980s electronic industries remained low: about 1.4 yuan (then U.S. 40 cents) per hour, compared to an average of U.S.$2 in Hong Kong or Taiwan, and U.S.$8 in Japan.[42]

A competitive semiconductor center was the Zhongguan Cun area in Haidian district, Beijing, which had a great deal of central support.[43] Shanghai's first major location for its own computer industry was Caohejing, near the western suburbs and the airport.[44] New companies were established in this area during 1989 to absorb investment in eight key fields: microelectronics, information technology, optical fibers, lasers, biological engineering, robotics, aviation, and new materials. Reports did not indicate which of these had been particularly funded. Beijing's clear hope was that financing for Shanghai would come from abroad—as finally it did by the 1990s, after local networks had forced taxes lower.

Shanghai in the 1990s enjoyed several technological success stories, some of which cannot be told well because they were rumored and military. The city's "Space Base" was the major manufacturer of Chinese rockets, especially the Long March IV type, in the early 1990s. These rockets were used by the army, but also for commercial launches of telecommunications and weather satellites. As a newspaper report said, "The improved rocket can shoulder the launching of multiple satellites for foreign clients."[45]

Think Tanks

Modern technological improvements do not come from thin air; they usually emerge from scientific laboratories. The most salient feature of civilian research labs in China and Shanghai was their cellularity. Engineering teams did not know what others in the same field were doing. Factories that might have used research findings failed to do so, perhaps because more efficiency would only have raised the fiscal extraction demanded by higher administrative levels.

This was a problem especially before the mid-1980s, when the structure of economic management had to change. According to a survey at the end of the previous decade, more than two-fifths of all new research projects in Shanghai's tertiary institutions and labs duplicated each other. Another third duplicated projects that had been tried as early as 1973–74.[46] The technical problems these labs were addressing may have been important, and duplication of effort might sometimes get them solved. But mainly, this pattern reflected a reluctance on the part of decision makers within labs to initiate new research on their own authority.

A national survey of several thousand scientific institutes in 1984 showed that less than 10 percent of their findings were actually being used in production. Research, according to another survey, was not a big budget item: a mere 0.5 percent of total expenditure in the metals industry, 1 percent in machines, 1.1 percent in chemicals, and 5.5 percent for electronics—well below international averages.[47] Part of the reason was that intellectuals, when they acted as state employees in government think tanks, might be paid somewhat better salaries than other intellectuals but still received very little. If they left the state sector to act as consultants for collectives, however, they made both more suggestions and more money. The nonstate managers were often more willing to try new ideas that could prove successful—and to fire workers who would not join such experiments.

The mid-1980s saw basic change in the link between technology and production in Shanghai. The state's role in this development, as in most reforms, was surprisingly peripheral (especially for a state run by Marxists). High officials were bystanders and commentators, sometimes helping and sometimes hindering basic reform; many of the effective actors were local. The Shanghai Industrial Technical Development Foundation, for example, was created in early 1985. By 1989, it was described as "half-official and half-civilian."[48] Part of its funds came from the government, but most came through "horizontal relations" with specialized banks, other foundations, and investment companies. This consortium-foundation aimed to support a policy of "three changes and one creation" (*san hua, yi chuang*): a change to more advanced technology in Shanghai laboratories, a change to better absorption of techniques by factories, a change to having more components produced within China, and the creation of more foreign exchange—especially by middle-sized and small Shanghai firms.

Financially, this consortium was a good success. In its first four years, it loaned 288 million yuan to roughly five hundred units for about as many projects. (The high numbers of units and projects suggest that this foundation's criteria for loans helped smaller firms than is usual in China.) For each yuan that the foundation invested in this way, 5 yuan were produced during the first four years. The average compound annual rate of return from the loaned money had been over 50 percent for some of the projects.[49] The rate of on-time loan repayments by 1989 had been 99 percent. A 1 percent bad debt rate is exceptional anywhere, and in reform China it was spectacularly low.

Many such organizations were established, often with titles that allowed them to take up almost any scientific or economic role during the mid-1980s. The Shanghai Culture Research Institute was a think tank not established by the government, but it was subordinate to the East China Chemical Engineering University and "run by the people" (*minban*).[50] Other such organizations were like the "dependent firms" (*guahu*) of large state or collective organizations.

These could claim to have some legal separation from the government. (The most famous example in Shanghai was not a think tank but a newspaper, the *World Economic Herald,* dependent on the Shanghai Academy of Social Sciences, whose status as state or nonstate became a matter of sharp controversy in May 1989.) Many consultancies were "dependent" on this academy or on the Shanghai Science and Technology Association. Of the "suggestion papers" (*jianyi shu*) sent to the municipal government by think tanks in the late 1980s, three-tenths were approved and distributed as "important documents."[51]

New technologies created variegated joint businesses, and some of their combinations were unexpected. Shanghai's Institute of Nuclear Research, for example, combined with the Shanghai Municipal Vegetable Company to found a factory in the mid-1980s that bought 35,000 tons of vegetables each year, and then kept them fresh by extinguishing nascent mold with radiation.[52]

As economic "takeoff" was achieved, first on the delta and then in Shanghai during reforms, scientific advice legitimated changes that conservatives tended to oppose. This pattern began outside the metropolis first, because the economic boom in surrounding areas came earlier there. Technical extension in Jiangsu took the form of a one-year "sparking plan," under which scientific research units and factories were supposed to pass modern technology "like sparks," to create new centers of rural industry.[53] Zhejiang also had this kind of program. That province in the mid-1980s had the second-highest output value in the country from its rural industries—after Jiangsu—and its "sparking plan" was aimed at furthering this record.[54] After controls loosened in Shanghai, especially in the 1990s, local exchanges of technology accompanied the economic boom. The modes and relations of production were changing, and these would be situational factors that could influence China's political form. There is little evidence that high Marxists in the government had any interest in taking these links seriously.

The Rise of Horizontal Trade and Regionalism

Domestic trade was a hallmark of China's reforms, and the speed and regionalism of its rise after 1970 struck directly at central planning. Self-sufficiency within small localities—the opposite of trade—had become a pillar of Chinese radical doctrine, but this tenet of autarky was decreasingly followed. All enterprises, according to radical statesmen, were supposed to "go to the local area to get materials, to process them, and to sell the products."[55] But ideal politics was not practical business, even in the early 1970s. So long as brigade and commune leaders openly proclaimed formal obeisance to leftist symbolic mantras, they could in practice create almost any markets they liked.

When material supplies decreased, or when rural industries on the delta expanded their operations, they sent buyers and sellers to other areas, establishing new markets. Economic connections of this sort were severely criticized—and the liaison offices arranging such trade had often been physically attacked—

during the height of Cultural Revolution violence in the late 1960s. But they developed strongly in the Shanghai delta during the first few years of the 1970s.

The early part of this decade saw a revival of horizontal (*hengxiang*) relations between rural enterprises and urban experts. "May 7 cadre schools" (*wuqi ganxiao*) at this time differed in certain respects from the camps for labor education (*laodong jiaoyu*) to which rightists had been sent since 1957. Some of the cadres sent there for brief periods still had reputable posts. Most of these respectable cadres did not stay very long in rural areas. They could get back into cities after a decent period of pretending to be peasants. But the attendance of some politically passable local leaders at the schools gave leeway for initiative. Also, many May 7 schools were located in better-off rural areas than most labor education settlements were. The May 7 cadres reportedly did little but read newspapers and drink tea during their stints in the countryside. But some in the Yangzi delta helped local peasants run new rural industries. These May 7 cadres of the early 1970s were the first "Sunday engineers" of the reform period, except that they stayed for the whole week. The Maoist schools taught more than what was official. They had unintended protocapitalist results. Radicals during the early 1970s criticized these rural-industrial technical connections. They argued that the cadre schools were supposed to teach city people about agriculture, not to teach peasants about industry and marketing.[56] But the trade prospered, and the traders saw no reason to explain themselves.

Liaisons of Individual Technicians with Rural Industries

In the thirty years after the mid-fifties, 1,400,000 Shanghai people—*not* counting rusticated youths—went to help other places in China. Of these, three-tenths were technicians.[57] Of all personnel specifically seconded from Shanghai jobs to help other places, a majority were workers, but many of these had technical skills and went to Jiangsu or Zhejiang. All of the nonstudent rusticates together accounted for about one-sixth of the total registered emigration from Shanghai over the three decades after 1949. This was a somewhat larger send-down than that of educated youths. It has received less scholarly attention because many of the workers and technicians went earlier and more gradually, and especially because the program's quasi-coercive aspects involved fewer intellectuals, fewer writers. In the second half of the 1950s, Shanghai light industries sent 145 whole factories to other provinces.[58]

Rustication policies inadvertently and slowly created a staff to connect nonstate rural firms with consumer markets. "Many people sent to rural areas from city offices, research agencies, and universities, as well as young intellectuals, brought science and technology, culture, knowledge, and economic information to the countryside. They linked city and countryside more closely. And because urban firms could not operate well to serve urban citizens' needs, rural industry found a market for its products."[59]

This outflow of technicians from Shanghai continued in the decade after 1978, usually on a voluntary basis as urban workers became aware that suburban and rich rural industries offered some good jobs. About 800,000 Shanghai personnel went at least for a period to other provinces for work. Most of these were nearby in Zhejiang or Jiangsu (especially in Suzhou, which is certainly not a hardship post). A lesser number of specialists went farther. By July 1980, in China as a whole, 3,400 joint enterprises across provincial jurisdictions had been registered; and more may have actually begun operations.[60] These were not organized according to the usual "vertical and horizontal" framework of supervision, but in various joint ways across geographical, functional, and ownership categories.

Past rustication policies, combined with continuing Shanghai residence controls, had the unintended effect of strengthening unofficial Shanghai connections with other rich cities in East China.

> Jiaxing has attracted many technicians and managers, especially those able to use its proximity to Shanghai. This has caused many technical personnel, who after 1949 flowed [from Shanghai] to various parts of the country and now find difficulty returning to Shanghai, to set up households in Jiaxing. Furthermore, their role in the development of Jiaxing's economy, through their personal (*siren*) connections, has caused many Jiaxing enterprises to establish links with relevant units in Shanghai.[61]

Thus Jiaxing, with the rest of the delta, came to be publicly considered as part of the "Shanghai economic circle." Some academics explicitly called for development of this "circle" around Shanghai "as a base" that would later and "gradually" spread its prosperity to farther parts of the country.[62] Although relations with the delta flourished, those with areas further inland did not.

Some of the connections of "Shanghai" firms with other places in East China were simply a matter of Shanghai businesspeople returning to their *gu xiang,* their ancestral homes. The immediate destinations of emigrants from Shanghai, in Mao's time and later, were far more frequently either small towns or large submetropolitan cities than medium-sized cities. The curve is U-shaped, on a graph of rates of flow by destination settlement sizes. Permanent emigration from Shanghai, according to a long-term survey, was more than six times more frequent to cities with over a million inhabitants than to smaller cities with more than half a million. More surprisingly, it was also about six times more frequent to *smaller* settlements of less than half a million.[63] In these locally controlled and less heavily taxed small cities and towns, professionals and technicians for rural industries most easily found niches.

These consultants came to be called "high-priced old men" (when they were not merely "Sunday engineers"), because they could earn 200 or 300 yuan for only four days of work each month—far more than their ordinary urban pay—usually for rural cooperative factories in small towns.[64] They were employed to solve technical problems, help maintain machines, give lessons, liaise with markets, and help manage. When they still had jobs in the city, often they kept such activities secret from their Shanghai units, partly to avoid others becoming jealous of the extra money they earned. But if such work was known, it might be approved by the Shanghai employers as a means of extending their own connections to rural sources of out-contracting and materials. Alternatively, it might be disapproved because it drained the energies of Shanghai technical employees. Since the trend could not be stopped, Shanghai local factory managers were usually wise to seek profits from it.

Links between specific Shanghai institutions and specific other places on the flatland began early. Before 1977, and continuing steadily thereafter, Shanghai's Jiaotong University had extensive connections with Shangyu (the largest Zhejiang city between Ningbo and Shaoxing). Apparently some Jiaotong engineers had family connections in Shangyu. They helped factories there to make refrigeration equipment, glass, metals, and electrical machines. Because of technical help from scientists at Shanghai's premier engineering university, the Shangyu Refrigeration Company was thus able to produce cooling towers that consumed one-quarter less power than units of this sort normally required. The three largest Shangyu factories that received such help from Jiaotong reciprocated by giving the university "cooperation fees" that totaled 700,000 yuan in the first seven years of the decade.[65]

The Shangyu Refrigeration Company increased its own technical staff, so that by 1986 one-fifth of the regular employees were involved in management. In the first two years of the decade, this factory sent forty workers to Jiaotong and Zhejiang universities for training.[66] These links began well before the central planners acknowledged the efficiency of "horizontal relations" in trade. They were publicized not at the time they began, but only later. They arose because of connections that particular people in Shanghai had with other East China places.

Conservatives Criticize the Technology Diffusion of Reform Rustication

Shanghai people made a great deal of money from technical consulting elsewhere. An extensive estimate for the period from 1977 to 1981 suggests that fifty-six of the city's largest research organizations, operating on commissions mostly for clients outside the city, earned about 20 million yuan for this engineering advice.[67] The pace of this development hastened as the state began to default more regularly on materials deliveries to the metropolis. In 1980, a Shanghai engineer named Han Kun was hired as a consultant by a Fengxian county enterprise in the suburbs. He received 2,000 yuan for this work. This became a *cause célèbre,* as sharp criticism came from cadres in the city who felt his compensation was too large. The critics' purpose was to discourage other Shanghai technicians from offering their services similarly. An explicit part of their complaint was that Shanghai's importance to China as a whole justified more control of personnel there than elsewhere. With consultancy becoming commonplace in other parts of China during the 1980s, and with so much technical talent in Shanghai, these conservatives fought a losing battle.

"Inopportune resignations" by technical personnel presented a problem to some Shanghai state-sector plants. From one company, four scientists left together "to work in a small factory. This withdrawal of expertise caused the key project on which they had been working to collapse. The case was even referred to by Premier Zhao Ziyang . . . . The publicity given to this case gave those who were opposed to the reform a weapon with which to counterattack."[68] Some Shanghai managers tried to restrict the employment of technicians and even retired people, preventing them from taking work in other provinces, apparently from a well-founded fear that an outflow of technology would create competitors there.[69] The long-term loser from this pattern, however, was the central government budget.

Motives of the Reform Rusticates

The people who left Shanghai to live in other places were not very numerous, but they were important because they provided links for development. Many were well schooled; a sample census showed that 80 percent had at least a secondary education. Many were young, although one-fifth to one-third were retired. About half left the city to do business elsewhere, usually in the Shanghai delta. At least one-tenth were traders. Some freely admitted that they left to escape the city's tough regulatory climate. As a local author said, "Since the open door and reforms, Shanghai has changed a great deal. But occupational mobility, especially in high positions, still is restrained by the personnel system."[70] Many talented people, especially those who had been in conflict with others in their Shanghai work units during earlier political campaigns, found comfort by moving away.

Other localities in China, some near Shanghai and some distant, generally welcomed this migration of talent. There was a continuing shortage of educated people in China, even in parts of its largest municipality. Meilong township, a suburban Shanghai county just on the border of the city, had a workforce in which, by 1988, a miniscule 0.6 percent had qualified as college-trained technicians. Surveying the whole labor pool in this town, which is so close to the city that the new rapid transit system runs there, a canvass of fourteen enterprises concluded that "skilled" workers made up just 28 percent of their total. "Among workers age 35 or more, the situation is more serious; about 25 percent are illiterate or semiliterate, and 30 percent merely had primary educations."[71] This did not render them unable to make basic political choices—or to make money. It did not mean they were unintelligent, and in reforms there is a great deal of evidence that most of these ex-peasants were not lazy. But it did mean they lacked the training necessary for technical management. For this, the metropolis could and did provide talent.

Many retired technicians and cadres from Shanghai have gone to Jiangsu or Zhejiang to live, and many others have remained in Shanghai but go to other delta cities for several days each month. Inland firms keep records, usually in card files, of contacts in Shanghai. These cover kinship ties and information about anyone else who may prove to be of use to a rural business.[72] Such a file would record the address, specialization, telephone, work unit, and other data about any possible consultant. At lunar New Year, and occasionally at other times, Shanghai contacts received cordial letters from the company, sending respects and sometimes asking for specific market information about selling products or obtaining materials, or asking whether the consultant might offer further introductions or perhaps come visit. Local authorities in Jiangsu or Zhejiang generally did not oppose links of this sort with Shanghai, especially when they could benefit from any trade that developed.

Business or technical people in the metropolis might try to establish links with their families' old hometowns. Often it was economically more rational to make liaisons with other places more appropriate for their particular economic aims. Local cadres in the hometowns of Shanghai entrepreneurs often had networks that could help make such linkages—for example, with a locality that might have a needed material. When such businesses prospered, money would frequently be donated to the towns of cadres who aided such connections. East China is now sprinkled with schools, clinics, and other institutions that have benefited from funds earned locally or elsewhere through the good offices of rural cadres who helped city-delta businesses near Shanghai.

This high-paid rustication, which was not organized by the state, also extended to somewhat more distant parts of China. Quick growth in southern Jiangsu and northern Zhejiang by the late 1980s affected adjacent areas, such as Jinhua in the mountains south of Hangzhou and nearby parts of Jiangxi and Anhui provinces.[73] These places supplied factors, notably cheap labor, to the faster-growing flatlands.

Pan'an county, the poorest in Jinhua, Zhejiang's poorest inland prefecture, by the mid-1980s still had "no industry and fewer resources." In 1983, its output value per capita was a mere 80 yuan. But the county head and CCP secretary were optimistic, because "in the past thirty years, a lot of university students came out of here. The county is poor, but people here emphasize their children's education. Now, the county has many connections with these university people. Many will come back to contribute to the rise of this poor county. These heads of the county also had university educations."[74]

The Shanghai delta's prowess in rural industrialization has led to envy in western China also—and thus to some consulting work there for Jiangnan people. In 1978, for example, a commune in Shanxi wanted to found an umbrella factory; so it compensated technicians from Zhejiang to help get it started.[75] But the economic effects of technical extension within Jiangnan were more evident during reforms, even though the central state almost surely served China's long-term interests by encouraging Shanghai connections to parts of the country that have low incomes.

"Horizontal" economic relationships within East China mutually reinforced old cultural ties. They arose because old markets over centuries had created a cultural region—which the Beijing politicians tried to weaken from 1949 to 1978 for the sake of revenues, but which still by the 1980s made a great deal of sense to many people in Jiangnan.[76] These liaisons benefited Shanghainese who participated in them more than they benefited the government. The expectations of Shanghai firms and companies in other areas when they entered into horizontal liaisons were often high. Inland companies would hope to garner Shanghai capital and technology, while Shanghai businesses often "felt that their own tasks under the state plan were already very heavy."[77] Both sides could gain advantages by cooperating on a local level.

Direct Liaisons Between Companies

The Shanghai Industrial Consulting Service Company was set up as early as 1979. It quickly made good profits and excellent foreign exchange earnings. Because this consultancy was under a regime of taxes and controls typical of all Shanghai companies, however, it ran into problems: "Because this company lacked decision making power in its internal management and in its disposal of its funds, plus the fact that its workers were not able to benefit even when they reaped handsome profits, the consulting company finally encountered difficulties in advancing its business."[78]

A sample survey of the company's transactions, conducted by another organization, determined that "every yuan spent in consulting fees by technology buyers enabled them to create 489 yuan worth of industrial output value per year. There were no specific rules, however, on the remuneration of the technicians who moonlighted and provided consulting services in their spare time." When the company clamped down on these moonlighters, "many of them quit the technological consulting firm." By 1986, the number of this company's new contracts was half that of 1985—and the company had to "suspend its business, because it could not break even."

Domestic Joint Ventures Cross the Planning Boundaries

Since 1980 especially, there have been a great many domestic "joint venture factories" (*lianying chang*) between Shanghai and other places, especially in southern Jiangsu.[79] The means of production—machines, capital, licenses, and the like—were supplied by Shanghai and were sometimes moved physically from plants in the metropolis. Many joint ventures reduced the bulk or weight of partially finished products that later were shipped to Shanghai for final processing. Universities and research centers, not just enterprises, could set up joint ventures that gave those institutions new revenues and the other cities new technology. Shanghai managers generally coordinated the packaging and selling of the products.[80]

In some fields, the supervising corporations encouraged these plans. From the beginning of 1981, the Shanghai Light Industrial Machines Company's sixteen factories developed "horizontal relations" with twenty-two plants in Wuxi, Wujin (a suburb of Changzhou), Shazhou (in Suzhou prefecture near the new foreign-trade harbor of Zhangjiagang), and elsewhere on the Shanghai delta. The production effects came quickly. Between 1979 and 1984, this Shanghai company increased its output by 44 percent. Its joint projects with factories in Suzhou created a 23 percent increase in just one year.[81]

Connections were often made directly between factories. Two printing machine plants in Shanghai and Wuxi combined in 1981. The press they coproduced was a market success, so another Shanghai plant in the same line soon set up similar arrangements with a factory in Changzhou.[82] Many Shanghai companies moved their activities only to the nearby suburbs. By 1984, fully 159 companies had been established on a joint basis between city firms and those in the suburbs, and nine-tenths were producing light industrial consumer products.[83] The greater availability of space in the suburbs was a major reason for such expansion. Among plants of the Garments Company of the city's Handicrafts Bureau by the end of 1985, for example, half of all factory space was outside Shanghai's urban districts. This was also a flight from the city's intensive bureaucratic monitoring. The supervising companies knew what was happening, of course—and they usually approved such arrangements, particularly after their own ability to manage input and product markets had collapsed anyway.

The autonomy of municipal governments throughout the delta (including Shanghai's) was somewhat reduced by this pattern; but if joint amalgamations of factories across borders was the best way for them to make money by the mid-1980s, local leaders could take a cut rather than objecting. Suzhou cadres reported that 80 percent of the firms in their city had Shanghai connections for raw materials or marketing. Three-quarters of the value of Suzhou's production was made or sold under arrangements with firms in Shanghai.[84]

Companies licensed by higher-level administrative jurisdictions apparently resisted horizontal linking more than fast-growth firms licensed by townships and especially villages, where the bills for taxes and bribes were local. In 1987 in Suzhou, only 27 percent of the firms licensed above the township level were involved in horizontal projects with other jurisdictions, mainly with Shanghai. The non-Suzhou capital that came to these projects was nonetheless 44 percent of their total assets.[85] More important, presuming this area was like others on the delta at that time, about half the value of all industrial production came from plants licensed at the township level or below.

In Wuxi, one-third of the township enterprises were joint with factories, schools, or research units in Shanghai. Some others were joint with larger plants in Wuxi or other cities. Competition was forcing even state firms to develop such ties. The number of large Shanghai firms with registered horizontal relations was 37 percent higher in 1987 than in 1986. Joint registrations with other units inside the municipality was up 18 percent, and with other provinces up 43 percent.[86] If medium-sized Shanghai industrial enterprises are counted along with large ones, more than 90 percent had subsidiaries or special relations with factories in other East China cities.[87]

Wuxi, sometimes called "Little Shanghai" before the Communist era, is the place with the largest production in Jiangsu. Wuxi is in many respects independent of both Shanghai and the provincial capital of Nanjing. One-third of all enterprises in adjacent Wuxi county by 1983 already had " 'private' trading links on a voluntary basis" with firms in seven other cities of the Shanghai delta.[88] Local leaders in the delta zone were creating regional institutions that integrated all of its large settlements.

Many kinds of cooperative links were established. Two-thirds of those involving Kunshan, for example, reportedly did not require major joint investments. Rather than money, these joint projects involved exchanges of technology, consultation services, marketing arrangements, or barter. Joint enterprises might most easily be licensed if new technology and equipment would be used, if management styles could be made more efficient, and if new kinds of products could result. But lack of official approval usually did not stymie cooperation between firms for profits from any of these changes. Especially for plants licensed at low levels, or by bureaucrats who could be bought, approvals were not hard to obtain when they were necessary. Rural Kunshan units by 1987 had more than 300 projects, of which 65 percent were with Shanghai universities, research units, and factories.[89] Kunshan also had connections with many other places, including Beijing, Tianjin, Fujian, Sichuan, and Zhejiang, and famous local products such as Kunshan honey were sold internationally.

Complementarity for Local Profits or for Central Profits

A conservative critic said the agreements for horizontal liaisons between companies were often just "short-term activities," joining companies that had comparative advantages in technology, materials, or markets. Linkages of this sort tended to be between firms in the same line of work, and each tended to develop for itself the capacities in which other partners originally had an advantage. So as time went on, this statist argued, the initial benefits from horizontal links beneath the state's radar should lessen; and he thought joint firms would become weaker. A more stable, longer-term kind of horizontal connection emerged (according to this critic) when such arrangements were set up between industrial, agricultural, and trade units, i.e., in different sectors supplying each other.[90] This centralist theory did not explain, however, why so many links were set up between similar plants: The aim was to save costs, especially taxes and other high-state rake-offs, by using whatever advantages could be found in different geographical places.

On the other hand, a minority of links were "arranged marriages," under which firms were "ordered to liaise." A Shanghai vegetable market, for example, was mandated to join with an inland trading company, setting up a new hotel. But the negotiations were between bureaucrats far above the levels of these two firms—and the local Shanghai partners were reported to disbelieve that the connection would be profitable. They were ordered to accept the proposal anyway. Business proved to be bad. The joint hotel lost money.[91]

In other cases, these marriages were between eager partners whose supervising bureaucrats disapproved. A Shanghai textile plant wanted to extend technical help to a shirt factory elsewhere in East China, for example, and municipal cadres favored the proposal too. But the supervising garment company, whose bureaucratic position was between these two levels, vetoed the proposal.[92] Such links could have been realized more quietly through trade and consultation anyway, and this may have occurred although it was not reported.

Horizontal connections were not publicized when they stirred opposition. Because so many different kinds of official units would have been involved, none was responsible for taking overall charge of this development. A PRC source reported that no comprehensive statistics on Shanghai links with Hangzhou and Jiaxing were available, for example. No one could keep tabs on all the links in Jiangnan. Many managers in small communities had interests in hiding these ties so that they could not be taxed. At least eight hundred specific connections between Shanghai and Hangzhou firms in the mid-1980s could nonetheless be documented.[93] Between Shanghai and Jiaxing, another two hundred links were also registered. Many of these were not with Jiaxing city as a whole, but with counties or townships there. One of the reasons for such cooperation was reportedly that Jiaxing's "price of land is cheap." Normally sales of land are difficult to arrange in China; but this attractive Zhejiang city is just 98 km from Shanghai by direct rail, and central procedures and taxes could be fudged there more easily than in the metropolis.

The Shanghai government in early 1986 classified horizontal links between the municipality and outside provinces into four categories: economic liaisons, compensation trade, new enterprises, and technical cooperation. These genres were needed for gathering statistics and then for monitoring the development of links that had long been unofficial and unplanned. A report was compiled, noting that most links were with areas near Shanghai; outreach to more distant regions was less frequent.[94] An attempt to catalogue such activity was most of what remained from socialist planning, but officials made no pretense that their record was complete.

Different jurisdictions within Shanghai had very different degrees of contact outside the municipality—and apparently some did not give complete reports of such links. Two of Shanghai's suburban counties (Baoshan and Chuansha) by mid-1987 had invested 9.5 million yuan in other provinces, but four other counties (Fengxian, Jinshan, Qingpu, and Songjiang) together reported such investments of only 2.7 million yuan. Shanghai county, also in the suburbs, had contracted or planned very extensive investments, totalling 11 million yuan. The data from Chongming county were said to be insufficient for analysis of "horizontal" activities from there.[95] Entrepreneurs had strong incentives to hide interactions that were unofficial and profitable. The wealth and productivity of various Shanghai counties of course varies somewhat—but not so radically as their reported horizontal investments. The main variation was almost surely in the degree to which their political leaders attempted to file full reports.

Consortia of Enterprises

When supervising industrial bureaus at Shanghai found it difficult to deliver materials at low state prices, "enterprise groups" began to form. These groups within industries would "work for the transfer of Shanghai's material-consuming industries to places where the materials are produced." Moving industries out of Shanghai solved the problems of executive cadres, who often took jobs with the new consortia. It did not, of course, provide jobs for Shanghai workers. The official and extremely hopeful claim was that "when some materials-consuming industries are shifted out of Shanghai, much space can be made available and much capital funnelled back for the development of hi-tech industries in the municipality." Those authorizations would depend, however, on fiscal and political decisions that were not guaranteed. Also, the whole plan neglected the value that local foremen placed on relations with their worker clients. So there was resistance, and it was expressed in strikes and complaints. As a Beijing newspaper reported in English:

> The effort has been merely confined to know-how transfer and granting use of [Shanghai] trade marks by local factories. There has been no real merger of capital and assets. As a result, the factories in the interior regions, which are supposed to be members of the Shanghai-based enterprise groups, actually work in the interest of the localities. In this way, Shanghai has only fostered competitors for its industry, much contrary to the original intention of making the best use of raw materials locally.[96]

Such competition would, however, be worse for Shanghai workers and tax collectors than for entrepreneurs in the city who had connections with nearby provinces. The economies of Shanghai and its delta were intertwined, even when central policies to separate them were overwhelmed by cumulative policies from local leaders to link them. Shanghai and Jiangsu, if taken as a single unit together in 1952, would have ranked only sixth among Chinese "provinces" in per-capita net value of industrial and agricultural output.[97] But by 1979, Shanghai and Jiangsu together ranked first in per-capita output among Chinese provinces, and Zhejiang had risen to sixth (and by 1984, to fourth). The big change was not in Shanghai but in its adjacent provinces. Government economic repression in the metropolis may have bred entrepreneurial habits that delivered big profits—on the delta outside Shanghai—as China's revolutionary centralization waned.

All major southern Jiangsu cities benefited from Shanghai connections at this time, and together they prospered enormously. The cities of Shanghai, Wuxi, and Changzhou contributed 87 percent of the combined output of Jiangsu and Shanghai in 1933; they still contributed 62 percent in 1982.[98] If *all* Chinese officially designated cities (*shi*) are ranked by their total gross product, counting both industry and agriculture, Suzhou and Wuxi in 1986 were respectively fourth and fifth—after only the three much larger province-level cities (Shanghai, Beijing, and Tianjin). As an analyst of the growth of these places put it, "No doubt these results are inseparable from their geographical proximity to Shanghai and their receiving the radiation and diffusion of Shanghai's economy."[99]

Joint ventures were the means of some of this diffusion, and enterprise groups accounted for more. Numbers of groups were published more frequently than their valuations, which would have been more revealing. The fifty-six enterprise groups of Changzhou in the first half of 1986, most of which also had members in Shanghai or some other non-Changzhou jurisdiction, accounted for one-third of Changzhou's industrial output and two-fifths of the remitted profits and taxes.[100] In the first nine months of 1986, Shanghai invested 850 million yuan in sixty-three joint projects, to make a total by that time of 507 such endeavors in "fraternal regions" (*xiongdi diqu*).

Many factories in Shanghai and its close hinterland developed profitable relations with similar plants in southern Jiangsu. The Tangqiao Towel Factory, founded toward the end of 1982 near Suzhou, began producing its wares in great quantity but then had problems selling them. So in 1984, it established liaisons (*lianxi*) with the Shanghai No. 15 Towel Factory, which sent technicians to Tangqiao to help raise the quality of the towels and to help market them. In 1983, a village of Tangqiao township signed a contract with the Shanghai-Wusong Chemical Fiber Factory, under which Shanghai provided equipment and some funds. This rural town put in more capital and provided factory space.[101] New Sunan factories could grow even faster if they had friends in Shanghai.

Ningbo and Shanghai: An Example of Old Relations

Cities along the coast of northern Zhejiang, from Ningbo to Hangzhou, also have long-standing connections with Shanghai. Businesspeople from that province had enormous influence in pre-1949 Shanghai. A 1920 survey of the most famous compradores in Shanghai showed that almost half were from Zhejiang.[102] Ningbo and the area around it contain the ancestral homes of many influential entrepreneurs in Shanghai. During the reform period, there were 300,000 overseas Ningbo people, mostly in Hong Kong or Southeast Asia, of whom some were very wealthy. Only one-tenth of these had actually visited Ningbo by October 1988—but their investment in the city was already enormous. PRC newspapers openly asked them in late 1988 to "help Ningbo."[103] Deng Xiaoping himself urged "mobilizing the whole world's 'Ningbo clique' to construct Ningbo." A Hong Kong shipping magnate named Bao Yugang (Sir Y. K. Pao) financed a large new university there in the 1980s. Shanghai also benefited from such generosity, but the high-tax climate mandated by Beijing was a major deterrent to investment. Few of these capitalists, if they wanted to make a profit, would put money into a city whose infrastructure had been underfinanced as badly as Shanghai's, especially when alternative sites for investment were available.

The Ningbo Association to Promote Economic Construction had its first general meeting in late 1988. A meeting of "directors" of this association included seven members from Shanghai, of whom the most notable was the group's deputy head, Li Chuwen. This high cadre was originally from Ningbo, and he had extensive experience in Hong Kong. But by late 1988, he was back in Shanghai as the main foreign affairs adviser to the municipal government. In early 1989, nine "Shanghai people with Ningbo origins" set up the Shanghai Association to Promote Ningbo Economic Construction, which was nongovernmental.[104]

Enterprise Groups, State Corporations, and Late-1980s Reformed Cadres

Local notables and state reformers alike found these traditional ties useful, though for different reasons. Just as "administrative cities" were the reformers' recipe for circumventing old conflicts between centralizers and decentralizers in China's geographical jurisdictions, "enterprise groups" became another way to change the structure of economic bureaucracies that suffered arthritis. As an economist's article claimed:

> The formation of enterprise groups will help remove barriers between different departments and regions, end the situation in which enterprises are "large and complete" or "small and complete," and rationalize enterprise structure. The past practice of "centralizing" and "decentralizing" power . . . failed thoroughly to improve the irrational product mix, [but] enterprise groups will help change the government's functions in economic management and . . . are the principal force for developing China's socialized large-scale production.[105]

This was a kind of local centralization, not a full devolution of power. It weakened the autonomy both of the central state and of most individuals. As with the "administrative cities" that centralized locally by taking over nearby geographical areas, "enterprise groups" assumed powers in economic functional fields that had, during the high tide of socialism, once been subject to ministries' plans. Such changes raised revenues, but not for the central state. The coteries behind them were local leaders who had many kinds of affective ties to each other.

A correlate of this reform was a change of symbols: economic cadres (*ganbu*) gave way to entrepreneurs (*qiye jia*). Shanghai's first major "Entrepreneurs' Club" was founded at a meeting attended by Mayor Wang Daohan in December 1984.[106] It first included 420 factory directors, managers, and chief engineers, but it was followed by many other such clubs—about forty large ones by the mid-1990s. Shanghai managers realized that they could be most effective in pressing for radical change if they acted together—and with businesspeople from other provinces.

The Golden Triangle Entrepreneurs' Club set up a 1988 "roundtable conference" in the Shanghai suburb of Jiading. Joint sponsors included the reformist Research Institute for Restructuring the Economic System and several newspapers (including the *Guangming Daily* and the *World Economic Herald*). Chief participants from Shanghai included many reformed cadres from very large state factories: the secretary of the Party committee at Baoshan Steel, the directors of both the Jiangnan and the Hudong shipyards, the heads at Shanghai Machine Tools, Shanghai Aircraft, Shanghai Bicycle, Shanghai Diesel Engines, Shanghai Solvents, Shanghai Petrochemicals, Shanghai Tunnel Engineering, and several other local power, petrochemical, and iron works. Other conferees came from Beijing, Shenzhen, Guangzhou, Yantai, Kailuan, Anshan, Shenyang, Dalian, Daqing, Haerbin, and elsewhere—heads of fifty-one huge state-owned companies.

These post-socialist taipans showed the extent of change by 1988, but even if they acted together, they may have done less to change the structure of Shanghai's political economy than "lower" levels of entrepreneurs had done. Partly because of their political stature, however, they had no need to mince words by the late 1980s in presenting their demands to other officials. They wanted to "open a road of genuinely separating two powers," so as to clarify "the administrative subordination of Party and mass organizations in enterprises."[107] They demanded the right to "participate in formulating plans." They wanted "to reduce the scope of mandatory planning and to gradually turn mandatory quotas into placement of state orders." They claimed freedom from short-term checks by supervising cadres in the ministries and bureaus above them so that they could "make independent decisions on investment." This also required that "the time limit on major enterprise contracts should be extended" so that they could plan their operations more than a few months in advance. They further demanded rights to "establish connections directly with foreign counterparts." They looked forward to more "industrial banking institutions," asking that "major enterprises and enterprise groups should be allowed to found industrial banks and group banks." They needed more serious laws, including a "free trade law" and a "corporation law." Just as vehemently, they demanded firmer "social norms to protect creditor rights and property rights" from political interference.

These ex-socialist tycoons insisted that "enterprise heads should no longer be put under serialized assessment management, as is the case with government cadres." And businesspeople should be duly compensated, so that "their social and economic position can rise along with the increase of their enterprise asset value and the expansion of their operations." They insisted on the right to set up "entrepreneurial organizations . . . through elections, to voice the demands of enterprises, particularly major ones, and to protect their interests." Finally, they required "administrative courts" that could "handle cases of government violations of the laws."

These managers were certainly not ideological liberals. Probably all of them were Communists—high-ranking ones, and unlikely to suffer dissent from their own subordinates. They were not a cowering, unproud lot. They had every reason for loyalty to the socialist system that had elevated them to posts of local power. But to maintain their enterprises, now that their supervisors in ministries and bureaus could no longer deliver materials or ensure markets, they declared independence. Whether they should properly be called an "interest group" or not, they clearly protested the parts of their own system (the state) that threatened their firms' survival. The system of small enterprises, which was effectively outside that system, was their real bane—but because they could not change that, they directed their fire at higher officials instead.

Common Interest Networks Among Entrepreneurs

The Golden Delta Entrepreneurs' Club (Jin Sanjiao Qiye Jia Julebu) took as one of its goals the networking of business firms with other kinds of units, especially in government.[108] This club hosted meals for city officials, cadres of the local Party Organization Department, officers of financial institutions, and lawyers to exchange ideas. They met regularly (on each workday that had a calendar date evenly divisible by five). The Golden Delta Entrepreneurs' Club also tried to link its members with scientists and university people. For example, the club held a seminar with academic economists about China's development strategy.

Another kind of linkage sponsored by this club was with entrepreneurs from foreign countries and other parts of China. The entrepreneurs wanted legitimation for their activities from the state offices, and they needed that particularly when they dealt with foreigners. But the presence of linkages between nonofficials and officials—especially when the nonpublic leaders organized the connections—did not show that power was flowing from the state. It flowed, along with funds, mostly in the opposite direction.[109]

The economic data networks affecting Shanghai might be analyzed in three parts, according to the size of the geographical units they covered. National-level exchanges were extensive for commercial and banking data. In all parts of China, there were hundreds of "information liaison stations" (*xinxi lianluo zhan*). At the regional level, in East China as a whole, data-exchange activities included the sending of statistics among the six provinces, a think tank for banks, another for electronic industries, another research center on production materials, and another in the office of the Shanghai Economic Zone (while this lasted). At the city level, Shanghai's municipal government in May 1984 established an Industrial Economy Information Exchange Station.[110] These were government organizations, but they were quite different from socialist planning offices. Businesspeople could call on them, or not, as they saw fit.

Technicians also established more regional and cross-regional organizations in the late 1980s, albeit with less permanent results because the period of breakneck reform at that time did not last long. The Shanghai branch of the Chinese Academy of Sciences established technical cooperation links with six hundred inland enterprises. A similar effort to develop cross-regional cooperation came under the aegis of the Shanghai Employees' Technical Association, which was linked to the Federation of Trade Unions.

The federation was not formally a government organization. Indeed, its importance in China's Communist movement goes back to the 1920s, long before the PRC government existed. But the Shanghai branch was mandated from Beijing to establish a link in 1986 with its counterpart in Yunnan province; in the next year, it expanded such connections to other border regions too.[111] These new public groupings of technicians and workers were more frequently reported as having far-flung links to distant Chinese places than did the entrepreneurs' clubs. But the managers' groups were more important—and more concentrated on the Shanghai delta. The resurgence of conservatism in late 1988, and then in mid-1989 when the government especially feared connections among workers and intellectuals, brought these developments to a temporary halt.

Commercial Embassies and Traveling Salespeople

The main effect of economic reform was that socialist offices no longer ensured factories their raw materials and product markets. Before 1979, Shanghai pharmaceutical makers already had increasing difficulty maintaining sales volumes inland, apparently because new factories in other provinces produced drugs from raw materials that the state had previously been able to requisition for high-tax Shanghai firms. In an attempt to restore the old pattern, the city got permission to establish a Pharmaceutical Management Bureau, whose head made sales trips to Zhejiang, Jiangsu, Fujian, and other places for market research.[112]

Permanent and temporary offices from Shanghai and its adjacent provinces were set up by all kinds of agencies to seek markets and raw materials not just in China but also abroad. In 1985, the Jiangsu provincial government set up a trade representative's office in Hong Kong.[113] Zhejiang established a Hong Kong trade office in 1988 (partly because the British colony was its largest overseas investor).[114] Commercial embassies flowed in all directions. By March 1985, offices from practically all of China's other provinces had "come to Shanghai to open stores and run factories."[115] Of the 307 such offices that were registered by that time, 46 percent came from within the Shanghai Economic Zone, including 18 percent each from Jiangsu and Zhejiang, and 5 percent each from Anhui and Jiangxi. When Shanghai agencies approved these offices, i.e., when the aim was not to reduce Shanghai's own supplies, units of the city provided about half the capital to them; so they were joint ventures.

Before 1986, there was a formal rule that allowed each jurisdiction outside the city to establish just one representative office in Shanghai. Under this restriction, seventy-six provinces and ministries had established embassies of this sort in the municipality by that year, but their subordinate units could not do so. When the restriction was abolished in the following year—apparently because it failed to ensure the registration of many such visitors—106 subprovincial agencies established their own offices to deal more directly with counterparts in Shanghai. Also, over a thousand branches of non-Shanghai factories and stores were approved for establishment within the city, and most of these opened almost immediately. Their total revenues exceeded 1.8 billion yuan, and their profits and tax remittances were worth 62 million yuan.[116]

The "embassies" of Shanghai municipality itself, as distinguished from those sent from companies within the city, have been limited in number. During the 1950s, the city ran only one such office (in Beijing). Not until the 1980s was this number raised. By 1987, Shanghai had quasi-consulates in five other PRC cities (Chongqing, Guangzhou, Haerbin, Wuhan, and Xi'an). These dealt with groups of provinces larger than the cities in which they were located, but there was an interesting discrepancy between Shanghai's relatively few offices elsewhere and the general representation in Shanghai of nearly every other province.

In 1987, Shanghai's centrally run government signed agreements "to protect the legal rights and interests of enterprises in horizontal economic relations" with a group of relatively distant places: Heilongjiang, Hunan, Jiangxi, Jilin, Sichuan (including a separate agreement with Chongqing), and Xinjiang.[117] Most sales teams, both to and from the city, nonetheless came and went from smaller units and lower administrative levels. The Beijing-run layers of the bureaucracy supported kinds of horizontal relations they could monitor. Administratively lower layers supported opposite kinds, which could operate freely under more local (not necessarily lighter) tax regimes.

A 1987 survey of over four thousand PRC travelers to Shanghai, which claimed to be random, showed that a majority (69 percent) came to the city for "connections," most of which were probably with families but part of which was for trade. Only 12 percent came for tourism, 6 percent for study, and 5 percent each to see friends or go to hospitals.[118] By 1988, 15 percent of the 1.1 million visitors in Shanghai each day came either to purchase materials or sell products.[119] The bulk were traveling salespeople. Since their activities were uncoordinated, outside any unified government control, they received little high-level official help. If banks would not finance their trade, these companies might barter in kind. As one conservative writer put it, "The state plan is flouted by barter arrangements which have very far-reaching administrative implications. They also have far-reaching implications for some of the familiar commonsense arguments for the encouragement of local industry, such as fortifying local self-sufficiency."[120]

The economic boom in localities simply overwhelmed these socialist concerns. Throughout the country, rural spending on consumer goods from 1978 to 1981 rose by 122 percent (a 30 percent annual growth rate). By 1987, three-fifths of all retail sales were in rural areas, and one-fifth of China's money supply was in the hands of peasants.[121] This exuberant new demand would be met. Since the state did not foster commercial channels that could fill it, nonstate and nominal low-state institutions did so.

Of Planners and Buttons

The most famous uncontrolled market in all China was not far from the Shanghai delta to the south. A Wenzhou township, Jiaotou, became the country's biggest button market. One-fourth of all buttons sold in China by the late 1980s came from that single town, and this is in fact a lot of buttons. The intellectuals who ran planning commissions had apparently not thought much about buttons, but newly rich rural Chinese wanted them for their post-Mao suit clothes. So three hundred Jiaotou households made these goods: "Every family opened a small factory to make buttons. Within less than one year, there were a lot of three-story buildings, and a street was formed. In each building, the first floor is the store, the second is a factory, and the third is the living room. . . . About a hundred thousand Wenzhou people now are scattered over the whole country. They form an information circuit, a business network."[122]

The southern Zhejiang economy complements the state sector, and that is why it could grow. Wenzhou's buttons became famous, but actually they contributed less than 5 percent of national trade from that prefecture in 1984. More important were appliances (28 percent), acrylic fiber clothes (23 percent), and plastic bags (19 percent). The prereform planned distribution system had failed to find wide markets for any of these particular commodities, even though many places in China produced them. Wenzhou traders, with their centuries-long tradition of emigration, seafaring, piracy, geographic isolation, and gross evasion of any inconvenient state policies, were well placed to fill niches the socialist allocation system did not serve. They got into many markets early, and they made a great deal of money.

The exceptionally free markets of Wenzhou were often located at spots where there had been traditional trading fairs. But they now traded nontraditional goods, ranging from plastics to computer chips. The freedom of these modern specialized markets attracted merchants on a nationwide basis, far beyond the old market area, even in China's far west and in foreign countries.[123] Buyers came to Wenzhou because the goods were more diverse and the prices were different—set more freely and usually lower for quality goods—than in their own places.[124]

"Materials Loans" and Barter in Commerce

If socialist credit crunches prevented monetized markets from developing, salespeople traded without money. Barter was a more common form of horizontal link than was investment, and exchanges often had to be documented in terms of "compensation trade" (*buchang maoyi*) even when they were ordinary sales, perhaps based on under-the-table money.[125] Rather than being a backward hindrance to reform, official support for barter was thus a pillar of modern change.

The reform process evinced many such ironies. As new industries grew up, especially in Shanghai's suburbs, barter was necessary as a means to obtain raw materials for the fresh factories. Inland suppliers often would not sell to these burgeoning rural industries at the low state prices, so the transactions had to be called "compensation trade" rather than purchases—even when the buyers compensated the sellers largely in money.

The terms of trade for Shanghai's suburban industries deteriorated in the mid-1980s, mostly because other rural industries in Jiangsu and Zhejiang would not send materials except at high prices. Four counties in Shanghai through 1985 had "compensated" places outside the municipality with a vast amount of money (53 million yuan) by June 1986, but in return they had received only 22 percent as much by value in "materials loans" (*wuzi daikuan*).[126] Baoshan county alone, from 1983 to 1986, had thirty compensation trade agreements, from which it received only 38 percent of the value it had supplied by then. This was intended "horizontal trade" by jurisdictions trying to obey the laws even after the state had left them in the lurch by abandoning socialist delivery plans it could not fulfill. This trade was contracted, but it largely did not occur. If inland suppliers had found higher prices elsewhere, they could in practice delay filling their contracts indefinitely.

Mixed Motives of State Cadres and Factory Managers in Horizontal Liaisons

Raw materials shortages gave Shanghai state cadres great incentives to make horizontal liaisons elsewhere, if only to preserve their own jobs by getting contract documents that could be reported upward in the bureaucracy. Firms under the Light Industrial Bureau, from 1979 to 1984, set up forty-eight "liaison enterprises." In the second half of 1984 and in 1985, the bureau allowed a tripling of the number of accounting units under its jurisdiction—mostly yet more liaison firms—of which it registered the establishment of no less than 241 in this period.[127] In some of these cases, the bureau may have done this under pressure from formally subordinate factory managers to whom it could not supply inputs it had promised. In any case, it is evident that not all the liaison agreements were clear successes. Many of the Shanghai firms still did not receive from inland places the materials for which they had contracted.

Shanghai managers, when they had personal connections with the inland towns that benefited from such arrangements, could have been content even if their firms in the high-tax urban environment were disadvantaged. By the mid-1980s, they could get permission from embarrassed procurement officials to sign almost any deal with inland places that *promised* materials—whether or not they would actually *deliver* materials. When these bargains worked to the advantage only of inland places where managers had or could form personal ties, these businesspeople might more willingly bear the consequent problems for their plants back in the city.

Shanghai factories before the 1990s did not stand a long-term chance of gaining anyway. Success in restoring Shanghai production had—always, like clockwork—led only to higher taxes and remittances. Local managers could not miss the overwhelming evidence for this. Their supervisors could not fire them, however, because sufficient personnel who might be competent and willing to replace many of these crucial hinge leaders were not available. For years, the supervising bureaucracies had made abundantly clear that they did not care about Shanghai firms except as sources of revenue, and Jiangnan managers in Shanghai with interests elsewhere could now follow this lead. The disruption of Shanghai supplies and markets provided a chance for managers with interests elsewhere to serve them. In this tense market, unintended industrial reforms could easily overwhelm the planned ones.

As commerce boomed to give a billion Chinese unprecedented supplies, commercial personnel still did not escape traditional ex-Confucian opprobrium. Their markets were crucial engines of reform—but so messy and unreliable, many had to break laws to get their business done. They did this, in fact and often; but they did not necessarily like doing it. Their norms and situations were in conflict. Salespeople during reforms have been objects of political schizophrenia. On China's early post-Mao stages, a surprising number of producers chose Arthur Miller's play *Death of a Salesman.* Its description of impersonal market pressures passed muster with conservatives as a critique of capitalism, and with reformers as a critique of alienation.[128] The play solved nothing, but it was an elegant means to explore a Chinese problem common at the time.

Commercial people were a large group. *Wenhui News* reported that by 1988 Shanghai had more than a hundred thousand salespeople in its ten thousand enterprises, although it is unclear how many of these were wholesalers. About an eighth of all visitors to Shanghai came as traders. As a radio broadcast put it:

> Some stay in luxury hotels and travel by taxi, while others wait for customers to come begging for the rare raw materials they can supply. But the majority are out all the time, trying their luck and getting their business done with popular brands of cigarettes and other small "bribes." It is a recognized fact that most salespeople enjoy low social status, even though some have helped their businesses achieve big profits. Some try to establish "connections" with those playing key roles in their companies by offering small bribes, small benefits, and other sorts of gifts. Others, especially those who look for state-controlled raw materials such as chemicals and iron, go from door to door, from one department to another, begging for what their factories need. Still others, people who work in small township factories and have little access to the urban administrative network, have to buy their way into each layer of the city's bureaucracy. They are willing to do whatever is necessary to make deals, occasionally at the cost of personal dignity and funds.[129]

"More channels and fewer links" (*duo qudao, shao huanjie*) is a reform slogan, calling for more horizontal trade and fewer vertical allocations. The economic advantages of letting producers sell directly to consumers, without going through higher state agencies, are clear. But laws to protect such trade have been easier to draft than to implement. This was like political reform—much simpler to discuss than to achieve. Horizontal trade was actually an endemic, structural kind of political reform. The rise of locally profitable trade lessened the power of high Party officials. Forty years of managerial tradition militated against direct channels of trade, but they could not prevent it. The resources generated by such commerce went mostly into local power networks.

The Rise and Fall of the Shanghai Economic Zone

China's largest plan for horizontal trade went through many forms, and it had many predecessors. In the 1950s, the East China Economic Coordination Zone (*Huadong jingji xiezuo qu*) was one of several organizations that Chen Yi's field army bequeathed to the region. In July 1957, the Shanghai Party called a conference on "economic coordination" for the provinces of Jiangsu, Zhejiang, Anhui, Fujian, Jiangxi, and Shanghai.[130] Many of the non-Shanghai enterprises either produced intermediate goods or extracted materials, especially in mining. "This coordination is expected to stimulate Shanghai's industry."[131]

One of the main early bases for regional cooperation and conflict was the East China electric grid.[132] This network came under the purview of the Shanghai Economic Zone, and a major aim was to ensure coal production in Anhui so that cities on the delta would have adequate energy. In return for capital and talent commitments to other parts of East China, the metropolis got something as valuable as credit: good markets for its own industries. The quid pro quo, from the viewpoint of Beijing planners, was that Shanghai could retain very few profits from these industries. The system remained stable only so long as the state remained strong.

The Zone's Stages

Already by 1970, national planning was decentralized so that the whole state plan was merely a sum of separate prospectuses for the "cooperation regions" (*xiezuo qu*), which worked independently of each other.[133] The economy in 1970 was therefore already regionalized. Interprovincial cooperation flourished in many fields during the first part of that decade—even though it was sometimes opposed by radicals.

An early example came not in the economy, but in the field of public health. Eight counties around the geographical point joining Shanghai, Jiangsu, and Zhejiang cooperated during the early 1970s in a local campaign against the disease usually called "liver fluke" or "snail fever." This debilitating and potentially fatal ailment, schistosomiasis, is caused by parasites that infect snails and workers in wet rice paddies. It remained a major medical problem in rural parts of East China even after communitarian campaigns had made progress against many other diseases. Interprovincial cooperation organized by local authorities had previously been rare, but by the spring of 1970, two medical organizations linked Shanghai with Jiangsu and with Zhejiang to combat schistosomiasis. They established thirteen "joint prevention areas" along their borders.[134] Cultural Revolution radicals at this time were running their own campaign against the "four pests,"[135] and they resented competition by local governments for medical resources. They reportedly "struggled against" the interprovincial antischistosomiasis campaign—but without much effect. Regional cadres called meetings, and when higher authorities sent down directives to quash these activities, the meetings simply continued anyway.[136]

Cooperation among these same eight Shanghai, Jiangsu, and Zhejiang counties extended from schistosomiasis to other fields. Local authorities in Wujiang, Jiangsu, promoted a particular kind of garbage-fermentation chamber for producing methane gas, which could be used by farm households for cooking. The leaders in all eight nearby counties adopted this as an agricultural extension project. Kunshan, Jiangsu, reportedly treated its "barefoot" doctors in a way that made them effective, so the other localities copied this too. Jiashan, Zhejiang, experimented with antisnail "firebreaks," and other counties reportedly contributed various kinds of scientific research.

These connections among localities developed because of actual similarities of problems and opportunities. Markets between counties and communes, which were convened at frequent fairs in the early 1970s, also involved traders from different sides of provincial borders. They were condoned by some central leaders and opposed by others. In all recent periods, Beijing has contained both reformers and conservatives.

At the end of 1978, an official fad emerged for an entirely different kind of zone, the "special economic zone" (SEZ) for foreign trade. Three of these were authorized in Guangdong, and one in Fujian. But in Shanghai, the premier taxpaying city, all such plans were delayed. Taiwan's "export processing zones" at Kaohsiung, Nantse, and Taichung had been highly successful in the 1970s, as had similar zones in other countries.[137] The three zones in Taiwan altogether comprised less than three square kilometers,[138] and they were sharply focused on external markets, with a very limited list of enterprises and borders that were easy to patrol. The Shenzhen SEZ alone was over a hundred times that size in area, it relied mostly on overseas Chinese rather than foreign capital, and its domestic interactions were at least as important as its effects on markets abroad. Shenzhen became a flagship and symbol of reform, as well as a specific plan to make money.

Some such development in Shanghai might have provided a better tax regime. The idea thus was welcomed locally. As two economists pointed out, the Shanghai delta covers one of the richest and most densely populated parts of China.

They called for something better than the old "cooperation zones" of the 1950s.[139] As late as the 1976–80 Five-Year Plan, the power of provincial jurisdictions had been firmly retained; but these reformers called for "breaking through provincial boundaries" so that these large areas could "both join together and compete."[140] From 1980, Shanghai mayor Wang Daohan began to hold regular joint meetings with the governors of Jiangsu and Zhejiang provinces and the mayors of Changzhou, Hangzhou, Jiaxing, Nantong, Ningbo, Shaoxing, Suzhou, and Wuxi cities. The office of the Shanghai Economic Zone emerged from these sessions, but it never had the authority to countermand provincial or municipal cadres. It existed only to coordinate them when they agreed.

In 1981, "more than one hundred experts" got together in Wuxi to confer on the economic future of the Shanghai delta. A report concluded that "Zhejiang, Jiangsu and Shanghai should cooperate to study the delta's agrarian areas, industrial network, and distribution of cities, and to make a new plan from a 'natural and economic' perspective." After this conference, the Shanghai Social Sciences Academy established a research group to make a more detailed report. On May 19, 1982, *Wenhui News* summarized proposals on founding an office to reconcile the economic plans of Jiangsu, Zhejiang, and Shanghai—not over their whole extent, but only "in the Yangzi delta, mainly in the Shanghai-Nanjing and Hangzhou areas." At this early date, northern Jiangsu and southern Zhejiang were omitted.

This initiative came from people in the region, although of course any plan over such a prosperous region would require bargaining for central allowances. Zhao Ziyang apparently began looking at maps centered on Shanghai, because he referred in several speeches to a "two-hundred-kilometer circle" that covers this natural market area. A Japanese economist, brought in by central reformers to analyze the proposal, specified that the Shanghai zone should "not be like the Guangzhou economic area, which mainly absorbs foreign money, but an economic zone given special powers to extend itself through cooperation within itself . . . not a closed but an open economy . . . a relatively independent part of the country as a big system."[141] This beneficence from Beijing was welcome but belated; economic liaisons within the delta had actually been booming for years.

As early as October 7, 1982, Zhao Ziyang proposed a Shanghai Economic Zone to overcome the "separation of horizontal from vertical management" (*tiaokuai fenge*). Zhao continued to be a patron of the zone into the mid-1980s, sending "instructions" (*pishi*) for many years to encourage conferences among local leaders. The upshot, however, was that regional and local jurisdictions were to become more important, and commands from Beijing less so. On December 22, 1982, the State Council in principle approved the zone, involving eight other cities with Shanghai.[142]

Yet the mandate remained vague, perhaps because central conservatives saw the disadvantages of this plan from their own viewpoint. Tax rates throughout the delta remained much higher than in most of China. Also, province-level governments on the delta did not have identical interests. Jurisdictions farther inland were clearly unsure they could benefit from this new arrangement. The less prosperous areas of East China could nonetheless agree with Shanghai politicians and economists that the city should specialize in high technology—and let them produce goods that had previously been Shanghai's strengths. A deputy mayor of Nanchang, Jiangxi, for example, argued that if more technology and investment came to his province, transport costs for the products could be lowered and Shanghai's own economic structure could be freed to develop in new areas.[143] This Jiangxi leader called for a shift of more processing industries inland. The problem was that such a strategy would require money for technical renovation in Shanghai. No one knew whence these funds would come, unless delta taxes fell. If that happened, the defense, hydraulic, and heavy industrial ministries in Beijing would have somehow to make their budgets without Shanghai.

In January 1983, the Planning Office of the Shanghai Economic Region nonetheless started its work. From the beginning, its independent authority was small. Most of its early efforts stressed construction projects that would help several jurisdictions, e.g., more ports on the lower Yangzi and better flood control for Lake Tai.[144] The zone's office mainly convened conferences of autonomous local leaders in various functional areas ranging from dikes to data collection. On some of the stated goals (for example, flood control around Lake Tai), progress was slow or absent.

The Shanghai Economic Zone in this early, compact form consisted of ten cities (the original nine plus Shaoxing, Zhejiang), along with the fifty-five rich counties covering the whole delta. These counties were all formally put under the administrations of the cities.[145] Although this zone comprises a tiny 0.7 percent of China's total land area and has only 2.7 percent of the country's arable land, its population (50 million then) is about 5 percent of the nation. These are small percentages. But this compact zone in 1984 produced about one-third of China's textiles, one-fourth of the machines, and one-fifth of the chemicals. Rural industries already accounted for 16 percent of the zone's total output value and a much higher portion of the nation's products from rural factories.[146] In terms of culture, or at least language, this zone coincided almost exactly with the Wu-speaking flatland.

This version of the Shanghai Economic Zone was grandly hailed as involving two "great breakthroughs in the thinking of the leadership." These two "new" insights were that Shanghai should pioneer a drive for the four modernizations, and that it should develop more foreign trade.[147] Both ideas were in fact very old, much mooted but for two decades less implemented. Actually, continued high taxation in Shanghai suggested that the central leadership was not united behind the zone, and the thinking of local leaders had made these breakthroughs long before. When investment was finally in prospect, however, there seemed no reason to quibble with pomp.

Interests in the zone of central leaders, provincial politicians, and individual managers were far from identical. Jiangsu's assent to the Shanghai Economic Zone was closely related to that province's hopes for more foreign trade. Most of the leaders in the provincial capital, Nanjing, came from poor parts of northern Jiangsu or neighboring Shandong. But the richest large parts of East China are on the delta, especially in southern Jiangsu. Competition for resources and markets was inevitable between the provincial authorities of Jiangsu, Zhejiang, and Shanghai—even when indigenous leaders tended to see this situation as less zero-sum.

In 1983, Wuxi city wanted closer connections with Shanghai than Jiangsu planners in Nanjing had allowed. By 1984, the Jiangsu government cut Wuxi's investment (in favor of parts of Subei), but the reason was not merely a political dispute. Instead, it lay in the fact that Shanghai's and Jiangsu's economies soon became more similar and less complementary. Both had advanced industries. As the open policy became more important, Shanghai's ability to market products abroad became a potential advantage for Jiangsu. This was sometimes an argument to include northern Jiangsu in the Shanghai Economic Zone, so that Shanghai might help export its products.[148] This strategy did not work well, however, for various reasons. The best Jiangsu enterprises (mostly in the south) soon found they could export directly, perhaps paying Shanghai consultants but not necessarily paying Shanghai officials. Also, northern Jiangsu industries still produced little that could compete internationally. Shanghai exports many products from Jiangsu—but the city was mainly connected (except in the part of the province nearest the metropolis) with relatively small Jiangsu firms, which were not strongly linked to the provincial government.

Economic zones nonetheless were a national trend by 1984, and all large regions pressed (or were pressed) to create them. All did so, at least nominally; the list of new zones in the mid-1980s is impressive on paper.[149] What the new economic administrations meant, however, differed enormously from place to place. Each zone was subject to flexible interpretation, not just by the central government but also by local networks and their leaders.

Added Layers for the Shanghai Zone

Announcement of the Shanghai Economic Zone's "readjustment" (expansion) came at a late-1984 symposium to discuss strategy for the development of agriculture. Northern Jiangsu and southern Zhejiang were now included, as well as all of Anhui and Jiangxi. The zone was thus divided into first and second "layers" (*cengci*). The "first layer" was the delta (*sanjiao zhou* from this time became a commonly used term), which was identical with the earlier compact zone. The "second layer" comprised all the rest of Jiangsu and Zhejiang, as well as all of Anhui and Jiangxi.[150] This second layer in 1985 had a population of almost 150 million people, while the first layer had a population of more than 50 million. The inner area had only 5 percent of the nation's people, but it still at that time produced 20 percent of the PRC's industrial output.

The local silence, after this central initiative, was deafening. Not a peep was heard, and not a thing was done. Perhaps delta leaders knew that such an enlargement would render the zone meaningless. They could make their own connections anyway; so as a purely symbolic gesture, in the mid-1980s crisis when the state was finally constructing other institutions that might replace its plans with less central arrangements, there was no political reason to object to a zone simply because it would be a fiction. Local leaders want to be loyalists even when their interests are hurt, and it may already have been evident that the new enlarged Shanghai Economic Zone was not going to harm anybody.

This was not, however, the conservatives' view, and they could express themselves in public. A member of the Central Advisory Commission, Zhang Pinghua, said that Shanghai should "set an example in modernizing agriculture . . . . This is its bounden duty and is expected by the people."[151] One analysis distinguished Shanghai's relations to near areas (which involved extensive professional cooperation) and its links to more distant areas (which tended to involve more extraction of raw materials).[152] Two subzones within the expanded zone were evident, and the delta was the most industrialized part.[153] In 1985, the portions of national income from industry in Jiangsu and Zhejiang were respectively 51 percent and 47 percent. But in Anhui and Jiangxi, this part was about 35 percent.[154] (In Shanghai, which is smaller and perhaps not comparable on this index, the industrial portion was 73 percent.)

The dominance of the Yangzi delta area—the "first layer" of the economic zone—is evident in Table 1.4–2. Jiangsu and Zhejiang are far richer than Jiangxi or Anhui, despite the relative poverty of northern Jiangsu and much of inland and southern Zhejiang. Jiangxi and Anhui had per-capita incomes below the national average. They rank in the upper half of provinces by wealth, but the national average is raised by a few coastal provinces—of which Shanghai, Jiangsu, and Zhejiang are among the most obvious.

Rough comparisons of gross and net output figures (even though they do not cover identical sets of activities) suggest that the degrees of vertical economic integration in these provinces correlate with their per-capita incomes. This variable also links to the rates at which all levels of government extract fiscal remittances and taxes from them. Shanghai's expanded 1984 economic zone was much larger than the previous version, but also less coherent. It had a population of 200 million, 19 percent of China's people. In the mid-1980s, this area's industrial and agricultural output value was 29 percent of China's total.[155] In comparison with the earlier, smaller zone, Shanghai was now being asked by the central government to take responsibility for four times the number of people—but to do that with an increase of resources less than twice as much. This was not, at first face, a very good deal; and in fact it did not last. Horizontal mutual advantages, not central decrees, determined fast or slow cooperation between areas. Regional plans were duly trumpeted, although they were implemented

Table 1.4-2

1983 Economic Indices for Provinces in the Expanded Shanghai Economic Zone (yuan per capita and a ratio)

	Shanghai*	Jiangsu*	Zhejiang*	Jiangxi	Anhui	*Shanghai Economic Zone*	All China
National income	2,553	621	556	369	357	612	481
Gross output	6,025	1,344	1,033	578	570	1,235	898
in industry	5,838	1,028	762	337	332	969	594
in agriculture	342	416	357	264	252	332	305
Retail sales	912	338	316	216	203	312	278
Sales/output	.15	.25	.31	.37	.36	.25	.31

Notes and Source: The three core provinces are asterisked. In order of per-capita wealth and industrial production, Shanghai, Jiangsu, Zhejiang, Jiangxi, Anhui is the ranking of provinces in the Shanghai Economic Zone. It is also (with a reversal of only of Anhui and Jiangxi) the order of the rate of fiscal remittance to government, or also the degree of vertical economic integration. (To estimate this last: the national income figure approximates a sum of values added, but the gross output figures involve extensive double-counting of values added. Their ratio roughly estimates vertical integration.) The retail sales figure is formally called the *shehui shangpin lingshou zong'e*. The last line of the table, a portion of retail sales in gross output, has been computed from the source and shows an inverse relation between provincial productivity and the rate at which value can be retained there. See *Shanghai jingji qu fazhan zhanlue chutan* (Preliminary Research on the Development Strategy of the Shanghai Economic Zone), *World Economic Herald* and Shanghai Economic Zone Research Society, eds. (Shanghai: Wuxi Branch of Shanghai Eighth People's Printers, 1986), p. 50, a book that is "distributed" (*faxing*), not on a limited-circulation basis but also without public sale. The second, third, and fourth lines on this table report gross output values: in total, in industry, and in agriculture. National income is a sum of values added. Gross output value statistics (which are less useful except for rough comparisons, but more available) sum the values simply from all accounting units.

only insofar as they met local interests. Especially in fields involving modern technology, competition between delta cities for investment was sharp. In the new and important optical fiber business, for example, the Shanghai Economic Zone generally had the best facilities in the nation. But each major city there wanted to develop this new field fully, and they did not coordinate with each other; they reportedly "fought" each other.[156]

This kind of conflict was between jurisdictions. Individual entrepreneurs could often maneuver between offices with fewer problems. Also, many cities on the delta had interests complementary to those of inland centers, including those of Jiangxi and Anhui. Conflicts between the delta and inland provinces were with high leaders there, who often doubted that the more advanced areas paid enough for what the inland places sold.

Shanghai has long made investments outside the city. In Anhui up the Yangzi from Nanjing, the Ma'anshan Iron Mine was a major Shanghai project. So were several mines at the Huainan colliery, as well as other Anhui extractive industries. The municipality owned factories making semifinished products for later work in Shanghai; but the usual purpose was to supply the metropolis with raw materials. Because of the advantages of operating in low-cost areas, Shanghai firms elsewhere have been profitable. Factories owned by the city, but located outside it, together sold as much output as each of six Shanghai counties did in 1980.[157] But by 1985, partly due to inland localization of ownership in some of these external enterprises, only three counties produced less than Shanghai's investments outside the municipality.[158] This localization came from political pressure by resurgent low-tax provinces to process their own resources during reforms.

Inland Complaints of Shanghai Imperialism

Anhui was a leading supplier of industrial raw materials. From 1952 to 1983, 60 percent of its coal production left the province, and one-third of its pig iron.[159] During the 1970s, Shanghai had invested in several PLA-related industries in Anhui, but these proved unprofitable because even the army did not want their products. These plants were therefore disbanded. The workers were not dismissed; many returned to Shanghai, and some found new work. Relations between Shanghai and Anhui agents—both offices and individuals—were complex. They involved complementary interests, but Shanghai was a metropolis that provincial leaders elsewhere feared could turn them into "colonies."[160]

A professor from Anhui complained in the mid-1980s that his province produced raw materials that were processed elsewhere (notably in Shanghai) and then were sold as finished goods back to Anhui at high prices. He demanded that "Shanghai, Jiangsu, and other developed provinces" should give Anhui more technical support in return.[161] He particularly suggested that Shanghai move some of its old equipment inland, so these places could develop and the metropolis could start new lines of business. A great many bridges, railways, and canals had been constructed in his province—as he put it, "built in Anhui, located in Anhui, but by no means just for the benefit of Anhui."[162] On the contrary, these facilities were mostly designed to take his province's minerals elsewhere.

A deputy mayor of Huaibei, Anhui, complained that his city's mining bureau sold almost a million tons of coal to Shanghai in 1983. But because of high production and transport costs—and a low fixed state price for coal—it lost 0.57 yuan on each ton. In the next year, Huaibei sold 10 percent more to Shanghai, so it lost more money. As this Anhui local leader complained, the price of Shanghai products in Anhui was high.[163] In fact, the metropolis did not profit much from these transactions because of its tax rate; the central government was making the money. But from the viewpoint of an inland East China city, Shanghai looked like a colonial metropole. At a 1988 meeting of ten thousand Anhui cadres, a provincial Party secretary said that Anhui would study Guangdong and Fujian far away, and Jiangsu and Zhejiang nearby—pointedly leaving out Shanghai.[164] In an article about Anhui's relation to the Shanghai Economic Zone, the provincial governor in 1985 slyly averred that Anhui was only a "Third World" place, without much technical capacity. But, as he pointed out, it had many resources that coastal areas lacked.[165]

Technical cooperation between Shanghai and Jiangxi, although subject to some of the same pressures, progressed well during reforms. The oddly named Sincere Discussion Society to Vitalize Jiangxi and the Shanghai Research Association to Vitalize Jiangxi got together in the metropolis for a meeting, which was attended by notables from both places.[166] Technical cooperation projects were at the center of these discussions. The meeting was held among organizations that had not been created by central fiat from Beijing, and its explicit goal was to spur "horizontal liaisons" (*hengxiang lianhe*) between Shanghai and Jiangxi. For Shanghai, the payoff was raw materials supplies; for Jiangxi, it was new technologies.

The viability of each connection depended on the particular proposal: whether local leaders or large bureaucracies could run the management, and the extent to which benefits would go to active participants. Governments, particularly at the provincial level but also at lower levels under some leaders, did not easily cooperate with each other. "In terms of ecology, artificial boundaries within the delta led to bad results, and these lines made it impossible to have a unified plan. An example is water. A program to control the level of Lake Tai has been on the agenda for several years, but because it involves several offices and local governments, a unified plan has not been agreed."[167] The Jiangsu-Zhejiang border runs through the lake, and provincial and local authorities could not easily agree on procedures for controlling the water level. Lacking a consensus, each jurisdiction did as it pleased.

There is also evidence that provincial authorities in Nanjing were less eager for close cooperation with Shanghai than were many entrepreneurs closer to the metropolis within Jiangsu province. The campaign for industrial reforms led to an all-province meeting, held at Zhenjiang, which resolved "to energetically improve southern Jiangsu and speedily develop northern Jiangsu." The southern (Sunan) area was the site of most past economic successes and current potentials, and its bureaucrats were urged to "break free from the limits of administrative divisions" within the province and especially to "step up port construction."[168] Riverine cities could develop deep-sea maritime facilities. The Nanjing International Container Shipping Company, established in late 1987, was a joint enterprise of the Nanjing Harbor Administration and the International Corporation of Alameda, California, which leased a container pier equipped with the latest in Wang computers.[169] Because of its decades-old role as a tax farm, Shanghai had trouble responding to such improvements elsewhere.

Nanjing bureaucrats wanted to unify their province, which was split by the Yangzi. In 1988, Jiangsu authorities developed a plan to improve Wuxi's communications with other parts of the province, specifically northern Jiangsu (Subei) by means of a bridge across the Yangzi at Jiangyang.[170] Realization of this concept was delayed, however. By the early 1990s, a "Sunan development area" was defined by Nanjing authorities as excluding Shanghai, so close across its border.[171] These boundaries did not, however, represent the connections that Jiangnan people had. Local ties between individuals and networks readily span the Shanghai-Jiangsu border—whose location is an administrative whim no more ancient than 1959. This line has no cultural meaning. Shanghai was, in imperial times, part of Jiangsu. Provincial officials on both sides pretended the border was important, but the people living near it have no such notion. The Shanghai delta, the flat part of the Yangzi floodplain where people speak Wu ("Shanghainese") dialects, is for them the natural unit.

Subprovincial Concerns and the Zone

Zhejiang authorities were more eager than those of Jiangsu in 1988 to make liaisons with Shanghai. The mayor of Hangzhou made a speech calling for closer links with Shanghai, calling the large metropolis the "head of the dragon" in the Yangzi and proposing Hangzhou-Ningbo-Shanghai cooperation to create a major export zone. He also suggested that joint ventures, material exchanges, and technical and personnel exchanges be intensified, as had happened in the newly prosperous areas of Guangdong.[172]

High officials at the province level (as in Beijing) had fluctuating and vague notions of what the Shanghai Economic Zone should be. What actually happened, however, showed these high leaders' partial irrelevance. After 1984, and especially in 1986, Shanghai's trade with both Jiangsu and Zhejiang accelerated quickly—at 40 to 60 percent per year, according to the estimate of one economist. Businesspeople could interpret their many mandates from on high in whatever ways would serve themselves. They could get like-minded government offices to support them. By 1985, the Shanghai Economic Association (Shanghai Shi Jingji Xuehui) sponsored the publication of a series of glossy books covering the whole economic zone, with detailed maps of counties, exhaustive lists of products and the factories whence they could be obtained, complete with pictures and company telephone numbers.[173]

Subprovincial units, whose leaders obtained their jobs locally, often cooperated more easily with each other. Members of the Changzhou City Planning Commission in mid-1984 expressed pleasure at the deals that had been done between their city, eight others, and Shanghai firms. They expressed confidence that Changzhou would be able to develop its own specialities within the region, especially in certain kinds of cloth and machines. Shanghai was expected to contribute technical expertise. But the Changzhou planners did not speak of major new investments to come from Shanghai, presumably because the metropolis's publicly solicitable money was still limited by demands from Beijing. They did not mention that Nanjing (their own provincial capital) also has economic planners.[174] In practice, some money as well as designs and personnel came from Shanghai.

Investments increasingly flowed in many directions. By 1987, units from other provinces ran more than 800 factories and shops in Shanghai (with gross revenues of 1,130 million yuan). Shanghai had financed, for its part, 579 projects in other provinces that generated raw materials for the city's factories (at a cost of more than 800 million yuan). The value of raw materials actually obtained from these plants during that year was, as prices rose quickly, half as much as the city's investment.[175]

Shanghai's urban districts had established "brotherly" (*xiongdi*) relationships with twenty-nine subprovincial cities and five counties in the Shanghai Economic Zone in the mid-1980s, and Shanghai's counties had set up links with twenty "fraternal counties" inland.[176] The government had to approve these links, but Shanghai individuals with particular interests in these other places were crucially involved. Nongovernmental organizations were recruited to help establish the links. For example, the Yangpu District Science and Technology Association organized nearly ten thousand engineers and technicians to help other places in East China. This association also set up twenty-eight work groups in functional fields such as chemical engineering, food processing, machinery, electronics, and bicycles.[177] The first kind of cooperation between Shanghai and hinterland places was usually technical cooperation.

The second kind was aimed at providing raw materials for the city's factories. Shanghai enterprises organized compensation trade with inland localities below the province level. Under these plans, firms in the city exchanged money and technical expertise for factors or out-processing. By 1985, the metropolis had financed 304 projects in the Shanghai Economic Zone for the purpose of exploiting raw material and labor sources for city factories. More than fifty kinds of inputs were involved, including coal, cement, iron, pig iron, nonferrous metals, and many other materials for light and chemical industries.[178]

A third kind of cooperation with subprovincial localities was based on the market value of Shanghai brands. Inland places provided factories and inputs to make more of these—and reap more sales for Shanghai companies, which expanded to use inland labor and materials. Capital seeks low labor costs in socialist economies, as in capitalist ones. In the first nine months of 1985, this kind of cooperation between Shanghai and all of China's other provinces (especially with those in East China) was estimated to have raised the total market value of their products by about 2 billion yuan.

A fourth kind of local cooperation involves professional liaisons. For example, 120 enterprises under the Shanghai First Electronics Bureau by 1985 had established "mid- or long-term fixed cooperation links" with 300 units outside the city.[179] A fifth kind of cooperation between Shanghai and other places in the zone arose when enterprises were financed jointly by different jurisdictions, either to avoid high taxes in Shanghai or to raise more capital. Sixth, scientific research institutes in the metropolis might establish profitable relations with inland companies; by the mid-1980s, over a thousand such links existed between specific Shanghai academic institutions and factories elsewhere. A seventh kind of cooperation involved the opening by outside jurisdictions of firms inside Shanghai. By the end of 1985, almost 700 such companies had been approved, of which 25 percent were retail outlets designed to sell local specialties of their areas (which presumably did not compete much with Shanghai products), 5 percent were service firms largely in consulting, 11 percent sold machines and building materials, 28 percent were involved in tourism or transport, and 31 percent sold garments and general goods that almost surely competed with Shanghai firms. Possibly because of resistance from retailers within the big city, only 326 of the approved companies actually opened. Among these, 59 percent were financed entirely from elsewhere, and the remaining 41 percent got some of their capital from the metropolis. Local investment in them was possible, despite their competition with Shanghai firms.[180]

Companies that stood to benefit were the initiators of such arrangements. The Shanghai Light Industrial Machines Corporation spurred horizontal links in particular with three counties of Jiangsu. Its "one city, three counties" committee in the mid-1980s involved the Shanghai corporation with counterparts in Shazhou, Wuxi, and Wujin.[181] This form of organization was novel, at least as a publicized model, because it was coordinated at the corporation and county levels. Each of these units was under a different midlevel jurisdiction, but horizontal links could be forged between them without regard to that.

Local officials increasingly acted like commercial boosters, as the reforms made Shanghai's border with southern Jiangsu much less hermetic. The head of Kunshan county in Jiangsu province, Wu Kequan, called in July 1988 for more economic cooperation with Shanghai. He pointed out that Jiading and Qingpu counties, which are now in Shanghai municipality, used to be subordinate to Kunshan—a place that is only forty minutes by train from the Shanghai station. One-third of the fifteen hundred nonprivate enterprises in Kunshan by 1988 were "horizontal liaison projects" (*hengxiang lianhe xiangmu*), and 60 percent of these were involved with Shanghai. Kunshan cooperated especially with the Shanghai Textile Bureau to establish an export base that sent cloth to twenty foreign countries. The Kunshan branch of the Shanghai First Television Plant regenerated its full capital within two and a half years. A Kunshan politician expressed a hope that his county would become the "supporting actor" or the "backyard" (*houyuan*) of Shanghai's outward development.[182] Such terms suggest a strong, even unctuous, sense of dependency on the metropolis in this nearby city—whose own famous cultural traditions might have led to more localism—and scant sense of conflict between this Jiangsu place and its big neighbor.

Regional links of this sort flourished throughout China in the mid-1980s, although the delta part of the Shanghai Economic Zone held perhaps the densest concentration of links over a large area. In all of China during late 1986, there were sixty-five thousand registered economic liaison organizations (*jingji lianhe zuzhi*). In addition, China at this time had seventy-five "economic cooperation zones" (*jingji hezuo qu*), of which the Shanghai Economic Zone in its large form, while it lasted, was just the most populous. The aims of cooperation included raising productivity and promoting the concentration of related enterprises into groups, as well as technical and financial help.[183]

Such an immense pattern of decentralization naturally entailed many problems. First, central and provincial governments that oversaw firms creating new "horizontal" entities generally remained reluctant to commit the scarcest resources (raw materials, capital, foreign exchange, or work space) to the cross-jurisdiction enterprises whenever their own solely controlled firms lacked any of these resources. Second, traditions of appointing cadres to ensure high central remittances, especially from Shanghai, reduced incentives for some governments to approve horizontal ventures outside their borders—unless that was necessary to obtain inputs—since the taxes on production elsewhere did not become part of the city's budget. Third, cross-provincial enterprises suffered from a lack of laws to protect them. These problems were counterbalanced by the benefits of less bureaucratic interference and budget extraction. The inadequate legal regime could, to some extent, be replaced by networks of personal relationships between local leaders.[184]

The Demise of the Zone

Most of this activity rose separately from the state's efforts to regulate it in zones. The plan for the Shanghai Economic Zone, as finally reformulated in 1987, remained long-term and vague. Shanghai was designated in State Council documents as the center of the region, and closer cooperation among all units of the region was vaguely mandated "by 1990."[185] Central politicians wanted to protect an important tax base, but they had insufficient resources to ensure this either by plans or by contracts. "Harmonization" in East China that was centrally organized did not work well because in the end it meant taxes. Local harmonization, outside the central system, worked well because it was based on preexisting connections between individual local elites in Shanghai and other parts of Jiangnan.

High agencies of the state gradually turned over their interests in regional trade to local officials and entrepreneurs, whether they wished to do so or not. An odd announcement proclaimed that the "industry cooperation networks" of the large Shanghai Economic Zone were already "basically established" by early 1988.[186] These were not offices staffed by central appointees, but instead were merely a habit of periodic meetings between economic leaders in all of the East China provinces that were supposed to cooperate. They met, but it is very unclear whether they had sufficient consensus to bring any economic results that would not have occurred because of purely local interests anyway. Shanghai top officials agreed to these meetings when the city's tax contribution was declining—as if they should make amends by instead "paying" in technical expertise. Because more local Shanghai interests prevailed in determining which interprovincial economic links were actually forged, these high politics had limited effects.

The zone still survived formally, but its name was mainly used for junkets and conferences, and the central politicians who boosted it never were able to specify its purposes. In April 1988, a delegation from the Shanghai Economic Zone visited Hong Kong to strengthen cooperation in electronics, computers, textiles, toys, microwave ovens, and sound equipment. By this time, Hong Kong had infused U.S. $440,000 into Shanghai—a total that was second only to the American investment there.[187] So one purpose of the zone was to garner foreign investment. But different—and somewhat conflicting—ideas came into different Party leaders' statements about the Shanghai Economic Zone as it declined. One was a hope of using such a large industrial base as Shanghai for the same purpose as the much smaller and newer "special economic zones" of Shenzhen, Zhuhai, and Xiamen, i.e., to raise hard currency through foreign investment, imports, and exports.

A concurrent and basically different concept of the zone, however, was that the metropolitan industrial center of Shanghai might generate the entrepreneurial energy to make the economies of China's domestic hinterlands more efficient. Economic advisers to Zhao Ziyang hoped that market centers might even break the incubus of some backward-looking rural cadres with their own administrative "kingdoms," and might weaken their links with the vertical network of planners that stifled trade. They applied this idea by placing most Chinese county administrations under the leadership of nearby cities. On a larger scale, the implication was clear: Whole provinces might be made more efficient if they were put under an industrial metropolis such as Shanghai.

This second notion of a "zone" was by no means restricted to coastal areas. The same concept was instituted in many different regions of China at this time. Sichuan's Chongqing (which was that province's largest city, but not its capital where Zhao Ziyang once ruled) was to coordinate a "Southwest Economic Zone" extending into Yunnan. Wuhan in Hubei was to be the industrial center of a "Central China Economic Zone." And Shanghai was to be the dynamo of the zone that bore its name.[188] All of these regional zones were encouraged from Beijing, although few finally had strong permanent effects in their areas.

They were not identical, however; they were divided into different official categories. Each of the zones centered on a large metropolis was conceived as a "comprehensive economic zone" (*zonghe jingji qu*), supposed to develop all kinds of goods and services; and the Shanghai Economic Zone was of this type. But the Guangdong and Fujian special areas were officially supposed to be only "sectoral economic zones" (*bumen jingji qu*), in these cases specializing in the foreign sector. Other zones in this category could be devoted to other sectors—and an economic zone was suggested for northeast China, to specialize especially in coal and electricity.[189] Shaanxi's comparative advantage was in energy and heavy industry. Even impoverished Guizhou was dubbed a "sectoral economic zone," to develop its energy resources. Zones were a much-publicized rage during China's reforms, but not all zones were created equal even though they were all centrally approved.

Comprehensive economic zones, such as Shanghai's, had a weakness that reflected the greater importance of less formal networks in their areas. This is clearest in their contrast with sectoral economic zones, whose head offices acquired powers to plan, in a definitive, legal, mandatory way, production of the goods in which they specialized. But the head offices of comprehensive economic zones were only supposed to "harmonize [*xietiao*] relations between other agencies," including geographical jurisdictions.[190] If one of these preferred not to cooperate, on any issue, a comprehensive zone's leadership could do little to bring it into line. This difference was clear in documents from Beijing, but it actually emerged from the potentials of different areas on account of their geographical locations and preexisting resources.

The Shanghai Economic Zone was comprehensive, but unlike the comprehensive zones centered on Wuhan or Chongqing, it was also coastal. It was supposed to have a role in attracting foreign capital, but it continued to pay much higher remittances and taxes than the zones in Guangdong and Fujian, which were specialized for that aim and had much lower imposts. The difference was not lost on foreign investors. The Shanghai zone was established only in the weak "comprehensive" mode. Something else was needed to bring in serious amounts of capital. Eventually, in the 1990s, Pudong received benefits that made development possible there. Such change came only after central conservatives realized, by the late 1980s, that China's new industrial structure would not allow Shanghai to perform its previous role for the central budget.

The Shanghai Economic Zone was never dubbed "special" (*tebie,* like Shenzhen), despite hopes among local entrepreneurs that it might become so. Zhang Jingfu, an important central economic bureaucrat, visited Guangdong in 1983, shortly after Shanghai had been given more autonomy to approve larger foreign investments. As he explained to his Cantonese audience, "This autonomy has a special meaning." He linked Chen Yun's "cage" to Shanghai: "Within this 'cage,' we would loosen the 'strings.' However the 'cage' has limits. We are not loosening the 'strings' in an abstract way . . . . As special economic zones, you [in Guangdong] have definitely more power than Shanghai."[191]

Shanghai firms received no import or export tariff preferences, no national subsidies to start new industries, and very few tax breaks except when such benefits could be arranged on a project-by-project basis. If there had been anything "special" about the Shanghai Economic Zone, it might have lasted as an organization. The name was a fishing license, but only for a shallow pool. By mid-1988, the Shanghai Economic Zone existed merely on paper. It had no office or permanent organization. After it became a central project, it never got off the ground. The zone did not die with fanfare but faded away.[192]

Regional Specialization and Market Efficiency

Two of the three provinces whose economies are mostly on the Shanghai delta began to have a faster growth than China's other provinces in 1972–73. Jiangsu, Zhejiang, and Shanghai together have maintained this record during most years since then. The right-hand column in Table 1.4–3 roughly shows the ratio of Shanghai delta output growth over other provinces' rates. In the period 1971–74, this ratio jumped to 1.16. The relatively high rate of coastal Shanghai growth in 1972—the highest figure in the right-hand column—suggests a 1972 beginning of reforms in the field of relative coastal growth.[193] In 1974–75 this index was again low; but by 1978–90, it receded to somewhat more stable rates between 1.0 and 1.5, dipping below this range in only three years.

One reason for these three provinces' good performance is that they trade with each other intensively. Even during the early 1980s, when Shanghai's total retail sales of manufactures scarcely changed, the city was involved in far more interprovincial trade than most other parts of China. The number of contracts for a wide variety of consumer goods that Shanghai enterprises signed in the second half of 1982 with other PRC companies was 48 percent of the national total.[194] Maoist policies had not uniformly discouraged trade. On the contrary, they had encouraged interjurisdiction trade that could be controlled and taxed. But when inputs to a production process could not be monitored, for example because of factors' small bulk, dispersed sources, or low-capital extraction, then Maoist policies reduced trade whenever they were followed. Such commodities are many, and their increased production is a major element of China's reforms.

Socialist economic structures remained evident in Shanghai city longer than in most other places, because of the delay in getting money for reform there. "Large and complete" (*da er quan*) self-sufficiency was no longer an ideal, but it was still built into Shanghai's economic institutions because of lack of funds to finance their change. Of 164 kinds of industries that were categorized for all of China in the mid-1980s, Shanghai had 90 percent of those types. This was a surprisingly low degree of specialization, even for a very large city.[195] Shanghai

Table 1.4-3

Shanghai Delta Growth Rates (billions of yuan of gross reported output value, and percentages)

Year	National	Change	Shanghai-Jiangsu-Zhejiang	Change	All other provinces	Change	Ratio, Shanghai-Jiangsu-Zhejiang to all other provinces
1970	380.0	19.35%	72.2	13.17%	307.8	20.90%	0.63
1971	420.3	10.61%	79.8	10.53%	340.5	10.62%	0.99
1972	439.6	4.59%	86.0	7.77%	353.6	3.85%	2.02
1973	477.6	8.64%	93.5	8.72%	384.1	8.63%	1.01
1974	485.9	1.74%	94.6	1.14%	391.3	1.88%	0.61
1975	537.9	10.70%	100.8	6.59%	437.1	11.70%	0.56
1976	543.3	1.00%	104.6	3.77%	438.7	0.37%	—
1977	600.3	10.49%	115.9	10.80%	484.4	10.42%	1.04
1978	684.6	14.04%	134.6	16.13%	550.0	13.54%	1.19
1979	764.2	11.63%	155.2	15.30%	609.0	10.73%	1.43
1980	853.4	11.67%	174.7	12.56%	678.7	11.44%	1.10

(continued)

Table 1.4-3 (continued)

1981	907.5	6.34%	187.8	7.50%	719.7	6.04%	1.24
1982	996.6	9.82%	202.5	7.82%	794.1	10.34%	0.76
1983	1,113.1	11.69%	222.6	9.93%	890.5	12.14%	0.82
1984	1,317.1	18.33%	267.1	19.99%	1,050.0	17.91%	1.12
1985	1,658.2	25.90%	345.2	29.24%	1,313.0	25.05%	1.17
1986	1,904.5	14.85%	404.8	17.26%	1,499.7	14.22%	1.21
1987	2,303.4	20.95%	497.7	22.96%	1,805.7	20.40%	1.13
1988	2,980.7	29.40%	644.3	29.46%	2,336.4	29.39%	1.00
1989	3,460.4	16.09%	698.6	8.43%	2,761.8	18.21%	0.46
1990	3,799.6	9.80%	791.3	13.27%	3,008.3	8.92%	1.49
1991	4,380.3	15.28%	920.8	16.37%	3,459.5	15.00%	1.09

Notes and sources: Growth in Shanghai municipality was often lower than in Jiangsu and Zhejiang, as other tables show. The outputs are at current prices. Data come or are calculated from *Zhongguo tongji nianjian, 1991*, p. 47, and 1992 edition, p. 47; *Shanghai tongji nianjian*, 1991, p. 39, and 1992 edition, p. 38; *Zhejiang tongji nianjian*, 1991, p. 27, and 1992 edition, p. 21; and *Jiangsu tongji nianjian*, 1991, p. 27, and 1992 edition, p. 27. See fn. 193.

made everything from steel to buttons—though other places clearly could do some things better. Mineral industries were practically the only ones that Shanghai lacked, because of its fine-grain sedimentary ground. Shanghai economists explicitly argued against the tradition of comprehensiveness. Not everything, they thought, should be "crammed into" their city. Because this had been attempted, the "special characteristics" of the local economy, and its comparative advantages, were reduced. Furthermore, this tradition in Shanghai had given a bad example to other places, which also wanted to engage in all kinds of production so that they would "not need to ask people for anything."[196]

Reforms have specialized more production locally. An economist has quantified this by calculating a ratio, e.g. for any commodity in any province, of the per-capita output there divided by the per-capita output in the rest of China. If this quotient is exactly 1, there is no local specialization; if it is greater than 1, the place specializes; and if it is less, then other places specialize in that product. Over time, if the ratio increases and is greater than 1 (or decreases and is less than 1), then specialization is rising. These tests have been made for Jiangsu.[197] It is no surprise that specialization continues in commodities for which this province has been traditionally famous. For silk, the ratio was 4.4 in 1988—very high for this statistic. But antispecialist policies of encouraging "self-reliance" (*zili gengsheng*) after 1957 affected Jiangsu. In practically all commodities for which the ratio could be calculated in both 1957 and 1970, it moved closer to one between those years, showing that the province became less specialized in Mao's time.

Comparing 1970 with 1978, however, the movement of about half the commodity ratios showed increased specialization then—showing that reforms toward specialized production, reversing the previous trend, began in the early 1970s. Between 1978 and 1988, this kind of comparison by the portion ratio movements for different commodities showed scarcely any difference from the 1970–78 comparison; about half the goods evinced higher specialization over both of these reform periods.[198] None had shown this between 1957 and 1970.[199] So the reforms (including the period 1970–78) led to increased provincial specialization.

Trade, too, was increasing sharply. By 1984, Shanghai exported 25 percent more industrial products to other Chinese provinces than it had in 1978.[200] This was, in both years, about 45 percent of all China's interprovincial trade in products from industry. Comparative advantages increasingly structured this trade. Shanghai's contribution of industrial products for daily use (*riyong gongye pin*) had been 19 percent in 1957; but because many places later found they had the resources to make simple commodities, and the metropolis had a comparative advantage in other fields, Shanghai's contribution of them decreased to 10 percent by 1983.[201]

It would be too easy to interpret this overall rise of horizontal trade in terms of increased efficiency. Not all of it was a matter of economic rationality, based on comparative advantages in production among different trading places. On the contrary, much horizontal trade arose in search of speculative profits based on artificial price differences, as central officials continued to resist scarcity prices in the reform period so that they could maintain remittances from state factories.

Horizontal trade nonetheless made Chinese markets more efficient, and this accounts for part of China's economic growth during reforms. As Audrey Donnithorne wrote in 1972, "China forms a Customs Union but not a Common Market. That is to say, the whole country has common trade barriers against the outside world, but it does not have free trade within its national boundaries."[202] Since then, internal barriers have been somewhat reduced. Further reductions of them, which are both possible and likely, will let growth expand yet more. If factors, technology, labor, capital, and retail goods all flow more easily between different places, the result over time will be more consumption. The ultimate reasons for such growth involve both greater economies of scale in production and greater competition in marketing. It is difficult to compute the increment of growth on the Shanghai delta in any recent year that can be attributed to horizontal trade among the three provinces there.[203] But the amount is surely large, and further regional integration has raised it.

Local Transport and Trade: Hindrances and Means

The benefits of trade, during reforms, went increasingly to local leaders rather than to state bureaucrats. Intellectual economists railed against this change. "Whereas Europe is pursuing an integrated and supranational market, China still has its 'kingdom economy' (*wangguo jingji*)," according to Shanghai's *World Economic Herald* in 1988. "Recently, while we are having our economy decentralized, such 'kingdom segments' or 'feudal segments' become more serious. . . . Local authorities try to have dominant influence and put up protective fences."[204]

In some rural areas of East China, counties charged "fees for road upkeep" (*yanglu fei*). In one Anhui region, an official regulation specified that only one such impost was to be made on any truck—but that rule did not effectively prevent counties and cities from charging more than once.[205] Regional disintegration of trade and investment created an "economy of dukes" (*zhuhou jingji*). This was the Billy Goat Gruff school of economic management. It was localist and not market-efficient, but in many small collectivities during China's reforms it was common. The more respectable school, based on a broader general equilibrium model, was espoused by central bureaucrats who wanted revenues collected in larger jurisdictions instead. Their tolls were high, too. Local reformers' commitment was to local profits, not to overall market efficiency. Yet these parochial extractors of rents were sometimes as production-efficient as the state's central extractors had been. They did, at least, inspire a good deal of local labor and enterprise.

Trade requires conveyances. Water transport remained crucial to growth on the delta, as it had been for centuries. The main inland waterway, toward Suzhou, was said to have a history of "more than 6000 years."[206] A 1930s survey reported "28,000 native cargo boats" in Shanghai's harbor. Other boat censuses by Chinese and Japanese researchers before 1949 indicated well over 100,000 junks in the whole Shanghai delta area—probably about two-thirds of the nation's total.[207] With reforms and more rural production, this system experienced a resurgence of use. Shanghai's canal network, for a while at least, carried a large portion of total trade, though surely not all of it was reported. Local newspapers praised the modern cost-efficiency of the ancient waterways. At least two major routes, through lakes west of Shanghai, received very heavy use. From 1980 to 1988, the traffic on these arteries rose 6 percent annually (an increase of about three-fifths in those years alone, for the reported tonnage). In the middle of the decade, the average daily number of ships on these waterways was more than four thousand, carrying 46 million metric tons. Canals brought more weight to and from Shanghai than railroads did.

Lines of boats, pulled by a tug, were called "waterborne trains" (*shuishang lieche*). They dominated Shanghai delta shipping since the official moves to collectivize local boat people in the 1950s. Monitoring the transport of raw materials to the metropolis had been, from the government's viewpoint, a prerequisite to socialist planning. Pressure on boat families to take up shore residence (and to educate their children in schools on land) had therefore been intense—and probably was effective only because state-subsidized tugboats put individually powered vessels at a severe cost disadvantage.[208]

The volume of reported boat transport in Shanghai municipality rose again between 1976 and 1982 by 17 percent. More important, the average distance of haulage became longer, so that the weekly number of ton-kilometers rose 55 percent in this period.[209] The beginning of this rise in regional trade thus preceded the 1978 announcement of reforms. Private transport firms (*geti yunshu hu*) continued to grow quickly in the 1980s, using trucks as well as boats.[210] These companies crossed provincial borders. By the late 1980s, boats from Jiangsu, Zhejiang, and Anhui accounted for 37 percent of the tonnage on Shanghai's inland rivers. They carried mainly construction materials, coal, nonferrous ores, and other industrial and agricultural inputs.

The economic efficiency of water transport was its decisive advantage. Capital costs for railroads or highways were far higher. Many of the canals had been dug long ago, with conscripted labor, and they required scant new investment because their depreciation was very slow. Cost-efficiency was also impressive for the main operating expense, fuel. On a per-ton basis, water transport took 60 percent less energy than trains and 88 percent less than trucks. Land-use efficiency in waterways was also great, because the canals doubled as sources of irrigation and fertilizer.[211] Each kilometer of railway, on the other hand, was estimated to remove more than 30 *mu* of land from any other use. Finally, the size of loads on canals could be huge; a single waterborne barge could handle a much larger weight or volume than many railroad cars or highway trucks.[212] The canals were a public good, mostly built long ago. But when officials in the 1980s could not stop the reemergence of unofficial, collective and private boat transport on these waterways, they lost a crucial means of planning Shanghai's economy.

A letter to the editor in the *Jiangsu Legal System News* in January 1989 complained that boat people asked for bribes, above the fixed transport prices, before they would agree to carry goods. For example, the price of hauling a ton from Xuzhou to Yancheng had been illegally raised in this way from 13 to 35 yuan. There were four basic problems, according to this analysis. First, unfair competition was alleged. "Individual transport households," i.e. families on boats, used gifts to establish relationships with companies that needed to have goods hauled.[213] Since the state-fixed price for haulage was too low to inspire the service, boat people were able to arrange higher fees. The transporters, for their part, had to pay tolls at the watergates of nine locks on this particular route. The amount of these payments inflated sharply during reforms. In 1982, a cheap pack of cigarettes was enough to get a boat through, but by the end of the decade, "great solidarity" (a ten-yuan bribe) was needed.[214]

A second reason for inflation in haulage was that the land-based heads of transport companies freely let boat households receive gifts and money (possibly taking a cut for themselves later).[215] A third cause was that the waiting time to open locks became longer, as local watchmen likewise wanted fees for this service. In sum, boat transport became slower. Before the reforms, it was possible for a boat to ply this route twice in a month—but by the end of the 1980s, a hauler had to press for service at each lock in order to make the trip just once a month. A fourth problem was that the boat people tended to "make chaos of the costs" (*luantan chengben*), refusing to haul unless they were offered much more than the state-fixed price. They demanded a "business fee" (*yewu fei,* which sounded valid and official despite its illegality). All these surcharges raised the cost above the bureaucratic level and toward a scarcity price. In 1990, the government announced a "Movement Against Three Arbitraries," namely, capricious impositions of fees, fines, and contributions.[216] Especially by that decade, however, a campaign was not enough to stop such habits.

"Horizontal Liaisons" against the Law

From nearby provinces, boats came to transport goods both legally and illegally. Shanghai firms needed inputs, and even during reforms subsidies persisted. In 1988, Shanghai waters were visited by 120,000 boats—more than during the previous year. Police tried to stop the smuggling of goods, but "some parts of the harbor were very disorderly."[217] In 1987, 72 percent of all "crimes" on rivers were committed by boatmen from outside the city. The local smugglers may have known which police to pay.

At the end of 1988, free-market rice in Shanghai's island county of Chongming could be sold for only 0.7 or 0.8 yuan per catty; but in Qidong, Jiangsu, a short boat trip away, it could be sold for 1.3 yuan, nearly twice as much. Its export from Shanghai was illegal. So a traveler who might transport 100 catties paying 0.8 yuan for the ferry ticket could make a handsome profit of more than 50 yuan for this short voyage.[218] In a temporary 1988 crackdown against this traffic, over two hundred peasants, private entrepreneurs, state employees, and teachers were arrested for trading rice regularly out of Chongming. In the period of about a week, some 360,000 catties of smuggled rice were confiscated by police. The profits on this rice, moving out of a single Shanghai county during just a few days, would have exceeded 200,000 yuan. The total extent of Shanghai's undetected boat trade is a mystery, but it was large.

As a newspaper pointed out, the government's "price basin" policies in Shanghai unintentionally financed wholesale smuggling:

> In 1988, the city's entire retail commodity value was 312 billion yuan, but 55 percent was purchased by non-Shanghai people in Shanghai. As a result, the contradiction between demand and supply rose. The government had to issue ration tickets for [local] people to get goods. So the Shanghai government spent several billion yuan to supply grain to outside people.[219]

Illegal transfers of industrial raw materials soared in Jiangnan as the 1990s approached. In the last month of 1988, for example, there was a campaign to arrest illegal materials traders in Suzhou. One-third more unauthorized industrial traders were found than in a similar movement in the same month one year earlier. The rate of arrests for illegal transfers of bulk materials in Suzhou during the second half of 1988 was five times higher than it had been the previous year. The value of the black market inputs increased 2.5 times in 1988 alone.[220] Many of the arrested criminals had previously worked in the organizations from which they had hijacked materials, so they were familiar with the easiest ways to obtain these. Some were buyers from Zhejiang rural industries, and their business was booming: "The more they steal, the bolder they become."[221]

Water transport remained crucial to Shanghai's expansion well into the 1990s at least, because the bureaucratic Ministry of Railways was unable to handle the bulk haulage that East China's booming economy required. Public roads, whenever bureaucracies were responsible for them, were also insufficient. So in 1992, less than 19 percent of the total tonnage of Shanghai trade came or left by railroad, and less than 32 percent by highway, but 49 percent by water.[222] Over the previous several years, the relative portion of tonnage by boat had risen. Railways and roads depended on medium- and high-level officials. Canals, rivers, and the sea were available to anyone who had a boat.

Notes

1. For these estimates of the age of Shanghai capital (rounded from more exact percentages in the source), see *Shijie xin jishu geming yu Shanghai de duice* (The Global Revolution in New Technology and Shanghai's Policies in Response), Shanghai Economic Research Center and Shanghai Science and Technology Committee, eds. (Shang-

hai: Shanghai Shehui Kexue Yuan Chuban She, 1986), pp. 35, 194–95, 205–6.

2. *Mubiao, zhongdian, duice—Tan Shanghai chuantong gongye de jishu gaizao* (Goals, Keypoints, and Policies—On the Technical Reform of Shanghai's Traditional Industries), Shanghai Municipal Enterprise Management Association, ed. (Shanghai: Shanghai Shi Qiye Guanli Xiehui, 1985) [limited circulation; referred to in *Shanghai qiye* (Shanghai Enterprise), August 1985, p. 5].

3. *Zhongguo shehui zhuyi chengshi jingji xue* (Chinese Socialist Urban Economics), Zhu Linxing, ed. (Shanghai: Shanghai Shehui Kexue Chuban She, 1986), p. 89.

4. The technological contribution to growth in Shanghai averaged 2.34 percent per year in this eighteen-year period, and 1.82 percent in China as a whole, according to *Shijie xin jishu,* p. 18.

5. Chen Minzhi and Yao Xitang, "Strategic Target Option for the Economic Development of Shanghai," in Zhang Zhongli et al., *SASS Papers* (Shanghai: Shanghai Academy of Social Sciences, 1986), p. 65.

6. Denis Fred Simon and Detlef Rehn, *Technological Innovation in China: The Case of the Shanghai Semiconductor Industry* (Cambridge: Ballinger, 1988), pp. 92–93.

7. For a report on this Beijing electronics area, see *La Chine en construction* 26:8 (August 1988), pp. 14–17.

8. Denis Fred Simon and Detlef Rehn, *Technological Innovation,* p. 74.

9. This "*Gui gu,*" named after Santa Clara, was in western Shanghai in the Caohejing area. See *XMWB,* January 29, 1989.

10. "Traditional industries" are *chuantong qiye. Shanghai qiye* (Shanghai Enterprise), August 1985, pp. 2–8. The only exception to the 1960s–1980s decline found in this thorough research was in plants under the city's Bureau of Chemical Industries—probably because of the effects of investment at Wujing. But even this index fell, precipitously, in the 1980s.

11. A complete list of the 1982 municipal bureaus is in Jiang Zemin et al., *Shanghai dangzheng jigou yange* (The Transformation of Shanghai's Party and Administration) (Shanghai: Shanghai Renmin Chuban She, 1988), pp. 226–30.

12. Only 3 percent each went into funds for employee benefits and bonuses. *Shanghai jingji, neibu ben: 1949–1982* (Shanghai Economy, Internal Volume: 1949–1982), Shanghai Academy of Social Sciences, ed. (Shanghai: Shanghai Shehui Kexue Yuan Chuban She, 1984), p. 134.

13. It is not clear that many of the workers (especially women) would surely be employed in the new industries. Chen Minzhi and Yao Xitang, "Strategic Target," pp. 73–74.

14. In 1983, Beijing reportedly had 167,642 engineers, and Shanghai had 166,701. Tony Saich, *China's Science Policy in the 80s* (Atlantic Highlands, NJ: Humanities Press, 1989), compare pp. 90 and 111.

15. Even impoverished Lanzhou had only a slightly lower density of technicians and scientists per 100 employees (*zhigong*) than Shanghai: 8.4 percent. *Shanghai shehui xiankuang he qushi, 1980–1983* (Situations and Trends in Shanghai Society, 1980–1983), Zheng Gongliang et al., eds. (Snanghai: Huadong Shifan Daxue Chuban She, 1988), p. 204.

16. Only 20,000 of Shanghai's young workers were said to be "illiterate or semiliterate," meaning they had not completed primary school; in such a large workforce in a developing country, this figure is not high. *Shijie xin jishu,* p. 394.

17. Lanzhou at this time was 0.64 percent university-educated—about the same portion as Shanghai, despite big differences in the quality and amount of capital and talented labor pools that needed to be managed in these two cities. *Shanghai shehui xiankuang,* p. 204.

18. Chen Benlin et al., *Gaige kaifang shenzhou jubian* (Great Change in the Sacred Land [China] During Reform and Opening) (Shanghai: Jiaotong Daxue Chuban She, 1984), p. 96.

19. *Shanghai jingji, 1987* (Shanghai's Economy, 1987), Xu Zhihe, Ling Yan, Gu Renzhang et al., eds. (Shanghai: Shanghai Renmin Chuban She, 1987), p. 12, indicates that the number of university students per 10,000 population rose from 46 in 1978 to 67 in 1980, and then to 95 in 1986.

20. *Shanghai jiaoyu fazhan zhanlue yanjiu baogao* (Research Report on the Strategy of Shanghai's Educational Development), Kang Yonghua, Liang Chenglin, and Tan Songhua, eds. (Shanghai: Huadong Shifan Daxue Chuban She, 1989), p. 3.

21. *Shehui* (Society), Shanghai, June 1985, p. 11.

22. "*Zichou zijin.*" The article also proposed research on ways of "unifying" the use of "self-generated funds"—a position that could please all comers, since factory managers liked to justify such funds and their supervising planners liked to tap them. *SHJJYJ,* April 1985, p. 32.

23. "*Waimao buyao neixiao yao; Shanghai buyao waidi yao.*" "Closure and guardedness" is *biguan zishou. WHB,* October 25, 1979.

24. Ibid.

25. Real revenues also fell. Between 1981 and 1982, for example, Shanghai's revenue from all domestic sales rose only 2 percent, and only 4 percent the next year—in nominal terms. In real terms these were decreases. *Shanghai jingji, neibu ben,* p. 553.

26. The Tianjin watches, mentioned below, could also be sold at a lower price. *WHB,* October 25, 1979.

27. *Zhongguo gongye de fazhan, 1949–1984* (China's Industrial Development, 1949–1984), Guojia Tongji Ju, Gongye Jiaotong Wuzi Tongji Si, ed. (Beijing: Zhongguo Tongji Chuban She, 1985), p. 57.

28. *JFRB,* April 27, 1988.

29. *Huadong xinxi bao,* January 28, 1989.

30. "*Xue Shanghai, shang shuiping.*" *Shanghai qiye* (Shanghai Enterprise), August 1985, pp. 34–35.

31. *SF,* March 26, 1990, for this and the following quotation. See also Cao Linzhang, Gu Guangqing, and Li Jianhua, *Shanghai shengchan ziliao suoyu zhi jiegou yanjiu* (Studies of Shanghai Production and Ownership Structure) (Shanghai: Shanghai Shehui Kexue Yuan Chuban She, 1987), p. 141.

32. *Hengxiang jingji lianhe de xin fazhan* (The New Development of Horizontal Economic Links), Shanghai Economics Association, ed. (Shanghai: Shanghai Shehui Kexue Yuan Chuban She, 1987), pp. 5–6.

33. The same phenomenon occurred in China's richest city, Hong Kong, whence many kinds of production have moved into Guangdong. But Hong Kong did not (yet) have Beijing restricting change in the structure of its economy.

34. G. Tian, "The Emergence of Shanghai's Role as an Entrepôt Centre Since the Mid-1980s," unpublished ms., especially p. 20.

35. Chen Minzhi and Yao Xitang, "Strategic Target," pp. 65–66.

36. Interview with Shanghai economists at the *World Economic Herald.*

37. Chen Yun, according to one source, "doted on Shanghai" and went there for consecutive lunar New Year celebrations—as did Deng Xiaoping in some eras, although the net benefit to the metropolis from these visits is not obvious in tax and expenditure tables. Southern journeys of emperors, since the Sui at least, could prove very expensive for the areas visited.

38. Chen Minzhi and Yao Xitang, "Strategic Target," p. 66.

39. Ibid., pp. 72–82.

40. "*Yong Shanghai ren de naodai, fa Wuxi ren de cai.*"

41. This amount was over 7 billion yuan. Li Cheng, "The Rise of Technocracy: Elite Transformation and Ideological Change in Post-Mao China" (Ph.D. Dissertation, Politics Department, Princeton University, 1991).

42. Interview with an economist at the Chinese Academy of Social Sciences, Beijing.

43. For a report on this Beijing electronics area, see *La Chine en construction* 26:8 (August 1988), pp. 14–17.

44. This place, using a direct translation of the California name, was informally called "Gui Gu." *XMWB,* January 29, 1989.

45. The Long March IV could launch warheads too, though this is not mentioned in *SF,* February 26, 1990.

46. Tony Saich, *China's Science,* p. 35.

47. Richard Conroy, "Technology and Economic Development," in *Reforming the Revolution: China in Transition,* Robert Benewick and Paul Wingrove, eds. (Basingstoke: Macmillan, 1988), p. 130.

48. This Shanghai Gongye Jishu Fazhan Jijin Hui foundation was called "*ban guan ban min*"—a most unusual term, which could be contrasted with the more traditional verbiage by which the government, then considered a more legitimate or moral actor than mere businesspeople could ever be, might deign to "attract merchants" (*zhao shang*). See *SHGYJJB,* February 2, 1989.

49. Calculated from ibid.

50. This Shanghai Wenhua Yanjiu Suo, reported in an interview, had an oddly unchemical name considering its sponsor.

51. Tao Yongkuan, *Dali fazhan disan chanye* (Vigorously Develop Tertiary Industry) (Shanghai: Shanghai Shehui Kexue Yuan Chuban She, 1986), pp. 40–41.

52. Tony Saich, *China's Science,* p. 70.

53. The budget for this technical outreach "sparking plan" (*xinghuo jihua*) in Jiangsu was 74 million yuan in 1986. *FBIS,* November 18, 1986, p. 4, reporting radio of November 15.

54. *FBIS,* November 3, 1986, p. 5, reporting radio of November 3.

55. "Self-sufficiency" is *zili gengsheng.* The three "go to the place" (*san jiu di*) norms were *jiudi qucai, jiudi jiagong,* and *jiudi xiaoshou.*

56. This material comes from interviews in Shanghai.

57. The number of technicians was specified as 410,000 in *Shanghai jingji nianjian, 1988* (Shanghai Economic Yearbook, 1988), Xiao Jun et al., eds. (Shanghai: Shanghai Renmin Chuban She, 1988), p. 11.

58. *Shijie xin jishu,* p. 195.

59. *Xin Zhongguo gongye jingji shi* (A History of New China's Industrial Economy), Wang Haibo, ed. (Beijing: Jingji Guanli Chuban She, 1986), pp. 361–63.

60. *Zhonghua renmin gonghe guo jingji dashi ji, 1949–1980* (Chronicle of Economic Events in the PRC, 1949–1980), Fang Weizhong et al., eds. (Beijing: Zhongguo Shehui Kexue Chuban She, 1984), p. 657.

61. *Chengshi wenti* (Urban Problems), January 1988, p. 25.

62. *Shanghai jingji quan.*

63. *Zhongguo 1986 nian 74 chengzhen renkou qianyi chouxiang diaocha ziliao* (Sample Survey Materials on 1986 Chinese Migration in 74 Cities and Towns), *Chinese Demography* Editorial Group, ed. (Beijing: *Zhongguo renkou kexue* bianji bu, 1988), p. 24.

64. *Gaojia laotou* is a term sardonically based on *gaojia guniang* (high-priced girls). "Sunday engineers" are *xingqiri gongcheng shi.* The information is from an interview with a researcher at the SASS.

65. This payment was given a nice joint socialist-capitalist name; it was called a "*xiezuo fei.*" *Hengxiang jingji,* pp. 168–70.

66. Ibid., p. 174.

67. Tony Saich, *China's Science,* p. 41.

68. Ibid., p. 133.

69. Hanson C.K. Leung and Kam Wing Chan, "Chinese Regional Development Policies: A Comparative Reassessment," paper prepared for Canadian Asian Studies Association, Winnipeg, June 6, 1986, p. 41, quoting Hong Kong *Dagong bao,* June 29, 1984.

70. Apparently temporary reasons for absence from Shanghai (travel and visiting relatives) were carefully accounted for by the census takers; but in the estimates above, the fractions indicate portions of the remainder. Di Juexian in *Shanghai liudong renkou* (Shanghai's Floating Population), Shanghai Statistics Bureau, ed. (Shanghai: Zhongguo Tongji Chuban She, 1989), pp. 187–97.

71. *Yige chengjiao xiangcun de jintian he mingtian: Shanghai shi Shanghai xian Meilong xiang jingji fazhan zongti guihua yanjiu* (A Suburban Village Today and Tomorrow: Comprehensive Plan for the Economic Development of Meilong Town, Shanghai County, Shanghai), Ling Yaochu and Zhang Zhaoan, eds. (Shanghai: Shanghai Shehui Kexue Chuban She, 1988), pp. 19–21.

72. A Shanghai interviewee whose hometown was in Zhejiang had seen his own name in such a file, along with these items of information for many other contacts in the metropolis.

73. Dong Fureng, "The Wenzhou Model for Developing the Rural Commodity Economy," *Market Forces in China: Competition and Small Business, The Wenzhou Debate,* Peter Nolan and Dong Fureng, eds. (London: Zed Books, 1990), p. 78.

74. Yao Shihuang, *Jin sanjiao de tansuo* (Search for the Golden Delta) (Chongqing: Chongqing Chuban She, 1988), pp. 35–68.

75. *RMRB,* October 7, 1978, quoted in Frank Leeming, *Rural China Today* (London: Longman, 1985), p. 116.

76. This borrows some ideas from G. William Skinner, *Marketing and Social Structure in Rural China* (Ann Arbor: Association for Asian Studies, reprinted from the *Journal of Asian Studies,* 1964–65).

77. *Hengxiang jingji,* p. 22.

78. *FBIS,* November 20, 1984, p. 3, reporting radio of November 20, for this and the next paragraph's quotations.

79. "Shanghai-Suzhou XX [product] Lianying Chang." This information comes from interviews.

80. Interview with an economist at the SASS.

81. *Fazhan zhong de hengxiang jingji lianhe* (Horizontal Economic Links in Development), Bureau for Economic System Reform, State Economic Commission, ed. (Beijing: Qiye Guanli Chuban She, 1986), p. 191.

82. *Shanghai qiye* (Shanghai Enterprise), February 1985, p. 12.

83. Cao Linzhang et al., *Shanghai shengchan,* p. 146.

84. Interview with a Shanghai economist who had personal experience with Suzhou leaders and Shanghai-Suzhou links.

85. *Hengxiang jingji,* p. 96, carries the story only to 1986.

86. *SHJJ,* April 1988, p. 63.

87. Interview with a Shanghai economist in 1989.

88. Huang Weixin, *Economic Integration as a Development Device: The Case of the EC and China* (Saarbrücken: Nijmegen Studies in Development, Breitenbach Verlag, 1992), p. 83.

89. *Hengxiang jingji,* pp. 143–45.

90. Ibid., p. 22.

91. "*Baoban hunyin,*" "*fengming lianhe.*" *Hengxiang jingji,* p. 243.

92. Ibid.

93. *Chengshi wenti* (Urban Problems), January 1988, p. 25.

94. *Jingji lianhe, buchang maoyi, kaidian banchang,* and *jishu xiezuo. Hengxiang jingji,* p. 206.

95. The hypothesis that differences in reporting data about "horizontal links" (not just differences in actual use of such links) may be responsible for these variations arises from very odd distributions in the available information. For example, the total industrial outputs of Jinshan and Qingpu counties were respectively the highest and lowest in the whole municipality, and it is reasonable to expect some correlation between output and trade or investment—yet these two counties were reported together in the low category for horizontal links. Officials in Jinshan could have done more than they told. See *Hengxiang jingji,* p. 207.

96. *CD,* March 9, 1988, quoting *World Economic Herald,* for this and the previous quotation.

97. Zhejiang at this time ranked twelfth. This method of combining the "directly ruled cities" with adjacent provinces renders a list of twenty-six jurisdictions. The more productive provinces in 1952 per capita were, in order: Heilongjiang, Liaoning, Inner Mongolia, Jilin, and the combination of Hebei, Beijing, and Tianjin. See Hanson C.K. Leung and Kam Wing Chan, "Chinese Regional Development Policies," Table 2.

98. Thomas G. Rawski, "The Economy of the Lower Yangtse Region, 1850–1980," 1985 ms., p. 40.

99. *Chengshi wenti* (Urban Problems), January 1988, p. 24. The surprisingly high rank, in total productivity, of Suzhou and Wuxi are confirmed by tables in *China: Urban Statistics, 1986,* State Statistical Bureau, PRC, comp. (Hong Kong: Longman, 1987), for an adjacent year. These statistics show that the crucial difference between Suzhou and Wuxi, on one hand, and the next-most-productive group (Guangzhou, Shenyang, and Wuhan) was the boom of Sunan rural industries. The national ranks of Suzhou and Wuxi in 1986 total population were very much lower. This surprising information is relegated here to a note, for just one reason: the geographical areas from which all such numbers are collected are administrative, and they imply merely an official definition of what a city is. Some "cities" include larger portions of farmers than others. But on this basis, just within Jiangsu alone, a great many mid-1980s cities (Huaiyin, Yangzhou, Nantong, Yancheng, and Xuzhou in that order) were more populous than Suzhou, and one more in addition (Nanjing, the capital) was larger than Wuxi. So the fourth and fifth *national* ranks of these two cities, for total production data collected on the same basis, are high indeed. In the next year or so, Wuxi's total production overtook even Suzhou's.

100. "Enterprise groups" are *qiye qunti,* sometimes also called *jituan. LW,* 5 (1987), p. 12.

101. Xu Yuanming and Ye Ding, *Tangqiao gongye hua zhi lu* (The Way to Industrialization in Tangqiao) (Shanghai: Shanghai Shehui Kexue Yuan Chuban She, 1987), pp. 40–41.

102. The number was 43 out of 90. See *Shehui kexue zhanxian* (Social Science Front) 4 (1984).

103. In a nice pun, this *Ningbo bang* was urged to *bang Ningbo;* see *JFRB,* October 20, 1988. The association was the Ningbo Jingji Jianshe Zujin Xiehui. The directors had a board, called a *lishi hui.*

104. These *Shanghai de Ningbo ji renshi* set up the Shanghai Shi Ningbo Jingji Jianshe Zujin Xiehui, which was a *qunzhong tuanti* rather than a branch of the state. *XMWB,* February 25, 1989.

105. *FBIS,* February 8, 1988, pp. 28–29, reporting *JJRB,* January 14.

106. *FBIS,* December 19, 1984, p. 4, reporting radio of December 17.

107. *FBIS,* March 9, 1988, pp. 33–36, reporting a journal of February 11.

108. *Shanghai jingji nianjian, 1988,* p. 160. The "overpass function" was called a *lijiao qiao.*

109. The Shanghai Entrepreneurs' Club (Shanghai Qiye Jia Julebu) was apparently somewhat less active, but its aims were similar. Its main sponsor was the *Economic Daily,* and its membership was more limited to the city. Many such clubs were formed in East China at this time, to foster "networking" among different kinds of local leaders.

110. On this Shanghai Gongye Jingji Jiaoliu Zhan, see Tao Yongkuan, *Dali fazhan,* p. 27.

111. The association was called the Zhigong Jixie for short. *Shanghai jingji nianjian, 1988,* p. 148.

112. *WHB,* October 27, 1979.

113. *Post,* August 29, 1988.

114. *CD,* October 10, 1988.

115. "*Lai Hu kaidian banchang.*" *Shanghai jingji qu fazhan zhanlue chutan* (Preliminary Research on the Development Strategy of the Shanghai Economic Zone), *World Economic Herald* and Shanghai Economic Zone Research Society, eds. (Shanghai: Wuxi Branch of Shanghai Eighth People's Printers, 1986), p. 316.

116. *Shanghai jingji nianjian, 1988,* p. 130, with slightly different figures on p. 144. These statistics report offices that had been officially acknowledged by the Shanghai municipal government; but others surely existed too, on a less formal basis.

117. *Shanghai jingji nianjian, 1988,* p. 32; see also pp. 144–45. It is unclear whether such agreements had previously been signed with Jiangsu or Zhejiang, and also whether the agreement with Chongqing or with Sichuan came first.

118. "Connections work" is *lianxi gongzuo. Shanghai jingji nianjian, 1988,* p. 54.

119. *FBIS,* March 11, 1988, pp. 30–31, reporting radio of March 11.

120. Frank Leeming, *Rural China,* p. 116, citing a 1979 *Jingji guanli* article by Wang Gengjin and future Shanghai mayor Zhu Rongji about flouting the plan and Dwight Perkins about self-sufficiency.

121. Jean C. Oi, *State and Peasant in Contemporary China: The Political Economy of Village Government* (Berkeley: University of California Press, 1989), p. 160.

122. The current author has often seen this three-story (commercial, industrial, residential) arrangement in Taiwan also; the family altars on the third floors in Wenzhou by 1988 may have been large. See Fei Xiaotong and Luo Yanxian, *Xiangzhen jingji bijiao moshi* (Comparative Model of the Village and Town Economy) (Chongqing: Chongqing Chuban She, 1988), pp. 5–9.

123. Zhang Lin, "Developing the Commodity Economy in the Rural Areas," *Market Forces in China,* Peter Nolan and Doug Furen, eds., p. 95.

124. Shanghai sales representatives in Wenzhou were fewer than those from some other cities; a compendium of offices in Wenzhou recorded just one from Shanghai, a cooperative—although that firm advertised it would arrange buying or selling of any product. See *Wenzhou qiye daquan, 1986* (Compendium of Wenzhou Enterprises, 1986), Wang Wence, ed. (Wenzhou: Wenzhou Shi Qiye Guanli Xiehui and Wenzhou Shi Gongye Pucha Bangong Shi, 1986), p. 385.

125. *Hengxiang jingji,* p. 207.

126. The language surrounding this trade had to be obscure in order to legalize it; so these inputs were "materials loans." The four counties were Baoshan, Fengxian, Jinshan, and Songjiang. Ibid.

127. Ibid., pp. 236–37.

128. Miller himself wrote a book entitled *Salesman in Beijing,* but the play was reportedly staged elsewhere too.

129. *FBIS,* March 11, 1988, pp. 30–31, reporting radio of March 11.

130. The conference met July 19–25; see *NCNA,* July 30, 1957.

131. See *NCNA,* March 12, 1958.

132. This grid was the *Huadong dianwang.* See *Shanghai jingji qu fazhan,* p. 11.

133. Jiang Zemin et al., *Shanghai dangzheng,* p. 132.

134. *Lian fang pian.* The last word, *pian,* is informal as an official designation for an administrative area, but these small areas that could cross interprovincial boundaries were unusual.

135. The *sihai* campaign, against mosquitos, flies, sparrows, and rats, began during the Great Leap Forward. In 1960, bedbugs replaced the sparrows. Radicals revived this movement in the early 1970s.

136. The counties were Jiading, Qingpu, and Jinshan in Shanghai; Taicang, Kunshan, and Wujiang in Jiangsu; Jiashan and Pinghu in Zhejiang. See *WHB,* December 12, 1977.

137. Based on a paper by George Fitting in the author's seminar at Princeton.

138. See Ezra Vogel, *One Step Ahead in China* (Cambridge: Harvard University Press, 1989), chap. 4.

139. On these "*xiezuo qu,*" see *Shanghai jingji qu fazhan,* pp. 213–14.

140. "*Dapo shengshi jiexian*" and "*you lian you jing.*"

141. Yao Shihuang, *Jin sanjiao,* pp. 82–88.

142. The cities, in addition to Shanghai, were Suzhou, Changzhou, Nantong, Wuxi, Hangzhou, Ningbo, Huzhou, and Jiaxing. Shaoxing was left off the original list of cities but was included later. See *Shanghai jingji qu de jianli yu fazhan* (The Establishment and Development of the Shanghai Economic Zone), *World Economic Herald* and Shanghai Economic Zone Research Society, eds. (Shanghai: Zhongguo Zhanwang Chuban She, 1984), pp. 8–20.

143. *Shanghai jingji qu fazhan,* p. 285.

144. Ibid., p. 5.

145. The number of counties is in parentheses after each city name: Shanghai (10), Suzhou (6), Wuxi (3), Changzhou (3), Nantong (6), Hangzhou (7), Jiaxing (5), Huzhou (3), Ningbo (7), and Shaoxing (5). Note that Nanjing (and Yangzhou and Zhenjiang) to the northwest were not included.

146. *Shanghai jingji qu de jianli,* pp. 1–2.

147. *Shanghai jingji qu fazhan,* p. 65.

148. Interview with a Shanghai economist.

149. As a PRC analysis put it, "Some economic zones came out of various equal negotiations, from the regions below upward; an example is the Southwest Economic Coordinating Association. . . . Some are second- or third-rank economic zones. By June 1986, there were 30 such economic associations. . . . Ten first-level economic areas can be identified: the Shanghai Economic Zone, including Shanghai, Jiangsu, Zhejiang, Anhui, and Jiangxi; the Northeast Economic Zone, including Liaoning, Heilongjiang, Jilin, and a part of Inner Mongolia; the North China Economic Zone, including Beijing, Tianjin, and Hebei; the Shandong Economic Zone; the Southeast Economic Zone, including Guangdong, Fujian and Guangxi; the Central China Economic Zone, including Hubei, Hunan and Henan; the Shanxi-centered energy base area; the Northwest Economic Zone, including Shaanxi, Gansu, Qinghai and Ningxia; the Xinjiang Economic Zone; and the Southwest Economic Zone, including Sichuan, Yunnan, Guizhou, Tibet and Chongqing." Chen Dongsheng and Chen Jiyuan, *Zhongguo diqu jingji jiegou yanjiu* (Studies on the Structure of China's Spatial Economy) (Taiyuan: Shanxi Renmin Chuban She, 1988), pp. 19–20.

150. *Shanghai jingji qu fazhan,* p. 32.
151. *FBIS,* December 7, 1984, p. 4, reporting radio of December 5.
152. *Shanghai jingji nianjian, 1988,* p. 139.
153. In Guangdong, the Pearl River's "small delta" (*xiao sanjiao zhou*) is contrasted with the "large delta" (*da sanjiao zhou*). See Ezra Vogel, *One Step,* chap. 5.
154. This difference would be greater if northern Jiangsu and southwestern Zhejiang prefectures not in the Shanghai delta were not included in data for those provinces. Quoted in Huang Weixin, *Economic Integration,* p. 119, from pp. 67–69 of the 1986 statistical yearbook for the zone.
155. Chen Dongsheng and Chen Jiyuan, *Zhongguo diqu jingji,* pp. 82–86.
156. *Zhongguo shehui zhuyi chengshi,* p. 155.
157. Baoshan, Chongming, Fengxian, Nanhui, Qingpu, and Songjiang, and the Shanghai factories outside, are covered in *Shanghai shi 1985 nian gongye pucha ziliao* (Materials from the 1985 Industrial Survey of Shanghai), Gu Delun et al., eds. (Shanghai: Zhongguo Tongji Chuban She, 1988), p. 514.
158. These three were Baoshan (because the steel mill was central and absorbed many resources there, but did not count as a Shanghai firm), Fengxian, and Qingpu.
159. *Shanghai jingji qu fazhan,* p. 149.
160. This tension is nothing new. A former governor of Zhejiang during the Cultural Revolution was irate about the "unified management and distribution" of hydroelectric power from Xin'an Dam to Shanghai, where the main East China electric authority is located. In 1969 he reportedly said, "If I get mad enough, I can destroy it [the dam] with an atom bomb." He summed up his complaint by declaring, "Zhejiang is not a colony of Shanghai." See Zhejiang Radio, Hangzhou, January 13, 1969, text of a *Zhejiang ribao* editorial, *Summary of World Broadcasts: The Far East* 2983 (January 25, 1969), pp. 11–14.
161. *Shanghai jingji qu fazhan,* pp. 174–76.
162. "*Jian zai Anhui, jia zai Anhui, liyi bing bu dou zai Anhui.*" Ibid., p. 177.
163. *Shanghai jingji qu fazhan,* pp. 147–48.
164. *JFRB,* February 7, 1988.
165. This article, by Anhui governor Wang Yushao, is in *Shanghai jingji qu fazhan,* pp. 138–47.
166. *JFRB,* June 28, 1988.
167. Yao Shihuang, *Jin sanjiao,* pp. 67–74.
168. *FBIS,* December 13, 1984, p. 2, reporting radio of December 11.
169. *FBIS,* December 9, 1987, p. 26, reporting radio of December 5.
170. *JFRB,* February 7, 1988.
171. *Sunan fada diqu jiaoyu fazhan zhanlue huanjing yanjiu baogao* (Research Report on the Environment for Educational Development Strategy in the Developed Region of Southern Jiangsu), Task Force on the Environment for Educational Development Strategy in the Developed Region of Southern Jiangsu, ed. and pub. Mimeographed "discussion draft" (*taolun gao*), n.p., 1991, p. 3.
172. *JFRB,* May 12, 1988.
173. *Shanghai jingji qu gongye gaimao* (General Description of Industry in the Shanghai Economic Zone), 30 vols., Shanghai Economic Association, ed. (Shanghai: Jiaotong Daxue Chuban She, 1985).
174. *Shanghai jingji kexue* (Shanghai Economic Science), May 1984, p. 3.
175. *Shanghai jingji nianjian, 1988,* p. 6.
176. It is linguistically interesting that counties were fraternal (*xiongdi*), while universities were sisterly (*jiemei*). Which was elder, and which younger, was left diplomatically undecided—though perhaps the Shanghai side had a viewpoint on this. See Cao Linzhang et al., *Shanghai shengchan,* p. 141.

177. Ibid. The association was the Yangpu Qu Kexue Jishu Xiehui.
178. Ibid., p. 142.
179. Ibid., p. 143, which used the term "*zhongchang qi dingdian xiezuo guanxi.*"
180. Ibid., p. 144.
181. Wuxi county is subordinate to the city of the same name; Shazhou county is under Suzhou; and Wujin is under Changzhou. *Shanghai qiye* (Shanghai Enterprise), February 1985, p. 13.
182. *Shanghai tan* (Shanghai Shore) 7 (July 1988), p. 1.
183. *LW* 5 (1987), p. 12.
184. This argument that *guanxi* networks substitute for laws has also been made to explain the oddly massive infusion of foreign direct investment to China, despite a striking lack of legal protections for property there. See Wang Hongying, "Transnational Networks and Foreign Direct Investment in China" (Ph.D. dissertation, Politics Department, Princeton University, 1996).
185. *Shanghai jingji qu fazhan,* p. 26.
186. The networks were *hangye xiezuo wangluo. JFRB,* April 18, 1988.
187. Shanghai–Hong Kong links grew faster than Shanghai–Shenzhen economic connections. Shanghai at this time had 120 offices and firms in Shenzhen. But other companies there reportedly did not take Shanghai enterprises or technologies very seriously. The Shanghai agencies in Shenzhen had not yet shown much strength. Although there was a flow of people to Shenzhen from Shanghai, there was scant flow of information or projects. Compared to other provinces' agencies in Shenzhen, the ones from Shanghai were relatively constrained by administrative rules, and they lacked "management autonomy." The Shanghai representatives were bound by "old attitudes" that made them unfit for competition in the special economic zone. Even in Shenzhen, "a majority of Shanghai firms lacked rights" to import and export as freely as other companies there did, and they "were run only like administrative offices." They tended to be there less for business than as "travel reception stations" (*lüyou jiedai zhan*). Although offices in Shenzhen from outside provinces may operate under Shenzhen laws, the supervising agencies in Shanghai restricted their branches more than those from other areas. The greater constraints on Shanghai business procedures were even more obvious in Shenzhen than in other places, because companies from all over China were together for comparison there. For material above also, see *JFRB,* April 19, 1988. The same paper on April 27, 1988, refers to deficient management autonomy (*jingying zizhu quan*) among Shanghai firms in Shenzhen.
188. The "Xinan Jingji Qu" and "Huazhong Jingji Qu" are mooted in *Shanghai jingji qu fazhan,* p. 79.
189. This "*Dongbei de jingji qu*" was not an institution's name, though it appears in *Shanghai jingji qu fazhan,* p. 94.
190. The Shanghai Jingji Qu Guihua Bangong Shi only had powers to "coordinate" such relations. Ibid., p. 94.
191. Quoted by Linda Li, "Central-Provincial Relations in the People's Republic of China" (Ph.D. dissertation, School of Oriental and African Studies, University of London, 1994), chap. 6, p. 5, from Zhang Jingfu's speech at the Shenzhen Party Committee, May 26, 1983.
192. Other economic zones disappeared at the same time. Ad hoc regional revivals sometimes took place, however, the most famous of which was in aviation. Shanghai-based China Eastern Airlines, like its regional counterparts elsewhere, was apparently established because of bad publicity caused by accidents involving the national carrier, CAAC (which disrespectful Western ways call "China Air Always Crashes"). Airplanes have military uses, and few developing countries have more than one international carrier.

By the spring of 1990, China Eastern Airlines flew not only to major cities in the Shanghai Economic Zone, but also to Hong Kong and four different cities in Japan. It had thirty new aircraft on order, and it advertised that its maintenance engineers were reliable and "most of the fleet's captains were trained in foreign countries." See *SF,* May 21, 1990.

193. The year 1976 is a clear outlier (the ratio is 10.19) and is probably best omitted from calculations about this subject until the underlying data are confirmed. The ratios before 1970 are also very erratic, probably in part because of reporting problems. These quantities, like others throughout this book, should not be taken as exact but should be read in qualitative terms, for clear trends over multiyear periods that may overwhelm the reporting problems. Thanks go to Peng Dajin for aiding the author with this table.

194. These statistics cover contracts for department store goods, cultural commodities, clothing, metals, and transport and electrical goods. *Shanghai jingji, neibu ben,* p. 562.

195. Tao Yongkuan, *Dali fazhan,* p. 21.

196. These places would not have to "*wanshi bu qiu ren.*" *Shijie xin jishu,* p. 9.

197. Penelope B. Prime, "Industry's Response to Market Liberalization in China: Evidence from Jiangsu Province," *Economic Development and Cultural Change* 41:1 (1992), especially p. 33.

198. This is based on ibid., p. 33, comparing the second, third, and fifth columns of Table 1. There is a difficulty with this kind of calculation, however, as Prime also suggests on p. 34, because Sunan (the economically dominant part of Jiangsu) became economically integrated with Shanghai and to some extent with Zhejiang during reforms. Markets can become more efficient, just as production can. Repeating the exercise with small groups of provinces and parts of them, to the extent this may be possible with the available data, might well reveal the trends suggested here more strongly. There is some evidence, based on a similar exercise covering Jiangsu's eleven administrative regions, that more specialization has also occurred among localities within the province.

199. Ibid., p. 33, comparison of Table 1, columns 1 and 2. Of about fifteen products, the sole exception in which Jiangsu "specialized" between 1957 and 1970, by producing less and apparently importing more, was paper. The province had much earlier run out of exploitable forests. In the 1978–88 period, the number of commodities for which the ratio indicated more specialization was roughly the same as in 1970–78, but in some commodities, the degree of Jiangsu's specialized production became great: radios, 9.9; woolens, 5.2; synthetic fibers, 5.0; pesticides, 4.0; and small tractors, 3.0. For small tractors, the 1988 ratio implied less specialization, relative to other provinces, than Jiangsu had in 1978 (although the 1978 figure implied more than in 1970).

200. Tao Yongkuan, *Dali fazhan,* pp. 8–9.

201. Ibid., p. 9.

202. Audrey Donnithorne, "China's Cellular Economy: Some Trends Since the Cultural Revolution," *China Quarterly* 52 (October-December 1972), p. 605.

203. Huang Weixin's *Economic Integration* comes as close to this as any research thus far. This economist admits not being close enough in quantitative terms to present any specific figure.

204. Based on a quotation from *SJJDB,* November 21, 1988, in Huang Weixin, *Economic Integration,* p. 5.

205. "Likin" (*lijin*) toll-taxes had been common in imperial times. For specific examples, see *Gaige mianlin zhidu chuangxin* (The Reforms Are Faced with System Innovation), Development Research Institute, ed. (Shanghai: Sanlian Shudian, 1988), p. 308.

206. This historical enthusiasm apparently ignored geology. The site of urban Shanghai had not yet emerged from the East China Sea six thousand years ago (although sedimentation had brought western reaches of the creek-and-slough system toward Suzhou above the waves by then). The import of *JFRB,* February 1, 1988, is its gusto, not its geology.

207. Thomas G. Rawski, "The Economy of the Lower Yangtse Region, 1850–1980," p. 21.

208. For more, see Lynn White, *Policies of Chaos* (Princeton: Princeton University Press, 1989), pp. 62 and 78.

209. *Shanghai jingji, neibu ben,* p. 498.

210. Interview in Hong Kong, 1990. In some areas of East China, such as the Zhoushan Archipelago of Zhejiang, private boats became numerous in the 1980s for both shipping and fishing. These were often larger than the boats used on canals, although the possibility of leased tugs apparently allowed more private canal barges too.

211. Algae grow on still canal water (as on paddies), and they use solar energy to fix nitrogen from the air, then fall to the bottoms of waterways. Dredged mud is used by peasants as fertilizer. The land area for sun catchment taken by canals is thus by no means fully wasted from an agricultural point of view. See Lynn White, "Agricultural and Industrial Values in China," in *Value Change in Chinese Society,* Richard Wilson, Sidney Greenblatt, and Amy Wilson, eds. (New York: Praeger, 1979), pp. 141–54.

212. *JFRB,* February 1, 1988, estimates that one standard large barge in the Shanghai region could, if necessary, handle more weight than a thousand of the rather small trucks that were usual there. This probably overstated a good point.

213. These households were called *geti yunshu hu;* apparently at least some of them were not formally private enterprises (which the term *geti* often implies), but were informally independent parts of state firms, collectives, larger private firms, or unregistered. The ambiguity of such a term may even add to the clarity of what is being described. Sharp lines are not realistic among the several categories of ownership that are allowed in China, and differences within these usual, official categories are at least as important as differences among them. The report is in *Jiangsu fazhi bao,* January 28, 1989.

214. The source, ibid., refers only to "great solidarity" (*da tuanjie*). The reporter for a police newspaper felt no need to define the phrase, since everybody knows it locally. An interviewee explained: One side of the old PRC ten-yuan note depicts a Han cadre, peasant worker, and soldier standing at the head of a crowd including people in minority costumes, all in warm solidarity with each other. But solidarity comes in local, not just all-China, forms. The state's slogan served smaller networks' use, as laws fell to humor and ten yuan became the uniform fixed price for a petty bribe.

215. These were the guarantors *(baocheng ren)* of the transport companies, and they "turned a blind eye" (*moxu*) on boat people accepting bribes. Ibid.

216. The *fan san luan* movement is mentioned in Wang Hongying, "Transnational Networks and Foreign Direct Investment in China," chap. 3, p. 7.

217. *XMWB,* March 22, 1989.

218. Calculated from *XMWB,* December 26, 1988—whose own figuring from the raw data slightly underestimated this profit, no doubt because of embarrassment about its size. Publication of this sort of information could well have spurred illegal traders to clear markets in Qidong and Chongming. Shanghai's borders were especially difficult to monitor along the wide river.

219. *XMWB,* March 24, 1989.

220. *Jiangsu fazhi bao,* January 21, 1989.

221. "*Yue tou, yue dan da.*" Ibid.

222. Calculated from *Shanghai shi duiwai jingji tongji nianjian, 1993* (Foreign Economic Statistical Yearbook of Shanghai, 1993), Shanghai Municipal Statistics Bureau, ed., "*neibu ziliao*" [internal materials] (Shanghai: Shanghai Tongji Ju, 1993), p. 11; but these figures include domestic as well as foreign trade.

Chapter 1.5

Local Situations Beyond the State

To be attached to the subdivision, to love the little platoon we belong to in society, is the first principle (the germ as it were) of public affections.

—Edmund Burke[1]

The context of China's reforms has affected individuals in ways that go beyond agriculture, industry, finance, and management—the topics of most usual interest to economists. In particular, China's cities have seen an enormous influx of ex-peasant laborers, domestic helpers, and retailers. Often the migrants have been young people who have yet to find families. But some come as couples, and others marry in cities. The long-term political effects of this massive population flow are difficult to predict. Perhaps urban migrants in China (like those in other developing countries) will make few political demands soon because the individuals most likely to do so will quickly join urban mainstream classes and status groups. The newcomers to Shanghai delta cities have already had major effects, however, and they are one of the groups deserving attention here.

Migration and Residence Controls

The main reform was economic growth, and it meant that more people changed their residences and jobs. Urbanization and migration have been salient aspects of economic development everywhere, because labor is the means by which capital wealth is accumulated. Arthur Lewis has explained the mechanism by which the capital-gathering sector grows for a long period before its prosperity begins to help most workers.[2] Output gains, at an early stage of modern growth, involve the migration of ex-agricultural wage labor into industry—and largely into towns. These workers create manufactured products at traditional low subsistence pay (plus a nominal markup) as long as the supply of them lasts. The value of what they make is greater than what they receive, and the capital-accumulating network takes the difference. Ex-peasant workers keep coming to towns even after urban factories are unable to hire them all, because their expected wages exceed what they would receive in farming—even after discounts for the fact that many are not employed quickly or steadily in cities.[3]

China's population living quite near subsistence was, until midreforms, a very large portion of all its people. Mao's state developed a political constituency of urban workers, for whom the wage markup that Lewis noted was guaranteed but low. The Maoist government set up urban residence controls and rural checks against migration. This controlled wage costs by "paying" high-productivity manufacturing workers partly with rights to city residence. This policy maximized state revenues, with Mao's socialist state serving exactly the role of Lewis's "capitalist sector." The effectiveness of this system began to decline in the 1970s and mostly collapsed in the mid-1980s, for reasons shown earlier in this book. But before then, it delayed the industrial—only partly urban—migration of labor that Lewis describes for early modern growth.

Extent of the Migration

China's largest metropolis and the "green city" surrounding it provide much evidence of these trends.[4] Shanghai is a settlement of "sojourners."[5] This place was already a populous transshipment center before the arrival of European settlers in the early 1840s. Immigrants came especially in three waves: Refugees fled the Taiping Rebellion during the late 1850s. Another tide to the International Settlement flowed because of the Japanese invasion in 1937. China's civil war of the late 1940s saw a further deluge of about two million.[6]

In the next four decades, however, this stream was reversed. From 1950 to 1992, a cumulative total of 11.2 million people had their household registrations removed from Shanghai. Fewer, 10.8 million, came legally into the city. During the years of greatest emigration, from 1955 to 1972, the net outflow was 2.2 million people. Table 1.5-1 on pages 410–411offers a survey of registered migration in and out of Shanghai, and it shows the strength of state efforts to move people away during Mao's time. The long-term limits of that policy would be more evident in the data, especially from the 1970s onward, if reliable statistics on unregistered migration could be included, but the table omits migrants who did not obtain police permission to live in Shanghai. The low net rates after 1970, and especially in the 1990s, show mainly that the state was somewhat effective in controlling registrations, if not migrations.

The table displays a great deal of political history. The huge 1950–51 roundups of "vagabonds" were almost completely balanced by an influx of Communist soldiers and others to the metropolis then. Chen Yi, the first PRC mayor of

Shanghai, nonetheless declared: "We must evacuate the population of the city systematically and transfer factories to the interior whenever possible."[7] The 1955 food shortages, along with pressure on urban people to "rusticate" to rural places just before the 1956 Transition to Socialism, caused the highest rate of net emigration Shanghai has seen since midcentury. The protoliberal Hundred Flowers of early 1957 created more immigration than the Anti-Rightist Campaign of late 1957 forced in emigration. The Great Leap Forward of 1958–59, with its subsequent depression, spurred high rates of emigration—but immigration was also fairly high in that chaotic time. The period of revolutionary China's most intensive state influence, in the early 1960s, saw many years with only slight net emigration. The Cultural Revolution of 1968–71 brought the most famous, though in comparison to 1955 or 1958 not the most massive, high tide of policy-generated emigration.[8]

During reforms, a new pattern of net migration emerged by the early 1970s. In 1973, for the first time in many years, the net inflow was positive. Its usual pattern throughout the reform years (positive but low) began then. Actual data on migration, as on many other topics, fly in the face of the often-repeated notion that 1966–76 should be conceived as a single period of Chinese history. A partial exception in the reform pattern was 1979, when great numbers of previously rusticated people could return to Shanghai (although only a minority took their parents' jobs, as will be shown below, despite policy announcements that they should do so). The 1979 migration ratio was the highest since 1957. It was in historical terms at a medium level, however, and was caused by a temporary political allowance to families that had suffered during the Cultural Revolution—at a time when the current state elite was blaming an earlier state elite for that injustice. After 1972, no year except 1979 showed a major net immigration of *registered* residents. Those who came without registrations will, of course, tell much of the story below.

Comparative Migration: Genders, Ages, and Settlement Sizes

If migration means movement between any settlements, then most migrants in the PRC (56 percent, according to a 1987 study) are women. This is unsurprising in a strongly patrilocal society, but in many other low-income countries, most migrants have been men.[9] Chinese women from poor areas during the 1970s were apparently more frequent migrants than in other periods, because they could obtain permissions from team or village leaders to take jobs in new industries that were developing rapidly. Young women, having a lower status than men in boondock areas, were more readily allowed to leave agricultural work and move to light industries elsewhere, whence they were expected to remit money to their families.[10]

Most people who moved during the whole reform period from Chinese rural areas to *large* cities, however, were men.[11] The influx to cities in coastal areas

Table 1.5-1

Registered Migration to and from Shanghai
(migrants in, out, and net; and their percentages of total population in the whole municipality)

	Total pop.	Immigrants	Immigrants as % of total pop.	Emigrants	Emigrants as % of total pop.	Net immigration	Net immigration as % of total pop.
1950	4,978,213	566,951	11.4	623,342	12.5	–56,391	–1.1
1951	5,224,621	1,004,032	19.2	566,208	10.8	437,824	8.4
1952	5,624,141	430,039	7.6	352,117	6.3	77,922	1.4
1953	5,939,367	487,806	8.2	255,492	4.3	232,314	3.9
1954	6,339,740	457,576	7.2	296,712	4.7	160,864	2.5
1955	6,429,039	260,430	4.1	847,293	13.2	–586,863	–9.1
1956	6,290,196	382,551	6.1	443,326	7.0	–60,775	–1.0
1957	6,623,157	418,474	6.3	134,833	2.0	283,641	4.3
1958	7,202,492	193,728	2.7	513,432	7.1	–319,704	–4.4
1959	8,895,972	323,163	3.6	322,050	3.6	1,113	0.0
1960	10,423,439	237,697	2.3	265,903	2.6	–28,206	–0.3
1961	10,576,449	192,723	1.8	335,522	3.2	–142,799	–1.4
1962	10,584,286	213,809	2.0	375,867	3.6	–162,058	–1.5
1963	10,657,542	152,565	1.4	238,262	2.2	–85,697	–0.8
1964	10,799,301	154,140	1.4	200,999	1.9	–46,859	–0.4
1965	10,900,050	161,679	1.5	206,458	1.9	–44,779	–0.4
1966	10,948,123	101,005	0.9	178,724	1.6	–77,719	–0.7
1967	11,007,744	39,983	0.4	73,385	0.7	–33,402	–0.3
1968	11,073,463	94,274	0.9	172,413	1.6	–78,139	–0.7
1969	11,014,847	77,488	0.7	352,535	3.2	–275,047	–2.5
1970	10,832,725	58,527	0.5	370,955	3.4	–312,428	–2.9
1971	10,698,848	126,392	1.2	253,829	2.4	–127,437	–1.2
1972	10,654,624	128,718	1.2	188,503	1.8	–59,785	–0.6
1973	10,670,592	171,298	1.6	158,909	1.5	12,389	0.1

(continued)

1974	10,718,962	166,509	1.6	161,670	1.5	4,839	0.0
1975	10,752,502	212,096	2.0	217,199	2.0	–5,103	0.0
1976	10,790,117	200,180	1.9	202,068	1.9	–1,888	0.0
1977	10,838,868	196,291	1.8	188,350	1.7	7,941	0.1
1978	10,923,759	248,335	2.3	181,288	1.7	67,047	0.6
1979	11,152,094	598,260	5.4	333,390	3.0	264,870	2.4
1980	11,465,200	287,559	2.5	210,834	1.8	76,725	0.7
1981	11,628,400	236,223	2.0	192,127	1.7	44,096	0.4
1982	11,805,100	234,601	2.0	196,557	1.7	38,044	0.3
1983	11,940,100	226,773	1.9	190,821	1.6	35,952	0.3
1984	12,047,800	196,551	1.6	174,842	1.5	21,079	0.2
1985	12,166,900	182,904	1.5	129,873	1.1	53,031	0.4
1986	12,323,300	197,700	1.6	135,000	1.1	62,700	0.5
1987	12,495,100	221,700	1.8	154,000	1.2	67,700	0.5
1988	12,624,200	221,100	1.8	170,200	1.3	50,900	0.4
1989	12,764,500	210,900	1.7	169,500	1.3	41,400	0.3
1990	12,833,500	188,700	1.5	174,100	1.4	14,600	0.1
1991	12,872,000	167,000	1.3	145,400	1.1	21,600	0.2
1992	12,893,700	175,300	1.4	149,200	1.2	26,100	0.2
1993	12,947,400	185,500	1.5	118,600	0.9	66,900	0.5
1994	12,988,100	199,600	1.5	125,400	1.0	74,200	0.6

Notes and sources: Percentages are calculated. Most figures after 1979 are rounded in the sources, as prior ones surely should have been. The basis for data collection has changed somewhat in certain years. Migrants to and from Shanghai have generally been registered; but increasingly after the mid-1980s, arrivals not counted here became numerous. Most migration has involved urban districts, although this also became less pronounced after the mid-1980s, when many migrants lived in suburban counties.

Administrative changes compromise the comparability of figures between specifiable periods. The population of the ten counties incorporated into Shanghai from Jiangsu in the late 1950s (by different decrees) was a noticeable fraction of the municipality's total at that time. This jurisdiction change, which mainly affects the first column, means that 1950–59 figures are not quite comparable to later ones. The reliability of reporting also varied over time: The 1958 and 1967–70 migration figures may be wrong by especially sizeable margins, overstating the net outflow; they are republished here from the source only to encourage in the reader a sense of critical humor about such things. Also, the first-column figures through 1987 are average populations during those years; but the best source found for 1988–90 does not specify this, and the increment rate of total population for the last two years may thus be slightly understated. But none of these problems affects the most important trends the table shows.

The raw data begin in *Zhongguo renkou: Shanghai fence* (China's Population: Shanghai Volume), Hu Huanyong et al., eds. (Beijing: Zhongguo Caizheng Jingji Chuban She, 1987), 77. Slightly different figures are in *Shanghai tongji nianjian, 1988* (Shanghai Statistical Yearbook, 1988), Li Mouhuan et al., eds. (Shanghai: Shanghai Shi Tongji Ju, 1988), 92 and 76. The last years' data are on pp. 60 and 67 of the 1990 Shanghai yearbook, pp. 60 and 68 of the 1991 edition, pp. 60 and 82 of the 1992 edition, pp. 64 and 70 of the 1993 edition, pp. 41 and 44 of the 1994 edition, and the latest source, pp. 47 and 50 of the 1995 edition. Some of the figures are separately confirmed (with slight differences) in Lin You Su, "Urban Migration in China: A Case Study of Three Urban Areas" (Ph.D. dissertation, Department of Geography, Australian National University, 1992), p. 72. The first source makes clear that these numbers come from police records on legal permanent and temporary residents. Illegal migrants are thus not counted; and their number was sometimes substantial even before the last years reported above.

was greatest; most provinces, which are inland, have shown net outflows of population.[12] In the years 1983–87, over thirty million people moved long distances between different cities, towns, or counties in China. That is about 3 percent of the national population. Such a figure would not be high in an industrialized nation, but it is very high for a developing country—and because of unregistered migrants, on whom data are scarce, this rate sharply increased in later years.

Migration volume correlated inversely with the distance the migrants moved. Comparative data from Shanghai, Shaoxing, and the smaller Zhejiang city of Xiashi all show this for the reform years. (Only the Shanghai city data do not show it for earlier years, because of the government's long-distance send-down programs then.) Also, young people tended to move farther than older people. Retirees often moved within the same county. Migrants who came from larger settlements tended to go farther to their new residences; those from small places traveled, on average, less far. Especially after 1970, most migration to Shanghai delta cities was toward fairly large settlements there, but an increasing majority of migrations were short-distance.[13] These patterns became more pronounced in China during the reforms, as state efforts to limit urbanization became less potent.

The sources of immigration to Shanghai have been mostly nearby, but previous send-downs to provinces far away have also brought many people back from a distance. A 1986 survey showed that 70 percent of interprovincial migration to Shanghai then came from five other provinces: Jiangsu, 31 percent; Zhejiang, 14 percent; Anhui, 11 percent; Jiangxi, 8 percent; and distant Heilongjiang, 7 percent.[14] But later, because of very fast economic growth in southern Jiangsu, which reduced the "push factors" for emigration from there more than from provinces farther inland, only one-fifth of Shanghai registered immigrants hailed from Jiangsu between 1986 and 1990.[15] Booming industries in Sunan kept many potential migrants out of Shanghai.

Construction teams (*jianzhu dui*) became very busy at Shanghai from 1986–90, when roughly two-thirds of the registered immigrants to the city were men.[16] This was typical of what comparativists call the "construction phase" of migration. Women, more liable to take jobs hawking in Shanghai and less likely to have work units register their residences, may well be underrepresented in these figures, but most of the migration to Shanghai was male.

To see what the overall pattern means politically—for the people who moved, for established residents, and for national and local leaders—it is useful to look not just at broad trends but also at the motives of individuals and families. In short, former "educated youths" wanted their places in Shanghai back, ex-agricultural workers wanted higher incomes, established city residents wanted domestic helpers and low-paid subalterns to justify better jobs for themselves, local managers and police could find clients by arranging urban household registrations, and state leaders needed fiscal revenues and political support.

Sent-Down "Educated Youth": Residential Justice and Children's Educations

Immigration to Shanghai and to smaller cities on the delta cannot be understood separately from the two main factors that have recently impelled it: the flow back from coercive rustications in the years 1955–58 and 1968–71, and the boom of rural industries that deeply affected the metropolis and its suburbs.

In the 1960s and 1970s throughout China, more than sixteen million young people went "up to the mountains and down to the villages" (*shangshan xiaxiang*).[17] In the 1970s, half of these people came back. By the 1980s, the cumulative portion who were no longer in rural areas was two-thirds. In Shanghai alone, roughly half a million (413,000 by 1985 and more later) were officially "returned" from this rustication—out of the approximately one million who had been sent down.[18] These received legal household registrations and jobs, usually in collectives. Many others came back to find work on their own.

Early 1970s Reverse Rustication

The return of sent-down people to Shanghai began well before Mao's death. "Educated youths" did not wait for state permission before reappearing in Shanghai. To prevent their return, the Chairman himself had ordered communes to treat urban rusticates well, in terms of housing and ration allowances; but interviewees report that peasant leaders generally ignored such calls, even from China's Great Helmsman and most distinguished (purely symbolic) peasant. Urban youths were generally unwelcome in the countryside. Unless they started factories or taught school, local farmers saw the city youths as a drain on resources, lazy contributors, inept field workers. The main exceptions were nubile ex-urban women who, if willing to remain in rural areas, were excellent marriage prospects for peasant men, because city families could not ask the high bride prices that most rural families demanded.

Many city youths had been reluctant to leave Shanghai, at least in the last two years of the 1960s, and most of their parents had strongly supported this attitude. For this reason, and because schools were disrupted, municipal leaders transferred the hard job of persuading families from school cadres to the work units of the parents. In the early 1970s, the rate of rustications dropped. "In major cities like Shanghai, the policy of sending youths to the frontiers was sharply cut back from 1974 onwards."[19] Before 1975, a return tide to cities had already risen, despite radicals' efforts to stem this flow.[20] Many parents held their own state employers, who had been important in pressing the younger generation out of Shanghai, responsible for the whole policy—and thus responsible for making amends when it ended.

In Shanghai urban districts, the second most common entry on police forms validating permanent residents, accounting for 21 percent of the approved household registrations from 1968 to 1977, was "educated youth returning to the city" (*zhiqing fancheng*). This all predated 1978. Youths who had been sent from huge metropolitan centers to villages, however, often first returned to medium-large cities in the early 1970s. Settlements having less than 1,000,000 but more than 500,000 people were affected first; to these places, the early-1970s reflux was very heavy. From about 1969 to 1972, gross immigration *trebled* to cities in this large-but-not-gigantic category. Such high rates were not matched for these cities even a decade later.[21] J-curve forms of migration have been evident in other countries, too.[22]

The rate of migration into China's cities of more than a million also climbed after 1970, doubling from that year to 1972 in comparison with 1967–68—and by 1971–72, achieving levels that had not been seen since the Great Leap Forward. After a slight dip in 1975–76, this rate soared to a new high in 1979, when many rusticates returned, and then it stabilized at a fairly high level. The influx to very large cities had begun somewhat earlier, even though 1979 showed a quantum leap in it, as the available percentages within periods of the total 1949–86 inflow show: 1969–70, 3.4; 1971–72, 4.4; 1973–74, 3.7; 1975–76, 5.5; 1977–78, 7.1; 1979–80, 12.3; 1981–82, 7.8; 1983–84, 8.3; and 1985–86, 8.1. Figures for later years are difficult to interpret, because unregistered immigration to big cities soared then.

The same figures for a sample of cities whose populations were over 500,000 but less than 1,000,000—where residence restrictions were less severe—show percentages of total 1949–86 immigration more heavily weighted toward the early 1970s: 1969–70, 10.5; 1971–72, 10.5; 1973–74, 5.7; 1975–76, 6.5; 1977–78, 5.4; 1979–80, 7.2; 1981–82, 6.9; 1983–84, 7.3; and 1985–86, 8.9.[23] For these cities the early reform rate, up until 1972, was never topped at least through the next decade and a half. Many youths and cadres sent to rural areas from very large cities found they could return to somewhat smaller cities then.

A Chinese source explains the reasons: "From 1973 on, more and more youths returned to cities. From 1976, the government carried out new policies toward these people and toward cadres who came back to cities."[24] A particular influx occurred in 1978–79, when thirteen million people crowded into urban places all over the country. In Shanghai, police still tried to enforce the household control system. But also, high state remittances and rising factor costs left companies little money for wage budgets, thus discouraging employment for many years after reforms began. Many migrants came, but their reasons can be more easily attributed to their own interests than to state policies, which both abetted and obstructed migration in uncoordinated ways.

Returns in 1979: With or Without Jobs

By 1979, public pressure in Shanghai to allow a return of rusticates was more than the state could contain. But in the same year, many cadres still tried to impel youths flowing into Shanghai to go back to their previous places. The Nanshi

District Office for Educated Youth called a meeting at which a "consolation team" (*weiwen tuan*) from Heilongjiang tried to propagandize youths who had returned from there.[25] By the time this Heilongjiang team's visit to Shanghai was finished, it had also held meetings in Nanpu, Putuo, Jing'an, Hongkou, and Changning districts, as well as in Shanghai county. The names of youths who volunteered to return north were published in newspapers.[26] Whether they actually went is less certain.[27] These procedures were almost identical to the rustication campaigns of the 1960s. But the reform context was different, and few of the potential rusticates complied.

A similar problem for state policy existed among university students, who were reluctant to leave the metropolis but in 1979–80 were still told "unconditionally to obey the state's requirements."[28] Cultural Revolution excesses had made the enforcement of such mandates very difficult. The Party was blaming previous leaders in the Gang of Four for past problems, and it could not at the same time effectively enforce Maoist migration policies. Anger not just against the old policies but also against the urban bureaucrats who had implemented them ran high among returning migrants. Everyone, including potential young recruits to the program, knew this. Occasionally in the early 1980s, "educated youths" back from rural areas went to their old schools in Shanghai and physically attacked their previous "teachers" (actually administrators), who had assigned them to permanent lives outside Shanghai.[29]

In late May 1979, there seems to have been a major battle in Shanghai, unreported in newspapers but apparently between returned youths and cadres at a police office that had arranged their deportation. The *Shanghai Public Security Yearbook*, 1988 edition, reached a Hong Kong bookstore despite its "internal circulation" status. It offers a list indicating that of the forty-six Shanghai police killed in the line of duty from 1949 to 1980, more than one-quarter (thirteen) died on a single day: May 30, 1979.[30] Of those killed, eight were members of the Communist Youth League, and five were in the Party. Information about collective violence in China has been generally treated as an official secret. The exact motives of this 1979 case are unclear, but it was lethal for state agents at Shanghai.

Returnees to the city peaked in that year. More than ninety thousand educated youths were reregistered at Shanghai in 1979. About twenty thousand of these received jobs in state units, but seventy thousand—the vast majority—found work in collectives.[31] This was the first year in which state factories were authorized to hold open recruitments (*gongkai zhaogong*), but most of the youths returned from inland were not hired in this way. The collective sector, which then employed 21 percent of Shanghai's total registered labor force, was able to absorb fully 78 percent of the new job seekers. The state sector, which in 1979 still had four-fifths of the workers, absorbed only one-fifth of the new influx.[32]

State officials had reasons to oppose the return of "educated youths" to Shanghai, but they could do nothing effective to stop the tide. To cap the wage budgets of state firms (whose materials costs were rising quickly at the same time), they announced a policy that youths could come back to take their parents' jobs if the older generation would retire. This was called "substitution" (*dingti*). But many youths came back and found jobs outside the state sector, and in fact their parents did not retire. Local managers of state-owned enterprises could set up "attached" collective firms, with personnel rosters that did not require high approvals, where ex-rusticates could get jobs. Nonstate enterprises were often related to "collective offices" (*jiti bangong shi*) at the city, district, or street levels.[33] They could induce local police to reregister the returnees in Shanghai. The problem of finding a more permanent job could be left until later.

A major criterion for employment was based on the applicant's "character." State managers may have doubted the character of some ex–Red Guards who were now still angry about their years in the bush. Only a small minority of the 600,000 educated youths who over the years filtered back to Shanghai received high-level jobs in state-owned institutions.[34] Ex-youths could not be prevented from returning, but they did not receive very desirable work.

Ex-Rusticates and Their Children

Many migrants to Shanghai during the reforms had lived there before. In a sample of people whose registrations between 1950 and 1985 had been moved out of Shanghai urban districts, 62 percent had returned by the mid-1980s. When their reasons for leaving had been politically correct, the portion of returnees was very large. For example, 91 percent of those who left to join the army were back in the metropolis. So were 69 percent of those who had gone for "adjusted" work assignments elsewhere. Fully 66 percent had returned among those who had left to "go up to the mountains and down to the villages."[35]

Other immigrants to Shanghai were the children of rusticated parents who remained outside the metropolis. They came to live with urban grandparents. Evidence for this unusual phenomenon (three-generation families in which the middle generation is absent) can be compiled from various sources. For example, although Shanghai primary school enrollments increased in the decade beginning 1978 by 3 percent, national enrollments decreased by 16 percent.[36] The reason for this sharp difference was not that Shanghai families went against the national demographic trend toward lower primary enrollments. Data show that primary enrollment in Shanghai had already been nearly universal by the early 1970s, and remained so thereafter; and birth rates in Shanghai were lower than the national average (for reasons that chapter 2.5 explains). Both these factors pushed against the rise of enrollments in Shanghai that nonetheless occurred. Other data indicate that two-thirds of permanently registered immigrants to Shanghai were, at the time of their arrival, in young age cohorts, 15 to 29; many were younger. Three-quarters were unmarried.[37] Many Shanghai registered immigrants were of school age.

Over three-fifths of all migrants listed as temporary in Shanghai in the mid-

1980s were either the children or, in more cases, the grandchildren of the household head.[38] Grandchildren were more frequent than children, especially grandsons. Their parents were presumably "educated youths," sent down in previous years. These people remained away from Shanghai, having established positions elsewhere; but in the 1980s they could send the youngest generation to attend schools in the metropolis.

The state long ago had forced these parents (one or both) out of their city. In many cases, they were now accustomed to their new places—marrying there, sometimes becoming "big fish in little ponds." They wanted a different future for their offspring, and education in Shanghai was the way to obtain it. They had done their bit for the state, and they now made decisions according to the interests of their families. The revival of the effective power of families to resist official pressures was real politics, and it made real policy outside official institutions, even though it did so quietly.

Ex-Peasant Workers and Suburban Managers: Better Jobs and Cheap Labor

Pressures impelling people toward industrial settlements were matched, in Mao's time, by state counterpressures to maintain the government's fiscal and political bases in large cities. Workers were split into two tiers: permanent and transient. The first postrevolution government in Shanghai, which was military, already stipulated that "directly employed temporary workers" (*zhijie guyong linshi gong*) should not exceed 20 percent of the authorized number of "regular workers" in each company.[39] When firms hired permanent employees, they were supposed to report to the city's Labor Bureau, which kept files on names and numbers. Soon the rules allowed that "according to the needs of production," temporary workers could be changed to regular status, but this was supposed to occur only when the result was an increase of state profits. Statistics during the First Five-Year Plan suggest that there were on average 160,000 temporary workers then in Shanghai—or about 10 percent of the regular, unionized force. During the depression after the Great Leap Forward, "when there were no production tasks," many contract workers were fired. The government ordered that they not be converted into regular workers. This limitation was not easy to enforce in cases where managers opposed it.

As the depression eased, construction teams again came to Shanghai, on the "both worker and peasant" (*yigong yinong*) program. Rural production brigades acted as labor contractors receiving money directly from urban companies that needed help. The builders were supposed to get only 40 percent of their work points from construction and the remaining 60 percent from farming—so they were called "four, six workers"—but this ratio was not applied uniformly.[40] New building projects were, by the early 1970s, even more common in small Shanghai delta cities than in the metropolis. For ex-peasants, as for ex-rusticates, the

Table 1.5-2

Migration to and from Shanghai Delta Cities: Shaoxing and Xiashi
(percentages of population)

	1949–60	1961–70	1971–80	1981–85
Shaoxing				
Immigration	3.3	1.5	1.3	2.7
Emigration	2.1	2.4	1.4	1.6
Net immigration	1.2	–0.9	–0.1	1.1
Xiashi				
Immigration	2.5	2.0	3.5	4.4
Emigration	1.4	2.5	2.4	1.8
Net immigration	1.1	–0.5	1.1	2.6

Source: Registration data of the Shaoxing and Xiashi public security bureaus, 1986, reported in Lin You Su, "Urban Migration in China: A Case Study of Three Urban Areas" (Ph.D. dissertation, Department of Geography, Australian National University, 1992), p. 75.

story of Shanghai immigration cannot be separated from the tale of migration to smaller places.

Medium-sized settlements on the Shanghai delta were affected, as the metropolis was, by official efforts to reduce urban populations. They were harder for central bureaucrats to monitor, however, and economic growth in them expanded the total number of adjacent industrial and agricultural jobs. Details are available from two Zhejiang places. The larger is Shaoxing, a very famous cultural center and prefectural capital with a 1986 population of just over 250,000. The smaller is Xiashi, a county seat containing about 40,000 people inland from the part of Hangzhou Bay's north shore that is in Zhejiang. As Table 1.5–2 shows, both these places showed some net outmigration between 1961 and 1970. The county seat in particular had net immigration at other times, especially during the 1980s—when Xiashi had lower emigration than in either of the earlier periods for which data are available. Much employment was available in small Shanghai delta cities during reforms.

The Employment Pull: Inland Workers to Village Collectives

Half the migrants to Shanghai suburban towns in the 1980s admitted they came "to change jobs."[41] People left rural China in droves to seek employment, in cities as large as Shanghai if they could. The level of absconding was surprisingly great from some boondocks. From one county in Henan, 190,000 people departed; if the county was of typical size, this was about two-fifths of its population.[42] Women especially sought jobs in housekeeping; men, in building. A survey showed that "after all expenditures are excluded, each person can have an average income of 500 yuan per year," i.e., far more than they could earn in the impoverished places they left. A popular saying put it in rhyme; "If you want to get rich, run to Shanghai!" (*Yao facai, pao Shanghai*). Another specified the city's fastest-growing part: "East, west, south, north, center; to find a job, go to Pudong!" (*Dong xi nan bei zhong, dagong dao Pudong*).

Most ex-agriculturalists "come to cities because they can make more money and because they are surplus in the countryside. Recently, the development of services and municipal engineering projects provide a lot of employment opportunities. These jobs generally are manual; and urban people, especially youths, are unwilling to do such work. So cities have to absorb skillful people from the countryside, towns, and small cities." Many transients also became domestic maids, and this trend was approved in publications: "In big cities, the family structure is being transformed. . . so family service workers are popular. . . . It is not an exaggeration to say that without them cities, especially big cities, would not operate well. . . . Another stable source of services is contract workers. They organize themselves voluntarily and contract with the units or companies that need them."[43]

The organization of these labor hiring systems was "voluntary" only in the sense that the state could no longer control it. Autonomous labor bosses of a sort known in many developing capitalist countries, including China before 1949, flourished.[44] Booming rural industries absorbed vast amounts of labor on the Shanghai delta. Different parts of the delta varied in their rates of change, as some of the examples above make clear. In Zhejiang by 1984 rural industry accounted for 46 percent of all product. Zhejiang factories then used 23 percent of the rural workforce. Even more ex-peasants had been displaced from field labor by new technologies and "responsibility" contracting in agriculture.

Many rural people, not working in either fields or local factories, "floated" to cities such as Ningbo and Hangzhou. From Zhejiang, many also left the province or moved from poor to rich areas within it. So by the mid-1980s,

> over 1.3 million [Zhejiang] laborers are working in other provinces. . . . Jinhua prefecture [the province's poorest] 'exports' about 200,000 workers, which is about 25 percent of the total agricultural labor power in that prefecture. . . . The local government of Yongjia county allowed 30,000 peasants to work at other places in 1983; this figure was about 15 percent of the county's total labor power. These [absentee] peasants had a total income of 56 million yuan that year, which was about 49 percent of the county's total agricultural [i.e., rural] income.[45]

Long-distance migration to rich cities such as Shanghai occurred because the supply of cheap rural labor near the metropolis was depleted. A Chinese economist has calculated the demand for labor in agriculture, in rural industries, and in other local activities. He charted these kinds of employment throughout rural Wuxi between 1975 and 1985, at each point deducting the county's demand from its total supply and calling the residual a surplus. He showed that "rural surplus labor" with Wuxi registration was already down to 55 percent of the workforce in 1975, and just 4 percent in 1985.[46] Inland migrants arrived to take jobs on the delta as local subsistence-wage labor disappeared.

Although the PRC government has traditionally attempted to prevent the formation of a national labor market, rising prosperity meant jobs and migrations.[47] Entrepreneurs in collectives promoted locals into desirable jobs or administrative posts—and imported inlanders to work for near-subsistence wages in either factories or fields. During 1985, Wuxi's permanent workforce in rural factories was still more than nine-tenths local. With an expansion of contract labor, this portion went down—but the management of nonstate rural enterprises in Wuxi remained overwhelmingly local. A sample showed that 93 percent of the managers were born in the township where their firms operated. Most of the well-paid workers were also local.

There was variation according to the administrative level that licensed a factory. Township (or higher) collective factories largely employed local labor. A survey near Jiading, Shanghai, indicated that district- and town-run enterprises (i.e, at the levels of *xiang* or *zhen*) seldom hired even temporary laborers who came from a distance, even as late as 1989. But the pattern was strikingly different for the nominally collective—de facto private—factories licensed by lower formal levels. Village-run (*cunban*) Jiading firms so often hired outside workers that 90 percent of the labor force in some of their factories came from Anhui or Jiangxi.[48]

Two-thirds of Shanghai's "agricultural" workers (over three million people) by the late 1980s were actually employed in suburban industries and services. Municipal officials publicly reckoned that the city then had "several hundred thousand" contract workers.[49] The vagueness of the estimate suggests that nobody was able to make a reliable count. Village factory managers, protected by local cadres against any effective state controls, had many reasons not to divulge their full lists of workers.

Labor Bosses and Urban Life

It was relatively easy during the reforms to justify labor exploitation. As a demographer wrote in 1987, "Some peasants have contracts with urban units. . . . Generally, the income of those doing temporary work in cities is much higher than of those working in rural areas. When peasants go to cities, they widen their vision, increase their knowledge, become familiar with life in cities. Especially, they learn what urban people need. Peasants see a lot of new products, which they produce following the city models. . . . Because of growing unofficial markets in cities, many surplus workers get jobs."[50]

The reason "floaters" came to Shanghai, according to a 1988 survey, was occupational for 68 percent and "social" for 23 percent. Over seven-tenths were men, and at least a quarter of the total came explicitly to work on construction projects. Nearly half (48 percent) of this nonpermanent influx had previously been farmers, and only 15 percent had been previously registered as industrial workers.[51]

A separate report indicated that seven-tenths of legal transients came to Shanghai seeking jobs, and they generally lived in accommodations provided by their employers, with relatives, "or in houses they made by themselves on areas just outside the city or on the streets."[52] These workers would often stay in Shanghai for several months while on a job, then go elsewhere, and perhaps return later for further work. A second, more affluent group of transients consisted of cadres and businesspeople, who generally lived in small hotels or reception stations (*zhaodai suo*), staying in Shanghai for relatively short periods but returning often. This group comprised one-fifth of the transients.

Labor-seekers who came to the metropolis did not remain second-class citizens forever. Three-fifths of the long-term permanent Shanghai immigrants since the regime's early years had, by the mid-1980s, acquired regular blue-collar jobs. More than a quarter had achieved managerial or professional posts. A larger portion of long-term permanent immigrants than Shanghai adults who had never been registered elsewhere held white-collar jobs. Some of these were political appointees into Shanghai during the PRC's early years, but many were ordinary migrants who had worked hard and done well.

Most newcomers on temporary household registrations took menial tasks. But people who had been in the city for a number of years made more money, on average, than nonmigrants (those born in Shanghai or living there before mid-century). They put up with harsh conditions to establish urban households. Later, many were economically successful. This was true not just in the metropolis, but also in smaller delta cities.[53] Economic pull is not just a demographic abstraction. From the viewpoint of the individual or the family, statistics show that migration to Shanghai—followed by years of work there—was in the long term a highly rational action.

Urban Managers and Police Interests: The Erosion of Household Controls

Managers try to hire cheap labor, so they have some interests that parallel migrants' hopes. In Shanghai, each large firm includes public security liaison officers, who generally must approve residence registrations for any new employee, either permanent or temporary. So long as the firm does not incur excessive costs for housing, and so long as the total number of new employees passes muster with higher officials, this system was designed to tie legal migration closely to state-approved work. What it also did, however, was to keep a power (albeit one of declining value) for the managements of state enterprises to recruit new personal clients. The result was a great deal of registered "temporary" migration among people who actually stayed in Shanghai on a permanent basis.

This was not supposed to happen, according to the official rules. All temporary household approvals were, at least by the mid-1980s, formally subject to police review for renewal or termination after three months. "Numerous officials have indicated, however, that these requirements for temporary registration are not always rigorously enforced, nor is careful attention given to the length of time that an individual has remained at a destination, provided that the individual does not become a burden on the community."[54] Such approvals are local.

Temporary Registration Procedures

Any rural migrant to a city is supposed to have a letter from police in the rural township. Urban police are supposed to require that document (among others) if the migrant applies for temporary or permanent registration. By no means, however, does every farmer leave a rural area with such a letter. Nor does every urban immigrant apply for the benefits of registration.

The most important of these incentives to comply—since food rationing and job allocation are now less effectively regulated than before the reforms—is the possibility of having an employer apply for housing space. Little new space was available for the state to distribute, however, because low urban rents discouraged residential construction. Housing reform (on which chapter 2.5 has more) largely became a matter of building at the edge of the city, so that the government could evict old downtown residents to build commercial structures that would bring high official rents. It did not much raise real rents for residents who stayed in their assigned housing. State enterprises during reforms had scant money to build new homes for staff. Cheap housing into the 1990s still created a strong tie between state-sector employees and their employers, because for most ordinary people in Shanghai space is the scarcest resource. Immigrants got little of this anyway. For registering, most migrants did not even receive temporary housing. They had to find shelter on their own.

They could apply for permanent (*changzhu*) registration. If the police did not issue this document, the effect on the newcomer's behavior was usually not great. Since most facilities, other than housing, are now available for money, many who prefer permanent registration in Shanghai nonetheless stay there without it. Manager-patrons, following their own interests (which can differ from those of the state), could keep better control both of their budgets and of their worker-clients by arranging less permanent documents.

Nonpermanent household registrations came in two kinds: Temporary (*zhanzhu*) documents have been legally required of any citizen staying in Shanghai for more than three days—though this rule is practically always unenforceable if the person moves from place to place within the city. Seconded (*jizhu*) registration is for officially sanctioned activities, e.g., in the economy or in government. Application for either kind of registry is supposed to be made within three days of arrival in the city.

These urban immigration forms usually go through either of two agencies: the city's Personnel Department for cadres, or the Labor Bureau for most people.[55] The effective sufficient criterion for approval is backing from a Shanghai employer. Professional cadres could move to Shanghai if they were sent by state units (including most companies). Returned youths were often helped by their parents' employers, whether or not they took jobs at those firms. The majority of rural migrants apparently arrived either under the auspices of a labor contractor or without papers.

The procedures became somewhat easier in the late 1970s, because of the demonstration effect on other groups of the insistent pressure from sent-down youths in 1979. People who attained permanent registrations often reached the city because a company gave a job and household warranty at the same time. A survey comparing large samples of 1958–76 immigrants with those of 1977–86 found that original hiring, not on the basis of previous references (as distinct from administrative seconding or transfers of jobs), was the main reason for the move to Shanghai of only 7 percent of immigrants in the Maoist years—but of 31 percent after that.[56] So leaders of established urban firms could populate their patronage networks with increasing ease during the reforms. They used their capacity to arrange Shanghai household registrations for new followers. This practice was traditionalist in an old Chinese sense, adding to "relationship networks" (*guanxi wang*), but it weakened Communist state organization in favor of local networks.

Greater freedom of movement for citizens within China is an aspect of reforms that many writers have neglected.[57] Urban intellectuals there generally doubt that freedom of movement is an unalloyed good. After the internal migration that accompanied the removal of bad labels in 1979, however, most Chinese could usually buy a train or bus ticket between cities without having to show as many official documents as had previously been required.[58] Already by the early 1980s, the arthritic Ministry of Railroads was left far behind, unable to meet the demand for passenger transport from newly rich entrepreneurs and ex-farmers, foreign tourists, Taiwanese, migrants, and other travelers. Getting tickets was difficult, and getting seats was exceptional, but at least citizens could travel.

Ordinary trains to Shanghai from Anhui, in particular, were densely stuffed with people. Anhui stations would sell tickets to would-be migrants, who might wait for days trying to get inside the slow trains (often climbing through windows, since the doors were blocked by other passengers). Train 311 reportedly was so full on one day that eight people stood in a single car's small toilet. Claustrophobic migrants were reported sometimes to have died as they jumped out of moving trains on the Anhui–Shanghai line. A survey of one such train found a high frequency of "mental disorders" because of crowding. On this run, 86 percent of the passengers were migrants.[59]

Nonetheless, "the large majority did not have official permission to change their registrations from rural to urban."[60] As a late 1980s source said, "The portion of the people who are 'temporarily resident' is getting higher and higher. Although the government has not recognized their urban citizenship, they are playing important roles in economic and social life."[61] Obtaining food and shelter depended less on state documents than it had in Mao's years.

Declining Effectiveness of Household Registers and Rations

During the 1980s, the registration and ration systems remained in force but lost their previous power over citizens' lives. Households with legal registry books (*hukou bu*) were entitled to grain certificates (*guliang zheng*) and supplementary food certificates (*fushi pin zheng*). Grain and food stores would mark the ration cards, selling specified amounts of provisions in set time periods. But during early reforms, urban food supplies rose nicely. The same products could all be bought at slightly higher prices, with better quality, on free markets. So the ration system largely lost its effectiveness as a means of residence control.[62]

Identification cards (*shenfen zheng*) for urban residents were thus issued by the PRC government in 1987, as an additional document for which police could ask. The Ministry of Public Security on September 15, 1989, decreed an "interim provision" that urban citizens should carry these cards at all times.[63] This revived a registration system like that used before 1949 by the KMT (and bitterly criticized then by the CCP). The identity cards ordinarily included the name, photo, home address, and ID number of the registrant—without information on employment or "class origins," as had earlier been used in China to aid or chastise people.

The ID cards were issued to individuals, not households. They did not in practice much raise state control over persons; they were more common, and thus permissive, replacements for the cards that had been previously issued by employers for purposes such as buying travel tickets. Household registration books still had to be presented for obtaining rations, school admissions, jobs, housing, moving vans, marriage licenses, or birth or death certificates (these last were occasions to edit the books). But household registration had also ceased to be an effective system of strict control. The new ID cards did not replace them in this role.

Police could ask individuals for ID cards, and technically could fine citizens for failure to show them, but in practice officers seldom held people strictly to these rules. The number of unregistered people in Shanghai was high, and police asked at random to see ID cards mainly during temporary campaigns. The municipal police by 1994 issued work certificates (*wugong zheng*). Their official hope was to limit migrants, approving only those who had sufficient backing from regular companies. This plan aimed at legalizing work permits in the city for employees who were needed—but only with strict expiry dates. When their construction projects were finished, they were supposed to leave. The floaters, however, understood these certificates differently: At last, they thought, the police were legitimating them in Shanghai. Because the documents were partly blue, they were popularly called "blue cards" (*lan ka,* or *lan hukou,* an analogy to the famous American "green cards"). That was not the official notion of them at all, but the state by the mid-1990s had neither the will nor the personnel to keep all the migrants out of Shanghai.

It was usually possible for people from outside Shanghai to remain there without any official permission.[64] As a PRC scholar wrote ruefully,

> With dramatic changes in Chinese society, the function of the household registration system actually no longer exists. In the early stages of the PRC, the system's main role was to control the mobility of population, in order to implement "unified purchases and sales," to limit the flow of peasants into cities, and to control the growth of urban populations. But now, because of reforms, we can no longer check the population's mobility. In Chinese cities, and especially in big cities, nonurban citizens have increased dramatically. They are an important part of the stable urban population and have had—and will have—a great impact on economic and social life.[65]

The migrants affected the views even of some who represented the state. Despite official efforts to reverse this trend, state power over residents simply declined.

Migrant Numbers and Houses

Three-tenths of migrant workers in the Shanghai suburbs during the mid-1980s had no fixed dwellings—and half had no fixed jobs.[66] Unregistered residents, to the extent they could be sampled in urban areas during late 1988, seem to have lived approximately as follows: 6 percent very literally "floated" by staying on boats; 16 percent were in "temporary work shacks, agricultural markets, terminuses, and docks"; 17 percent resided in hospices or hotels; and 61 percent had beds in permanently registered collectives or families. Fully 85 percent of these "floaters" in the urban districts hailed from outside Shanghai, not from nearby counties.[67]

Another survey of the flow to Shanghai showed that in 1984, more than 700,000 people were immigrants without permanent registrations. But in the next year, the number had risen to 1,110,000, and the influx continued at about the same level in 1986. Over 30 percent stayed in reception houses or hotels, and many of these had come to do business. More than 20 percent were classed as "transport workers," and this apparently included construction carriers (coolies, to use the old term). Slightly less than half in this sample came into individual or collective households.[68]

The total registered and unregistered floating population of Shanghai has been difficult to estimate, but the municipal police (who know quite well that their records are incomplete) periodically enlist the support of academics to conduct censuses. In 1988, one such survey tried to cover people without fixed abodes:

Table 1.5-3

Transient Populations of PRC Cities in Mid-Reforms
(thousands of persons)

	Shanghai	Beijing	Tianjin	Wuhan	Guangzhou	24 Cities
1978		300				
1985		900			600	
1986	1,340				880	
1987	2,000	1,150	860	800	1,000	10,000

Notes and sources: Chengshi wenti (Urban Problems), March 1988, p. 64, and (for 1987) *Shanghai jingji* (Shanghai Economy), June 1988, p. 6. The twenty-four cities were *all* those with total populations in excess of one million. More recent figures using a standard definition of transience are difficult to find, even in publications such as the *Zhongguo chengshi tongji nianjian* (Chinese Urban Statistics Yearbook), where they might be expected to appear.

those living in hotels, markets, boats, and transport stations. This survey reached the conclusion that on October 20, 1988, only 2 percent of Shanghai's population was floating—which was surely a sharp underestimate. Unregistered persons in Shanghai have no incentive to make themselves available when the census takers arrive. Of the illegal respondents, three-fifths alleged they had applied for legal temporary or permanent registration in Shanghai.[69]

A further source claimed that by 1988 Shanghai had "the country's biggest floating population."[70] Another suggests that the portion of floaters in the urban districts rose in the mid-1980s.[71] At least up to 1987, as Table 1.5–3 suggests, Shanghai had more unauthorized immigrants than any other Chinese city (even Guangzhou). By about this time, migrants already comprised one-fifth of the population in China's twenty-four largest cities—and probably more than that in the built-up parts of Shanghai.[72] In the urban districts of Shanghai, according to an early 1989 estimate, one of every four persons lacked permanent household registration.[73] Toward the beginning of the 1990s, diverse reports suggest that one-fifth of the people were migrants, but these guesses may be somewhat low. Comprehensive and comparable figures from many cities have not yet been found for later years, but Shanghai sources indicate that by 1994 the portion of recent arrivals in the population rose quickly. One mid-1990s report estimated that Shanghai's "floating population" was 3.3 million.[74] Over one-quarter of Shanghai's whole population was migrant by that time.

Jobs and Immigration

The portion of floaters who were unregistered—i.e., who had no employers to arrange documents—in most Shanghai delta cities rose quickly after the mid-

1980s.[75] Working-age persons (ages 15 to 59) in a 1988 census of migrants made up 81 percent. Males were 62 percent. Only 52 percent were in the urban districts; so almost half (mostly from Jiangsu or Zhejiang) lived in the suburbs. Illiterates and semi-illiterates comprised 15 percent of the total, but those with middle school educations were 45 percent (and with university educations, 2 percent—higher than in the legally resident population). These immigrants, self-reporting their former occupations, were 48 percent farmers, 15 percent workers, 8 percent technicians, 4 percent businesspeople, 3 percent cadres, and 20 percent unemployed. Many worked in construction and transport. Of the women (a 38 percent minority of the total), 51 percent were married. Fully 68 percent were of childbearing age; 24 percent had actually given birth to babies in Shanghai, and another 5 percent were pregnant during this census. At least 14 percent of all the floating population worked as domestics, apparently full time. One-third of the floaters came from Jiangsu, and a strong majority hailed from either Jiangsu or Zhejiang.[76]

Many who were unregistered, or who were supposed to be only temporary in the city, could nonetheless make satisfactory livings. Some did so illegally. A man from Xinghua in northern Jiangsu, for example, came to Shanghai and "stole" materials from factory rubbish bins. He could in this way make a high income of 70 or 80 yuan per day. Legal activities were less profitable, but they still paid far more than migrants had previously received as peasants. A 25-year-old legal migrant from Henan to Suzhou explained in 1994 why he was so much more productive on the delta: "We used to spend three months doing farm work, one month celebrating the Spring Festival, and eight months in idle time every year." Now he was a restaurant waiter, working fourteen hours each day, seven days a week—but receiving 400 yuan (about U.S. $50 per month), which was four times his previous Henan wage. When asked whether he thought he was working too hard, he replied with great eloquence, showing the human motives that are needed to complement the economic theory about subsistence wage labor. He explained not so much why he migrated, but what his hard work meant for change in his life:

> No, it is better than sitting idly by watching people in cities getting rich. The conditions here are not bad at all. Color TV, electric heating, free meals—these are great. What I like most here is that I can take a shower every day. I was not able to take a bath during the entire winter at home. It would be too cold to do so in the river.[77]

Normalization of the End of Residence Controls

A report from the mid-1990s indicated that one of every six people in Shanghai had "recently arrived" from rural areas. This immigrant labor force was said to number 2.5 million, but only three-fifths had reliable jobs. One million had to forgo money or else look for a job each day. Most immigrants with steady work came from other places in the Shanghai delta, and many of these had relatives already in the metropolis. As one construction team chief from Jiangsu said, "We hire workers from our hometown and from neighboring towns, so that we can be sure of our credibility."[78] These were the fortunate migrants.

Many others, who came disproportionately from Anhui, Henan, Jiangxi, and Sichuan, took Shanghai jobs without residence permits and thus broke the law. So they lacked any medical or injury benefits, despite the dangerous work many of them had to do. They also lacked recourse to police if their labor contractors did not pay them. Many of these lived on the edge of the city. Their shacks looked like storage sheds, made of corrugated metal, with asphalted canvas for roofs, bamboo for pillars to hold the structures up, and cardboard or woven straw mats to separate the "rooms." The Pengpu area became one of several major centers for the "tide of migrant workers" (*min gong chao*). When they were not hired by construction or stevedore teams, they took up individual work selling food on the streets, repairing shoes or bicycles, or picking rubbish.

Places just on the edge of Shanghai city, such as Zhenru (which has a train stop) or the suburbs of Wujiaochang or Wanshanbang, became the abodes of many ex-peasant migrants without urban registrations. These newcomers wanted to make money, but as illegal residents they could not obtain business licenses. So they set up factories and shops without official blessing. During a 1990 raid at Wanshanbang, police found thirty "underground" food processing factories, which baked and catered mainly for people living in Shanghai's central districts.[79]

Women domestic workers came especially from Anhui to Shanghai. Already in the 1970s, they had organized a housemaids' union informally called the "Anhui group." Authorities of the inland province were so perturbed by this exodus, which reduced both economic production and political control in their area, they prevailed on the Shanghai government to ship some migrants back to Anhui by train.[80] Domestic helpers and family relatives, however, were generally welcomed by Shanghai residents, and bureaucrats usually gave up hope of monitoring all their goings and comings. About three-fifths of Shanghai's temporary migrants, according to a mid-1980s study, lived in the households of permanent residents. When they were not members of the same family, they were usually in Shanghai to work. When they were relatives, they frankly told pollsters they were there to visit or live—even though such activities have no status in state planning documents.[81]

Many migrants stayed for long periods in the city. Contract work for building projects usually justified half a year or more. Of Shanghai's "floating population" without permanent residence permits, at least one-fifth of the estimated total were in building trades. These formed more than four hundred construction teams, a larger force than the city's legally registered population in that industry. Two steady facts about these near-subsistence-wage laborers were that they were cheap and they worked very hard.

Local Shanghai construction teams were less profitable, when they did jobs in the city, than were those brought from other provinces. The outside teams also in practice paid lower taxes, so the state's uneven fiscal structure was, for this group if not others, an unintended spur to urban immigration. In the late 1980s, *Labor News* reported that half the construction teams working in Shanghai had been recruited within the municipality. This was especially true in Pudong (i.e., Chuansha county), where the sharp objections of local peasants to confiscation of their land were partly allayed by giving their construction teams a great deal of lucrative work. But in the city as a whole, locals ran fewer teams than those brought from a distance.[82] Although the skills of the Shanghai builders were deemed better, local contractors' costs were higher, and they tended to lose money. As the newspaper politely put it, the "competitive opportunities" of non-Shanghai teams were better. Their tax and remittance costs were also lower—even for work on the same project.

Migrants did a great variety of other jobs, too. "Almost all the tea-egg salesgirls . . . are from northern Jiangsu. . . . Many of them earn 15 to 20 yuan a day, about six times a government employee's daily pay."[83] Other trades in which illegal and impermanent residents predominated were furniture repair, quilt making, and knife grinding. These functions, and the services of house-maids, were appreciated by permanent Shanghai residents even when performed by illegals.

The Interests of Police, Long-Term Residents, and Officials

Urban immigrants called themselves "free people" (*ziyou ren*; the old English term is "freemen"). They broke the bonds rural cadres had previously placed on them.[84] Established residents in Shanghai benefited from migrants in some ways, but at the same time often looked down on them—and tended to think them libertines. Open disdain between subethnic groups in Shanghai, especially toward people from Subei (northern Jiangsu), is an old story.[85] During reforms, immigrants as a group became convenient social scapegoats. They often lived in flimsy housing, were said to compete with long-term residents for jobs, and were actually numerous among criminals. Many were already violating registration laws; so it was a short step to break others.

Young rural immigrants to Shanghai often could not obtain living space in the crowded central city. But peasants on the outskirts offered them space—at high rents, and without the blessings of any official authority. The lifestyles of these young people were often unstable. Largely because of their influx, suburban economic crime soared in 1984, rising by 60 percent above the 1983 rate.[86] Although only 7 percent of Shanghai crime was committed by unregistered people in 1983, this portion rose to 11 percent in 1984 and 1985, 18 percent in 1986, 20 percent in 1987, 30 percent in 1988, and 31 percent in 1989—and this is just the floaters' portion. The total crime rate also rose rapidly over these years.[87]

At the end of the decade, an estimated 3 percent of all temporary residents had been arrested for crimes. The portion among the permanently registered was 1 percent. Shanghai had seven million bicycles in 1993, of which 150,000 were stolen (despite locks, police, and bicycle watchers) in that year alone. Four-fifths of the bike thieves who were caught in 1993 turned out to be migrants to Shanghai.[88] Victims of these crimes, not just perpetrators, tended also to be in the city unofficially. Migrants were regularly dunned for "taxes," payable to violent "protection" gangs, often from their own home provinces. One such group was called the "Vegetable Knife Gang" (Caidao Bang), indicating its members' favorite weapon.[89]

Permanent residents could disdain such behavior while at the same time benefiting from migrants. The attitudes of established families to the influx were generally negative but complex. Even beyond the useful maids and construction workers, there was a grudging acceptance of migrants. As one writer put it by 1989, the "floaters. . . do not live in Shanghai temporarily; they are 'actual' Shanghai residents." Locals also had a new (illegal) source of income from the migrants: "Now, because a lot of peasants came, Shanghai citizens could sell surplus grain [from ration coupons] to them. . . . Some outsiders are working for Shanghai residents. They did not want to be paid in cash but in rice."[90]

The monthly legal grain quota per Shanghai resident had not been lowered since the 1950s (despite nondeliveries in bad times, and despite the much greater availability of meat and vegetables since the early 1970s). But because many kinds of meats and vegetables could now be had, Shanghai legal residents could easily forgo some of their grain. A newspaper suggested, "If we reformed this policy, the problem [for official budgets] would be solved."[91] But nothing happened. The matter was politically sensitive. Top socialist administrators apparently thought that a reduction of Shanghai legal residents' traditional food entitlement could stir resentment among workers in state factories. PRC leaders may occasionally remind themselves that workers in cities like Shanghai do not lack revolutionary histories.

A Shanghai author claimed that in sum: "We should have a positive attitude toward the current floating population." He admitted that migrants brought big problems. Among Shanghai crimes "in the water area, 72 percent were perpetrated by the transient population. These people were also responsible for 32 percent of the burglaries, 34 percent of frauds, and 22 percent of rapes and homicides. . . . Many women in the floating population gave birth illegally. Among those who did so in Shanghai, 13 percent had two children, and 4 percent had three or more." Despite all this, the migrants were helping to construct a modern metropolis. "Without them, it would be difficult to imagine so many new buildings in today's Shanghai. A quarter million laborers from other places work in the textile industry and in environmental sanitation."[92] Such a sanguine attitude was not shared by all, but state leaders' interests in immigration, even the illegal kinds, were very mixed.

The influx brought cheap labor, and apparently managers supposed it would not directly bring unrest among permanent workers, whose worst jobs could thus be staffed by outsiders. Migrant proletarians, even if they lived under extraordinarily cramped conditions, were often in their own "communities outside the system" (*tizhi wai qunluo*). One young unmarried man had arrived in early 1994 at a "Sichuan village" in the Pengpu area. He lived with five hundred other Sichuan migrants in a 300–square-meter asphalt-roofed shack—but he expressed some contentment: "I like to stay with my fellow Sichuan people. We take care of each other like brothers. We shoulder our hardships together, just as we share our dreams."[93]

It is as yet unclear whether strong traditional organization among temporary laborers in China—which has correlated with past unrest among contract laborers—will provide forums through which immigrants may make political demands. Comparative research from other cultures, especially on the politics of migrants to Mexico City, Lima, Rio de Janiero, and other developing cities, has suggested that ex-peasant urban villages in Latin America have not become hotbeds of political unrest—at least not for the first generation of "urban villagers."[94] New arrivals to big cities from rural areas, reproducing their traditional communities separate from the surrounding metropolitan environments, have been politically quiescent. Even when sanitation, water supply, and other urban services for them have been minimal, as is currently the case for many in Shanghai, they are not a direct threat to the political order.[95] Indirectly, however, their presence may create such a threat because of the reactions of more established residents.

The migration to cities of millions of unlicensed migratory workers in the 1980s and 1990s has been unpopular with some long-term Shanghai residents, who fear their jobs are endangered by immigrant labor. The state's public policy has often called for migrants' expulsion back to the countryside. Official sermons with this theme please most state-sector workers. Long-term residents readily believe that official coercion has a rightful role, at least for keeping vagrants in line. Migrants provide many occasions for police to prove their constabulary worth. Officials can publicize the expulsion of relatively few unregistered migrants while actually allowing most to stay, and the police since 1989 need as much legitimacy as they can muster.[96] But effective enforcement, except in random campaigns, is quite another matter. So long as migrants provide low-cost help to many state enterprises with tightly constrained budgets, they will not be leaving Shanghai.

Urban intellectuals in China have long fulminated against "blindly flowing population" (*mangliu renkou*). When a book entitled *The History of Chinese Hooliganism* was published in 1993, it traced in loving detail the state's efforts to control migrants from before the First Emperor to 1911.[97] Planners, who want to tell citizens where to live, suggest that intellectuals linked to the state know how ordinary people should conduct their lives better than the people themselves do. This is not a silly opinion, because there is no sure way of knowing the general conditions under which small groups' (or individuals') benefits come from collective arrangements—or the general conditions under which they do not. There is a chance the planners may plan sagely and fairly; the state has promoted any discourse that suggests this possibility. But urban intellectuals with good state jobs tend to live in choice spots already. Even if would-be migrants fully obeyed whatever China's leaders decreed, it would be hard for an outside observer to believe that such officials give much weight to the interests of people quite different from themselves.

Green Revolution, Floods, Income Equality, and Migration

Agricultural modernization was, until recently, thought to be a potential disaster for most peasants. It might free labor from backbreaking field work, but it also seemed likely to liberate them from their sources of income. These portents of disaster were not realized. Green revolution in practice has brought many migrants in developing countries (including China) from impoverished areas to richer ones, where their presence has raised production, income inequality, and obvious exploitation. They fare better economically in these new places than in the villages they left.

Inland poverty pushes young people away from the places they leave, as much as coastal wealth pulls them. Recurrent temporary floods combine with the steady growth of demand for industrial labor to bring people toward Shanghai. Severe summer flooding struck the middle Yangzi in several years of the mid-1990s, for example 1996. Much of the water came from rain that hit ground east of the Three Gorges, in the watersheds of the Xiang, Gan, and Huai rivers, so that many doubted the dam could solve this problem. The Shanghai delta was also affected, especially in Jiangsu. Sometimes the deluge was almost as bad there as in large parts of Hunan, Jiangxi, and Anhui, where millions of farmers saw their crops, factories, and houses ruined by water. Many were washed out in more than one year during the 1990s. These events gave them compelling occasion to migrate elsewhere, trying to find a better life.

Migrants' own expectations that their incomes would later rise have, in past years, actually been realized. The inland places suffer a talent drain, but average farm sizes there will increase if China follows the pattern of other countries after green revolutions.[98] The chief buffering factor against social disaster, after the seminal reform of farm techniques, is migration. Arthur Lewis, writing in the early 1950s, could not have predicted the effects of then-future agronomy, but the green revolution has done in fields what the capital-accumulating sector did in factories: It has speeded the decline of the supply of subsistence-wage labor.

So workers have moved because the opportunities in their situation have changed. Migration has the effect of a political decision, taken in parallel by many actors but not just according to the interests of any one size of collectivity. The real liberation of China, which occurred after the 1970s when many peasants became workers, threatened both the patronist state and intellectuals' ideals of plans in power. Migration is a concomitant of development, and increased income has been such a strong interest of so many Chinese, the state can no longer control where people live.

Services and Collective or Private Enterprises

Chinese Marxist and statist theories alike place a high value on one service: government. Other services have received less consistent support. Whatever rational justifications might be offered for commerce, insurance, finance, tourism, brokerage, or advertising, in Mao's time radicals deemed these activities "nonproductive," frivolous at best and exploitative at worst. A crucial aspect of China's reforms has been the revival of services, after fifteen years of official discrimination against them. A closely related correlate of reform has been the growth of collectives and the revival of individual and private firms, which mostly sold services.

Services in the Early Reforms

Service firms in Shanghai numbered about 140,000 during the 1950s, but only 10,000 by the mid-1970s. This reduction of 93 percent was not just a result of business mergers, creating larger socialist corporations with many branches, although that caused much of it. As the city's population grew in these years, the absolute number of service employees also went down.[99] Shanghai's rich tradition in all services (except government) was sharply degraded. But service-sector productivity had by 1970 already recovered from a sharp recession after 1957. Pricing and capital allocation policies against services still remained, but demand for them was growing. Only in 1975 did service productivity regain its 1957 level, although it had been growing since 1970, as Table 1.5–4 shows. Then it rose quickly—especially in 1980 and 1985, during periods of inflation and movements to register service firms so they could be taxed.[100]

Shanghai's industrial sector, which is mostly state-owned, showed a slow labor productivity increase during the early 1970s. Then it jumped during the quasi–Great Leap of 1978—but suffered a decline from 1979 to 1983, partly because of lower incentives to state workers than to those in other sectors, but also because of the expanding supply of registered labor (as sent-down Shanghai youths and ex-peasants came from rural places to the metropolis). The advance after 1984 was slower than inflation. Both output and workers were almost surely underreported in Shanghai's most dynamic sector, suburban collectives. At some times (such as 1985 and 1988) higher incentives to report output probably affected the apparent results. The situation is further complicated because some workers straddled different sectors, sometimes in manufacturing and sometimes in services.

Table 1.5-4

Labor Productivity in Shanghai by Sector
(reported gross output per worker in yuan; annual percentage increases)

	Tertiary services	% Change	Secondary manufactures	% Change
1957	*2,600*		3,070	
1962	*2,185*	–4	3,960	5
1965	*2,174*	0	5,150	9
1970	2,538	3	*5,244*	0
1975	2,884	3	5,687	2
1978	3,407	6	6,900	7
1979	3,518	3	*6,724*	–3
1980	4,106	17	*6,669*	–1
1981	4,157	1	*6,533*	–2
1982	4,206	1	*6,442*	–1
1983	4,559	8	*6,320*	–2
1984	5,197	14	6,541	3
1985	6,235	20	7,367	13
1986	6,690	7	7,418	1
1987	7,594	14	7,930	7
1988	8,682	14	9,375	18
1989	9,252	7	10,174	9
1990	10,516	14	10,458	3
1991	12,030	14	11,861	13

Note and sources: Inflation affects these results, but finding appropriate factors with which to adjust these sectoral figures would not be easy, so the table reports them unadjusted. Calculated from *Shanghai tongji nianjian, 1988* (Shanghai Statistical Yearbook, 1988), Li Mouhuan et al., eds. (Shanghai: Shanghai Shi Tongji Ju, 1988), p. 41 for the gross national product (*guomin shengchan zongzhi*) and p. 97 for the laborers (*shehui laodong zhe*); and for later years, calculated from ibid., 1990, pp. 71 and 34; 1991, pp. 72 and 34; 1992, pp. 86 and 35 (each book reporting the previous year). The denominator is supposed to include not only regular, unionized laborers but also others. For clarification on the numerator, see *Tongji cidian* (Statistical Dictionary), Jia Hongyu, ed. (Shanghai: Shanghai Renmin Chuban She, 1986), pp. 293–95.

The revival of services was very bumpy, and in some of the most obvious fields it related to changes of lifestyle. Services were revived partly by overseas trade from the early 1970s, but then more powerfully by domestic demand. The Shanghai government did not set up a bureau for tourism until 1978, although many visitors had come under various auspices before then. From that year until 1982, the number of foreign tourists increased on average by 30 percent yearly. Many domestic travelers found Shanghai, with its low consumer prices, to be good for shopping. By 1982, more than half the city's revenues from tourism came through retail commodity purchases, especially from domestic travelers.[101]

To take a small example in the field of design: As early as 1975, Shanghai clothing began to diversify away from baggy blue. Miniskirts (then called *chaoduan qun*) were seen in parks; their appearance was officially condemned by radicals, and the women wearing them were few but noticeable at this time. Collars were also deemed by conservative arbiters of taste to have become unnecessarily large. Fabrics of distinctive colors, and especially cloth that was partly transparent, came in for puritanical criticism; these were considered products of capitalism. But the Cultural Revolution was finished by that time, and some people wore such clothes by 1975 without incurring violent struggle against themselves. The new styles were of some popular interest to Shanghai residents then, partly because they were striking early symbols against the radical tradition.[102] Some people wearing these "strange clothes" were "individual peddlers"—the predecessors of later private firms.

Employment and Services

Young people often could find jobs only in service firms or by individual initiative. In 1976, Shanghai's urban districts had nearly a million youths age 21 to 30. Because so many returned from the countryside in the next few years, this number by 1983 was up 86 percent.[103] Such a sharp swell in the 21-to-30 age cohort was much higher than the rise in all of Shanghai's population during the same years (16 percent).[104] At the end of 1982, all of Shanghai had 11,000 collectives, employing 1,030,000 people (22 percent of the city's labor force). They made only 8 percent of the industrial product, but these collectives were most important in services, where they comprised 28 percent of the registered firms. Their tax payments were only 4 percent of the city's revenues.[105] In all of China, the portion of service workers rose from 12 percent in 1980 to 16 percent in 1985.[106]

Employment was what drove the revival of the service sector. The government needed to make sure that youths, often ex-rusticates, got off the streets and into jobs. The slowness of employment in China's large cities had correlated before 1970 not just with send-downs, but also with "steel-eating" industrial investments, which absorbed much money but little labor. To the extent that Shanghai and other cities could support many small service firms in the 1980s, they grew because the new, more labor-absorbing service companies could hire people.

Service employment growth until the middle of reforms was nonetheless almost incredibly snail-like. In *the whole Shanghai financial sector from 1952 to 1984,* the average number of new employees had been only ten persons annually.[107] Such a rate is not just low. In a developing city whose average size in this period was roughly ten million, it is grotesque. By 1983, the finance and insurance industries still contributed only 3 percent of Shanghai's gross product—though Shanghai had once been China's financial center.

Local cadres attempted to make jobs available to approved persons while not taking the state's normal responsibility for housing, health, rations, pensions, and benefits. The main parts of the tertiary sector, as defined in Chinese accounts, are commerce, finance, technology, consulting, and hotels and restaurants. The government and the military—along with education, which in China is associated with the government—are not included.[108] Hawking and illegal services are also not included, so the available data are almost surely underreports.

For years, as Table 1.5–5 shows on a long-term basis, state policies had effectively discouraged growth in Shanghai services. The tertiary sector of the economy employed 28 percent of the city's workers in 1952, but the mid-1950s transition to socialist management and the post–Great Leap Forward depression reduced this to about 21 percent. It stayed at that level for more than two decades. Its rise in the 1980s, however, was steady, and by 1989 services employed the same portion of Shanghai workers as in 1952. The service sector rose from two-tenths to three-tenths of all registered employment from the mid-1970s into the 1990s.[109]

The portion of laborers in the service sectors of other cities internationally, in the mid-1980s for example, was much higher than in Shanghai. This was true for a wide variety of cities in both developed and developing countries, both socialist and capitalist: Tokyo, 69 percent; Singapore, 66 percent; Chicago, 64 percent; Mexico City, 60 percent; Warsaw, 57 percent; Cairo, 49 percent—and Shanghai, 24 percent.[110] Services remained severely underpriced in Shanghai through the late 1980s at least.

Service Subsectors

Commerce was the most important absorber of labor, but for many years nonstate stores in Shanghai had difficulty obtaining physical space to show their wares. Despite this problem, collective trade developed in Shanghai at a quick rate because these quasi-private firms often offered better goods at lower prices than the state stores. By 1984, collectives sold about 40 percent of all products (while in the manufacturing sector, they still produced only 14 percent of commodity values).[111] State stores had largely stopped searching the whole country for better items to sell.

In some service trades, such as insurance, Shanghai could establish agencies beyond its boundaries. In that field, these firms were particularly active on the delta in Changzhou, Hangzhou, Ningbo, Suzhou, and Wuxi.[112] The proliferation of local state companies competing with each other, combined with new collectives that were also licensed locally, provided by the late 1980s a greater choice of service providers than China had seen for many decades.

The mid-1980s intensification of local reforms, especially for small companies, can be illustrated in the travel business. All Shanghai had only thirteen travel agencies in 1983; but by the end of 1984, the number was sixty, and in the

Table 1.5-5

Fall and Rise of Shanghai's Service Sector, 1952–1992
(percentages of product, and [in bold italics] of registered employees, in designated primary, secondary, and tertiary sectors)

	Services	Industry	Agriculture
1952	42, ***28***	54, ***30***	4, ***42***
1957	37, ***27***	59, ***36***	4, ***37***
1975	19, ***21***	77, ***42***	5
1978	18, ***21***	76, ***44***	5
1983	22, ***24***	72, ***52***	6, ***24***
1986	28, ***26***	69, ***59***	3, ***15***
1987	29, ***27***	67, ***60***	4, ***13***
1989	29, ***28***	67, ***60***	4, ***12***
1990	31, ***28***	65, ***60***	4, ***11***
1991	32, ***29***	64, ***60***	4, ***11***
1992	33, ***30***	64, ***60***	3, ***11***

Notes and source: Good data were not, unfortunately, found for the 1960s or early 1970s. Figures for agricultural employment in some years are highly misleading (and reports for industry are too low) because persons registered as peasants were working in factories licensed by rural units. The tertiary sector comprises services, including trade (but not the government or military), the secondary sector is manufacturing industry, and the primary sector is agriculture and extraction (small in Shanghai). Compiled from separate but consistent accounts in Cao Linzhang, Gu Guangqing, and Li Jianhua, *Shanghai shengchan ziliao suoyu zhi jiegou yanjiu* (Studies of Shanghai Production and Ownership Structure) (Shanghai: Shanghai Shehui Kexue Yuan Chuban She, 1987), 127; *Shanghai tongji nianjian, 1988*, p. 44; and *Shanghai jingji yanjiu* (Shanghai Economic Research), May 1985, p. 46. For 1988 and 1990, see *Shanghai tongji nianjian, 1990* (Shanghai Statistical Yearbook, 1990), Shanghai Shi Tongji Ju, ed. (Beijing: Zhongguo Tongji Chuban She, 1990), pp. 34, for product data and 71 for number of workers by sector; and ibid., 1991 edition, respectively, pp. 34 and 72. For 1991 and 1992, see the same yearbook, 1993 edition, pp. 37 and 74.

next year it rose to eighty. Many were at first unable to establish efficient connections inland, because most transport was still run by state bureaucracies. So in 1986, the number of agencies fell again, to sixty-seven. Tourists coming in or out of Shanghai each day in 1985 averaged almost a hundred thousand. Half of them stayed for several days.[113] Tourism is an archetypal "nonproductive" sector from the viewpoint of Party conservatives, but that opinion no longer could stop Shanghai agencies from booking tours.

Suzhou and Hangzhou were, for the expansion of this service industry, two of Shanghai's biggest attractions. Shanghai's economic interests in this field, as in others, overlapped strongly with the interests of Jiangsu and Zhejiang. Economic cooperation in these areas was speedy; by 1980, Shanghai, Jiangsu, and Zhejiang had established a "regional tourism coordination small group." This organization was later expanded to cover all of East China, and it was said thus to "escape the administrative cage" of provincial jurisdictions.[114] But local agents did not need this official advice; they were already arranging trips wherever they could.

Shanghai's tourism was expected to develop first by providing more expeditions to close scenic cities on the delta, and later to more distant sites such as Huangshan and Lushan inland.[115] Actual development in this sector was not mainly organized by the city or central authorities. It resulted from the efforts of collective and private travel agencies, and especially from the new wealth of their clients. Agencies established "horizontal" links with private and collective counterparts in other East China places. In this service sector, as in others, the reforms were a boom time.

Hawkers

In many developing cities, the most common providers of services and the most obvious individual enterprises are street peddlers. Hawkers have never mixed well with statism. During the height of the Cultural Revolution, when police efforts to ban them were effective because of support from activists against petty capitalism, hawkers were seldom seen in Shanghai. They reappeared gradually during the 1970s, closing their stands and packing their wares quickly, in the ancient ritual, whenever enforcers of the ban came near.

General licenses for hawking were implicit in the idea of "specialized agricultural households" that could freely sell their over-quota goods. Not until February 1983, however, did the Shanghai city government finally declare that peasants, after making their deliveries to the state for fixed sums, could sell any agricultural products (except cotton) at whatever prices the market would bear. A consequence was that profits from individual trading had to be recognized as legal. Hawkers had actually done business in Shanghai for many years before that, however. Officially announced policies about hawking, even more than about other topics, were especially reactive and variable.

Often consumer goods prices in regular Shanghai state stores (and in collectives, after more were established in the mid-1980s) were more heavily subsidized and lower than elsewhere. Low state prices reduced hawking of these goods far more effectively than police could. But this system broke down in the 1980s. Shanghai officials ruled that suburban farmers could sell their over-quota grain "freely"—so long as they did so in Shanghai, where the prices were low. By mid-July 1983, just a few months after legalizing individual trade, the government held a campaign to punish Shanghai farmers who sold their surplus crops elsewhere at a profit.[116] The reform state wanted to maximize incentives to produce, but it also wanted an official monopoly of profitable commerce. This was a contradiction. Households went very easily into trade. Once they did so, private commerce over time became increasingly difficult for the government to prohibit.

By the 1990s, there were at least a hundred thousand hawkers in Shanghai who lacked legal licenses—and this figure was about equal to the number of licenses the local government had issued.[117] Some unregistered salespeople were officially counted among the unemployed (*daiye,* "waiting for vocations"), including many youths who had returned from the countryside. Others were retired. Newspapers castigated many for being simply "lazy," apparently because they refused to take temporary nonunion jobs at low wages in state-owned firms. But many hawkers also had regular state jobs; their illegal salesmanship was moonlighting to raise their incomes. Some were quoted with frank complaints against their inadequate salaries in regular jobs. According to one, hawking was "better than going to work."

Policies for dealing with illegal hawking, like those for dealing with migrants, threatened the municipal benefits these activities brought. Officials admitted in print that many of the unemployed needed their hawking jobs for livelihood. Local governments therefore began to issue such people "temporary business licenses" (*linshi jingying xuke zheng*). Retirees, however, were encouraged to get out of trade, live on their pensions, and participate in "social charity."[118] Younger people who had returned to Shanghai from rural assignments could also apply for temporary business licenses—and when they did this, they would be given a hard time if they lacked Shanghai household registrations, which they might acquire at this point if they were well connected.

Food vendors were common among hawkers, but the postsocialist context bred new trade sectors, too. At least ten thousand Shanghai women by 1989 were estimated to be professional purchasers of surplus ration tickets. This activity was illegal, so they used the standard cover of peddling tea-boiled eggs. A newspaper guessed they made at least 10 yuan a day on average—a quite respectable wage.[119] The main influx of these hawkers to Shanghai came largely from Anhui and Henan, as well as northern Jiangsu. Plainclothes police could stop some of this trade without difficulty, but officials knew that it would soon emerge in another form, if they moved seriously against the tea-egg/coupon industry.

It was not difficult for them to find worse problems in both manufacturing and commerce. Child laborers as young as 15 years reportedly heard they could clear 200 yuan a month working in Shanghai. They would come from impoverished provinces to Shanghai, often sleep outside small hotels, and work in order to eat. Some joined gangs or became pickpockets. Teenagers reportedly made railroad stations and docks somewhat dangerous. Sixty percent of all injuries near railways, according to a 1989 estimate, were caused by people who had "blindly flowed" into Shanghai.[120] Considering what some of them earned, especially in comparison with the wages of state employees, they were actually not blind. Many were part-time hawkers, and their workaday illegality in commerce did not dispose them to obey any laws.

June 1989 conservatism led to a campaign against unlicensed street hawkers, on whom very "incomplete statistics" counted "about forty thousand" in Shanghai. As authorities admitted, even legally licensed vendors did a great deal of trade they failed to report for taxation. Common commodities in Shanghai's gray economy ranged widely: from cigarettes and transport tickets to bulk industrial goods. More than eight hundred scalpers were caught selling train tickets illegally at the new Shanghai station in a July 1989 campaign, because the Railroad Ministry would neither raise its prices to improve service nor keep up with the demand for transport that the booming economy generated.

The Shanghai Public Security Bureau had a campaign at this time, in which it arrested 236 entrepreneurs for 134 cases. In each of these, the illegal transactions had exceeded 10,000 yuan during the first half of 1989. Gold ingots, cultural relics, calligraphic scrolls, and many kinds of Chinese and foreign currency were involved, having a total value in excess of 4 million yuan.[121] This was just the tip of an iceberg of illegality. The police did not catch most traders who broke the law. High bureaucrats found hawkers unbecoming in China's largest city, and other illegal private traders were difficult to stop. Their threat to the regime was political, but it was indirect and cumulative rather than specific or immediate. Many citizens found their services convenient.

The 1991–95 Five-Year Plan scheduled an increase of only 10 percent in the number of officially recognized free markets in China, over the late 1990 number.[122] The state could scarcely enforce such a low limit on the growth of the economy's most dynamic service sector. Fewer markets would be easier than many to monitor. The limit on planned growth, however, was mainly an admission that state cadres were stretched thin trying to keep track of trade. Conservatives clearly wanted to restrict the growth of unmonitored markets. High-level reformers saw the opposite result, not because of their own preferences but because they knew millions of small traders wanted to make money.

Individual and Private Firms

The renaissance of the service sector meant mainly a rise of small collectives. Formally private enterprise in Shanghai revived more slowly. The era before

1949 provided the main precedents, and the story of Shanghai's early capitalist development need not be retold here. Private ownership has long been severely discouraged by Communist hard-liners in the PRC.[123] Change in the individually owned service sector can be discussed together with industry, since until the 1990s both in Shanghai were very small-scale if private. The Transition to Socialism of 1956 eliminated private firms in manufacturing, and the Great Leap Forward made a practical end of private commerce. During 1958 alone, the number of Shanghai private firms shrank from twenty-two thousand to six thousand.[124] Less than 1 percent of retail products in the city was sold by private firms. In manufacturing, less than one-tenth of 1 percent of legally registered and priced industrial value came from private firms by 1959.

In the early 1960s, a few private firms reappeared, so that ten thousand of them actually existed in Shanghai by 1965. The Cultural Revolution, for all its ideological communism, was not sufficiently organized to nationalize the remaining private firms. But it criticized them and scared their operators. Hawkers, with no fixed abode, were never totally eliminated—although the Cultural Revolution went far toward this end. Later, by the end of 1975, the number of employees in these very local firms was reportedly thirteen thousand—about the same as during the early 1960s.[125] In a city of Shanghai's size, this had become a trivially small sector.

The recent history of quasi-private lane and street industries is not well known. "Street industries" first emerged in Shanghai under that name after the Great Leap Forward, on the basis of efforts by individual entrepreneurs. They long predated 1978. In 1963, after the economic depression, they were nominally put under district- or street-level administration. Their productivity was reported to rise most quickly when these firms were legitimated by street offices (rather than by smaller neighborhood committees), and they had more success in some urban districts than in others. In the relatively poor and densely populated district of Nanshi, for example, the product value from enterprises under street committees in 1976 was seven times that in 1963. In Hongkou or Putuo, however, this rise was over forty times. On average in the whole city, it was over twenty times. These firms responded to newly available technologies more flexibly than did state-owned companies. Fully 43 percent of the total value of street-level enterprises by 1977 (and 28 percent of the workforce employed at this level) was in electronics. Parallel 1977 portions for registered street-level factories in other sectors may be summarized as follows:[126]

	% of value	% of workers	% of firms
Electronics	43	27	23
Handicrafts	22	28	31
Machines	21	26	24
Arts and co-ops	11	13	15
Technical support	3	7	7

Firms legitimated by local neighborhood committees hired more than twice as many workers as those under street companies by the mid-1970s—or 250,000 on a regular permanent basis, and probably many more on nonunion and temporary bases. These neighborhood bodies, unlike street committees, were not formally offices of the government. The reported product value from these lane industries expanded more slowly than the number of workers they employed, after the 1963 watershed policies that first attempted to put such plants under materials supply plans. But they may well have left part of their output off the official books. In lane factories, the increase of gross product from 1965 to 1978 reportedly rose five times, and in the shorter period from 1978 to 1982, it rose again more than three times.[127] The productivity of labor in street-committee-run enterprises was ten times that in lane-run plants[128] — on the very unlikely premise that the latter reported all their output. The purpose of the small plants, at least for the people who worked there and the neighborhood cadres who got them jobs, was not just production but also employment in Shanghai.

Individual Enterprises in the 1970s

"Individual" (*geti*) and especially "private" (*si*) are somewhat pejorative words in Chinese. Firms in these categories existed on a small scale in Shanghai even during the early 1970s, although the political shadow over them makes reports of them inconsistent. One source, for example, indicates that eight thousand Shanghai private entrepreneurs were registered in 1976.[129] Another reports that private enterprises, in the form of small "individual households," were not legally revived in Shanghai until 1979.[130] There is extensive evidence that private vendors and small factories never quite completely disappeared. The history of these firms has been distorted because some writers have taken high-state pronouncements about their nonexistence at face value. Private enterprises became very small, sometimes nominally collective, and occasionally underground—but they did exist.

These were supposed, by the late 1970s, to be ex-peasant agricultural households that had signed contracts to specialize in other work. In fact, they were small private entrepreneurs who could usually operate with or without a license, because traders from whom they were nearly indistinguishable had been legalized. Open markets for sellers of handicrafts, agricultural produce, and then increasingly other goods became very common. These expanded sharply in the late 1970s and early 1980s. By 1983, the number of registered households in Shanghai on such markets was thirty-four thousand. Unlicensed vendors made the total higher.

The Privatist Model, Wenzhou, and Economic Legitimacy in Shanghai

Wenzhou, predictably, was the PRC's most brazen experiment with free markets. Mountains cut off this Zhejiang port from the Shanghai delta, making

Wenzhou the China coast's most isolated major city. This place speaks a dialect of Shanghainese, however. Wenzhou's largely unsocialist economic institutions by the late 1970s echoed the unbridled capitalism, exploitation, ambition, and economic tumult of pre-1949 Shanghai. Many observers reported this—causing others, who liked it, to publish apologies claiming practically the opposite: that Wenzhou was a "socialist market experiment." Conservatives in Beijing had more doubts about this pattern than did reformers in the Shanghai delta, many of whom clearly hoped that allowances accorded to the "Wenzhou experimental zone" might flow northward onto their flatlands.

Shanghai's *Liberation Daily* was the first major medium to publicize a "Wenzhou model."[131] This formulation allowed it to be distinguished from the "Sunan model"—but also made it legitimate to be studied, or conceivably even emulated after statist intellectuals discussed it enough. Wenzhou firms had great economic success, and management aspects of their experience are treated in previous chapters. Shanghai exponents of the "Wenzhou model" were second only to those from Wenzhou itself.

The fly in the ointment, in the view of Party conservatives, was the prominence of private enterprises in Wenzhou. Private ownership could be adopted by very few Shanghai firms. Publicity in the metropolis about Wenzhou nonetheless lent some political legitimacy to collective companies that paid their executives high salaries. Street collectives in Shanghai could be accorded public attention during the early 1980s; they made profits, but they appeared less unsocialist than much-publicized firms in Wenzhou. Four Shanghai street collectives, which each contributed more than 100 million yuan in profits to the government, were praised in the lead article of *Xinmin Evening News* on New Year's Day, 1982. They dealt in electrical supplies, plastics, instruments, and semiconductors.[132] Before reforms, firms that came in for public praise had practically always been in the state sector.

Public legitimacy was slowly extended even to workers in nonstate firms. Almost a thousand "labor models" (*laodong mofan*) and 360 "model collectives" (*mofan jiti*) were chosen by an office of the municipal government in 1987.[133] For the first time, both state cadres and nonstate enterprise workers were eligible. Titles for individuals correlated highly with bonuses, so the inclusion of nonstate workers involved material incentives as well as symbols. Still, of all the people selected, 81 percent were members of the CCP (and 36 percent had a university-level education). Reformers and entrepreneurs were supposed to be favored for these honors. Local conservatives resisted changing the criteria for these public awards. In earlier years, a very large rally had been held to fête the model workers, but in 1987, a relatively modest audience of 1,700 attended the celebrations.

The nonstate sector, which was still overwhelmingly collective in Shanghai, involved less equal salaries and fewer communal benefits than the state sector. Income inequality can be measured by a high Gini coefficient. This statistic for the households of employees in Shanghai state units, by the second quarter of

1984, was 0.0755; but for "nonemployees" (i.e., mostly workers or farmers in collectives), the coefficient was 0.2149—showing much greater inequality in the nonstate group. Independence from the official system also meant higher absolute earnings. People working for state firms or offices got an average of only 78 yuan per month in 1984, but "nonemployees" (i.e., those who were independent or under nongovernmental managers) averaged 94 yuan.[134]

Shanghai's unemployed flocked to quasi-private collectives because they were profitable and could offer jobs. But small commercial operations cut the profits of state shops heavily, so that government policies encouraged laid-off and unemployed workers to join established firms rather than to found their own. The official employment agencies would help almost anybody with local registration to seek a job and get a "waiting for work certificate" (*daiye zheng*). But any unemployed person who wanted to start a private firm had first to turn in that certificate before applying for a business license.[135] The reaction of many was simply to ignore the bureaucrats, start enterprises directly, and make money as long as possible, without the benediction of the state.

The mid-1980s saw the start of a serious expansion beyond the collective sector. Private "individual households" (i.e., small companies) numbered 85,000 in Shanghai by the end of 1986, and they employed almost 120,000 people according to very incomplete reports. Fifty-three percent of these workers, and 47 percent of the firms, were in the suburbs. These companies were restricted, because they were not supposed to hire more than five people on a regular basis. Not until 1987 did the central government restore legal status to "private enterprises" (*siying qiye*), which could employ more than five. The average reported monthly income of these licensed individual enterprises was 312 yuan, and the average income of those that paid taxes was over 400 yuan. This rate was 2.7 times the average reported income of Shanghai cooperative workers, and also more than twice that in state factories, stores, and offices.[136]

A survey determined that 7 percent of these Shanghai private companies were "ten-thousand-yuan households," receiving that much yearly. A separate survey estimated that 10 percent made that much. (For comparison, the very highest-paid state employee, the premier of China, each month was supposed to receive just 530 yuan.)[137] The scale of these private firms was kept small. By 1988, Shanghai still had only a thousand private enterprises employing eight or more people. The registered amounts of fixed and operating capital were surprisingly large, considering the reported incomes. Those who worked in urban markets were especially prosperous. At the Fumin Street Market, 19 percent of the firms surveyed in the mid-1980s were ten-thousand-yuan households, and another 42 percent made at least half as much. At the Liuling Road Clothes Market, a 1985 survey showed that 34 percent of the firms had net incomes greater than ten thousand yuan. By 1986 this had *reportedly* decreased to less than 30 percent. The Municipal Tax Bureau estimated that more than 85 percent of Shanghai's private firms presented false accounts in order to evade taxes.[138]

Laws Slowly Catch Up with Private Enterprise

Private property is not among the many topics on which the *Communist Manifesto* leaves room for interpretation. It says, "The theory of the Communists may be summed up in the single sentence: abolition of private property . . . i.e., that kind of property which exploits wage labor."[139] Reform Communists in China increasingly violated this tenet. They arguably chose the best available policies for China and for the Party as an organization in its context, but formally they were no longer Communists. Their country prospered as it postponed solutions to the problems created by so much support for making labor an ordinary market commodity.

The official PRC sequence for legitimation of any public activity is that it should be first approved in principle through national decrees, then registered with regional governments, and only afterward begun in an institutional sense. The actual sequence for private firms (and many other activities in the reform era) was the exact inverse: local establishment first, municipal registration second, and national legislation last. A law was drafted in 1988 to set the rights and duties of private firms that hired more than eight employees—even though these had actually begun earlier, often in the form of collectives that were de facto private. Formally, for symbolic reasons, the private sector was still small. There were at this time a hundred times as many "individual" firms that employed fewer than eight workers, and some of these also used contract workers.[140]

Discussion among economists and lawyers centered on the question of whether large private firms should have the status of legal persons. Sizeable private enterprises seemed more threatening to state conservatives than were individuals' businesses, although large collectives were in fact more corrosive of the state sector. The cumulation of reforms and models made a positive difference for private firms as such. These factors were more important for their expansion than were state laws.

By the end of 1985, before the 1988 law, Shanghai had 86,000 individual firms, employing 134,000 people (already more, by half, than similar companies had hired immediately after Liberation in 1949).[141] The number of such firms had risen ten times from 1979 to 1985, and the number of employees was up by sixteen times. Of these companies in 1985, more than 98 percent were apparently registered under the names of single owners, although some were run by more than one person. Multi-entrepreneur businesses were less than 2 percent by number, but they employed 15 percent of the sector's workers. The private economy's total revenues were reported as 700 million yuan, of which 61 percent were in retail sales. This may have been an underreport; it represented only 2.4 percent of the city's total retail revenues. The private sector was small but changing.

Individuals could apply to establish new firms in Shanghai, but only if certain requirements were met. The entrepreneur needed permanent residence in the city. Cadres or state employees (i.e., most workers) were legally disqualified from receiving business licenses, but suburban farmers, retired cadres, and the unemployed could try to start private firms. The types of businesses they could legally found were specified in long lists, and different criteria and procedures were published for each trade.[142] The regulations contained vague wording to the effect that the state might prohibit some kinds of enterprise. This proviso gave local bureaucrats power to stop the legal establishment of enterprises they did not like. But at least in the reform period more of the rules were public.

An aspiring entrepreneur would first apply to the local trade and commerce administrative office (*gongshang xingzheng guanli suo*). The prospective businessperson would show an ID card and proof of not being a current cadre or state employee. The office was supposed to decide on each application within ten days, forwarding the file to the city's Industry and Commerce Administrative Management Bureau, which was supposed to make a further ruling within twenty days. These procedures were relatively clear, although the criteria for approval were less so. For each kind of trade, many other kinds of documents were required from specific city offices. Obtaining space for business was particularly difficult in Shanghai. The procedure involved so many red-seal chops on so many documents, many entrepreneurs began their operations first as "dependent households" (*guahu*) under larger state or collective enterprises, using their space or bank accounts or other facilities for convenience, and presumably waiting for rules that might legitimate them later.

"Dependent Households" and Camouflaged Privatization

The distinction between public and private organizations in China became blurred during midreforms, because advantages given to nonprivate nonstate firms discouraged the formally private category. Laws on private businesses were formalized in the 1980s, and courts and cadres alike gave private businesspeople many incentives to disappear. So they registered as collectives instead, "for reasons of protective coloration."[143] The name of a collective enterprise, especially if it could be extenuated to become a "dependent firm," could allow local prosperity. The legitimating company could charge a rent for this political service, but it did not have to manage or take economic risks. De facto private firms increasingly presented themselves as parts of collective or state agencies. They received "red caps" from collectives or small state firms. They were thus legitimated and enjoyed low taxes. Their local patrons might demand kickbacks, but this kind of clientelism weakened rather than strengthened state control. As a saying put it, "Li wears Zhang's crown" (*Zhang guan Li dai*).[144] Local state cadres could keep all the official symbols while substantially abandoning the state's interests.

Throughout China, private firms near the end of the 1980s employed more than 200,000 CCP members, as well as many model workers and delegates to people's congresses and political consultative committees at various levels.[145]

The Tiananmen disaster had only a temporary effect in slowing the replacement of state companies by assorted flavors of nonstate companies. The number of registered private businesses in China by the end of 1990 had climbed 7 percent over the end of 1989, and the number of workers reported in private firms rose 8 percent.

Such companies did not provide sure job security for their employees. These firms were not line items on any large budget, they were founded in a time of tumultuous economic change, and they could go under. Officials complained in the early 1990s that three million private firms had gone bankrupt nationwide in the period since a late 1988 austerity program against inflation. But the total registered number of such companies at the start of 1990 was thirteen million and rising.[146] There were high birth and death rates among such companies—and perhaps both these rates were higher on a reported basis than on an actual basis, because small companies had incentives to register publicly during reformist periods (raising the number of foundings) when they could best prosper, but then to deregister, declare bankruptcy, or go underground (or at least go collective) during conservative spells when they would also be most likely to founder on economic grounds.

Private Taxes

The socialist state's main reason for registering private enterprise was to tax it. According to a temporary national law on private businesses, they had to pay 60 percent of earnings in taxes on the first 30,000 yuan of profits, and 84 percent on any profits above that.[147] Small firms could try to avoid these high corporate tax rates by not filing registration papers, which might classify their income (to the extent they had to report it) as personal earnings. This main extraction was very heavy, and it did not include many other enterprise taxes and management fees, which were additional. Such steep corporate taxes meant that private firms remained small for many years, registered as collectives whenever possible, and could practically never make money if all the laws were strictly enforced. This tax code was written so that the state and its collectors could use it as a hunting license. It was not a coherent instrument of fiscal policy. Nobody, apparently, expected these laws would be followed to the letter.

Deregistration was often the only way for private Shanghai business people to make a profit. Fully 110,000 private entrepreneurs were on the city's official rosters at the start of 1988—but by August of that year, as government constraints against such businesses grew, "nearly 10,000 of them had returned their registration certificates to the government." This trend served municipal cadres' interests, because they could report on their prowess enforcing the policy to reduce firms that were not socialist. It also served the interests of entrepreneurs, whose removal from the tax and inspection lists was welcome. But it was, of course, a shell game. As a Chinese paper reported in the spring of 1989, "While the number of registered self-employed people is decreasing, the number of those without licenses is on the increase. According to a survey, certified self-employed people account for less than one-third of the total self-employed people in more than 400 markets in Shanghai."[148]

The tax law was revised later, but the rates remained near the extortion range for private enterprises, and the government clearly expected illegal underreporting. These firms had to pay a high "accumulation tax" (*leijin shui*). Enforcement problems caused the rate schedule to be progressive, since private enterprises were very difficult to monitor. For firms making over 50,000 yuan a year, the basic profits tax rate became 60 percent, with surcharges of 10 to 40 percent of that portion for larger profits.[149] It was reported that some Shanghai firms actually paid the maximal 84 percent of their profits in taxes. This impost was not out of line for state plants, counting both their remittances and taxes, but it inspired truly creative initiatives in private accounting.

Other places in the Shanghai delta generally enjoyed lower nonstate tax rates. Jiangsu in the late 1980s reported only a 20 percent income tax (*suode shui*) and another 5 percent business tax (*yingye shui*) for many enterprises there. Shanghai private-sector managers were reported to complain the taxation they faced was "heavy and diverse." The manager of a metal-punching factory in Shanghai's Jiading county figured that if he moved his plant a few kilometers into Jiangsu province, his profits would rise by 50,000 or 60,000 yuan each year, simply because of lower official extractions. Prohibitive levies in the metropolis were the main reason why—until the 1990s—private enterprise there remained scarce.

The Shanghai Coral Knitting Factory in the first quarter of 1988 had an effective tax rate on the reported profits of 89 percent. The *Wenhui News* reported, "Some self-employed people complain that after registration they are asked for more than 20 kinds of taxes by different government departments. Another reason cited for the increase in market chaos is the lack of a sound legal system and the lack of professional ethics on the part of individual business people and government officials." The entrepreneurs did not stop work, however. "They take advantage of the technology and transportation in Shanghai, producing along with factories elsewhere, and selling outside Shanghai. Lenient economic policies and loopholes of management in other places make life easy for these self-employed businessmen. . . . They get commissions and bonuses from factories outside Shanghai. In order to make a sale, they sometimes bribe shop managers and assistants."[150] Imposts and rules against private businesses within the metropolis were so strict, it is hardly surprising that entrepreneurs went elsewhere.

New personal income tax rules had been in force at Shanghai for eighteen months when a survey in mid-1988, showed that the portion of households with earnings over the minimum threshold was one of every forty. Nonetheless,

> there are still a lot of people who fail to pay their income taxes according to the tax law, including some well-known personalities, leading cadres, and ordinary citizens. Some don't know about the tax law, while some know about

> it but fail to abide by it. In literary and art circles in Shanghai, for example, only 250 people paid their income taxes last year, just 0.02 percent of the total number of people in those circles. Some people who intentionally evaded their taxes said they did so because the tax law was grossly unfair.[151]

The rates were high, and the implementation was uneven. If the whole of Shanghai's population had a tax compliance rate like that of the group mentioned in this quotation, then one out of each five thousand taxpayers complied with the law. Actual compliance was probably higher than this, but it was still very low.

Surtaxes were added onto private profits, depending on the kind of trade. The tax scheme was published in tabular form, but it was complex enough to be subject to a good deal of administrative interpretation.[152] Official policy swung like a pendulum, even though it did not always affect the practical operations of private firms. The reasons for the high taxes were mainly political, not economic or fiscal.

Enterprise and Politics: Two Environments Interact

Private entrepreneurs were criticized after the Tiananmen disaster, although most prominent dissidents were student intellectuals instead. The *Economic Daily* argued, "It is true that in a private enterprise, employees' pursuit of personal interests may bring about high efficiency. [But] in a country like China, with a short supply of resources, the creation of too many private enterprises would lead to an unbalanced economic structure." In this conservative view, "government policies" had "put the public economy in a disadvantaged position, losing ground to the private sector. That is what we are going to reform."[153]

The state affected the legal ownership types of nonstate enterprises. It had less effect on their presence, absence, or overall growth. This political phenomenon was evident also in other countries that underwent a deflation of socialism. János Kenedi describes three kinds of house contractors in Hungary: the state builders who have low prices but low reliability, the licensed private ones who do the job well at high prices, and the illegal ones who do the job well at very low prices (partly because those builders steal materials from the state).[154] The private and illegal economies in China, as in Hungary, depend on the state sector and would be structured differently if it did not exist. They are deeply affected by tax laws, bureaucrats, and the existence of a large state sector. But they do not always react to this environment as conservative officials intend they should.

The same point is true in an inverse form: In a context of more enterprise and hard work, socialist politics also change. Markets among Communist traders, connected to each other through the Party, have not worked to spur growth; nor have Chinese socialists recently been able to inspire much hard work within the state sector. But traders and managers who are really independent actors, i.e. capitalists, have done this in China lately—and their obvious prosperity tends to delegitimate socialism. Richard Smith argues from a Marxist viewpoint that "it was precisely the failure of market reform to transform the 'socialist' state sector that forced the reform leadership . . . to tolerate the growth of an initially small but rapidly growing private capitalist sector." He adds with regret, "Today, this dynamic and increasingly powerful capitalist 'economy within the economy' is threatening to bring down the entire bureaucratic social order and restore capitalism in China."[155] Smith's evaluation of the educated bureaucrats' order is easy to question. But his analysis of a political danger to state socialism calls a spade a spade. If leaders ultimately cannot deliver goods, many will eventually seek other local and then perhaps national leaders who can.

Notes

1. Edmund Burke, *Reflections on the Revolution in France* (Harmondsworth: Penguin, 1982), p. 135.

2. The fact that the capital-accumulating sector in China was long run by a "socialist" state is irrelevant to this theory. Arthur Lewis, "Economic Development with Unlimited Supplies of Labour," *The Manchester School of Economic and Social Studies* (1954), pp. 139–99.

3. This follows work by Michael P. Todaro, whose ideas on migration are most succinctly put in his textbook *Economic Development* (New York: Longman, 1994).

4. The "green city" description of Shanghai's suburbs is detailed in Lynn White's "Shanghai-Suburb Relations, 1949–1966," in *Shanghai: Revolution and Development in an Asian Metropolis,* Christopher Howe, ed. (Cambridge: Cambridge University Press, 1981), pp. 241–68.

5. See *Shanghai Sojourners,* Frederic Wakeman Jr. and Wen-hsin Yeh, eds. (Berkeley: University of California Institute of Asian Studies, 1992).

6. Lin You Su, "Urban Migration in China: A Case Study of Three Urban Areas" (Ph.D. dissertation, Department of Geography, Australian National University, 1992), p. 71.

7. Rhoads Murphey, *Shanghai: Key to Modern China* (Cambridge: Harvard University Press, 1953), p. 27.

8. Intellectuals have previously received almost exclusive scholarly attention. The 1955 event was roughly similar in scale to the 1969–70 rustications and was quicker. But the portion of writers in the early send-downs was low, so these events have been nearly omitted from written history. The reversal of c. 1970–73 is also missed, because many high intellectuals still fared badly then.

9. Migration theorists moot the likelihood of a broad trend in several developing countries toward more female migrants, because women work in light industries that trade internationally.

10. The author's student and friend Solomon Karmel reports his interviewees talking about "bachelor villages" in destitute parts of inland provinces, whence many young women had left.

11. See Li Wen-Lang, "Migration, Urbanization and Regional Development," in *Forces for Change in Contemporary China,* Lin Bih-jaw and James T. Myers, eds. (Taipei: Institute for International Relations, 1992), p. 153.

12. See *JFRB,* March 16, 1988.

13. Except as noted, these relationships tend to hold regardless of the size of destination settlement (as shown in the three delta cases of Shanghai, Shaoxing, and Xiashi). See Lin You Su, "Urban Migration," pp. 81–84 and 184.

14. Beijing supplied only 3 percent; Xinjiang, 2 percent; Yunnan, 2 percent; Fujian, 3

percent; and Shandong, 4 percent; all other provinces were less. *Zhongguo 1986 nian 74 chengzhen renkou qianyi chouxiang diaocha ziliao* (Sample Survey Materials on 1986 Chinese Migration in 74 Cities and Towns), *Chinese Demography* Editorial Group, ed. (Beijing: *Zhongguo renkou kexue* Bianji Bu, 1988), p. 14.

15. Jiangsu and Zhejiang migrants to Shanghai reportedly tended to have somewhat less difficulty being registered than migrants from elsewhere—but because of proximity, they also could make repeated trips to the city from their previous homes more easily than others could. Most of the basic data, and the sex ratios on immigrants reported later, come through the generosity of Dr. Ronald Skeldon, Department of Geography, University of Hong Kong. But the base for the estimated portions comes from figures in Table 1.5–1.

16. There were then 213 men for each 100 women from Jiangsu. They were nearly as high a proportion from Zhejiang and Anhui (199 and 181 men per 100 women, respectively). These data were provided by the geographer Ronald Skeldon, who has nationwide statistics on migration in the PRC.

17. With these rusticates went many older people who had been attacked during the Cultural Revolution, although their number has been estimated with so much variance that it is hard to know. See Chen Benlin et al., *Gaige kaifang shenzhou jubian* (Great Change in the Sacred Land [China] During Reform and Opening) (Shanghai: Jiaotong Daxue Chuban She, 1984), pp. 65–66. For background, see Thomas Bernstein, *Up to the Mountains and Down to the Villages: The Transfer of Youth from Urban to Rural China* (New Haven: Yale University Press, 1977).

18. This is based on a rough calculation from figures in *Shanghai jingji, neibu ben: 1949–1982* (Shanghai Economy, Internal Volume: 1949–1982), Shanghai Academy of Social Sciences, ed. (Shanghai: Shanghai Shehui Kexue Yuan Chuban She, 1984), p. 961.

19. See the informative article by Jonathan Unger, "China's Troubled Down to the Countryside Campaign," *Contemporary China 3:3* (1979), p. 88 and passim.

20. The rustication program, by stirring the residential pot, quickened migration then and later between all sizes of cities—including from rural to urban places. If all China's approximately three hundred officially designated "cities" are ranked by size (Shanghai is at the top of this list), the falloff by population for midsize settlements is not steep when compared to most other countries, even many large ones. Young rusticates from medium and small cities, if they absconded from rural posts, often went to large cities such as Shanghai rather than back to the places whose authorities had rusticated them. They were illegal in either case and saw little to lose in trying the metropolitan chance. For these "rusticates," the effect of policy was opposite to what the state had intended. A different but compatible argument has been easier to document: Rustication sent many, at least temporarily, from very large to medium-sized cities in the early 1970s. Send-down campaigns made migration a live option.

21. A graph, showing these changes clearly but with an accompanying text that avoids any interpretation of them for the early 1970s, is in *Zhongguo 1986 nian,* p. 340. The immigration line for "large-sized [500,000–1,000,000] cities" soars in an absolutely unmistakable way for 1970–72. This change in the early 1970s is stunning, and the sample contains no provincial capitals (which tend to have relatively high taxes and strong residence controls). The Chinese text below the graph merely speaks of "reeducation in rural areas" and "transfer to a lower level" during the "ten years of upheaval" (1966–76). The graphed findings about actual behavior are spectacular, but they are not really "found." It boggles the mind to see PRC scholars doing arduous survey work, coming up with unexpected results, graphing them so that they have to strike any viewer between the eyes, and then blithely ignoring them because 1966–76 is officially a single homogeneous period. As everyone knows, nothing really new can possibly have happened in the early 1970s.

22. In Japan, individuals could move from villages to very large cities (Tokyo, Osaka) for most of their careers, but then retire to medium-sized places often near but not identical to the places from which they originated. This pattern (which also appears in Shanghai) can be pictured in the form of an inverted and reversed J. The text above describes migration from metropolis to village to medium city: merely a reversed J. For help with such matters, the author is very grateful to the geographer Dr. Ronald Skeldon.

23. *Zhongguo 1986 nian,* p. 334.

24. Zhe Xiaoye, *Chengshi zai zhuanzhe dianshang* (Cities at a Turning Point) (Beijing: Zhongguo Funü Chuban She, 1989), pp. 30–31.

25. Nanshi district had this *zhishi qingnian bangong shi. Weiwen tuan* had been common in 1964–65 also. See *WHB,* May 20, 1979.

26. *WHB,* May 29, 1979.

27. See a 1976 photo by Lynn White, reproduced in Thomas Bernstein, *Up to the Mountains,* showing a bulletin board in a Wuxi silk factory that differentiated young migrants (offspring of the factory's workers) who had volunteered from those whose registrations had legally been changed, and also from those who had actually gone.

28. *WHB,* May 24, 1979.

29. *Post,* October 12, 1981, and *XDRB,* October 14, 1981. Reports about this (and a list of other subjects such as strikes) could not be printed in PRC papers, but they appeared in Hong Kong.

30. The police martyrs are listed by name, with birth dates and other particulars to honor them, in *Shanghai gongan nianjian, 1988* (Shanghai Public Security Yearbook, 1988) (*neibu,* photocopy reprint sold in Hong Kong, 515 pages), *Shanghai Gongan Nianjian* Editorial Department, ed. (Shanghai: Shanghai Shehui Kexue Chuban She, 1988), pp. 99–101. Thanks go to a British friend for showing me this source.

31. *WHB,* October 30, 1979.

32. These portions are calculated from raw data in *SHTJNJ86,* p. 70. Interviewees report that from the mid-1950s to 1979, new hires to Shanghai state factories were "distributed" there by organizations above or outside the factories.

33. Interview with a student at Fudan University.

34. *JFRB,* December 20, 1979.

35. *Shangshan xiaxiang.* Few people whose first regular work assignment was outside of Shanghai were allowed back, however. Among Shanghainese who married elsewhere, only one-quarter had returned. *Zhongguo renkou qianyi yu chengshi hua yanjiu* (Studies on Chinese Migration and Urbanization), Editorial Group for Studies on Chinese Migration and Urbanization, ed. (Beijing: Zhongguo Shehui Kexue Yuan Renkou Yanjiu Suo, 1988), p. 296.

36. See *SHTJNJ88,* p. 327, and *Zhongguo tongji zhaiyao, 1988* (A Statistical Survey of China, 1988), State Statistical Bureau, ed. (Beijing: Zhongguo Tongji Chuban She, 1988), p. 105.

37. The first datum is based on a survey of long-term immigrants by the Population Research Institute of the Chinese Academy of Social Sciences, and the second reports 1977–86 migrations. To the much smaller Shanghai delta city of Xiashi, fewer (just below half) of the 1977–86 immigrants were unmarried. See Lin You Su, "Urban Migration," pp. 111 and 115.

38. See Alice Goldstein, Sidney Goldstein, and Guo Shenyang, "Temporary Migrants in Shanghai Households, 1986," *Demography* 28 (1991), p. 275.

39. Regular workers were "formal," *zhengshi gong. Shanghai jingji, neibu ben,* p. 965.

40. These *yigong yinong* workers were thus also called *siliu gong. Shanghai jingji, neibu ben,* p. 965.

41. *Zhuanhuan gongzuo. Zhongguo yanhai diqu xiao chengzhen fazhan yu renkou*

qianyi (Migration and the Development of Small Cities and Towns on the China Coast), Liu Zheng et al., eds. (Beijing: Zhongguo Caizheng Jingji Chuban She, 1989), p. 195. Interesting in this respect is Sidney Goldstein, "Forms of Mobility and Their Policy Implications: Thailand and China Compared," *Social Forces* 65:4 (1987), p. 915.

42. The county was, unfortunately, not identified in the source. *FBIS,* December 17, 1987, p. 30, reporting radio of December 16, for the quotation below and the number of departing ex-peasants.

43. Zhe Xiaoye, *Chengshi zai zhuanzhe dianshang,* pp. 23–29.

44. On labor contractors in old Shanghai, see Jean Chesneaux, *The Chinese Labor Movement, 1919–1927,* tr. Hope M. Wright (Stanford: Stanford University Press, 1968), among other sources.

45. *Zhongguo renkou qianyi* (Population Shifts in China), Tian Fang and Ling Fatong, eds. (Beijing: Zhishi Chuban She, 1987), pp. 248–59.

46. This is based on work by Meng Xin; see graphs in *China's Rural Industry: Structure, Development, and Reform,* William A. Byrd and Lin Qingsong, eds. (Washington: World Bank, 1990), p. 300, and pp. 326–27 for the end of the next text paragraph. Wuxi's portion of permanent workers was higher than a comparable county in Anhui, and much higher than one in Guangdong for which data have been gathered—but this does not report contract labor.

47. See the main argument, showing the same phenomenon for a much earlier period, in Lynn White, *Careers in Shanghai* (Berkeley: University of California Press, 1978).

48. Interview with anthropologist Lu Feiyun, who has done fieldwork in the Shanghai delta. See also Hua Daming, "Xiangban chang dui nonggong de guofen bodu ying yinqi zhuyi" (The Overexploitation of Peasant Workers by Township-run Factories Calls for Attention), *Shehui* (Society) 2 (1990), Shanghai, pp. 12–13.

49. The exact figure is probably unknown to anyone. See *FBIS,* December 21, 1987, p. 42, reporting radio of December 10.

50. *Zhongguo renkou qianyi,* pp. 19–21.

51. Only 8 percent of the registered floaters were of school age, and 16 percent were retirees. Of the remaining tenth, half reportedly came to Shanghai for adult training and half for other reasons. For these and the following figures, see *Liudong renkou dui da chengshi fazhan de yinxiang ji duice* (Policies on the Influence of Transient Population for the Development of Large Cities), Li Mengbai et al., eds. (Beijing: *Jingji ribao* Chuban She, 1991), p. 153, and for the following data to p. 156.

52. Zhe Xiaoye, *Chengshi zai zhuanzhe dianshang,* pp. 23–29.

53. The main survey, a 1986 effort by the Chinese Academy of Social Sciences, oddly omits to report temporarily registered migrants or illegal migrants. But see Lin You Su, "Urban Migration," pp. 96, 98, and 103. Long-term migrants to Shanghai were surprisingly like those to the smaller city of Xiashi in terms of occupations.

54. Ibid., p. 93.

55. The two bureaus are the Laodong Ju and Renshi Ju. There is also a procedure by which unmarried members of Shanghai families can be brought back to the city, but the conditions for this are written restrictively: The single member applies to return home, but the application is approved only if older relatives in Shanghai are "severely sick" and have no able-bodied younger family members to care for them (especially if the offspring outside Shanghai is an only child). Actual practice has been less restrictive than the rule in *Shanghai shimin banshi zhinan* (Citizen's Practical Guide to Shanghai), Shanghai Municipal Government, ed. (Shanghai: Shanghai Renmin Chuban She, 1989), p. 2 on the previous paragraph; and here, pp. 91–92.

56. The difference between these figures may be exaggerated because the later sample includes nonpermanent immigrants who had a long time to establish permanent status. Lin You Su, "Urban Migration," p. 173.

57. An exception is Guilhem Fabre, "The Chinese Mirror of Transition," *Communist Economies and Economic Transformation* 4:2 (1992), p. 263. Foreign travel, as he points out, was still severely restricted. Research ought to be done on changes over time in the criteria for entering special zones such as Shenzhen; apparently by 1996 they had somewhat relaxed.

58. Not since the brief period of "revolutionary tourism" in the late 1960s had there been such freedom of movement. Red Guard travelers did not need authorizing documents to buy tickets; they did not even need tickets! They declared pilgrimage goals and hopped on trains. For more, see Gordon A. Bennett and Ronald N. Montaperto, *Red Guard: The Political Biography of Dai Hsiao-ai* (Garden City, NY: Doubleday, 1972).

59. For this, from *LW* 36 (1993), p. 18, and *XMWB,* April 21, 1994, thanks go to Professor Li Cheng.

60. Alice Goldstein and Guo Shenyang, "Temporary Migration in Shanghai and Beijing," *Studies in Comparative International Development* 27:2 (Summer 1992), p. 42, cites three different PRC authors on this point.

61. Zhe Xiaoye, *Chengshi zai zhuanzhe dianshang,* pp. 23–29.

62. This development was the main prediction in Lynn White, *Careers in Shanghai,* concluding chapter.

63. Margaret Y. K. Woo, "Legal Reforms in the Aftermath of Tiananmen Square," *Review of Socialist Law* (1991), p. 59.

64. This conclusion comes from a combination of interviews and *Shanghai shimin banshi zhinan.*

65. Zhe Xiaoye, *Chengshi zai zhuanzhe dianshang,* pp. 23–24.

66. Their *zhufang* and *jiuye* were *mei jiejue* in an extensive 1986 survey. *Zhongguo yanhai diqu,* p. 205.

67. The "temporary work shacks" were *linshi gongpeng*. All the portions are calculated from raw data of the sample that could be found by surveyors for *Liudong renkou,* p. 152.

68. Data on itinerants' housing are based on a Fudan University survey. Only 3 percent were boat people (some of whom may have obtained legal Shanghai residence in earlier campaigns to settle on land, because they could help the state gather economic information). Just 1 percent came officially as rural traders or representatives of rural market fairs. "Reception houses," *zhaodai suo,* are the most common form of hotel. *Shanghai jingji nianjian, 1988* (Shanghai Economic Yearbook, 1988), Xiao Jun et al., eds. (Shanghai: Shanghai Renmin Chuban She, 1988), p. 25.

69. Police census efforts by 1988 were aided by the Statistics Bureau, Fudan University, East China Normal University, and the Population Institute of the Academy of Social Sciences. The pollsters asked each adult's name, sex, age, education level, former job, and reason for coming to Shanghai. In 1988, they added questions about number of children, method of birth control, and (of women) whether pregnant. For some queries, as for the census as a whole, it would have been hopeful to expect complete coverage. See Zhu Ci in *Shanghai liudong renkou* (Shanghai's Floating Population), Shanghai Statistics Bureau, ed. (Shanghai: Zhongguo Tongji Chuban She, 1989), pp. 11–16.

70. Ibid., p. 11.

71. The 1982 census found only 246,000 transients in Shanghai's urban districts, which would be only about 4 percent of their population then, but later reports are all much higher. Beijing claimed a 3 percent rate as late as 1988, but this may well be an underreport. The portion for Guangzhou was so high that different census-taking methods may make such rates incomparable. Zhe Xiaoye, *Chengshi zai zhuanzhe dianshang,* pp. 23–24.

72. *Chengshi wenti* (Urban Problems), Shanghai, March 1988, p. 64.

73. *LDB,* March 19, 1989.

74. *Shanghai Star,* March 22 and April 15, 1994, suggested that about one-quarter of

the migrants were in construction work, and another quarter were not working. Found by Prof. Li Cheng.

75. For example, in Hangzhou, migrants were 11 percent of that city's population in 1985 and had already been 9 percent in 1975, but only 4 percent in both 1965 and 1955. See *Liudong renkou,* p. 281.

76. Zhu Ci, in *Shanghai liudong renkou,* pp. 11–16.

77. This interview was by Prof. Li Cheng in 1994, and it offers the perspective of individuals and families that contemporary Chinese studies has too often lacked.

78. See the report by journalist T. S. Rousseau in *Eastern Express* (Hong Kong), February 23, 1994.

79. Prof. Kate Xiao Zhou reports this information from Huang Wanwei, *Zhongguo de yinxing jingji* (China's Hidden Economy), a 1993 source from Hebei.

80. This information on the Anhui *bang* comes from Prof. Kate Xiao Zhou, who cites a Shanghai 1991 book entitled *Food Is the Basis of People: Report from Rural China.*

81. Alice Goldstein, Sidney Goldstein, and Guo Shenyang, "Temporary Migration," p. 275, gives details on methods in the 1984 Shanghai Temporary Migration Survey.

82. The 346 registered Shanghai local teams at the start of 1989 employed 358,000 workers, and the 300 teams from elsewhere used 370,000. It is very likely that unregistered contractors were also at building sites in the city. *LDB,* January 31, 1989, reports data amassed on this topic by Shanghai's local Construction Bank. This lead article particularly mentioned projects to build new hotels, and it amounted to a complaint against unfairly high extraction from Shanghai firms.

83. The Population Institute of Fudan University directed a census on October 20, 1988, for policy makers who wanted to reduce the floating population. See *CD,* November 25, 1988. Later estimates of the portion of migrants in construction varied but were not sharply different from one-fifth or one quarter. Many registered for construction jobs supplemented their incomes in other activities.

84. See Edward Friedman, "Deng vs. the Peasantry: Recollectivization in the Countryside," *Problems of Communism* 39 (September–October 1991), pp. 30–49.

85. See Emily Honig, *Creating Chinese Ethnicity: Subei People in Shanghai, 1850–1980* (New Haven: Yale University Press, 1992).

86. Data from *FBIS,* December 14, 1984, p. 3, reporting radio of December 13.

87. *Liudong renkou,* p. 160. A similar and compatible report is *XMWB,* March 24, 1989.

88. *Eastern Express* (Hong Kong), February 23, 1994.

89. See Solomon M. Karmel, "The Neo-Authoritarian Contradiction: Trials of Developmentalist Dictatorships and the Retreat of the State in Mainland China" (Ph.D. dissertation, Politics Department, Princeton University 1995), p. 142, using work by Zhou Daming, especially on Hunan and Sichuan gangs in Guangzhou. This pattern is old and is recorded in various books by Jean Chesneaux, especially *The Chinese Labor Movement.*

90. The price of rationed rice in April 1989 at Shanghai (.55 yuan per *jin*) was 27 percent less than on the free market. So the state subsidy was still heavy—and costly—though many unrationed foods were available. This and the quotation are from Sheng Li and Fu Qiping in *XMWB,* April 18, 1989.

91. Ibid.

92. The number of such laborers was specified at 240,000. See Mao Zhongwei and Zhou Zigeng in *Shanghai liudong renkou,* pp. 47–57.

93. Prof. Li Cheng mentioned the phrase and provided this interview quotation about community.

94. Latin Americanists reporting the slums of São Paolo, Lima, and Mexico City have provided the earliest and best material. See works by anthropologist Oscar Lewis on Mexico and sociologist François Borricauld on Peru; by political scientist Wayne Corne-

lius, especially "Urbanization and Political Demand Making," *American Political Science Review* 9:74 (September 1974), pp. 1125–46, with data from Mexican barrios; and for theoretical background, the classic "tunnel effect" article by economist Albert Hirschman, "Changing Tolerance for Income Inequality in the Course of Economic Development," *World Development* 1:12 (1973), pp. 24–36.

95. The best student of labor unrest in China has orally suggested that Latin American and African experiences may not be replicated there. Chinese organizational traditions, especially in same-place associations, seem strong. But the present author still supposes the main threat migrants pose to the state is indirect, through their interactions with political networks of older urban residents, rather than direct through their own capacities for political organization. The jury is still out on this question.

96. Similar arguments appear in a superb essay about the national situation by Dorothy Solinger, "China's Transients and the State: A Form of Civil Society?" *Politics and Society* 21:1 (1993), pp. 91–122.

97. Chen Baoliang, *Zhongguo liumang shi* (The History of Chinese Hooliganism) (Beijing: Zhongguo Shehui Kexue Chuban She, 1993).

98. See *Modern Rice Technology and Income Distribution in Asia,* Cristina C. David and Keijiro Otsuka, eds. (Boulder: Lynne Rienner, 1994).

99. *SHJJYJ,* May 1985, p. 46.

100. These figures on productivity are difficult to interpret exactly, because in periods when any sector is legitimated/registered for extraction, both output and the number of workers are reported more fully (whereas in periods of repression, both are reported less fully). These two numbers are the numerator and denominator of the productivity ratio. Any difference in the extent to which they move separately affects the rate of productivity change. Data on the smaller primary sector (practically all agriculture in Shanghai, whose sedimentary geology precludes mining) are also reported in the source; but these are especially unreliable, because it was easier for rural units to obscure the amount of time rural workers were spending in factories than to hide marketed output. This overestimation of the actual labor force working in fields, the denominator, almost surely made the reported agricultural productivity ratios inaccurately low until the early 1980s (when they show inaccurately high increases from the previous levels that had been underreported). The author made calculations to show these effects, but they are not presented because they tell more about data gathering than about productivity. Readers should be aware that at many places in this book, the author uses statistical series qualitatively, looking at directions of change (when the data reporting problems do not seem insurmountable) more than at the absolute levels. The only purpose is to draw conclusions about politics. This caveat is repeated occasionally in the book, but readers are asked to have it in mind when looking at any figures here.

101. *Shanghai jingji, neibu ben,* pp. 869–71.

102. *WHB,* September 12, 1975.

103. The 1976 figure was 908,000, and the 1983 number was 1,690,000. *Shanghai shehui xiankuang he qushi, 1980–1983* (Situations and Trends in Shanghai Society, 1980–1983), Zheng Gongliang et al., eds. (Shanghai: Huadong Shifan Daxue Chuban She, 1988), p. 21.

104. Calculated from data in *SHTJNJ86,* p. 52.

105. *Shanghai jingji, neibu ben,* p. 96.

106. *Zhongguo shehui tongji ziliao, 1987* (Chinese Social Statistics, 1987), Social Statistics Office, State Statistical Bureau, ed. (Beijing: Zhongguo Tongji Chuban She, 1987), p. 1.

107. Tao Yongkuan, *Dali fazhan disan chanye* (Vigorously Develop Tertiary Industry) (Shanghai: Shanghai Shehui Kexue Yuan Chuban She, 1986), p. 13.

108. Zhang Zhongli, Zhu Qingzha et al., *Disan chanye de lilun yu shixian: Jianlun*

Shanghai disan chanye fazhan zhanlue (Theory and Practice of the Tertiary Sector: On the Development Strategy of Shanghai's Tertiary Sector) (Shanghai: Shanghai Shehui Kexue Yuan Chuban She, 1986), p. 16.

109. The rise was more if unregistered service workers were included. These figures may also misrepresent the change, because persons registered as peasants sometimes worked in rural factories, and also because some producers of agricultural output were (often illegal) migrants not recorded in the population. PRC definitions of the three sectors do not exactly match Western ones, with differences that are unimportant here. The terms "tertiary," "secondary," and "primary" in Chinese sources generally stand for services, manufacturing, and agriculture (there is almost no mining in Shanghai, although there is some fishing). The increase in the primary sector on the table is mainly caused by an addition of more rural areas to the municipality in 1958–59. But the decline of agricultural employment, the rise of manufactures as speeded by state policies, and the decline and then rise of service employment are all valid stories, despite these reporting problems.

110. *Shanghai shehui xiankuang,* pp. 31 and 36.

111. Cao Linzhang, Gu Guangqing, and Li Jianhua, *Shanghai shengchan ziliao suoyu zhi jiegou yanjiu* (Studies of Shanghai Production and Ownership Structure) (Shanghai: Shanghai Shehui Kexue Yuan Chuban She, 1987), p. 217.

112. *Shanghai jingji nianjian, 1988*, p. 84.

113. Yan Tingchang, Cai Beihua, Xu Zhihe et al., *Shanghai lüyou ye de jintian he mingtian* (Shanghai Tourism Today and Tomorrow) (Shanghai: Shanghai Shehui Kexue Yuan Chuban She, 1987), pp. 98 and 103.

114. This small group was the "*quyu lüyou xiezuo xiaozu,*" and what it did was expressed in strong words, "*baituo xingzheng kuangkuang,*" because the word *kuangkuang,* meaning "frame" or "coffin," has a long history of use in Shanghai by authors as varied as Ba Jin and Yao Wenyuan. It is the coffin in which radicals want bourgeois kept, and the frame that liberals want to see broken. See *Hengxiang jingji lianhe de xin fazhan* (The New Development of Horizontal Economic Links), Shanghai Economics Association, ed. (Shanghai: Shanghai Shehui Kexue Yuan Chuban She, 1987), pp. 182–85.

115. Yan Tingchang, Cai Beihua, Xu Zhihe et al., *Shanghai lüyou,* pp. 2–3.

116. The exception of cotton was very important, because many Shanghai jobs and much state revenue depended on state factories' ability to buy cotton at a low price. Dorothy J. Solinger, *China's Transition from Socialism: Statist Legacies and Market Reforms, 1980–1990* (Armonk, NY: M.E. Sharpe, 1993), p. 76.

117. *XWB,* February 2, 1989.

118. *Shehui gongyi* is recommended in *XWB,* February 2, 1989.

119. *LDB,* March 19, 1989.

120. Ibid.

121. *Xianggang jingji bao* (Hong Kong Economic Journal), July 21, 1989, for this and the previous paragraph.

122. Legally registered free markets at the end of 1990 numbered 72,130 throughout the country. But of course, trading occurred elsewhere too. *CD,* December 14, 1990.

123. See Lynn White, *Policies of Chaos* (Princeton: Princeton University Press, 1989), chap. 2, e.g., Table 1 on p. 76, and other works cited there, e.g. by Robert Loh and by John Gardner.

124. Cao Linzhang, Gu Guangqing, and Li Jianhua, *Shanghai shengchan,* p. 193. The number of employees in these many small shops during the same period fell somewhat less spectacularly, from 31,100 to 14,500—but this counted only the legally registered employees, and many other workers (as well as firms) were unregistered until the post-Leap depression dried up their supplies and markets.

125. Ibid.

126. *Shanghai jingji, neibu ben,* pp. 255–58. This reports both on "street factories" (*jiedao gongchang*) and on smaller "lane production groups" or "street industries" (*lilong shengchan zu* or *jiedao gongye*).

127. Ibid., p. 260. Calculations of marginal increments of labor productivity in these industries from 1963 to 1965 can also be made on a district-by-district basis from a table in ibid., p. 259.

128. Calculation from figures on the numbers of workers and gross output in the mid-1970s in ibid., pp. 258 and 260.

129. *Dangdai Zhongguo de jingji tizhi gaige* (Reform of the Economic System in Contemporary China), Zhou Taihe et al., eds. (Beijing: Zhongguo Shehui Kexue Chuban She, 1984), p. 564.

130. Interview with a Shanghai economist, November 1988.

131. Alan P. L. Liu, "The 'Wenzhou Model' of Development and China's Modernization," *Asian Survey* 22:8 (August 1992), p. 704.

132. *XMWB,* January 1, 1982.

133. Many less prestigious awards, especially for "civilized units" (*wenming danwei*), were also given to agencies at any level that did salient public service such as planting trees on streets, offering good service, or keeping premises clean. Plaques could often be seen in neighborhood offices, factories, and schools that boasted this title. *JFRB,* May 11, 1988.

134. *Shanghai shehui xiankuang,* pp. 100 and 106, does not give time series Gini coefficients.

135. *Shanghai shimin banshi zhinan,* p. 82.

136. *Tansuo yu zhengming* (Investigation and Debate), March 1988, p. 50. Incomes are presented in monthly terms, because that is the usual PRC way of figuring them.

137. This does not, of course, include his expense accounts and perquisites. Report from an interviewee.

138. *Tansuo yu zhengming* (Investigation and Debate), March 1988, p. 51.

139. Karl Marx and Friedrich Engels, *Manifesto of the Communist Party* (Beijing: Foreign Languages Press, 1965), pp. 48–49.

140. Calculated in figures from *FBIS,* March 11, 1988, p. 26, reporting radio of March 10. Partly based on interviews.

141. Cao Linzhang, Gu Guangqing, and Li Jianhua, *Shanghai shengchan,* p. 194. These figures in the text are rounded to the nearest thousand for readability.

142. *Shanghai shimin banshi zhinan,* pp. 105–6.

143. See Alison W. Conner, "To Get Rich Is Precarious: Regulation of Private Enterprise in the People's Republic of China," *Journal of Chinese Law* 5:1 (Spring 1991), especially p. 3.

144. This phrase is reported by Prof. Kate Zhou Xiao, one of the author's students, on the basis of interviews in China. For much more on "dependent firms," see an article that Zhou and White coauthored, "Quiet Politics and Rural Enterprise in Reform China," *Journal of the Developing Areas* 29 (July 1995), pp. 461–90.

145. *CD,* March 11, 1989.

146. *CD,* April 16, 1991.

147. This law was passed before the 1988 announcement that such businesses were legal in Shanghai. A full table of rates (from 7 percent on incomes less than 1,000 yuan; already 25 percent on twice that) is in "Temporary Income Tax Regulations for Urban and Rural Private Businesses in the PRC (Jan. 7, 1986)," in *Chinese Private Enterprises,* State Council Investigation Team, ed. (Beijing: Reform Press, 1990).

148. *CD,* April 18, 1989, based on a *WHB* report.

149. Some of this comes from *Zhongguo shuiwu baike quanshu* (*Encyclopedia of Chinese Taxation*), Encyclopedia of Chinese Taxation Editorial Group, ed. (Beijing: Jingji Guanli Chuban She, 1991), p. 286.

150. *CD,* April 18, 1989, based on a *WHB* report.

151. *CD,* August 5, 1988.

152. *Shanghai shimin banshi zhinan,* pp. 120–22. The complex tables of rates on different trades would be reproduced in the text if private Shanghai businesspeople did not so widely ignore them.

153. *CD,* July 14, 1989.

154. Barrett L. McCormick, *Political Reform in Post-Mao China: Democracy and Bureaucracy in a Leninist State* (Berkeley: University of California Press, 1990), p. 86, quoting János Kenedi, *Do It Yourself* (London: Pluto Press, 1981).

155. Richard Smith, "The Chinese Road to Capitalism," *New Left Review* 199 (1993), pp. 60–61.

Sources

Bibliography

Most books cited in the footnotes are on the list below. Chinese newspapers and journals, especially those on the roster of abbreviations near the Table of Contents, were essential for this study because these are often less thoroughly censored than books. Other essential bases for this study were interviews in Shanghai, Beijing, Hong Kong, Taipei, Princeton, and elsewhere.

Many materials that would have been of great relevance to this study are available only in Chinese publications that are limited-circulation (*neibu*). But daily newspapers sometimes provide materials on topics similar to those covered in confidential sources. The contemporary China field is in any case not plagued by a dearth of materials; it suffers on the contrary from a surfeit. No one will ever read all the good materials about the Shanghai delta from the 1970s into the 1990s, because there are far too many.

Materials in Languages other than Chinese

Aberle, D.F., et al. "The Functional Prerequisites of a Society," Indianapolis: Bobbs-Merrill reprint, 1966; from *Ethics* 60, pp. 100–10.

Alexis de Tocqueville on Democracy, Revolution, and Society. John Stone and Stephen Mennell, eds. Chicago: University of Chicago Press, 1980.

Almond, Gabriel A., and G. Bingham Powell, Jr. *Comparative Politics: A Developmental Approach* (Boston: Little, Brown, 1966).

Almond, Gabriel A., and Sidney Verba. *The Civic Culture*. Princeton: Princeton University Press, 1963.

Anagnost, Ann S. "The Beginning and End of an Emperor: A Counterrepresentation of the State," *Modern China* 11:2 (April 1985), pp. 147–76.

Anderson, Benedict. *Imagined Communities: Reflections on the Origin and Spread of Nationalism*, rev. ed. London: Verso, 1991.

Anderson, Benedict. "Studies of the Thai State: The State of Thai Studies," consulted in MS but published in Eliezer B. Ayal, ed. *The Study of Thailand*. Athens, OH: Ohio University Southeast Asia Program, 1978.

Andrews, Julia F. *Painters and Politics in the People's Republic of China, 1949–1979*. Berkeley: University of California Press, 1994.

The Anglo-Dutch Moment: Essays on the Glorious Revolution and its World Impact. Jonathan I. Israel, ed. Cambridge: Cambridge University Press, 1991.

Antier, Gilles. "New Planning Trends in Shanghai." Paris: Institut d'Aménagement de d'Urbanisme de la Région d'Ile-de-France, 1993.

Arnold, Walter. "Japan and the Development of Shanghai's Pudong Area. *Pacific Review* 5:3 (September 1992), pp. 241–49.

Atkinson, A.B. *Unemployment Insurance and Economic Reform in China.* London: Development Research Program, 1990.

Aubert, Claude. "The Agricultural Crisis in China at the End of the 1980s," in Jørgen Delman, et al., eds. *Remaking Peasant China: Problems of Rural Development and Institutions at the Start of the 1990s.* Aarhus: Aarhus University Press, 1990, pp. 16–37.

Ayer, A. J. *Language, Truth, and Logic.* New York: Dover, 1952.

Bachman, David M. *Bureaucracy, Economy, and Leadership in China: The Institutional origins of the Great Leap Forward.* Cambridge: Cambridge University Press, 1991.

Bachman, David M. *Chen Yun and the Chinese Political System.* Berkeley: Center for Chinese Studies, 1985.

Bakken, Børge. "Crime, Juvenile Delinquency, and Deterrence Policy in China." *Australian Journal of Chinese Affairs* 30 (July 1993), pp. 29–60.

Bakvis, Herman, and William M. Chandler, eds. *Federalism and the Role of the State.* Toronto: University of Toronto Press, 1987.

Barlow, Tani E., and Donald M. Lowe. *Teaching China's Lost Generation: Foreign Experts in the People's Republic of China* [at the Shanghai Foreign Languages College]. San Francisco: China Books and Periodicals, 1987.

Barmé, Geremie. "Liu Dahong: Artist Laureate of China's Reform." *Far Eastern Economic Review* (March 4, 1993), p. 60.

Barmé, Geremie, and John Minford, eds. *Seeds of Fire: Chinese Voices of Conscience.* New York: Noonday, 1989.

Bates, Robert H. *Markets and States in Tropical Africa: The Political Basis of Agricultural Policies.* Berkeley and Los Angeles: University of California Press, 1981.

Baum, Richard. *The Cycles of Reform: Chinese Politics in the Age of Deng Xiaoping.* Princeton: Princeton University Press, 1994.

Bei Dao (Zhao Zhenkai). *Notes from the City of the Sun.* Bonnie S. MacDougall, tr. Ithaca: Cornell University China-Japan Program, 1983.

Belden, Jack. *China Shakes the World.* New York: Parthenon, 1970.

Belich, James. *Victorian Interpretation of Racial Conflict: The Maori, the British, and the New Zealand Wars.* Montreal: MacGill-Queen's University Press, 1989.

Benda, Julien, tr. R. Aldington. *The Treason of the Intellectuals* (La trahison des clercs). New York: Norton, 1969 [1928].

Bendix, John, Bertel Ollman, Bartholomew Sparrow, and Timothy Mitchell. "Going Beyond the State." *American Political Science Review* 86:4 (December 1992), pp. 1007–20.

Bendix, Reinhard. *Max Weber: An Intellectual Portrait.* Garden City: Doubleday, 1960.

Bendix, Reinhard, John Bendix, and Norman Furniss. "Reflections on Modern Western States and Civil Societies." *Research in Political Sociology* 3, pp. 1–38.

Benewick, Robert, and Paul Wingrove, eds. *Reforming the Revolution: China in Transition.* Basingstoke: Macmillan, 1988.

Bennett, Gordon A. and Ronald N. Montaperto, *Red Guard: The Political Biography of Dai Hsiao-ai.* Garden City: Doubleday, 1972.

Bergère, Marie-Claire. " 'The Other China:' Shanghai from 1919 to 1949," in Christopher Howe, ed., *Shanghai: Revolution and Development in an Asian Metropolis.* Cambridge: Cambridge University Press, 1981, pp. 1–34.

Bernstein, Thomas. *Up to the Mountains and Down to the Villages: The Transfer of Youth from Urban to Rural China*. New Haven: Yale University Press, 1977.

Berry, Chris, ed. *Perspectives on Chinese Cinema*. Ithaca: Cornell China-Japan Program, 1985.

Bertrand, Jacques. *Compliance, Resistance, and Trust: Peasants and the State in Indonesia*. Princeton University Politics Department Ph.D. Dissertation, 1995.

Bialer, Seweryn. *Stalin's Successors*. Cambridge: Cambridge University Press, 1980.

Binder, Leonard, James S. Coleman, Joseph LaPalombara, Lucian W. Pye, Sidney Verba, and Myron Weiner. *Crises and Sequences in Political Development*. Princeton: Princeton University Press, 1971.

Birnbaum, H. Philip, and Gilbert Y. Y. Wong. "Cultural Values of Managers in the People's Republic of China and Hong Kong." Hong Kong: University of Hong Kong, Department of Management Studies Working Paper 13, n.d.

Blecher, Marc, and Vivienne Shue. *Tethered Deer: Government and Economy in a Chinese County*. Stanford: Stanford University Press, 1995.

Blendon, Robert J. "Can China's Health Care be Transplanted without China's Economic Policies?" *New England Journal of Medicine*, 300:1453–58.

Bond, Michael Harris. *The Psychology of the Chinese People*. Hong Kong: Oxford University Press, 1986.

Bonnin, M., and Y. Chevrier. "Autonomy during the Post-Mao Era," *China Quarterly* 123 (1991), pp. 569–593.

Boorman, Scott. *The Protracted Game: A Wei-ch'i Interpretation of Maoist Revolutionary Strategy*

Bosco, Joseph, "*Yi Guan Dao*: 'Heterodoxy' and Popular Religion in Taiwan," unpublished manuscript.

Bosco, Joseph. "Factions versus Ideology: Mobilization Strategy in Taiwan's Elections," *China Quarterly* (March 1994).

Bosco, Joseph. "Taiwan Factions: *Guanxi*, Patronage, and the State in Local Politics." *Ethnology* 31:2 (1992), pp. 157–83.

Brady, James P. *Justice and Politics in People's China: Legal Order or Continuing Revolution?* New York: Academic Press, 1982.

Bramall, Chris. "Origins of the Agricultural 'Miracle': Some Evidence from Sichuan." *China Quarterly* 143 (September 1995), pp. 731–55.

Brewer, John, and John Styles, eds. *An Ungovernable People: The English and their Law in the Seventeenth and Eighteenth Centuries*. London: Hutchinson, 1980.

Bringing the State Back In. Evans, Peter B., Dietrich Rueschemeyer, and Theda Skocpol, eds. Cambridge: Cambridge University Press, 1985.

The Broken Mirror: China After Tiananmen. Hicks, George, ed. London: Longmans, 1990.

Bunce, Valerie. *Do New Leaders Make a Difference? Executive Succession and Public Policy under Capitalism and Socialism*. Princeton: Princeton University Press, 1981.

Burke, Edmund. *Reflections on the Revolution in France*. Edited by Conor Cruise O'Brien. London: Penguin, 1968.

Burns, John P. "China's *Nomenklatura* System." *Problems of Communism* (September-October 1987), pp. 30–41.

Burns, John P. "Rural Guangdong's Second Economy." *China Quarterly* 88 (December 1981), pp. 629–44.

Burns, John P., and Stanley Rosen, eds. *Policy Conflicts in Post-Mao China*. Armonk: M. E. Sharpe, 1986.

Burton, Charles. *Political and Social Change in China Since 1978*. Westport, Conn.: Greenwood Press, 1990.

Butler, Steven. *Agricultural Mechanization in China: The Administrative Impact*. New York: East Asian Institute, Columbia University, 1978.

Byrd, William A. *China's Financial System: The Changing Role of Banks*. Boulder: Westview, 1983.

Byrd, William A., and Lin Qingsong, eds. *China's Rural Industry: Structure, Development, and Reform.* Washington: World Bank, 1990.

Byres, T. J., and Peter Nolan. *Inequality: China and India Compared, 1950–70.* Milton Keynes, UK: Open University, 1976.

Calder, Kent E. *Crisis and Compensation: Public Policy and Political Stability in Japan, 1949–1986*. Princeton: Princeton University Press, 1988.

Calder, Kent E. *Strategic Capitalism: Private Business and Public Purpose in Japanese Industrial Finance*. Princeton: Princeton University Press, 1993.

Calder, Kent E. *The State and Selective Credit Programs in Japan, 1946–1986.* Draft of book manuscript; Woodrow Wilson School, Princeton University, 1988.

Cannon, Terry, and Alan Jenkins, eds., *The Geography of Contemporary China: The Impact of Deng Xiaoping's Decade*. London: Routledge, 1990.

Carr, Raymond and Juan Pablo Fusi. *Spain: Dictatorship to Democracy*, second edition. London: George Allen and Unwin, 1981.

Carrère D'Encausse, Hèléne. *Stalin: Order Through Terror*. London: Longman, 1981.

Chan Ka Yan. "The Role of Migration in China's Regional Development: A Local Study of Southern China." M.Phil. Thesis, Department of Geography, University of Hong Kong, 1990.

Chan, Anita. *Children of Mao: Personality Development and Political Activism in the Red Guard Generation*. Seattle: University of Washington Press, 1985.

Chan, Anita. "Dispelling Misconceptions about the Red Guard Movement: The Necessity to Re-Examine Cultural Revolution Factionalism and Periodization." *Journal of Contemporary China* 1:1 (1992), pp. 61–85.

Chan, Anita. "Revolution or Corporatism? Workers and Trade Unions in Post-Mao China." *China's Quiet Revolution: New Interactions Between State and Society*. David S. G. Goodman and Beverley Hooper, eds. New York: St. Martin's, 1994, pp. 162–90.

Chan, Anita, Richard Madsen, and Jonathan Unger. *Chen Village*. Berkeley: University of California Press, 1984.

Chan, Joseph. "The Asian Challenge to Universal Human Rights: A Philosophical Appraisal," in James T. H. Tang, ed. *Human Rights and International Relations in the Asia Pacific Region*. London: Pinter, 1995.

Chang Ta-kuang. "The Making of the Chinese Bankruptcy Law: A Study in the Chinese Legislative Process." *Harvard International Law Review* 28:2 (Spring 1987), pp. 333–72.

Chang, Arnold. *Painting in the People's Republic of China: The Politics of Style*. Boulder: Westview, 1980.

Chen Jialing. *Hua* (Transformation). Hong Kong: Plum Blossoms, 1990.

Chen, Nancy N. "Urban Spaces and Experiences of Qigong," in Deborah S. Davis, et al., eds., *Urban Spaces in Contemporary China*. Washington: Woodrow Wilson International Center, 1995, pp. 347–361.

Chen Ta. *Chinese Migrations: With Special Reference to Labor Conditions*. New York: Paragon, 1967 (orig. 1923).

Cheng Hsiao-shih. *Party-Military Relations in the PRC and Taiwan: Paradoxes of Control*. Boulder: Westview, 1990.

Cheng Hsiao-shih. *Party-Military Relations in the PRC and Taiwan: Paradoxes of Control*. Boulder: Westview, 1990.

Cheng Kai Ming. "Reform in the Financing of Education in Mainland China." *Chinese Education: A Journal of Translations* 25:2–4 (1992), three whole issues.

Cheng Xiaonong. "The Structure of Economic Growth in China: An Approach to Measuring the Contribution of the Public and Non-Public Sectors, and Some Estimations." Unpublished paper, Princeton University, 1993.

Chesneaux, Jean. *The Chinese Labor Movement, 1919–1927.* Trans. Hope M. Wright. Stanford: Stanford University Press, 1968.

Child, John, and Xu Xinzhong. "The Communist Party's Role in Enterprise Leadership at the High Water of China's Economic Reform." Beijing: China-EC Management Institute Working Paper, September 1989.

Childs, John. *The Army of Charles II.* London: Routledge & Kegan Paul, 1976.

China: Urban Statistics, 1986. State Statistical Bureau, PRC, compiler. Hong Kong: Longman, 1987.

China at Forty: Mid-Life Crisis? Goodman, David, and Gerald Segal, eds. Oxford: Clarendon Press, 1989.

China Deconstructs: Politics, Trade, and Regionalism. David Goodman and Gerald Segal, eds. London: Routledge, 1994.

China in Transformation. Tu Wei-ming, ed. Cambridge: Harvard University Press, 1994.

China Reflected: An Anthology from Chinese and Western Sources, ed. Iain Orr et al. London: Foreign and Commonwealth Office, 1986.

China Review, 1991. Kuan Hsin-chi and Maurice Brosseau, eds. Hong Kong: Chinese University Press, 1991.

China Review, 1992. Kuan Hsin-chi and Maurice Brosseau, eds. Hong Kong: Chinese University Press, 1992.

China Under Deng. Kwan Ha Yim, ed. New York: Facts on File, 1991.

China's Economic Reforms. Joseph C. H. Chai and Chi-Keung Leung, eds. Hong Kong: University of Hong Kong Centre of Asian Studies, 1987.

China's Education and the Industrialized World. Marianne Bastid and Ruth Hayhoe, ed. Armonk: M.E. Sharpe, 1987.

China's Fifth Modernization: The Human Rights Movement, 1978–1979. Seymour, James D., ed.

China's Industrial Reform. Tidrick, Gene, and Chen Jiyuan, eds. New York: Oxford University Press, 1987.

The Chinese People's Movement: Perspectives on Spring 1989. Saich, Tony, ed. Armonk: M.E. Sharpe, 1990.

Chinese Society on the Eve of Tiananmen: The Impact of Reform. Davis, Deborah S., and Ezra Vogel, eds. Cambridge: Harvard Council on East Asian Studies, 1990.

Chirot, Daniel, ed. *The Crisis of Leninism and the Decline of the Left: The Revolutions of 1989.* Seattle: University of Washington Press, 1991.

Chomiak, Theodora B. "First Government, Then Power: The Lviv [L'vov] City Council, 1990." Princeton Politics Department Senior Thesis, 1991.

Chow, Gregory C. *The Chinese Economy.* New York: Harper & Row, 1985.

Chow, Gregory C. *Understanding China's Economy.* Singapore: World Scientific Press, 1994.

Chūgoku no toshika to nōson kensetsu (Chinese Urbanization and Rural Construction). Kojima Reeitsu, ed. Tokyo: Ryûkei Shosha, 1978.

Chui, Victor Chi-leung. *Chinese Perception of Organization and Authority.* Hong Kong: M.B.A. Thesis, University of Hong Kong Department of Management Sciences, 1987.

Clark, Paul. "Official Reactions to Modern Art in China Since the Beijing Massacre." *Pacific Affairs* 65:3 (Fall, 1992), pp. 334–352.

Clark, Paul. *Chinese Cinema: Culture and Politics Since 1949*. Cambridge: Cambridge University Press, 1987.

Clarke, Donald C. "Dispute Resolution in China." *Journal of Chinese Law* 5:2 (Fall 1991), pp. 245–296.

Clarke, Donald C. "Regulation and its Discontents: Understanding Economic Law in China." *Stanford Journal of International Law* 28:2 (1992), pp. 283–322.

Clarke, Donald C. "What's Law Got to Do with It? Legal Institutions and Economic Reform in China." *UCLA Pacific Basin Law Journal* 10:1 (Fall 1991), pp. 1–76.

Clavel, Alex B. "Law and Authoritarianism in China, 1978–1995." Princeton University, East Asian Studies Senior Thesis, 1995.

Cleverly, John. *The Schooling of China: Tradition and Modernity in Chinese Education*. Sydney: George Allen and Unwin, 1985.

Coady, Dave, et al. *Production, Marketing, and Pricing of Vegetables in China's Cities*. London: Development Research Program, 1990.

Coale, Ansley J., et al. "Recent Trends in Fertility and Nuptiality in China." *Science* 251 (1991), pp. 389–93.

Coble, Parks M., Jr. *The Shanghai Capitalist Class and the Nationalist Government, 1927–37*. Cambridge, Mass.: Harvard University East Asian Studies Center and Harvard University Press, 1986.

Cohen, Jerome Alan. "Chinese Law: At the Crossroads," *China Quarterly* 53 (January-March, 1973), p. 138–43.

Cohen, Joan Lebold *The New Chinese Painting, 1949–1986*. New York: H. N. Abrams, 1987.

Cohen, Paul, "The Post-Mao Reforms in Historical Perspective," Journal of Asian Studies 47:3 (August 1988), 518–40.

Cohen, Stephen F. *Rethinking the Soviet Experience: Politics and History Since 1917*. New York: Oxford University Press, 1985.

Coleman, D. C. *The Economy of England, 1450–1750*. Oxford: Oxford University Press, 1977.

Comparative Politics: A Reader. Eckstein, Harry, and David Apter, eds. Glencoe: Free Press, 1963.

The Comprehensive Plan of Shanghai. Bureau of Shanghai Urban Planning and Building Administration, ed. [No titlepage, but Shanghai: Bureau of Shanghai Urban Planning and Building Administration, apparently 1986.]

Conner, Alison W. "To Get Rich is Precarious: Regulation of Private Enterprise in the People's Republic of China." *Journal of Chinese Law* 5:1 (Spring 1991), pp. 1–57.

Connor, Walter D. *Deviance in Soviet Society: Crime, Delinquency, and Alcoholism*. New York: Columbia University Press, 1972.

Cook, Chris and John Stevenson. *Modern European History, 1763–1985*. New York: Longman, 1987.

Cornelius, Wayne A. *Politics and the Migrant Poor in Mexico City*. Stanford: Stanford University Press, 1975.

Coser, Lewis. *The Functions of Social Conflict*. New York: Free Press, 1956.

Cries for Democracy. Han Minzhu (pseud.), ed. Princeton: Princeton University Press, 1990.

Croll, Elisabeth. *Changing Identities of Chinese Women: Rhetoric, Experience, and Self-Perception in Twentieth-century China*. Hong Kong: Hong Kong University Press, 1995.

Cromer, Alan. *Uncommon Sense: The Heretical Nature of Science*. New York: Oxford University Press, 1993.

Cui Zhiyuan. "Getting the Prices and Property Rights Wrong? The Chinese Reform in the

Schumpeterian Perspective and Beyond," in *China: A Reformable System?*, Gan Yang and Cui Zhiyuan, eds. New York: Oxford University Press, 1995.

Cumings, Bruce. *The Origins of the Korean War*. Princeton: Princeton University Press, 1990.

Dahl, Robert A. *Modern Political Analysis*. Englewood Cliffs, NJ: Prentice-Hall, 1963.

Dahl, Robert A. *Polyarchy*. New Haven: Yale University Press, 1971.

Dahrendorf, Ralf. *Class and Class Conflict in Industrial Society*. London: Routledge & Kegan Paul, 1959.

Dai Houying. *Stones of the Wall*. London: Sceptre, 1987.

Dalai Lama (Tenzin Gyasto). *Freedom in Exile: The Autobiography of the Dalai Lama*. New York: Harper Collins, 1990.

Daniels, Robert V. *Soviet Communism from Reform to Collapse*. Lexington, MA: Heath, 1995.

Darnton, Robert. *The Great Cat Massacre and Other Episodes in French Cultural History*. New York: Basic Books, 1984.

David, Cristina C., and Keijiro Otsuka, eds. *Modern Rice Technology and Income Distribution in Asia*. Boulder: Lynne Rienner, 1994.

Davidson, Donald. *Essays on Actions and Events*. Oxford: Oxford University Press, 1980.

Davis, Deborah S. "Housing and Family Life in Shanghai." *China Update* 11:3 (Fall 1991), pp. 8–13.

deBary, William Theodore. *The Liberal Tradition in China*. New York: Columbia University Press, 1983.

Deng Xiaoping. *Fundamental Issues in Present-Day China*. Beijing: Foreign Languages Press, 1987.

Deng Xiaoping. *Selected Works of Deng Xiaoping, 1975–1982*. Beijing: Foreign Languages Press, 1984.

Derbyshire, Ian. *Politics in China: From Mao to Deng*. Cambridge: Chambers, 1987.

Des Forges, Roger, et al., eds. *China: The Crisis of 1989, Origins & Implications*. Buffalo: Council on International Studies, SUNY Buffalo, 1990.

Deutsch, Karl. *The Nerves of Government: Models of Political Communication and Control*. Glencoe: Free Press, 1963.

Dicker, Richard. "A Law for Change—With Loopholes." *Human Rights Tribune* III:2 (Summer 1992), pp. 7–9.

Dikötter, Frank. *The Discourse of Race in Modern China*. Stanford: Stanford University Press, 1992.

Ding Xueliang. *The Decline of Communism in China: The Legitimacy Crisis, 1979–1989*. New York: Cambridge University Press, 1994.

Dittmer, Lowell. "Ideology and Organization in Post-Mao China." *Asian Survey*, 24:3 (March 1984), 3:349–69.

Domes, Jürgen. *Socialism in the Chinese Countryside: Rural Societal Policies in the People's Republic of China, 1949–1979*, tr. Margritta Wendling. London: C. Hurst, 1980.

Domestic Law Reforms in Post-Mao China. Pitman Potter, ed. Armonk: M.E. Sharpe, 1993.

Donnithorne, Audrey. "China's Cellular Economy: Some Trends Since the Cultural Revolution." *China Quarterly* 52 (October-December 1972), pp. 605–619.

Donnithorne, Audrey. *China's Economic System*. New York: Praeger, 1967.

Dorfman, Robert, Paul A. Samuelson, and Robert Solow. *Linear Programming and Economic Analysis*. New York: McGraw-Hill, 1958.

Doyle, Michael. "Kant, Liberal Legacies, and Foreign Affairs," *Philosophy and Public Affairs* 12:3–4 (Summer and Fall, 1983), 205–35 and 323–52.

Dreyer, June Teufel, "The Demobilization of PLA Servicemen and their Reintegration into Civilian Life," in June Dreyer, ed. *China's Defense and Foreign Policy*. New York: Paragon, 1988, 297–349.

Dreyfus, Hubert, and Paul Rabinow. *Michel Foucault: Beyond Structuralism and Hermeneutics*, 2nd ed. Chicago: University of Chicago Press, 1983.

Dreze, J., and A. Sen, *Hunger and Public Action*. Oxford: Clarendon Press, 1989.

Du Ruiqing. *Chinese Higher Education*. New York: St. Martin's Press, 1992.

Duara, Prasenjit. *Culture, Power, and the State: Rural North China, 1900–1942*. Stanford: Stanford University Press, 1988.

Duke, Michael. *Blooming and Contending: Chinese Literature of the Post-Mao Era*. Bloomington: Indiana University Press, 1985.

Dutton, Michael R. *Policing and Punishment in China: From Patriarchy to "the People."* Cambridge: Cambridge University Press, 1992.

Duverger, Maurice. *Political Parties: Their Organization and Activity in the Modern State*, tr. B. and R. North. New York: Wiley, 1954.

Dworkin, Ronald M. *Taking Rights Seriously*. London: Duckworth, 1978

Dye, Thomas. *American Federalism: Competition among Governments*. Lexington, MA: Heath, 1990.

Eberstadt, Nick. "Population and Economic Growth." *Wilson Quarterly* X:5 (1986), pp. 95–127.

Eckstein, Harry. "Case Study and Theory in Political Science," in F. Greenstein and N. Polsby, eds. *Handbook of Political Science*, vol. 7. Reading, MA: Addison-Wesley, 1975, pp. 79–137.

Eckstein, Harry. "The Idea of Political Development: From Dignity to Efficiency," in Ikuō Kabashima and Lynn T. White III, eds., *Political System and Change*. Princeton: Princeton University Press, 1986, pp. 311–46.

Education in Mainland China. Lin Bih-jaw and Fan Li-min, eds. Taipei: Institute of International Relations, 1990.

Eftimiades, Nicholas. *Chinese Intelligence Operations*. Hong Kong: Naval Institute Press, 1994.

Eisenstadt, S. N., and René Marchand, eds. *Political Clientelism, Patronage, and Development*. Beverly Hills: Sage, 1981.

Elkins, David, and Richard Simeon. "A Cause in Search of its Effect, or What Does Political Culture Explain?" *Comparative Politics* 11 (January, 1979), 127–46.

Engelstein, Laura (with reactions from Rudy Koshar and Jan Goldstein, and a reply by Engelstein). "*AHR* Forum; Combined Underdevelopment: Discipline and the Law in Imperial and Soviet Russia." *American Historical Review* (April 1993), pp. 338–81.

Entrepreneurship, Economic Growth, and Social Change. David Schak, ed. Brisbane: Griffith University Centre for the Study of Australian-Asian Relations, 1994.

Erro, Davide. "The Crisis of Argentine Political Economy and the Breakdown of Corporatism, 1966–1989." Princeton University, Woodrow Wilson School Senior Thesis, 1991.

Etzioni, Amitai. *A Comparative Analysis of Complex Organizations*. New York: Wiley, 1961.

Evans, Grant. *Lao Peasants Under Socialism*. New Haven: Yale University Press, 1990.

Evans, Peter. *Dependent Development: The Alliance of Multinational, State, and Local Capital in Brazil*. Princeton: Princeton University Press, 1979.

Fabre, Guilhem. "Le réveil de Shanghaï: Stratégies Économiques 1949–2000" (The Awakening of Shanghai: Economic Strategies, 1949–2000). *Le courrier des pays de l'est*, No. 325 (January 1988), pp. 3–40.

Faligot, Roger and Rémi Kauffer. *The Chinese Secret Service*. Tr. Christine Donougher. London: Headline, 1989.

Faure, David. "The Lineage as a Cultural Invention: The Case of the Pearl River Delta." *Modern China* 15:1 (1989), pp. 4–36.

Fei Xiaotong. *Small Towns in China: Functions, Problems, and Prospects*. Beijing: New World Press, 1986.

Feinerman, James V. "Chinese Constitutionalism." Unpublished paper, 1993.

Fenwick, Ann. "Equity Joint Ventures in the People's Republic of China: An Assessment of the First Five Years." *Business Lawyer* 40:3 (May 1985), pp. 839–78.

Fenwick, Ann. "Evaluating China's Special Economic Zones." *International Tax and Business Lawyer* 2:2 (Fall 1984), pp. 376–97.

Fewsmith, Joseph. *Dilemmas of Reform in China: Political Conflict and Economic Debate*. Armonk: M.E. Sharpe, 1994.

Fewsmith, Joseph. Review of "Leninger's" *Disan zhi yanjing kan Zhongguo* (Looking at China Through a Third Eye) in *Journal of Contemporary China* 7 (Fall 1994), p. 100–04.

Field, Robert Michael, Kathleen McGlynn, and William Abnett. "Political Conflict and Industrial Growth in China, 1965–77," in *Chinese Economy Post-Mao*, vol. 1. Washington: Government Printing Office, 1978, pp. 239–283.

Finnane, Antonia. "The Origins of Prejudice: The Malintegration of Subei in Late Imperial China," *Comparative Studies in Society and History* 35:2 (April 1993), pp. 211–38.

Fischer, David Hackett. *Albion's Seed: Four British Folkways in America*. New York: Oxford University Press, 1989.

Fitzgerald, John. *The Irony of the Chinese Revolution*. Stanford: Stanford University Press, 1992.

Forces for Change in Contemporary China. Lin Bih-jaw and James T. Myers, eds. Taipei: Institute for International Relations, 1992.

The Formation of National States in Western Europe. Tilly, Charles, ed. Princeton: Princeton University Press, 1975.

Forster, Keith. "The Politics of Destabilization and Confrontation: The Campaign against Lin Biao and Confucius in Zhejiang Province, 1974." *China Quarterly* 107 (September 1986), pp. 433–62.

Forster, Keith. *Rebellion and Factionalism in a Chinese Province: Zhejiang 1966–76*. Armonk: M. E. Sharpe, 1990.

Fortescue, William. *Revolution and Counter-Revolution in France, 1815–1852*. Oxford: Basil Blackwell, 1988.

Foster, Frances Hoar. "Codification in Post-Mao China." *American Journal of Comparative Law* 30 (Summer 1982), pp. 395–428.

Foucault, Michel. *Discipline and Punish: The Birth of the Prison*. New York: Pantheon, 1977.

Frankenstein, John. "The People's Republic of China: Arms Production, Industrial Strategy, and Problems of History," in *Arms Industry Limited*. Herbert Wulf, ed. Oxford: Oxford University Press, 1993, pp. 271–319.

Fransman, Martin. *Technology and Economic Development*. Boulder: Westview, 1986.

Friedberg, Aaron. *Creating Power: The American State and the Conduct of the Cold War*. Princeton: Princeton University Press, 1996.

Friedman, Edward. "Deng vs. the Peasantry: Recollectivization in the Countryside." *Problems of Communism* (September-October 1991), pp. 30–49.

Friedman, Edward. "Reconstructing China's National Identity: A Southern Alterbative to Mao-era Anti-Imperialist Nationalsim," *Journal of Asian Studies*, 53:1 (February 1994), pp.67–87.

Friedman, Edward. "Reconstructing China's National Identity: A Southern Alternative to Mao-era Anti-Imperialist Nationalism," *Journal of Asian Studies* (February 1994), 67–91.

Friedman, Edward, Paul G. Pickowicz, and Mark Selden. *Chinese Village, Socialist State*. New Haven: Yale University Press, 1991.

Frolic, B. Michael. *Mao's People: Sixteen Portraits of Life in Revolutionary China*. Cambridge: Harvard University Press, 1980.

Fu Gangzhan, et al., *Unemployment in Urban China: An Analysis of Survey Data from Shanghai*. London: Development Economics Research Programme, 1992.

Fu Poshek. *Passivity, Resistance, and Collaboration: Intellectual Choices in Occupied Shanghai, 1937–1945*. Stanford: Stanford University Press, 1993.

Fu Zhengyuan, "The Sociology of Political Science in the PRC," in *The Development of Political Science: A Comparative Study*, D. Easton, J. Gunnell, and L. Graziano, eds. London: Routledge, 1991, 223–51.

Fuegi, John, et al., eds. *Brecht in Asia and Africa: The Brecht Yearboook XIV; Brecht in Asien und Afrika, Brecht-Jahrbuch XIV* (in English and German). Hong Kong: University of Hong Kong Department of Comparative Literature, 1989.

Gallin, Bernard. *Hsin Hsing, Taiwan: A Chinese Village in Change*. Berkeley: University of California Press, 1966.

Gannon, Martin J., et al. *Understanding Global Cultures: Metaphorical Journeys Through 17 Countries*. Thousand Oaks, CA: Sage, 1994.

Gargan, Edward. *China's Fate: Reform & Repression, 1980–90*. New York: Doubleday, 1990.

Gates, Hill. *China's Motor: A Thousand Years of Petty Capitalism*. Ithaca: Cornell University Press, 1996.

Geertz, Clifford. *Agricultural Involution: The Processes of Ecological Change in Indonesia*. Berkeley: University of California Press, 1963.

Geertz, Clifford. *Islam Observed: Religious Development in Morocco and Indonesia*. New Haven: Yale University Press, 1968.

Geertz, Clifford. *Negara: The Theatre State in Nineteenth-Century Bali*. Princeton: Princeton University Press, 1980.

Geertz, Clifford. *The Interpretation of Cultures*. New York: Basic Books, 1973.

Geertz, Clifford. *The Interpretation of Cultures*. New York: Basic Books, 1973.

Gelatt, Timothy A. "Book Review." *China Law Reporter* VII: 3–4 (1993), pp. 231–41.

Gellner, Ernest. *Civil Society and its Rivals*. New York: Penguin, 1994.

Gerschenkron, Alexander. *Bread and Democracy in Germany*. Berkeley: University of California Press, 1943.

Gerschenkron, Alexander. *Economic Backwardness in Historical Perspective: A Book of Essays*. Cambridge: Harvard University Press, 1962.

Gipouloux, François. *Les cent fleurs à l'usine: Agitation ouvière et crise du model sovietique en Chine, 1956–1957*. Paris: L'école des hautes études en sciences sociales, 1986.

Gleick, James. *Chaos: Making a New Science*. New York: Penguin, 1987.

Gold, Thomas B. "Urban Private Business and Social Change," in Deborah Davis and Ezra Vogel, eds., *Chinese Society on the Eve of Tiananmen: The Impact of Reform*. Cambridge: Harvard University Press, 1990, pp. 157–78.

Goldblatt, Howard, ed. *Chinese Literature for the 1980s: The Fourth Congress of Writers and Artists*. Armonk: M. E. Sharpe, 1982.

Goldman, Merle. *China's Intellectuals: Advise and Dissent*. Cambridge: Harvard University Press, 1981.

Goldman, Merle. *Literary Dissent in Communist China*. Cambridge: Harvard University Press, 1967.

Goldman, Merle. *Sowing the Seeds of Democracy in China: Political Reform in the Era of Deng Xiaoping*. Cambridge: Harvard University Press, 1994.

Goldstein, Alice, and Guo Shenyang. "Temporary Migration in Shanghai and Beijing," *Studies in Comparative International Development* 27:2 (Summer 1992), pp. 39–56.

Goldstein, Alice, Sidney Goldstein, and Shenyang Guo. "Temporary Migrants in Shanghai Households, 1984." *Demography* 28:2 (1991), pp. 275–91.

Goldstein, Avery. *From Bandwagon to Balance-of-Power Politics: Structural Constraints, 1949–78.* Berkeley: University of California Press, 1991.

Goldstein, Sidney. "Forms of Mobility and their Policy Implications: Thailand and China Compared." *Social Forces* 65:4 (1987), pp. 915–42.

Goldstein, Sidney, and Alice Goldstein. "Population Movement, Labor Force Absorption, and Urbanization in China." *Annals of the American Academy of Political and Social Science* 476 (1984), pp. 90–110.

Goldstein, Sidney, and Alice Goldstein. "Varieties of Population Mobility in Relation to Development in China." *Studies in Comparative International Development.* 22:4 (1987–88), pp. 101–24.

Goldstein, Steven M. "Reforming Socialist Systems: Some Lessons of the Chinese Experience." *Studies in Comparative Communism* 21:2 (summer 1988).

Goodman, David. *Beijing Street Voices: The Poetry and Politics of China's Democracy Movement.* London: Marion Boyars, 1981.

Goodman, David. *China's Regional Development.* London: Routledge, 1989.

Gorbachev, Mikhail. *Perestroika: New Thinking for Our Country and the World.* New edition. London: Fontana, 1988.

Gramsci, Antonio. *Letters from Prison*, tr. Lynne Lawner. New York: Harper and Row, 1973. Another edition is *Prison Notebooks*, New York: International Publishers, 1971.

Granick, David. "China's Multiple Labour Markets." *China Quarterly* (November-December 1991), pp. 269–89.

Granick, David. *Chinese State Enterprises: A Regional Property Rights Analysis.* Chicago: University of Chicago Press, 1990.

Granovetter, Mark. "Economic Action and Social Structure: The Problem of Embeddedness." *American Journal of Sociology,* 91 (November 1985), pp. 481–510.

Grant, Joan. *Worm-eaten Hinges: Tensions and Turmoil in Shanghai, 1988–89, Events Leading up to Tiananmen Square.* Melbourne: Hyland House, 1991.

Habermas, Jürgen. *Legitimation Crisis.* Boston: Beacon Press, 1973.

Habermas, Jürgen. *The Structural Transformation of the Public Sphere: An Inquiry into a Category of Bourgeois Society.* Cambridge, MA: MIT Press, 1989.

Habermas, Jürgen. *Toward a Rational Society: Student Protest, Science, and Politics.* Boston: Beacon Books, 1970.

Hall, Peter A. *Governing the Economy: The Politics of State Intervention in Britain and France.* New York: Oxford University Press, 1986.

Hankiss, Elemér. *East European Alternatives.* Oxford: Clarendon Press, 1990.

Hansen, Chad. "Chinese Language, Chinese Philosophy, and 'Truth.' " *Journal of Asian Studies* XLIV:5 (May 1985), pp. 491–520.

Hansen, Chad. "Do Human Rights Apply to China? A Normative Analysis in Comparative Ethics" (unpublished paper, Philosophy Department, University of Hong Kong, 1994).

Harding, Harry. *China's Second Revolution: Reform After Mao.* Washington: Brookings Institution, 1987.

Harding, Harry. *A Fragile Relationship: The United States and China since 1972.* Washington: Brookings, 1992.

Harrell, Stevan. "Men, Women, and Ghosts in Taiwanese Folk Religion," in Caroline Bynum, Stevan Harrell, and Paula Richman, eds. *Gender and Religion: On the Complexity of Symbols.* Boston: Beacon Press, 1986, pp. 97–116.

Harsanyi, J.C. "Rational-Choice Models of Political Behavior vs. Functionalist and Conformist Theories." *World Politics* 21:1 (July 1969), pp. 513–38.
Hayhoe, Ruth. *China's Universities and the Open Door*. Armonk: M.E. Sharpe, 1989.
Hays, Samuel P. *The Response to Industrialism, 1885–1914*. Chicago History of American Civilization. Chicago: University of Chicago Press, 1957.
Hill, Christopher. *Reformation to Industrial Revolution*. Harmondsworth, Middlesex: Penguin, 1969.
Hirschman, Albert. *Exit, Voice, and Loyalty*. Cambridge, MA: Harvard University Press, 1970.
Ho, Samuel P. S., and Ralph Huenemann. *China's Open Door Policy: The Quest for Foreign Technology and Capital*. Vancouver: University of British Columbia Press, 1984.
Ho, Samuel. *Rural China in Transition: Non-agricultural Development in Rural Jiangsu, 1978–90*. New York: Oxford University Press, 1994.
Hobsbawm, Eric J. *Primitive Rebels*. Manchester: University of Manchester Press, 1959.
Hobsbawm, Eric J. *The Age of Revolution, 1789–1848*. New York: Mentor, 1962.
Hodder, Rupert N. W. *The Creation of Wealth in China*. London: Belhaven Press, 1992.
Hodder, Rupert N. W. "China's Industry—Horizontal Linkages in Shanghai." *Transactions of the Institute of British Geographers* 1990: 15, pp. 487–503.
Hodder, Rupert N. W. "Exchange and Reform in the Economy of Shanghai Municipality: Socialist Geography under Reform." *Annals of the Association of American Geographers* 83:2 (1993), pp. 303–19.
Hong Kong Trade Union Education Centre. *A Moment of Truth: Workers' Participation in China's 1989 Democracy Movement and the Emergence of Independent Unions*. Hong Kong: Hong Kong Trade Union Education Centre, 1990.
Honig, Emily. *Creating Chinese Ethnicity: Subei People in Shanghai, 1850–1980*. New Haven: Yale University Press, 1992.
Hood, Marlowe. "Mystics, Ghosts, and Faith Healers." *Los Angeles Times Magazine*, April 19, 1992, pp. 20–35.
Hood, Marlowe. "On the Use and Abuse of the Print Media by China's Leaders during the 1980s." Paper for a conference on "Voices of China," University of Minnesota, 1991.
Horgan, John. "Can Science Explain Consciousness?" *Scientific American* 271:1 (July 1994), pp. 72–78.
Hosking, Geoffrey. *The Awakening of the Soviet Union*. Cambridge: Harvard University Press, 1990.
Hoston, Germaine A. *Marxism and the Crisis of Development in Prewar Japan*. Princeton: Princeton University Press, 1986.
Howard, Pat. *Breaking the Iron Rice Bowl: Prospects for Socialism in China's Countryside*. Armonk: M. E. Sharpe, 1988.
Howell, Jude. "The Poverty of Civil Society: Insights from China." Norwich: University of East Anglia School of Development Studies, 1993.
Hsieh Chiao-min. *Atlas of China*. New York: McGraw-Hill, 1973.
Hsu Kai-yu. *Literature of the People's Republic of China*. Bloomington: Indiana University Press, 1980.
Hu Hsien-chin. *The Common Descent Group in China and its Functions*. New York: Viking Fund, 1948.
Hua Junwu. *Cartoons from Contemporary China*. Beijing, New World Press, 1989.
Hua Sheng, Zhang Xuejun, and Luo Xiaopeng. *China: From Revolution to Reform*. London: Macmillan, 1993.
Huang Weixin. *Economic Integration as a Development Device: The Case of the EC and China*. Saarbrücken: Nijmegen Studies in Development, Breitenbach Verlag, 1992.

Huang Yasheng. "Information, Bureaucracy, and Economic Reforms in China and the Former Soviet Union." *World Politics* (forthcoming).
Huang, Philip C. C. *The Peasant Family and Rural Development in the Yangzi Delta, 1350–1988.* Stanford: Stanford University Press, 1990.
Huang, Philip C. C. "The Paradigmatic Crisis in Chinese Studies: Paradoxes in Social and Economic History." *Modern China* 17:3 (July 1991), pp. 299–341.
Huang, Philip C. C. " 'Public Sphere'/'Civil Society' in China? The Third Realm Between State and Society." *Modern China* 19:2 (April 1993), pp. 216–40.
Hughes, H. Stuart. *Consciousness and Society*. New York: Vintage, 1961.
Huntington, Samuel H. "Political Development and Political Decay," in Ikuō Kabashima and Lynn T. White III, eds., *Political System and Change.* Princeton: Princeton University Press, 1986, pp. 95–139.
Huntington, Samuel P. *American Politics: The Promise of Disharmony.* Cambridge, Mass.: Harvard University Press, 1981.
Huntington, Samuel P. *Political Order in Changing Societies.* New Haven: Yale University Press, 1968.
Huntington, Samuel P. *The Third Wave: Democratization in the Late Twentieth Century.* Norman: University of Oklahoma Press, 1991.
Huntington, Samuel P., and Joan M. Nelson. *No Easy Choice: Political Participation in Developing Countries.* Cambridge, Mass: Harvard University Press, 1976.
Hussain, Athar and N. Stern. *On the Recent Increase in Death Rates in China.* London: Development Research Program, 1990.
Hussain, Athar. *Chinese Enterprise Reforms.* London: Development Research Program, 1990.
Hussain, Athar, et al. *The Chinese Television Industry.* London: Development Research Program, 1990.
Hutton, Ronald. *The Restoration: A Political and Religious History of England and Wales, 1658–1667.* Oxford: Clarendon Press, 1985.
Imai, Hiroyuki. "China's Business Cycles." *China Business Review*, January-February 1994, pp. 14–16.
Inkeles, Alex, and David Smith. *Becoming Modern: Individual Change in Six Developing Countries.* London: Heinemann, 1974.
Ishida Hiroshi. *Chūgoku nōson keizai no kiso kōzō: Shanhai kinkō nōson no kōgyōka to kindaika no ayumi* (Rural China in Transition: Experiences of Rural Shanghai toward Industrialization and Modernization). Kyōto: Kōyō Shobō, 1991.
Jameson, Fredric. *The Political Unconscious: Narrative as a Socially Symbolic Act.* Ithaca: Cornell University Press, 1981.
Jane's Information Group. *China in Crisis: The Role of the Military.* Coulsdon, Surrey: Jane's Defense Data, 1989.
Jing Jun. "The Working Press in China." Unpublished paper, 1985.
Joffe, Ellis. *The Chinese Army after Mao.* London: Weidenfeld and Nicolson, 1987.
Johnson, Chalmers A. *Peasant Nationalism and Communist Power: The Emergence of Revolutionary China, 1937–1945.* Stanford: Stanford University Press, 1962.
Johnson, Chalmers A. *Revolutionary Change.* Boston: Little Brown, 1966.
Johnson, Kay. "Chinese Orphanages: Saving China's Abandoned Girls." *Australian Journal of Chinese Affairs* 30 (July 1993), pp. 61–87.
Johnston, Tess, and Deke Erh. *A Last Look: Western Architecture in Old Shanghai.* Hong Kong: Old China Hand Press, 1993.
Jones, Andrew F. *Like a Knife: Ideology and Genre in Contemporary Chinese Popular Music.* Ithaca: Cornell East Asia Series, 1992.
Jose, Nicholas. "Next Wave Art." *Art and Asia Pacific Quarterly* 1 (1993), pp. 25–30.

Joseph, William, Christine Wong, and David Zweig, eds. *New Perspectives on the Cultural Revolution*. Cambridge: Harvard University Press, 1991).

Jowitt, Kenneth. "An Organizational Approach to the Study of Political Cultures in Marxist-Leninist Systems." *American Political Science Review* 68:3 (September 1974), 1171–88.

Jowitt, Kenneth. "Soviet Neo-traditionalism: The Political Corruption of a Leninist Regime." *Soviet Studies* 35:3 (July 1983), pp. 275–97.

Jowitt, Kenneth. "Soviet Neotraditionalism: The Political Corruption of a Leninist Regime." *Soviet Studies* 25:3 (1983), pp. 275–97.

Jowitt, Kenneth. *New World Disorder: The Leninist Extinction*. Berkeley: University of California Press, 1992.

Kahneman, Daniel. "New Challenges to the Rationality Assumption." *Journal of Institutional and Theoretical Economics*, 150:1 (1994), pp. 18–36.

Kaple, Deborah. *Dream of a Red Factory: The Legacy of High Stalinism in China*. Oxford: Oxford University Press, 1994.

Karmel, Solomon M. "Capitalism with Chinese Characteristics." MS, Princeton, NJ, August 1993.

Karmel, Solomon M. "The Neo-Authoritarian Contradiction: Trials of Developmentalist Dictatorships and the Retreat of the State in Mainland China." Princeton University Politics Department Ph.D. Dissertation, 1995.

Kelliher, Daniel. *Peasant Power: The Era of Rural Reform, 1979–1989*. New Haven: Yale University Press, 1993.

Kelliher, Daniel. "The Political Consequences of China's Reforms." *Comparative Politics*, July 1986, pp. 480–81.

Kenyon, Daphen A. & John Kincaid, eds. *Competition Among States: Efficiency and Equity in American Federalism*. Washington: Urban Institute, 1992.

Kenyon, John P. *Stuart England*. Second Edition; Harmondsworth: Penguin, 1985.

Key, V. O., Jr. *Southern Politics*. New York: Vintage, 1949.

Kim, Samuel S. *China, the United Nations, and World Order*. Princeton: Princeton University Press, 1989.

Kindermann, G., "An Overview of Sun Yat-sen's Doctrine." C. Y. Cheng, ed. *Sun Yat-sen's Doctrine in the Modern World*. Boulder: Westview, 1989, pp. 52–78.

King, Richard. "'Wounds' and 'Exposure:' Chinese Literature After the Gang of Four." *Pacific Affairs* (Spring 1981): 82–99.

Kinkley, Jeffrey, ed. *After Mao: Chinese Literature and Society, 1978–81*. Cambridge: Harvard University Press, 1985.

Kleinberg, Robert. *China's Opening to the Outside World: The Experiment with Foreign Capitalism*. Boulder: Westview, 1990.

Kohli, Atul. *Democracy and Discontent: India's Growing Crisis of Governability*. Cambridge: Cambridge University Press, 1990.

Kohli, Atul. *The State and Poverty in India: The Politics of Reform*. New York: Cambridge University Press, 1987.

Kojima Reeitsu. *Chūgoku no keizai kaikaku* (China's Economic Reforms). Tokyo: Keisō Shobō, 1988.

Kojima Reeitsu. *Urbanization and Urban Problems in China*. Tokyo: Institute of Developing Economies, 1987.

Kojima, Reiitsu. "The Growing Fiscal Authority of Provincial-Level Governments in China," *The Developing Economies* 30:4 (December 1992), pp. 315–46.

Kornai, János. *The Economics of Shortage*. Amsterdam: North Holland, 1980.

Kornai, János. "The Hungarian Reform Process: Visions, Hopes, and Reality." *Journal of Economic Literature* (December 1986): 1687–1737.

Kornai, János. *The Road to a Free Economy: The Example of Hungary*. New York: Norton, 1990.

Kornai, János. *The Socialist System: The Political Economy of Communism*. Princeton: Princeton University Press, 1992.

Kouwenhoven, Frank. "Developments in Mainland China's New Music," *China Information*, "Part I: From China to the United States," 7:1 (Summer 1992), pp. 17–39; "Part II: From Europe to the Pacific & Back to China," 7:2 (Autumn 1992), pp. 30–46.

Krasner, Stephen D. *Defending the National Interest*. Princeton: Princeton University Press, 1978.

Kraus, Richard. *Brushes with Power: Modern Politics and the Chinese Art of Calligraphy*. Berkeley: University of California Press, 1991.

Kraus, Richard. "China's 'Liberalization' and Conflict over the Social Organization of the Arts." *Modern China* 9:2 (April 1983), pp. 212–27.

Kueh, Y. Y. *Economic Planning and Local Mobilization in Post-Mao China*. London: SOAS Contemporary China Institute, 1985.

Kuhn, Philip A. *Soulstealers: The Chinese Sorcery Scare of 1768*. Cambridge: Harvard University Press, 1990.

Kuhn, Thomas. *The Structure of Scientific Revolutions*. Chicago: University of Chicago Press, 1964.

Kuisel, Richard. *Seducing the French: The Dilemma of Americanization*. Berkeley: University of California Press, 1993.

Kwok, Daniel W. Y. *Scientism in Chinese Thought, 1900–1950*. New Haven: Yale University Press, 1965.

Kwok, Reginald Yin-wang. "Metropolitan Development in China: A Struggle Between Contradictions." *Habitat International* 12:4 (1988), pp. 201–12.

Kwong, Julia. *Cultural Revolution in China's Schools, May 1966–April 1969*. Stanford: Hoover Institution Press, 1988.

Laing, Ellen. *The Winking Owl: Art in the People's Republic of China*. Berkeley: University of California Press, 1988.

Lakoff, George. *Women, Fire, and Dangerous Things: What Categories Reveal about the Mind*. Chicago: University of Chicago Press, 1988.

Lam, Willy Wo-Lap. *The Era of Zhao Ziyang: Power Struggle in China, 1986–88*. Hong Kong: A.B. Books, 1989.

Lam, Willy Wo-Lap. *Toward a Chinese-style Socialism: An Assessment of Deng Xiaoping's Reforms*. Hong Kong: Oceanic Cultural Service, 1987.

Lamb, Franklin P. "An Interview with Chinese Legal Officials," *China Quarterly* 66 (June 1976), pp. 323–27.

Lampton, David M. *Paths to Power*. Ann Arbor: Center for Chinese Studies, University of Michigan, 1986.

Lampton, David M. *Policy Implementation in Post-Mao China*. Berkeley: University of California Press, 1987.

Lane, Ruth. "Concrete Theory: An Emerging Political Method." *American Political Science Review* 84:3 (September 1990), pp. 927–40.

Langer, Suzanne. *Feeling and Form*. Scribner's: New York, 1943.

Langer, Suzanne. *Philosophy in a New Key: A Study in the Symbolism of Reason, Rite, and Art*. New York: Penguin, 1942.

Lanternari, Vittorio. *Religions of the Oppressed: Studies of Modern Messianic Cults*. New York: Knopf, 1963.

LaPalombara, Joseph. *Democracy, Italian Style*. New Haven: Yale University Press, 1987.

Lardy, Nicholas R. *Agriculture in China's Modern Economic Development*. Cambridge: Cambridge Univ. Press, 1983.

Lardy, Nicholas R. "Consumption and Living Standards in China, 1978–1983," *China Quarterly* (1984): 847–65.
Lawrence, Susan. "Democracy, Chinese Style." *The Australian Journal of Chinese Affairs* 32 (July 1994), pp. 61–68.
Leadership on the China Coast. Göran Aijmer, ed. London and Malmö: Curzon Press for the Scandinavian Institute of Asian Studies, 1984.
Lee Hong Yung. *From Revolutionary Cadres to Party Technocrats in Socialist China*. Berkeley: University of California Press, 1991.
Lee, Peter N. S. *Industrial Management and Economic Reform in China, 1949–1984*. Hong Kong: Oxford University Press, 1988.
Lee, Peter N. S. "Reforming the Social Security System in China." Stewart Nagel and Mariam Mills, eds. *Public Policy in China*. Westport, CT: Greenwood Press, 1993, pp. 33–51.
Leeming, Frank. *Rural China Today*. Harlowe, UK: Longman, 1985.
The Lenin Anthology. Robert C. Tucker, ed. New York: Norton, 1975.
Leung Chi Yan. "The Politics of Economic Leap Forward and Readjustment: A Case Study of Economic Policy Making in China, 1977–1980." University of Hong Kong, Political Science Department M.Phil. Thesis, 1992.
Leung Yuen-sang. *The Shanghai Taotai: Linkage Man in a Changing Society, 1843–90*. Honolulu: University of Hawaii Press, 1990.
Leung, Beatrice. *Sino-Vatican Relations: Problems in Conflicting Authority, 1976–1986*. Cambridge: Cambridge University Press, 1992.
Levenson, Joseph. *Confucian China and its Modern Fate: The Problem of Monarchical Decay*. Berkeley: University of California Press, 1964.
Levi, Carlo. *Christ Stopped at Eboli*. New York: Farrar, Straus, 1947.
Levy, Jr., Marion J. *The Family Revolution in Modern China*. New York: Atheneum, 1948.
Levy, Jr., Marion J. "Structural-Functional Analysis," in *International Encyclopaedia of the Social Sciences*. London: Macmillan, 1968, pp. 21–28.
Levy, Jr., Marion J. *The Structure of Society*. Princeton: Princeton University Press, 1952.
Levy, Marion J., Jr. *Modernization and the Structure of Societies*. Princeton: Princeton University Press, 1966.
Lewin, Moshe. *The Gorbachev Phenomenon: A Historical Interpretation*. Berkeley: University of California Press, 1988.
Lewis, W. Arthur. *Politics in West Africa*. London: Allen and Unwin, 1965.
Lewis, W. Arthur. *The Theory of Economic Growth* (Homewood, Ill.: Irwin, 1955.
Li Cheng. "The Rise of Technocracy: Elite Transformation and Ideological Change in Post-Mao China" (Ph.D. Dissertation, Politics Department, Princeton University, 1992).
Li Cheng. "University Networks and the Rise of Qinghua Graduates in China." *Australian Journal of Chinese Affairs* 32 (July 1994), pp. 1–32.
Li Cheng and David Bachman. "Localism, Elitism, and Immobilism: Elite Transformation and Social Change in Post-Mao China." *World Politics*, 42 (October), pp. 64–94.
Li Cheng and Lynn White. "The Army in the Succession to Deng Xiaoping: Familiar Fealties and Technocratic Trends." *Asian Survey* 33:8 (August 1993), pp. 757–86.
Li Cheng and Lynn White. "China's Technocratic Movement and the *World Economic Herald*." *Modern China* 17:3 (July 1991), pp. 342–388.
Li Cheng and Lynn White. "Elite Transformation and Modern Change in Mainland China and Taiwan." *China Quarterly* 121, March 1990, pp. 1–35.
Li Cheng and Lynn White. "The Thirteenth Central Committee of the Chinese Communist Party: From Mobilizers to Managers." *Asian Survey* 28:4 (April 1988), pp. 371–99.

Li Lianjiang and Kevin J. O'Brien. "Villagers and Popular Resistance in Contemporary China." *Modern China* 22:1 (January 1966), pp. 28–61.

Li Maoguan, "Why 'Laws Go Unenforced," *Beijing Review* (September 11–17, 1989), 17–19 and 26–27.

Li, Victor. "Law and Penology: Systems of Reform and Correction," in Michel Oksenberg, ed., *China's Developmental Experience* (New York: Praeger, 1973), pp. 144–56.

Lieberthal, Jane Lindsay. "From Cooperative to Commune: An Analysis of Rural Administrative Policy in China, 1955–58." M.A. Thesis, Political Science, Columbia University, 1971.

Lieberthal, Kenneth. *Governing China*. New York: Norton, 1995.

Lieberthal, Kenneth, and Michel Oksenberg. *Policymaking in China: Leaders, Structures, and Processes*. Princeton: Princeton University Press, 1988.

Lijphart, Arend. "Consociation and Federation: Conceptual and Empirical Links," *Canadian Journal of Political Science* 7:3 (September 1979), pp. 499–515.

Li, Linda Chelan. "Central-Provincial Relations in the People's Republic of China, Nature and Configurations: The Administration of Fixed Assets Investment in Shanghai and Guangdong since 1978." Ph.D. Dissertation, School of Oriental and African Studies, University of London, 1994.

Lin You Su. "Urban Migration in China: A Case Study of Three Urban Areas." Ph.D. Dissertation, Department of Geography, Australian National University, 1992.

Lindblom, Charles E. *Democracy and Market System*. Oslo: Norwegian University Press, 1988.

Lindblom, Charles E. *The Policy-Making Process*, 2nd ed. Englewood Cliffs: Prentice-Hall, 1980.

Lindenbaum, Bradley. "The Bifurcated State: Chinese Fiscal Structure and the Most Favored Nation Debate." Princeton University Senior Thesis, Woodrow Wilson School, 1992.

Link, Perry. *Evening Chats in Beijing: Probing China's Predicament*. New York: Norton, 1992.

Link, Perry. *Stubborn Weeds: Popular and Controversial Chinese Literature After the Cultural Revolution*. Bloomington: Indian University Press, 1983.

Linz, Juan. "Authoritarian and Totalitarian Regimes," in Fred Greenstein and Nelson Polsby, eds., *Handbook of Political Science*, vol. 3. Reading, MA: Addison-Wesley, 1975.

Lipset, Seymour Martin. *Political Man*. London: Heinemann, 1969.

Little, Daniel. *Understanding Peasant China: Case Studies in the Philosophy of Social Science*. New Haven: Yale University Press, 1989.

Little, Daniel. *Varieties of Social Explanation: An Introduction to the Philosophy of Social Science*. Boulder: Westview, 1991.

Liu Binyan. "People or Monsters," in *People or Monsters*, Perry Link, ed. Bloomington: Indiana University Press, 1983.

Liu Dahong. *Paintings, 1986–1992*. Hong Kong: Schoeni, 1992.

Liu Ya-ling. "Reform from Below: The Private Economy and Local Politics in Wenzhou." *China Quarterly*, 130 (June 1992), pp. 293–316.

Liu, Alan P. L. "Communications and Development in Post-Mao Mainland China." *Issues and Studies* 27:12 (December 1991), pp. 73–99.

Liu, Alan P. L. "The 'Wenzhou Model' of Development and China's Modernization." *Asian Survey* 22:8 (August 1992), pp. 696–711.

Lo, Leslie Nai-kwai. "State Patronage of Intellectuals in Chinese Higher Education." *Comparative Education Review* 35:4 (November 1991), pp. 690–720.

Lord, Bette Bao. *Legacies: A Chinese Mosaic*. New York: Knopf, 1990.

Lord, Bette Bao. *Spring Moon*. New York: Harper and Row, 1981.

Lull, James. *China Turned On: Television, Reform, and Resistance*. London: Routledge, 1991.

Lü Xiaobo. "Organizational Involution and Official Deviance: A Study of Cadre Corruption in China, 1949–93." Ph.D. Dissertation, University of California at Berkeley, Political Science, 1994.

Lyons, Thomas P. *Economic Integration and Planning in Maoist China*. New York: Columbia University Press, 1987.

Ma Xia. "On the Temporary Movement of the Rural Population." *Chinese Society and Anthropology* XXI:2 (1988–89), pp. 78–84.

McCormick, Barrett L. "Democracy or Dictatorship?" *AJCA* 31 (January 1994), pp. 91–105.

McCormick, Barrett L. *Political Reform in Post-Mao China: Democracy and Bureaucracy in a Leninist State*. Berkeley: University of California Press, 1990.

MacDougall, Bonnie S., ed. *Popular Chinese Literature and Performing Arts in the People's Republic of China, 1949–1979.* Berkeley: University of California Press, 1984.

Machiavelli, Niccolò. *The Prince*. Luigi Ricci, tr.; Christian Gauss, intro. New York: Mentor, 1952.

MacInnis, Donald E. *Religion in China Today: Policy and Practice*. Maryknoll, NY: Orbis, 1989.

Mackerras, Colin, and Amanda Yorke, eds. *Cambridge Handbook of Contemporary China*. Cambridge: Cambridge University Press, 1991.

Macleod, Roderick. *China, Inc.: How to do Business with the Chinese* [by an American businessman in Shanghai]. New York: Bantam, 1988.

Madison, James. "Federalist Paper No. 10," *The Federalist Papers*. Roy P. Fairfield, ed. Garden City, NY: Anchor, 1961, pp. 16–23.

Madsen, Richard. *Morality and Power in a Chinese Village*. Berkeley: University of California Press, 1984.

Madsen, Richard. "The Public Sphere: Civil Society and Moral Community." *Modern China* 19:2 (April 1993), pp. 183–198.

Malhotra, Angelina. "Shanghai's Dark Side: Army and Police Officers are Once Again in League with Vice." *Asia, Inc.* 3:2 (February 1994), pp. 32–39.

Manion, Melanie. *Public Policies, Social Norms, Private Interests: Cadre Retirement in Communist China*. Princeton: Princeton University Press, 1993.

Mannheim, Karl. *Ideology and Utopia: An Introduction to the Sociology of Knowledge*. London: Routledge, 1936.

March, James G., and Johan P. Olsen. "The New Institutionalism: Organizational Factors in Political Life." *American Political Science Review* 78:3 (March 1984), pp. 734–49.

Martz, John. Taiwanese Campaigning and Elections, 1991: An Outsider's View," *Studies in Comparative International Development* 27:2 (Summer 1992), pp. 84–94.

The Marx-Engels Reader, Second Edition. Robert C. Tucker, ed. New York: Norton, 1972, pp. 594–617.

Marx, Karl, and Frederick Engels. *Manifesto of the Communist Party*. Beijing: Foreign Languages Press, 1965.

Marx, Karl. "The Eighteenth Brumaire of Louis Bonaparte," in Robert C. Tucker, ed., *The Marx-Engels Reader*. New York: Norton, 1972, pp. 436–525.

Mayer, Arno J. *Dynamics of Counterrevolution in Europe, 1970–1956*. New York: Harper Torchbooks, 1971.

Mayer, Arno J. *The Persistence of the Old Regime: Europe to the Great War. New York: Pantheon, 1981.*

Meaney, Connie Squires. "Market Reform in a Leninist System: Some Trends in the Distribution of Power Strategy and Money in Urban China." *Studies in Comparative Communism* 22:2–3 (Summer-Autumn 1989), pp. 203–20.

Meyer, John W., and Brian Rowan. "Institutional Organizations: Formal Structure as Myth and Ceremony." *American Journal of Sociology* 83 (1977), pp. 340–363.

Michael Cohen, et al. "A Garbage Can Model of Organizational Choice." *Administrative Science Quarterly* (March 1972), pp. 1–25.

Migdal, Joel S. *Strong Societies and Weak States: State-Society Relations and State Capabilities in the Third World*. Princeton: Princeton University Press, 1988.

The Military Balance, 1988–1989. IISS, ed. London: International Institute for Strategic Studies, 1988.

Miller, H. Lyman. *Ideology, Science, and Authority in Dengist China*. Forthcoming.

Miller, Robert, ed. *The Development of Civil Society in Communist Systems*. London: Allen and Unwin, 1991.

Mitchell, Timothy. "The Limits of the State: Beyond Statist Approaches and their Critics." *American Political Science Review* 85:1 (March 1991), pp. 77–96.

Modern Western Ideologies and the May 4 Movement in China. Liu Guisheng, ed. Beijing: Qinghua Daxue Chuban She, 1989.

Moerman, Michael. "A Thai Village Headman as a Synaptic Leader," in *Modern Thai Politics*, rev ed. Clarke Neher, ed. London: Schenkman, 1979.

Mok Chiu Yu and J. Frank Harrison, eds. *Voices from Tiananmen Square: Beijing Spring and the Democracy Movement*. Montreal: Black Rose Books, 1990.

Morgan, Stephen L. "City-Town Enterprises in the Lower Changjiang (Yangtze) River Basin." M.A. Thesis in Asian Studies, University of Hong Kong, 1987.

Mosca, Gactano. *The Ruling Class*. New York: McGraw-Hill, 1939.

Moss, Hugh. *Some Recent Developments in Twentieth Century Chinese Painting. A Personal View*. Hong Kong: Umbrella, 1982.

Mote, Frederick W., and Lynn White. "Political Structure," Chapter 9, in Gilbert Rozman, *The Modernization of China*. New York: Free Press, 1981, pp. 255–351.

Mount, Ferdinand. *The Subversive Family: An Alternative History of Love and Marriage*. New York: Free Press, 1992.

Munro, Donald J. *The Concept of Man in Contemporary China*. Ann Arbor: University of Michigan Press, 1977.

Murphey, Rhoads. *Shanghai: Key to Modern China*. Cambridge: Harvard University Press, 1953.

Mushkat, Miron, and Adrian Faure. *Shanghai—Promise and Performance: Economic and Stock Market Review*. Hong Kong: Baring Securities, 1991.

Myers, James T. *Enemies Without Guns: The Catholic Church in the People's Republic of China*. New York: Paragon, 1991.

Nathan, Andrew J. *China's Crisis: Dilemmas of Reform and Prospects for Democracy*. New York: Columbia University Press, 1990.

Nathan, Andrew J. *Chinese Democracy*. Berkeley: University of California Press, 1985.

Nathan, Andrew J., and Shi Tianjian. "China's Ideological Landscape." *World Politics* (forthcoming).

Nathan, Andrew J., and Shi Tianjian. "Cultural Requisites for Democracy in China: Findings from a Survey." *Daedalus* (Spring 1993), pp. 95–123.

Naughton, Barry. "Industrial Policy during the Cultural Revolution," in W. Joseph et al., eds., *New Perspectives on the Cultural Revolution*. Cambridge: Harvard University Press, 1991, pp. 153–81.

Naughton, Barry. "False Starts and the Second Wind: Financial Reforms in China's Industrial System," in *The Political Economy of Reform in Post-Mao China*. Elizabeth

J. Perry and Christine Wong, eds. Cambridge: Harvard University Press, 1985, pp. 223–52.

New Directions in the Social Sciences and Humanities in China. Michael B. Yahuda, ed. New York: St. Martin's Press, 1987.

The New Institutionalism in Organizational Analysis. Walter W. Powell and Paul J. DiMaggio, eds. Chicago: University of Chicago Press, 1991.

Nicholas, Ralph W., "Factions: A Comparative Analysis." In Michael Banton, ed., *Political Systems and the Distribution of Power* (London: Tavistock, 1968), pp. 21–58.

Nolan, Peter & Dong Fureng, eds. *Market Forces in China: Competition & Small Business, The Wenzhou Debate*. London: Zed Books, 1990.

Nolan, Peter. *Growth Processes and Distributional Change in a South Chinese Province: The Case of Guangdong*. London: SOAS Contemporary China Institute, 1983.

Nolan, Peter. *The Political Economy of Collective Farms: An Analysis of China's Rural Reforms since Mao*. Cambridge: Polity Press, 1988.

Nolan, Peter, and Robert F. Ash. "China's Economy of the Eve of Reforms," *China Quarterly* 144 (December 1995), pp. 980–98.

North, Douglass C. *Institutions, Institutional Change, and Economic Performance*. Cambridge: Cambridge University Press, 1990.

Nozick, Robert. *Anarchy, State, and Utopia*. London: Blackwell, 1974.

O'Brien, Kevin J. *Reform Without Liberalization: China's National People's Congress and the Politics of Institutional Change*. New York: Cambridge University Press, 1990.

O'Brien, Kevin. "Chinese People's Congresses and Legislative Imbeddedness: Understanding Early Institutional Development." Draft of paper for *Comparative Political Studies*.

O'Brien, Kevin. "Implementing Political Reform in China's Villages." *The Australian Journal of Chinese Affairs* 32 (July 1994), pp. 33–59.

Oi, Jean C. "Fiscal Reform and the Economic Foundations of Local State Corporatism in China." *World Politics* 45:1 (October 1992), pp. 99–126.

Oi, Jean C. *State and Peasant in Contemporary China: The Political Economy of Village Government*. Berkeley: University of California, 1989.

Oksenberg, Michel and Bruce Dickson. "The Origins, Process, and Outcomes of Great Political Reform: A Framework for Analysis," in *Comparative Political Dynamics: Global Research Perspectives*, Dankwart Rustow and Kenneth Erickson, eds. New York: Harper and Row, 1991, pp. 235–61.

Oksenberg, Michel, and James Tong. "The Evolution of Central-Provincial Fiscal Relations in China, 1971–1984: The Formal System." *China Quarterly* 125 (March 1991), pp. 1–32.

Oksenberg, Michel. "Chinese Policy Process and the Public Health Issue: An Arena Approach." *Comparative Studies of Communism* (Winter 1974), pp. 375–412.

On Socialist Democracy and the Chinese Legal System. Anita Chan, Stanley Rosen, and Jonathan Unger, eds. Armonk: M.E. Sharpe, 1985.

Orr, Robert G. *Religion in China*. New York: Friendship Press, 1980.

Paltiel, Jeremy T. "China: Mexicanization or Market Reform," in James A. Caporaso, ed., *The Illusive State: International and Comparative Perspectives* (Newbury Park, CA: Sage, 1989), pp. 255–78.

Pan, Lynn. *The New Chinese Revolution*. Revised and updated ed. London: Penguin, 1987.

Pareto, Vilfredo. *The Rise and Fall of Elites*, intro. by Hans Zetterberg. New York: Arno Press, 1979.

Parish, William L., Xiaoye Zhe and Fang Li. "Nonfarm Work and Marketization of the Chinese Countryside." *China Quarterly* 143 (September 1995), pp. 697–728.

Parish, William L., and Martin K. Whyte. *Village and Family in Contemporary China*. Chicago: University of Chicago Press, 1978.

Parker, Geoffrey. *The Dutch Revolt*. Revised edition; Harmondsworth: Penguin, 1985.

Parsons, Talcott. *The Evolution of Societies*. Jackson Toby, ed. Englewood Cliffs: Prentice-Hall, 1977.

Parsons, Talcott. *The Social System*. Glencoe: Free Press, 1951.

Parsons, Talcott. *Societies: Evolutionary and Comparative Perspectives*. Englewood Cliffs: Prentice-Hall, 1966.

Parsons, Talcott. *The Structure of Social Action*. New York: Magraw-Hill, 1937.

Pas, Julian, ed., *The Turning of the Tide: Religion in China Today*. Hong Kong: Oxford University Press, 1989.

Pearson, Margaret M. "The Janus Face of Business Associations in China: Socialist Corporatism in Foreign Enterprises." *Australian Journal of Chinese Affairs* 31 (January 1994), pp. 25–46.

Pearson, Margaret M. *Joint Ventures in the People's Republic of China: The Control of Foreign Direct Investment Under Socialism*. Princeton: Princeton University Press, 1991.

Pearson, Veronica. "Law Rights, and Psychiatry in the People's Republic of China." *International Journal of Law and Psychiatry*, 15:1992, pp. 409–423.

Pearson, Veronica. *Mental Health Care in China*. London: Gaskell, 1995.

Pei Minxin. *From Reform to Revolution: The Demise of Communism in China and the Soviet Union*. Cambridge: Harvard University Press, 1994.

Peng Xizhe. *Demographic Transition in China: Fertility Trends since the 1950s*. Oxford: Oxford University Press, 1991.

Pensley, Danielle S. "The Socialist City?" [about Neubaugebeit Berlin-Hellersdorf]. Senior Thesis, Woodrow Wilson School, Princeton University, 1993.

Pepper, Stephen. *World Hypotheses: A Study in Evidence*. Berkeley: University of California Press, 1970.

Pepper, Suzanne. *China's Education Reform in the 1980s*. Berkeley: Center of Chinese Studies, University of California, 1990.

Perkins, Dwight, et al. *Rural Small-Scale Industry in the People's Republic of China*. Berkeley: University of California Press, 1977.

The Permanent Revolution: The French Revolution and its Legacy, 1989–1989. Geoffrey Best, ed. London: Fontana, 1988.

Perry, Elizabeth J. "Rural Violence in Socialist China." *China Quarterly*, No. 103 (September 1985), pp. 414–40;

Perry, Elizabeth J. "Labor Divided: Sources of State Formation in Modern China," in Joel S. Migdal, Atul Kohli, and Vivienne Shue, eds., *State Power and Social Forces*. New York: Cambridge University Press, 1994, pp. 143–73.

Perry, Elizabeth J. *Rebels and Revolutionaries in North China, 1845–1945*. Stanford: Stanford University Press, 1980.

Perry, Elizabeth J. *Shanghai on Strike: The Politics of Chinese Labor*. Boulder: Westview, 1995.

Perry, Elizabeth J. "The Shanghai Strike Wave of 1957." (Seen in manuscript form.)

Perry, Elizabeth J. and Li Xun. *Proletarian Power: Shanghai in the Cultural Revolution*. Boulder: Westview, 1996.

The Philosophy of Social Explanation. Alan Ryan, ed. Oxford: Oxford University Press, 1973.

Piven, Frances Fox, and Richard A. Cloward. *Poor People's Movements*. New York: Vintage, 1979.

Polanyi, Karl. *The Great Transformation: The Social and Economic Origins of our Time*. New York: Rinehart, 1944.

The Political Economy of Reform in Post-Mao China. Perry, Elizabeth J., and Christine Wong, eds. Cambridge: Harvard University Press, 1985.

The Politics of China, 1949–1989. Roderick MacFarquhar, ed. Cambridge: Cambridge University Press, 1993.

The Politics of the Developing Areas. Almond, Gabriel A., and James S. Coleman, eds. Princeton: Princeton University Press, 1960.

Polumbaum, Judy. "In the Name of Stability: Restrictions on the Right of Assembly in the People's Republic of China." *Australian Journal of Chinese Affairs* 26 (July 1991), pp. 43–64.

Popkin, Samuel L. *The Rational Peasant: The Political Economy of Rural Society in Vietnam*. Berkeley: University of California Press, 1979.

Popper, Karl R. *Conjectures and Refutations: The Growth of Scientific Knowledge*. New York: Harper, 1965.

Portes, Alejandro, Manuel Castells, and Lauren A. Benton, eds. *The Informal Economy*. Baltimore: Johns Hopkins University Press, 1989.

Poston, Jr., Dudley L., and Saochang Gu. "Socioeconomic Development, Family Planning, and Fertility in China," *Demography* 24:4 (November 1987), pp. 531–49.

Potter, Pitman B. "Riding the Tiger: Legitimacy and Legal Culture in Post-Mao China," *China Quarterly* 138 (June 1994), pp. 225–58.

Potter, Sulamith Heins and Jack M. Potter. *China's Peasants*. Cambridge; Cambridge University Press, 1990.

Prime, Penelope B. "Industry's Response to Market Liberalization in China: Evidence from Jiangsu Province." *Economic Development and Cultural Change* 41:1 (1992), 23–50.

The Pro-Democracy Protests in China; Reports from the Provinces. Unger, Jonathan, ed. Armonk: M.E. Sharpe, 1991.

Przeworski, Adam. *Democracy and the Market: Political and Economic Reforms in Eastern Europe and Latin America* (New York: Cambridge University Press, 1991).

Psychiatric Rehabilitation in China; Models for Change in a Changing Society. Michael R. Phillips, Veronica Pearson, and Ruiwen Wang, eds. Supplement 24 to the *British Journal of Psychiatry*, vol. 165 (August 1994), pp. 1–142.

Putnam, Robert. *Making Democracy Work*. Princeton: Princeton University Press, 1993.

Putterman, Louis. "Institutional Boundaries, Structural Change, and Economic Reform in China," *Modern China* 18:1 (January 1992), pp. 3–13.

Pye, Lucian W. *The Mandarin and the Cadre: China's Political Cultures*. Ann Arbor: Center for Chinese Studies, University of Michigan, 1988.

Rabb, Theodore K. *The Struggle for Stability in Early Modern Europe*. New York: Oxford University Press, 1975.

Rae, Douglas. *The Political Consequences of Electoral Laws*.

Ragin, Charles C. *The Comparative Method: Moving Beyond Qualitative and Quantitative Strategies*. Berkeley: University of California Press, 1987.

Rawski, Thomas. *Economic Growth and Employment in China*. New York: Oxford University Press, 1979.

The Re-emergence of the Chinese Peasantry. Saith, Ashwani, ed. London: Croom Helm, 1987.

Reform and Reaction in Post-Mao China: The Road to Tiananmen. Baum, Richard, ed. New York: Routledge, 1991.

Reform in China's Political System [special spring issue of *Chinese Law and Government*]. Stavis, Benedict, ed. Armonk: M.E. Sharpe, 1987.

Reforms and State Capacity: Changing Central-Local Relations in China. Jia Hao and Lin Zhiyuan, eds. Boulder: Westview, forthcoming.

Reinhard Bendix. *Nation-Building and Citizenship*. New York: Wiley, 1964.
Religion under Socialism in China. Luo Zhufeng, ed. Armonk: M. E. Sharpe, 1991.
Remaking the Economic Institutions of China and Eastern Europe. Nee, Victor, and David Stark, eds. Stanford: Stanford University Press, 1991.
The Restored Monarchy, 1660–1668. J. R. Jones, ed. London: Macmillan, 1979.
Reynolds, Bruce. *Reform in China: Challenges and Choices*. Armonk: M. E. Sharpe, 1987.
Richman, Barry. *Industrial Society in Communist China*. New York: Random House, 1969.
Rigger, Shelley. "Electoral Strategies and Political Institutions in the Republic of China on Taiwan." *Fairbank Center Working Papers*, No. 1. Cambridge, Mass.: Harvard University Fairbank Center, 1993.
Riker, William H. *Federalism: Origin, Operation, Significance*. Boston: Little, Brown, 1964.
Robert Michael Field, Nicholas R. Lardy, and John Philip Emerson. *Provincial Industrial Output in the People's Republic of China: 1949–75*. Washington: U.S. Department of Commerce, Bureau of Economic Analysis, 1976.
Rocca, Jean-Louis. "Corruption and its Shadow: An Anthropological View of Corruption in China." *China Quarterly*, 130 (June 1992), pp. 402–16.
Rocca, Jean-Louis. "Réprimer et rééduquer: Le traitement de la délinquance juvénile dans la municipalité de Shanghai," in *Shanghai dans les anneés 1980: études urbaines*, C. Henriot, ed. Lyon: Université Jean Moulin, Centre Rhônalpin de Recherche sur l'Extrême Orient Contemporain, 1989, pp. 106–144.
Roney, Jennifer. "Relaxing the Iron Hand: Crime under Perestroika." Senior Thesis, Politics Department, Princeton University, 1991.
Rosen, Stanley. "The Chinese Communist Party and Chinese Society: Popular Attitudes Toward Party Membership and the Party's Image," *Australian Journal of Chinese Affairs* 24 (July 1990), pp. 51–92.
Rosen, Stanley. "The Effect of Post-June 4 Re-education Campaigns on Chinese Students." Paper for the American Association of China Studies, 1992.
Rosen, Stanley, and David Chu. *Survey Research in the People's Republic of China*. Washington: United States Information Agency, 1987.
Roseneau, Pauline Marie. *Post-modernism and the Social Sciences: Insights, Inroads, and Intrusions*. Princeton: Princeton University Press, 1992.
Rowe, William T. *Hankow: Conflict and Community in a Chinese City, 1796–1895*. Stanford: Stanford University Press, 1989.
Rowe, William T. "The Problem of Civil Society in Late Imperial China," *Modern China* 19:2 (April 1993), pp. 139–157.
Rozelle, Scott. "Decision-making in China's Rural Economy: The Linkages between Village Leaders and Farm Households." *China Quarterly* 137 (March 1994), pp. 99–124.
Rozelle, Scott, and Richard N. Boisvert. "Quantifying Chinese Village Leaders' Multiple Objectives." *Journal of Comparative Economics* 18 (1994), pp. 25–45.
Rubin, Vitaly A. *Individualism and the State in Ancient China*, Steven Levine, ed. New York: Columbia University Press, 1976.
Rudé, George. *Revolutionary Europe, 1783–1815*. London: Fontana, 1964.
Rueschemeyer, Dietrich, et al., *Capitalist Development and Democracy*. Chicago: University of Chicago Press, 1991.
Rustow, Dankwart. "Transitions to Democracy: Toward a Dynamic Model," *Comparative Politics* 2:3 (1970), pp. 337–63.
Ryan, Alan. "Why Democracy?" *New York Times Book Review*, January 1, 1995, pp. 8–9.
Saich, Tony. *China's Science Policy in the 80s*. Atlantic Highlands, NJ: Humanities Press, 1989.

Saith, Ashwani, ed. *The Re-emergence of the Chinese Peasantry: Aspects of Rural Decollectivization*. London: Croom Helm, 1987.
Sangren, Stevan. "Traditional Chinese Corporations: Beyond Kinship." *Journal of Asian Studies* 43:3, pp. 391–415.
Sartori, Giovanni. "Concept Misformation in Comparative Politics," in *American Political Science Review* 64:4 (December 1970), pp. 1033–53.
Saso, Michael R. *Taoism and the Rite of Cosmic Renewal*. Pullman, WA: Washington State University Press, 1989.
SASS Papers (2). Zhang Zhongli et al., eds. Shanghai: Shanghai Academy of Social Sciences, 1988.
SASS Papers. Zhang Zhongli et al., eds. Shanghai: Shanghai Academy of Social Sciences, 1986.
Schattschneider, E.E. *The Semi-Sovereign People: A Realist's View of Democracy in America*, intro. by David Adamany. Hinsdale, IL: Dreyden Press, 1975.
Schelling, Thomas C. *Micromotives and Macrobehavior*. New York: Norton, 1978.
Schmitter, Philippe. "Still the Century of Corporatism?" in F. Pike and T. Stritch, eds., *The New Corporatism*. South Bend: Notre Dame, 1974.
Schneider, Ben Ross. *Politics Within the State: Elite Bureaucrats and Industrial Policy in Authoritarian Brazil*. Pittsburgh: University of Pittsburgh Press, 1991.
Schoeck, Helmut, and James W. Wiggins, eds. *Scientism and Values*. Princeton: D. Van Nostrand Co., 1960.
Schoenhals, Michael. "The Organization and Operation of the Central Case Examination Group (1966–1979): Mao's Mode of Cruelty." *China Quarterly* 145 (March 1996), pp. 87–111.
Schoenhals, Michael. *The Paradox of Power in a People's Republic of China Middle School*. Armonk: M.E. Sharpe, 1993.
Schoppa, Keith. *Xiang Lake [N. Zhejiang]: Nine Centuries of Chinese Life*. New Haven: Yale University Press, 1989.
Schorske, Carl E. *Fin-de-Siècle Vienna: Politics and Culture*. New York: Vintage, 1981.
Schram, Stuart, ed. *Chairman Mao Talks to the People*. New York: Pantheon, 1974.
Schumpeter, Joseph. *Capitalism, Socialism, and Democracy*, 3rd ed. , 1950.
Schurmann, Franz. *Ideology and Organization in Communist China*. Berkeley and Los Angeles: University of California Press, 1966.
Schwarcz, Vera. "Memory, Commemoration, and the Plight of China's Intellectuals." *Wilson Quarterly* (Autumn 1989), pp. 120–29.
Schwarcz, Vera. *The Chinese Enlightenment: Intellectuals and the Legacy of the May Fourth Movement of 1919*. Berkeley: University of California Press, 1986.
Scott, Ian. *Political Change and the Crisis of Legitimacy in Hong Kong*. Oxford: Oxford University Press, 1989.
Scott, James C. *Domination and the Arts of Resistance: Hidden Transcripts*. New Haven: Yale University Press, 1990.
Scott, James C. "Everyday Forms of Resistance," in Forrest D. Colburn, ed., *Everyday Forms of Peasant Resistance*. Armonk: M.E. Sharpe, 1989, pp. 3–30.
Scott, James C. *Weapons of the Weak: Everyday Forms of Peasant Resistance*. New Haven: Yale University Press, 1985.
Segal, Gerald. *China Changes Shape: Regionalism and Foreign Policy*. London: International Institute of Strategic Studies Adelphi Paper, 1994.
Seligman, Adam. *The Idea of Civil Society*. New York: Free Press, 1992.
Selznick, Philip. *The Organizational Weapon: A Study of Bolshevik Strategy and Tactics* (New York: McGraw-Hill, 1952).

Semsel, George S., ed. *Chinese Film: The State of the Art in the People's Republic*. New York: Praeger, 1987.

Seymour, James D. "China's Democracy Movement: What the Agenda has been Missing." Paper at the conference on "Rights in China: What Happens Next?" in London, June 28–29, 1991.

Seymour, James D. *China's Satellite Parties*. Armonk: M.E. Sharpe, 1987.

Shanghai dans les anneés 1980: études urbaines. Christian Henriot, ed. Lyon: Université Jean Moulin, Centre Rhônalpin de Recherche sur l'Extrême Orient Contemporain, 1989.

Shanghai Sojourners. Wakeman, Frederic, Jr., and Wen-hsin Yeh, eds. Berkeley: University of California Institute of Asian Studies, 1992.

Shanghai Statistical Yearbook, 1988 Concise Edition. Municipal Statistical Bureau of Shanghai. Beijing: China Statistical Publishing House, 1988.

Shanghai Statistical Yearbook, 1989 Concise Edition. Municipal Statistical Bureau of Shanghai. Beijing: China Statistical Publishing House, 1989.

Shapiro, Ian, and Donald P. Green. *Pathologies of Rational Choice Theory: A Critique of Applications in Political Science*. New Haven: Yale University Press, 1994.

Shirk, Susan L. *Competitive Comrades: Career Incentives and Student Strategies in China*. Berkeley: University of California Press, 1985.

Shirk, Susan L. *The Political Logic of Economic Reform in China*. Berkeley: University of California Press, 1993.

Shortell, Troy. "The Party-Building Campaign in China." Princeton University Senior Thesis, 1991.

Shue, Vivienne. "Beyond the Budget: Finance Organization and Reform in a Chinese County." *Modern China* 10:2 (April 1984), pp. 147–86.

Shue, Vivienne. "Emerging State-Society Relations in Rural China," in Irgen Delman, et al., eds. *Remaking Peasant China: Problems of Rural Development and Institutions at the Start of the 1990s* (Aarhus: Aarhus University Press, 1990), pp. 60–80.

Shue, Vivienne. "Grasping Reform: Economic Logic, Political Logic, and the State-Society Spiral." *China Quarterly* 144 (December 1995), pp. 1174–85.

Shue, Vivienne. "State Power and Social Organization in China." In Joel Migdal, Atul Kohli, and Vivienne Shue, eds. *State Power and Social Forces: Domination and Transformation in the Third World*. Cambridge: Cambridge University Press, 1994.

Shue, Vivienne. "State Power and Social Organization in China," in Joel S. Migdal, Atul Kohli, and Vivienne Shue, eds., *State Power and Social Forces*. New York: Cambridge University Press, 1994, pp. 65–88.

Shue, Vivienne. *The Reach of the State: Sketches of the Chinese Body Politic*. Stanford: Stanford University Press, 1988.

Siddiqul, Kamal. "The Emergence of Local Self-Government in Rural China." *The Journal of Social Studies* 64 (April 1994), pp. 48–72.

Silin, Robert, and Edwin A. Winckler. *China Provincial Economic Briefing Series: Guangdong*. Hong Kong: Consulting Group, BankAmerica Asia, Ltd., 1981.

Simon, Dennis Fred, and Detlef Rehn. *Technological Innovation in China: The Case of the Shanghai Semi-Conductor Industry*. Cambridge, Mass.: Ballinger, 1988.

Simon, Dennis Fred, and Merle Goldman, eds. *Science and Technology in Post-Mao China*. Cambridge: Harvard University Press, 1989.

Siu, Helen F. *Agents and Victims in South China: Accomplices in Rural Revolution*. New Haven: Yale University Press, 1989.

Siu, Helen F. *Furrows: Peasants, Intellectuals, and the State*. Stanford: Stanford University Press, 1990.

Siu, Helen F. "Recycling Rituals: Politics and Popular Culture in Contemporary Rural China." In *Unofficial China: Popular Culture and Thought in the People's Republic*, Perry Link, et al., eds. Boulder: Westview Press, 1989, pp. 121–37.

Siu, Helen F. "Socialist Peddlers and Princes in a Chinese Market Town." *American Ethnologist* 16:2 (May 1989), pp. 195–212.

Skilling, H. Gordon, and Franklyn Griffiths, eds. *Interest Groups in Soviet Politics*. Princeton: Princeton University Press, 1971.

Skilling, H. Gordon. *Samizdat and an Independent Society in Central and Eastern Europe*. Houndmills: Macmillan, 1989.

Skinner, G. William. *Leadership and Power in the Chinese Community of Thailand*. Ithaca: Cornell University Press, 1958.

Skinner, G. William. "Overseas Chinese Leadership: Paradigm for a Paradox," in Gehan Wijeyewardene, ed., *Leadership and Authority: A Symposium*. Singapore: University of Malaya Press, 1968, pp. 191–203.

Skinner, G. William, and Edwin A. Winckler. "Compliance Succession in Rural Communist China: A Cyclical Theory," in Amitai Etzioni, ed., *A Sociological Reader in Complex Organizations*, 2nd. ed. New York: Holt, Rinehart & Winston, 1969, pp. 410–38.

Skocpol, Theda. *States and Social Revolutions*. Cambridge: Cambridge University Press, 1979.

Smart, Alan. "Gifts, Bribes, and *Guanxi*: A Reconsideration of Bourdieu's Social Capital." *Cultural Anthropology* 8:3, pp. 388–408.

Smelser, Neil J. "The Rational Choice Perspective: A Theoretical Assessment," *Rationality and Society* 4:4 (October 1992), pp. 381–410.

Smelser, Neil J., and Talcott Parsons. *Economy and Society*. Glencoe, IL: Free Press, 1956.

Smil, Vaclav. *The Bad Earth: Environmental Degradation in China*. Armonk: M.E. Sharpe, 1984.

Smith, Karen. "In With the New: China's New Art, Post-1989." *Asian Art News* 3:1 (January-February 1993), pp. 32–39.

Smith, Richard. "The Chinese Road to Capitalism." *New Left Review* 199 (May-June 1993), pp. 55–99.

Solinger, Dorothy J. "China's Transients and the State: A Form of Civil Society?" *Politics and Society* 21:1 (March 1993).

Solinger, Dorothy J. "China's Urban Transients in the Transition from Socialism and the Collapse of the Communist Urban Public Goods Regime." *Comparative Politics* (January 1995), pp. 127–46.

Solinger, Dorothy J. *China's Transition from Socialism: Statist Legacies and Market Reforms, 1980–1990*. Armonk: M.E. Sharpe, 1993.

Solomon, Andrew. "The Fine Art of Protest." *Post Magazine*, January 23, 1994.

Solomon, Richard H. *Mao's Revolution and the Chinese Political Culture*. Berkeley: University of California Press, 1971.

Spruyt, Hendrik. *The Sovereign State and Its Competitors*. Princeton: Princeton University Press, 1995.

Stalinism. Robert C. Tucker, ed. New York: Norton, 1977.

State and Society in China: The Consequences of Reform. Rosenbaum, Arthur Lewis, ed. Boulder: Westview, 1992.

Stavis, Benedict. *Agricultural Mechanization in China*. Ithaca: Cornell University Press, 1978.

Stavis, Benedict. *China's Political Reforms: An Interim Report*. New York: Praeger, 1988.

Stepan, Alfred. *Rethinking Military Politics*. Princeton: Princeton University Press, 1991.

Stepan, Alfred. *The State and Society: Peru in Comparative Perspective*. Princeton: Princeton University Press, 1978.

Stone, Lawrence, and Jeanne C. Fawtier Stone. *An Open Elite? England, 1540–1880*, abridged ed. New York: Oxford University Press, 1986.

Strand, David. *Rickshaw Beijing: City People and Politics in the 1920s*. Berkeley: University of California Press, 1989.

Strecker, Erica. "The One-Child Campaign in Rural China: Limits on its Implementation and Success." Thesis for the Program in East Asian Studies, Georgetown University, 1994.

Streeck, Wolfgang, and Philippe Schmitter. "Community, Market, State - and Associations? The Prospective Contribution of Interest Governance to Social Order," in Streeck and Schmitter, eds. *Private Interest Government: Beyond Market and State*. Newbury Park, CA: Sage, 1985.

Street, John. "Popular Culture = Political Culture? Some Thoughts on Postmodernism's Relevance to Politics." *Politics* 11:2 (1991), pp. 20–25.

Su Xiaokang and Wang Luxiang. *Deathsong of the River: A Reader's Guide to the Chinese TV Series, Heshang*, tr. Richard W. Bodman and Pin P. Wang. Ithaca: Cornell University East Asia Program, 1991.

Suleiman, Ezra N. *Private Power and Centralization in France: The Notaires and the State*. Princeton: Princeton University Press, 1987.

Sung Yun-Wing. *Explaining China's Export Drive: The Only Success Among Command Economies*. Hong Kong: Chinese University Hong Kong Institute of Asia-Pacific Studies, 1991.

Suttmeier, Richard P. "Party Views of Science: The Record from the First Decade." *China Quarterly* 44 (October-December 1970), pp. 146–68.

Swire, Peter M. "The Onslaught of Complexity: Information Technologies and Developments in Legal and Economic Thought." Princeton University Senior Thesis, Woodrow Wilson School, 1980.

Tai Hung-chao. "The Oriental Alternative: An Hypothesis on Culture and Economy," in *Confucianism and Economic Development: An Oriental Alternative*. Washington: The Washington Institute Press, 1989.

Tai, Jeanne, ed. and tr. *Spring Bamboo: A Collection of Contemporary Chinese Short Stories*. New York: Random House, 1989.

Tanner, Murray Scot. *The Politics of Lawmaking in Post-Mao China: Institutions, Processes, and Democratic Prospects* (forthcoming).

Tatlow, Antony and Tak-Wai Wong, eds. *Brecht and East Asian Theatre*. Hong Kong: Hong Kong University Press, 1982.

Taylor, Charles. *Philosophy and the Human Sciences*. Cambridge: Cambridge University Press, 1985.

Thurston, Anne F. *Enemies of the People*. New York: Alfred Knopf, 1987.

Tian, G. "The Emergence of Shanghai's Role as an Entrepôt Centre Since the Mid-1980s," unpublished MS .

Tilly, Charles. *Big Structures, Large Processes, Huge Comparisons*. New York: Russell Sage Foundation, 1985.

Tilly, Charles. *From Mobilization to Revolution*. Reading, Mass.: Addison Wesley, 1978.

Tillyard, E. M. W. *The Elizabethan World Picture: A Study of the Idea of Order in the Age of Shakespeare, Donne and Milton*. New York: Vintage Books, n.d.

Todaro, Michael P. "A Model of Labor Migration and Urban Unemployment in Less Developed Countries." *American Economic Review* 59 (1969), pp. 138–48.

Tong Yanqi. "State, Society, and Political Change in China and Hungary." *Comparative Politics* 26:3 (April 1994), pp. 333–53.

"Towards Dominance of Technocrats and Leadership Stability: The Shanghai Leadership Change, 1976–1993" (anonymous article seen in manuscript form).
Towery, Britt. *The Churches of China*. Hong Kong: Amazing Grace Books, 1986.
Trimberger, Ellen Kay. *Revolution from Above: Military Bureaucrats and Development in Japan, Turkey, Egypt, and Peru*. New Brunswick, N.J.: Transaction Books, 1978.
Turner, Victor. *The Forest of Symbols: Aspects of Ndembu Ritual*. Ithaca: Cornell University Press, 1967.
Twentieth-Century Chinese Painting. Kao Mayching, ed. Oxford: Oxford University Press, 1988.
U.S. and Asia Statistical Handbook, 1993 Edition. Richard D. Fisher and Jason Bruzdzinski, eds. Washington: Heritage Foundation, 1993.
U.S. Congress, Joint Economic Committee. *China: A Reassessment of the Economy*. Washington: Government Printing Office, 1975.
U.S. National Foreign Assessment Center. *China: Gross Value of Industrial Output, 1965–77*. Washington: National Foreign Assessment Center, 1978
UNESCO. *Chinese Paintings: Catalogue of the Thirteenth UNESCO Travelling Exhibition*. Paris: UNESCO, 1979.
Unger, Jonathan. "China's Troubled Down to the Countryside Campaign." *Contemporary China* (1979), pp. 79–92.
Unger, Jonathan. "The Decollectivization of the Chinese Countryside: A Survey of Twenty-eight Villages." *Pacific Affairs* 58:4 (Winter 1985–86), pp. 585–606.
Unger, Jonathan. " 'Rich Man, Poor Man': The Making of New Classes in the Countryside." *China's Quiet Revolution: New Interactions Between State and Society*. David S. G. Goodman and Beverley Hooper, eds. New York: St. Martin's, 1994, pp. 43–63.
Unger, Jonathan, and Anita Chan. "China, Corporatism, and the East Asian Model." *Australian Journal of Chinese Affairs* 32 (January 1995), pp. 29–53.
Urban Spaces in Contemporary China: The Potential for Autonomy and Community in Post-Mao China. Deborah S. Davis, Richard Kraus, Barry Naughton, and Elizabeth Perry, eds. Cambridge: Cambridge University Press, 1993.
Urban, Michael E. *More Power to the Soviets: The Democratic Revolution in the USSR*. Worchester, UK: Elgar Publishing, 1990.
Ure, John. "Telecommunications with Chinese Characteristics." Unpublished paper, Hong Kong University Centre of Asian Studies, November 1993.
Versenyi, Laszlo. *Socratic Humanism*
Vogel, Ezra F. *One Step Ahead: Guangdong Under Reform*. Cambridge: Harvard University Press, 1989.
Wagner, Rudolf G. *The Contemporary Chinese Historical Drama: Four Studies*. Berkeley: University of California Press, 1990.
Wakeman, Frederic, Jr. "The Chinese Mirror," in Michel Oksenberg, ed. *China's Developmental Experience*. New York: Praeger, 1973, pp. 208–219.
Wakeman, Frederic, Jr. "The Civil Society and Public Sphere Debate: Western Reflections on Chinese Political Culture," *Modern China* 19:2 (April 1993), pp. 108–38.
Wakeman, Frederic, Jr. *History and Will:*
Wakeman, Frederic, Jr. "Models of Historical Change: The Chinese State and Society, 1839–1989," in Kenneth Lieberthal, Joyce Kallgren, Roderick MacFarquhar, and Frederic Wakeman, Jr., eds., *Perspective on Modern China: Four Anniversaries*. Armonk: M.E. Sharpe, 1991, pp. 68–102.
Wakeman, Frederic, Jr. *Policing Shanghai*. Berkeley: University of California Press, 1994.
Wakeman, Frederic, Jr. *Strangers at the Gate: Social Disorder in South China, 1839–1861*. Berkeley: University of California Press, 1966.

Walder, Andrew. *Communist Neo-Traditionalism: Work and Authority in Chinese Industry*. Berkeley: University of California Press, 1986.
Wang Hongying. "Transnational Networks and Foreign Direct Investment in China." Ph.D. Dissertation, Politics Department, Princeton University, 1996.
Wang Shaoguang. *Failure of Charisma: The Cultural Revolution in Wuhan*. Hong Kong: Oxford University Press, 1995.
Wang Shaoguang. "The Rise of the Second Budget and the Decline of State Capacity in China." Unpublished paper, apparently 1993.
The Waning of the Communist State. Andrew G. Walder, ed. Berkeley: University of California Press, 1995.
Wasserstrom, Jeffrey. *Student Protests in 20th C. China: The View from Shanghai*. Stanford: Stanford University Press, 1991.
Watson, Andrew. "New Structures in the Organization of Chinese Agriculture: A Variable Model." *Pacific Affairs* 57 (Winter, 1984–85), pp. 621–45. Waxman, Chaim ed. *The End of Ideology Debate*. New York: Funk and Wagnalls, 1968.
Weber, Eugen. *Peasants into Frenchmen*. Berkeley: University of California Press, 1977.
Weber, Max. *From Max Weber: Essays in Sociology*, H.H. Gerth and C. Wright Mills, eds. New York: Oxford University Press, 1958.
Weber, Max. *The Protestant Ethic and the Spirit of Capitalism*. New York: Scribner's, 1958.
Weber, Max. *The Religion of China*. Glencoe: Free Press, 1951.
Wei Lin and Arnold Chao, eds. *China's Economic Reforms*. Philadelphia: University of Pennsylvania Press, 1982.
Wei, Betty Pei t'i. *Shanghai: Crucible of Modern China*. Hong Kong: Oxford University Press, 1987.
Weldon, Thomas. *The Vocabulary of Politics*. Harmondsworth: Penguin, 1960.
Weller, Robert P. *Resistance, Chaos, and Control in China: Taiping Rebels, Taiwanese Ghosts, and Tiananmen*. Seattle: University of Washington Press, 1994.
Weller, Robert P. *Unities and Diversities in Chinese Religion*. Seattle: University of Washington Press, 1987.
White, Barbara-Sue. *Turbans and Traders: Hong Kong's Indian Communities*. Hong Kong: Oxford University Press, 1994.
White, Gordon. "Prospects for Civil Society: A Case Study of Xiaoshan City." *China's Quiet Revolution: New Interactions Between State and Society*. David S. G. Goodman and Beverley Hooper, eds. New York: St. Martin's, 1994, pp. 194–215.
White, Lynn and Li Cheng. "China Coast Identities: Region, Nation, and World," in Lowell Dittmer and Samuel Kim, eds. *China's Quest for National Identity*. Ithaca: Cornell Univ. Press, 1993, pp. 154–93.
White, Lynn. "A Political Demography of Shanghai after 1949," *Proceedings of the Fifth Sino-American Conference on Mainland China* (Taipei: Kuo-chi kuan-hsi yen-chiu so, 1976), reprinted serially in *Ming bao* (Bright News), Hong Kong, November 1976.
White, Lynn. "Agricultural and Industrial Values in China," in R. Wilson, S. Greenblatt, and A. Wilson, eds. *Value Change in Chinese Society*. New York: Praeger, 1979.
White, Lynn. "Bourgeois Radicalism in the 'New Class' of Shanghai," in James L. Watson, ed. *Class and Social Stratification in Post-Revolution China*. Cambridge: Cambridge University Press, 1984, pp. 142–74.
White, Lynn. *Careers in Shanghai: The Social Guidance of Individual Energies in a Developing Chinese City*. Berkeley and Los Angeles: University of California Press, 1978.
White, Lynn. "Changing Concepts of Corruption in Communist China," in Yu-ming

Shaw, ed. *Changes and Continuities in Chinese Communism: The Economy, Society, and Technology*. Boulder: Westview, 1988, pp. 316–53.

White, Lynn. "Deviance, Modernization, Rations, and Household Registration in Chinese Cities," in R. W. Wilson, S. Greenblatt, and A. Wilson, eds. *Deviance and Social Control in Chinese Society*. New York: Praeger, 1977, pp. 151–72.

White, Lynn. "Joint Ventures in a New Shanghai at Pudong," in Sally Stewart, ed., *Advances in Chinese Industrial Studies: Joint Ventures in the PRC*. Greenwich, CT: JAI Press, 1995, pp. 75–120.

White, Lynn. "Leadership and Participation: The Case of Shanghai's Managers," in Victor C. Falkenheim, ed., *Citizens and Groups in the People's Republic of China*. Ann Arbor: University of Michigan Press, 1986, pp. 189–211.

White, Lynn. "Leadership in Shanghai, 1955–69," in Robert A. Scalapino, ed. *Elites in the People's Republic of China*. Seattle: University of Washington Press, 1972, pp. 302–77.

White, Lynn. "Local Autonomy in China during the Cultural Revolution: The Theoretical Uses of an Atypical Case." *American Political Science Review* 70 (June 1976), pp. 479–91.

White, Lynn. "Low Power: Small Enterprises in Shanghai," *China Quarterly* 73 (March 1978), pp. 45–76.

White, Lynn. "Non-Governmentalism in the Historical Development of Modern Shanghai," in Laurence J.C. Ma and Edward W. Hanten eds., *Urban Development in Modern China*. Boulder: Westview, 1981, pp. 19–57.

White, Lynn. *Policies of Chaos: The Organizational Causes of Violence in China's Cultural Revolution*. Princeton: Princeton University Press, 1989.

White, Lynn. *Shanghai Shanghaied? Uneven Taxes in Reform China*. Hong Kong: Centre of Asian Studies, University of Hong Kong, 1989.

White, Lynn. "Shanghai's Polity in Cultural Revolution," in John W. Lewis, ed. *The City in Communist China*. Stanford: Stanford University Press, 1971, pp. 325–70.

White, Lynn. "Shanghai-Suburb Relations, 1949–1966," in Christopher Howe, ed. *Shanghai: Revolution and Development in an Asian Metropolis*. Cambridge: Cambridge University Press, 1981, pp. 241–68.

White, Lynn. "The Cultural Revolution as an Unintended Result of Administrative Policies," in W. Josephs, C. Wong, and D. Zweig, eds., *New Perspectives on the Cultural Revolution* (Cambridge: Harvard University Press, 1991), pp. 83–104.

White, Lynn. "The Liberation Army and the Chinese People." *Armed Forces and Society* I:3 (May 1975), pp. 364–83.

White, Lynn. "The Political Effects of Resource Allocations in Taiwan and Mainland China," *The Journal of the Developing Areas* 15 (October 1980), pp. 43–66.

White, Lynn. "The Road to Urumchi: Approved Institutions in Search of Attainable Goals." *China Quarterly* 79 (October 1979), pp. 481–510.

White, Lynn. "Workers' Politics in Shanghai." *Journal of Asian Studies* XXVI:1 (November 1976), pp. 99–116.

Whiting, Allen S. *The Chinese Calculus of Deterrence*. Ann Arbor: University of Michigan Press, 1975.

Whitson, William W. (with Huang Chen-hsia). *The Chinese High Command: A History of Military Politics*. New York: Praeger, 1973.

Who's Who in the People's Republic of China. Wolfgang Bartke, ed. Armonk: M. E. Sharpe, 1981.

Whyte, Martin K. and William Parish. *Urban Life in Contemporary China*. Chicago: University of Chicago Press, 1984.

Wickeri, Philip L. *Seeking the Common Ground*. New York: Orbis, 1988.

Wickham, Carrie Rosefsky. "Political Mobilization Under Authoritarian Rule: Explaining Islamic Activism in Mubarak's Egypt." Doctoral dissertation, Politics Department, Princeton University, 1996.

Wilkinson, Rupert. *Gentlemanly Power: British Leadership and the Public School Tradition, A Comparative Study in the Making of Rulers*. Oxford: Oxford University Press, 1964.

Williams, Howard. *Concepts of Ideology*. Sussex, UK: Wheatsheaf, 1988.

Wittgenstein, Ludwig. *Philosophical Investigations*. London: Blackwell, 1953.

Wittgenstein, Ludwig. *Tractatus Logico-Philosophicus*. London: Blackwell, 1973 reprint.

Wolf, Margery. *The House of Lim*. New York: Appleton, Century, Crofts, 1968.

Wolin, Sheldon S. *Politics and Vision*. Boston: Little, Brown, 1960.

Womack, Brantly. "Editor's Introduction: Media and the Chinese Public." *Chinese Sociology and Anthropology* 18 (1986), pp. 6–53.

Wong Siu-Lun. *Emigrant Entrepreneurs: Shanghai Industrialists in Hong Kong*. Hong Kong: Oxford University Press, 1988.

Wong, Christine. "Between Plan and Market: The Role of the Local Sector in Post-Mao China." *Journal of Comparative Economics* (1987), pp. 385–98.

Wong, Christine. "The Economics of Shortage and Problems of Reform in Chinese Industry." *Journal of Comparative Economics* (1986), pp. 363–87.

Wong, Christine. "Fiscal Reform and Local Industrialization." *Modern China* 18:2 (April 1992), pp. 197–227.

Woo, Margaret Y. K. "Legal Reforms in the Aftermath of Tiananmen Square." *Review of Socialist Law* 1991, pp. 51–74.

World Bank. *China: Revenue Mobilization and Tax Policy*. Washington: World Bank, 1990.

World Bank. *World Development Report, 1994*. New York: Oxford University Press, 1994.

The Wounded: New Stories of the Cultural Revolution. Geremie Barmé and Bennett Lee, eds. Hong Kong: Joint Publishing Company, 1979.

Wright, Joseph J., Jr. *The Balancing Act: A History of Modern Thailand*. Oakland: Pacific Rim Press, 1991.

Wu Dingbo and Patrick D. Murphy, eds. *Science Fiction from China*. New York: Praeger, 1989.

Wu Guanzhong. *Painting from the Heart: Selected Works of Wu Guanzhong*. Chengdu: Sichuan Art Publishing House, 1990.

Wu Guoguang. "Hard Politics with Soft Institutions: China's Political Reform in 1986–1989." Ph.D. Dissertation, Politics Department, Princeton University, 1995.

Wu, Victor. *Contemporary Chinese Painters 1*. Hong Kong: Hai Feng Publishing Co., 1982.

Xu Lilai. "China's Financial Reform in the 1990s: A Case Study of Financial Environment in Pudong New Area, Shanghai." *Journal of Asian Economics* 2:2 (Fall 1991), pp. 353–71.

Yabuki Susumu. *China's New Political Economy: The Giant Awakes*. Tr. Stephen M. Harner. Boulder: Westview, 1995.

Yan Yunxiang. *The Flow of Gifts: Reciprocity and Social Networks in a Chinese Village*. Stanford: Stanford University Press, 1995.

Yang Dali, "Making Reform: The Great Leap Famine and Rural Change in China." Princeton University Ph.D. Dissertation, Politics Department, December 1992.

Yang, Mayfair Mei-hui. "The Art of Social Relationships and Exchange in China." University of California, Berkeley, Ph.D. Dissertation in Anthropology, 1986.

Yang, Mayfair Mei-hui. *Gifts, Favors, & Banquets: The Art of Social Relationships in China*. Ithaca: Cornell University Press, 1994.

Yearbook on PLA Affairs, 1987. Richard H. Yang, ed. Kaohsiung: Sun Yat-sen Center for Policy Studies, 1987.

Yin Qiping and Gordon White. *The "Marketization" of Chinese Higher Education: A Critical Assessment.* Sussex, UK: University of Sussex, Institute of Development Studies, 1993.

You Long Gong, et al. "Cigarette Smoking in China." *Journal of the American Medical Association* 274:15 (October 18, 1995), pp. 1232–34.

Young, Iris M. *Justice and the Politics of Difference.* Princeton: Princeton University Press, 1990.

Young, Susan. *Private Business and Economic Reform in China.* Armonk: M.E. Sharpe, 1995.

Yu Jing Jie, et al. "A Comparison of Smoking Patterns in the People's Republic of China and the United States: An Impending Health Catastrophe for the Middle Kingdom," *Journal of the American Medical Association*, vol. 264, no. 12, pp. 1575–1579.

Yu Shiao-ling Shen. "The Cultural Revolution in Post-Mao Literature." University of Wisconsin, Madison, Ph.D. Dissertation, 1983.

Zafanolli, Wojtek. "China's Second Economy: Second Nature?" *Revue d'Etudes Est-Ouest*, 14:3 (September 1983), pp. 103–51.

Zang Xiaowei. "The Fourteenth Central Committee of the Chinese Communist Party." *Asian Survey* 33:8 (August 1993), pp. 787–803.

Zhang Mingwu, et al. *Chinese Qigong Therapy.* Jinan: Shandong Science and Technology Press, 1985.

Zhang Qingwu. "Basic Facts on the Household Registration System." *Chinese Economic Studies* 22:1 (1988).

Zheng Yongnian. "Institutional Change, Local Developmentalism, and Economic Growth: The Making of a Semi-Federal System in Reform China." Ph.D. Dissertation, Politics Department, Princeton University, 1995.

Zhou Xueguang. "Unorganized Interests and Collective Action in Communist China." *American Sociological Review* 58 (February 1993), pp. 54–73.

Zhou, Kate Xiao. *How the Farmers Changed China.* Boulder: Westview, 1996 (and Ph.D. Dissertation, Politics Department, Princeton University, 1994).

Zhou, Kate Xiao, and Lynn White. "Quiet Politics and Rural Enterprise in Reform China." *The Journal of the Developing Areas* 29 (July 1995), pp. 461–90.

Zweig, David. *Agrarian Radicalism in China, 1968–1981.* Cambridge: Harvard University Press, 1989.

Zweig, David. "Rural Industry: Constraining the Leading Growth Sector in China's Economy," in Joint Economic Committee, *China's Economic Dilemmas in the 1990s: The Problems of Reforms, Modernization, and Interdependence.* Washington: Government Printing Office, 1991, pp. 418–36.

Materials in Chinese

Bao Ligui. *Jinxian dai difang zhengfu bijiao* (Comparative Modern Local Government). Beijing: Guangming Ribao Chuban She, 1988.

Baoshan xian zhi (Baoshan County Gazetteer). Zhu Baohe, ed. Shanghai: Shanghai Renmin Chuban She, 1992.

Bo Fengcheng. "*Zhonggong nongye xiandai hua zhengce zhi fenxi*" (An Analysis of CCP Rural Modernization Policy). Taipei: National Chengchi University M.A. Thesis, 1978.

Cao Linzhang, Gu Guangqing, and Li Jianhua. *Shanghai shengchan ziliao suoyu zhi jiegou yanjiu* (Studies of Shanghai Production and Ownership Structure). Shanghai: Shanghai Shehui Kexue Yuan Chuban She, 1987.

Chen Baoliang. *Zhongguo liumang shi* (The History of Chinese Hooliganism). Beijing: Zhongguo Shehui Kexue Chuban She, 1993.

Chen Benlin, et al. *Gaige kaifang shenzhou jubian* (Great Change in the Sacred Land [China] During Reform and Opening). Shanghai: Jiaotong Daxue Chuban She, 1984.

Chen Dongsheng and Chen Jiyuan. *Zhongguo diqu jingji jiegou yanjiu* (Studies on the Structure of China's Spatial Economy). Taiyuan: Shanxi Renmin Chuban She, 1988.

Chen Minzhi, et al. *Shanghai jingji fazhan zhanlue yanjiu* (Studies of Shanghai's Economic Development Strategy). Shanghai: Shanghai Renmin Chuban She, 1985.

Chen Minzhi, Xue Chao, and Gu Jirui, et al. *Gaige de zuji: Nanjing jingji tizhi zonghe gaige jishi* (Footprints of Reform: Notes on the Comprehensive Reform of Nanjing's Economic System). Shanghai: Shanghai Shehui Kexue Yuan Chuban She, 1988.

Chen Yifei. *Chen Yifei huigu zhan* (Chen Yifei: A Retrospective). Hong Kong: Plum Blossoms, Ltd., 1992.

Chengshi he jingji qu (Cities and Economic Regions). Li Zhongfan, et al., eds. Fuzhou: Fujian Renmin Chuban She, 1984.

Chengshi shengtai jingji lilun yu shixian (The Theory and Practice of Urban Environmental Economics). Chen Yuqun, ed. Shanghai: Shanghai Shehui Kexue Yuan Chuban She, 1988.

Chongming dongtan tanyu ziyuan kaifa liyong shishi guihua zonghe yanjiu baogao (Summary Research Report on the Plan to Realize and Opening and Use of Beach Resources on the Chongming East Coast). Shanghai Environmental Economics Society, ed. Shanghai: Shanghai Shi Shengtai Jingji Xuehui, 1990.

Chongming xian zhi (Chongming County Gazetteer). Zhou Zike, ed. Shanghai: Shanghai Renmin Chuban She, 1989.

Chuansha xian jianshe zhi (Chronicle of Construction in Chuansha County). Wu Side, ed. Shanghai: Shanghai Shehui Kexue Chuban She, 1988.

Chuansha xian zhi (Chuansha County Gazetteer). Zhu Hongbo, ed. Shanghai: Shanghai Renmin Chuban She, 1990.

Dalu hunyin jicheng fa (Mainland Marriage and Inheritance Law). Xu Penghua and Chang Feng, eds. Taibei: Weili Falü Chuban She reprint of a PRC case book, 1989.

Dalu ruhe jiejue minshi jiufen (How the Mainland Solves Civil Disputes). Chang Feng, Yang Jiandong, and Qiu Haiyang, eds. Taibei: Weili Falü Chuban She reprint of a PRC case book, 1988.

Dangdai Zhongguo de guangbo dianshi (Radio and Television in China Today), two volumes. Li Hua, et al., eds. Beijing: Zhongguo Shehui Kexue Chuban She, 1987.

Dangdai Zhongguo de guding zichan guanli (Fixed Asset Investments and Management in Contemporary China). Zhou Daojiong, ed. Beijing: Zhongguo Shehui Kexue Chuban She, 1989.

Dangdai Zhongguo de Jiangsu (Jiangsu in Today's China). Liu Dinghan et al., eds. Beijing: Zhongguo Shehui Kexue Chuban She, 1989.

Dangdai Zhongguo de jingji tizhi gaige (Reform of the Economic System in Modern China). Zhou Taihe, et al., eds. Beijing: Zhongguo Shehui Kexue Chuban She, 1984.

Dangdai Zhongguo de nongye jixie hua (Agricultural Mechanization in Contemporary China). Wu Shaowen, ed. Beijing: Zhongguo Shehui Kexue Yuan, 1991.

Dangdai Zhongguo de renkou (Population in China Today). Xu Dixin, et al., eds. Beijing: Zhongguo Shehui Kexue Chuban She.

Ding Richu, "*Xinhai geming qian Shanghai ziben jia de zhengzhi huodong*" (The Political Activities of Shanghai Capitalists before the Xinhai Revolution). In *Jindai Zhongguo zichan jieji yanjiu* (Studies on China's Capitalist Class in Recent Times), Fudan History Department, ed. Shanghai: Fudan Daxue Chuban She, 1983, 501–23.

Fahui guangrong chuantong, minrong shehui kexue (Develop the Glorious Tradition, Let

Social Science Prosper). Guo Jiafu et al., eds. Shanghai: Shanghai Shehui Kexue Yuan Chuban She, 1985.

Fang Litian. *Zhongguo Fojiao yu chuantong wenhua* (Chinese Buddhism and Traditional Culture). Shanghai: Renmin Chuban She, 1988.

Fazhan zhong de hengxiang jingji lianhe (Horizontal Economic Links in Development). Bureau for Economic System Reform, State Economic Commission, ed. Beijing: Qiye Guanli Chuban She, 1986.

Fei Xiaotong and Luo Hanxian. *Xiangzhen jingji bijiao moshi* (Comparative Models for Rural and Township Economies). Chongqing: Chongqing Chuban She, 1988.

Fengxian xian zhi (Fengxian County Gazetteer). Yao Jinxiang, ed. Shanghai: Shanghai Renmin Chuban She, 1987.

Fengxian yanzheng zhi (Gazeteer of the Salt Monopoly in Fengxian). Liu Guolun, ed. Shanghai: Shanghai Shehui Kexue Chuban She, 1987.

Fudan Daxue de gaige yu tansuo (Reforms and Explorations at Fudan University). Fudan Daxue Gaodeng Jiaoyu Yanjiu Suo, ed. Shanghai: Fudan Daxue Chuban She, 1987.

Gaige mianlin zhidu chuangxin (The Reforms are Faced with System Innovation). Development Research Institute, ed. Shanghai: Sanlian Shudian, 1988.

Gaige zhong de funü wenti (Women's Issues in the Reforms). Zhang Lianzhen, ed. Nanjing: Jiangsu Renmin Chuban She, 1988.

Gaige zhong de shehui zhuyi suoyou zhi (Socialist Ownership Systems in the Middle of Reforms). Shanghai Economics Association, ed. Shanghai: Shanghai Shehui Kexue Yuan Chuban She, 1987.

Gaige: Women mianlin de wenti yu silu (Reforms: The Problems and Options that Face Us). Research Institute for the Reform of China's Economic Structure, ed. Beijing: Jingji Guanli Chuban She, 1987.

Ge Xiangxian and Qu Weiying, *Zhongguo mingong chao: "Mangliu" zhenxiang lu* (China's Tide of Labor: A Record of the True Facts about the "Blind Floaters"). Beijing: Zhongguo Guoji Guangbo Chuban She, 1990.

Gonghui jichu zhishi (Basic Knowledge about Trade Unions). All-China Federation of Trade Unions, ed. Beijing: Jingji Kexue Chuban She, 1987.

Guangdong sheng tongji nianjian (Guangdong Province Statistical Yearbook), various years, Guangdong Province Statistics Bureau, ed. Beijing: Zhongguo Tongji Chubanshe.

Guangzhou jingji, 1988 (The Economy of Guangzhou, 1988). Survey Office, Guangzhou People's Government, ed. Guangzhou: Zhongshan Daxue Chuban She, 1988.

Guangzhou tongji nianjian (Guangzhou Statistical Yearbook), various years. Guangzhou Municipal Statistics Bureau, ed. Beijing: Zhongguo Tongji Chuban She.

Gufen jingji yanjiu (Studies in the Economics of Shares). Shanghai Economics Association, ed. Shanghai: Shanghai Shehui Kexue Yuan Chuban She, 1987.

Guomin shouru tongji ziliao huibian, 1949–1985 (Collected Statistical Materials on National Income, 1949–1985). State Statistical Bureau, ed. Beijing: Zhongguo Tongji Chuban She, 1987.

He Mengbi and Duan Haoran. *Zhongguo gongchan dang liushi nian* (Sixty Years of the CCP). Beijing: Jiefang Jun Chuban She, 1984.

Hengxiang jingji lianhe de xin fazhan (The New Development of Horizontal Economic Links). Shanghai Economics Association, ed. Shanghai: Shanghai Shehui Kexue Yuan Chuban She, 1987.

Hong Ze, et al. *Shanghai yanjiu luncong: Di yi ji* (Papers on Studies of Shanghai: First Set). Shanghai: Shanghai Shehui Kexue Yuan Chuban She, 1988.

Hongliu zhong de renmen: Jiangsu qiye jia baogao wenxue ji (People in the Torrent [of reforms]: The Report Literature on Jiangsu Entrepreneurs). Shanghai: Shanghai Shehui Kexue Yuan Chuban She, 1988.

Hou Jun. *Piruan de yulun jiandu* (The Worn-Out Guidance of Public Opinion). Beijing: Zhongguo Funü Chuban She, 1989.

Hu Fanzhu. *Yumo yuyan xue* (The Linguistics of Jokes). Shanghai: Shanghai Shehui Kexue Yuan Chuban She, 1987.

Hua Daming. "*Xiangban chang dui nonggong de guofen bodu ying yinqi zhuyi*" (The Overexploitation of Peasant Workers by Township-run Factories Calls for Attention). *Shehui* (Society), No. 2, 1990 (Shanghai), pp. 12–13.

Huadong tongji nianjian, (Statistical Yearbook of East China), various years to 1993. Statistical Information Network of the East China Region, ed. Beijing: Zhongguo Tongji Chuban She.

Jiading xian shedui gongye zhi (Records of Industry in Communes and Teams of Jiading County [Shanghai]). Group to Edit the Records of Industry in Communes and Teams of Jiading County, ed. Shanghai: Shanghai Shehui Kexue Yuan Chuban She, 1988.

Jiading xian zhi (Jiading County Gazetteer). Yang Yubai, ed. Shanghai: Shanghai Renmin Chuban She, 1992.

Jiangsu jingji he shehui fazhan gaikuang (The Development of Jiangsu's Economy and Society). Jiangsu Sheng Renmin Zhengfu Jingji Yanjiu Zhongxin [Yang Jiaxiang, et al.], ed. Nanjing: Jiangsu Renmin Chuban She, 1984.

Jiangsu jingji nianjian (Jiangsu Economic Yearbook), various years. *Jiangsu jingji nianjian* Bianji Weiyuanhui, ed. Nanjing: Jiangsu Renmin Chuban She, same year.

Jiangsu sheng dashi ji, 1949–1985 (Chronology of Jiangsu, 1949–1985). "Dangdai Zhongguo de Jiangsu" Editorial Committee and Jiangsu Provincial Records Bureau, eds. Nanjing: Jiangsu Renmin Chuban She, 1988.

Jiangsu tongji nianjian 1991 (Jiangsu Statistical Yearbook, 1991), various years. Jiangsu Statistical Bureau, ed. Nanjing: Zhongguo Tongji Chuban she, 1991).

Jiangsu xiangzhen gongye fazhan shi (History of the Development of Jiangsu Rural Industry). Mo Yuanren, ed. Nanjing: Nanjing Gongxue Yuan Chuban She, 1987.

Jiaoyu jingfei yu jiaoshi gongzi (Educational Funds and Teachers' Salaries). State Education Commission, Educational Funds Research Unit, ed. Beijing: Jiaoyu Kexue Chuban She, 1988.

Jihui youxing shiwei fa jianghua (Talking about the Law on Assemblies, Parades, and Demonstrations). Propaganda Office of the Judicial Department of the People's Republic of China, ed. Beijing: Falü Chuban She, 1990.

Jindai Shanghai da shi ji (Chronology of Modern Shanghai [1840 to 1918]). Tang Zhijun, ed. Shanghai: Shanghai Cisu Chuban She, 1987.

Jingji fazhan zhanlue wenti lunwen ji (Collection of Essays on Issues of Economic Development Strategy). Shanghai Municipal Economic Association, ed. Shanghai: Shanghai Shih Jingji Xuehui, 1984.

Jingji tizhi gaige tansuo wenji (Collection of Documents Exploring the Economic System Reform). Shanghai Municipal Economic Association, ed. Shanghai: Shanghai Shi Jingji Xuehui, 1985.

Jingji xue tansuo de fengshuo chengguo: Shanghai shi jingji xuehui 1979–1985 nian huojiang sunwen ji (Rich Fruits from Explorations in Economics: Collected Prizewinning Shanghai Economics Association Theses, 1979–1985). Shanghai: Shanghai Shehui Kexue Yuan Chuban She, 1988.

Jinshan xian zhi (Jinshan County Gazetteer). Zhu Yanchu, ed. Shanghai: Shanghai Renmin Chuban She, 1990.

Jiu Zhongguo de Shanghai guangbo shiye (Broadcasting Enterprises in the Shanghai of

Old China, 1923–49). Liu Guangqing, ed. Shanghai: Zhongguo Guangbo Dianshi Chuban She, 1985.

Jushi zhumu de banian (1978–1986): Zhongguo fazhan yu gaige jishi (Eight Years Attracting Attention Worldwide [1978–1986]: A Chronicle of China's Development and Reforms. Chinese Economic System Reform Research Institute, ed. Chengdu: Sichuan Renmin Chuban She, 1987.

Lei Ge. *Fansi gongping* (Reflections on Justice). Beijing: Zhongguo Funü Chuban She, 1989.

Li Pan, Li Douheng, and Chu Zhongxin, et al. *Gaige yu kaifang xin wenti yanjiu* (Studies of New Questions in Reform and Opening). Shanghai: Shanghai Shehui Kexue Yuan Chuban She, 1987.

Liao Mei. *Shinian lai Fudan daxue xuesheng shetuan de fazhan qi qushi* (The Development and Tendency of Fudan University Student Associations over the Past Ten Years), a proposal for academic exchange among Fudan University, Taiwan National University and Hongkong University students, January, 1989.

Lin Qibing and Chen Hua. *Fu-Ri de shengchan fangshi* (The Fujian-Japan Method of Production). Shanghai: Shanghai Shehui Kexue Yuan Chuban She, 1987.

Liu Gang, et al. *Shanghai chengshi jiti suoyou zhi gongye yanjiu* (Studies of Shanghai's Urban Collective Industries). Shanghai: Shanghai Renmin Chuban She, 1980.

Liu Guoguang. *Zhongguo jingji fazhan zhanlue wenti yanjiu* (Studies on Issues of China's Economic Development Strategy).

Liudong renkou dui da chengshi fazhan de yinxiang ji duice (Policies on the Influence of Transient Population for the Development of Large Cities). Li Mengbai, et al., eds. Beijing: *Jingji ribao* Chuban She, 1991.

Liuwu qijian woguo chengzhen jumin jiating shouzhi diaocha ziliao (Survey of Residential Families' Incomes and Expenditures in Our Country's Cities and Towns during the Sixth Five-Year Plan). State Statistical Bureau, Urban Survey Group, ed. Beijing: Zhongguo Tongji Chuban She, 1988.

Lu Feiyun. "*Zhuanye chengbao zhe—Yige xin jieceng de quqi*" (Specialized Contractors—The Origins of a New Stratum). *Shehui* (Society), No. 3, 1990 (Shanghai), pp. 30–31.

Luo Zhufeng, et al. *Zhongguo shehui zhuyi shiqi de zongjiao wenti* (Problems of Religion in China's Socialist Period). Shanghai: Shanghai Shehui Kexue Yuan Chuban She, 1987.

Ma Hong and Sun Shangqing. *Zhongguo jingji jiegou wenti yanjiu* (Studies on China's Economic Structure). Beijing: Renmin Chuban She, 1980.

Min Qi. *Zhongguo zhengzhi wenhua: Minzhu zhengzhi nanchan de shehui xinli gusu* (China's Political Culture: Social-Psychological Factors Inhibiting the Birth of Democratic Politics). Kunming: Yunnan Renmin Chuban She, 1989.

Minzhu shengyue duchang gequ xuan (Selection of Folk Music Solos). Shanghai: Shanghai Yinyue Chuban She, 1990.

Mubiao, zhongdian, duice—Tan Shanghai chuantong gongye de jishu gaizao (Goals, Keypoints, and Policies - On the Technical Reform of Shanghai's Traditional Industries). Shanghai Municipal Enterprise Management Association, ed. Shanghai: Shanghai Shi Qiye Guanli Xiehui, 1985.

"Pipan" Beijing ren?! ("Criticize" Beijing Man?!). Luo Shuang, et al., eds. Beijing: Zhongguo Shehui Chuban She, 1994.

Qi Shaohua. *Guanliao zhuyi zhongzhong* (Various Kinds of Bureaucratism). Shanghai: Renmin Chuban She, 1988.

Qingpu xian zhi (Qingpu County Gazetteer). Feng Wenxue, ed. Shanghai: Shanghai Renmin Chuban She, 1990.

Qiye gaige yu fazhan xinlu: Shanghai gongye qiye hengxiang lianhe diaocha baogao ji (The Reform of Enterprise and the New Road to Development: A Collection of Investigation Reports on Horizontal Integration in Shanghai Industrial Enterprises). Fudan University Economic Research Center, ed. Shanghai: Fudan Daxue Chuban She, 1988.

Quanguo ge sheng zizhi qu zhixia shi lishi tongji ziliao huibian, 1949–1989 (Historical Statistics Collection on Provinces, Autonomous Regions, and Municipalities Throughout the Country, 1949–1989). State Statistical Bureau, ed. Beijing: Zhongguo Tongji Chuban She, 1990.

Shanghai chuanshu (Shanghai Encyclopedia). Chu Dawei, ed. Shanghai: Xuelin Chuban She, 1989.

Shanghai dangzheng jigou yange, 1949–1986 (The Evolution of Shanghai Party and Government Organization, 1949–1986). Cao Jin, ed. Shanghai: Shanghai Renmin Chuban She, 1988.

Shanghai difang shi ziliao (wu): Xinwen, chuban (Materials on the Local History of Shanghai [5]: Journalism and Publishing). Shanghai Literary History House, ed. Shanghai: Shanghai Shehui Kexue Yuan Chuban She, 1986.

Shanghai dixia dangzhi yuan Huazhong kang-Ri genju di (Shanghai's Underground Party Branches Helping the Anti-Japanese Base Areas in Central China). Zheng Gongliang, ed. Shanghai: Huadong Shifan Daxue Chuban She, 1987.

Shanghai Duiwai Kaifang de "Kaifang Du" Yanjiu Keti Zu (Research Group on Shanghai's "Degree of Openness" to the Outside), *Shanghai duiwai kaifang de "kaifang du" yanjiu* (Study of the Degree of Shanghai's Openness to the Outside), (Shanghai: Shanghai Shehui Kexue Yuan, 1988).

Shanghai gaoji zhuanjia minglü (Who's Who of Shanghai High-Level Specialists). Liu Zhenyuan, ed. Shanghai: Shanghai Kexue Jishu Chuban She, 1992.

Shanghai gongan nianjian, 1988 (Shanghai Public Security Yearbook, 1988) (*neibu*, photocopy reprint sold in Hong Kong, 515 pages). "Shanghai Gongan Nianjian" Editorial Department, ed. Shanghai: Shanghai Shehui Kexue Chuban She, 1988.

Shanghai gongye jiegou lishi yange ji xiankuang (The Historical Evolution and Present Situation of Shanghai's Industrial Structure). Shanghai Statistical Bureau, ed. Shanghai: Shanghai Tongji Ju, 1987.

Shanghai guoji yinyue bisai, 1987 Zhongxi bei, Zhongguo fengge gangqin qu, Huojiang zuopin ji (Shanghai International Music Competition, 1987 China-West Album of Prizewinning Piano Competitions in Chinese Style). Shanghai: Shanghai Yinyue Chuban She, 1989.

Shanghai Jiaotong Daxue guanli gaige chutan (Preliminary Research on the Management Reform at Shanghai's Jiaotong University). Shanghai Jiaotong University, Communist Party Committee Office, ed. Shanghai: Jiaotong Daxue Chuban She, 1983.

Shanghai jiaoyu fazhan zhanlue yanjiu (Research on a Strategy for Shanghai's Educational Development). Task Force on Shanghai Educational Development Strategy, ed. Shanghai: Fudan Daxue Chuban She, 1988.

Shanghai jiaoyu fazhan zhanlue yanjiu baogao (Research Report on the Strategy of Shanghai's Educational Development). Kang Yonghua, Liang Chenglin, and Tan Songhua, eds. Shanghai: Huadong Shifan Daxue Chuban She, 1989.

Shanghai jiaoyu, 1988 (Shanghai Education, 1988). Wang Shenghong, ed. Shanghai: Tongji Daxue Chuban She, 1989.

Shanghai jingji 1949–1982 (Shanghai's Economy, 1949–1982). Xu Zhihe, Ding Richu, Jin Liren, Wang Zhiping et al, eds. (Shanghai Academy of Social Sciences). Shanghai: Shanghai Renmin Chuban She, 1983.

Shanghai jingji 1983–1985 (Shanghai's Economy, 1983–1985). Xu Zhihe, Ling Yan, Gu

Renzhang et al, eds. (Shanghai Academy of Social Sciences). Shanghai: Shanghai Renmin Chuban She, 1986.

Shanghai jingji 1987 (Shanghai's Economy, 1987). Xu Zhihe, Ling Yan, Gu Renzhang, et al., eds. (Shanghai Academy of Social Sciences). Shanghai: Shanghai Renmin Chuban She, 1987.

Shanghai jingji nianjian (Shanghai Economic Yearbook, various years). Often Xiao Jun, et al., at the Shanghai Academy of Social Sciences, ed. Shanghai: Shanghai Renmin Chuban She or "Shanghai Jingji Nianjian" Chuban She, published in the same year.

Shanghai jingji qu de jianli yu fazhan (The Establishment and Development of the Shanghai Economic Zone). World Economic Herald and Shanghai Economic Zone Research Society, co-eds. Shanghai: Zhongguo Zhanwang Chuban She, 1984.

Shanghai jingji qu fazhan zhanlue chutan (Preliminary Research on the Development Strategy of the Shanghai Economic Zone). World Economic Herald and Shanghai Economic Zone Research Society, co-eds. Shanghai: Wuxi Branch of Shanghai Eighth People's Printers, 1986.

Shanghai jingji qu gongye gaimao (General Description of Industry in the Shanghai Economic Zone), thirty volumes. Shanghai Economic Association, ed. Shanghai: Jiaotong Daxue Chuban She, 1985 and 1986.

Shanghai jingji qu qiye jituan gaixian (Summary on Enterprise Groups in the Shanghai Economic Zone). Shen Jianzheng, Tong Wensheng, and Dai Xianru, eds. Shanghai: Baijia Chuban She, 1988.

Shanghai jingji, neibu ben: 1949–1982 (Shanghai Economy, Internal [i.e. classified] Volume: 1949–1982). Shanghai Academy of Social Sciences, ed. Shanghai: Shanghai Shehui Kexue Yuan Chuban She, 1984.

Shanghai keji, 1949–1984 (Shanghai Science and Technology, 1949–1984). Wei Hu and Fang Kaibing, eds. Shanghai: Kexue Jishu Wenxian Chuban She, 1985.

Shanghai liudong renkou (Shanghai's Floating Population). Shanghai Statistics Bureau, ed. Shanghai: Zhongguo Tongji Chuban She, 1989.

Shanghai nongcun shehui jingji (The Economy of Shanghai Rural Society). Shanghai Municipal Statistics Bureau, ed. Shanghai: Shanghai Shehui Kexue Chuban She, 1989.

Shanghai Pudong kaifa yu touzi (Development and Investment in Pudong, Shanghai). Hong Kong: Jingji Daobao Chuban She, n.d. apparently 1990.

Shanghai Pudong Xinqu fazhan qianjing yu touzi zhengce (Development Prospects and Investment Policies in Shanghai's Pudong New Area). Economic Information Center, ed. Shanghai: Kexue Jishu Chuban She, 1990.

Shanghai Pudong xinqu tongji nianbao, 1991 (Annual Statistical Report of the Pudong New Area). Shanghai Municipal Government Statistics Bureau, ed. Shanghai: Shanghai Kexue Jishu Chuban She, 1991.

Shanghai qiye jia (The Shanghai Entrepreneur). Zhou Bi, ed. Beijing: Zhongguo Jingji Chuban She, 1987.

Shanghai qiye jituan: Jianli yu fazhan (Shanghai Enterprise Groups: Their Establishment and Development). Dai Jinde and Li Gengchun, eds. Shanghai: Kexue Puji Chuban She, 1988.

Shanghai shehui kexue (Social Science in Shanghai), Institute of Information Studies of the Shanghai Social Science Academy, ed. Shanghai: Shanghai Shehui Kexue Chuban She, 1988.

Shanghai shehui tongji ziliao, 1980–1983 (Statistical Materials on Shanghai Society, 1980–1983). Group on the Shanghai Social Situation and Trends, ed. Shanghai: Huadong Shifan Daxue Chuban She, 1988.

Shanghai shehui xiankuang he qushi, 1980–1983 (Situations and Trends in Shanghai

Society, 1980–1983). Zheng Gongliang, et al., eds. Shanghai: Huadong Shifan Daxue Chuban She, 1988.

Shanghai shengli de shinian, 1976–1985 (Shanghai's Ten Years of Victory, 1976–1985). Shanghai CCP Propaganda Department and Shanghai Municipal Statistics Bureau, eds. Shanghai: Shanghai Renmin Chuban She, 1986.

Shanghai shi 1985 nian gongye pucha ziliao (Materials from the 1985 Industrial Survey of Shanghai). Gu Delun et al., eds. Shanghai: Zhongguo Tongji Chuban She, 1988.

Shanghai shi di sanci renkou pucha ziliao huibian (Compendium of Materials from the Third Census in Shanghai Municipality). Shanghai Census Office, ed. Shanghai: Shanghai Renkou Pucha Bangong Shi, 1984.

Shanghai shi duiwai jingji tongji nianjian, 1993 (Foreign Economic Statistical Yearbook of Shanghai, 1993). Shanghai Municipal Statistics Bureau, ed., *neibu ziliao*. Shanghai: Shanghai Tongji Ju, 1993.

Shanghai shi fagui huizhang huibian, 1949–1985 (Compendium of Laws and Regulations of Shanghai City, 1949–1985). Shanghai: Shanghai Renmin Chuban She, 1986.

Shanghai shi gaoxiao zhuanye jieshao (Introduction to the Professions in Shanghai's University-level Academies). Fang Ren, ed. Shanghai: Jiaotong Daxue Chuban She, 1988.

Shanghai shi jiaoqu gongye qiye daquan (Compendium on Industrial Enterprises in the Shanghai Suburbs). Gu Delun and Xie Jinhuai, eds. Shanghai: Zhongguo Tongji Chuban She, 1988.

Shanghai shi jingji dili (Shanghai Economic Geography). Cheng Lu, ed. Beijing: Xinhua Chuban She, 1987.

Shanghai shi liyong waizi gongzuo shouce (Shanghai Overseas Investment Utilization Handbook). Shanghai Municipal Foreign Economic Trade Committee, ed. Shanghai: Shanghai Fanyi Chuban Gongsi, 1985. (Also, a second edition in 1988).

Shanghai shi nongye jixie hua fazhan zhanlue yanjiu (Studies on Strategy for Developing Agricultural Mechanization in Shanghai Municipality). Xie Zifen, ed. Shanghai: Shanghai Kexue Puji Chuban She, 1991.

"Shanghai shi qingshaonian baohu tiaolie" lifa jishi (Record on the Legislation of the 'Rules for Protection of Youths and Infants in Shanghai'). Drafting Office for the "Rules for Protection of Youths and Infants in Shanghai," ed. Shanghai: Shanghai Shehui Kexue Yuan Chuban She, 1987.

Shanghai shi waishang touzi qiye gaikuang (Shanghai Enterprises with Foreign Investment). Shanghai Translation and Publishing Centre, ed. Shanghai: Shanghai Fanyi Chuban Gongsi, 1988.

Shanghai shi wenxue jiang huojiang zuopin ji (1982–1984 nian baogao wenxue shige) (Collection of Prizewinning Works in Shanghai Literature [Reportage and Poems, 1982–1984]), two vols. Shanghai: Shanghai Shehui Kexue Yuan Chuban She, 1986.

Shanghai shi wenxue jiang huojiang zuopin ji (1982–1984 nian zhong duan bian xiaoshuo) (Collection of Prizewinning Works in Shanghai Literature [Novellas and Short Stories, 1982–1984]), two vols. Shanghai: Shanghai Shehui Kexue Yuan Chuban She, 1986.

Shanghai shi wenxue jiang huojiang zuopin ji (1982–1984 nian lilun pinglun) (Collection of Prizewinning Works in Shanghai Literature [Theory and Criticism, 1982–1984]). Shanghai: Shanghai Shehui Kexue Yuan Chuban She, 1986.

Shanghai shi Xuhui qu diming zhi (Gazeteer of Shanghai City's Xuhui District). Shanghai: Shanghai Shehui Kexue Yuan Chuban She, 1990.

Shanghai shi zixun fuwu gongsi minglu (Catalogue of Shanghai Consultancy and Service Companies). Jin Zixin, ed. Shanghai: Xuelin Chuban She, 1985.

Shanghai shi difang xing fagui huibian, 1980–1985 (Compendium of Local Laws of

Shanghai Municipality, 1980–1985). Secretariat of the Standing Committee of the Shanghai People's Congress, ed. Shanghai: Shanghai People's Congress, 1986.

Shanghai shimin banshi zhinan (Citizen's Practical Guide to Shanghai). Shanghai Municipal Government Administrative Office, ed. Shanghai: Shanghai Renmin Chuban She, 1989.

Shanghai tongji nianjian, various years to 1993 (Shanghai Statistical Yearbook). Shanghai Shi Tongji Ju, eds. Beijing: Zhongguo Tongji Chuban She.

Shanghai touzi zhinan (Shanghai Investment Guide). Shanghai Investment and Trust Corporation, ed. Shanghai and Hong Kong: Shanghai Fanyi Chuban She and China Information Source Co., 1984.

Shanghai wenhua (Shanghai Culture). Liu Zhengyuan, ed. Hong Kong: Jingji Daobao She, n.d. [1989?].

Shanghai wenhua nianjian, 1987 (Shanghai Culture Yearbook, 1987). Liu Zhenyuan et al., eds. Shanghai: Zhongguo Da Baike Chuban She, 1987.

Shanghai yu Xianggang de jingji hezuo (Shanghai-Hongkong Economic Cooperation). China Economic Research and Development Consultants, eds. Hong Kong: Zhongguo Jingji Yanjiu Zixun Gongsi, 1988.

Shanghai zhigong tiaojian ziliao shouce (Handbook on the Conditions of Shanghai Employees). Shanghai Statistics Bureau, ed. Shanghai: Shanghai Tongji Chuban She, 1985.

Shanghai ziben zhuyi gongshang ye de shehui zhuyi gaizao (The Socialist Transformation of Shanghai's Capitalist Industry and Commerce). Shanghai Academy of Social Sciences, ed. Shanghai: Shanghai Renmin Chuban She, 1980.

Shanghai: Gaige, kaifang, yu fazhan, 1979–87 (Shanghai: Reforms, Opening, and Development, 1979–87). Shanghai Statistical Bureau, ed. Shanghai: Sanlian Shudian, 1988.

Shangpin jingji yu rencai ziyuan peizhi (The Commodity Economy and Allocation of Talents and Resources). Shanghai Municipal Personnel Bureau and Shanghai Municipal Scientific and Technical Cadres Bureau, eds. Shanghai: Shanghai Shehui Kexue Yuan Chuban She, 1988.

Shanguang de zuyi: Shanghai shi gongchan dangyuan xianjin shiyi xuan (Flashing Footprints: Selected Progressive Deeds by Shanghai Communist Party Members). Shanghai: Shanghai Renmin Chuban She, 1986.

Shehui zhuyi jingji wenti xinlun (New Ideas on Questions of the Socialist Economy). Shanghai Economics Association, ed. Shanghai: Shanghai Shehui Kexue Yuan Chuban She, 1987.

Shehui zhuyi shangpin jingji tantao (Inquiries into the Socialist Commodity Economy). Shanghai Economics Association, ed. Shanghai: Shanghai Shehui Kexue Yuan Chuban She, 1987.

Shenhua qiye gaige tansuo (Explorations on Deepening Enterprise Reforms). Shanghai Economics Association, ed. Shanghai: Shanghai Shehui Kexue Yuan Chuban She, 1987.

Shi Huanzhang, et al. *Huadong Zhengfa Xueyuan faxue shuoshi lunwen ji* (Collection of Master's Theses in Law from the East China Institute of Politics and Law). Shanghai: Shanghai Shehui Kexue Yuan Chuban She, 1988.

Shi Tianchuan. *Guangbo dianshi gailun* (General Outline on Broadcasting and Television). Shanghai: Fudan Daxue Chuban She, 1987.

Shidai de zuowei yu lilun de xuanze: Xifang jindai sichao yu Zhongguo "Wusi" qimeng sixiang (Theoretical Selections from a Time Out of Joint: Modern Tides of Thought in the West and the Enlightenment Thought of China's "May 4"). Liu Guisheng, ed. Beijing: Qinghua Daxue Chuban She, 1989.

Shijie shida zongjiao (Ten Great Religions of the World). Huang Xinchuan, ed. Beijing: Dongfang Chuban She, 1988.

Shijie xin jishu geming yu Shanghai de duice (The Global Revolution in New Technology and Shanghai's Policies in Response). Shanghai Economic Research Center and Shanghai Science and Technology Committee, eds. Shanghai: Shanghai Shehui Kexue Yuan Chuban She, 1986.

Shuiwu gongzuo shouce (Tax Work Handbook). Zou Yunfang, ed. Beijing: Nengyuan Chuban She, 1987.

Song Qiang, et al. *Zhongguo keyi shuo bu* (China Can Say No). Beijing: Zhonghua Gongshang Lianhe Chuban She, 1996.

Songjiang nianjian, 1987 [and 1988] (Songjiang Yearbook, 1987 [and 1988]). Shanghai: Shanghai Shehui Kexue Yuan Chuban She, 1987 [and 1988].

Songjiang xian xianqing: Xiandai hua jincheng diaocha (The Current Situation in Songjiang County: An Investigation of the Modernization Process). Yao Xitang, ed., vol. II. Shanghai: no publisher but probably the Shanghai Academy of Social Sciences, n.d.

Songjiang xian zhi (Songjiang County Gazetteer). He Huimin, ed. Shanghai: Shanghai Renmin Chuban She, 1991.

Songjiang zhenzhi (Gazeteer of Songjiang Town). Che Chi et al., eds. Shanghai: Shanghai Renmin Chuban She, 1988.

Su Shaokang, Wang Luxiang, and Xia Jun. *Heshang* (River Elegy). Reprint; Hong Kong: Sanlian Shudian, 1988.

Sunan fada diqu jiaoyu fazhan zhanlue huanjing yanjiu baogao (Research Report on the Environment for Educational Development Strategy in the Developed Region of Southern Jiangsu). Task Force on the Environment for Educational Development Strategy in the Developed Region of Southern Jiangsu, ed. and pub. Mimeographed "discussion draft" (*taolun gao*), n.p., 1991.

Tao Yongkuan, et al. *Dali fazhan disan chanye* (Vigorously Develop Tertiary Industry). Shanghai: Shanghai Shehui Kexue Yuan Chuban She, 1986.

Tao Youzhi, et al. *Sunan moshi yu zhifu zhi dao* (The South Jiangsu Model and Road to Prosperity). Shanghai: Shanghai Shehui Kexue Yuan Chuban She, 1988.

Tao Youzhi. *Jishu gaige xinlun* (New Ideas on Technical Reform). Shanghai: Shanghai Renmin Chuban She, 1987. Tian Yinong, Zhu Fulin, and Xiang Huaicheng. *Zhongguo caizheng guanli tizhi de gaige* (The Structural Reform of Chinese Fiscal Management). Beijing: Jingji Kexue Chuban She, 1985.

Tianjin tongji nianjian, (Tianjin Statistical Yearbook,), various years. Tianjin Statistical Bureau, ed. Beijing: Zhongguo Tongji Chuban She.

Tongji cidian (Statistical Dictionary). Jia Hongyu, ed. Shanghai: Shanghai Renmin Chuban She, 1986.

Tongyi gongzuo shouce (Handbook of Unification Work). Office of Unification Studies and Voice of Jinling Broadcasting Station, eds. Nanjing: Nanjing Daxue Chuban She, 1986.

Tongzhan gongzuo shouce (Handbook of United Front Work). Ma Fen et al., eds. Shanghai: Shanghai Renmin Chuban She, 1989.

Wang Anyun and Bo Xiangyuan. *Shanghai Da Shijie* (Shanghai's Great World [entertainment center]). Wuhan: Changjiang Wenyi Chuban She, 1988.

Wang Hongxun, et al. *Fenghuang sanshi nian, 1958–1988* (Thirty Years of Phoenix [Bicycle Factory, Shanghai], 1958–1988). Shanghai: Shanghai Shehui Kexue Yuan Chuban She, 1988.

Wang Yu, et al. *Da juanbian shiqi* (The Era of Great Transformation). Shijiazhuang: Hebei Renmin Chuban She, 1987.

Wenhui bao dashi ji, 1938.1–1939.5, 1945.8–1947.5 (Record of Major events at the *Wenhui Daily* [to 1947]). Wenhui Bao Baoshi Yanjiu Shih, ed. Shanghai: Wenhui Chuban She, 1986.

Wenhui bao shilüe, 1938.1–1939.5, 1945.8–1947.5 (Outline History of the *Wenhui Daily* [to 1947]). Wenhui Bao Baoshi Yanjiu Shih, ed. Shanghai: Wenhui Chuban She, 1988.

Wenhui bao wushi nian, 1938–1988 (Fifty Years of the *Wenhui Daily*, 1938–1988). Wenhui Bao She, ed. Shanghai: Wenhui Chuban She, 1988.

Wenzhou moshi de lilun tansuo (Theoretical Exploration of the Wenzhou Model). Lin Bai et al., eds. Nanning: Guangxi Renmin Chuban She, 1987.

Wenzhou qiye dachuan, 1986 (Compendium of Wenzhou Enterprises, 1986). Wang Wence, ed. Wenzhou: Wenzhou Shi Qiye Guanli Xiehui and Wenzhou Shi Gongye Pucha Bangong Shi, 1986.

Wenzhou shiyan qu (The Wenzhou Experimental Zone). Pan Shangeng. ed. Beijing: Nengyuan Chuban She, 1988.

Wu Yantao, et al. *Shanghai de gupiao he zhaijuan* (Shanghai Shares and Bonds). Shanghai: Shanghai Shehui Kexue Yuan Chuban She, 1988.

Xian de jingji yu jiaoyu de diaocha (Survey of County Economies and Education). Task Force for Research on China's Rural Education, ed. Beijing: Jiaoyu Kexue Chuban She, 1989.

Xiandai hua yu Zhongguo wenhua yantao hui lunwen huibian (Proceedings of the Conference on Modernization and Chinese Culture). Chiao Chien, ed. Hong Kong: Xianggang Zhongwen Daxue Shehui Kexue Yuan ji Shehui Yanjiu Suo, 1985.

Xiandai Zhongguo de yibai xiang jianshe (One Hundred Projects in Modern China). "One Hundred Projects in Modern China" Editorial Group, eds. Beijing: Hongqi Chuban She, 1985.

Xiao Zhenmei. "*Dalu huatan sishi nian*" (Mainland Painting for Forty Years). *Zhongguo dalu yanjiu* 35:11 (November 1992), pp. 89–98.

Xiao Zhenmei. "*Zhongguo dalu de xiandai hua*" (Contemporary Painting on the Chinese Mainland). *Zhongguo dalu yanjiu* 36:4 (April 1993), pp. 75–86.

Xiao Zhenmei. *Xian jieduan zhi dalu nongjing biange* (The Transformation of the Mainland's Rural Economy at the Present Stage). Taibei: Juliu Tushu Gongsi, 1988.

Xie Zifen, et al. *Shanghai xiangzhen qiye jingji, keshu fazhan zhanlue he zhengce wenti yanjiu* (Strategy and Policy Studies for the Economic and Technical Development of Shanghai Rural Enterprises). Shanghai: Shanghai Shehui Kexue Yuan, 1988.

Xie Zifen, Li Wuwei, et al. *Quyu jingji yanjiu: Zhanlue guihua yu moxing* (Regional Economic Studies: Strategies, Plans, and Models). Shanghai: Shanghai Shehui Kexue Yuan Chuban She, 1988.

Xin xiaoshuo zai 1985 (New Novellas in 1985). Wu Liang and Cheng Depei, eds. Shanghai: Shanghai Shehui Kexue Yuan Chuban She, 1986.

Xin Zhongguo gongye jingji shi (A History of New China's Industrial Economy). Wang Haibo, ed. Jingji Guanli Chuban She, 1986.

Xin Zhongguo shangye shigao, 1949–1982 (Outline History of New China's Commerce, 1949–1982). Ministry of Commerce, ed. Beijing: Zhongguo Caizheng Jingji Chuban She, 1984.

Xinwen xiaoshuo zai '86 (News Novellas, '86). Wu Liang and Cheng Depei, eds. Shanghai: Shanghai Shehui Kexue Yuan Chuban She, 1988.

Xinwen ziyou lunji (Collection of Essays on Journalistic Freedom). Shanghai: Wenhui Chuban She, 1988.

Xu Chongqi and Tang Yanbo. "*Shanghai Pudong jihua de fazhan he pinggu*" (Development and Assessment of Shanghai's Pudong Plan). *Zhongguo dalu yanjiu* (Mainland China Studies) 36:8 (August, 1993), pp. 29–44.

Xu Riqing, et al. *Shehui zhuyi chengshi caizheng xue* (Socialist Urban Finance). Shanghai: Shanghai Shehui Kexue Yuan Chuban She, 1986.

Xu Yiren and Cheng Pu. *Falü de shihxiao wenti* (Issues of Legal Prescription). Shanghai: Shanghai Shehui Kexue Yuan Chuban She, 1988.

Xu Yonglu, Chu Yugen, and Yu Zhuwen. *Jingji qiangren zhi lu* (An Economic Strong Man's Way). Shanghai: Shanghai Shehui Kexue Yuan Chuban She, 1987.

Xu Yuanming and Ye Ding. *Tangqiao gongye hua zhi lu* (The Way to Industrialization in Tangqiao). Shanghai: Shanghai Shehui Kexue Yuan Chuban She, 1987.

Xu Zhenliang. "*Shanghai caizheng shouru "huapo" de xiankuang, chengyin ji qi duice*" (The "Slide" of Shanghai's Financial Income: Situation, Reasons, and Countermeasures). In *Caijing yanjiu* (Financial and Economic Studies), March 1988, pp. 18–23.

Yan Jiaqi and Gao Gao. *Wenhua dageming shinian shi* (Ten Years of the Great Cultural Revolution). Tianjin: Tianjin Renmin Chuban She, 1986.

Yan Jiaqi. *Lianbang Zhongguo gouxiang* (Plan for a Federal China). Hong Kong: Mingbao Chuban She, 1992.

Yan Tingchang, Cai Beihua, Xu Zhihe, et al. *Shanghai lüyou ye de jintian he mingtian* (Shanghai Tourism Today and Tomorrow). Shanghai: Shanghai Shehui Kexue Yuan Chuban She, 1987.

Yang Dongping. *Chengshi jifeng: Beijing he Shanghai de wenhua jingshen* (City Monsoon: The Cultural Spirit of Beijing and Shanghai). Beijing: Dongfang Chuban She, 1994.

Yanhai jingji kaifang qu: Jingji yanjiu he tongji ziliao (Coastal Open Economic Zones: Economic Research and Statistical Materials). State Statistical Bureau, ed. Beijing: Zhongguo Tongji Chuban She, 1989.

Yao Shihuang. *Jin sanjiao de tansuo* (Search for the Golden Delta). Chongqing: Chongqing Chuban She, 1988.

Yige chengjiao xiangcun de jintian he mingtian: Shanghai shi Shanghai xian Meilong xiang jingji fazhan zongti guihua yanjiu (A Suburban Village Today and Tomorrow: Comprehensive Plan for the Economic Development of Meilong Town, Shanghai County, Shanghai). Ling Yaochu and Zhang Zhaoan eds. Shanghai: Shanghai Shehui Kexue Chuban She, 1988.

Yu Ning and Li Deming. *Zenyang xie xinwen pinglun* (How to Write News Editorials). Beijing: Zhongguo Xinwen Chuban She, 1987.

Yu Tijun and Shi Hejun. *Baocheng, zulin, gufen zhi* (The System of Responsibility, Leasing, and Shares). Shanghai: Shanghai Fanyi Chuban She, 1988.

Yu Youwei. *Shanghai jindai Fojiao jianshi* (Concise History of Modern Buddhism in Shanghai). Shanghai: Huadong Shifan Daxue Chuban She, 1988.

Yuan Enzhen, et al. *Wenzhou moshi yu fuyu zhi lu* (The Wenzhou Model and Way to Affluence). Shanghai: Shanghai Shehui Kexue Yuan Chuban She, 1987.

Zhang Linlan, "*Women de tansuo—jiefang hou de Shanghai 'Xinmin bao'* " (Our Exploration - Shanghai's *Xinmin News* After Liberation," in Chen Mingde, et al., *"Xinmin bao" chunqiu* (The Spring and Autumn of the "*Xinmin News*"). Chongqing: Chongqing Chuban She, 1987. Pp. 405–30.

Zhang Shanmin, Li Xin, and Wu Zhangnan, et al. *Zou xiang chenggong* (Marching to Accomplishments). Shanghai: Shanghai Shehui Kexue Yuan Chuban She, 1988.

Zhang Sui. *Zongjiao gujin tan* (Religion Yesterday and Today). Shanghai: Shanghai Shehui Kexue Yuan Chuban She, 1985.

Zhang Zhanbin, et al. *Xin Zhongguo qiye lingdao zhidu* (Leadership Systems for New China's Enterprises). Beijing: Chunqiu Chuban She, 1988.

Zhang Zhongli, Zhu Qingzha, et al. *Disan chanye de lilun yu shixian: Jianlun Shanghai disan chanye fazhan zhanlue* (Theory and Practice of the Tertiary Sector: On the Development Strategy of Shanghai's Tertiary Sector). Shanghai: Shanghai Shehui Kexue Yuan Chuban She, 1986.

Zhang Zuan. *Shanghai diming xiaozhi* (Précis on Shanghai Placenames). Shanghai: Shanghai Shehui Kexue Chuban She, 1988.

Zhangjiagang Bureau of Rural Industries, *Zhangjiagang shi xiangzhen gongye zhi* (Gazeteer of Zhangjiagang Rural Industries). Shanghai: Shanghai Renmin Chuban She, 1990.

Zhe Xiaoye. *Chengshi zai zhuanzhe dianshang* (Cities at a Turning point). Beijing: Zhongguo Funü Chuban She, 1989.

Zhejiang jingji nianjian (Zhejiang Economic Yearbook) various years. Zhejiang CCP Committee Policy Research Office and Zhejiang People's Government Economic, Technical, and Social Development Research Center, eds. Hangzhou: Zhejiang Renmin Chuban She, same years.

Zhong-Ying duizhao Zhonggong changyong ciyu lubian (A Chinese English-Lexicon of Chinese Communist Terminology), Institute of Current China Studies, ed. (Taipei: Institute of Current China Studies, 1993).

Zhonggong zhengquan sishi nian de huigu yu zhanwang (Recollections and Prospects on the Forty Years of CCP Power). Wu An-chia, ed. Taipei: Guoji guanxi yanjiu zhongxin, 1991.

Zhongguo 1986 nian 74 chengzhen renkou qianyi chouxiang diaocha ziliao (Sample Survey Materials on 1986 Chinese Migration in 74 Cities and Towns). *Chinese Demography* Editorial Group, ed. Beijing: *Zhongguo renkou kexue* bianji bu, 1988.

Zhongguo 1987 nian 1% renkou chouxiang pucha ziliao: Shanghai shi fence (Chinese 1987 1% Sample Survey: Shanghai Municipality Volume) Shanghai City Statistical Bureau, ed. Beijing: Zhongguo Tongji Chuban She, 1988.

Zhongguo 1987 nian 1% renkou chouxiang pucha ziliao: Zhejiang sheng fence (Chinese 1987 1% Sample Survey: Zhejiang Province Volume), Zhejiang Province Statistical Bureau, ed. Beijing: Zhongguo Tongji Chuban She, 1988.

Zhongguo 1987 nian 1% renkou chouxiang pucha ziliao: Jiangsu sheng fence (Chinese 1987 1% Sample Survey: Jiangsu Province Volume), Jiangsu Province Statistical Bureau and Jiangsu Province Census Office, eds. Nanjing: Zhongguo Tongji Chuban She, 1988.

Zhongguo 1987 nian 1% renkou chouxiang pucha ziliao: Quanguo fence (Tabulations of China 1% Population Sample Survey: National Volume), Department of Population Statistics, State Statistical Bureau, ed. Beijing: Zhongguo Tongji Chuban She, 1988.

Zhongguo baike nianjian 1990 (Encyclopedic Yearbook of China, 1990). Luo Luo, ed. Shanghai: Zhongguo Dai Baike Quanshu Chuban She, 1990.

Zhongguo caizheng tongji, 1950–1985 (Chinese Fiscal Statistics, 1950–1985). Comprehensive Planning Office of the PRC Ministry of Finance, ed. Beijing: Zhongguo Caizheng Jingji Chuban She, 1987.

Zhongguo chengshi jiating (The Chinese Urban Family). Five Cities Family Research Project, ed. Jinan: Shandong Renmin Chuban She, 1985.

Zhongguo chengshi jingji shehui nianjian (Economic and Social Yearbook of China's Cities, various years). Zhongguo Chengshi Jingji Shehui Nianjian Lishi Hui, ed. Beijing: Zhongguo Chengshi Jingji Shehui Chuban She, various years.

Zhongguo chengshi jingji tizhi gaige xuexi wenxuan (Selected Studies of China's Urban Economic System Reforms). Shanghai Academy of Social Sciences, ed. Shanghai: Shanghai Shehui Kexue Yuan Chuban She, 1984.

Zhongguo chengshi tongji nianjian (Statistical Yearbook of Chinese Cities), various years. State Statistical Bureau, ed. Beijing: Zhongguo Tongji Xinxi Zixun Fuwu Zhongxin and Xin Shijie Chuban She.

Zhongguo chengshi tongji nianjian (Statistical Yearbook of Chinese Cities, various years). State Statistical Bureau, ed. Beijing: Zhongguo Tongji Xinxi Zixun Fuwu Zhongxin & Zhongguo Jianshe Chuban She, various years.

Zhongguo chuban nianjian, 1985 (China Publishing Yearbook, 1985). China Publishers' Association, ed. Beijing: Shangwu Yinshu Guan, 1985.

Zhongguo falü nianjian (China Law Yearbook), various years, 1986–90. Chengdu: Zhongguo Falü Nianjian Chuban She, published the following year.

Zhongguo funü gongzuo shouce (China Women's Work Handbook). Editorial Group for the *China Women's Work Handbook*, ed. Shanghai: Shanghai Renmin Chuban She, 1988).

Zhongguo funü tongji ziliao, 1949–1989 (Statistical Materials on Chinese Women, 1949–1989). Research Institute of the All China Women's Federation and Research Office of Shaanxi Provincial Women's Federation, eds. Beijing: Zhongguo Tongji Chuban She, 1991.

Zhongguo gaige da cidian (Dictionary of Chinese Reforms), Dictionary of Chinese Reforms Editorial Group, ed. (Haikou: Hainan Chuban She, 1992.

Zhongguo gaige quanshu (Complete Book of Chinese Reforms). Six vols., separate editorial committee for each. Dalian: Dalian Chuban She, 1992.

Zhongguo Gongchan Dang dangyuan da cidian (Dictionary for CCP Members). Cheng Min, ed. Beijing: Zhongguo Guoji Guangbo Chuban She, 1991.

Zhongguo Gongchan Dang qishi nian (The Chinese Communist Party's Seventy Years). Hu Sheng, ed. Beijing: Zhonggong Dangshi Chuban She, 1991.

Zhongguo Gongchang Dang renming da cidian, 1921–1991 (Who's Who of the CCP, 1921–1991). Sheng Ping, ed. Beijing: Zhongguo Guoji Guangbo Chuban She, 1991.

Zhongguo gongye de fazhan, 1949–1984 (China's Industrial Development, 1949–1984). Guojia Tongji Ju, Gongye Jiaotong Wuzi Tongji Si, ed. Beijing: Zhongguo Tongji Chuban She, 1985.

Zhongguo gongye jingji tongji ziliao, 1987 (Statistical Materials on China's Industrial Economy, 1987). Guojia Tongji Ju, Gongye Jiaotong Wuzi Tongji Si, ed. Beijing: Zhongguo Tongji Chuban She, 1987.

Zhongguo jianzhu ye tongji ziliao, 1952–1985 (China Construction Statistics, 1952–1985). Guojia Tongji Ju, Guding Zichan Touzi Tongji Si, ed. Beijing: Zhongguo Tongji Chuban She, 1988.

Zhongguo jiaoyu chengjiu: Tongji ziliao, 1949–1983 (Achievement of Education in China: Statistics, 1949–1983). Department of Planning, PRC Ministry of Education, ed. Beijing: Zhongguo Jiaoyu Chuban She, 1984.

Zhongguo jiaoyu chengjiu: Tongji ziliao, 1980–1985 (Achievement of Education in China: Statistics, 1980–1985). Department of Planning, PRC State Education Commission, ed. Beijing: Zhongguo Jiaoyu Chuban She, 1986.

Zhongguo jiaoyu tongji nianjian (China Education Statistics Yearbook). State Education Committee, ed. Beijing: Zhongguo Jiaoyu Chuban She, 1991 for 1990 edition, and 1992 for 1991–92 edition.

Zhongguo jiaoyu tongji nianjian, 1987 nian (Statistical Yearbook on Chinese Education, 1987). Guojia Jiaoyu Weiyuan Hui, Jihua Caiwu Ju (Planning and Finance Bureau of the State Education Commission), ed. Beijing: Beijing Gongye Daxue Chuban She, 1988.

Zhongguo jingji jiegou wenti yanjiu (Studies on Issues of Chinese Economic Structure). Ma Hong and Sun Shangqing, eds. Beijing: Renmin Chuban She, 1981.

Zhongguo jingji nianjian (China Economic Yearbook, various years). Compilation Committee for China Economic Yearbook, ed. Beijing: Jingji Guanli Chuban She, various years.

Zhongguo laodong gongzi tongji ziliao, 1949–1985 (Statistical Materials on Chinese Labor and Wages, 1949–1985). Beijing: Zhongguo Tongji Chuban She, 1987.

Zhongguo minzhu dangpai: lishi, zhenggang, renwu (China's Democratic Parties: Histories, Platforms, and Personages). Qin Guosheng and Hu Zhisheng, eds. Jinan: Shandong Renmin Chuban She, 1990.

Zhongguo qingshaonian fanzui yanjiu nianjian, 1987 (Yearbook on Chinese Juvenile Delinquency Studies, 1987). Chinese Juvenile Delinquency Studies Association, ed. Beijing: Chunqiu Chuban She, 1988).

Zhongguo renkou dili (Demographic Geography of China). Hu Huanyong and Zhang Shanyu; *neibu*. Shanghai: Huadong Shifan Daxue Chuban She, two vols., *shang ce* 1984, *xia ce* 1986.

Zhongguo renkou nianjian, 1985 (China Population Yearbook, 1985). Population Research Center, CASS, ed. Beijing: Zhongguo Shehui Kexue Chuban She, 1986.

Zhongguo renkou qianyi (Population Shifts in China). Tian Fang and Ling Fatong, eds. Beijing: Zhishi Chuban She, 1987.

Zhongguo renkou qianyi yu chengshi hua yanjiu (Studies on Chinese Migration and Urbanization). Editorial Group for Studies on Chinese Migration and Urbanization, ed. Beijing: Zhongguo Shehui Kexu Yuan Renkou Yanjiu Suo, 1988.

Zhongguo renkou tongji nianjian (China Population Statistics Yearbook), various years. State Statistics Bureau, comp. Beijing: Zhongguo Zhanwang Chuban She, the same year.

Zhongguo renkou: Jiangsu fence (China's Population: Jiangsu Volume). Du Wenzhen et al., eds. Beijing Zhongguo Caizheng Jingji Chuban She, 1987.

Zhongguo renkou: Shanghai fence (China's Population: Shanghai Volume). Hu Huanyong et al., eds. Beijing Zhongguo Caizheng Jingji Chuban She, 1987.

Zhongguo renkou: Sichuan fence (China's Population: Sichuan Volume). Liu Hongkang et al., eds. Beijing Zhongguo Caizheng Jingji Chuban She, 1988.

Zhongguo renming da cidian: dangdai renwu juan (Who's Who in China: Volume on Contemporary Personages). Editorial Group for the Who's Who in China, ed. Shanghai: Shanghai Cishu Chuban She, 1992.

Zhongguo shehui tongji ziliao, 1987 (Chinese Social Statistics, 1987). Social Statistics Office, State Statistical Bureau, ed. Beijing: Zhongguo Tongji Chuban She, 1987.

Zhongguo shehui zhuyi chengshi jingji xue (Chinese Socialist Urban Economics). Zhu Linxing, ed. Shanghai: Shanghai Shehui Kexue Chuban She, 1986.

Zhongguo shinian gailan (Summary of China's Ten Years of Reform). Gu Changchun and Deng Derong, eds. Beijing: Zhongguo Zhanwang Chuban She, 1989.

Zhongguo shuiwu baike chuanshu (Encyclopedia of Chinese Taxation). Encyclopedia of Chinese Taxation Editorial Group, ed. Beijing: Jingji Guanli Chuban She, 1991.

Zhongguo tongji nianjian (China Statistical Yearbook), each year, 1980–93. State Statistical Bureau, ed. Beijing: Zhongguo Tongji Chuban She, 1980–93.

Zhongguo tongji zhaiyao, 1986 (A Statistical Survey of China, 1986). State Statistical Bureau, ed. Beijing: Zhongguo Tongji Chuban She, 1986.

Zhongguo tongji zhaiyao, 1988 (A Statistical Survey of China, 1988). State Statistical Bureau, ed. Beijing: Zhongguo Tongji Chuban She, 1988.

Zhongguo wujia tongji nianjian (Statistical Yearbook of Chinese Prices), various years. Urban Society and Economy Survey Group, ed. Beijing: Zhongguo Tongji Chuban She.

Zhongguo wujia tongji nianjian, 1988 (Statistical Yearbook of Chinese Prices, 1988). Urban Society and Economy Survey Group, ed. Beijing: Zhongguo Tongji Chuban She, 1988.

Zhongguo xinwen nianjian (Yearbook of Chinese Journalism, various years). An Gang et al., eds. Beijing: Zhongguo Shehui Kexue Chuban She.

Zhongguo xinwen nianjian, 1982 (Yearbook of Chinese Journalism, 1982). News Studies Institute of the Chinese Social Science Academy, ed. Beijing: Zhongguo Shehui Kexue Chuban She, 1982.

Zhongguo xueshu jie dashi ji, 1919–1985 (Chronicle of Chinese Academic Circles, 1919–1985). Wang Yafu and Zhang Hengzhong, eds. Shanghai: Shanghai Shehui Kexue Yuan Chuban She, 1988.

Zhongguo yanhai diqu xiao chengzhen fazhan yu renkou qianyi (Migration and the Development of Small Cities and Towns on the China Coast). Liu Zheng, et al., eds. Beijing: Zhongguo Caizheng Jingji Chuban She, 1989.

Zhongguo yinyue nianjian, 1990 [also 1988 and 1989] (China Music Yearbook, 1990). Jinan: Shandong Jiaoyu Chuban She, 1990 Beijing: Wenhua Yishu Chuban She for 1988 and 1989.

Zhongguo youhua zhan xuanji (Selection from an Exhibition of Chinese Oil Paintings), portfolios 1 and 2. Shao Chuangu, ed. Shanghai: Shanghai Renmin Meishu Chuban She, 1988.

Zhongguo Zhenjiang hezi, hezuo, buchang maoyi xiangmu mulu (A List of Projects for Joint Venture, Coproduction, and Compensation Trade in Zhenjiang, China). Zhenjiang Municipal Planning and Economic Committee and Zhenjiang Municipal Foreign Economic Trade Committee, eds. Zhenjiang, Jiangsu: no publisher, 1988.

Zhongguo zhuming daxue gailan (A Brief Overview of China's Famous Universities). Huang Zhanpeng, ed. Jinan: Shandong Renmin Chuban She, 1990.

Zhonghua Renmin Gonghe Guo jingji dashi ji, 1949–1980 (Chronicle of Economic Events in the PRC, 1949–1980). Fang Weizhong, et al., eds. Beijing: Zhongguo Kexue Chuban She, 1984.

Zhonghua Renmin Gonghe Guo jingji guanli dashi ji (Chronicle of PRC Economic Management). *Dangdai Zhongguo Jingji Guanli* Editorial Dept., ed. Beijing: Zhongguo Jingji Chuban She, 1986.

Zhonghua Renmin Gonghe Guo renkou tongji ziliao huibian, 1949–1985 (Compendium of PRC Materials on Population Statistics, 1949–1985). Population Office of the State Statistical Bureau and Third Bureau of the Ministry of Public Security, eds., *neibu*. Beijing: Zhongguo Caizheng Jingji Chuban She, 1988.

Zhonghua Renmin Gonghe Guo tongji dashi ji, 1949–1991 (A Chronicle of Statistics in the PRC, 1949–1991). Zhang Sai, ed. Beijing: Zhongguo Tongji Chuban She, 1992.

Zhonghua Renmin Gonghe Guo xianfa (Constitution of the People's Republic of China [1982]). Beijing: Falü Chuban She, 1986.

Zhonghua Renmin Gonghe Guo xingzheng susong fa jianghua (Talking about the PRC's Administrative Litigation Law). Propaganda Office of the Judicial Department of the People's Republic of China, ed. Beijing: Falü Chuban She, 1990.

Zhongwai lishi renwu cidian (Who's Who of Historical World Figures). Wang Banghe et al., eds. Changsha: Hunan Renmin Chuban She, 1987.

Zhou Yongcai. *Jiang Zhe Hu mingtu techan zhi* (Special Products of Jiangsu, Zhejiang, and Shanghai). Nanjing: Nanjing Daxue Chuban She, 1987.

Zhu Linxing, et al. *Zhongguo shehui zhuyi chengshi jingji xue* (China's Socialist Economics of Cities). Shanghai: Shanghai Shehui Kexue Yuan Chuban She, 1986.

Zou Yunfang, et al. *Shui wu gongzuo shouce* (Tax Work Handbook). Shanghai: Nengyuan Chuban She, 1987.

Zuo Chuntai, Song Xinzhong, et al. *Zhongguo shehui zhuyi caizheng jianshi* (Sketch History of China's Socialist Finance). Beijing: Zhongguo Caizheng Jingji Chuban She, 1988.

Some of the Interviewees

Chen Haowen, Chief, Materials Group, *Qingnian bao* (Youth News).

Chen Shenshen, Assistant Director, Institute of National Economy Research, Shanghai Academy of Social Sciences.

Chen Yuqun, Head, Shanghai Society of Ecological Economics.
Fu Qiangguo, Judge, Shanghai High People's Court.
Gu Mingyuan, President, China Society for Comparative Education.
Harris, Norma, U.S. Consul for Press and Cultural Affairs, U.S. Consulate General, Shanghai.
He Deyu, Researcher, Population Institute, Shanghai Academy of Social Sciences.
Li Wuwei, Shanghai Investment Consulting Corporation; and Deputy Director, Institute of National Economics, Shanghai Academy of Social Sciences.
Li Xuecheng, Reporter, Shanghai Radio and Television Bureau.
Lin Hao, Correspondent, *Shijie jingji daobao* (World Economic Herald).
Lin Lu, Chief Editor, *Shehui kexue bao* (Social Sciences Information).
Lin Quanshui, Associate Professor, Institute of Economics, Chinese Academy of Social Sciences.
Lü Zheng, Institute of Industrial Economics, Chinese Academy of Social Sciences.
Ma Da, Editor-in-Chief, *Wenhui bao*, and Standing Committee, Shanghai Municipal People's Congress.
Norris, John, U.S. Consul for Economic Affairs, U.S. Consulate General, Shanghai.
Orr, Iain, Former British Consul General, Shanghai.
Qin Jianxun, Correspondent, *Shijie jingji daobao* (World Economic Herald).
Shi Qingkai, Graduate Student in Economic Law and Chief of the Academic Department of the Postgraduates' Union, Shanghai Academy of Social Sciences.
Shi Qingsheng, researcher on professionalization, People's Liberation Army, Beijing.
Shih, H.Y, Professor of Fine Arts, University of Hong Kong.
Shu Hanfeng, Journalist, *Shijie jingji daobao* (World Economic Herald).
Shu Renqiu, Chief Editor, *Xinmin wanbao* (Xinmin Evening News).
Song Jun, Director, Shanghai News Research Institute.
Su Songxing, Deputy Chief Editor, *Social Sciences Information* (Shehui kexue bao).
Tatlow, Antony, Professor of Comparative Literature, University of Hong Kong.
Wang Chongfang, Assistant Professor, Department of International Politics, Fudan University.
Wang Shaoyun, International Department, Shanghai Television Station.
Williams, Adam, Jardine Mathieson, Shanghai.
Xia Jinxiong, Institute of World Economics, Shanghai Academy of Social Sciences.
Yang Sizheng, Member, Shanghai Committee of the Chinese People's Political Consultative Conference.
Yao Liang, Assistant Director, Institute of International Economics, Jiaotong University, Shanghai.
Yao Tinggang, Deputy Director, Institute of World Economy, Shanghai Academy of Social Sciences.
Yen Chengzhong, Associate Research Professor, Shanghai Academy of Social Sciences.
Yu Shutong, Vice-President, China Law Society.
Zhang Linlan, Deputy Editor, *Xinmin wanbao* (Xinmin Evening News).
Zhang Yongwei, Graduate Student in Political Sociology, Shanghai Academy of Social Sciences.
Zhou Ji, International Department, Shanghai Television Station.
Zhou Jianping, Deputy Director, Economic, Legal, and Social Consultancy Center, Shanghai Academy of Social Sciences.
Zhou Ruijin, Deputy Editor-in-Chief, *Jiefang ribao* (Liberation Daily).
Zhu Xingqing, Deputy Chief Editor, *Shijie jingji daobao* (World Economic Herald).
Zhuang Ming, Editor, *Shehui kexue bao* (Social Sciences Information).
Zou Fanyang, Former Director, Shanghai Radio and Television Bureau.

Index

A

Agency theory, 32
Agricultural Bank of China, 144, 310, 312, 328
Agriculture
  capital investment in, 107
  compensation system in, 89, 95
  decollectivization of, 93-95, 96
  evasion of state authority in, 108-109, 110-111
  extension activities in, 88-89, 91
  flooding, 432
  household contracting, 87, 95-97, 105, 107
  income, 92, 103, 109
  independent farmers, 133
  labor, 89-90, 102, 107, 167-168
  and land reform, 84-85
  and Leap policies, 86-87
  markets for products, 98, 100, 186
  modernization, 9, 83, 85, 87-88, 89, 107, 109-110, 432
  monoculture, 93
  and peasant power, 97-98
  population in, 89-90
  prices, 95, 96, 98, 98-100, 109, 129-130
  production, 85, 90, 91, 95, 103, 107, 108, 130
  responsibility fields, 87
  shift to rural industry, 100-107, 129-130, 137-138, 150, 407-408
  and state bureaucracy, 107-110
Agriculture *(continued)*
  triple-cropping, 90-93, 110
Aijian Credit and Investment Company, 312
Almond, Gabriel, 24
Aluminum industry, 180
Anhui, 379
  in Shanghai Economic Zone, 377, 378, 380-381
  Shanghai investment in, 179, 380
  textile industry in, 345
Articulation, political, 37-43
Authority. *See* Leadership; Power
Aviation, 404-405n.192

B

Bachman, David, 24
Bai Hua, 68n.5
Bank of Communications, 310, 311–312
Bank of Industry and Commerce, 310
Bankruptcy, of state enterprises, 191-192, 196, 311
Banks
  central bank, 148, 227, 232, 306, 310, 313, 319, 328
  deposits, 306, 314-319
  interest rates, 305-306, 314-315
  loans, 143-144, 286, 304-306, 309, 310, 312, 313-314
  local, 306, 308, 312-314
  Party groups in, 308-309
  profits, 232, 308

Banks *(continued)*
reform of, 310-312
and state bonds, 227
Baoshan Steel Plant, 194, 229, 238, 348-349
Bao Yugang, 365
Barter agreements, 170, 182-185, 369, 370-371
Bates, Robert, 84
Beijing
approach to reform in, 55-56
economic conference in, 223
raw materials purchases of, 185
taxation of, 205-206
technological development in, 342, 343
Bicycle industry, 187, 346-347
Birth planning, 322, 430
Birth rate, 137, 416
Black market, 289-290, 395
Blue cards, 425
Bonds
market, 319-310
treasury, 320, 321
wage, 227
Brigade enterprises, 113-118
Business cycles, 326-330
Butler, Steven, 120
Button market, in Wenzhou, 370

C

Canals, 393, 406n.211
Capital investment. *See* Investment, capital
Capital stock depreciation, 228-229, 263-264, 271, 300-301
Causation
circumspect approach to, 51-53
defined, 78n.129
humanist approach to, 48-49
and individual preference, 51
naturalist approach to, 49-50
rational-action approach to, 43-48
and research design, 50-51, 58-59
Central policy, reform defined as, 8, 9, 10
Chan, Anita, 14
Changchun, 233
Changzhou, 138, 141, 212, 360, 364, 383, 436
Charismatic campaigns, 33, 34, 35, 47
Chelan Li, Linda, 201
Chemical industry, shortages in, 194
Chengdu, 233
Cheng Xiaonong, 331n.26
Chen Yi, 219, 408-409
Chen Yun, 196, 349, 387
Child labor, 440
China Eastern Airlines, 404-405n.192
Chinese Communist Party (CCP), 19, 36, 86, 168
in banks, 308-309
decline of rural organization, 132-133, 149
and Enterprise Law, 282-283
Chongqing, 386
City planning, 286
Cleaning Class Ranks Campaign, 134
Clothing, styles of, 434-435
Cloward, Richard A., 29, 84
Coal, 193, 381
Collectives
efficiency of, 135-136
labor in, 122-123, 138, 142, 162n.194
land contracting from, 287
and local cadres, 118-119, 141
production of, 130, 132
prosperity of, 127
shift to, 117, 141-142
urban, 265-266
credit to, 309
food retailers, 267
labor in, 443-444
profit retention in, 304
restrictions on, 270
Wenzhou model for, 146-147
Commercial papers, 320-321
Commune enterprises, 113-118
Communist Manifesto, 445
Communist Youth League, 415
Computer development, 342, 351
Concrete theory, 7
Consciousness, scientific basis of, 79n.134
Constitution of 1982, 286
Construction
migrant labor in, 428-429
mortgage loans for, 286
nonstate capital for, 299-300
and planning, 273-274, 286
residential, 145, 287-288
slowness of, 171-172
Construction Bank, 320
Consultants, technology, 356-357, 359

Consumer goods
  domestic exports of, 187-188
  prices of, 82, 187, 434-435, 436, 439
  production of, 170-171, 213-214
  retail sales of, 267, 281-282
  rural spending on, 369-370
  shortages of, 187, 188
Contract responsibility system, 275-278, 282, 283
Corruption
  and black market, 289-290
  by wholesalers, 293
  cost of, 294
  definitions of, 290, 291, 294, 335n.99
  embezzlement, 290-291
  rural and suburban, 293-294
  speculation, 291-293
Credit
  cards, 313
  commercial papers, 320-321
  cooperatives, 309, 327
  expansion of, 309-310, 328-329
  from private loans, 318, 322
  and savings, 314-319
  self supply, 327
  to rural industry, 143-144, 148, 308, 318
  to state industry, 171, 235, 263, 286, 304-306, 309, 311, 312
  to urban collectives, 309
  See also Banks
Crime
  embezzlement, 290-291
  hawking, 439-440
  hijacking, 395
  smuggling, 394-395
  unregistered migrants in, 429-430
  youth, 440
Cultural Revolution, 36, 41, 68n.3, 137, 354
  aftermath of, 18
  end of, 13-14, 16, 89, 134
  investment policy of, 135
  periodization of, 11, 12-13, 15, 16
  and private enterprises, 441
  in Shanghai, 214-215, 218-219
  violence in, 76n.103, 86

D

Dahl, Robert, 27, 63
Dahrendorf, Ralf, 42, 63
Decollectivization, rural, 93-95, 96
Deng Xiaoping, 9, 10, 11, 89, 119, 134, 219, 323, 364-365
  inconsistency of policies, 27-29
  periodization of reform, 14-15
  on rural industry, 96
Depreciation rate, 300-302
Disease
  hepatitis epidemic, 189-190, 191, 227
  regional campaign against, 373-374
Documentary sources, 55
Domestic workers, 419, 428
Donnithorne, Audrey, 19, 201-202, 392
Duara, Prasenjit, 35

E

East China Economic Coordination Zone, 373
Easton, David, 24
Economic Daily, 193-194, 244, 449
Economic growth, 82-83, 170-171, 326-327, 328
Economic reform
  authority during, 35-36, 37
  causal hypotheses of, 3-7
  central and local origins of, 8-11, 28
  fiscal, 212, 218-219, 222-228
  "Four Don'ts" of, 28
  impetus of rural industrialization, 9-10, 85-86, 110-112, 151
  models for, 120, 145-148
  and ownership types, 257-258, 265-266
  periodization of, 11-16, 134-135
  rural, 93-95
  short vs long-term factors in, 4
  and statist ends, 23-24
  See also Collectives; Private enterprises; Rural industry; State enterprises
Economic zones, 374, 386-387, 402n.149
  See also Shanghai Economic Zone
Education
  cadre schools, 354
  primary school enrollment, 416
  and technological development, 343-344, 357
Electricity, shortages of, 193
Electronics industry, 342, 349-351
Eleventh Party Congress, Third Plenum of, 96-97

Embezzlement, 290-291
Emerson, John Philip, 202
Employment. *See* Labor force
Energy, shortages of, 193-194
Enterprise Bankruptcy Law, 192
Enterprise Law, 282-283
Entrepreneurs
  organizations of, 365-368
  in rural industry, 115, 126-129
  in state enterprises, 295-296
  See also Private enterprises
Exports. *See* Trade

F

Fabre, Guilhem, 294
Famine of 1959-1961, 86-87, 95
Federation of Trade Unions, 368
Fei Xiaotong, 90, 106, 118, 138, 140, 142, 150, 178
Field, Robert Michael, 202
Floods, 432
Food
  collectives, 267
  hawkers, 439
  markets, 98, 100
  rationing, 424, 439
  supply, 83, 90, 409
Foreign currency, speculation on, 291-292
Foreign investment, 212, 324, 386
Foreign trade, 185-186, 347-348, 374
Forever bicycles, 346
Foshan, 267
Foucault, Michel, 29, 65
"Four Don'ts," 28
Friedman, Edward, 97
Fudan University, 273-274
Fujian, 181, 187, 374, 387
Functionalism, 52, 79n.139
Fuyang model, 146

G

Gang of Four, 9, 13, 14, 169, 214, 298, 415
Geertz, Clifford, 62, 68n.1
Ge Hongsheng, 147
Golden Triangle Entrepreneurs' Club, 366, 367
Goldstein, Avery, 24
Granovetter, Mark, 289
Great Leap Forward, 86-87, 95, 112, 113, 202, 409, 441
Great Third Front, 202, 205
Green revolution, 85, 88-89, 91, 110, 432
Guangdong, 56, 143, 181, 187, 205, 242, 243
  in economic zone, 374, 387, 388
  spending/revenue for, 216-217, 218
  state ownership in, 267, 268
Guangming Daily, 366
Guangzhou, 56, 212, 216-217, 218, 267
Guizhou, 96, 387

H

Hangzhou, 236, 436, 438
Hankiss, Elemér, 39
Han Kun, 356
Harding, Harry, 9
Hawkers, 438-440, 441
Health. *See* Disease
Hepatitis epidemic, 189-190, 191, 227
Hinge leaders, 20, 30-33, 35, 39, 141, 275, 276, 283
Hirschman, Albert, 243
Hong Kong
  influence of, 56
  investment in Shanghai, 386
  investment in Zhejiang, 364-365
  in joint ventures, 324
  regime legitimacy in, 72n.45
  trade representatives in, 368
Household contracting, 87, 95-97, 105, 107
Household registration, 137, 408, 414
  decline in effectiveness, 424-425
  temporary, 422-424
  unregistered migrants, 425-431
Housing
  construction, 145, 287, 422
  rental, 287-288, 422
  for unregistered migrants, 426, 429, 454n.68
Hua Guofeng, 11, 13, 114, 134, 169-170
Huang, Philip, 110
Hundred Flowers campaign, 409
Hungary, private enterprises in, 449
Huntington, Samuel, 8, 21, 38

Hu Qiaomu, 6, 68n.5
Hu Yaobang, 68n.5

I

Identification cards, 424-425
Imports. *See* Trade
Income
  and consumption, 315, 316
  national, 22, 169, 170, 177, 235, 245n.11
  personal, 101-102, 103, 109
Indonesia, agricultural technology in, 110
Industry
  and ownership types, 257-258, 265-266, 273
  See also Collectives; Private enterprises; Rural industry; State enterprises
Inflation, 186, 187, 192, 196, 319, 326, 328
Intellectuals, 23, 30, 34, 134
  in Beijing, 56
  harassment of, 11, 41, 69n.12
  political articulation of, 38
  statist, 111
  in think tanks, 352
Interest rates
  on bank loans, 305-306
  on bonds, 320
  on deposits, 314-315, 317
Investment
  in bonds, 319-310, 321
  capital
    agricultural, 107
    during Cultural Revolution, 135, 215
    and depreciation, 228-229, 263-64, 271, 300-302, 341
    extrabudgetary, 299
    fixed, 307, 308
    in heavy industry, 302, 348-349
    inland, 135, 179-180, 204-205, 298-299
    on noneconomic grounds, 298
    nonstate funding, 299-300, 302-303
    -output ratio, 202-203
    in rural industry, 129, 140
    in technology, 341-342, 344, 348
  foreign, 212, 324, 364-365, 386
  in gold and silver, 319
  in money market, 321-322
  in stocks, 322-326

J

Jiang Qing, 298
Jiangsu, 112, 121
  commune enterprises in, 114-115, 116, 117
  consumer goods in, 188
  corruption in, 294
  credit in, 318-319
  economic growth of, 83, 236-237, 363, 379, 388, 389-390
  in enterprise groups, 364
  entrepreneurs in, 128-129, 141
  exports of, 348
  in joint ventures, 361
  local leadership in, 119-120, 141
  management in, 283-284
  markets in, 144
  private enterprises in, 146, 448
  production in, 125, 141, 142
  in regional public health campaign, 373-374
  savings in, 318
  service sector in, 438
  in Shanghai Economic Zone, 374, 375, 377, 378, 381 382, 384
  silk trade in, 175, 178
  stock investment in, 326
  taxation in, 221, 236, 448
  technological development in, 353, 354, 355
  trade representatives of, 368
Jiangxi, 181, 377, 378, 379
Jiang Zemin, 10, 175, 220, 240, 298, 350
Jiaotong University, 356
Jiaxing, 344, 355, 362
Ji'nan, 233
Jinshan Chemical Factory, 238
Jiujiang, 345
Joint ventures
  domestic, 359-363
  foreign, 324

K

Kang Shien, 76n.107
Kelliher, Daniel, 97, 110
Kenedi, János, 449
Kornai, János, 8
Krasner, Stephen, 21
Kunshan, 361, 384-385

L

Labor force
agricultural, 89-90, 102, 107, 167-168
central-associated, 214
child, 440
costs of, 187, 351
domestic workers, 419, 428
education of, 343-344, 354, 357
ex-rusticates in, 416, 435
in private enterprises, 442, 443-444, 446
productivity, 433, 434, 456n.100
and raw material shortage, 186, 193-194
in rural industry, 136, 140, 420
at township level, 115, 137, 138
at village level, 114, 115, 117-118
collectives, 122, 122-123, 138, 142, 162n.194
exploitation of, 139-140
part-time, 162n.194
and rustication, 211, 354-358
size of, 151
technicians, 354-358
temporary/contract, 138-139
in service sector, 435-436, 438-440
shift from agriculture, 103-104, 117, 129-130, 407-408
stock share sales to, 283
unregistered migrants in, 426-429, 431
urban migration of, 417-425
See also Wages
Land
auctions, 288
leased, 286, 288-289
reform, 84-85
rural and suburban, 286-288
Langfang model, 146
Lanzhou, 233
Lardy, Nicholas, 201, 202
Leadership
charismatic, 33, 34, 35, 47
inconsistency of, 27-29, 123
medium-level, 26, 34, 37
one-man model, 3
during reform, 35-36, 37
strata of, 19
synaptic, 32, 35
traditional-clientalist, 29-33, 34-35, 47
types of authority, 33-34
See also Local leadership; Management
Leeming, Frank, 92
Lewis, Arthur, 203, 407-408, 432
Liberation Daily, 180-181, 182, 185, 324, 443
Li Chuwen, 365
Lieberthal, Kenneth, 27
Lin Biao, 13
Li Peng, 42, 76n.107
Li Tieying, 28
Little, Daniel, 51
Liu Binyan, 76n.106
Loans
bank, 143-144, 286, 304-306, 309, 310, 312, 313-314
private, 318, 322
Local leadership
and agricultural reform, 96-98
allegiance to state, 32
and collective norms, 20
coordinated vs. cellular, 19-20
effectiveness of, 36-37
entrepreneurs, 126-129, 136
evasion of state authority, 29, 33, 39, 108-109, 110-111, 118, 120
ex-officials, 128
and famine of 1959-1961, 86-87
flexibility of, 28
hinge, 20, 30-33, 35, 39, 141, 275, 276, 283
patron-client groups, 31, 32, 35-36
structure of, 33-36

M

MacDougall, Bonnie, 14
Madsen, Richard, 39
Management
authority of, 172-173, 261-263, 275-276, 285
centrally managed plants, 214, 232, 258, 259, 271, 284
of collective enterprises, 270
and corruption, 291-293
and decentralization, 282-85, 294-295
entrepreneurial, 295, 297
functions of, 168
incentives, 193, 261-263
localization of, 227, 232-237, 258
and production quotas, 261-262
and raw materials procurement, 189, 190
responsibility, 261

Management *(continued)*
in rural industry, 115, 126-129, 135, 136, 283-285
and supervising agencies, 260-261, 264-265, 276
top-heavy system of, 259-60
Mao Zedong, 3, 10, 86, 92, 168, 298
Markets. *See* Trade
Marx, Karl, 40
Mergers, of state enterprises, 192-193, 272, 274
Migdal, Joel, 20, 22
Migration. *See* Population migration
Miller, Arthur, 372
Modernization theory, 38
Money market, 321-322
Money supply, 326-329
Moody's Investors' Service, 314

N

Nanjing, 212, 220, 233, 361, 381-382
Nantong, 141, 236
National income, 22, 169, 170, 177, 235, 245n.11
Naughton, Barry, 14, 202
Nee, Victor, 37
Newspapers, and paper shortage, 180-182
Ningbo, 212, 267, 364, 436
Nonstate networks, 19, 23
North China Agricultural Conference, 118

O

Oi, Jean, 128
Oksenberg, Michel, 27
One-man model, 3
Ownership
land, 286-289
types of, 257-258, 265-266, 273

P

Paper, shortage of, 180-182
Pareto, Vilfredo, 63
Parsons, Talcott, 64, 79n.139
Peasants
and collective action, 40
displacement of, 85
housing construction by, 287
Peasants *(continued)*
inarticulate power of, 110-111
See also Agriculture
People's Bank of China, 148, 227, 232, 306, 310, 313, 319, 323
People's Construction Bank, 310
Pharmaceutical industry, 368
Pickowicz, Paul G., 97
Piven, Frances Fox, 29, 84
Political reform
and articulation, 37-43
individual context for, 43-48
rural industry as impetus for, 110-112, 151
Pollution, 348, 349
Population migration
extent of, 161n.174, 408, 410-411
motives for rustication, 357-358
patterns of, 408-409, 412
and residence controls, 408, 414, 421-425, 431-432
reverse rustication, 409, 413-417
and rustication policy, 211, 354-355, 409, 451n.20
and technology diffusion, 356-357
to rural industry, 136, 140, 211, 354-356
to urban industry, 417-421, 426-429, 431
unregistered migrants, 425-431
Population policy, 322
Power
and authority relations, 33-34
defined, 27
informal, 33
resistance related to, 29
traditional, 29-33
See also Leadership
Press freedom, 41
Prices
agricultural, 95, 96, 98, 98-100, 109, 129-130
black-market, 289-290
consumer, 82, 187, 434-435, 436, 439
inflation, 186, 187, 192, 196, 319, 326, 328
multiple, 263, 297
of raw materials, 175, 178, 181, 184, 231-232
and revenue decline, 231-232
state-fixed, 82, 168-169, 178, 187, 188, 197-98, 201, 263
state/market divergence in, 178

Prices *(continued)*
subsidies, 191, 195
Private enterprises
camouflaged, 446
credit to, 318
ex-rusticates in, 416
hawkers, 438-440, 441
impact on state, 449-450
labor force in, 442, 443-444, 446
legal status of, 445-446
number of, 447
revival of, 268-270, 440-441
service sector, 436
state campaign against, 195
street-committee-run, 441-442
taxation of, 211-212, 444, 447-449
Wenzhou model for, 120-121, 146-148, 270, 442-443
Private plots, 93
Production
agricultural, 85, 90, 91, 95, 103, 107, 108, 130
costs, 186-187
decline in, 82-83, 195
growth of, 12, 176
light, 170-171, 174, 195
and management autonomy, 285
by ownership sector, 331–332n.26
quotas, 174, 261-262
in rural industry, 135, 140-141
for warehouse, 280-281
Profits
bank, 232, 308
retention of, 230, 304
and taxation, 209, 230-231, 232-237
Public health, regional cooperation in, 373-374

R

Railroads, 393, 423, 440
Rational-action theory, 5-6, 43-48, 52
Raw materials
barter agreements for, 170, 182-185
foreign imports of, 185-186
illegal transfers of, 241, 395
liaison agreements for, 371
price of, 175, 178, 181, 184, 189, 231-232, 319
procurement of, 178, 186, 190-191, 241, 327, 368
Raw materials *(continued)*
shortages
in chemical industry, 194-195
and delivery shortfalls, 171, 174, 176, 189
for electrical products, 186, 190
energy, 193-194
labor force impact of, 186, 193-194
of paper, 180-182
State Council priorities on, 190
of textiles, 175
state allocation of, 174, 176, 177, 191
and vertical integration, 179-180
Real estate market, 286-289
Reference Information, 13
Regional cooperation
and economic zones, 374, 386-387, 402n.149
in public health, 373-374
in tourism, 438
in trade, 361, 371-373, 388, 391-392
See also Shanghai Economic Zone
Rehn, Detlef, 342
Research Institute for Restructuring the Economic System, 366
Residence controls. *See* Household registration
Responsibility fields, 87
Retail sales
in collectives, 267
farm markets, 98, 100, 186
hawking, 438-440
in private enterprises, 441
in state stores, 281-282, 434-435, 439
Roseneau, James, 65
Rural industry, 5-6, 29, 82, 83, 116
beginnings of, 112-113
brigade and commune enterprises, 113-118
capital investment in, 129, 140
credit to, 143-144, 148, 318
growth of, 10, 100-107, 113, 115, 150-151, 328
geographical differences in, 123-126
periodization in, 133-135
vs agricultural growth, 130, 131
illegal plants, 118-123
as impetus for reform, 9-10, 85-86, 110-112, 151
inefficiency of plants, 135-136

Rural industry *(continued)*
labor in. *See* Labor force, in rural industry
local cadre support for, 118-122, 123
managers of, 115, 126-129, 135, 136, 283-285
markets for, 145, 195, 238, 353-354, 371
ownership type, 117, 130, 132
and party membership, 132-133
productivity of, 135, 140-141
state policy toward, 119-120, 140, 146-147, 148-150, 195, 328
tax revenue from, 142-143, 148, 177
technology in, 150, 353, 354-358
village and township, 117, 130-131, 132, 137, 138, 284-285
wages in, 130, 136-137
Wenzhou model, 120, 146-148
See also Collectives
Rustication policy, 354-356, 413, 451n.20

S

Sales tax, 209
Savings, 314-319
Schistosomiasis, public health campaign against, 373-374
Schumpeter, Joseph, 295, 297
Schurmann, Franz, 63, 202
Scientific institutes, 351-353
Scott, James, 36
Selden, Mark, 97
Semiconductors, 342, 351
Service sector
hawkers, 438-440
private enterprises in, 436
state-owned firms in, 433, 434-436, 437
tourism, 436, 438
Shaanxi, 387
Shamanism, 155n.71
Shanghai
agricultural mechanization in, 87
banks in, 311-312, 316-317, 319
black market in, 289-290
bond market in, 319-320
collective industries in, 211, 267-270
consumer-goods shortages in, 187, 188
crime in, 429-430, 440
during Cultural Revolution, 214-215, 218-219

Shanghai *(continued)*
decollectivization in, 94
documentary sources on, 55
economic circle of, 355
economic control of, 212-213
economic development plan for, 272-274, 348-349
economic growth of, 82-83, 170, 185, 379, 388, 389-390
education in, 344, 416
emigration from, 211, 354-358, 408, 410-411
foreign investment in, 386
GNP share of, 267
hepatitis epidemic in, 189-190, 191, 227
housing in, 229-230, 287-288
immigration to, 408-412, 413-417, 419, 421, 425-430
labor productivity of, 433, 434
nonbudget spending in, 206, 207-208
political leadership in, 14, 206, 219-221, 226, 240, 273
private enterprises in, 211, 269, 270, 440-442, 443-446, 447-449
rural industry in
brigade and commune enterprises, 113-117
collectives, 122, 141-142
costs of, 142-143
entrepreneurs, 127-128
growth of, 100-107, 112, 123-125
labor force of, 137-138, 139
markets of, 144-145, 371
savings in, 315, 316-317
smuggling in, 394-395
state industry in
bankruptcies of, 191-192
capital investment in, 202-203, 204-206, 215, 229, 298, 299-300, 302, 303, 348-349
capital stock depreciation of, 228-229, 263-264, 271, 300-301, 341
centrally managed, 214, 232, 259
competition from other provinces, 174, 231, 232, 345-347
consumer sector growth, 82, 170-171, 213-214
and contract responsibility system, 276-278, 282
credit to, 298, 311, 312, 314

Shanghai
 state industry in *(continued)*
  domestic markets for, 176, 187-188, 231, 347, 369, 391-392. *See also* Shanghai Economic Zone
  embezzlement in, 290-291
  in enterprise groups, 363-364
  entrepreneur organizations of, 365-368
  foreign markets for, 347-348
  in joint ventures, 359-363
  labor emigration from, 211, 354-358
  labor force of, 343-344, 356-357, 417, 421-422, 435-436
  liaison enterprises of, 371-372
  mergers of, 192-193, 272, 274
  nonmonetary extractions from, 209, 211
  and prices, 168-169, 178, 187, 188
  production of, 170-171, 176, 186-187, 195
  regional ties of, 364-365
  resistance to reform, 193
  service sector of, 433, 434-440
  specialization of production, 391
  subsidies to, 191
  and technological development, 342-353
  terms of trade, 184-185
  traditional industries, 342
  vertical integration of, 179-180. *See also* Management; Raw materials; Taxation
 stock market in, 322-323, 324, 325
 studies of, 80n.146
 Subei people in, 220
 suburban population growth in, 137, 286-288
 technology consultants in, 356-357, 359
 telephone system in, 230
 tourism in, 438
 traders in, 369, 372-373
 water transport in, 392-394, 395
Shanghai Academy of Social Sciences, 231, 274, 353
Shanghai Culture Research Institute, 352
Shanghai Economic Association, 382
Shanghai Economic Research, 172
Shanghai Economic Zone
 demise of, 385-388
 economies of provinces in, 378, 379
 expansion of, 377-378, 380
 inland-Shanghai conflicts in, 380-382
Shanghai Economic Zone *(continued)*
 stages of, 373-377
 subprovincial cooperation in, 382-385
 trade offices in, 368
Shanghai Electric Cable Factory, 186
Shanghai Employees' Technical Association, 368
Shanghai First Electronics Bureau, 384
Shanghai Handicrafts Bureau, 170, 176
Shanghai Industrial Consulting Service Company, 359
Shanghai Industrial Technical Development Foundation, 352
Shanghai Insurance Investment Company, 312
Shanghai Joint Development Corporation, 179
Shanghai Light Industrial Machines Company, 360, 384
Shanghai Light Industries Bureau, 347, 371
Shanghai Materials Bureau, 186
Shanghai Production Materials Service Company, 170
Shanghai Public Security Yearbook, 415
Shanghai Research Association to Vitalize Jiangxi, 381
Shanghai Science and Technology Association, 353
Shanghai Textile Bureau, 229
Shanghai Vacuum Electrical Appliance Co., 323
Shangyu, 356
Shaoxing, 236, 418
Shazhou, 138, 360, 384
Shenzhen, 187, 243, 374, 387, 404n.187
Shirk, Susan, 35
Silk industry, 175, 178, 293
Simon, Denis Fred, 342
Sincere Discussion Society to Vitalize Jiagxi, 381
Singapore, regime legitimacy in, 72n.45
Skinner, G. William, 30, 34, 202
Skocpol, Theda, 22, 23, 24
Smith, Richard, 449
Smuggling, 394-395
Solinger, Dorothy, 22, 23
Sources, documentary, 55
South Korea, regime legitimacy in, 72n.45
Sparrow, Bartholomew, 52

Special economic zone (SEZ), 374, 387-388
Speculation, 291-293
Speech freedom, 41
State
  capacity, 21-24, 32, 73n.63
  contraction of power, 17-19, 38
  defining, 17, 24-26, 74n.73
  and hinge leaders, 19-21, 30, 32, 33, 141
  legitimacy of, 31
  parasitism, 32
  patronism, 31, 33
  political networks in, 26-27, 31-32
  and society, 17, 24-25
  vs nonstate networks, 19, 23, 31
  See also Leadership
State enterprises
  bankruptcies of, 191-192, 196, 311
  contract responsibility system in, 275-278, 282, 283
  corruption in, 290-293
  and costs, 186-187, 264
  credit to, 171, 235, 263, 286, 304-306
  decline of, 12, 141-142, 191-196
  efficiency of, 135
  in enterprise groups, 363-364, 365
  in entrepreneur organizations, 365-368
  evasion, 237
  growth of, 133, 169, 176, 284
  in joint ventures, 359-363
  lease system in, 282
  light-industry, 13, 70n.32, 82, 112, 170-171, 174-175, 186-187, 195, 206, 213
  markets for, 176, 187-188, 231, 232, 345-347
  mergers of, 192-193, 272, 274
  and prices, 82, 168-169, 178, 187, 188
  profit retention of, 130, 304
  regional ties of, 364-365
  service sector, 433, 434-440
  shift to private sector, 268-269
  size of, 121
  and state control, 169-170, 178, 2 70-272
  stocks in, 323-325
  subsidies to, 191
  trading firms, 281-282
  wages in, 167, 172, 227
  warehoused waste in, 280-281
State enterprises *(continued)*
  See also Investment; Labor force; Management; Production; Raw materials; Shanghai, state industry in; Taxation; Technology
Steel industry
  development strategy for, 348-349
  raw materials for, 175, 176, 194
Stepan, Alfred, 17-18
Stock market, 322-326
Street industries, 441-442
Student protest, 23, 28, 42
Sunan, 138, 141, 146, 148-149, 220-221
Sun Zi, 275, 333n.43
Suzhou, 114, 138, 141, 267, 360, 364, 395, 400n.99, 436, 438

T

Taiwan
  democratization in, 70n.26
  economic zones in, 374
  regime legitimacy in, 72n.45
Taiyuan, 233
Tangqiao, 114-115, 116
Taxation
  extractions by province, 198-199
  fragmented system of, 201-202
  grain, 92
  and profits, 209, 230, 232-237
  reform, 212, 218-219, 222-228, 239-240, 241
  of rural industry, 142-143, 148
  of Shanghai, 82, 83, 172, 198-99
    comparison with other cities, 206-209, 210
    during Cultural Revolution, 215, 218
    as economic control, 213
    fairness debate over, 242-244
    and hidden accounts, 201, 203, 206, 212, 228
    impact on capital investment, 228-229, 230, 271
    impact on housing, 229-230
    and implicit subsidies, 197-198
    incomplete data on, 201-202
    for inland investment, 112, 202, 204-205
    under national guarantee system, 241
    on private industry, 211-212, 444, 447-449

Taxation *(continued)*
reasons for high extraction, 213-215, 218-221
reform of, 222-228, 239-240
relation to spending, 206, 209, 216-217, 218
and revenue decline, 230-32, 233, 237-239
sales tax, 209
state vs city extraction, 197
and technological development, 343
in Shanghai Economic Zone, 375
Technology
agricultural, 9, 83, 85, 87-88, 89, 107, 109-10
capital investment in, 341-342, 344, 348
consultants, 356-357, 359
and electronics industry, 342, 349-351
from research organizations, 351-353
and industrial growth, 341
and labor force education, 343-344, 357
national allocation for, 343, 350
in rural industry, 150, 353, 354-358
in Shanghai Economic Zone, 376
and trade competition, 174, 345-348
Telephone system, 230
Television, 9
Textile industry
capital stock depreciation in, 228-229
and clothing styles, 435
competition in, 345
decline in production, 196
raw material shortage in, 175, 179
state management of, 270-271
Think tanks, 352-353
Three Gorges Dam, 135, 329, 432
Tiananmen disaster, 447, 449
Tianjin, 218
Tianshui model, 146
Tobacco industry, 180
Tocqueville, Alexis de, 81
Tourism, 434, 436, 438
Townsend, James R., 202
Trade
barriers, 392
barter, 170, 182-185, 369, 370-371
black market, 289-290, 395
competition, 174, 231, 232, 345-347
Trade *(continued)*
and economic growth, 388
foreign, 185-186, 347-348, 374
horizontal, 361, 371-373, 388, 391-392. *See also* Shanghai Economic Zone
illegal, 291, 293
localist control over, 392
in raw materials, 38, 185-186, 395
representatives, 368-369
of rural industry, 145, 195, 238, 353-354, 371
Shanghai exports, 187-188, 347, 391
smuggling, 394-395
and technological development, 174, 345-348
and transportation, 392-394
traveling salespeople, 369, 372-373
Wenzhou button market, 370
See also Retail sales
Transportation
railroads, 393, 423, 440
water, 392-394
Treasury bonds, 319, 321
Triple-cropping, 90-93, 110
Tu Yuesheng, 155n.71

U

Universities
hinge leaders in, 30
student protest in, 23, 28, 42
technical education in, 344
Urban migration, 409-412, 413-417

V

Violence, youth, 415
Volkswagen, 183

W

Wages
agricultural, 103
bonds, 227
in brigade teams, 101-102
in private enterprises, 444
in rural industry, 130, 136-137
in state enterprises, 167, 172, 227
subsistence, 408
Wang Bingqian, 243-244

Wang Daohan, 365, 375
Wang Hongwen, 298
Wang Shaoguang, 21
Wan Li, 111
Warehouses
  leasing of, 287-288
  production for, 280-281
Water transport, 392-394
Weber, Max, 47, 62
Wei Jingsheng, 68n.5
Wenhui News, 181, 182, 345, 372, 375, 448
Wenzhou
  button market in, 370
  collectives and private enterprises in, 120-121, 146-148, 270, 442-443
  money market in, 321-322
Wholesalers, corruption of, 293
Wolin, Sheldon, 65
Women
  domestic workers, 419, 428
  hawkers, 439
  migration patterns of, 409
Workers. *See* Labor force
World Economic Herald, 220, 343, 353, 366, 392
Wuhan, 56, 386
Wujin, 360, 384
Wujing Chemical Factory, 194-195
Wu Kequan, 384
Wuxi, 377, 382, 384, 436
  credit in, 143-144
  electronics industry in, 350-351
  industrial growth in, 140-141, 284, 364, 400n.99
  joint ventures in, 360-361
  labor force in, 420
  taxation of, 304

X

Xi'an, 233, 350
Xiashi, 418
Xinmin Evening News, 443
Xu Jiatun, 119-120

Y

Yang Shangkun, 219
Yao Yilin, 239

Z

Zhang Chunqiao, 88, 92, 113, 120, 252n.158, 298
Zhang Jingfu, 387-388
Zhang Pinghua, 378
Zhao Ziyang, 28, 93, 239, 357
  and Shanghai Economic Zone, 375, 386
  and Shanghai taxation, 240
Zhejiang
  collective industry in, 267, 268, 270
  corruption in, 293
  decollectivization in, 96, 108-109
  economic growth of, 83, 236, 363, 379, 388, 389-390
  entrepreneurs from, 364
  exports of, 348
  Hong Kong investment in, 364-365, 368
  in joint ventures, 362
  labor force in, 139-140, 354, 355, 356, 358
  population migration in, 418, 419
  reformer managers in, 283-284
  in regional public health campaign, 373-374
  rural industry in, 112-113, 120-121, 125, 141, 142, 353
  savings in, 318
  service sector in, 438
  in Shanghai Economic Zone, 374, 375, 377, 378, 382
  silk trade in, 175, 178
  stock investment in, 326
  technological development in, 344, 353
  Wenzhou model in, 120-121, 146-148, 270, 442-443
Zhou Enlai, 10, 119, 167, 258
Zhou Xueguang, 31, 42
Zhu Rongji, 10, 212, 219, 226, 328
Zweig, David, 95

Lynn T. White III is a professor in the Woodrow Wilson School and the Politics Department at Princeton University, frequently visiting the University of Hong Kong's Centre of Asian Studies for research. His previous books include *Careers in Shanghai*, which mostly concerns the 1950s, and *Policies of Chaos*, dealing with the causes of the Cultural Revolution in the same city during the 1960s. *Unstately Power* follows these studies into the era of China's reforms and into Shanghai's hinterland. For each of these periods, White tries to explain political patterns by a combination of unintended and policy factors, both among individuals and at larger sizes of organization.

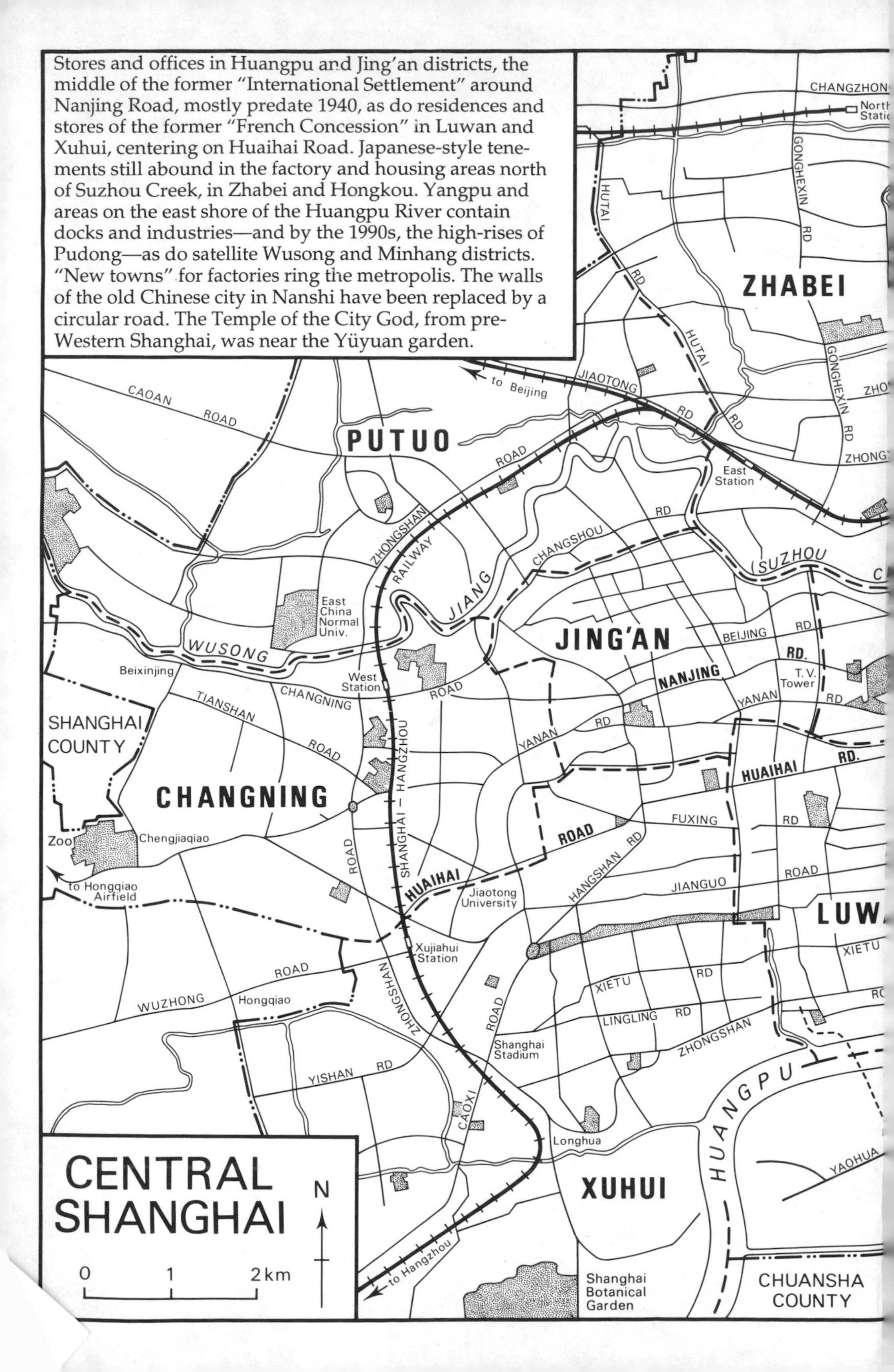

Stores and offices in Huangpu and Jing'an districts, the middle of the former "International Settlement" around Nanjing Road, mostly predate 1940, as do residences and stores of the former "French Concession" in Luwan and Xuhui, centering on Huaihai Road. Japanese-style tenements still abound in the factory and housing areas north of Suzhou Creek, in Zhabei and Hongkou. Yangpu and areas on the east shore of the Huangpu River contain docks and industries—and by the 1990s, the high-rises of Pudong—as do satellite Wusong and Minhang districts. "New towns" for factories ring the metropolis. The walls of the old Chinese city in Nanshi have been replaced by a circular road. The Temple of the City God, from pre-Western Shanghai, was near the Yüyuan garden.